PITTSBURGH

THE STORY OF AN AMERICAN CITY

Fourth Edition

updated and enlarged

in 1988

BOOKS BY STEFAN LORANT

I Was Hitler's Prisoner (1935)

Lincoln, His Life in Photographs (1941)

The New World: The First Pictures of America (1946)

(revised edition in 1965)

FDR, A Pictorial Biography (1950)

The Presidency: The History of Presidential Elections (1951)

Lincoln, A Picture Story of His Life (1952)

(revised and enlarged editions in 1957 and 1969)

The Life of Abraham Lincoln (1954)

The Life and Times of Theodore Roosevelt (1959)

The Glorious Burden: The American Presidency (1968)

(revised and enlarged edition in 1977)

Sieg Heil!: An Illustrated History of Germany

from Bismarck to Hitler (1974)

Pittsburgh, The Story of an American City (1964)

(revised and enlarged editions in 1975, 1980, and 1988)

PITTSBURGH

THE STORY OF AN AMERICAN CITY

STEFAN LORANT

With Contributions by

Henry Steele Commager   Oscar Handlin

J. Cutler Andrews   Sylvester K. Stevens

John Morton Blum   Henry David

Gerald W. Johnson   David Lawrence

AUTHORS EDITION, INC.   LENOX, MASSACHUSETTS

Layout and Design by Stefan Lorant

Updated and enlarged edition, Library of Congress Catalog Card Number CCN75-24970
Copyright © 1964 by Stefan Lorant
Copyright © 1975 by Stefan Lorant
Copyright © 1980 by Stefan Lorant
Copyright © 1988 by Stefan Lorant

Printed and bound in the United States of America by Arcata Graphics/Kingsport

FIRST EDITION
1964
First printing of 25,000 copies — October 1964
Second printing of 25,000 copies — November 1964

SECOND EDITION
1975
First printing of 25,000 copies of the revised and updated
Bicentennial edition — October 1975
Second printing of 10,000 copies — November 1975
Third printing of 10,000 copies — December 1975
Fourth printing of 10,000 copies — May 1977

THIRD EDITION
1980
First printing of 20,000 copies of the enlarged and updated
third edition — November 1980

FOURTH EDITION
1988
First printing of 20,000 copies of the enlarged and updated
fourth edition — October 1988

ISBN 0–685–92012–7

CONTENTS

FOREWORD TO THE FOURTH EDITION

This is the third time that I update and enlarge upon this book. In 1964, when the first edition came out, the volume had 520 pages. Eleven years later, in 1975, the updated second edition had 608 pages. In 1980, the third edition had 672 pages. And now, in 1988, the fourth edition grew to 736 pages. As Pittsburgh expanded so did the book.

I have been asked many times how it came about that I—a non-Pittsburgher—did a book on Pittsburgh's history. It is a curious tale, worth retelling.

It began with a telephone call from my friend Edgar Kaufmann in the early days in 1953. Edgar called from his Palm Springs winter home and asked me to visit him. There seemed to be an urgency in his voice when he repeated the words: "I must talk to you."

I guessed why he wanted to see me. A few weeks before, his wife Liliane, committed suicide and Edgar needed a friend to whom he could unburden his soul. So I flew to Palm Springs. While staying there, a group of Pittsburghers came to see Edgar. General Sommerville, President of Koppers Company, flew them to California in his company's plane. David Lawrence, the Mayor of Pittsburgh, was one of them, Park Martin, Director of the Allegheny Conference was another. And there were a number of younger people in the group: Jack Robin, John Grove, Theodore Hazlett and others. They came to persuade Edgar to increase his gift for the erection of the Civic Arena so that the building could be used not only in warm weather, but in the winter as well.

After they left the house, the floor of the living room was littered with blueprints and architectural sketches.

Edgar looked at the blueprints and asked: "What do you think?" speaking more to himself than to me. "Shall I do it?" I replied: "Do you have the money?" Edgar nodded. "Would the thing give you pleasure?" and, again, he nodded. "So what are you waiting for?"

We burst out in laughter and it was not difficult to see that his mind was made up. He was to give the additional money for the building of the Arena.

In the evening there was a dinner party for the Pittsburgh visitors at the Racquet Club. Celebrities of stage and screen mingled with the men from Pittsburgh. William Powell was there, as were Dinah Shore and Rhonda Fleming. Gussy Moran, the glamorous tennis star, sat between David Lawrence and me. The Mayor, eager to make conversation asked Gussy "What do you do?" and she answered: "I play tennis." "Is that all?" said the puzzled Lawrence. Gussy whispered in my ear: "This Pittsburgher is perhaps the only one in the world who never heard of my lace panties, which scandalized Wimbledon."

Next morning—after the visitors left for greener pastures—I was sitting with Edgar at the side of the pool. He began talking about Pittsburgh and for the rest of the morning he went on praising the city he loved. Little did I think that his talk at that time would eventually lead to my doing a book on Pittsburgh.

A year later, in the Spring of 1954 Edgar phoned me in my Massachusetts home and invited me to spend the weekend with him at Bear Run.

He was waiting for me at the airport and on the drive to *Fallingwater* he explained why he asked me to come.

"I want you to do a book on Pittsburgh, a big book with a lot of illustrations—'a de-luxe book.'" His eyes were glowing as he repeated the word "de-luxe."

His proposal surprised me. I had no knowledge of Pittsburgh; I was a stranger to the city; I was there only once and that was many years ago. I arrived in the late morning—but the streets were as dark as at night, and the air was full of grime. I could not breathe. I soon had enough of the unpleasant place; I took the next train away from it.

During our drive to *Fallingwater* Edgar spoke of the great transformation that had taken place in the city since my last visit and how things had changed. I listened but I showed little interest. Still Edgar was adamant. So next morning I consented to look at Pittsburgh on my own and "case the joint."

Harold Jones, Edgar's chauffeur, was to drive me around the city. I asked him to show me Pittsburgh as he knew it. So we went. We drove through the North Side and through the South Side; we drove through Oakland, through Squirrel Hill, through Shady Side, through Fox Chapel. Jones showed me the shacks on the Hill and he took me to the Carnegie Museum and to Phipps Conservatory.

Then we went to see the J & L Mills, the Heinz Plants—we visited Westinghouse, Pittsburgh Screw and Bolt and other places of manufacture. I saw hot steel poured, glass blown, nails made, soup canned. I saw the homes of the rich and the dilapidated shacks of the poor. I watched students rehearsing a play in the theater of Carnegie Tech and researchers working at the Mellon Institute. For three full days I explored the city and its neighborhoods. I floated down the Monongahela on a coal barge and up the Allegheny in a motorboat. And before the three days were over I was in love with Pittsburgh and excited about the project. I saw that the story of Pittsburgh was the story of America; a microcosm of the history of the whole country. So I was ready to do the book.

When I began work on it in 1954 the Renaissance was in full swing. The skies were already clear of smog; the rivers were already controlled; the demolition of slum areas were on the way, some of the Gateway Buildings at the Point already built. Pittsburghers were thrilled about their future, about the great things that were to come. Civic spirit was soaring. Personal and political differences that made effective action in the past well-nigh impossible vanished. Republican industrialists and financiers joined hands with Democratic politicians for the good of their city. Led by banker Mellon on the one side and Mayor Lawrence on the other, they were to transform Pittsburgh into a beautiful city. Their enthusiasm infected other leaders of business, of finance and industry. The Allegheny Conference on Community Development became a catalyst of all these activities.

I expected to complete the "de-luxe" book within a year. But as it happened it took ten full years of research and writing before I was finished with it.

I had barely begun my work when Edgar died in his sleep on April 14, 1955. Were it not for the Allegheny Conference and for some of the Pittsburgh Foundations, the project would have been abandoned. But Edgar's friends were determined to make the book a reality. Foremost among them was Theodore L. Hazlett, Jr., solicitor of the Allegheny Conference.

Ted took on where Edgar left off; he sustained me when the sledding turned tough and offered a helping hand when things were near collapse.

I began my research in 1954 in the Historical Room of the Carnegie Library in Oakland and in the Pennsylvania Room of the Carnegie Library on the North Side, then went through the files of the Historical Society of Western Pennsylvania and the photographic collection in the University of Pittsburgh. I soon found that the authoritative source material on the city's history was sporadic and sparse. I realized that I had to look for material outside the city—so I went to the Library of Congress in Washington, to the New York Public Library, to the Widener Library at Harvard, to the Antiquarian Society at Worcester, to the Libraries in Philadelphia and Harrisburg.

As the standard histories on Pittsburgh were not too reliable I began the compilation of the events during the city's two hundred years history. Helped by historians and newspapermen, we went through the pages of the local newspapers, from the early issues of the *Pittsburgh Gazette* to the latest numbers of *The Pittsburgh Press*. The data culled from these sources make up the Chronology.

The search for illustrations turned out to be equally difficult. Pittsburgh had no comprehensive picture collection on its past. When I asked my friends about this, their answer was: "We had to work, we had to make money, we had no time for such things."

The Carnegie Library had boxes of photographs and a file of portraits of those who lived in the city and left their mark on it. The University of Pittsburgh had albums on the post-World War II period; the Historical Society had some interesting historical paintings; the libraries of the newspapers had some good pictures, but not enough for a comprehensive work.

I had to search for illustrations and pictures one by one. William Block, the publisher of the *Pittsburgh Post-Gazette*, kindly allowed me to enlist the cooperation of his readers. Scores of them responded with old family photographs.

I extended my research to foreign countries. The original plans of Fort Pitt came from the British Museum in London. To reproduce the drawings of Charles Alexandre Lesueur, which he made on his visit to the city in 1825, I sent a photographer from Paris to the Natural History Museum at LeHavre, where the drawings reposed. The contemporary account describing the burning of Fort Duquesne I found in the Newport *Rhode Island Mercury* at the American Antiquarian Society in Worcester, Massachusetts. Illustrations of early industrial buildings I discovered in a Spanish promotion booklet of 1889 printed in Madrid. And so on and on.

I went through the issues of the early American pictorial weeklies. In *Gleason's Pictorial Drawing Room Companion* and in *Ballou's Pictorial* I came upon renderings of life in Pittsburgh during the eighteen-fifties. In *Frank Leslie's Illustrated* (1855–1922) and *Harper's Weekly* (1857–1916) I came upon excellent woodcuts on life in Pittsburgh after the Civil War. *Every Saturday*, the New England weekly, printed a special Pittsburgh issue in 1871, with interesting drawings on the city's industries. *The Library*, published in Pittsburgh at the turn of the century, yielded many illustrations, as did the *Bulletin Index*, another Pittsburgh publication during the early years of the presidency of Franklin D. Roosevelt.

The *Illustrated London News* in London and the *Illustrierte Zeitung* of Leipzig preserved photographs of Pittsburgh in their archives. The editors were kind enough and sent me the material I asked for. My gratitude to them.

To illustrate early events, I held an art contest in which artists of the city—William Libby, Roy Hilton, Edwin Anderson, Edgar Roth, Harry Scheuch, Marty Cornelius, Idabelle Kleinhans and others participated. Some of their paintings are printed in the early chapters of the book.

I hoped that photographs of events in the twentieth century would be easier to find. They were not. In the 1936 flood, the picture collections of the city's newspapers were inundated by the waters, and what water and mud did not destroy, efficiency experts did. To create more space for staff and equipment, much of the authentic photographic material was thrown into wastebaskets.

To present life as it was in the nineteen-fifties, I engaged W. Eugene Smith to capture the moods of the city. He responded to my requests and did what I asked him to do. His photographs taken specially for the book became famous and won him later a Guggenheim fellowship.

So-after ten years of research and writing the "de-luxe" book of Edgar's dream was in the stores. Within a short time the 50,000 copies of the first edition were sold out.

After the book was out of print for many years, I started to compile a revised and updated edition. As the original plates of the first edition were lost, I had to collect all the pictures anew; all the color plates had to be remade. A new chapter of eighty pages was added with many new photographs taken by Joel Librizzi. This revised Centennial edition came out in 1975 and again it was not before long that the 55,000 copies printed had been sold out. Once again we were out of print. Thus, in 1980 I did another enlarged and updated edition. I thought it would be the final one. It was not.

Now in 1988, thirty-four years after I begun working on the book, here is the fourth enlarged edition.

To be able to complete the volume I was helped and assisted by many friends, foremost among them Bruce D. Campbell, Gregory D. Curtis and William Pietragallo II. My heartfelt thanks to them.

I have interviewed a number of leading Pittsburghers and they shared with me their thoughts about the city and of its future. Mayor Caliguiri talked to me at length— it was probably his last interview. I have talked to Anthony J. F. O'Reilly, the brilliant Chief Executive Officer of the Heinz Company, and to John F. Donahue, the founder of Federated Investors and listened to their views. I interviewed the Presidents of Pittsburgh's great Universities: Richard W. Cyert of Carnegie Mellon and Wesley W. Posvar of the University of Pittsburgh and they both were generous with their time. I talked to some of Pittsburgh's financial and business leaders, to Howard M. Love, Chairman and C.E.O. of National Intergroup, to Thomas H. O'Brien, President and C.E.O. of PNC Financial Corporation, to Alan Fellheimer, Chairman of Equibank, also to Howard W. Hanna III, the head of the State's largest real estate company and to Edward J. Lewis, the most aggressive real estate developer in the Golden Triangle. I had a delightful interview with "Woman of the Year" Elsie Hillman, and had talks with Robert B. Pease of the Allegheny Conference and John P. Robin of the Urban Redevelopment Authority, with Timothy Parks of the High Technology Council, with Dr. Thomas Detre, the

inventive genius of medical services and with many others. My profound thanks for sharing their thoughts with me.

In completing this volume I was helped and assisted by a number of experts.

Most of the new color pictures were taken by Norman W. Schumm. The quality of his work places him among the top of the country's great photographers.

My deep bow to Pamela Z. Bryan for her memorable representations of the old steel mills.

In preparing the chronological events of the eighties I was assisted by John Benson, Dean Campbell and Raymond Martin. My dear friend Roy McHugh, the great newspaperman, Maria Zini from the Pennsylvania Room of the Carnegie Library and Gail Campbell checked the entries and suggested changes and corrections. If any mistakes have crept in, the responsibility is mine.

The "mechanicals" have been done by Lynne Foy, one of the best in her trade. The separations for the color photographs were the work of John Schechterle and his firm in Greenfield, Massachusetts. Nadine Margaret Landers typed and retyped the manuscript with patience and good humor. Leslie Sullivan typed the final draft. The index was prepared by Mrs. Joan Whitman.

I dedicate this (no doubt final edition of this book compiled by me) to the memory of Edgar J. Kaufmann (d. in 1955), Theodore L. Hazlett, Jr. (d. in 1979) and to the memory of my beloved son Mark (d. in 1984), who adored Pittsburgh and who lost his life in a car accident a fortnight after his 19th birthday.

STEFAN LORANT

"Farview"
Lenox, Massachusetts
June 25, 1988

Chapter 1

FORTS IN THE WILDERNESS...

by Henry Steele Commager

THREE MAJESTIC themes focus on the Forks of the Ohio and the city that was to grow up along its silver fingers: the prodigious struggle for the continent between England and France; the desperate warfare between the Indians and the whites; the westward movement and the planting of civilization in the great valley. The first, fought from Louisbourg to Michilimackinac, from the Ohio to New Orleans, reached one of its great climacterics in the struggle that began with Colonel Washington's ill-fated stand at Fort Necessity and ended four years later with the burning of Fort Duquesne and the retirement of the French from the Forks. The second, fought out from Jamestown and Cape Cod to the bloody tracks of Chief Joseph and the Nez Percé three hundred years later, reached one of its climacterics in the savage warfare from Braddock's Field to Bushy Run. The third, a constant in our history, saw one of its great triumphs when pioneers first surmounted the Appalachian barrier and planted civilization along the banks of the Youghiogheny, the Monongahela, and the Cheat; it was the forerunner of those successive frontiers that carried the American people to the Pacific in another century.

The historical significance of Pittsburgh was determined, from the beginning, by geography. Whoever commanded the Forks of the Ohio commanded the great interior of the continent—the rich Ohio Valley, drained by a dozen flashing rivers, the Great Lakes, and the mighty Mississippi. The swift Allegheny and the brawling Monon-

gahela met here to form what the French well called the Belle Rivière; and then flowed westward, absorbing as it went the Beaver, the Muskingum, the Scioto, the Miami, the White, and the Wabash, and from the south the Kanawha, the Guyandot, the Sandy, the Licking, the Kentucky, the Green, the Cumberland, the Tennessee; all pouring into the Father of Waters. The city that was to rise at this strategic point on the threshold of the Forks was at once the bridge from the East and the gateway to the West, the most western of the great cities of the seaboard, the most eastern of the great cities of the valley: it is no accident that it has commanded this position now for a century and a half; its sovereignty is still unchallenged.

The full significance of control of the Forks and of the land below first emerged in connection with the century-long struggle between England and France for North America. By the early years of the eighteenth century France was firmly established in Canada and at the mouth of the Mississippi, and, somewhat uncertainly, in the Ohio and Illinois country between. The English were as firmly planted along the Atlantic coast, but hemmed in there by the most formidable mountain range that any migrating people had encountered since the barbarian invasions of Italy and Spain. France had but to strengthen the two great bastions at either end of the great angle formed by the St. Lawrence and the Mississippi rivers, and spin a web of communication in the vast area between, and the

largest and richest part of the continent was hers. All the odds of history and of geography were in her favor. There were five gateways to the great interior: the St. Lawrence and the Mississippi which formed the two angles; the Mohawk River and the southern Appalachians, roughly at thirty degrees of the angle; and the difficult and formidable approach along the tributaries of the Susquehanna and the Potomac, roughly at the center. France controlled both the outer approaches—the St. Lawrence and the Mississippi. The warlike Iroquois and their allies barred the approach from the Mohawk, and the equally warlike Cherokee and Creek the approach around the Appalachians. There remained only the central route—if it can be called that—up the rivers north and south that flowed into the Chesapeake Bay—the intricate network of streams that made up the Susquehanna and linked it by forbidding portages to the headwaters of the Allegheny; or the network of streams of the upper Potomac which linked up, no less inhospitably, with the Youghiogheny, the Monongahela, and the Cheat. For the French the approach to the Forks was far easier: they had only to shift their line of communication from the Lake Michigan-Wisconsin or the Lake Erie-Wabash routes a bit to the east: by easy portages from Lakes Ontario or Erie to the Ohio. If they

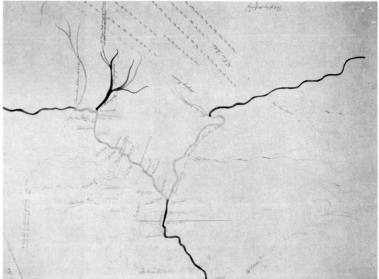

ONE OF THE EARLIEST ENGLISH MAPS of the Ohio Company lands. Made by John Mercer, secretary of the company, in 1752, it was later used in support of the company's land claims.

The original map is in the Public Record Office in London, a copy of it is in the Darlington Library, Pittsburgh.

THE ANTAGONISTS: The English pushed their settlements west of the Allegheny Mountains. English traders, sent by the newly formed Ohio Land Company, traded in the territory that the King of France claimed through discovery and exploration.

Original drawing of an eighteenth-century English foot soldier, made specially for this book by Douglas Gorsline.

could weave a network of forts and trading posts and Indian alliances along this easterly route, they would hem in the English behind the Appalachian barrier and win indisputable dominion over the great valley.

From the beginning of the century the French had set up posts deep in the interior—Fort Miami in 1704, Fort Ouatanon on the Wabash in 1719, Fort Vincennes in 1724. It was none too soon. As early as the 1730s intrepid English traders were venturing across the Appalachians and following the waters of the Ohio deep into the interior; another decade and the English were everywhere challenging French dominion over the forest and its furs, outbidding them, underselling them, weaning away their Indian allies, impudently setting up posts in the very heart of country that belonged by discovery, exploration, and possession to the King of France. ("All the resources of the state will never preserve Canada if the English are once settled at the head of these western rivers," said Captain Dumas—he was later to command at Fort Duquesne and to smite the hapless Braddock, and live to see his prophecy come true.) By the 1740s the indefatigable George Croghan—"King of the Traders"—had set up trading posts at Logstown, below the Forks; at Sandusky Bay; and at the wonderfully named Pickawillany on the Miami, thus tap-

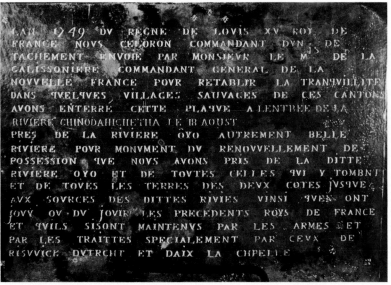

ONE OF THE LEADEN PLATES which a French expedition under the leadership of Céloron de Blainville buried in the Ohio Country in 1749, claiming the land for the French King Louis XV.

The contemporary leaden plate, found near the mouth of the Great Kanawha River, is in the Virginia Historical Society.

THE ANTAGONISTS: The French resisted the challenge of the English. In 1749 they sent an expedition under Céloron de Blainville to the New World to reassert their claims to the Ohio Country, oust the English traders, and stir up the Indians against them.

Original drawing of an eighteenth-century French soldier, made specially for this book by Douglas Gorsline.

ping the fur trade of the Great Lakes and of the Wabash country as well.

From Montreal the French struck back with trade, diplomacy, and arms. As early as 1744 the Marquis de Beauharnois wrote to the Comte de Maurepas in Paris:

> On receiving intelligence this spring of the different settlements and magazines the English have formed on the Beautiful River, I issued my orders and sent belts to the Detroit nations to drive them thence by force of arms and to plunder the stores they have there; I gave like orders to the Commandant among the Ouiatanons and the Miamis. Therefore . . . I have reason to presume that these will act against the English settled on the Beautiful River and also against the other settlements the latter may possibly form in that vicinity, and which the former will not suffer, as independent of the war that I have had chanted in all the villages, they have accepted the belts presented on that occasion.

The Indians, however, were by no means eager to drive out the English traders; after all, their goods were cheaper, better, and more certain than any the French could manage to send down the long rivers and lakes. King George's War

(turn to page 15)

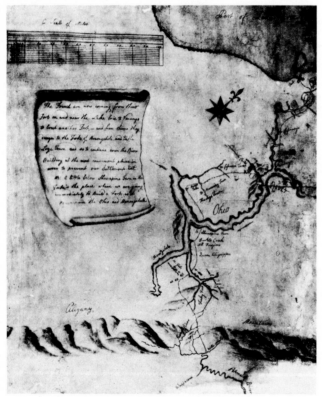

Courtesy Pennsylvania Historical and Museum Collection.

THE MAP OF GEORGE WASHINGTON shows the route that he and his five companions took into the Ohio Country in 1753.

ON NOVEMBER 23, 1753, George Washington, the twenty-one-year-old major in the Virginia Militia sent by Governor Robert Dinwiddie to deliver a warning to the commandant of the French forces on the Ohio, reached the spot where Pittsburgh is built today. Observing the territory, Washington noted in his *Journal* that the land at the fork was "extremely well situated for a Fort, as it has the absolute Command of both Rivers."

Original drawing made specially for this book by William Libby.

and *John Mac-Quire*, Indian Traders, *Henry Steward*, and *William Jenkins* ; and in Company with those Persons, left the Inhabitants the Day following.

The excessive Rains and vast Quantity of Snow which had fallen, prevented our reaching Mr. *Frazier's*, an Indian Trader, at the Mouth of *Turtle*-Creek, on *Monongahela* [River] till *Thursday* the 22d. We were informed here, that Expresses had been sent a few Days before to the Traders down the River, to acquaint them with the *French* General's Death, and the Return of the major Part of the *French* Army into Winter Quarters.

The Waters were quite impassable, without swimming our Horses ; which obliged us to get the Loan of a Canoe from *Frazier*, and to send *Barnaby Currin*, and *Henry Steward*, down the *Monongahela*, with our Baggage, to meet us at the Forks of *Ohio*, about 10 Miles, there to cross the *Aligany*.*

As I got down before the Canoe, I spent some Time in viewing the Rivers, and the Land in the Fork ; which I think extremely well situated for a Fort, as it has the absolute Command of both Rivers. The Land at the Point is 20 or 25 Feet above the common Surface of the Water ; and a considerable Bottom of flat, well-timbered Land all around it, very convenient for Building : The Rivers are each a Quarter of a Mile, or more, across, and run here very near at right Angles : *Aligany* bearing N. E. and *Monongahela* S. E. The former of these two is a very rapid and swift running Water ; the other deep and still, without any perceptible Fall.

About two Miles from this, on the South East Side of the River, at the Place where the *Ohio*

* The *Ohio* and *Aligany* are the same River.

Company

Company intended to erect a Fort, lives *Shingiss*, King of the *Delawares* : We called upon him, to invite him to Council at the *Loggs*-Town.

As I had taken a good deal of Notice Yesterday of the Situation at the *Forks*, my Curiosity led me to examine this more particularly, and I think it greatly inferior, either for Defence or Advantages ; especially the latter : For a Fort at the *Forks* would be equally well situated on the *Ohio*, and have the entire Command of the *Monongahela* ; which runs up to our Settlements and is extremely well designed for Water Carriage, as it is of a deep still Nature. Besides a Fort at the *Fork* might be built at a much less Expence, than at the other Place.—

Nature has well contrived this lower Place, for Water Defence ; but the Hill whereon it must stand being about a Quarter of a Mile in Length, and then descending gradually on the Land Side, will render it difficult and very expensive, to make a sufficient Fortification there.—The whole Flat upon the Hill must be taken-in, the Side next the Descent made extremely high, or else the Hill itself cut away : Otherwise, the Enemy may raise Batteries within that Distance without being exposed to a single Shot from the Fort.

Shingiss attended us to the *Loggs*-Town, where we arrived between Sun-setting and Dark, the 25th Day after I left *Williamsburg*. We travelled over some extreme good and bad Land, to get to this Place.—

As soon as I came into Town, I went to *Monakatoocha* (as the Half-king was out at his hunting-Cabbin on little *Beaver*-Creek, about 15 Miles off) and informed him by *John Davison* my *Indian* Interpreter, that I was sent a Messenger to the *French* General ; and was ordered to call upon the Sachems of the *Six Nations*, to acquaint them with it.—

WASHINGTON'S JOURNAL was printed in 1754 in Williamsburg on the behest of Governor Dinwiddie of Virginia, who hoped that it would influence the Virginia Burgesses to appropriate funds for military expenditures large enough to subdue the French. Within a few months the thirty-two page *Journal* was reprinted in London.

The paragraph beginning "As I got down before the Canoe, I spent some Time in viewing the Rivers, and the Land in the Fork ..." is George Washington's often-quoted description of the spot where the city of Pittsburgh arose afterwards.

Courtesy Darlington Memorial Library, Pittsburgh.

The painting of William S. Mount (1807–1868) is reproduced through the courtesy of Miss Kate W. Strong.

CROSSING THE ALLEGHENY. Late in December 1753, Washington and Gist reached Shannopin's town, a Delaware village about two miles above the fork. This is Washington's description of the event:

"There was no Way for getting over but on a Raft: Which we set about, with but one poor Hatchet, and finished just after Sun-setting. This was a whole Day's Work: we next got it launched, and went on Board on it: . . . Notwithstanding all our Efforts we could not get the Raft to either Shore; but were obliged, as we were near an Island, to quit our Raft and make to it.

"The Cold was so . . . severe, that Mr. Gist had all his Fingers, and some of his Toes frozen . . ."

Painted specially for this book by Roy Hilton.

THE GOVERNOR'S EMMISSARY. At a trader's house in Logstown, George Washington enters the day's events in his *Journal*. With him are his companions, the Dutchman Jacob Van Braam and the Ohio Company scout Christopher Gist. About a month later the young major stood before the commander of Fort Le Boeuf and demanded to know "by what Authority he had made Prisoners of sev- eral of our English Subjects." The French- man replied firmly, "that no Englishman had a Right to trade upon those Waters," and that if he found any of them in the Ohio Country they would be apprehended.

ended, inconclusively, in 1748; Aix-la-Chapelle was an uneasy truce; more to the point was the Treaty of Logs- town that same year, where George Croghan and Conrad Weiser won the Delaware, the Shawnee, and the Wyandot Indians over to the English and wrung from them (what they had neither right nor power to give) the privilege of trading all the way to the Mississippi.

To the French this was intolerable, and they moved at once to win back the Indians and oust their aggressive rivals. Technically England and France were at peace, and the use of force could not be countenanced. Instead, the Marquis de la Galissonière, Governor of New France, launched an expedition designed to reassert the legal claims of the French to the Ohio country, oust the English traders, and stir up the savages to hostilities short of war. In mid-June 1749 the Captain Céloron de Blainville (often spelled Bienville), a chevalier de St. Louis, with fourteen officers and cadets, twenty French soldiers, and some two hundred Canadians and Indians, set out in twenty-three swift birchbark canoes for the Ohio country. They carried with them leaden plates roundly asserting the sovereignty of the King of France over the Ohio, and an adequate supply of royal arms to nail up on convenient trees. A month later the colorful expedition beached at the Lake Erie portage of Chautauqua (a town on the little lake still bears the name Céloron); all that summer they swept in colorful array down the Allegheny, down the Ohio, up the Miami, by portage to the Maumee, and back through the lakes to Montreal. Everywhere Céloron buried his leaden plates and nailed up his coats of arms; everywhere he rallied the Indians to their ancient allegiance; but every- where, alas, the woods swarmed with English trappers, and English traders had set up shop as if the continent belonged to them, and—what was worse—"under the protection of

15

Original drawing made specially for this book by William Libby.

16

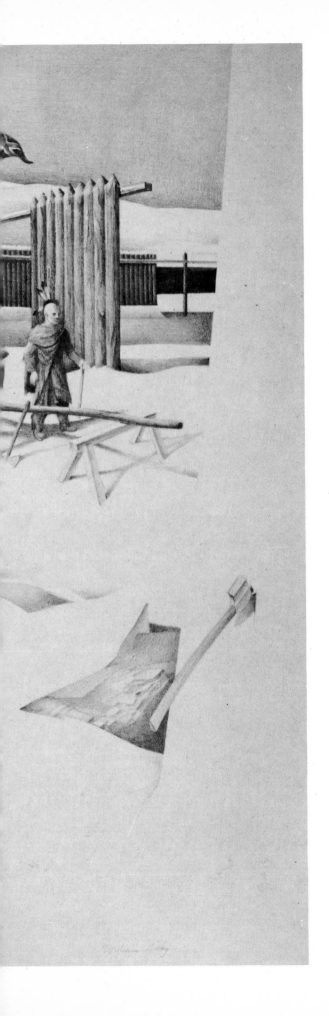

a crowd of savages whom they have drawn over to them." Solemnly Blainville warned his Indian allies against the treacherous English. "They intend to rob you of your country," he admonished, "and that they may succeed they begin by corrupting your minds." It was all true enough, but the Indians were like reeds shaken by the wind. And as for the English, they were not to be scared off by harsh words or even by royal proclamations.

In 1747 a group of Virginia gentlemen (Lawrence Washington among them and, in a small way, his half brother George) formed the Ohio Company to engage in land speculation and Indian trade, and petitioned for half a million acres or more; the following year an acquiescent Privy Council granted them two hundred thousand acres between the Forks of the Ohio, and they moved at once to explore and survey their lands. In 1750 that incomparable frontier scout, Christopher Gist, was exploring the grant—and the land to the west for good measure. He set up a supply post where Wills Creek flows into the Potomac and where Cumberland now stands; with the help of an Indian, who achieved thereby a curious immortality, he hewed out the Nemacolin Road; he built storehouses on the Monongahela and the Youghiogheny. Going on to the Muskingum he found George Croghan there, and together they journeyed far into the West, beyond Ohio Company land to the flourishing trading post of Pickawillany on the Miami. Croghan had preferred a fort at the Forks of the Ohio: there was nothing there but a straggling Delaware village called Shannopin's Town, and the Indians themselves (so they said) wanted a post and a fort, "that in case of war we may have a place to secure our wives and children and our brothers that come to trade with us." It was the first hint of Pittsburgh. Croghan tried in vain to interest the Pennsylvania Quakers, but they would have none of it. Then, instead of withdrawing to the east, he had established himself on the distant Miami, where he reigned like a monarch. "We entered with English colors before us, and were kindly received by their king," wrote Gist; "then all the white men and traders that were there came and welcomed us." The local king was a stout Miami, who rejoiced in two names: La Demoiselle and Old Britain, both eloquent enough. This was the center of Croghan's empire; it swarmed with English traders who

THE BUILDING OF FORT PRINCE GEORGE — the first English fortification west of the Allegheny Mountains. When in the early weeks of 1754 the French learned that a small group of Virginians was erecting a fort at the forks of the Ohio, they dispatched a large force "with sixty boats and 300 canoes and 18 pieces of artillery." On April 17, 1754, Claude de Contrecoeur, the French commander, ordered the Virginians "to retreat peaceably," leave the lands of the French King, "and not to return." As there were only 41 Virginians against half a thousand French, Ensign Edward Ward, in charge of the detachment, was forced to obey the French summons and retreat to Virginia with his men.

tapped the furs of the Wabash and the Erie; it might have been called Fort Croghan. But as Captain de Raymond, commandant at distant Kiskakon on the Maumee, asserted, "If the English stay in this country, we are lost. We must attack and drive them out."

In 1752 the blow fell, the first blow of the great war for empire that was to rage intermittently for nine years through the forests and lakes of North America, on the plains of Silesia, on the waters of the Caribbean and the Mediterranean, along the tropic shores of Africa, and in distant Bengal, until in the end France was driven from the American continent and Britain—for a short hour—ruled supreme in the Western world. As with most great historic events, the preliminaries were almost comically modest. Up on Green Bay was a young French trader, Charles Langlade by name. He had taken a squaw to wife and won the esteem of the savages of his country. Early in June 1752 he set out with 250 painted warriors of the Ottawa and Ojibway tribes; they paddled along the shore of Huron to Detroit; then to Lake Erie and down the Maumee to the fort of that Captain de Raymond, who had already sounded a warning. Early on the morning of June 21 they reached Pickawillany. Most of the traders were away, and the Miami warriors too; the attack was swift and decisive; the Miami were scattered, the fort burned to the ground, and La Demoiselle boiled and eaten.

Now it was the English who were on the defensive, or in retreat, for the fickle Indians began to desert their temporary allies and return to their older allegiance. And now, too, there was a firm hand at the helm in Montreal, the Marquis Duquesne. He was not content with leaden plates and proclamations hanging from trees, and when Langlade reached Montreal with the story of his military and gastronomic triumph, Duquesne rewarded him handsomely and promptly enlisted him in a larger and bolder project. England and France were still at peace; nevertheless, in the spring of 1753 Duquesne launched the most formidable expedition which the Indians of the West had yet seen. An advance party went out, found the wonderful harbor of Presque Isle—where Erie now stands—threw up a fort of chestnut logs, cut a road through the woods to French Creek, and hastily put up another fort called Le Boeuf. From here it was possible, at high water, to float down to the Allegheny and on to the Belle Rivère itself. By late spring the armada was on the way, 1500 strong; there were delays, at the rapids of LaChine, at the Niagara portage. Not until frost was in the air and the foliage yellow and red did the armada reach its destination. Then winter closed in; disease and exhaustion took a heavy toll; and all but three hundred of the expeditionary force were sent back to Montreal to recuperate. The little army under a new commander, Legardeur de St. Pierre, dug in until spring.

So much for prologue. Now the pace quickens. When Pennsylvania's Governor Hamilton heard of the building of Fort Le Boeuf, he wrote to the Assembly that "So

alarmed an occasion has not occurred since the first settlement of the Province, nor any one thing happen'd that so much deserves your serious attention." The Quakers of Pennsylvania did not indulge their attention but the Virginians did, especially those connected with the Ohio Company—and who, after all, was not? That October, Governor Dinwiddie—himself a member—commissioned the young Major Washington (he was just twenty-one) "to visit and deliver a letter to the commandant of the French forces on the Ohio."

It is by now a familiar, almost a hackneyed story: how Washington set out, on the edge of winter, with the cunning Christopher Gist, who knew the country better than anyone else, and with his French interpreter, Jacob Van Braam; how he trekked from Wills Creek over the Great Divide along the Youghiogheny, and to the Forks of the Ohio ("which I think extremely well situated for a Fort, as it has the absolute Command of both Rivers," he wrote), and on to Logstown; and how, as winter was closing in on him, pelted by rain and snow, he fought his way across the Allegheny wilderness to Venango and Le Boeuf to deliver his letter. The French officer Philippe Thomas Joncaire commanded at Venango (it had been one of Croghan's posts), and welcomed the young Major with warm hospitality.

The Wine, as they dosed themselves pretty plentifully with it, soon banished the Restraint which at first appeared in their Conversation; and gave a Licence to their Tongues to reveal their Sentiments more freely.

They told me, That it was their absolute Design to take Possession of the *Ohio*, and by G— they would do it: For that altho' they were sensible the *English* could raise two Men for their one; yet they knew, their Motions were too slow and dilatory to prevent any Undertaking of theirs.

When Washington recovered, he made his way northward to Le Boeuf and on December 12 presented his letter to the commandant, Legardeur de St. Pierre—"an elderly Gentleman" with "much the Air of a Soldier." "I must desire you," Dinwiddie had written in lordly fashion,

. . . to acquaint me, by whose Authority and Instructions you have lately marched from *Canada*, with an armed Force; and invaded the King of *Great-Britain's* Territories, in the Manner complained of? . . . in Obedience to my Instructions, it becomes my Duty to **require** your peaceable Departure; and that you would forbear prosecuting a Purpose so interruptive of the Harmony and good Understanding, which his Majesty is desirous to continue and cultivate with the most Christian King.

I persuade myself you will receive and entertain Major *Washington* with the Candour and Politeness natural to your Nation . . .

This St. Pierre was quite willing to do, but further than this he would not go. "As to the Summons you send me to retire," he wrote firmly, "I do not think myself obliged to obey." The French, in short, were there to stay: that is the message Washington carried back with him to Williamsburg—stumbling along the frozen banks of French Creek, shot at by a treacherous Indian at the well-named Murdering Town, immersed in the icy waters of the Allegheny, plodding, day after day, through the tangled

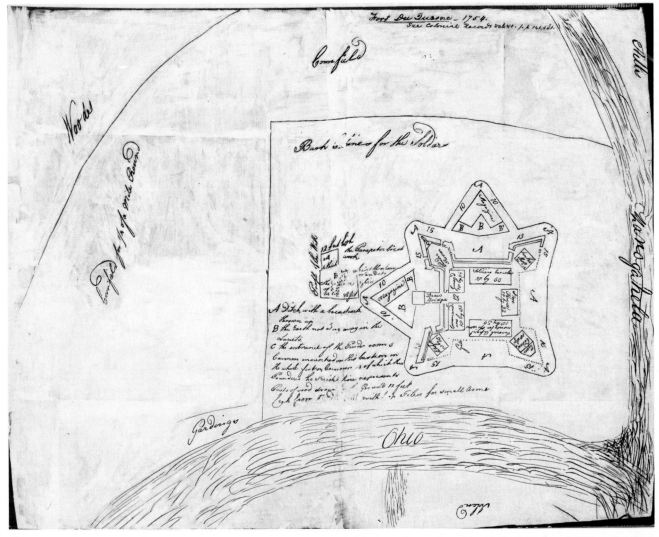

From Robert Stobo's 1754 letter-map in the Darlington Memorial Library, Pittsburgh.

A SKETCH OF FORT DUQUESNE. At Fort Necessity, where George Washington was defeated, the French took two hostages to be held until the prisoners taken at the Battle of Great Meadows were returned to them. The hostages—the French speaking Jacob Van Braam, and the easygoing Scotsman Robert Stobo—were taken to Fort Duquesne, which the French erected at the spot where Fort Prince George stood before.

Inside the fort, Robert Stobo kept his ears and eyes wide open. On July 28, 1754, he sent a letter with the friendly Indians Moses and Delaware George to James Innes, the commandant of the English forces. Stobo not only told of the rumors, gossip, and happenings inside the compound, but enclosed an accurate sketch of the fort. "I would die a thou-sand deaths, to have the pleasure of possessing this Fort but one day," he wrote. "They [the French] are so vain of their success at the Meadows it is worse than death to hear them." The following day he sent another letter, smuggled out by Delaware George, the Indian chief. "Haste to strike," Stobo urged the English commander. But it took a full year before English forces moved towards Fort Duquesne.

forests, over the mountains, to Gist's outpost, and then on, by easier stages, to the bright little capital of Virginia.

Were the English indeed "too slow and dilatory"? Not Governor Dinwiddie. He was a man of parts and a man of energy. Much of his energy, to be sure, had been exhausted in a needless quarrel with the burgesses, but there was enough left to accept the French challenge. Even as Washington was setting out from Gist's fort to Williamsburg—it was January 6—he met an advance contingent headed for the Forks, and along with them a straggling group of settlers. Determined to anticipate the French, Dinwiddie—and the Ohio Company—had sent out William Trent and Thomas Cresap to build a fort, pre-sumably at the Forks. So ambitious were the seaboard gentry that they had authorized Trent to lay out a town as well, all provided with a "school for the education of the Indian children." Trent was supposed to have one hundred men, but actually he had only twenty when in mid-February '54 he reached the Forks. Others drifted in, but there were never enough to do the job. Sometime in March the work got under way. It was the beginning of what was to be Pittsburgh.

Alas, the boasts of the French proved right. What Dinwiddie did (or was it the Ohio Company?) was too little and too late. On April 17, with the fort only half built and less than half manned (even the commanders were

19

away, trying to beat up reinforcements, leaving the fort under the dubious command of young Ensign Ward), an advance body of the French, five hundred strong, appeared. That veteran of many a campaign, Pierre de Contrecoeur was in command. "Nothing," he wrote—for there was still no war and it was all very formal—"nothing can equal my surprise at seeing you attempt an establishment on the lands of the King . . . and that is the reason I am come to find out from yourselves by whose order you have come here to establish a fort on the domain of the King. It is an incontestable fact that the land situated along Belle Rivière belong to his most Christian Highness." Poor Ensign Ward, left holding the bag, was given an hour in which to surrender. As he had only forty-one men against Contrecoeur's hundreds, the decision was not difficult. He gave up as gracefully as he could and marched back to Virginia. The French dismantled what the English built and began to build a proper fort, designed to be the Louisbourg of the West. They baptized it after their Governor, the Marquis Duquesne.

Meantime, Dinwiddie pushed ahead with his plans to re-establish the English at the Forks of the Ohio. It was a Virginia enterprise; it was, he fondly hoped, a colonial enterprise as well. His hopes were vain. He called upon his sister colonies, and they were hostile or indifferent. There was some aid from the mother country—a few regiments in the end and supplies—but for the most part Virginia was left to shoulder the burden alone. That spring of '54 Colonel Joshua Fry and his second in command, the veteran George Washington, raised a regiment at Alexandria. On April 2 Washington set out with an advance force of two companies, hoping to win the race for the Forks. On the way reliable reports reached him that he had already lost; what was to have been the English Fort Prince George was now the French Fort Duquesne. Undaunted, Washington decided to push on. He fought his way through underbrush and swamps, over Laurel Hill and Chestnut Ridge, across turbulent streams, on toward Gist's station on the Redstone. On May 24 he reached the Great Meadows, not far from the Youghiogheny, fifty miles south of the Forks. Three days later Gist himself rode into camp with news that a small French reconnaissance force under Ensign Joseph Coulon de Jumonville was on the march. That day Washington felt out the enemy and found him. At sunrise the next morning he struck. It was all over in fifteen minutes, a dozen French killed, among them poor Jumonville, and the rest prisoners. It was the formal beginning of the French and Indian war.

"If the whole detachment of the French behave with no more resolution than this chosen party did, I flatter myself we shall have no great trouble in driving them to . . . Montreal," wrote Washington. It was his first engagement, and he was very young. The French, he was shortly to learn, were not wanting in resolution. He moved on to Gist's settlement, hewing out a road over some of the most formidable terrain in the East, and brought up his miniature army now dubiously reinforced by a company of South Carolina regulars. There he learned that the French and their Indian allies, a thousand strong, were on the warpath. Gist's settlement was indefensible, and prudently the young colonel (Fry was dead now and Washington had been promoted) decided to pull back to Great Meadows. By the time the soldiers had struggled back over the wretched roads, carrying not only the baggage but their swivel guns, his force had been reduced to less than three hundred.

July 3, 1754, dawned hot and steamy; the rain began early and poured down all day. The French attacked at noon, Coulon de Villiers, brother to the unfortunate Jumonville, in command. Washington's half-built stockade afforded little protection; the trenches filled with water, ammunition ran low, the powder was wet, and the swivel guns proved all but useless. "We continued this unequal fight," wrote Washington, "with an enemy sheltered behind the trees, ourselves without shelter, in trenches full of water, in a settled Rain, and the Enemy galling us on all Sides incessantly from the woods, till eight o'clock at Night." Then the French offered to discuss terms and Washington accepted. The terms of capitulation seemed honorable—the English were to march home with drums beating and all the honors of war—but there was an awkward reference to the "assassination" of Jumonville, which Washington signed unwittingly, that was to embarrass him for years to come. Villiers and his Indian allies returned to Fort Duquesne, burning Gist's settlement on the way. In all the Ohio country France was supreme. When Benjamin Franklin heard the news of Fort Necessity he published his famous cartoon of the snake cut into thirteen pieces: "Unite or die."

The Albany Congress met that very summer, but it did not bring union. Clearly the colonies were incapable of driving the French from the Forks, or even of protecting their own borders against raids by the Indians now flocking to the victorious fleur-de-lis. Though there was as yet no formal war, the British Ministry acted as if war was a reality and planned an elaborate series of counteroffensives designed to push the French back all along the frontiers from Acadia to the forks of the Ohio. With characteristic fatuousness where America was concerned, the Duke of Newcastle appointed Major General Edward Braddock to the command in North America. In the course of the eighteenth century Britain chalked up a fascinating record of mistakes in her American commanders; even in a list that included Loudoun, Clinton, and Howe, General Braddock has a lurid conspicuousness. Yet he was not so much a bad soldier as an unfortunate one.

He had fought at Fontenoy; he had governed at Gibraltar; he was a friend of the brutal Duke of Cumberland; now sixty, he confessed to forty-five years of military experience. He had command of all the forces in America, and it was an indication of the importance assigned to the Ohio that he chose to lead in person the expedition

(turn to page 22)

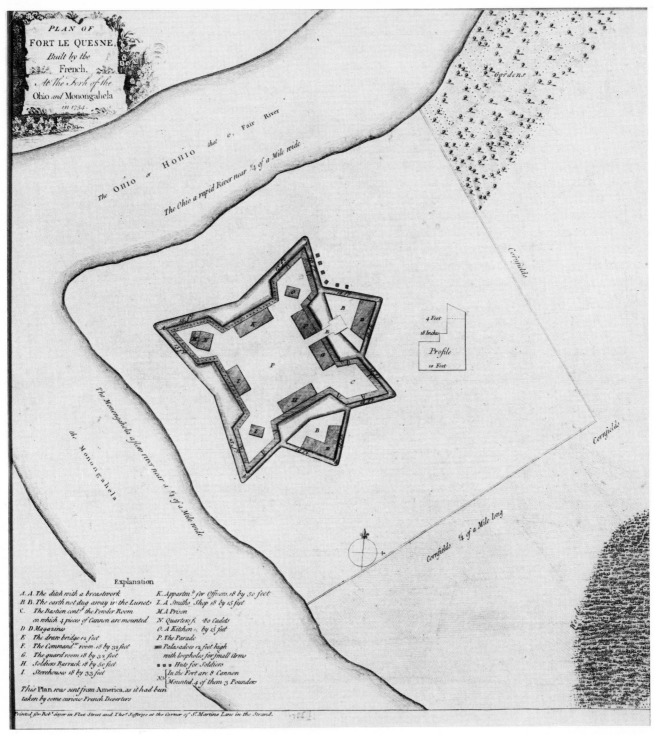

The image shows a "PLAN OF FORT LE QUESNE, Built by the French, At the Fork of the Ohio and Monongahela in 1754."

Map labels include:
- The Ohio or Hohio that is Fair River
- The Ohio a rapid River near ¼ of a Mile wide
- The Monongahela a clear river near a ⅓ of a Mile wide
- the Monongahela
- Gardens
- Cornfields
- Cornfields
- Cornfields ¼ of a Mile long
- 4 Feet / 18 Inches / Profile / 10 Feet

Explanation

A. A. The ditch with a breastwork
B. B. The earth not dug away in the Lunets
C. The Bastion cont.d the Powder Room on which 4 pieces of Cannon are mounted
D. D. Magazines
E. The draw bridge 12 feet
F. The Command.t room 18 by 32 feet
G. The guard room 18 by 32 feet
H. Soldiers Barrack 18 by 50 feet
I. Storehouse 18 by 33 feet
K. Appartm.o for Officers 18 by 50 feet
L. A Smiths Shop 18 by 15 feet
M. A Prison
N. Quarters f. 80 Cadets
O. A Kitchen 15 by 15 feet
P. The Parade
▬ Palasadoes 12 feet high with loopholes for small Arms
▪▪▪ Huts for Soldiers
In the Fort are 8 Cannon Mounted 4 of them 3 Pounders

This Plan was sent from America, as it had been taken by some curious French Deserters.

Printed for Rob.t Sayer in Fleet Street and Tho.s Jefferys at the Corner of S.t Martins Lane in the Strand.

Courtesy British Museum, London.

"THIS PLAN WAS SENT FROM AMERICA, AS IT HAD BEEN TAKEN BY SOME CURIOUS FRENCH DESERTERS," reads the legend on the drawing, which was printed in England in 1755.

Fort Duquesne, with its four protruding bastions, was protected by a massive 12-foot-high log stockade on the water, and by ravelins, ditch, and glacis on the land sides.

The Parade (P) was surrounded by five buildings. To the right from the drawbridge (E) as one entered the fort stood the commandant's house (F). To the left was the guardhouse (G). Opposite the entrance were the storerooms (I), while on the northern side were the "apartments" for officers (K). On the southern side were "barracks" for the soldiers (H).

Within three of the bastions were buildings; within the fourth was the "Powder Room on which 4 pieces of cannon are mounted" (C). In the northwest bastion were the barracks for 80 cadets (N), and next to it the prison (M); in the northeast bastion was the kitchen (O); in the southeast bastion was the blacksmith shop (L).

Though the fort made a magnificent appearance, it was of little military value. General Montcalm knew it when he wrote in June, 1756: "Fort Duquesne is not worth a straw. A freshet nearly carried it off a short time ago." The Marquis de Vaudreuil, governor of Canada, knew it when he said a year later: "Fort Duquesne in its present condition, could not resist the enemy. It is too small to lodge the garrison necessary for such a purpose. A single cannon shot would be sufficient to set it on fire, which could not be extinguished because the houses are too close together."

against Fort Duquesne. In February '55 he disembarked in Virginia with two regiments, set up camp at Alexandria, and assembled an army, equipment, and supplies. By April he was ready to advance along the Potomac into the West; on May 10 his stout expeditionary force, twenty-two hundred strong, reached the rendezvous at Fort Cumberland, where Wills Creek flows into the Potomac. For a month Braddock, with his aides, Governor Shirley and Colonel Washington (now serving with the rank of captain), whipped the army into shape, built wagons, and made ready for the invasion; and on June 10 began to march over the mountains that form the Great Divide. After a week of slow and back-breaking advance, Braddock was induced to push on toward the fort with a picked force of twelve hundred. Picture a long column, toiling painfully across the mountains and through the dense forest glades. The greatest of our historians has described the scene:

The music, the banners, the mounted officers, the troop of light cavalry, the naval detachment, the red-coated regulars, the blue-coated Virginians, the wagons and tumbrils, cannon, howitzers, and coehorns, the train of packhorses, and the droves of cattle, passed in long procession through the rippling shadows, and slowly entered the bordering forest. (turn to page 24)

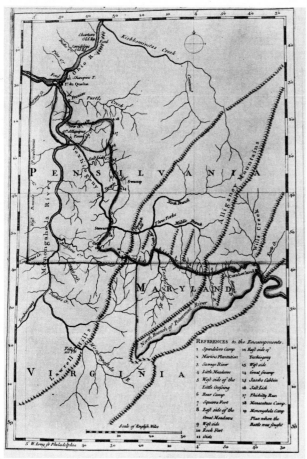

BRADDOCK'S ROUTE FROM WILLS CREEK. The march was begun on June 10, 1755. George Washington wrote in desperation: "instead of pushing on with vigor . . . they were halting to level every mole-hill and to erect bridges over every brook, by which means we were four days in getting twelve miles."

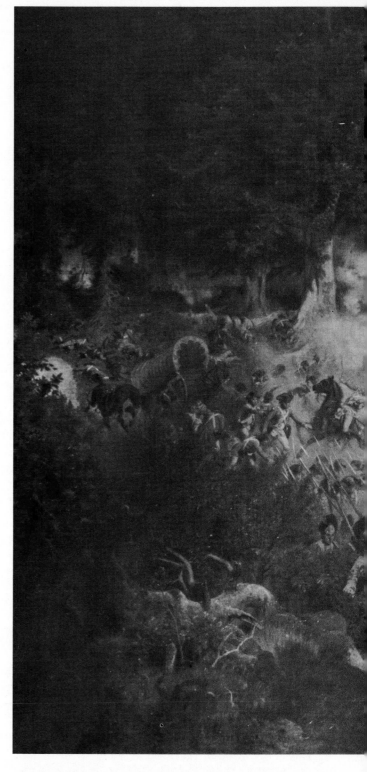

THE ATTEMPT OF THE ENGLISH TO WREST FORT General Edward Braddock (1695-1755), in command of the British forces in North America drew near Fort Duquesne with some 1400 regulars, 700 provincials, and 50 sailors, but divided his army, leaving 750 men and the heavy equipment to proceed more slowly. On the night of July 8, 1755, his soldiers encamped at a site where McKeesport is today. To avoid the narrow pass on the east bank of the Monongahela, Braddock ordered his troops to ford the river, then recross it just below Turtle Creek.

The commandant at Fort Duquesne, Claude de Contrécoeur, was aware that Braddock was moving against him. On July 8 his scouts brought him the news that the English were only eight

The imaginative painting of Braddock's defeat by Emmanuel Leutze (1816–68) was bought by the pennies of school children and given to the Carnegie Library, Braddock.

DUQUESNE ENDED IN FAILURE. IN THE BATTLE miles away. The next day he dispatched Captain Daniel Beaujeu with 250 French and 600 Indians to intercept the attackers.

The battle was fought on July 9. Captain Robert Orme, of Braddock's staff, described the scene vividly: "It was now near two o'clock, and the advanced party under Lieutenant Colonel Gage and the working party under Sir John St. Clair were ordered to march on 'till three. No sooner were the pickets upon their respective flanks, and the word given to march, but we heard an excessive quick and heavy firing in the front. The General imagining the advanced parties were very warmly attacked, . . . ordered Lieutenant Colonel Burton to reinforce them with the vanguard,

GENERAL BRADDOCK WAS MORTALLY WOUNDED. and the line to halt. . . . The advanced detachments soon gave way and fell back upon . . . Burton's detachment. . . . The General ordered the officers to endeavor to form the men, but neither entreaties nor threats could prevail. . . . When the men had fired away all their ammunition and the General and most of the officers were wounded, they by one common consent left the field, running off with the greatest precipitation."

The casualties of the English were heavy. Braddock's army had 456 dead, 421 wounded. The general himself was mortally wounded; he died four days later, uttering, according to tradition: "We shall better know how to deal with them another time."

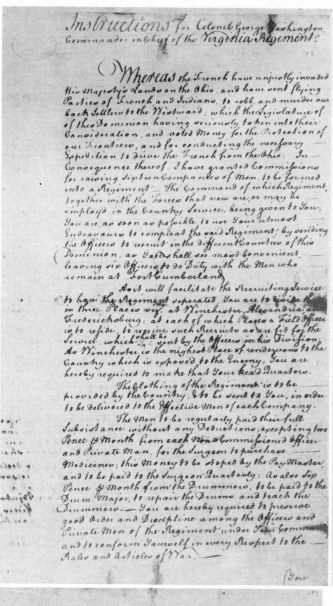

COMMANDER IN CHIEF AT 23. Four weeks after the defeat of General Braddock in July 1755, Governor Robert Dinwiddie appointed the twenty-three-year old Colonel George Washington as commander in chief of a newly formed Virginia regiment. In this three-page letter of instruction the governor spells out in detail the responsibilities of the new commander, and concludes with the sincere desire "that you will inculcate Morality and Virtue among your men, to punish Drunkenness and Swearing."

On the morning of July 9 the long column forded the Monongahela at Turtle Creek, just eight miles below the Forks. Then, at midafternoon, the French and their Indian allies struck. Dumas was there, and Charles Langlade with his Ojibways, and Ottawa chief, Pontiac, not yet a name to conjure with. It was the worst possible place, a narrow ravine along the edge of the swift river, commanded by forest thickets on both sides. There was no surprise, no ambuscade; there was confusion, mismanagement, terror, panic, and flight. The officers fought with utmost heroism, but the troops disintegrated into a mob, broke, and fled: of eighty-six officers, sixty-three were killed or wounded,

GEORGE WASHINGTON
(1732–99), fought against the
French at Fort Necessity in 1754
and again under General Braddock a year later. This portrait,
probably by Charles W. Peale,
shows him as he looked about the
time he was moving against Fort
Duquesne with General Forbes.

Painting by Charles W. Peale (1741–1827)
in the Metropolitan Museum of Art, N. Y.

HENRY BOUQUET
(1719–65), the Swiss professional
soldier who came to the New
World in the spring of 1756,
served under General Forbes on
his campaign against Fort Duquesne. Seven years later he won
the Battle of Bushy Run, which
raised the Indian siege of Fort Pitt.

Attributed to Benjamin West (1738–1820)
in the Historical Society of Pennsylvania.

Courtesy Carnegie Library, Pittsburgh.

"I IMMEDIATELY DIRECTED ALL YOUR ORDERS TO BE EXECUTED,"
writes George Washington to Colonel
Bouquet, who was organizing the English
campaign against Fort Duquesne. The letter is dated July 9, 1758—the third anniversary of General Edward Braddock's
failure to accomplish the same mission.

and of fourteen hundred privates only four hundred fifty-nine escaped unhurt. The flight itself was a shambles.
"The shocking scenes which presented themselves," wrote
Washington, "are not to be described. The dead, the
dying, the groans, the lamentations and crys along the
Road of the wounded for help . . . were enough to pierce
a heart of adamant. The gloom and horror of which was
not a little encreased by the impervious darkness occasioned by the close shade of thick woods which in places
rendered it impossible for the two guides which attended
to know when they were in, or out, of the track but by
groping on the ground with their hands." The Indians

celebrated their victory by roasting their prisoners at the
stake, then departed with their booty, leaving Fort Duquesne almost defenseless. Colonel Dunbar, left behind
at Little Meadows, might have rallied his forces and resumed the offensive; had he done so, he might have won
Fort Duquesne and immortality. Instead, he, too, gave
way to panic, burned his wagons, scattered his powder,
jettisoned his provisions, abandoned his provincial allies,
and ran all the way to Philadelphia. Braddock, shot
through the lungs, was carried in a litter to Gist's farm.
He died on the thirteenth at Orchard Camp nearby.
Washington wrote his epitaph:

Thus died a man whose good and bad qualities were intimately blended. He was brave even to a fault, and in regular Service would have done honor to his profession. His attachments were warm, his enmities were strong, and having no disguise about him, both appeared in full force. He was generous and disinterested, but plain and blunt in his manner.

"We shall know better how to deal with them another time," said Braddock with his dying breath. The prophecy was true enough, but next time was a long way off.

For three years the fleur-de-lis fluttered in the breezes over Fort Duquesne, and over a score of other forts and outposts, all the way from fogbound Isle Royale to the warm waters of the lower Mississippi; Louisbourg, Beauséjour, Quebec, Montreal, Frontenac, Niagara, Presque Isle, Detroit, Vincennes, Chartres, New Orleans, and Duquesne. For the English colonies, quarreling and divided, the situation was desperate. Oswego fell, and Fort George

(turn to page 28)

AN EYEWITNESS REPORTS THE FALL OF THE FORT. The draft of a note by Colonel Joseph Shippen, one of the British officers in the attack on Fort Duquesne, to his father on November 27, 1758, after the French blew up the fort. Shippen speculates that "the chief matter which might possibly induce them to act so infamously was their Consciousness of having basely violated all the Laws of Humanity, in encouraging their Savage allies to perpetrate so many barbarous Acts of Cruelty upon the innocent Prisoners that have during the War Fallen into their Hands."

Original drawing made specially for this book by William Libby.

THE TAKING OF FORT DUQUESNE. On November 24, 1758, Captain François le Marchand de Ligneris, the commander of Fort Duquesne, ordered the destruction of the fort. Thus, when the British regiments under their ailing General Forbes—who throughout the campaign had to be carried on a litter—reached the spot, all that they saw were the charred and burned-out walls of the bastion. The French soldiers left the forks of the Ohio without giving battle; the British took it without firing a single shot.

26

NEW YORK, December 13. 1758.

Early on Monday Morning laft, an Exprefs arrived here from the Weftward, and brought fundry Letters, which gave an Account, that General Forbes was in Poffeffion of Fort Du Quefne: One of thefe Letters fay, That the 'Monfieurs did not ftay for the Ap-'proach of our Army, but blew up the Fort, fpiked 'their Cannon, threw them into the River, and made 'the beft of their Way off, carrying with them every 'thing that was valuable, except the fpot where the 'Fort ftood." And Yefterday another Exprefs arrived here with other Letters confirming the foregoing, and directed from the Fort itfelf; the moft Particular of which, are as follows, viz.

Fort Du Quefne, Nov. 26. 1758.

"I HAVE now the Pleafure to write you from the Ruins of the Fort. On the 24th at Night, we were informed by one of our Indian Scouts, that he had difcovered a Cloud of Smoke above the place: And foon after another came in with certain Intelligence, that it was burnt and abandoned by the Enemy. We were then about 15 Miles from it. A troop of Horfe was fent forward immediately, to extinguifh the Burning; and the whole Army followed. We arrived at fix o'Clock laft Night, and found it in a great Meafure deftroyed.

There are two Forts about 20 Yards diftant; the one built with immenfe Labour; fmall, but a great deal of very ftrong Works collected into little Room, and'ftands on the Point of a narrow Neck of Land, at the Confluence of the two Rivers: It is fquare, and has two Ravelins, Gabions at each Corner, &c. The other Fort ftands on the Bank of the Allegany, in the Form of a Parallelogram, but nothing fo ftrong as the other; Several of the Outworks are lately began, and ftill unfinifhed. There are, I think, 30 Stacks of Chimneys ftanding, but the Houfes are all deftroyed. They fprung a Mine, which ruined one of their Magazines; in the other we found 16 Barrels of Ammunition, a prodigious Quantity of old Carriage Iron, Barrels of Guns, about a Cartload of Scalping Knives, &c. They went off in fo much Hafte, that they could not make quite the Havock of their Works they intended. We are told by the Indians, that they lay the Night before laft at Beaver-Creek, about 40 Miles down the Ohio from here. Whether they buried their Cannon in the River, or carried them down in their Battoes, we have not yet learnt. A Boy about 12 Years old, who has been their Prifoner about 2 Years, and made his Efcape the 2d Inftant, tells us, they had carried a prodigious Quantity of Wood into the Fort; that they had burnt five of the prifoners they took at Major Grant's Defeat, on the Parade, and deliver'd others to the Indians, who were tomahawk'd on the Spot. We found Numbers of Bodies within a Quarter of a Mile of the Fort, unburied, fo many Monuments of French Humanity! A great many Indians, moftly Delawares, were gathered together on the Ifland laft Night and this Morning, to treat with the General, and we are making Rafts to bring them over. Whether the General will think of repairing the Ruins, or leaving any of the Troops here, I have not yet learnt. Mr. Batie is appointed to preach a Thankfgiving Sermon for the Superiority of His Majefty's Arms. We left all our Tents at Loyalhanning, and every Conveniency except a Blanket and a Knapfack.

Another Letter mentions, that only about 2500 picked Men marched from Loyalhanning; that the Garrifon confifted of about 400 Men, Part of which are gone down the Ohio, 100 by Land, fuppofed to Prefque Ifle, and 200 with the Governor, Monf. Delignier, to Venango, and to ftay there till the Spring, and then return, and difpoffefs our People. That 200 of our People are to be left at Fort Du Quefne, now Pittfburgh, to keep Poffeffion of the Ground, 100 of the oldeft Virginians, the other of our oldeft Pennfylvanians; That the new raifed Levies are all difcharged; and that at the laft Affair at Loyalhanning, the French loft ten Indians in the Field, and carried off four mortally wounded: This an Indian now in our Camp informs, who was in the engagement.

Fort Du Quefne, November 30. 1778.

AFTER much Fatigue and Labour, we have at laft bro't the Artillery to this Place, and found the French had left us nothing to do, having on the 24th inftant blown up their Magazine, and burnt their Fort to the Ground. Their Indians had, either thro' fear, or to atone for their many Barbarities, deferted them; and as they depended on them to attack us in the Woods (the only chance they had of beating us,) the French judged rightly in abandoning a Fort the front of whofe Polygon is only 150 feet, and which our Shells would have deftroyed in three Days. We have fired fome Hawitzer Shells into the face of the Work, which is made of nine Inch Plank, and ramm'd between with Earth; and found that in firing but a few Hours, we muft have deftroyed the entire face. [All this, confirms the Account we receiv'd two Weeks paft, that the Fort furrender'd without Refiftance!]

HOW FORT DUQUESNE FELL. A description of the event in a December 1758 issue of the Newport, R. I., Mercury.

THE MAN WHO NAMED PITTSBURGH, General John Forbes (1710-59), commanded the British expedition against Fort Duquesne. During the campaign he was ailing and had to be carried in a hurdle slung between two horses, or on a litter carried by his men, every move causing him severe pain. After taking possession of the fort, Forbes, "looking like an emaciated old woman of eighty," was taken to Philadelphia, where he died a few weeks later.

The pastel portrait of Forbes was made by an unknown artist in 1751, and is in the possession of William Hamilton Robertson-Arkman of the Ross at Hamilton, Scotland. John O'Connor, Jr. found it there.

and Fort William Henry: the whole Mohawk Valley was uncovered and the Iroquois alliance shaken. From the headwaters of the Susquehanna to the headwaters of the Potomac and the Greenbrier, the French and their savage allies ravaged the borderlands with tomahawk and torch. From Duquesne and from Kittanning on the Allegheny, the Delawares, the Shawnees, the Mingos, the Miamis, the Wyandots swarmed out like hornets onto the hapless frontiersmen of Pennsylvania and Virginia. They butchered hundreds of men and women; they laid scores of tiny settlements in ashes; they rolled back the frontier a hundred miles, penetrating all the way to Fort Cumberland and even to Reading. "It is not possible to conceive of the situation and danger of this miserable country," wrote Washington. "Such numbers of French and Indians are all around that no road is safe." Sometimes, in desperation, the frontiersmen struck back. Thus in the summer of '56 Colonel Armstrong with three hundred men destroyed the Indian town of Kittanning; it is an interesting commentary on the esteem in which young Washington was held that the raid was officially ascribed to *"le général Washington."* Mostly the English stood sullenly on the defensive. Virginia put up scores of puny forts; the Pennsylvania Assembly bickered and quarreled; New York did nothing; even the Mother Country seemed paralyzed

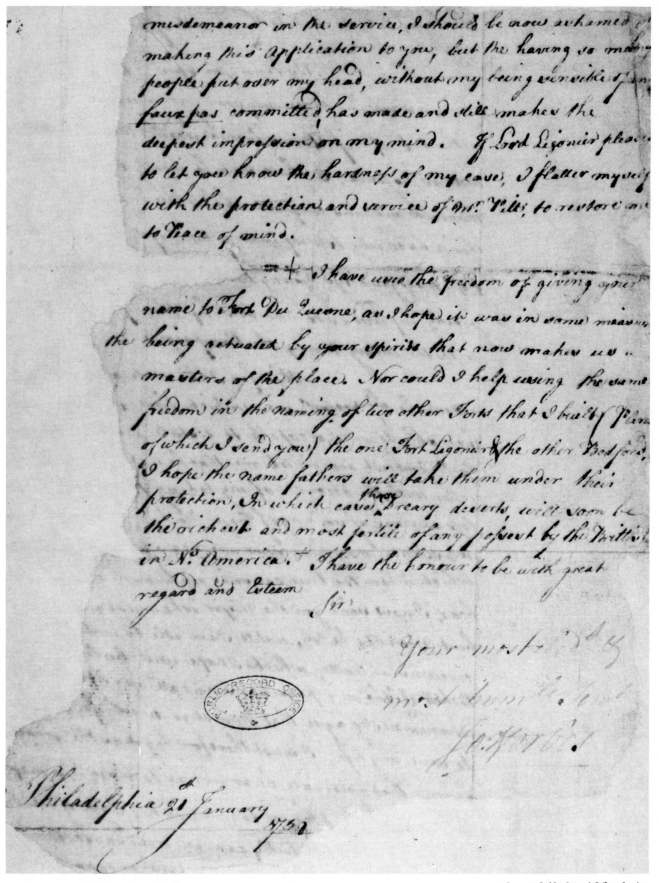

THE NAMING OF PITTSBURGH. The last page of General John Forbes' letter, dated January 21, 1759, to William Pitt, the English prime minister. Writing from Philadelphia, Forbes tells Pitt: "I have used the freedom of giving your name to Fort Duquesne, as I hope it was in some measure the being actuated by your spirits that now makes us masters of the place."

with incompetence and indecision. It was high tide for the French in America, and it seemed that at long last the dream of a great empire stretching from the St. Lawrence to the Caribbean, from the Appalachians to the Rockies and beyond, was to be realized.

And so it might have been but for two men of genius: Frederick II of Prussia, called the Great, and William Pitt. In 1756 France, eager for hegemony on the European as on the American continent, joined hands with Austria and Russia in a supreme effort to destroy Prussia. England, seeking allies against France, promptly subsidized Frederick, and thus bought the sharpest sword in Europe. While British soldiers were stumbling back through the forests of America and British sailors suffering defeat on the Atlantic and in the Mediterranean, Frederick was winning victory after victory. This curious mixture of despot and philosopher, of warrior and dilettante, audacious and resolute, implacable and resourceful, speedily proved himself one of the great soldiers of history. In '56 he conquered Saxony; in '57 he struck the Austrians at Prague and at Leuthen and routed the French at Rossbach; in '58 he shattered the Russians at Zorndorf. Even when his own army was destroyed and his capital seized he did not give up, but raised new armies and fought on until his enemies fell out among themselves and singly sued for peace.

As for England, in her dark hour she turned to the Great Commoner, William Pitt. It was, wrote Parkman, "an event pregnant with glorious consequences.... The passion for power and glory subdued in him all the sordid parts of humanity, and made the power and glory of England one with his own." Upright, steadfast, incorruptible, a statesman rather than a warrior, closer to Cato than to Machiavelli, he was unlike Frederick in everything but patriotism and courage. He was determined to humble France; he was determined to make England supreme wherever on the globe he chose to go. "I am sure that I can save this country and that nobody else can," he said, and the accuracy of the boast justified its arrogance. Almost at once he infused into his people a new courage, and into the conduct of the war a new energy.

Pitt planned to resume the offensive everywhere—in America, in Africa, in India, and on the high seas. In America the new spirit made itself felt at once. Parliament voted to pay the colonies most of the costs of the war and raised new levies for the American campaigns; Pitt decreed that hereafter colonial officers would rank with regulars. He planned to recapture Louisbourg and Ticonderoga; he recalled the incompetent Loudoun, promoted Colonel Jeffery Amherst to a major generalship and gave him command in America; he assigned to General John Forbes the task of retaking Duquesne.

A Scotsman, trained to medicine, Forbes was a veteran of the War of the Austrian Succession and the Louisbourg campaign; cautious, prudent, and slow, he was at the same time fair, resolute, and brave. He commanded a formidable army: some two thousand regulars, twenty-five hundred men from Pennsylvania, fifteen hundred from Virginia, and small segments from other colonies—altogether between six and seven thousand soldiers. Early in March '58 he began preparations for what he hoped would be a permanent advance. At the outset he faced a crucial decision: should he use the old Braddock's Road, narrow and circuitous but *there*, or should he hack a new one through the forests and over the mountains of Pennsylvania? It was a question of logistics but it had political and economic implications, for a permanent road to the Forks of the Ohio would be an immense asset to a colony. Over the anguished protests of Washington, who thought the decision fatal, General Forbes decided on the Pennsylvania road. That meant that most of the summer and the fall was given over to road building. Not until September did the road—and therefore the army—reach Bedford; it took another two months to get across the mountains to Ligonier. "Nothing now but a *miracle*," wrote Washington, "can bring this campaign to a happy issue." There would be no miracle, but the will of Pitt served as effectively.

Already the tide had turned and French power was on the ebb. The mighty fortress of Louisbourg fell to Boscawen and Wolfe; Colonel Bradstreet crossed Ontario, destroyed the French fleet on that lake, and took Frontenac; the fickle savages were sending wampum belts to the English, and the extraordinary Moravian missionary, Frederick Post, won the Delawares and the Shawnees over to peace. Fort Duquesne, too, pivot of the French empire of the West, was falling into decay. "In its present condition," wrote Governor Vaudreuil, "the Fort could not resist the enemy. It is too small to lodge the garrison necessary for such a purpose. A single cannon shot would be sufficient to set it on fire, which could not be extinguished because the houses are too close together. The garrison would then find itself in the sad necessity of abandoning the fort." There was some exaggeration here, as the bold commandant at the Forks was to prove, but the general argument was sound enough.

The fort was falling into decay; the savage allies were deserting; but there was still fight in the French. Early in September the hotheaded Major James Grant persuaded Forbes to let him take eight hundred Highlanders on a reconnaissance to the Forks. He reached the hill overlooking the fort on the morning of September 13 and, infatuated with the notion of capturing Duquesne all by himself, had his drums beat the reveille—presumably to frighten the enemy. At once the French and their Indian allies swarmed out to the attack; it was Braddock's Field over again, in miniature. One third of the British force was killed or captured, among them the hapless Grant. The Indians burned some at the stake; others they decapitated, neatly arranging the heads on stakes tucked up with kilts outside the fort.

Not until November did the main army reach Fort Ligonier; by then it was so late that the ailing Forbes decided to dig in for the winter; clearly Washington had

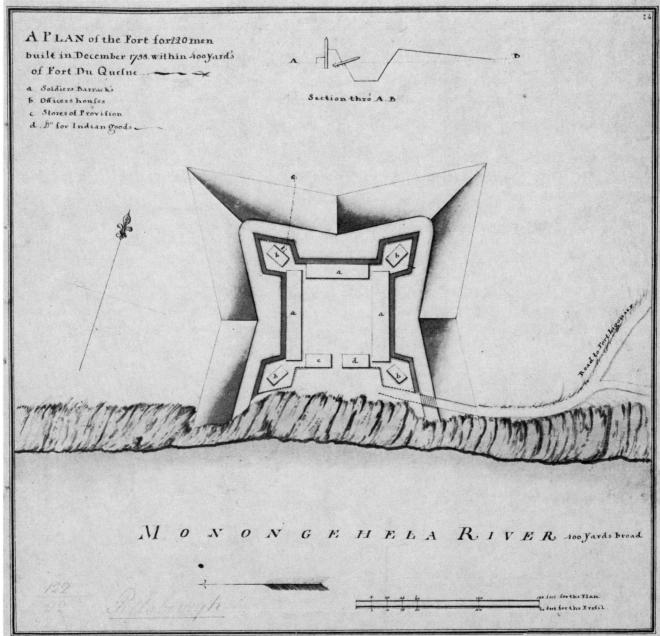

A PLAN of the Fort for 220 men built in December 1758 within 400 Yards of Fort Du Quefne

a Soldiers Barracks
b Officers houses
c Stores of Provifion
d D° for Indian goods

Section thró A.B

Road to Fort Ligonier

MONONGEHELA RIVER 400 Yards broad

Section thró A.B

THE TEMPORARY ENGLISH FORT built in the vicinity of the burned-out Fort Duquesne. Erected near the bank of the Monongahela, it left the Point area free for a more elaborate fortification. The commander of the English forces, Colonel Hugh Mercer, who had under him 200 Virginians and Pennsylvanians, anticipating a renewed French attack, was pushing forward feverishly with the building of the fort. On December 19, 1758, he reported: "We are now employed in raising a Magazine, in hanging the Gate and Raising the Bankets. I expect in four Days to have the

Place made capable of a tolerable Defence, and am fully determined to maintain the Post, or at least make it as dear a Purchase to the Enemy as Possible."

With the coming of 1759 the temporary fort, designed by Harry Gordon, was pretty nearly completed. By then 280 men lived inside its walls; in February this number, with the arrival of a detachment of Highlanders and Royal Americans, increased to 400. But for Colonel Mercer this was still not enough—he asked for more troops—he wanted at least 1000, preferably 1500, so that if the French de-

cided to attack, the fort should be able to withstand it.

General Jeffery Amherst, the commander of the British forces in America, was not worried. He was confident that the French would not be able to move against Mercer's men, and that there would be plenty of time to build the formidable new fort without being molested by the enemy. His opinion proved to be right; no French troops attacked the temporary fort. "Mercer's Fort" stood for a year and a half, proving that the position of England at the forks was impregnable.

been right. Then spies brought word that Fort Duquesne was ripe for the picking. Unable to feed his voracious Indian allies, Ligneris had sent them home with their booty; only a few hundred defenders were left, and they were

at the point of starvation. The weather was frightful; the rain and snow incessant, the roads had turned to mud, but Forbes determined to push on. Washington went ahead, cutting a road to the fort; on the 24th he reached

(turn to page 34)

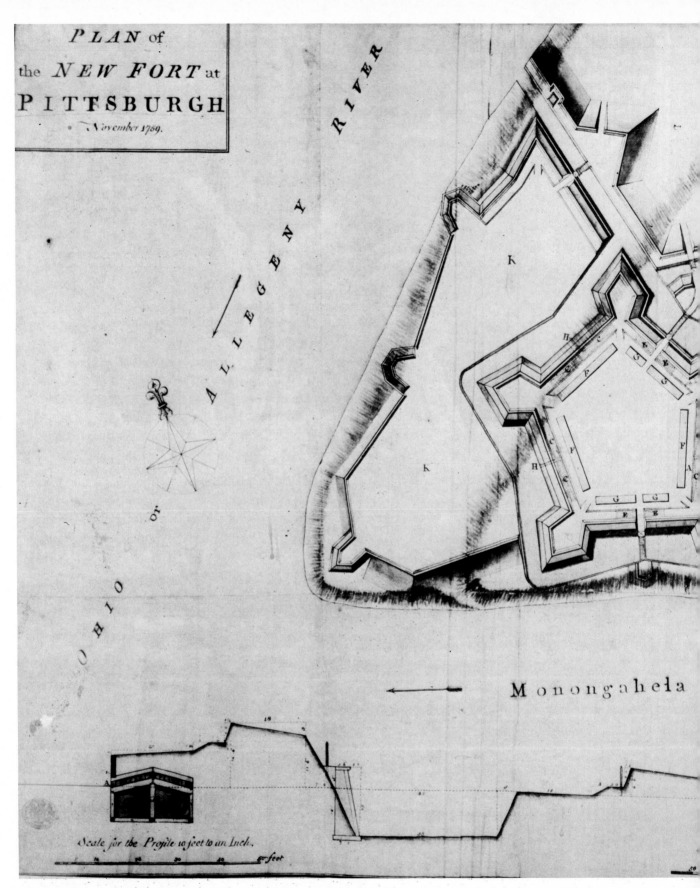

PLAN of
the *NEW FORT* at
PITTSBURGH
November 1759.

ALLEGENY RIVER

OHIO or ALLEGENY

K

K

H

Monongahela

Scale for the Profile 10 feet to an Inch.

A CONTEMPORARY PLAN of the fort. Fort Pitt was the most elaborate English bastion on the American frontier. Within the walls the area measured over two acres, while the entire fort, with all its out-works, occupied 17½ acres.

Toward the land the fort's 15-foot-high earth ramparts were supported by walls of brick and stone. Brigadier General John Stanwix, who succeeded General John Forbes in command at the forks and who directed the construction of Fort Pitt, reported to General Jeffrey Amherst, commander of the British forces in North America, in September 1759 that his bas-

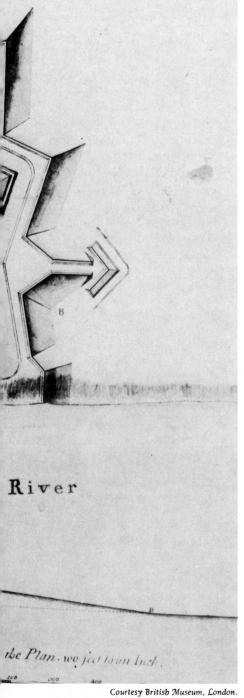

Explanation.

C . *Casemates under the Curtains.*
D . *Powder Magazines.*
E . *Laboratories for the Artillery.*
F . *Barracks for 700 Men.*
G . *Barracks for Officers.*
H . *Sally Ports from the Casemates.*
K . *Low Town.* L. *The Guard .*

River

the Plan. 100 feet to an Inch .

FORT PITT

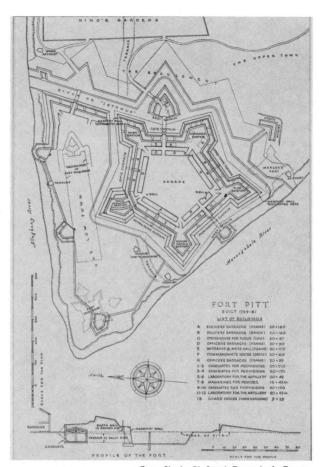

A MODERN RECONSTRUCTION OF FORT PITT by architect Charles M. Stotz, the indefatigable student of early forts.

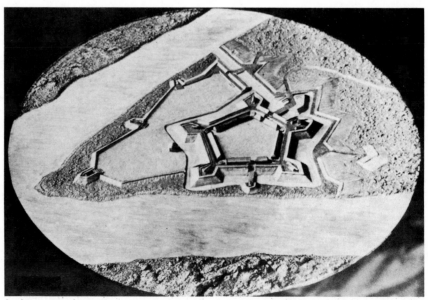

tion "will be of Sufficient Strength and every way adequate to the great importance of its several Objects," the main among them to secure for the English the undisputed possession of the Ohio territory.

A MODERN MODEL OF FORT PITT in the Historical Society of Western Pennsylvania shows the fort at the junction of the Monongahela and Allegheny rivers.

the heights overlooking the Forks. The next morning the army marched down to the Forks to find the fort in ashes and the enemy fled. Duquesne had fallen without a shot! The next day a Presbyterian divine, the Reverend Charles Beatty, preached a thanksgiving sermon. General Forbes came in, borne on a litter; he found strength to dictate a letter to William Pitt. It was dated:

Pittsbourgh, 27 Novem. 1758

Sir, I do myself the honour of acquainting you that it has pleased God to crown His Majesty's Arms with Success over all His Enemies upon the Ohio. . . .

Concluding his letter in Philadelphia on January 21, 1759, Forbes wrote:

"I have used the freedom of giving your name to Fort Du Quesne as I hope it was in some measure the being actuated by your spirits that now makes us Masters of the place. Nor could I help using the same freedom in the naming of two other Forts that I built, the one Fort Ligonier & the other Bedford. I hope the name Fathers will take them under their Protection. In which case these dreary deserts will soon be the richest and most fertile of any possest by the Brittish in No. America.

So, too, thought an anonymous correspondent to the *Pennsylvania Gazette:*

Blessed be God, the long look'd for Day is arrived, that has now fixed us on the Banks of the Ohio with great Propriety called La

THE EARLIEST PITTSBURGH ACCOUNT BOOK that is preserved is the ledger of trader George Allen, who had been appointed as Indian agent in March 1759. The entries for June of that year, less than half a year after the French burned and destroyed Fort Duquesne, show that Allen had a prosperous business.

Belle Rivière, in the quiet and peaceable Possession of the finest and most fertile Country of America, lying in the happiest Climate in the Universe. This valuable Acquisition lays open to all his Majesty's subjects a Vein of Treasure which, if rightly managed, may prove richer than the Mines of Mexico, the Trade with the Numerous Nations of Western Indians: It deprives our Enemies of the Benefits they expected from their deep laid Schemes, and breaks asunder the Chain of Communication betwixt Canada and Louisiana, a Chain that threatened this Continent with Slavery. . . ."

Within a few weeks poor Forbes went back to die, and Colonel Hugh Mercer took over as commandant; he had fought with Prince Charlie at Culloden; he was to fight alongside Washington and to die, heroically, at Princeton. Most of the immense army that had conquered the Forks returned home, and Mercer was left with less than three hundred men to guard the strategic point, overawe the Indians, and rebuild the fort and the village. Marauding bands of Indians still terrorized the frontier—even Fort Ligonier was besieged for a short time—but with the fall of Niagara in July '59, the French abandoned all their outposts east of Detroit, and something like peace returned to the war-torn borderlands. That summer, and the next, "King" Croghan presided over immense Indian conferences—as many as one thousand Indians were there in 1760—designed to re-establish trade and to get back prisoners. As the soldiers hurriedly put up log cabins to shelter them against the storms and cold of winter, the traders and the trappers returned. Soon the fur trade was flourishing with all its old vigor; had suffered during the years of war, and the market was eager. George Allen, who ran the provincial store at Pittsburgh, kept a record of the furs brought in that first year. There were 15,000 skins, to the value of over 4000 pounds sterling: only 658 were the prized beaver; 300 were bear; mink—it is interesting to note—were valued at a shilling each!

Along with Allen was another storekeeper, James Kenny; he was Pittsburgh's first diarist, and he had an eye for the ordinary and transcribed it with austere faithfulness. Thus, for 1759:

August 20th: Croghan has a black eye this morning, and I have been informed, that he was drunk and fought with ye Indians, and that Teedyuscung gave him ye black eye. . . . This day are come a party from Virginia of great Sutlers, brought some cattle and sheep.
24th. They have set to build a saw mill on ye other side of ye main river, down in sight of ye Fort, being on ye South side, and there are 9 saws going in one pit at ye old fort.
27th. This day came here about 100 horses loaded with oats chiefly. . . . I measured a fish, being a Pike, and it was four feet long and weighed 20 lbs. ye inwards being cleaned out.
29th. This day ye General arrived here witih his Train and set of music — he was very plainly dressed and seems not proud.

This was General John Stanwix come to carry out Pitt's order to build a fort "strong enough to assure the undisputed possession of the Ohio." He brought with him army engineers and skilled workmen from the East, and soon the Forks was a hive of industry: sawmills, quarries, clay pits, tan yards, coal mines, forges—a faint anticipation of the Pittsburgh that was to come. By March 1760

(turn to page 38)

ANOTHER PAGE FROM ALLEN'S ACCOUNT BOOK.

Pittsburgh. Anno, 1759.

Contra ... Cr:

				£	s	d
June	30th	By 246. Fallskins ... Wt. 1042¼ ... @ sundry prices ...	£	77	14	4½
	ditto	115. Summer do. ... 279½ ... @ 20/7 p^r lb		23	5	10
	.	24. Shav'd do. ... 67¼ ... @ 20 Do.		5	12	1
	.	4. Indian drest do. ... 3¾ ... @ 3/ do.		—	11	3
	.	14. Parchment do. ... 15 ... @ diff^t. Prices		1	17	11
	.	32. Bears do. ... @ Various prices ...		7	10	6
	.	5. Beaver do. ... Wt. 6½ ... @ 7/6 lb		2	8	9
	.	171. Racoons do. ... @ sundry prices ...		15	5	—
	.	11. Fox's do. ... @ do.		1	—	—
	.	13. Cats do. ... @ do.		1	5	6
	.	3. Otter Do. ... @ 6/ Each		—	18	—
	.	1. Fisher do. ...		0	3	6
	.	1. Martin do. ...		—	3	—
	.	By Cash, of Sundry Indians to this Day		26	5	7
		Profit & Loss ... this Month			—	10
			£	164	2	1½

Contra ... Cr:

				£	s	d
July	31st	By 379. Summerskins ... Wt. 1011 lb ... @ sundry prices ...	£	85	5	6
	ditto	53. Fall do. ... 184 ... @ 1/6 p^r lb		13	16	0
	.	96. Shav'd do. ... 247¼ @ 1/8 do.		20	12	1
	.	20. Indian drest do. ... 23¼ @ 3/ do.		3	9	9
	.	14. Parchment do. ... 17½ @ 2/6 do.		2	3	9
	.	62. Bears do. ... @ Various prices		10	19	1
	.	92. Beaver do. ... Wt. 149¼ lb @ do.		55	16	6½
	.	146. Racoons do. ... @ do.		12	0	9
	.	6. Fox's do. ... @ 2/ Each		—	12	0
	.	9. Cats do. ... @ diff^t. prices		—	17	6
	.	3. Otters do. ... @ 6/ Each		0	18	—
	.	2. Fishers do. ...		—	7	0
	.	1. Wolf do. ...		—	2	—
	.	2. Elks ...		0	16	—
	.	By Cash, of Sundry Indians to this Day ...		64	17	5
		Profit & Loss ... this Month		—	—	6¼
			£	272	13	10¾

18.
1761
8 mo 6

I receiv'd a Letter from Frederick Post dated ye 27th of last month at Tuscorawas Town, in which he informs me that the Indians are not all willing to deliver up ye Prisoners as yet — & that he has hard living amongst them any Provis'n they have being so dear a Bushell Corn being forty Shillings one quart Milk, two Shill: & Six pence One Pound Butter Ten Shill: & for washing one Shirt Two Shill: & Six Pence & Venison ye . th pence, he also adds that he hops of being of Service amongst them, & signifies that he was in fear some time agoe when ye Beaver took Six Keggs Rum there & they were Drunke Six Days, —
that they talk of going to Philad a soon to hold a treaty there

7th Had some little Trade to Day tho, trade is very dull here now —

8th Was Invited to a Barbacue of Tortle this Day by Levy ye Jew & Crafford ye Trader but had no appetite for ye feast to being held on ye Island, & they came over about dusk like so many Drunken Indians —

9 My Namesake Indian, returned from his Hunt last Night having brought thirty Skins with him & deal't them with me this Day, had some more of some Shawanas being brought to me & Jno: Owen, who is desirous to serve ye Commiss:

10. The Indians that deal at our Store, often want to stay in ye House at Nights, while they remain here, & often wants Victuals, they also want to bring Sole Squas to lie with at Night, which I object against letting them know that they shall bring none such to Sleep in our House, & having shut out two such Squas last Night they kept throwing Stones on ye House & Door after we went to Bed, untill we went out & threatend them away, so many Roberies Commited here at Nights that all Noise tends to keep one from Sleep & ye Sleeps together that I got but Little Sleep &c

Courtesy Historical Society of Pennsylvania, Philadelphia.

JOURNAL OF JAMES KENNY, written during the years of 1759, 1761, and 1763, gives a vivid picture of Pittsburgh's early life. Kenny, a Chester County Quaker, came to the forks in 1759, but left soon thereafter. He returned in 1761 as an assistant to Josiah Davenport, the Indian agent at Fort Pitt. The entries in his diary are highly entertaining. One, dated August 10, 1761 reads: "The Indians that deal at our Store, often want to Stay in ye House at Nights . . . & often wants Victuals, they also want to bring . . . Squas to lie with at Night, which I Object against letting them know that they shall bring none such to Sleep in Our House."

Summer in ye South East Corner ye Roof being now aputing
on, having fine Steps at ye Bon of Hewn free Stone, a Cellar
all under it, at ye Back Side of ye Barracks opens ye Doors
of ye Magazines Vaults & Dungeons lying under ye great
Banks of Earth thrown out of ye Great Trinches all Round
in these are kept ye Stores of Amunition &c & Prisoners
that are to be tried for thier Lives, in these Vaults are no light
but as they carry Lanthorns, on ye South East Bastion stands
a High Poal like a Mast & top Mast to Hoist ye flag on
which is Hoisted on every first Day of ye Week from about
Eleven to One oClock & on State Days &c there are three
Wells of Water wall'd in ye fort, & a Square of Clear Ground
in ye inside of about 2 Acres.

20. I have been Informd by a Young Man that was orderd by ye Commanding Officer Collonel Bouquet this Sumer to Number all ye
Dwelling Houses without ye Fort marking the number on each
Door that there was above one Hundred Houses but ye Highest
number I have seen to take notice of by taley out there is 150 Housses
these being ye Inhabitants of Pittsburgh, where two years ago I
have seen all ye Houses that were without ye little fort they had
then, thrown Down, only One, which stands yet, also two that
was within that little fort is now standing being ye Hospital
now, all ye rest being Built since, which if ye Place continues
to Increase near this manner it must soon be very large
which seems likely to me,

21 As to ye Government of ye Place at present ye Chief Laws have been
Out by ye Generals Orders, which are Viz 1th that all Subjects may by
applying to ye Chief Engineer Build Houses, but none to Sell or Rent
any, that no person Shall buy of ye Indians Horses nor Bells &c

Courtesy Historical Society of Pennsylvania, Philadelphia.

ANOTHER PAGE OF KENNY'S JOURNAL, with entries from
November 19 to 21, 1761. On November 20, Kenny notes that
a "Young Man" had been ordered by "Collonel" Bouquet "to
Number all ye Dwelling Houses without ye Fort," and records
that there was above one Hundred Houses." (In Colonel Henry
Bouquet's papers the number of houses is given as 160 and the
number of people living in Pittsburgh, including the soldiers, is
given as 332.) Kenny makes the prediction that "if ye Place continues to Increase near this manner it must soon be very large
which seems likely to me," a prophecy borne out by the future.

the shell was up; in another year the fort was completed and inevitably named Fort Pitt. It was a formidable affair, a veritable Louisbourg of the West. In shape it was a somewhat irregular pentagon. It had high walls, those nearest the river of earth, those facing the land of brick—over a million bricks went into its making. A moat which encircled it made its eight acres virtually an island, reached only by drawbridges and bastions. The bastions nearest the Point were known as the Monongahela and the Ohio, while guarding the main entrance on the east was the Grenadier bastion. The other two bastions bore the names of The Music and The Flag; the latter boasted a "High Poal" from which fluttered the Union Jack.

A census taken in 1760 discovered a settlement of 146 "houses" and 36 "huts," but a population of only 149—88 men, 29 women, 18 girls and 14 boys; clearly the garrison was not included in the enumeration. A count in the next year disclosed a population of 332: this number probably included some of the garrison. When at the outbreak of Indian hostilities two years later Captain Ecuyer ordered all whites into the fort, the total who found refuge there was no less than 630: 330 men, 104 women and 196 children; the frontier settlement was doing well on children!

It was well that Fort Pitt was finished, for it was needed. Already by 1762 the Indians were restless and ready to send around the war belt. They had—so they thought—grievances. Amherst had stopped the customary presents—a gesture of economy that drove both George Croghan and Robert Rogers from the Indian service. With French competition all but eliminated, many of the traders took merciless advantage of the Indians. Rogers described it in his tragedy, *Ponteach*:

> A thousand Opportunities present
> To take Advantage of their Ignorance;
> But the great Engine I employ is Rum, . . .
> That cooling Draught well suits their scorching Throats.
> Their Fur and Peltry come in quick Return;
> My Scales are honest, but as well contriv'd,
> That one small Slip will turn Three Pounds to One;
> Which they, poor silly Souls! Ignorant of Weights
> And Rules of Balancing, do not perceive.

Far more serious was the invasion of the Indian hunting lands by land speculators and settlers. "For two years past," wrote Colonel Bouquet, "these lands have been run over by a number of Vagabonds, who under pretense of hunting, were making Settlements in several parts of them, of which the Indians made grievous and repeated Complaints." Bouquet forbade settlement in the west but in vain; in vain, too, solemn treaties with the Indians, the laws of the colonial assemblies and the proclamations of the Royal Government. "I have learned from experience," wrote Governor Dunmore, "that the established Authority of any government in America, and the policy of government at home, are both inefficient to restrain the Americans; and that they do and will remove as their avidity and restlessness incite them. . . . Wandering about seems engrafted in their Nature; and it is a weakness incident to it that they should forever imagine the Lands further off are Still better than those upon which they are already Settled."

The Conspiracy of Pontiac, as the Indian uprising of 1763-64 is traditionally and somewhat erroneously known,
(turn to page 40)

Painted specially for this book by Stephen James Kubisak.

THE FLOODED POINT. On January 8, 1762, James Kenny noted in his *Journal* "that ye Ice broke up this Evening & ye River Rose very fast." Some of the cabins near the fort were almost washed away. Next day the flood got so bad that "by Noon ye Street fronting our door" was under water. By dusk the "water got to power into our Celler increasing with ye Same progress as at first ye Celler having no Wall but mud banks we conclud'd to shut all ye Doors...& make our escape..."

Original drawing made specially for this book by William Libby.

PREPARING FOR INDIAN ATTACK.
When in the summer of 1763 Chief Pontiac made a last attempt to clear the land of the English, the commander of Fort Pitt ordered the people in the surroundings to take shelter within the fort.

The siege lasted for five days. Simon Ecuyer, who commanded Fort Pitt, noted that the Indians "threw fire arrows to burn our works, but . . . only two arrows came into the fort, one of which had the insolence to make free with my left leg."

The besiegers withdrew when they learned that Colonel Henry Bouquet was on the way with a large force. On August 5 and 6 in the Battle of Bushy Run Bouquet's army defeated the Indians. Never again had Fort Pitt to fear their attack.

affected Pittsburgh briefly but powerfully. The Ottawa chief, Pontiac, had persuaded most of the tribes north of the Ohio to join in a concerted attack on English forts and settlements; it was perhaps the most formidable of many desperate and hopeless efforts to drive the English back over the mountains. The first blows came early in May 1763; within a few months every western fort but Detroit, Niagara, and Pitt had fallen to the Indians; hundreds of soldiers and settlers had been butchered; and the frontier was once more ebbing back to the East.

A Swiss soldier of fortune, Captain Simeon Ecuyer, was in command at Fort Pitt: a braver or more resourceful soldier could not have been found. He realized at once the peril to which the little outpost was exposed and moved to overcome it. First he called on General Amherst for help. That lordly soldier did not take the Indian danger seriously and wrote somewhat condescendingly that "I am persuaded this alarm will end in nothing more than a rash attempt at what the Senecas have been threatening and which we have heard for some time past. . . . The post of Fort Pitt, or any of the others commanded by officers, can

certainly never be in danger from such a wretched enemy as the Indians are, at this time, if the garrisons do their duty." Amherst did, however, start Colonel Bouquet westward with a small force; meantime he proposed a more effective if somewhat slower method of dealing with the savages. "Could it not be contrived," he wrote Bouquet, "to send the *Small Pox* among those disaffected tribes of Indians? We must on this occasion use every stratagem in our powers to reduce them." And, again: "You will do well to try to inoculate the Indians by means of blankets, as well as to try every other method that can serve to extirpate this execrable race."

Meantime Ecuyer put the fort in shape for a prolonged siege. He leveled all the outlying houses; gathered all the whites of the neighborhood within the protection of the ramparts; accumulated immense stores of food and supplies: 100,000 pounds of flour, 300 barrels of beef and 66 of pork, 332 bushels of salt, 238 oxen and 76 sheep, and even 1000 pounds of butter! "I believe that I am surrounded by Indians," he wrote; "I neglect nothing to give them a good reception." He gave them so warm a recep-

(turn to page 42)

Painted specially for this book by Wilma Wellens.

THE ENGLISH TRADING POST in the confines of Fort Pitt to which the Indians brought their furs and venison to exchange them for clothing, powder, shot, vermilion, brooches, ribbons, mirrors, knives, buttons, and ornaments.

Exchange prices were reckoned in bucks—a buck was one fall male deerskin.

For one buck one got two does, or two spring bucks, or six raccoons, or four foxes. For a blanket one had to give four bucks, for a tin kettle three bucks, for a shirt two bucks, while four small knives or a pair of stockings cost a single buck. But bucks were even then hard to come by.

Fort Pitt . . . . May 13th 1765 .

Gunpowder in Compy . . . . Dr

To George Croghan Esq: his Acco proper

For 200 lb . . . . . a £20 ⅌ Ct . . 40 .

George Croghan Esqr Dr to Sale of Goods
Inv? Cost, for the Crown . viz:

450 lb Lead . . . . . . a 83/ ⅌ Ct . . 18 . 15 . 9
10 Strouds, Deliv. Mr McKee . a 22/6 . 11 . 5 . —
1 Large Arm band . . . . 1 . 15 . —
2 Strouds . . . . a 22/6 . 2 . 5 . —
2 Shirts . . . . a 12/ . 1 . 4 . —
1 French Matchcoat . . . . 12 . —
1 m Black Wampum . a . . . 2 . 5 . —   *38 . 1 . 9*

Expence Acco: . . . . Dr

To Cash paid Capt:n Will:m Long . . . . 1 . 10 . —

14th
George Croghan Esqr Dr to Sale of Goods Inv: Cost
for the Crown . viz:
4 Beaver Traps . . . a 30/ . . . . 6 . —
3 Ruffled Shirts . . a 14/ . . . . 2 . 2 . —
1 half do . do . . a 12/ . . . . 12 . —
15 200 White Wampum a 30/ . 22 . 16 . —   *31 . 10 . —*

Cash Dr to Sundries . . . viz:
To Doctor Anthony . . . . 3 . 6
To Major Smallman . . . . 9 . 6   *. 13 .*

George Croghan Esq:r Dr to Sale of Goods Inv: Cost
for the Crown . viz:
2 Gun Locks . . . . . a 4/6 . . . . 9 . —
1 Small pen knife . . . . 6 .   *9 . 6*

Cash . . . . Dr
To John Reed . . . . 1 . — . —

Major Smallman Dr to Sale March 12th &c

THE ACCOUNT BOOK OF GEORGE CROGHAN, one of the legendary figures of the Ohio Country and the greatest of the Pennsylvania traders. Croghan, a true Irishman, was with George Washington in the battle of Fort Necessity, served under General Braddock, and marched with General Forbes' troops to Fort Duquesne. As Deputy Superintendent of Indian Affairs with headquarters at Fort Pitt, he bought furs, sold goods, made and lost money. He was an attractive man, hot-tempered, a lover of wine and women.

tion that the Indians desisted from their first attacks and tried diplomacy instead. Ecuyer countered with stories of immense armies marching over the mountains and then— so Captain William Trent tells us in his journal:

June 24th. The Turtles Heart a principal Warrior of the Delawares and Mamaltee a Chief came within a small distance of the Fort. . . . They made a Speech letting us know that . . . Ligonier was destroyed . . . that out of regard to us they had prevailed on 6 Nations (not to) attack us but give us time to go down the Country and they desired we would set off immediately. The Commanding Officer thanked them, let them know that we had everything we wanted, that we could defend it against all the Indians in the Woods. . . . Out of our regard to them we gave them two Blankets and a Handkerchief out of the Small Pox Hospital. I hope it will have the desired effect.

Desultory fighting continued all through July; at the end there was a major attack, which the defenders beat off without too much trouble. Meantime Colonel Bouquet had reached Ligonier and was pushing on to the beleaguered fort. At Bushy Run, some twenty-five miles to the east of the Forks, the Indians tried to surprise and destroy him as they had destroyed Braddock. Bouquet was made of sterner stuff, and he was, besides, a veteran of backwoods warfare; it was the Indians who were outwitted, thrown into confusion, and destroyed. Let Captain Trent tell how the news reached the fort:

August 10th. at Break of day in the Morning, Miller, who was sent Express the 5th with two others came in from Col. Boquet, who he left at the Nine Mile Run, he brings an Account that the Indians engaged our Troops for two days, that our People beat them off. About 10 o'clock a detachment from the Garrison under the Command of Capt. Philips marched out to meet the Troops and returned about 2 o'Clock have joined the Col. at Bullocks Hill. The following is the best Account I have been able to learn of the Action which happened the 5th about a Mile beyond Bushy Run. Our Advanced Guard discovered the Indians where they were lying in Ambush and fired on them about 3 o'Clock in the Afternoon. This brought on a General Engagement which continued the rest of the next day and night. Our People behaved with the greatest bravery as well as the Indians who often advanced within a few steps of our People. The Action continued doubtful till the Enemy by a stratagem was drawn into an Ambuscade when they were entirely routed, leaving a great many of their People dead on the Spott.

Sullenly the Indians withdrew from the Forks. Never again would they threaten Fort Pitt.

With the collapse of Pontiac's "conspiracy" in the summer of 1763, two of the three grand themes that we associate with the early history of Pittsburgh reached their climax. The struggle for the continent had ended with the victory of the English; the contest between red men and white, with the defeat of the Indians. As Francis Parkman so eloquently says, "England had crushed her hereditary foe; and France, in her fall, had left to irretrievable ruin the savage tribes to whom her policy and self-interest had lent a transient support." Now the third theme opens in full strength: the westward movement of the American people, the transplanting of civilization across the Appalachians and into the great interior.

Gradually peace returned to the stricken borderlands. As the Indians put away their tomahawks and scalping knives, dazed prisoners, released from an incredible captivity, stumbled back through the Forks on their way to their old homes; refugees from years of frontier wars moved back to their abandoned farms; and new settlers poured in by the hundred. Swiftly Pittsburgh was metamorphosed from a military to a trading post: in just a few

(turn to page 44)

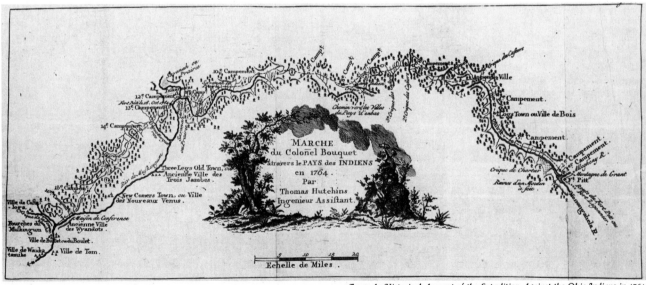

From An Historical Account of the Expedition Against the Obio Indians in 1764.

BOUQUET'S MARCH from Fort Pitt to the forks of the Muskingum in the heart of Indian country, where Coshocton, Ohio, now stands. In 1764, Colonel Henry Bouquet, who the year before had lifted the siege against Fort Pitt with his victory at Bushy Run, led an expedition to pacify the rebellious Indians. He marched 130 miles with 1500 men, built a fort and a treaty house, and forced the savages to agree to peace and the surrender of prisoners. This campaign, during which not one shot was fired, made the area safe for English occupation.

The contemporary map shows the army's route. It may have been drawn by Dr. William Smith (1727–1803) from a survey by Captain Thomas Hutchins (1730–89), a military engineer and geographer of the United States, for *An Historical Account of the Expedition Against the Ohio Indians in 1764.* The account, including the map, was translated into French—therefore the French names.

BY THE HONOURABLE

JOHN PENN, Esquire,

Governor and Commander in Chief of the Province of *Pennsylvania*, and Counties
of *New-Castle*, *Kent* and *Suffex*, on *Delaware*,

A PROCLAMATION.

WHEREAS I have received Information that his Excellency the Earl of *Dunmore*, Governor-General in and
over His Majesty's Colony of *Virginia*, hath lately issued a very extraordinary Proclamation, setting forth,
" That the rapid Settlement made on the West of the *Alleghaney* Mountains by His Majesty's Subjects,
" within the Course of these few Years, had become an Object of real Concern to His Majesty's Interest in that
" Quarter;——that the Province of *Pennsylvania* had unduly laid Claim to a very valuable and extensive Quantity of His
" Majesty's Territory, and the executive Part of that Government, in Consequence thereof, had most arbitrarily and
" unwarrantably proceeded to abuse the laudable Adventurers in that Part of His Majesty's Dominions, by many
" oppressive and illegal Measures in Discharge of their imaginary Authority, and that the antient Claim laid to that
" Country by the Colony of *Virginia*, founded in Reason, upon Pre-occupancy, and the general Acquiescence of all
" Persons, together with the Instruction he had lately received from His Majesty's Servants, ordering him to take that
" Country under his Administration;——and as the evident Injustice manifestly offered to His Majesty, by the immode-
" rate Strides taken by the Proprietaries of *Pennsylvania*, in Prosecution of their wild Claim to that Country, demanded
" an immediate Remedy, he did thereby, in His Majesty's Name, require and command all His Majesty's Subjects, West
" of the *Laurel-Hill*, to pay a due Respect to his said Proclamation, thereby strictly prohibiting the Execution of any Act
" of Authority on Behalf of the Province of *Pennsylvania*, at their Peril, in that Country; but, on the contrary, that a
" due Regard and entire Obedience to the Laws of His Majesty's Colony of *Virginia*, under his Administration, should
" be observed, to the End that Regularity might ensue, and a just Regard to the Interest of His Majesty in that Quarter,
" as well as to His Majesty's Subjects, might be the Consequence." AND WHEREAS, although the Western
Limits of the Province of *Pennsylvania* have not been settled by any Authority from the Crown, yet it has been sufficiently
demonstrated, by Lines accurately run by the most skilful Artists, that not only a great Tract of Country West of the
Laurel-Hill, but *Fort-Pitt* also, are comprehended within the Charter Bounds of this Province, a great Part of which
Country has been actually settled, and is now held, under Grants from the Proprietaries of *Pennsylvania*, and the Juris-
diction of this Government has been peaceably exercised in that Quarter of the Country, till the late strange Claim set up
by the Earl of *Dunmore*, in Behalf of His Majesty's Colony of *Virginia*, founded, as his Lordship is above pleased to say,
" in Reason, Pre-occupancy, and the general Acquiescence of all Persons;" which Claim to Lands within the said Charter
Limits must appear still the more extraordinary, as His most gracious Majesty, in an Act passed the very last Session of
Parliament, " for making more effectual Provision for the Government of the Province of *Quebec*," has been pleased, in
the fullest Manner, to recognize the Charter of the Province of *Pennsylvania*, by expressly referring to the same, and bind-
ing the said Province of *Quebec* by the Northern and Western Bounds thereof: Wherefore there is the greatest Reason to
conclude, that any Instructions the Governor of *Virginia* may have received from His Majesty's Servants, to take that
Country under his Administration, must be founded on some Misrepresentation to them respecting the Western Extent of
this Province. In Justice therefore to the Proprietaries of the Province of *Pennsylvania*, who are only desirous to secure
their own undoubted Property from the Encroachment of others, I HAVE thought fit, with the Advice of the Council, to issue this my Proclamation, hereby requiring all Persons, West of the *Laurel-Hill*, to retain their Settlements as
aforesaid made under this Province, and to pay due Obedience to the Laws of this Government; and all Magistrates, and
other Officers, who hold Commissions or Offices under this Government, to proceed as usual in the Administration of
Justice, without paying the least Regard to the said recited Proclamation, until His Majesty's Pleasure shall be known in
the Premises; at the same Time strictly charging and enjoining the said Inhabitants and Magistrates to use their utmost
Endeavours to preserve Peace and good Order.

GIVEN under my Hand, and the Great Seal of the said Province, at Philadelphia,
the Twelfth Day of October, *in the Year of our Lord One Thousand Seven Hundred
and Seventy-four, and in the Fourteenth Year of the Reign of our Sovereign Lord*
GEORGE *the Third, by the Grace of* GOD, *of* Great-Britain, France *and*
Ireland, *King, Defender of the Faith, and so forth,*

JOHN PENN.

By His Honour's Command,
JOSEPH SHIPPEN, junior, Secretary.

GOD Save the KING.

PHILADELPHIA: PRINTED BY HALL AND SELLERS. 1774.

Courtesy Darlington Memorial Library, Pittsburgh.

AFTER VIRGINIA PROCLAIMED her title to the territory west of the Alleghenies, John Penn issued this counterproclamation on October 12, 1774.

It was in January of that year that Dr. John Connolly arrived at Fort Pitt and in the name of Virginia's governor, Lord Dunmore, took possession of it. The Penn-sylvania authorities were not willing to tolerate such interference; they arrested Connolly. But when they released him on bail, he returned with a 150-man armed force and reclaimed the fort.

In response to Lord Dunmore's assertion, John Penn stated in his proclamation that "although the Western Limits of the Province of Pennsylvania have not been settled by any Authority from the Crown," the land was within the bounds of his colony.

The boundary controversy continued with varying intensity until 1779, when the two colonies were united by their common struggle against the mother country.

years proud Fort Pitt was to be dismantled, its massive materials sold for a paltry fifty pounds, its garrison dispersed. Once again log cabins went up along the Monongahela and the Allegheny, and surveyor John Campbell—how the Scots names echo down through the history of the city!—laid out four blocks and streets along the lower river. Quickly, too, stores and warehouses and taverns sprang up, for Pittsburgh was the entrepôt for the whole West, for traders and settlers alike.

Or, in any event, it would be if trade were resumed, if settlement were permitted. Pontiac was still at large, unregenerate and implacable, and his loyal followers still held the forests and the streams west of the Miami. To conciliate him and his warriors and to open up trade all the way to the Wabash and the Illinois country—English now, every acre of it—the new commander, General Thomas Gage, turned once again to the ubiquitous and indispensable George Croghan. In the lush spring of 1765 Croghan set off down the Ohio with two bateaux loaded down with presents, with articles of trade, and with money, for the farthest interior. When he reached the Wabash he was attacked by the fierce Kickapoos; a tomahawk bit into his scalp, but he was tough and survived the wound. He moved on to Vincennes, where he smoked pipes of peace; then on to Fort Chartres, where he met the mighty Pontiac. The great chieftain, who saw that the game was up, was ready now to make peace; soon Croghan could write in his journal that "Pontiac and I are on extreme good terms." Accompanied by Pontiac now, Croghan circled around to Detroit, where he met a vast council of the chiefs of thirty tribes who agreed to return all prisoners, reopen trade, and recognize the English as their Fathers. Then on to Niagara and a conference with the Senecas; to Ontario for a conference with the Onondagas—everywhere the Indians were eager for peace and for trade.

Soon Pittsburgh was astir with preparations for western trade. The Philadelphia firm of Baynton, Wharton and Morgan was first in the field, closely followed by David Franks and Company, which had London connections. The House of Morgan had ambitious plans for western trade; they put up a great warehouse, brought in carpenters and shipbuilders to build scores of bateaux, and hired hundreds of rivermen to row them: no less than 600 packhorses were employed to carry supplies and trading goods across the mountains. The next year Morgan's traders had penetrated deep into Kentucky and Illinois in their search for pelts.

The mortal enemy of both traders and Indians was, of course, the settler. Lord Barrington, the new Secretary of War in Rockingham's Ministry, put this with brutal candor: "The Country on the Westward of our Frontier quite to the Mississippi," he said, "was intended to be a Desert for the Indians to hunt in and inhabit." This was official policy; it was the policy of the Proclamation of 1763; it was the policy of the Pennsylvania Assembly which voted the death penalty to those who settled illegally on lands south or west of the Forks; it was the policy of the military commanders at Fort Pitt, who sent out one expedition after another, to disperse the settlers. All in vain. In October 1767 Croghan could write that "notwithstanding all the trouble that has been taken to move the People settled on Redstone Creek and Cheat River I am well assured there are double the number of inhabitants in those two settlements than ever was before." By 1768, it was estimated, over two thousand pioneers had settled south of the Forks. That year government gave up the vain effort to command the tides of settlement. By the Treaty of Fort Stanwix the Iroquois surrendered whatever claims they had to the lands west of the Allegheny; the Proclamation Line of '63 still outlawed settlement south of the Forks, but from then on it was forgotten. Now the dam burst and settlers poured in and took up land all along the Youghiogheny, the Monongahela, and the Cheat. In 1769 the Penns opened a land office at Pittsburgh; on the first day 2790 applicants filed for farms of three hundred acres each, and within a few months the proprietors had disposed of over a million acres. Meantime Virginia was making even more lavish grants, and settlers from Virginia and Maryland were swarming out along the old Braddock and Nemacolin roads to the sunset side of the Appalachians. By 1770 there were probably five thousand settlers south of the Forks; five years later the population of this first transAppalachian west had increased tenfold. It was the most rapid and the most massive western settlement in the history of the American colonies.

Already a new conflict was in the making, a forerunner of those sectional conflicts which were to loom so large in the history of the next century. Was Pittsburgh, was the country south of the Forks, part of Pennsylvania or of Virginia? Clearly Virginia had the better claim. Her charter designated her boundaries as northward and westward from sea to sea, and even after the Quebec Act that certainly took in the country north to the Ohio; as for Pennsylvania, so reluctant were her Quakers to involve themselves in any military expense that they actually had refused to appropriate money for the defense of Pittsburgh on the ground that the Forks lay outside her boundaries! It was Virginia's Ohio Company that had surveyed the area; Washington spoke for Virginia at Fort Le Boeuf and fought for Virginia at Fort Necessity. Not only did Virginia have the better legal claim; she had better material claims as well. Nature herself seemed to include this region in Virginia, for the headwaters of the Potomac interlaced with those of the Cheat and of the Youghiogheny. Most of the settlers had come by those routes, bringing with them their Virginia speech and manners, and—most important of all—their Virginia land titles. So persuasive were the Virginia claims that George Croghan, always something of a weathervane—shifted allegiance to the Virginia camp.

In 1773 Governor—or "Lord"—Dunmore (he had just named a daughter "Virginia") was out at the Forks on a personal reconnaissance of his lands. He ordered a new fort built, and modestly named it Fort Dunmore; he appointed the speculator and adventurer, Dr. John Connolly, "captain commandant" of "Pittsburgh and its dependencies," whatever that meant. Connolly—a nephew to Croghan—had just returned from a trip to Kentucky and was full of large plans for speculation and settlement in that country. In '74 Dunmore organized the whole area as the District of West Augusta, and later divided it into Yohogania, Monongalia, and Ohio counties. Pennsylvania, of course, resisted, and for a time there was a bloodless civil war on this frontier. The swashbuckling Connolly managed, or mismanaged, things with a high hand; Arthur St. Clair—later to achieve melancholy fame in the West—resisted him; there were arrests and counterarrests; nothing was settled. Then, as if to complicate things further, Dunmore and Connolly between them excited a quarrel with the Indians which has come down in history under the sonorous name of Lord Dunmore's War. It was scarcely that; it was a continuation of the endless series of scalpings and ambuscades and treacheries that marked the early history of the Ohio country. In June '74 Dunmore called out the militia for an expedition against the

Shawnee towns of the Ohio; St. Clair raised another force to patrol the northern borderlands in order to prevent war. Colonel Andrew Lewis—he had fought with Washington at Fort Necessity, with Braddock, and with Forbes—led a force of eight hundred Virginia militia into Kentucky, met the Shawnees at the Kanawha, and in the hotly fought battle of Point Pleasant whipped them soundly. It was the end of Lord Dunmore's War, and seemed to strengthen the Virginia claims.

Clearly everything favored Virginia—everything but fate. Alas for Virginia's claim; it was inextricably interwoven with the fortunes of Lord Dunmore and of his lieutenant, Dr. Connolly—that is, of the royal cause and of loyalism. With the approach of open conflict between colonies and mother country, the Virginia cause became shaky; with open conflict it became desperate. That the shot fired at Concord Bridge was heard around the world is a poetic fancy, but that it was heard at Fort Pitt is historical fact, and there its reverberations echoed down through history.

There can be no doubt that Virginians and Pennsylvanians enjoyed quarreling with each other, but they much preferred to quarrel with the mother country. Thus as early as October 1774 Valentine Crawford, then in Dunmore's little force in Kentucky, wrote Colonel Washing-

ON JUNE 3, 1776, a month before the Declaration of Independence, Colonel George Morgan (1747–1810), who was appointed by Congress as Indian Agent for the Middle Department of the United States with headquarters at Pittsburgh, protested strongly the effort of the Virginia Convention to engage Indians in the fight for independence. George Morgan, a partner in Baynton, Wharton, and Morgan, was largely responsible for keeping the western tribes allied with the colonists.

45

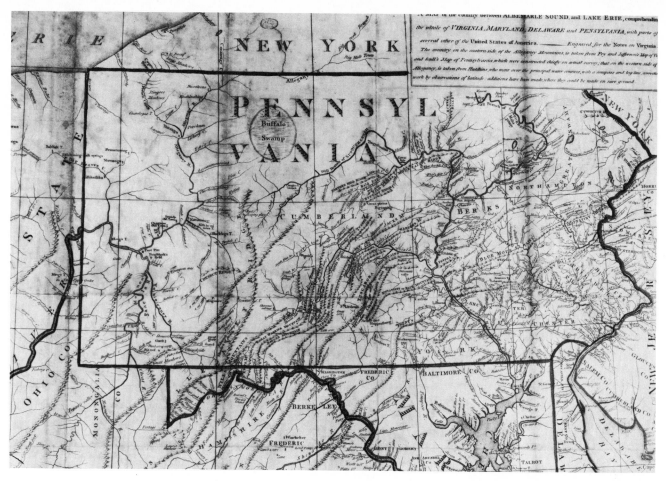

THE BOUNDARY DISPUTE between Virginia and Pennsylvania was settled the last day of August in 1779. On that date the two contesting parties agreed in Baltimore "to extend Mason and Dixon's line due west five degrees of longitude, to be computed from the river Delaware, for the southern boundary of Pennsylvania, and that a meridian, drawn from the western extremity thereof, to the northern limit of said State, be the western boundary of said State forever."

The following year the Virginia and Pennsylvania legislatures ratified the agreement; the citizens of the states found it more opportune to resist England than to fight against each other. Thus the bitter contest over the boundary line was ended.

ton that he hoped for a quick peace with the savages "in order that we may be able to assist you in relieving the poor distressed Bostonians. If the report is true," he added, "that General Gage has bombarded the city of Boston, this is a most alarming circumstance and calls on every friend of the liberty of his country to exert himself in its cause."

The report was not true, but soon there came one that was. News of Lexington and Concord reached Pittsburgh on May 16—how the couriers must have flown!—and the quarreling factions closed ranks and rallied to the support of the American cause. That very day the inhabitants of Pittsburgh adopted resolutions pledging resistance to "invaders of American rights and privileges" and moved to organize military help for beleaguered Boston; the next day the Pennsylvanians of nearby Hannastown fell in line. Soon every town and county was organized. "We have nothing but musters and committees all over the country, and everything seems to be running into wildest confusion" wrote Arthur St. Clair, and the English traveler, Nicholas Cresswell, wrote in disgust that "the people here

are Liberty mad, and nothing but War is thought of."

It was not the Americans who first thought of war, it was their English cousins. But war came, and soon Pittsburgh threw in her lot with Massachusetts and Virginia and their sister colonies. Local issues were not drowned out—the dispute between the adherents of Pennsylvania and of Virginia, the agitation for a new state (it was to be named Westsylvania), the organization of local government, the struggle with the Indians—but were subordinated to the larger issues of the Revolution. Soon companies from the Monongahela and the Youghiogheny were marching to the relief of Boston, or to Valley Forge, or northward along the Allegheny to smite the Senecas, or westward to Detroit; soon there were expeditions into the Illinois country, and even to distant New Orleans for powder and supplies. Pittsburgh, long the westernmost outpost of the seaboard, became now, by a great convulsion, the easternmost outpost of the vast hinterland which, with the triumph of American arms, stretched to the Mississippi. It was a revolution which fixed her place firmly in the history of the new nation.

Chapter 2

GATEWAY
TO THE WEST

by Stefan Lorant

THE PIONEER village on the confluence of the two rivers grew at a safe and steady pace. The seed planted in the area where the Monongahela joined with the Allegheny was a hearty one; it flowered and blossomed with apparent ease. In less than a generation, the virgin forests gave way to rows of homes, spreading factories, and bustling business establishments. The idyllic picture of the primeval landscape faded away; the wilderness retreated before the axe of the woodsman, and the shape of the city became apparent. One could see the transformation with the naked eye, as day after day new buildings and new settlements were added to the older ones.

That the place had a bright future was evident from the beginning. Pittsburgh grew because Providence endowed the area with fabulous riches. There was wood in the forests, coal in the hills, limestone, sandstone, clay in the soil, flax and cotton in the fields. Iron ore, though not in the immediate neighborhood, was readily available. The timber that covered the land supplied logs for the building of homes and charcoal for iron-making; it gave material for barrels and casks in which goods were preserved and shipped; it was made into rafts, boats, and barges, those early means of transportation that took the produce down the river, steadily expanding the market and laying the foundation for the town's future industries. Limestone and sand were used for glassmaking, clay for bricks, flax and cotton for textiles; iron ore for nails, utensils, and implements.

Pittsburgh grew because of the rich farmland that surrounded it. The fertile soil yielded more than those who tilled it could consume. Soon there was a surplus, and this surplus was sold or exchanged for other necessities. It was mainly because of this farm wealth that Pittsburgh would become a manufacturing town. Within its confines the mills turned grain into flour; tanneries made leather goods out of the hides of animals; iron works, textile mills, glasshouses sprung up, using the raw materials of the nearby countryside.

Pittsburgh grew because of its sturdy, hard-working citizens. Though early descriptions damn it as wicked, the town was nonetheless a religious place. "A compound of worship on Sunday and whiskey on Monday, thus blending the spirits," went the saying. Presbyterianism ran strong in the veins of the men and women who settled on the Western Pennsylvania frontier; it formed a mould for their thinking; the Presbyterian Church, the Scotch-Irishman's bulwark in legislative, social and moral matters, was the prominent force in Pittsburgh. There was a story about John Knox, who had prayed, "O! Lord give me Scotland," and God had not only granted the request, but had thrown in Pittsburgh for good measure. And one repeated the saying of the little Pittsburgh girl who, when asked about her religious affiliation, replied: "Mama says it is sinful to boast, but I am a Presbyterian." The strength of Presbyterianism was the result of the early labors of their missionaries and the determination of their followers to hold on to their Scotch-Irish traditions. Their pastors, courageous, freedom-loving men, came from a hearty breed. During the week they worked in the fields; they were one with their flock; they had their respect and confidence. Thus, despite the numerous Methodist and Baptist communities, despite the strong Catholic and Quaker influences, it was Presbyterianism that took hold of the town and gave Pittsburgh its moral fiber.

Pittsburgh grew because of its superb geographical location. The mountains in the eastern part of the state formed a formidable barrier, making transportation from the seaboard not only hazardous, but also expensive. Thus the people of the town had to rely on themselves to produce the things they needed. The two great rivers —most vital arteries of communication and trade—that flowed together at Pittsburgh's heart, gave a great boost to the town's development. The Allegheny, coming from the north, connected northern Pennsylvania with the southern part of the state, while the Monongahela, flowing from the south, tapped the commerce of northern Virginia and the eastern corner of western Pennsylvania. It was in Pittsburgh that overland and river traffic met. It was here that the goods brought over the mountains on the backs of packhorses or in Conestoga wagons were put on the river boats which transported them and the region's agricultural produce down the Ohio and the Mississippi. The Frenchman, François Michaux, visiting the town in 1802, observed: "Corn, hams and dried pork are the principal articles sent to New Orleans, whence they are re-exported into Carribees. They also export for the consumption of Louisiana, bar-iron, coarse linen, bottles manufactured at Pittsburgh, and salt butter. . . ." And while these goods moved down river, up river came quantities of hemp, tobacco, cotton, lead, copper, glazed powder, hides, whiskey, linen, sugar, saltpeter, and a wide variety of West Indian produce.

Pittsburgh grew because America grew and expanded. After the adoption of the federal constitution and the passage of the ordinance for government of the Northwest Territory in 1787, the tide of immigration into the West swelled. And as the newcomers moved to their future homes in the Ohio Valley, in Kentucky, or in Indiana, they halted at the Forks, where they built or bought their boats and where they acquired their equipment and tools. A flatboat in the Pittsburgh boatyards could be purchased for no more than a dollar for a foot in length, and goods and implements were sold there cheaper than in the stores of the eastern cities. The money of the immigrants was one of the largest sources of western cash; it helped to bring prosperity to the people of Pittsburgh. Between October 1786 and December 1788, according to the *Pittsburgh Gazette*, 16,203 immigrants passed through the town on their way West; their migration, in the words of an early historian, "converted the wilderness into a garden and made the valleys to bloom as a rose." It was like a great tidal wave. Leaving the crowded cities of the Atlantic Seaboard, where taxes were high and where the conservatism of the Federalists damped their spirits, the pioneers moved westward in pursuit of a freer life.

Finally, Pittsburgh grew because the diplomatic achievements of the nation pushed the frontier back. Jay's Treaty in 1795 secured the northwestern posts to which the English had held on so tenaciously while the Louisiana Purchase in 1803 procured vast new lands, giving the United States control and jurisdiction over the entire Mississippi and the harbor of New Orleans. More land meant a larger trading area; it meant more settlers, and this in turn meant more production and more profits.

If only the Indians could be subdued! They were a constant menace to the growth of commerce, a steady threat to the lives and possessions of the inhabitants. Though the tribes signed the treaties at Fort Stanwix in 1784 and at Fort McIntosh in 1785 (in which the powerful confederacy of the Northwest surrendered all its land claims in that territory and also sold Pennsylvania for $5000 all the unceded land in that state), yet, as the white man moved into the area, the Indians resisted his advance.

In 1790, his first year in the Presidency, George Washington sent out General Josiah Harmar with fifteen hundred men to subdue the hostile tribes at the Maumee River. At the outset the campaign went well, but as the troops were on their homeward march, the Indians wellnigh wiped out the entire force.

To avenge the defeat, the President dispatched General Arthur St. Clair the following year. St. Clair fought the Indians at the headwaters of the Wabash. He had no more luck than Harmar. Losing two thirds of his men, he was forced to retreat. For a long time thereafter the balladeers chanted the sad tale:

" 'Twas November the fo-urth, in the year of ninety-one
    We had a sore engag-e-ment, near to Fort Jefferson;
  Sinclair was our command-er, which may remember'd be,
    For there we lost nine hundred men in the Western Ter'torie."

The third expedition that marched against the resisting red men was that of General Anthony Wayne. "Mad Anthony" trained his soldiers with minute care at Legionsville; but the supplies of the troops came from nearby Pittsburgh. In the summer of 1794 he moved into battle and defeated the tribes on the battlefield of Fallen Timbers, where Toledo, Ohio, is today. His victory secured the frontier. No longer had the settlers to fear the raids of the Indians; no longer need they dread the attacks on life and property. The success of his armies paved the way for the undisturbed growth of the West and of Pittsburgh.

*

This period in Pittsburgh's history is a period of change, a period of transformation. During these decades—from the end of the Revolutionary War in 1783 up to 1816, when Pittsburgh was incorporated as a city—the agricultural village changed into an industrial town whose growth kept pace with that of the rapidly expanding nation.

(turn to page 50)

PITTSBURGH GAZETTE

Price Six-Pence.]   SATURDAY, AUGUST 12, 1786.   [VOL. I.

Foreign Intelligence.

HAGUE. *April 18.*

WE are assured that the emperor of Morocco has offered their high mightinesses the exclusive privilege of the port of Larache, for the trade of the inhabitants of the United Provinces.

PARIS. *April 18.*

We have just now an express arrived from Pera, which mentions a dangerous insurrection at Constantinople, that raged so much as to occasion all the gates and avenues of the city to be shut up, and no person suffered to pass but under proper restriction; all the ambassadors had shut themselves up in their hotels; the French consul at Pera despatched this news.

MADRID. *April 4.*

For some weeks past two Americans have been at this place, who were presented to his majesty and the royal family, on Tuesday last. They are a Mr Barclay, consul general of the United States, at l'Orient, and an officer named Franks. They are going to Morocco, to negociate a peace with the emperor of Barbary and the states of America. Two other Americans have been here these two months, one of them an officer by the name of Randal. They have set off from Barcelona for Algiers, with a view to effect a conciliation between that power & the United States.

NAPLES, (Italy) *March 15.*

A few days since an occurrence took place in this city, shocking to human nature, though it happily had not its full effect. A young man of quality being violently enamoured of a girl of inferior rank, determined to marry her. The marquis of —— took measures to prevent so disadvantageous an alliance, which so irritated the son that he took the horrid resolution of depriving the author of his existence of life, and for that purpose bribed a servant to put some poison into a bottle of the wine which the marquis was accustomed to drink. Upon taking a glass of the wine, the marquis and a friend who was at dinner with him observed, that it had a very particular taste; and a physician being sent for, he found it to be impregnated with poison. Medicines for counteracting the poison were administered with success; but the precipitate flight of the youth convinced the unhappy father of a truth more painful than the effects of the poison.

March 18. His Sicilian majesty's deputy has had several conferences with the dey of Algiers; but according to the dispatches received, nothing has yet been concluded upon, and indeed there are not much hopes of success; notwithstanding which, the deputy expressed himself with all the force and energy that belongs to a polished nation when treating with a country of pirates;—he answered the dey, " that before the king his master would consent to pay the odious tribute which he dared to demand under the name of presents, he would use all the force of his country, not only to defend his subjects against the piracies of the Algerines, but to force him to make compensation for the damage done by the corsairs."

LONDON, *April 27.*

According to the accounts at the Bullion Office it appears, that there has been remitted from America in specie, that is, dollars of silver, since the conclusion of the late peace, upwards of one million two hundred and sixty thousand pounds sterling. This is one proof that America is not in a despicable situation, at least to such a degree as has been industriously circulated, in order to depreciate the value of a commercial connection with them.

During the late war, Mr. Fox, a merchant of Falmouth, had a share in a ship, which the other owners determined to fit out as a letter of marque, very much against the opinion and inclination of Mr. Fox, who was of the society of Quakers. The ship had the luck to take two French merchantmen; and the share of the prize money due to Mr. Fox amounted to the sum of 1500l. At the close of the war Mr. Fox sent his son to Paris with the 1500l. which he faithfully repaid to the owners of the ships taken. The young gentleman, to discover the owners of the vessels, was obliged to advertise them in the Paris gazette. In consequence of this advertisement, he received a letter from a small village near Nismes, in the province of Languedoc, acquainting him, that a society of Quakers was established in that remote part of France, consisting of about 100 families. That they were so

much struck with this true instance of generosity in one of their sect, that they were very desirous to open a correspondence with their friends in England. Since this accident, a count of Marsilliac, who is one of the heads of the society, has been in London to pay his friends there a visit, and is returned highly pleased with his reception. The society of French Quakers has subsisted in their present residence more than a century, without maintaining a correspondence with any other society. They are supposed to be a remnant of the ancient Albigenses, against whom several persecuting crusades were instituted in the reign of Philip the second, towards the close of the twelfth century. The count de Marsilliac was a captain of horse before he became a Quaker.

Copy of a letter from lord George Gordon, to the marquis of Carmarthen, one of his majesty's principal secretaries of state, &c. &c.

My Lord,

Mr. TUFFTS, an American gentleman, now in London, is possessed of undeniable intelligence, that John Adams, esquire, (who is received by the king as ambassador from the United States of America) has his salary paid him quarterly by the compte d'Adhemar, the French ambassador. I thought it my duty to acquaint your lordship with Mr. Tuffts's communication to me, for the immediate information of his majesty's council and government, that you may beware of Mr. Adams.

" I have the honor to be, &c.
" Ten o'clock, Saturday   G. GORDON.
night, Welbeck street."

The Marquis of Carmarthen's answer addressed to the right honorable lord George Gordon, Welbeck street, and subscribed " Carmarthen."

Monday night, May 1, 1786.

" LORD CARMARTHEN presents his compliments to lord George Gordon, and returns his lordship thanks for the note received from him yesterday.

" Right Hon. Lord George Gordon."

May 3.

To the Printer of the Public Advertiser.

SIR,

" Having seen in your paper of this day, a copy of a letter, &c. signed G. Gordon, asserting that I was possessed of undeniable intelligence, that John Adams, esquire, has his salary paid him quarterly by the compte d'Adhemar, the French ambassador: please to inform your readers of the true state of the case, which is as follows:

" I had the honor of being introduced by an acquaintance, by mere accident, to lord George Gordon, in Bond-street. We stept into the Blenheim coffee-house, where, in the course of conversation, I happened to mention that I heard from a gentleman, whose name I have mentioned to the parties, that the American ambassador, as he heard, was paid through the French ambassador.

" Without any further authority the above publication appeared. I leave the world to judge how far his lordship's conduct is consistent with propriety.

I am, sir, your humble servant,
May 3, 1786.   S. TUFFTS.

Doctor Priestly has lately found that water is essential to the production of inflammable air, and that charcoal and iron when intensely hot have so strong an affinity to water, that they will attract it in the midst of the greatest fire, and even through the pores of a glass retort. This discovery, it is thought, will be of great importance in the several branches of chemistry.

Extract of a letter from the Hague, April 11.

" The report prevails again here, that in the first sittings of the states of Holland, the command of the garrison of this city will be offered to the prince stadtholder, and it is assured that the stadtholderian family will certainly not fail to be here by the 15th of May next, the day of the annual review of the burghers. This festival would certainly not take place without the presence of his serene highness, who is in some measure the object of it, as first citizen of the city, and to whom the military honors of the citizens are rendered exclusively on that day.

" The citizens of Wyck in the province of Utrecht, shew the firmest countenance, and brave openly the severest resolutions of the states. There is not the least appearance that the other provinces (Gueldres alone perhaps excepted) will grant any of their troops to that of Utrecht, to make the burghers submit; now the province of Utrecht has not a sufficient number of regiments, any more than that of Gueldres, for such

an undertaking; therefore, it is naturally concluded that the citizens will probably attain their ends, and that, finally, the regulations of the Regency will pass in the affirmative on the 20th of October next."

May 7. The most authentic accounts from Dublin, by the last packet, inform us, that there is at present a greater prospect of an union between Great-Britain and Ireland, than has appeared in any former period; the most distinguished patriots having given the strongest assurance to government, that they are ready to meet in any impartial plan for a lasting alliance between the two islands in the most cordial manner. An event most devoutly to be wished, as it is only by an union between the sister islands that the success of the one can become the interest of the other, and that the riches and strength of either kingdom can become the property of both.

DUBLIN, *April 22.*

A curious trial will come on next month before the parliament of Limoges, in France. An adventurer of the masculine gender, who travelled through most parts of the kingdom, sometimes as a lady, and sometimes as a gentleman, had long made a practice of forming matrimonial connexions with either sex. He had a carriage and suit agreeable to the pretensions of a person of quality; and managed his designs so artfully, either in a male or female character, that several of both sexes have become dupes to his art. He always made it a practice to decamp early the morning after the ceremony was performed, and carried with him the most valuable portable articles that were to be found.

A letter received yesterday by a gentleman of this city from London, on whose authenticity we have every reason to rely, contains the following very important intelligence: That Mr. Pitt and a nobleman of this kingdom, now in London, have had of late several conferences touching the affairs of Ireland, the result of which is a determination, as soon as the British parliament rise, to resume the business of a commercial adjustment between the kingdoms on the broadest bottom; for which purpose three members of the Irish privy council are to be in London in July next: The British minister being determined, says the letter writer, to carry this, his favorite measures, through the Irish houses, *let it cost what it will.*

On NEGROES. A FRAGMENT.

WHEN Tom, an't please your honor, got to the shop, there was nobody in it, but a poor negro girl, with a bunch of white feathers slightly tied to the end of a long cane, flapping away flies—not killing them.

'Tis a pretty picture! said my uncle Toby.—She had suffered persecution, Trim, and had learnt mercy—

—She was good, an't please your honor, from nature, as well as from hardships; and there are circumstances in the story of that poor, friendless slut, which would melt a heart of stone, said Trim; and, some dismal winter's evening, when your honor is in the humor, they shall be told you, with the rest of Trim's story, for it makes a part of it—

Then do not forget, Trim, said my uncle Toby.

A negro has a soul, an't please your honor, said the corporal—doubtingly.

I am not much versed, corporal, quoth my uncle Toby, in things of this kind; but I suppose God would not leave him without one, any more than thee or me—

—It would be putting one sadly over the head of another, quoth the corporal—

—It would so, said my uncle Toby.

Why, then, an't please your honor, is a black wench to be used worse than a white one?

I can give no reason, said my uncle Toby—

—Only, cried the corporal, shaking his head, because she has no one to stand up for her.—

'Tis that very thing, quoth my uncle Toby, which recommends her to protection, and her brethren with her.—'Tis the fortune of war which has put the whip into our hands now—where it may be hereafter, Heaven knows! but be it where it will, the brave, Trim, will not use it unkindly.

God forbid, said the corporal.—Amen, responded my uncle Toby, laying his hand upon his heart.

STERNE.

THE FIRST NEWSPAPER west of the Alleghenies was *The Pittsburgh Gazette,* founded in the summer of 1786 by John Scull and Joseph Hall. It took the two young men ten full hours to turn out the required 700 copies of the four-page paper, which at the beginning was issued fortnightly. Yearly subscription was 17 shillings and sixpence.

The first number contained an enthusiastic article by Hugh Henry Brackenridge, the eminent lawyer and civic leader, praising the advantages of the city.

49

At the end of the Revolution, Pittsburgh's population was somewhat over three hundred. Dr. Johann Schoepf, the German doctor who came to America as the chief surgeon of the Ansbach mercenaries, noted during his visit in 1783 that the town consisted of "perhaps 60 wooden houses and cabins, in which live something more than 100 families." The buildings were neither elaborate nor were they beautiful; they were simple structures made of unsquared logs. The streets before them were unpaved, dirty, littered with refuse, with dogs and hogs roaming through the mire. On rainy days one waded through the mud, in dry weather the dust rose in clouds.

Early travelers were not complimentary in the description. A man wrote to his wife back East that the town was "excellent to do pennance in." True enough, Pittsburgh was a crude place, tough and rowdy. John Wilkins, who later became one of the town's foremost citizens, recalled that in the Pittsburgh of that day "all sort of wickedness were carried on to excess, and there was no morality or regular order."

Life was simple and uneventful. In the countryside—and everything outside the few blocks around the Point belonged to the countryside—social activities were limited. People met at church services, they met at weddings and funerals, at house raisings or house warmings; otherwise they saw little of each other.

The pioneer family was a self-supporting unit—a complete world in itself. Father was a man of a thousand trades; he built his house, he made his plowshares, buckets, tubs and tankards. Mother spun flax, wove linen, cut and sewed the clothes for the family. And the children split brooms, helped make candles, and made themselves useful in many other ways. Every member of the family worked either in the fields or at home; no one was idle.

The room of their cabins offered little comfort. It was drafty and smoky. The bearskins and blankets on the beds bred fleas. At night rats and snakes crawled on the floor.

They dressed simply; the men wore a tan or red hunting shirt. Breeches and leggings were made of deerskin or linsey. Though better materials were brought over the mountains for the women, only a few were able to afford them. The little money the pioneer family possessed was used for salt, nails, gunpowder, and bullets rather than for clothing.

They ate what the Lord provided—game and birds of the forest: wild turkeys, woodcock, grouse, quail, wild pigeon, deer, elk, squirrel; fish from the streams: catfish, sturgeon, bass, eel, and turtle; bushes, plants, and berries from the woods: forest berries, nuts, crabapples.

Bread was not a daily fare; at times the family went for long periods without it, but there was always dried pumpkin ground into meal or cornmeal johnnycake made from Indian corn. Milk was plentiful, as was mush, usually mixed with sweetened water, molasses, or maple syrup. Hominy, made from whole corn soaked overnight in lye water, was a popular dish, particularly with the children.

Coffee was introduced after the Revolution; but beer remained a luxury.

Behind each house there was a truck patch with corn, pumpkin, squash, beans, potatoes, cabbage, turnips, watermelon and muskmelon. The chief crops were maize, wheat, rye, flax, Irish potatoes, in that order, and also buckwheat, millet, oats, barley, hay, peas, tobacco, and melons. All farming was carried on by hand, with the ax, the hoe, the scythe, and plows made of wood. But with the coming of better tools, and better cultivation methods, the farmers were able to hire servants, most of them signing a bond for their services. These farm hands, "washed, lodged, and boarded" by their masters, were paid ten to sixteen pounds a year.

In Pittsburgh itself life had more diversions. There the women visited each other and worked together in the evenings while the men ambled to the taverns searching for company. It was good to find solace in drink after a hard day's work—so good in fact that the place soon acquired a reputation as "the drinkingest town" in the West.

Accounts of the early visitors speak in derogatory tones about the inhabitants. To Dr. Schoepf, the people of Pittsburgh, who "gained their living hitherto by farming and trafficking in skins and furs," appeared not only poor "but also extremely inactive and idle; so much so that they are recalcitrant when given work and an opportunity to earn money, for which, however, they hanker." The German doctor must have had a bad experience in the place, for he noted that "the people here do not grow rich by industry and fair prices but prefer rather to deal extortionately with strangers and travellers; and shunning work charge the more for it, their comfortable sloth being interrupted."

It was in 1784 that the town was laid out. Once the Penns decided to sell part of their manor of Pittsburgh they asked George Woods of Bedford to make a survey of it. Woods' assistant, Thomas Vickroy, recalled the event some half a century later. "We arrived in Pittsburgh in the month of May, 1784," wrote Vickory in his deposition.

And the first thing we did was to circumscribe the ground where we intended to lay the town out. We began up about where Grant Street now is, on the bank of the Monongahela, and proceeded down the Monongahela, according to the meanderings of the river, to its junction with the Allegheny River. Then up the Allegheny River on the bank, keeping on the bank a certain distance, up to about Washington's Street; from thence to Grant's Hill, thence along Grant's Hill to the place of the beginning. I made a draft of it in Mr. Woods' presence, throwing it into a large scale to see how it would answer to lay out into lots and streets. After that there was a good deal of conversation, and the ground was viewed by Mr. Woods and the persons who lived at the place to fix on the best plan to lay out the town with the greatest convenience. There had been lots laid out before, as I understand, called military lots, said to be laid out by Mr. Campbell.

The military lots which Vickroy mentions—four blocks on the banks of the Monongahela, with borders at Ferry,

Painting by Gilbert Stuart.

H. H. BRACKENRIDGE

(1748-1816), one of the city's prominent early citizens, came to Pittsburgh in 1781 where he began a law practice.

He was instrumental in chartering the Pittsburgh Academy in 1787 and the erection of Allegheny County in 1788. In 1799 he became a justice of the State Supreme Court. He was the author of *Modern Chivalry*.

WHAT ONE COULD BUY IN PITTSBURGH

There was a wide variety of goods in the stores. On July 18, 1788, Elliot, Williams, and Company advertised in *The Pittsburgh Gazette* that they had just received a large assortment of European and West Indian merchandise.

The store, located at Front and Ferry Streets, offered "Dry Goods, Hardware, and Cutlery" and advertised broadcloths in blue, green, scarlet, claret, brown, bottle green, mixed and in drab colors. The customers could choose from the jeans and corduroys, chintzes, linens, silks, muslins, and calicoes to their heart's desire.

They could buy coarse or fine hats for men, elegant fans and mantuas for women, and all kinds of shoes for children.

Toothbrushes, combs, shaving boxes and brushes, snuff in bottles, playing cards, and gunpowder were among the goods.

On the grocery counter the spices of the Orient were displayed; tea, coffee, chocolate, molasses, and sugar were on the shelves, as were West Indian rum; Madeira, claret, and port.

Conditions of sale were simple. The store was offering not only to sell merchandise for cash, but also to exchange for "poultry, bacon, beef, cattle on foot, whiskey, flour, butter, cheese, tallow, candlewick, hard soap, and vinegar."

Second, Market, and Water Streets—were mapped out by Colonel John Campbell in 1764, a year after Pontiac's uprising, when most of the buildings in "the upper town" were destroyed. Campbell, attempting to bring order into the chaos, drew a plan for the orderly development of the fort's neighborhood, a plan which served well for two decades. Now, Woods and Vickroy proposed "to new model those small streets and lots so as to make them larger" and to widen Market Street to 60 feet. But the people who had their houses there, objected; they would not hear of any such innovation. They were apprehensive that the widening of the roads would diminish the value of their properties, so the surveyors kept the layout as they had found it. However, they continued Campbell's plan to Grant Street and they laid out Liberty and Penn running parallel to the Allegheny and leading to Fort Pitt, while on Market they created a public square, the Diamond.

In the very year that the town was laid out, Arthur Lee, a member of the celebrated Virginia family and one of the three commissioners who were sent to Fort McIntosh (the present Beaver) to negotiate a treaty with the Indians, passed through Pittsburgh. And what Lee noted was no more laudatory to Pittsburghers than were the observations of Dr. Schoepf the year before. An entry in his journal, dated December 17, 1784, reads:

> Pittsburgh is inhabited almost entirely by Scots and Irish who live in paltry log-houses, and are as dirty as in the north of Ireland, or even Scotland. There is a great deal of small trade carried on; the goods being brought at the vast expense of forty-five shillings per cwt., from Philadelphia and Baltimore. They take in the shops, money, wheat, flour and skins. There are in the town four attorneys, two doctors, and not a priest of any persuasion, nor church, nor chapel; so that they are likely to be damned, *without the benefit of clergy* . . . The place, I believe, will never be very considerable.

But despite such prophecy, Pittsburgh kept growing at a steady pace. Before long it even had its newspaper. On July 29, 1786, the first issue of the *Pittsburgh Gazette* appeared. Published by two young men, John Scull and Joseph Hall, "the first newspaper west of the mountains" mirrored the ideas of western Federalism. It was printed on a hand press in the back of a rude building on the corner of Water Street and Chancery Lane, and its subscription price was 17 shillings and sixpence for the year. Joseph Hall died a few months after the *Gazette* made its first appearance; his successor, John Boyd, troubled by his wife's alleged infidelity, hanged himself on the hill which bears his name, but the newspaper kept on prospering under the guidance of the new partner, John Scull.

For the first issue the lawyer Hugh Henry Brackenridge penned an enthusiastic article on the virtues of the town. The Princeton-educated Brackenridge, who came to the Forks five years earlier, fell in love with the area and was determined to make Pittsburgh the best place in the West. He was greatly responsible for the founding of the Pittsburgh Academy, which later grew into the University of

Pittsburgh, and he was instrumental in the erection of Allegheny County.

"The town consists at present of about an hundred dwelling houses with building apurtenant. More are daily added, and for some time past it has improved with an equal but continual pace," asserted Brackenridge in his article, even though *Niles' Weekly Register* for the same year counted only "36 log houses, one stone house, one frame house, and five small stores." In his ardor, the lawyer included the population of the entire surrounding area when he claimed that 1500 people lived in Pittsburgh, for in reality their number was hardly one fifth of that. But whether the town was small or large, to Brackenridge no other on earth surpassed it. He waxed lyrical as he continued:

> As I pass along, I may remark that this new country is in general highly prolific; whether it is that the vegetable air, if I may so express it, constantly perfumed with aromatic flavor, and impregnated with salts drawn from the fresh soil, is more favorable to the production of men and other animals than decayed grounds.
>
> There is not a more delightful spot under the heaven to spend any of the summer months than at this place. . . .
>
> Nor is the winter season enjoyed with less festivity than in more populous and cultivated towns. The buildings warm, fuel abundant, consisting of the finest coal from the neighboring hills, or of ash, hickory or oak brought down in rafts by the river. In the meantime, the climate is less severe at this place than on the other side of the mountain.

Everything was better in Pittsburgh, even the fog:

> It may be observed that, at the junction of these two rivers, until 8 o'clock of summer mornings a light fog is usually incumbent; but it is of a salutary nature, inasmuch as it consists of vapor, not exhaled from stagnant water but which the sun of the preceding day had extracted from trees and flowers, and in the evening had sent back in dew, with it rising from a second sun in fog, and becoming of aromatic quality, it is experienced to be helpful.

In the subsequent issues of the newspaper—on August 19 and August 29, 1786—Brackenridge continued his eulogy and made the prophecy:

> This town in future time will be the place of great manufactory. Indeed the greatest on the continent, or perhaps in the world. The present carriage from Philadelphia is six pence for each pound weight and however improved the conveyance may be, and by whatever channel, yet such is our distance from either of the oceans that the importation of heavy articles will still be expensive. The manufacturing of them will therefore become more an object here than elsewhere. It is a prospect of this with men of reflection which renders the soil of this place so valuable.

The advertisements in the early numbers of the *Gazette* give a good picture of the village's life. In November 1786 a Mrs. Pride advertised that in her boarding and day school for young ladies she would teach English, reading and knitting. A store in the following year announced that it was ready to exchange "at the most reasonable terms for good merchantable flour, beef, cattle, butter or cash," the following merchandise: broadcloth, corduroys, velvets and velverets, beaver pillows, cotton denims, quilting, Irish linen, cambrics, muslins, gauzes of all kinds, coffee mills, Bibles, spelling books, and primers. With the gradual disappearance of the Indian traders, Pittsburghers asked for diversified and better quality merchandise, imported from New Orleans or Philadelphia. There was a market for pewter dishes and plates, for Indian and Roman handkerchiefs, for ribbons, buttons, threads, chintz, calico and flannels, for combs, shoes, hats and stockings; they were looking for scissors, thimbles, writing paper, sealing wax, ink powder, and inkstands. The farmer on the land needed cross cut saws, carpenter's and wheelwright's axes, wagon tools, sickles, scythes, saddles, powder and lead. And he wanted sugar, salt, coffee, tea, chocolate, nutmegs and pepper. According to an advertisement, all these articles could be bought "on the lowest terms, for cash, flour, rye, bacon, ginseng, snake-root, deer-skins, furs and all kinds of certificates."

It was a year later, in 1788, that the first regular mail service began between Pittsburgh and Philadelphia. Not many took advantage of this opportunity; letter writing was still a hard task for the ordinary citizen. In 1790, the town's postal receipts for the full year amounted to only $110.99; Pittsburgh was at that time still a modest village, and the year-old United States still a small country, with a population of only 3,900,000 of which 700,000 were slaves. The two largest cities on the eastern coast were Philadelphia with 42,000 and New York with 32,000 inhabitants. About nine tenths of all Americans earned their livelihood through agriculture; the main industries worth noting were shipping and fishing. Money, capital, and free labor were scarce. Industrial goods were brought over from England, the workshop of the world.

Yet changes were in the air. Gradually America began to rely on its own strength; it began to produce goods. Artisans, who came to Pittsburgh in growing numbers, manufactured articles at the backs of the stores—mostly clothing, utensils, and implements. By 1792, so the *American Museum* noted, there were in the town:

1 Clock and Watch Maker, 2 Coopers, 1 Skin Dresser and Breeches maker, 2 Tanners and Curriers, 4 Cabinet-makers, 2 Hatters, 2 Weavers, 5 Blacksmiths, 5 Shoemakers, 3 Saddlers, 1 Malster and Brewer, 2 Tinners, 3 Wheelwrights, 1 Stocking-Weaver, 1 Ropemaker, 2 White-smiths.

The influx of these skilled workmen stimulated trade and kept business conditions improving. The half a dozen stores at the end of the Revolution grew to seven times as many a decade later.

The fall of 1788 saw the creation of Allegheny County. Until then Pittsburgh was part of Westmoreland, with Hannastown, the county seat, some thirty miles away from the Fork. Pittsburghers, tired of traveling to Hannastown or Greensburg to do their county business, wanted a county seat that would be nearer to their homes. The Commonwealth of Pennsylvania had already reserved a tract of 3000 acres north of the Ohio and the Allegheny opposite Pittsburgh for such a purpose, and the Supreme

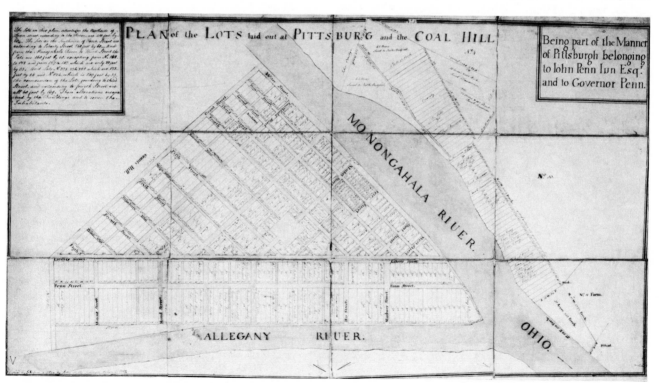

SURVEY OF THE PITTSBURGH LOTS, made by John Hill in 1787, the year of the framing of the Constitution and the passage of the Northwest Ordinance. The streets of the town had been laid out three years earlier by George Woods and Thomas Vickroy.

At this time the entire population of Pittsburgh consisted of less than 400 souls. *Niles Weekly Register* counted 38 houses

and only five stores for 1786.

But as immigration increased, as settlers provided for an ever-expanding market, the town of Pittsburgh grew into an industrial center—the Birmingham of America.

TRANSPORTATION AND MANUFACTURING.

EARLY TRANSPORTATION of goods was done by pack-horse trains. Usually 12 to 20 horses with packsaddles made up a train, each horse carrying a load of 150 to 200 pounds. Travel was slow and costly; it took a train 20 days to travel from Philadelphia to Pittsburgh.

RIVER TRAFFIC. Flatboats, keelbo[...] and barges carried agricultural produ[...] on the rivers; they took immigrants a[...]

THE BLACKSMITH was one of the most important men of the frontier. He wrought bar iron into horseshoes, made all kinds of tools and utensils, wagon wheels, nails, sickles, and scythes. Until 1790 the iron he used was transported over the mountains by horse and wagon.

THE KITCHEN FIREPLACE was t[...] central part of a frontier home. He[...] mother cooked the food in the utens[...]

Executive Council had already issued an order that this tract should be laid out in lots and put up for sale, with sections set aside for a court house, gaol, market house, churches, a burial ground, and a common pasture.

On February 19, 1788, David Redick, who helped to lay out the future town of Allegheny, wrote to Benjamin Franklin, president of the executive council:

On Tuesday last I went with several other gentlemen to fix on the spot for laying out the town opposite Pittsburgh, and at the same time took a general view of the tract, and found it inferior to expectations, although I had been no stranger to it. There is some pretty low ground on the rivers Ohio and Alleghenia, but there is but a small proportion of it dry land which appears anyways valuable, either for timber or soil; but especially for soil; it abounds with high hills, deep hollows, almost inaccessible to a surveyor. I'm of the opinion that if the inhabitants of the moon are capable of receiving the same advantages from the earth as we do from their world, I say if it be so, this same far-famed tract of land would afford them a variety of beautiful lunar spots, not unworthy the eye of a philosopher. I cannot think that 10-acre lots on such pits and hills will profitably meet with purchasers, unless, like a pig in a poke, it be kept out of view.

On September 24, of the same year, an Act of Assembly

heir possessions to new lands in the West. From the outset, Pittsburgh was a key city in this constantly increasing commerce.

SHIPS OF INLAND COMMERCE, as the Conestoga wagons with the six-horse teams were called, offered safer transportation than the horse trains. Early in the nineteenth century it cost about $5.00 for a hundred weight to send goods from Philadelphia to Pittsburgh.

anging over the fire and baked bread in he oven on the left. The family often en- oyed its warmth on long winter evenings.

From The Planting of Civilization in Western Pennsylvania, *by S. and E. Buck (University of Pittsburgh Press.)*

FORGE. The crank at the wheel, on the right, operated the two tub bellows, on the top, which in turn furnished the blast for the forge. The shaft entering the building furnished the power for the tilt hammer. In 1800, there were only 11 furnaces in the entire Pittsburgh area.

created Allegheny County out of the parts of Westmoreland and Washington, adding to it a large area north and west of the Ohio. But the people of Pittsburgh petitioned the government to allow them to erect the county buildings on their own ground instead of on the reserved tract. Their appeal to the legislature was successful, and on April 13, 1791, that part of the former act which authorized the erection of a court house and gaol on the reserved tract was repealed; the buildings could be erected in Pittsburgh.

It was at that time that Major Samuel Forman visited the town and described it as "the muddiest place I ever was in; and by reason of using so much coal, being a great manufacturing place and kept in so much smoke and dust, as to effect the skin of the inhabitants." This is amusing if one bears in mind that in 1790 the entire population of Pittsburgh was no more than 376. As manufacturing was still in its infancy, with only a few establishments producing goods, one wonders how a handful of factories could have made so much smoke and dust as to affect the skin of the inhabitants.

*

The year 1794 was a milestone in the history of Western

Pennsylvania, a momentous year for Pittsburgh. It was the year when the Monongahela farmers took up arms to fight the excise on whiskey distilling; it was the year when General Anthony Wayne defeated the hostile Indian tribes and freed the frontier of their menace.

The troubles about the whiskey excise began brewing when Congress adopted the tax in 1791. The new government was badly in need of money so that the finances of the nation could be put in order and the debts which the states contracted during the Revolutionary War could be repaid. At the adoption of the Constitution the debt of the United States ran to $54,000,000. Of this sum $12,000,000 was owed to France and Holland, while the rest was owed domestically. Alexander Hamilton, the first Secretary of the Treasury, pleaded for both the payment of the national debt and the assumption by the central government of the indebtedness which the individual states had incurred during the Revolution and which amounted to over $20,000,000. To meet the interest on such a vast sum the government needed an annual revenue of $4,500,000 and to raise this, Congress put an excise on distilled liquors and a tariff on imported goods.

The tax on whiskey alarmed the farm communities around Pittsburgh, where every fifth man had a still. The people held that the excise was not only unjust but impossible to meet. For the farmers in the country, whiskey was not only a commodity, not only a drink, not only a medicine for all ills, not only a source of nourishment, but also a bartering agent in lieu of money.

The docket was discovered in 1955 by Clerk of Court Thomas E. Barrett.

FROM THE FIRST DOCKET of the Allegheny County Criminal Court, dated September 1789. Most of the cases tried between 1789 and 1793 involved assault and battery. Those found guilty were fined up to five pounds, and were jailed until the fine was paid. There were no paroles or probations in those days. The Court exercised jurisdiction over Pittsburgh and the townships of Pitt, Moon, Plum, St. Clair, Mifflin, Elizabeth, and Versailles.

HOMES IN PITTSBURGH AND IN ITS VICINITY CONSTRUCTED DURING THE LAST PART OF THE EIGHTEENTH

Courtesy Pittsburgh Architectural Survey.

BUILT IN 1785: THE PRESLEY NEVILLE HOUSE

Courtesy Pittsburgh Architectural Survey.

BUILT IN 1787: JOHN TURNER'S LOG HOUSE

During the Revolution and the years afterward, money was scarce; specie was hard to come by; country folk saw little of it. A farmer of this period recalled that besides his taxes he never laid out "more than 10 dollars a year, which was for salt, nails and the like; nothing to wear, eat or drink was purchased, as my farm provided all." And while money was in short supply, whiskey was plentiful and as its value kept stable it was used as a medium of exchange.

In the Monongahela country, rye, from which whiskey was made, grew aplenty. Though a bushel fetched only 40 cents—that was the sum the Army paid for it in 1794—at even such a rate there was little demand for it. To sell the rye, the farmers had to send it to the East. But as a packhorse could only carry four bushels, the three-hundred-mile journey to Philadelphia with only a dollar and sixty cents' worth of rye could not be made into a profitable undertaking. However, if the rye were distilled into whiskey the picture changed. A bushel and a half of rye gave a gallon of whiskey, and as a gallon sold in the eastern cities for a dollar, it was evident that by shipping rye in a liquid state one would be able to make money on it. As a packhorse carried two eight-gallon gourds, the shipment on the back of a single horse brought $16, or ten times more than one received for the four bushels that the packhorse carried before.

Thus on the face of it the farmer had little reason to complain against the excise. He made enough to pay the tax; the rub was that the money appeared only on paper. In reality the people did not receive cash for their prod-

Courtesy Criminal Court, Pittsburgh.

ANOTHER PAGE OF THE EARLIEST RECORD of the Allegheny County Criminal Court. These entries for September 1789 report the names of persons "who were sworn a Grand Inquest for the Body of the County," and list "Tavern Keepers Recommended." Judge Alexander Addison presided over the Court; he was assisted by Judges George Wallace, John Wilkins, Jr., John McDowell, and John Gibson, stern jurists who insisted on order.

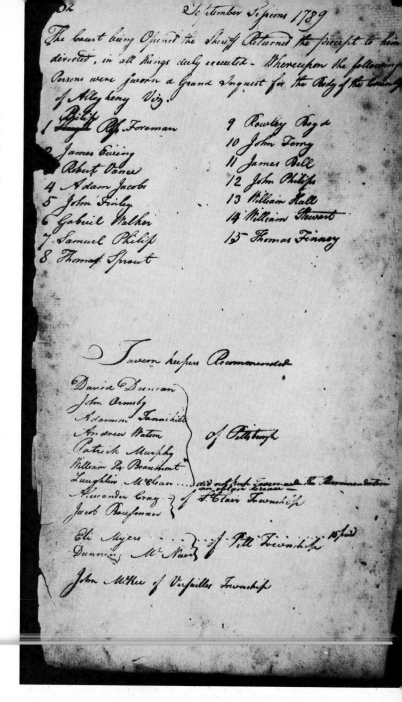

CENTURY SHOW A MARKED EUROPEAN INFLUENCE AND THE AMERICAN DESIRE FOR COMFORTABLE LIVING.

Courtesy Pittsburgh Architectural Survey.

BUILT IN 1800: MAJOR DANIEL LEET'S TAVERN

Courtesy Pittsburgh Architectural Survey.

BUILT BEFORE 1800: JOHN WOOD HOMESTEAD.

JAMES O'HARA (1754-1819), one of the earliest industrialists of the town, came from Liverpool to Pittsburgh as a young man. At first he clerked for Simon and Campbell, then he joined the Indian traders Devereux Smith and Ephraim Douglass. From 1784 on, his task was to provision the western forces. As deputy quartermaster-general under Isaac Craig, he procured the supplies for the armies fighting the Indians. O'Hara had manifold business interests. He had a retail store; he imported salt from the Onandoga salt works; he built a brewery; he owned a sawmill, a tanyard, and a gristmill; he also had his hand in shipbuilding; he erected the town's first glasswork, built houses, exported goods and held huge parcels of real estate, which became the foundation of several large Pittsburgh fortunes.

uct; they bartered their whiskey to the merchant, who either sold it to the army or shipped it downriver and sold it to the Spaniards in New Orleans. For the money the merchants purchased goods in the East which were sorely needed in the West. So the farmers faced the insoluble problem: How to pay the excise without cash.

The western farm communities had troubles enough without being burdened with the new tax on liquor as well. Their list of complaints was a long one; the main among them was that they were far from the markets, thus to transport their goods where they could sell them was costly, and the government would not ease their lot by building new roads. Therefore, they proposed a land tax as a more equitable source of revenue, a suggestion which was indignantly rejected by the East, where land values were high.

To the complaints of the westerners the East retorted that those who moved into the new country knew of the conditions they were to face. They knew that there was no adequate road system to carry their produce so that it could be sold advantageously in the East—yet they went there because western land was cheap and western life was attractive. Now if they were dissatisfied, if they felt that the excise on whiskey was unjust, they must appeal to Congress instead of threatening to take matters into their own hands. The laws of the country had to be obeyed by all; they were made for all of the United States, not for one section only. People must carry their responsibilities in the East, South, North, and West alike. But the farmers of western Pennsylvania would not listen to such arguments. They felt abused by the government, and they were determined to fight for their rights.

Shortly after the imposition of the tax, Albert Gallatin, a leading spokesman of back-country democracy, introduced to the legislature of Pennsylvania a resolution against the excise. From then on the issue was kept alive; the farming communities held one protest meeting after the other; they adopted resolutions and submitted petitions. And as the controversy deepened, their dissent turned into physical violence. On September 9, 1791, Robert Johnson, the collector of revenue for Washington and Allegheny counties, was waylaid by a gang of sixteen who cut his hair off, tarred and feathered him. During the following months the attacks on revenue collectors multiplied. If the assailants were caught they had to pay heavy fines. There was a constant tension, a steady challenge of federal authority. Newspapers in the East began to refer to the anti-excise movement in the West as the "Whiskey Rebellion," a term far too strong for the discontent, but a term which served the Federalist politicians well.

On September 15, 1792, President Washington warned those who signed a resolution against the excise collectors "to desist from all unlawful combinations and proceedings whatsoever having for object or tending to obstruct the operation of the laws." George Clymer, supervisor from the Treasury, was sent to Pittsburgh to investigate the complaints, but his heavy handed attitude only caused further irritation. In the back country the farmers burned the effigy of General John Neville, the collector of revenue for Allegheny, Bedford, Washington, and Westmoreland counties.

And were it not for events in Europe, the discontent in Monongahela Country probably might have subsided and the resentment of the farmers might have quieted down. But curiously enough, the events of the French Revolution became closely related to the happenings in the Pittsburgh area.

At the outbreak of the French Revolution, most Americans sympathized with its aims. However, by 1793 the sentiment had shifted; the execution of Louis XVI in January of that year and the declaration of war on Great Britain, Spain, and Holland the following month had a sobering effect on the country. On April 22, President Washington issued his neutrality proclamation: the United States was not going to take sides in the European war. And while America was officially neutral, the Americans were not. The feelings of the Federalists, the merchants, the shipbuilders, the financiers, in short, the well-to-do, were with the English while the wage earners, the workers, artisans, and farmers were behind the French revolutionists. These latter classes drew together in clubs; they acclaimed Citizen Gênet, the French minister who attempted to use American ports as bases for an attack on Spanish and British territories in the Western Hemisphere, and they offered him a triumphant welcome the minute he set foot on American soil.

President Washington castigated the activities of the democratic clubs. He said that they were sowing jealousy and distrust among the people and that, if they were allowed to operate , "they would shake the government to its foundation." But how could they be stopped? How could the government forbid their existence?

The most powerful democratic club in the Monongahela area was the one at Mingo Creek, soon to be known as "the cradle of the Whiskey Rebellion." Its three hundred members urged the replacement of the corrupt tax collectors by honest and reputable men. Angered by those distillers who were willing to pay the excise, they riddled with bullets the still of James Kiddoe and shot holes in William

Coughran's still. When John Holcroft, who led the attack on Coughran's still, was asked what he was doing, he replied jestingly that he and his friends were only "tinkering" with it. The expression stuck. From then on, resolutions, broadsides, and notices against the excise bore the signature of "Tom the Tinker" or "Tom the Tinker's men."

The destruction of stills posed a powerful challenge to the federal government. If raids on the property of law-abiding citizens could not be suppressed, how could law and order be maintained? Alexander Hamilton urged his followers to pass a bill which would allow the state courts to deal with those who refused to pay the tax. Such a bill was voted upon and received the President's signature on June 5. Now the machinery of the government began to grind. David Lenox, a United States marshal, left Philadelphia for the Pittsburgh area with writs to be served on the recalcitrants. Reaching the district in the middle of July, he asked General Neville, the tax collector for the district, to accompany him on the mission. And soon the two men were riding into Monongahela County ready to do their duty.

The farmers were at harvesting; the marshal and the collector of revenue could not have chosen a worse time.

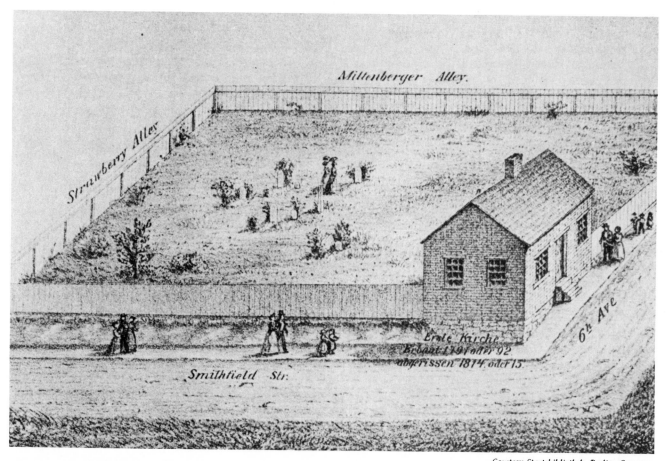

Courtesy Staatsbibliothek, Berlin, Germany.

THE FIRST PROTESTANT CHURCH west of the Allegheny Mountains was the German Reformed Church on the corner of Sixth Avenue and Smithfield Street. Erected early in the 1790s on land donated by John Penn, the building was demolished in 1814 or in 1815, making room for a more elaborate church. For eighteen years the new place of worship served the community; in 1833 a third building was erected which stood until 1875 when another more sumptuous edifice replaced it.

As they attempted to serve William Miller, a member of the Mingo Creek Democratic Society, with a writ, Miller refused to accept it. "I felt myself mad with passion. I felt my blood boil, at seeing General Neville along to pilot the sheriff to my very door," he said. In no time, Miller's neighbors appeared on the scene, whereupon the marshal and general took to the woods.

The community was seething with anger. Rumors spread that the marshal had come not only to serve writs but also to make arrests and to take those whom he arrested to Philadelphia. So it was resolved to capture him. How this was to help the farmers' cause is not easy to understand, but the time for clear thinking had passed; the people in the Monongahela country were swayed by their emotions. They may have felt that once the marshal became their prisoner the government would no longer harass them. Whatever their reason, a party of forty, led by John Holbrook, set out for Bower Hill, the estate of General Neville, assuming that the marshal was staying there. At daybreak of July 16 they drew a ring around the mansion and asked for the papers of the marshal and the tax collector. And when their request was refused, they began to fire at the house. Fortunately, no one was harmed.

There was very little sleep that night in Monongahela County. Next morning the farmers met at Couch's Fort, and when they heard that Pittsburgh militiamen were on the way to defend Bower Hill, the five hundred men at the meeting resolved to move to the mansion and force a showdown. As it happened, the rumor turned out to be false; there were no militiamen on the way to the Neville estate. Still, the farmers were on the march. As they reached Bower Hill, they sent David Hamilton into the house to ask for Neville's resignation. Abraham Kirkpatrick, the brother-in-law of Neville who was left in charge of the estate, replied that he had no authority to give such a promise without the General's consent, and as Neville was in Pittsburgh, one must wait until his return. The farmers outside the mansion were not satisfied with the answer; they insisted on seeing Neville's tax papers. And when Kirkpatrick refused to entertain this demand, they commenced firing at the house. The men inside the mansion responded and for a while the shooting went on. During a lull James McFarlane, the leader of the attackers, left the shelter of a tree and was hit by a bullet. Now the enraged attackers set fire to the slave-cabins which surrounded the mansion, and soon the flames engulfed the main house.

Next day, the men of Mingo Creek buried McFarlane. The mood of the community was ugly. The people were determined to prevent the return of the writs as they believed that once the writs were returned the government would confiscate their land. David Hamilton rode to Pittsburgh, asking for the surrender of the writs and for Neville's resignation. But Marshal Lenox would not budge; Hamilton had to leave the city without a promise.

On July 21, another meeting was held at Mingo Creek to which Hugh Henry Brackenridge from Pittsburgh was invited. The lawyer accepted the invitation and came in the company of prominent Pittsburgh citizens. Chief Burgess George Robinson was there, as were the Assistant Burgesses Josiah Tannehill, William H. Beaumont, Peter Audrian, and William Semple. Addressing the meeting, Brackenridge said that in his opinion President Washington would pardon those who were involved in the attack on Bower Hill, therefore he suggested that no further disturbance should be caused. But the meeting would not listen to him; the men were swayed by the firebrand David Bradford, who demanded a show of strength and the interception of the mail from Pittsburgh. Bradford's suggestion was taken. A few days later a post rider from Pittsburgh was caught and relieved of his mail pouch in which were letters from Presley Neville, the general's son, to General Daniel Morgan; from General John Gibson to Governor Thomas Mifflin; from Edward Day to Alexander Hamilton, all urging armed intervention and strong action against the "rebels."

As Bradford read the letters, he called out, "They shall be hung" and his words were taken up by the others. But to hang the culprits one had to catch them. So it was agreed to move against Pittsburgh, whose Federalist merchants were considered as the enemy of the back-country democracy, arrest the men and burn the place. The date for the city's destruction was set for the first day of August.

Pittsburgh was panic-stricken. When the ominous day arrived, twenty-one of the town's leading citizens rode out to Braddock's Field where a few thousand farmers assembled and remonstrated with them that the destruction of the city would give them no benefits. Brackenridge passed from group to group and did his best to calm the excited spirits.

Describing the events in his *Incidents of the Insurrection*, the lawyer recounts a dialogue with one of "Tom the Tinker's men."

"Are we to take the garrison?" asked the man, meaning the capture of Fort Fayette in Pittsburgh, and Brackenridge replied, "We are."

"Can we take it?"

"No doubt of it."

"But of a great loss?"

"Not at all," said Brackenridge. "Not above a thousand killed and a five hundred mortally wounded."

The questioner's jaw dropped; he was ready to destroy the fort and burn the city, but to give up his life for it was another matter.

In the end the men from Pittsburgh were able to persuade the farmers to march into the town and show their strength—but not to do any harm to it. "The people of Pittsburgh wish to see the army," Brackenridge orated, "and you must go through it. . . . It will convince the government that we are no mob, but a regular army, and can preserve discipline, and pass thro' a town, like the French and American armies, in the course of the last war, without doing the least injury to persons or property."

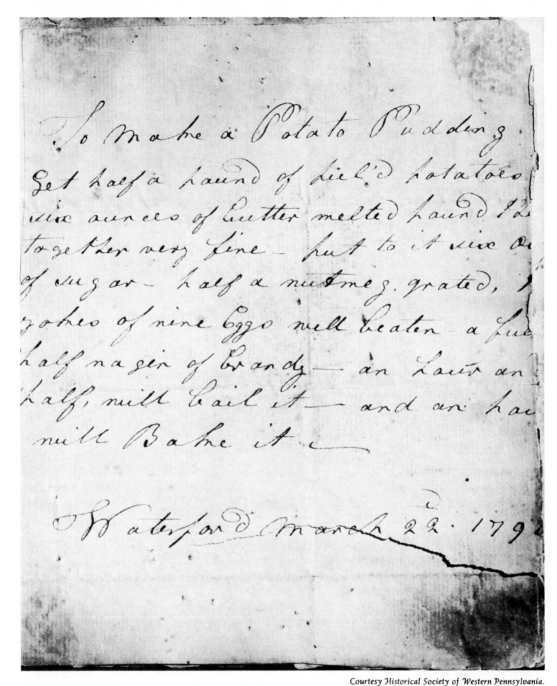

To Make a Potato Pudding

Get half a pound of piel'd potatoes
six ounces of butter melted pound them
together very fine — put to it six ou
of sugar — half a nutmeg, grated,
yokes of nine Eggs well beaten — a full
half nagin of brandy — an hour an
half, will boil it — and an hou
will Bake it

Waterford march 22 · 179

A RECIPE BOOK FROM 1790, which came down to us, gives directions for the preparation of potato pudding. In it the pioneer woman advises her readers: "Get half a pound of piel'd potatoes six ounces of butter melted pound them together very fine—put to it six ounces of sugar—half a nutmeg, grated, yokes of nine Eggs well beaten—a full half nogin of brandy—an hour and half, will boil it—and an hour will bake it."

So it was to be. As the invaders entered, they were offered whiskey, barrels of it. Brackenridge reasoned: "I thought it better to be employed in extinguishing the fire of their thirst, than of my house." By nightfall the troops left and Pittsburgh was free. No damage was caused; nothing was burned, nothing was looted, no one was killed, no one was arrested. The march into the city, so a leader of the farmers proclaimed, was "a glorious revolution accomplished without bloodshed." The boasting words may have reassured the county folk that their move on Pittsburgh was helpful in their fight against the excise. But was it really?

To the country, the march looked like a challenge to the powers of the central government. In Philadelphia, President Washington called a Cabinet meeting and pledged to use every measure at his disposal to subdue the "rebellion." On August 4, Chief Justice Wilson issued a certificate declaring that "the enforcement of the laws in Western Pennsylvania was being obstructed by combinations too powerful to be suppressed" by judicial pro-

(turn to page 64)

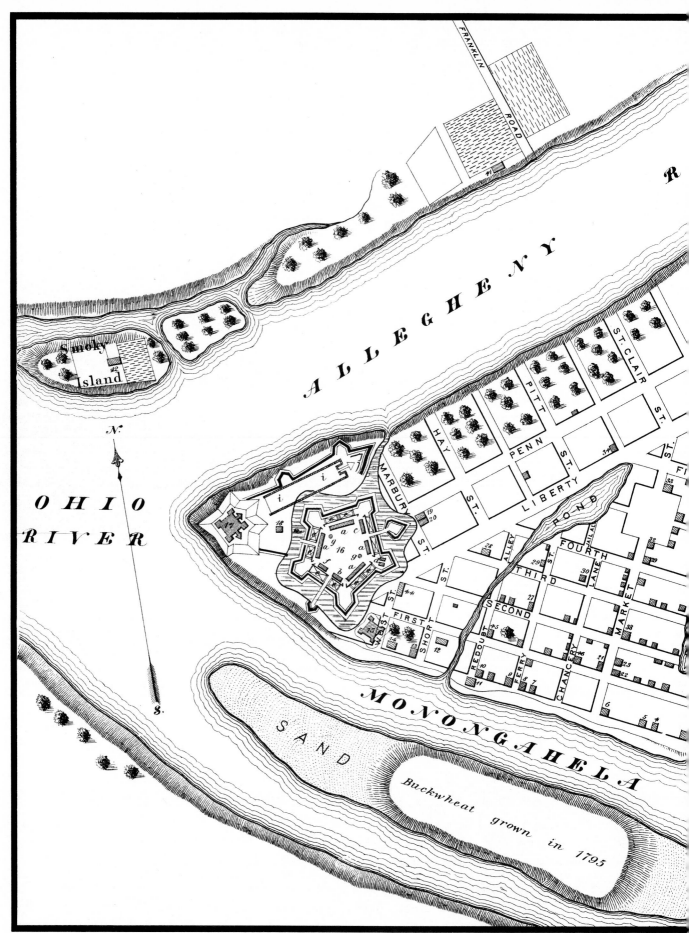

FRANKLIN ROAD

ALLEGHENY R

Smoky Island

OHIO RIVER

N.

S.

ST. CLAIR ST.

PITT ST.

PENN ST.

HAY ST.

MARBURY ST.

LIBERTY ST.

POND

ST.

19
20

i
i
i

18

16
a
g
a c
a
g
a
f
b
a

44

WEST ST.

FIRST ST.

SHORT ST.

14
15
12

REDOUBT ALLEY

10
11

FERRY

9
7

CHANCERY LANE

8

28

THIRD ST.

SECOND ST.

27

45

46
21
23
22

FOURTH ST.

MARKET ST.

29
30

6
5

38

RAILWAY LANE

33

35

MONONGAHELA

SAND

Buckwheat grown in 1795

From History of Allegheny County (1876).

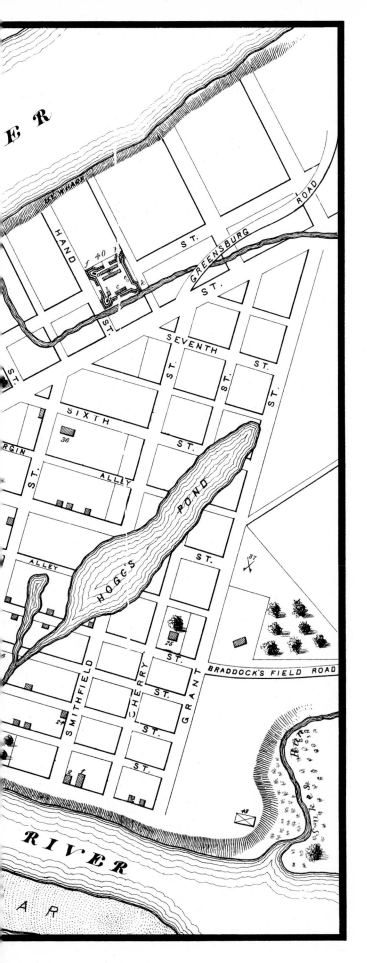

PITTSBURGH IN 1795. A plan of the city, showing the position of the forts, the homes of the citizens, and the public buildings.

Starting out at Cherry and going toward the west along the Monongahela were the homes of Peter Audrian (1) and James Ross (2); and also the place of Robert Henderson from where he operated his ferry (3); William Morrow's "Sign of the Green Tree Tavern" (4); Adamson Tannehill's house (5); the homes of Samuel Ewalt (6) and John Ormsby (7); Samuel Semples' Tavern, where George Washington stopped in 1770 (8); the residences of John Neville (9) and Isaac Craig (10), two of the city's most outstanding citizens; and the Redoubt constructed in 1765 (11). At Short Street was the site of the boatyard (12), farther on were the homes of Abraham Kirkpatrick (13) and James O'Hara (14).

Near the Point was the site of the temporary fort built by Colonel Mercer after Fort Duquesne was destroyed (15).

The plan of Fort Pitt (16) shows the barracks (a), the commandant's house (b), the storehouse (c), powder magazine (d), casemates (e), storehouse for flour (f), wells (g), and the southeast bastion (i). To the northeast stood Fort Duquesne (17).

Between Fort Duquesne and Fort Pitt is Colonel Bouquet's Redoubt (18), the city's celebrated blockhouse, still standing today. Built in 1764, it was converted into a dwelling 20 years later and for a time was occupied by Isaac Craig.

On the corner of Marbury and Penn were the houses of the widows of Colonel William Butler (19) and General R. Butler (20).

Near the corner of Market and First lived John Scull. In his house (21) he printed *The Pittsburgh Gazette* and kept the town's post office. Further on were Andrew Watson's Tavern (22), where the first Court of Quarter Sessions of Allegheny and the first Court of Oyer and Terminer were held; and Hugh Henry Brackenridge's residence (23).

At the corner of Smithfield and Second was the house of Alexander Addison (24). At Fourth between Grant and Cherry lived Jean Marie (25). General John Wilkins resided at the corner of Wood and Third (26). A tavern kept by the Negro Charles Richard was situated at the corner of Second and Ferry (27).

At the western end of Third Street stood Major John Irvine's home (28). In the next block, facing Ferry, lived John Gibson (29). Near the corner of Third and Chancery was the house of the colored man Benjamin Richard (30), and at the intersection of Fourth and Wood lived John Wilkins (31).

Irvine's Hall was on the eastern side of Market Street near Diamond (32), not far from the Black Bear Hotel (33).

In the area laid out along the Allegheny stood the homes of William Cecil on Liberty opposite Fifth (34); and Dr. Nathaniel Bedford, bounded by Liberty, Penn, and Irvine (35).

The First Presbyterian Church stood on Wood near Sixth (36).

East of Grant near the end of Fifth was the site of Major Grant's defeat before the English took Fort Duquesne (37).

Public buildings along Market Street were the Market House at the corner of Second (38), and the jail at the corner of Fourth (39).

Fort Fayette was at Hand Street (40). Inside it were the two story blockhouse (a), the powder magazine (b), the officer's quarters (c), barracks for the men (d), the flagstaff (e), salient angles (f and h), the guardhouse (i), and the southeast bastion (k).

Across the Allegheny near Franklin Road was James Robinson's home (41); on Smoky Island lived J. Lichtenberger (42).

General Wayne's stables were near the junction of Suke's Run and the Monongahela (43); his headquarters during 1792 were located at the corner of West and Second (44).

George Adams lived at the corner of Redoubt Alley and First Street (45). The post office moved here in 1794.

John Johnston, the grandfather of William G. Johnston, had his home at the northeast corner of First and Chancery Lane (46).

63

ceedings. This certificate gave the government free rein to use military units against the opponents of the excise. On August 5, Alexander Hamilton issued a report recounting the story of the uprising. Proclamations of the President and the Governor of Pennsylvania followed. The Secretary of War asked the governors of Pennsylvania, New Jersey, Maryland, and Virginia to call up 13,000 militiamen and be ready to march against the Monongahela farmers.

Hamilton, realizing the political advantage of firm action, urged the instant dispatch of the military. The burning of Bower Hill and the march on Pittsburgh afforded an excellent opportunity to bear down on the opposition and crush the rebellious democratic societies.

However, before the troops began their march, commissioners were sent to western Pennsylvania to attempt a peaceful settlement. Those who were involved in the "rebellion" were asked to sign a declaration solemnly promising that in the future they would submit to the laws of the United States and that they would not "directly or indirectly, oppose the execution of the acts for raising a revenue on distilled spirits and stills," and that they would support "as far as the law required, the civil authority in affording the protection due to all officers and other citizens." All those who signed the declaration were to receive a pardon.

Yet, while the farmers began to take the oath of submission, the government moved its army over the mountains to subdue the uprising that at this time was already over. The troops, under the command of Governor Henry Lee and accompanied by a federal judge, a federal attorney, and a federal marshal, reached Pittsburgh at the end of October. For three weeks they stayed in the town, arresting some of those who took part in the burning of Bower Hill and those who led the upheaval. On November 19, the first detachment of soldiers left the city with the prisoners, forcing them to march on foot all the way to Philadelphia. At their trials, all of those arrested, save two, were acquitted, and even those two men received their pardons not long thereafter.

President Washington named February 19, 1795, as a day of thanksgiving for "the seasonable controul which has been given to a spirit of disorder in the suppression of the late insurrection."

With this the story of the "Whiskey Rebellion" came to an end. It was basically an uprising of the small farmers against the commercial and business classes; a desperate stand of the small agriculturists against the big producers. It brought into the political picture the opponents of the Federalists' policies. Within a few years the dissatisfied elements were strong enough to send Thomas Jefferson to the White House in "the glorious revolution of 1800." With Jefferson in the presidency, the excise was repealed, but even while it was in force the farmers of the Pittsburgh area found subtler means than taking up arms to evade it.

*

After the exciting year of 1794, life in Pittsburgh once more ran on an even keel.

The village—comprising from the Point to Grant Street on the Monongahela, to Washington Street (now Eleventh) on the Allegheny side—was incorporated into a borough on April 22, 1794. Borough officers were elected a year later. George Robinson and Josiah Tannehill became chief burgesses; Nathaniel Irish, John Johnston, George Adams, and Nathaniel Bedford assistant burgesses; Samuel Morrison, high constable; James Clow, town clerk; William Amberson and Abraham Kirkpatrick, assessors; and William Gray and John McMasters, supervisors. About that time Thomas Chapman described Pittsburgh as "a thriving town containing . . . about two hundred Houses, fifty of which are brick and framed & the remainder log." The taxes collected in 1794 amounted to £253/19/9. As expenditures came to £190/4/9 there remained a surplus of £63/15/0, hardly enough to make the much needed improvements on the streets. Therefore, between the years of 1794 and 1801 almost four thousand additional dollars were levied for such purposes. Five hundred seventy dollars a year in the average for street improvements was a paltry sum, but that was all the borough would spend. In 1801, an ordinance was passed "that pathways of brick, stone or gravel, bounded by curbstones or square pieces of timber should be constructed." Even more pressing than curbstone walks was the water problem. The town needed "a more effective supply of water," more wells and pumps. Five new pumps were installed, one on Market, one between First and Second Street, one between Second and Third, one between Third and Fourth, and one at the Court House. Better streets, better water supply, and other municipal improvements helped the town's growth and furthered the expansion of its industries.

During the last years of the century, several manufacturing establishments sprang up. Boatbuilding, which had flourished ever since Pittsburgh's beginning, expanded vigorously. In 1792, the sloop Western Experiment was completed on the banks of Monongahela and floated down to New Orleans. In 1797, when war with France was imminent, Congress ordered two vessels in Pittsburgh for use at the lower Mississippi. These boats—the President Adams and the Senator Ross—were launched in the spring of 1799. By 1800 the production of the boatbuilders was estimated to reach the sum of $12,000. Some of the boatyards, like Tarascon Brothers and James Berthoud & Company which began a mercantile and shipbuilding business in Pittsburgh in 1802, were large establishments with smith shops and rigging and sail lofts next to the main store and warehouse. At the turn of the century, the Pittsburgh boatyards already constructed sturdy vessels, seaworthy enough to cross the ocean. The first transatlantic sailing of a western boat with a cargo of cotton was presumably that of the 170-ton brig Dean. This vessel, built on the banks of the Allegheny, left Pittsburgh in January 1803 and arrived in Liverpool on England's shores some weeks later.

(turn to page 69)

THE FIRST SKETCH OF PITTSBURGH was drawn in 1790 by Louis Brantz, a Philadelphia merchant. He wrote of the forks that "the view from this spot is in truth the most beautiful I ever beheld." Seth Eastman redrew Brantz's original (now in Carnegie Library) for Schoolcraft's *Information Respecting the Indian Tribes of the United States.*

PITTSBURGH IN 1804 as painted by George Beck, the English artist who in that year made a tour of the western country and passed through Pittsburgh on his way to Kentucky. Some 50 buildings in the painting were identified by Lois Mulkearn, who wrote a well-documented article about her findings for the spring 1948 issue of the *Pitt Magazine.*

Painted specially for this book by Marty Cornelius.

THE FIRST POST OFFICE. In 1787 the town's post office was located in the home of John Scull, the first postmaster of Pittsburgh, on the corner of Market and First Streets. Scull continued as the city's postmaster until late in 1796.

Painted specially for this book by George W. Mengelson.

THE FIRST ISSUE OF *THE PITTSBURGH GAZETTE* appeared at the end of July 1786. The fortnightly publication was printed on a Ramage handpress in the rear of John Scull's house, which also served as post office for the city.

Painted specially for this book by Edwin R. Anderson.

THE FIRST DEPARTMENT STORE. Thomas Perkins, the jeweler opened a store in 1800 at Third and Market, where all kinds of goods could be bought. In the same building was the establishment of John Hammond, the shoemaker.

THE
FIRST
GLASS
WORK

*Painted
specially
for this book
by
Edgar A. Roth*

67

Watercolor made specially for this book by Walter A. Gasowski.

THE FIRST IRON FURNACE. In 1793, George Anshutz's small furnace on Two Mile Run, the present Shadyside, produced mainly casting of stoves and grates. It lasted only a year; there was not enough iron ore or timber near by.

Watercolor made specially for this book by Walter A. Gasowski.

RIVER COMMERCE. In the last decades of the eighteenth century, the main arteries of commerce were the rivers. Produce was sent down the Ohio mostly in flatboats. The journey to Louisville and back took about three months.

Other boats sailed to Lisbon, to St. Thomas in the Virgin Islands and to other ports of the world. Before long the crossing of the Atlantic from Pittsburgh became a commonplace event, it amounted to little more than a paragraph in the local newspapers.

For the world it was hard to believe that a boat could set out from Pittsburgh, so far inland, and sail all the way to the shores of Europe. The Pittsburgh *Almanac* relates an amusing anecdote about such an occurrence. According to the story, Henry Clay told in the House of Representatives of a Pittsburgh-built vessel that sailed into an Italian harbor. When the master presented his papers, the customs officer told him: "Sir, your papers are forged; there is no such place as Pittsburgh in the world! Your vessel must be confiscated!" Whereupon the American captain "laid before the officer a map of the U.S., directed him to the Gulf of Mexico; pointed out the mouth of the Mississippi; led him a thousand miles up it to the mouth of the Ohio, and thence another thousand miles up to Pittsburgh. 'There, Sir, is the port whence my vessel cleared out!'" The officer was too startled to say a word.

But while the building of boats that crossed the ocean was noteworthy, the making of small craft in the Pittsburgh yards grew to an everyday occurrence. The completion of a small boat that carried immigrants and produce down the Ohio took not much longer than the forging of an implement by the blacksmith. A few logs, a bucketful of nails, and the craft was finished.

The boatyards turned out a great variety of vessels; they made them in different sizes and shapes, and they were called by different names, but generally all these craft fitted into three categories: flatboats, keelboats, and barges.

The most convenient way to transport goods downstream was by flatboat. It was also the cheapest. These boats were called Kentucky or New Orleans boats according to their destination, or arks and broadhorns because of their wide-bladed sweep and because they seemed to resemble the ancient craft of Noah, and they were called tobacco, horse, or cattle boats after the produce and animals they carried. But however different their given names were, in the main they were very much alike. Their length varied between twenty and one hundred feet, their width between twelve and twenty feet. A twelve-foot-wide flatboat in Pittsburgh cost about one dollar a foot, a fourteen-foot-wide one ran to a dollar and a half; the price for the whole boat usually included one steering and four rowing oars. On the average, a flatboat carried forty to fifty tons of merchandise or, measuring it in a different way, four to five hundred barrels. The better ones were built of oak, the cheaper ones from pine and other woods. Flatboats had one great advantage; at the end of the trip they could be dismantled and their lumber sold in the Southern cities where lumber was much desired.

While downstream traffic was done by flatboats, for upstream hauls keelboats were used. Keelboats were long

narrow crafts of light draft, easily navigable in shallow waters. Their characteristic was the cleated running board on which the boatmen walked from bow to stern, pushing their long poles against the bottom of the stream and thus moving the boat against the current. They were on the average forty to eighty feet long and from seven to ten feet in beam. Built on a three-inch-deep and four- to five-inch-wide keel, they carried fifteen to fifty tons of merchandise. In 1805 fifty keelboats of thirty-ton capacity moved regularly between Pittsburgh and Cincinnati; a decade later there were three times as many. The trip by keelboat from New Orleans to Pittsburgh took four months; downriver the 1950-mile passage was made in four to six weeks. Freight rates varied. For a hundredweight of goods shipped from New Orleans to Pittsburgh the charge was eight dollars; from Louisville to Pittsburgh it cost three dollars. The downriver rate was only a dollar or two for a hundredweight.

Barges were the larger brothers of the keelboats. These crafts drew more water; their draft was about three to four feet, thus they were used in the deeper waters of the Mississippi. Their length was about seventy-five to one hundred feet, their width twelve to twenty feet. Barges had a cabin and a mast and sails; they were propelled by oars and poles and steered by a rudder; in difficulties they were towed by a line from the shore.

The boatmen, boisterous, bragging, cantankerous, and hard drinking, were the heroes of the rivers. After the war of 1812 there were about 3000 of them on the western waters. Perhaps the best known of them was the Pittsburgh-born Mike Fink, a legendary figure whose escapades became part of American folklore. Fink would swear:

I'm a salt river roarer; and I love the wimming, and how I'm chock-full of fight . . . I can out-run, out-dance, out-jump, out-dive, out-drink, out-holler, and out-lick any white thugs in the shape o' human that's ever put foot within two thousand miles o' the big Mississippi. Whoop! holler, you varmints!—holler fur the Snapping Turkle! or I'l jump right straight down yer throats, quicker nor a streak o' greased chain-lightning can down a nigger's!

The stories about Mike Fink are legion, they abound in thrills and humor and they give a vivid picture of the keelboat age and the life on the rivers before the advent of the steamboat.

The river traffic stimulated manufacturing; the factories of Pittsburgh produced goods not only for home consumption but for shipment as well. The expansion of industries brought prosperity to the town.

One of the earliest industries of Pittsburgh—next to boatbuilding—was glassmaking. General James O'Hara, in association with Major Isaac Craig, began a glassworks in 1795 on the south side of the Monongahela. Its superintendent was the German-born Peter William Eichbaum, who gave the name to Oakland. When after numerous unsuccessful trials Eichbaum produced a bottle, O'Hara noted: "To-day we made the first bottle at a cost of $30,000." Five years later, in 1800, General James Wilkinson, Dr. Hugh Scott, John Wilkins, and others built a window pane factory on the north side of the Ohio, known after the product's selling agents as Denny and Beelen. And by 1807, the most famous of the town's glassworks was established—Bakewell's Glass House. Its products were bought by the wealthy of the world. Meals on Bakewell plates were served in the White House by Dolly Madison and also in luxurious French and English châteaux.

The pressing need for tools, implements, and clothing called for better and faster methods of production. In due time the home spinning wheel and the village smithy disappeared and were replaced by factories where goods were no longer made by hands alone.

In 1801, George Cochran started a chair work; William Cecil made saddles, bridles, and other leather goods; in 1802 Jeffery Scaife, together with his future father-in-law, William Barrett, and William Gazzam, opened a tin-plate business; in 1803, John Parkin began to manufacture iron ware. By then printing was established, as was cording and spinning. In 1804, Peter Eltonhead built the area's first cotton factory.

The earliest iron foundry, established at Shadyside by the Alsace-born George Anshutz, sprang up in 1793, but it turned out to be a failure, as the price of the iron ore which had to be brought over the mountains was prohibitive. Within two years the furnace closed down. Not until 1805 did John McClurg, Joseph Smith, and John Gormly set up a foundry. It was this work that supplied Commodore Perry's fleet on Lake Erie in 1812 with cannon, howitzers, shells, and balls, and furnished material for Andrew Jackson's army at New Orleans.

While Pittsburgh had no furnaces and forges at this time, the surrounding area was studded with them. Iron products—from small utensils to huge sugar kettles for Louisiana—were made in Fayette and Westmoreland counties, from where they were sent to the Pittsburgh market and to the Pittsburgh wharves. These early furnaces made nails, shovels, tongs, spades, scythes, sickles, hoes, axes, frying pans, knives, and other implements for the pioneer household.

Pittsburgh's manufacturing establishments increased at a speedy rate. In 1808 Cramer's *Navigator* listed for the previous year: 1 cotton factory, 1 green glass work, 2 breweries, 1 air furnace, 4 nail factories, 7 coppersmiths, 1 wire manufactory, 1 brass foundry, 6 saddlers, 2 gunsmiths, 2 tobacconists, 1 bell maker, 1 scythe and sickle maker (five

(turn to page 72)

HARSH PRESSURE was applied to collectors and to all those who paid the whiskey tax. This column of *The Pittsburgh Gazette* prints the resignation of tax collector Robert Johnson, while John Reed, who complied with the law, found this notice near his distillery. It was signed by Tom the Tinker, the name adopted by those resisting authority, because of the way they "mended" the stills of some farmers.

Painted specially for this book by Idabelle Kleinhans.

THE WHISKEY REBELLION. During the summer of 1794 the Monongahela country was seething with excitement. The tempers of the backwoods farmers were at a high pitch; discontent and rebellion were in the air. On July 16 five hundred men marched toward Bower Hill, General John Neville's country estate.

Neville, the erstwhile commander of Fort Pitt, was now revenue collector for Bedford, Washington, Westmoreland, and Allegheny counties, and as was his duty, he set out to collect the excise tax on whiskey distilling. A day before, a writ was served on one William Miller, ordering him to appear before the district court of far-away Philadelphia as he had resisted paying the excise. This sparked the flame of rebellion. Led by Major James MacFarlane, the enraged neighbors of Miller marched against the revenue collector's home, demanding General Neville's books and asking for his resignation. When the request was refused, shooting began. MacFarlane was killed by a bullet; in retaliation, his supporters

set fire to the buildings on the estate.

The attack on Bower Hill was one of the numerous incidents in the Western Pennsylvania farmers' struggle against the unpopular tax. Ever since 1791, when Congress had adopted Alexander Hamilton's financial proposals including an excise on spirits distilled from grain, the small distillers in the farm area were disturbed. They tarred and abused excise collectors and riddled with bullets the stills of those who obeyed the law and paid the duty.

"The small distillers consider themselves wronged by this tax," wrote Hugh Henry Brackenridge not long after the burning of Bower Hill, "which in truth takes away their profit if they bear the expense of its transportation below . . . and if they keep it here they must trade it for Country produce and never see in a year enough hard cash to pay the assessment—large distillers, who sell to the Army, think to use the Law in trading down the little fellow. . . ."

In reality, the root of the trouble was

deeper than being a quarrel over the excise tax. It was, as Brackenridge put it, "a stand of the democratic, poverty-ridden West against the encroachments of the aristocratic Money Bags of the East; of a people who feel themselves taxed in order to fasten the yoke of Plutocrats about their necks."

A fortnight after the attack on Neville's home, some 5000 men assembled at Braddock's Field, ready to burn down the town of Sodom—Pittsburgh. Fortunately men of good will were able to persuade them to desist.

When news of the upheaval reached the federal government, President Washington dispatched a militia numbering 13,000 to restore order; but long before the soldiers reached Pittsburgh the rebellion spent itself. To the country on the whole, it appeared that it was the strong military force that succeeded in crushing the rebellion; it seemed a victory for the federal government, which forced the recalcitrant elements in the countryside to obey the laws of the land.

miles up the Allegheny), 2 soap boilers and tallow chandlers, 1 brush maker, 1 trunk maker, 5 coopers, 10 blue dyers, 13 weavers, 1 comb maker, 7 cabinet makers, 1 turner, 6 bakers, 8 butchers, 2 barbers, 6 hatters, 2 potteries, 2 straw bonnet makers, 1 reed maker, 2 spinning wheel makers, 1 wool and cotton cord manufacturer, 4 plane makers, 6 miliners, 12 mantua makers, 1 stocking weaver, 1 glass cutter, 2 book binderies, 4 house and sign painters, 2 tinners, 1 sail maker, 2 mattress makers, 1 upholsterer, 5 wagon makers, 5 watch and clock makers and silversmiths, 5 bricklayers, 4 plasterers, 3 stone cutters, 5 boatbuilders, 2 ship builders, 1 saddle tree maker, 1 flute and jewsharp maker, 1 pump maker, 1 bell hanger, 2 looking glass makers, 1 ladies lace maker, 1 lock maker, 7 tanners, 2 rope walks, 1 gardner and seedsman, 17 blacksmiths, 1 machinist and whitesmith, 1 cutter and tool maker, 32 house carpenters and joiners, 21 boot and shoemakers, 1 ladies' shoemaker, 5 windsor chair makers, 1 split bottom chair maker, 13 tailors, 3 spinning-wheel spindle and crank makers, 1 breeches maker, 1 glove maker, 33 tavern keepers, 50 store keepers or merchants, 4 printing offices, 1 copper plate printer, 5 brick yards, 3 stone masons, 2 booksellers, 1 harness maker, 1 horse farrier, 1 starch maker, 3 board and lumber yards. The enumeration of the professions, the manufactories, and the master workmen in each particular branch also included 12 schoolmistresses and 4 physicians but unfortunately omitted the number of ministers.

The invention of the steam engine gave a fresh impetus to manufacturing; it changed the methods of production and transportation. In 1809, Oliver Evans founded the first steam gristmill west of the mountains; two years later Nicholas Roosevelt, a partner in the firm of inventor Robert Fulton, ordered the building of a steamboat, the *New Orleans,* in a Pittsburgh yard; in 1812, the first rolling mill powered by a steam engine was established by Christopher Cowan. By then the works of Oliver Evans were already making steam engines.

How fast manufacturing grew one realizes if one compares the town's production figures of 1802 with those of 1810.

Zadok Cramer's *Almanac for 1803* estimated that the total value of goods turned out in Pittsburgh for the preceding year was about $350,000. The breakdown of this sum was as follows:

Iron	$56,548
Textiles	46,825
Boatbuilding	40,000
Leather	34,165
Wood	33,900
Liquor	32,100
Brick and stone	17,800
Brass and tin	15,600
Hat and cap	14,675
Glass	13,000

Eight years later—in 1810—the U. S. Census reported the following figures:

PITTSBURGH IN THE YEAR OF 1796. The French Minister to the United States, M. Adet, asked General Victor Collot, who served in the Revolutionary War under Marshal Rochambeau, to furnish him with "a minute detail of the political, commercial and military state of the western part" of the United States and the Ohio and Mississippi valleys.

On March 21, 1796, General Collot

A LITHOGRAPH BY TARDIEU AFTER A DRAWING BY JOSEPH WARIN, WHO ACCOMPANIED GENERAL COLLOT

and his companions set out on their journey. For nine months they traveled through the land, gathering information, making notes, and drawing pictures. One of the men in the general's group was Joseph Warin, and it was he who signed this water color drawing of Pittsburgh, the second known view of the place. It is an excellent and obviously correct pictorial representation of the town. The French artist Tardieu copied the drawing later and published it in Paris as a lithograph.

General Collot died in 1804. The account of his travels remained in manuscript until 1826, when it was printed in a French edition of 300 copies, and an English translation limited to 100 copies. An atlas of 36 views and plans was included to illustrate the work.

In his book the general described Pittsburgh as a town of 150 houses, some of them built of brick, the rest of mud. "This town," predicted Collot with accuracy in 1796, "when the Indian Frontier is thrown back, and the roads are rendered practicable, will certainly become one of the first inland cities of the United States."

73

Iron	$94,890
Leather	81,378
Glass	63,000
Boatbuilding	43,000
Brass and tin	25,500
Hats and caps	24,507
Brick and stone	22,400
Wood	19,674
Soap, candles	14,500
Textiles	14,248

In less than a decade glass manufacturing increased five fold, leather two and a half fold, and iron production almost doubled!

The expanding manufacturing establishments brought about an increase of population. The 376 inhabitants of 1790 grew into 1565 by 1800, and by 1810 this figure had risen to 4768.

A book called *The Stranger in America*, published in London in 1807 described Pittsburgh as a well-built town which "has a swanky appearance, and contains about five hundred houses." Another report, three years later, counted 11 stone, 283 brick, and 473 frame and log buildings. Pittsburgh was on the march.

*

Politics was a popular pastime at the Forks. The political leaders of Westmoreland, from which Allegheny grew, came mainly from the farm communities; they were Republicans, followers of Thomas Jefferson. The outstanding among them were William Findley, John Baird, and William Todd, two Scotch-Irishmen and an Irishman. The Swiss-born Albert Gallatin, who under Jefferson became Secretary of the Treasury, carried the banner of Democracy in the legislature.

Pittsburgh itself had no outstanding political figure. The majority of the merchants and businessmen were Federalists. General John Neville and his "connections," his son Presley, his brother-in-law Abraham Kirkpatrick, his son-in-law Isaac Craig, were staunch supporters of President George Washington. So were most of the traders, men like William Semple or John Gibson. But there grew among the merchants and professional men a small yet strong opposition to Federalism. The core of it was the Clapboard Junto—men who lived in clapboard houses on Market Street. Dr. Hugh Scott, William Gazzam, Thomas Baird, Samuel Ewalt, Adamson Tannehill, and Nathaniel Irish were among them; politicians like Tarleton Bates, Henry Baldwin, and Walter Forward already laid the grounds for the future success of democratic Jeffersonianism.

*

Wars have always boosted Pittsburgh's economic growth. From its earliest days, the town was a supplier of war materiel, a manufacturer of guns and bullets, of rigging and cordage. From each war, Pittsburgh emerged bigger and richer. The War of 1812 benefited the town in many ways; it opened up new avenues for its trade and commerce, and it forced the production of goods on a larger scale. The tariff on foreign goods and the British blockade not only stimulated domestic manufactures, they also caused a reversal in the direction of western commerce. Trade from South to North was forced to go inland, and it flowed through Pittsburgh. Southern cotton, sugar, lead, peltry, hemp, saltpeter, and hides coming up the Mississippi and the Ohio were put into wagons in the town, from where they were carried to Philadelphia and the eastern seaboard. By 1813, some 4000 wagonloads of goods—each wagon carrying 3000 to 4000 pounds of merchandise—crossed the mountains; two years later this number grew to 5800.

During the war years the flow of goods from Europe ebbed to a trickle, and Americans were compelled to manufacture goods that formerly came from overseas.

(turn to page 77)

HOMES IN THE PITTSBURGH AREA. THESE WERE BUILT IN THE EARLY YEARS OF THE NINETEENTH CENTURY

Courtesy Pittsburgh Architectural Survey.

THE HUGH JACKSON HOUSE, near Mount Lebanon, was erected in 1808, with material coming from the land nearby.

Courtesy Pittsburgh Architectural Survey.

THE JAMES MILLER HOUSE in South Park, Allegheny County, a beautiful stonewall building, was built about 1808.

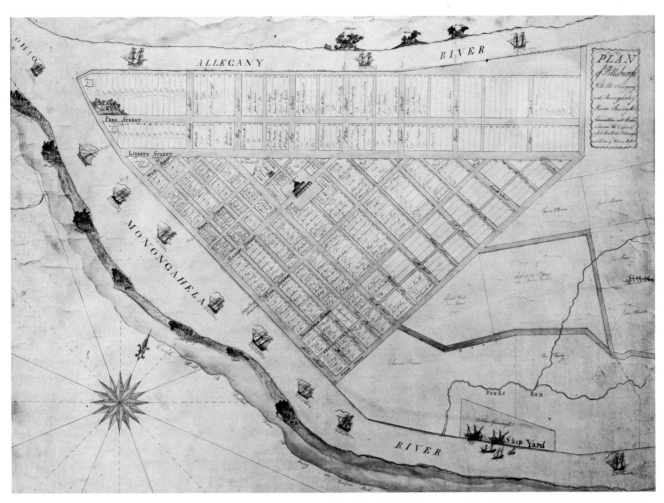

Courtesy Historical Society of Western Pennsylvania.

THE PLAN OF THE CITY IN 1805, when Pittsburgh's population was about 3000. In 1764, a year after the houses clustered outside Fort Pitt were destroyed in preparation for an Indian attack, a plan was drawn by Colonel John Campbell so the future town could be built in an orderly way. The boundaries on the plan were Water, Second (now Boulevard of the Allies), Ferry, and Market Streets.

Twenty years later, in 1784, Colonel George Woods and Thomas Vickroy, his assistant, made another plan for the Penns. They continued Campbell's plan to Grant Street, then laid out two streets, Penn and Liberty, running parallel to the Allegheny and at angles to the thoroughfares running parallel to the Monongahela.

It was two decades after this, that William Mason drew this plan in 1805, basing his drawings mainly on the former surveys of Campbell and that of Woods and Vickroy. Emphasizing the city's importance as shipping and shipbuilding center, Mason put a number of vessels, which were built in Pittsburgh, into his sketch. There were the schooners *Amity* and *Conquest*, the brigs *Allegheny*, *Ann Jane*, *Bison*, *Fayette*, and *Nanina*, the ships *Western Trader*, *General Butler*, and *Pittsburgh*.

Courtesy Pittsburgh Architectural Survey.

THE JAMES ROSS HOUSE near Aspinwall, built around 1810, adapted the sumptuous Georgian style to the needs of the frontier.

Courtesy Pittsburgh Architectural Survey.

THE JOHN WAY HOUSE in Edgeworth built in 1838, was a charming home with an English basement and large windows.

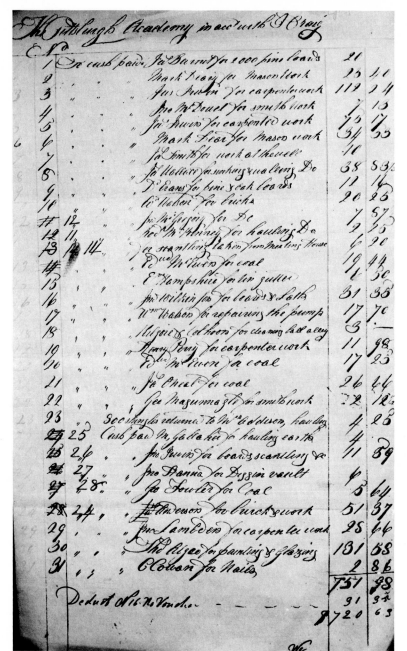

Courtesy Historical Society of Western Pennsylvania.

EBENEZER DENNY (1761-1822), a prominent merchant and director of the Bank of Pennsylvania, was a veteran of both the Revolutionary and Mexican wars. He was elected in 1816 as Pittsburgh's first mayor.

TO THE PUBLICK

THE public are hereby informed, that the subscribers have entered into partnership and will hereafter conduct business under the firm or denomination of

"The Pittsburgh Steam Engine Company."

They carry on the manufacturing of STEAM ENGINES, and all kinds of MACHINERY, together with wrought iron work and castings, &c. &c. Such as all kinds of wrought and cast iron-work appertaining to merchant, flour mills, rolling and slitting mills, forges, tilts, furnaces, sugar, paper and saw mills, &c. and all work of a similar kind, together with every other description of castings that may be wanted.

They will also make patterns, and do boring, and turning in iron, &c. From their preparations, and practical knowledge, in the various branches mentioned, they expect to be able to execute any piece of work, however large or difficult.

They have also under their controul the making of

Oliver Evans's Patented Steam ENGINES,

and the power of granting license to use them.

The superiority of these engines, over all others yet invented, is great. Their power to others, is as 100 to 10. They are infinitely more simple and durable, require less fuel, occupy less room, are less expensive. They require as little water, and being made to supply themselves by their own operations, with distilled water, that they may be set almost in any situation where an ordinary well may be had. A well is sufficient for a 100 horse-power. These last peculiar properties will be found particularly beneficial in this country, where water is scarce and of a quality injurious to Steam-Engines not thus ordered. An ordinary capacity can be taught in two weeks to manage one of those engines completely.

They do also hereby caution all manner of persons from infringing on the principles of the aforesaid patented engine, as they are determined to defend their rights therein. Any person using elastic steam, above the power of the atmosphere, will infringe, however dissimilar may be the form of the engine.

GEO: EVANS,
MAHLON ROGERS,
MARK STACKHOUSE,
LUTHER STEPHES.

Pittsburgh, March 11, 1813.   tfq.

CRAMER, SPEAR & EICHB....

Courtesy Historical Society of Western Pennsylvania.

ACCOUNT OF THE PITTSBURGH ACADEMY WITH ISAAC CRAIG, dated July 27, 1818. Craig, one of Pittsburgh's prominent citizens, arrived in the city during the Revolutionary War. At one time he was commander of Fort Pitt; in 1791 and the year after he supervised the construction of Fort Fayette.

He was an astute and successful businessman. In 1797 he formed a partnership with General James O'Hara, under whom he served as deputy quartermaster general, and the two men built the first glassworks of the town. Craig had many interests, he built ships, invested in manufacturing, made a fortune in real estate.

*

right:

A STEAM ENGINE ADVERTISEMENT IN THE PITTSBURGH *MERCURY* On March 11, 1813, the Pittsburgh Steam Engine Company, formed by George Evans, Mahlon Rogers, Mark Stackhouse, and Luther Stephes, announced the manufacturing of steam engines and all kinds of machines. In their notice they boasted of the superior quality of the Oliver Evans steam engines. "Their power to others, is as 100 to 10. They are infinitely more simple and durable, require less fuel, occupy less room, are less expensive. They require as little water, and being made to supply themselves by their own operations, with distilled water, that they may be set almost in any situation where an ordinary well may be had."

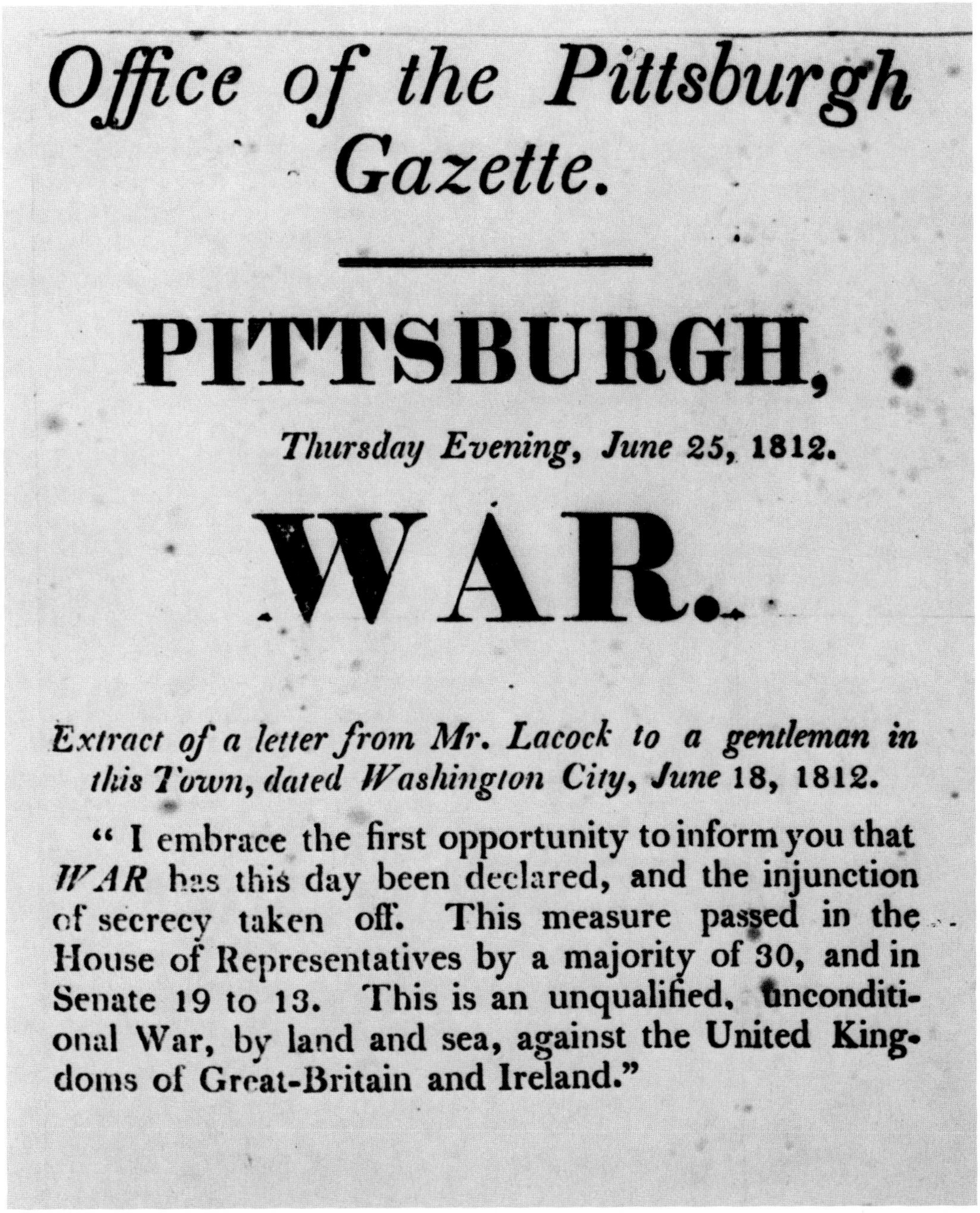

Office of the Pittsburgh Gazette.

—————

PITTSBURGH,

Thursday Evening, June 25, 1812.

WAR.

Extract of a letter from Mr. Lacock to a gentleman in this Town, dated Washington City, June 18, 1812.

" I embrace the first opportunity to inform you that *WAR* has this day been declared, and the injunction of secrecy taken off. This measure passed in the House of Representatives by a majority of 30, and in Senate 19 to 13. This is an unqualified, unconditional War, by land and sea, against the United Kingdoms of Great-Britain and Ireland."

THE DECLARATION OF THE WAR OF 1812—A *PITTSBURGH GAZETTE* BROADSIDE

By 1815, Pittsburgh produced:

Iron	$764,200
Brass and tin	249,633
Glass	235,000
Leather	215,000
Wood	144,900
Hat and cap	122,000
Textiles	115,500
Red & white lead	110,000
Liquor	91,050
Tobacco	45,850

Thus, within half a decade, brass and tin production increased tenfold, iron and textile eightfold, glass manufacturing fourfold. Pittsburgh was now a vastly different place from the village of the decade before. Travelers who passed through it could hardly recognize it, so vast was the transformation. Manufacturing, said Zadok Cramer's *Almanac for 1817*, "has almost rendered us as independent of the eastern states, as those states have been rendered by the war independent of the Old World." The 37 mechanics working in 16 factories in 1792 increased to 1657 workmen toiling in 259 factories by 1817, and turning out two and one-half million dollars worth of goods yearly. One hundred hands were employed in the copper and tinsmith trade, 92 in the green glass factories, 87 in the iron foundries, 70 made steam engines, and 109 produced shoes and boots.

*

Courtesy American Antiquarian Society, Worcester, Mass.

WHAT THEY ADVERTISED IN JULY 1813. In the advertising columns of *The Mercury*, a master asked for the return of his two runaway apprentices, offering six cents reward "to whoever will bring the said runaways or either of them to their master, or for lodging them in any jail"; a subscriber announced that he had found a pocket book "containing a quantity of money"; the Pittsburgh Steam Mill offered flour for exportation "for the Orleans market"; while the general store of J. Johnston & Co. advertised the recent arrival of a "General Assortment of Goods."

On March 18, 1816, Pittsburgh was incorporated a city. The city government consisted of a mayor—to which post the merchant Ebenezer Denny was chosen—the select council (James Ross (President), Samuel Douglass, Richard Geary, William Hays, James Irwin, William Lecky, John Rosebergh, Mark Stackhouse, and Dr. George Stevenson), the common council to which the people elected many of the town's leading citizens, (William Wilkins was the Council's first president; while the other councilmen were Paul Anderson, James Brown, James R. Butler, John Caldwell, John Carson, George Evans, David Hunter, Alexander Johnston, John W. Johnston, Thomas McKee, Richard Robinson, John P. Skelton, James B. Stevenson, and J. W. Trembley), a recorder (Charles Wilkins, the son of General Wilkins), and twelve aldermen (Ebenezer Denny, John Darragh, William Steele, Phillip Mowry, Lazarus Stewart, Thomas Enoch, Phillip Gilland, James Young, Robert Graham, John Hannan, John M. Snowden, Matthew B. Lowrie).

The *Boston Yankee* duly noted the election of Ebenezer Denny, even though the Massachusetts editors were not quite sure where Pittsburgh was located. They thought it was in Ohio. *The Commonwealth* of Pittsburgh, which came into being after the demise of the town's second newspaper *The Tree of Liberty* in 1806, was furious about the Massachusetts newspaper's ignorance. How could they make a mistake about "a city containing ten thousand inhabitants—possessing a manufacturing capital of many millions—having three banking institutions, and a commerce extending to every part of the union—a town which has long been considered perhaps the most important one in the west, and place it in the state of Ohio?" As sure as the Allegheny joined the Monongahela, Pittsburgh was a fine Pennsylvania town, and proud of it.

Pittsburgh may have been a fine town for those who lived there, but for strangers it was not a stimulating place. To David Thomas, who journeyed through the western country in 1816, Pittsburgh seemed gloomy because "dark dense smoke was rising from many parts, and a hovering cloud of this vapour" obscured the view. He also noted: "Wooden buildings, interspersed with those of brick, mar the beauty of its streets; and as few of these are paved, mud, in showery weather, becomes abundant."

Cramer's *Navigator* of 1817 admitted that life in Pittsburgh was drab, but explained that

the character of the people is that of enterprising and perservering industry; every man to his business is the prevailing maxim, there is therefore little time devoted to amusements or to the cultivation of refined social pleasures. . . . Luxury, pomp and parade are scarcely seen, there are perhaps, not more than one or two carriages in the place. There is a public academy, but not in a flourishing state, where the Latin and Greek classics are taught. . . . The amusements of these industrious people are not numerous, a few balls during the winter season; there is also a small theatre where a company from the eastern cities sometimes performs.

Palmer's Journals of Travels asserted a year later:

Water color made specially for this book by Walter A. Gasowski.

THE NEW ORLEANS, the first steamboat on western waters, was built on the Pittsburgh waterfront in 1811 and launched in March of that year. Ordered by Nicholas Roosevelt, a partner in the firm of inventor Robert Fulton, the construction of the 150-feet-long boat came to $40,000. The capacity was 450 tons.

The maiden voyage down the rivers began on October 25. Three days later the boat was in Louisville, Kentucky, having made the trip from Pittsburgh in 64 hours.

But because of low water, it took another month before the boat could leave Louisville and steam toward New Orleans.

"From the number of manufactures, and the inhabitants burning coal, the buildings have not that clean appearance, so conspicuous in most American towns." And *Darby's Emigrant's Guide for 1818* complained: "Pittsburgh is by no means a pleasant city to a stranger. The constant volume of smoke preserve the atmosphere in a continued cloud of coal dust."

Such complaints remained with the town for a century and a half. The soot kept the sky dark; it covered the landscape; it killed the vegetation. Yet the darkness of the sky was not an unmitigated scourge. It was also an indication that the inhabitants of Pittsburgh were working, that the factories were producing goods.

In the year of its incorporation as a city, Pittsburgh numbered 960 houses and a population of six thousand. Counting the inhabitants of the expanding suburbs, such as Birmingham on the South side, Allegheny on the North side, Bayardstown and Lawrenceville, this figure rose to 10,000. The town had eight churches, among them an attractive octagon Episcopal Church and a spacious Presbyterian Church. It had three banks (The Bank of Pennsylvania, The Bank of Pittsburgh, and the Farmers and Mechanics Bank), a theatre, a Masonic Hall, three market houses (one in the Diamond and two on Second Street), a courthouse and a jail. Its first two bridges were already chartered—one to connect the city with Birmingham, the other with Allegheny.

Pittsburgh was no longer an insignificant frontier village; within a generation it grew into a vital manufacturing center, into the "Birmingham of America." One spoke of it as "the Capital and Emporium of the Western Country." It was regarded as the "Gateway to the West."

PITTSBURGH IN 1817—AFTER A SKETCH BY MRS. GIBSON, THE WIFE OF A PHILADELPHIA LAWYER.

The previous year Pittsburgh was incorporated as a city, to be governed by a mayor, a select and a common council, a recorder, and 12 aldermen.

The war—when vitally needed European goods could not be imported and Americans were forced to manufacture their own—helped Pittsburgh's growth.

Manufactories expanded; the iron foundries produced implements; in the glass houses green glass and flint glass were blown; boatbuilding, engine construction, shoemaking were flourishing enterprises.

At this time, Birmingham, on the South Side—the first borough created in the county after Pittsburgh—had about 50 houses and some factories; Allegheny town, across the river, the site of the Scott, Denny, and Beelen glassworks, was expanding; Northern Liberties (Bayardstown), located to profit from the first canals and railroads, had been laid out; and Lawrenceville, site of the Allegheny Arsenal, received settlers by the dozens.

Painted specially for this book by Edgar A. Roth.

THE PRESIDENT IN PITTSBURGH. In the fall of 1817, the year he took office, James Monroe, fifth President of the United States, visited Pittsburgh. He was met outside the city by distinguished Pittsburghers and "conducted to the ferry where an elegant barge, rowed by four sea captains awaited his approach." In the city the President was entertained at the house of William Wilkins, was thanked by the citizens for his efforts on behalf of the Western Country, particularly for the opening up of the Mississippi; he inspected the Arsenal, saw some factories, attended in one day the services of both the Episcopal and Presbyterian Church, caused a social whirl with the ladies and was "gratified by the friendly reception."

Chapter 3

THE CITY GROWS

by Oscar Handlin

BETWEEN THE two wars—the War of 1812 and the Civil War—Pittsburgh became a modern city. Gone was the frontier village—the wilderness edged farther and farther away; the outlines of a great metropolis took form.

In these decades, the expanding trade supplied the town with a solid commercial basis for economic prosperity; and the lusty beginnings of manufacturing showed clearly the nature of its future industrial destiny. A thriving community sought appropriate ways of expressing its culture. A rising population, self-conscious about its own and the city's interests, played a significant part in politics. By the end of the Civil War, Pittsburgh was ready to move into the era in which it would reach full maturity.

*

In 1816, Pittsburgh ceased to be legally a mere borough with only limited powers of self-government. In that year it became a full-fledged city. It had, by then, a population of about 10,000, including the adjoining communities, and every expectation that it would continue to grow rapidly.

At that time the town still enjoyed a rustic quality. Looking upward from the spot where the Monongahela joined with the Allegheny, one could see the tightly clustered wooden two-story residences of the inhabitants, with here and there a church spire rising above the general level. Nature still dominated the scene. The rolling wooded hills rose abruptly behind the houses and there was shrubbery on the waterfront. Indeed, one of the city's first ordinances had permitted the planting of ornamental shade trees along the banks of the Monongahela, "provided that they do not incommodate the passage" and "that they be set on the side of the street next to the water, and so as not to stop or obstruct the passage of water along the gutters."

It was true, as a traveler observed, that it was no longer common to see Indians in Pittsburgh. But the countryside was not further than a stone's throw and rustic habits survived among the people. In Hall's *Letters from the West*, written in 1828, one can read: "The city lay beneath me, enveloped in smoke—the clang of hammers resounded from its numerous manufactories." Yet, "behind me were all of the silent soft attractions of rural sweetness." The law was still concerned lest horses, oxen, and hogs run at large in the streets; and provisions for municipal services were still primitive.

The population had just emerged from the first stages of settlement and had little time for amusement or refinement. There was not much visible evidence of luxury, pomp or parade. Aside from a few balls and the occasional visits of itinerant theatrical companies there was little to relieve the monotony of life.

All the new city's energies focused upon its economy. The river craft and the wagons that linked it with the outer world were the carriers of a commerce upon which Pittsburgh's capacity to grow depended. Nor did it matter that a pall of smoke was depriving its buildings of "that clean appearance so conspicuous in most American towns."

That smoke, issuing forth from a rising number of furnaces, was evidence of the birth of industry that would make Pittsburgh great. The inhabitants consoled themselves that property values had increased tenfold in the decade ending in 1817. An expanding economy would be the key to the city's development in the next half-century.

*

As the war of 1812 came to its close, commerce was still the primary element in Pittsburgh's prosperity. The city had by then become the main eastern gateway to the whole trans-Allegheny west. Overland traffic from the Atlantic seacoast to the interior was not only difficult and time consuming but costly. Whatever roads existed were poor, seas of mud in the spring, dusty in the summer and obstructed by snow in the winter. Shippers therefore preferred to send their goods by water and Pittsburgh was the node of a river system which gave it an incomparable advantage over any rival. Here the two branches of the Ohio River came together to flow unimpeded into the Mississippi and southward to the Gulf. Almost without interruption from this point, men and freight could move by cheap water transportation to the very heart of the continent and to the ocean at New Orleans.

The city was also tied to the East. The great mountain chain that stretched from New England to Georgia had very few gaps in it, and almost all of them led directly or indirectly to Pittsburgh. The only break in the barrier of significance that did not, that of the Mohawk River Valley, would in time create a potent rival in Buffalo. But Pittsburgh, at the start of the nineteenth century, had the superior inland situation.

As the settlement of the west proceeded, the importance of Pittsburgh's commercial facilities grew. Since the turn of the century a service to Cincinnati had been established and the constantly rising number of boats moving down the river were an index of the town's prosperity. The War of 1812, which removed the Indian and British threat to the Northwest, stimulated the flow of settlers into the region and increased the volume of business.

The appearance of the steamship on the western waters quite naturally added to the volume of commerce. Before the steamship era, most of the traffic had gone down the river; to move a vessel upstream had been a laborious and time-consuming task, managed by hauling against ropes attached to a nearby tree. It took as much as a month to make the distance between Cincinnati and Pittsburgh. Thus, trade moved through Pittsburgh mainly in one direction—downstream. It was easier and cheaper to ship from New Orleans by sea to Philadelphia and across the mountains to Pittsburgh than to come directly up the river against the current. The steamboat changed all this. As steam propelled boats became numerous, goods moved

PITTSBURGH IN 1825: A CONTEMPORARY SKETCH BY JOSHUA SHAW, THE EMINENT ENGLISH PAINTER.

PITTSBURGH IN 1825, AS PRESERVED ON AN ENGLISH DINNER PLATE MADE IN STAFFORDSHIRE.

upstream with the same ease as they did downstream.

The War of 1812 also helped the city's commercial situation. Pittsburgh emerged from the war robust, ready for expansion.

The return of peace brought a tremendous speculative boom. Everyone expected further growth; thus prices rose rapidly and merchants were extending their business. But the boom turned out to be of short duration. The inevitable collapse came, bringing about a depression which dragged on for years. Though the stores were stuffed with all kinds of English goods, from men's coats and ladies gowns to whips and oyster knives, there were few buyers. This situa-

tion lasted until the last years of the twenties, and the setback was felt as long as a decade after that period.

Recovery was slow because the city felt the effects of competition for trade on the part of potent rivals. With the completion of the National Road, Wheeling suddenly had better connections to the markets of the East; thriving trading centers also developed downstream at Cincinnati, Louisville and St. Louis. The completion of the Erie Canal in 1825 put Buffalo and the lake system in a position to draw the interior trade to the northward. Such developments, as the *Pittsburgh Statesman* pointed out, threatened to turn the city into a deserted village. In response to these challenges, Pittsburghers tried to strengthen their own position by improving the means of transportation that linked them to their markets. Unfortunately they had to work through the state government; and as the interests of Philadelphia and the East were not identical with their own, progress in their direction was slow and halting.

The Pennsylvania Turnpike (completed in 1820) provided a road by which wagons could come over the mountains. It proved a substantial boon to Pittsburgh, for it reduced the journey from Philadelphia to less than two weeks. Though the tolls were high, the roads rarely returned a profit. Still, they facilitated the course of trade with the East. The yearly report of one of the gates for 1834 reveals the character of the traffic—in that year and on a single gate these were the figures:

broad wheel wagons	6,359
narrow wheel wagons	374
single horse wagons	1,243
two horse wagons	779
carriages	107
gigs	18
carts	60
riding horses	2,817
draft horses	42,330

cattle	6,457
sheep	2,853
hogs	40

Since each Conestoga wagon carried as much as 4000 pounds in goods, the total amount of goods sent to the East was substantial.

While on land transportation the progress was great, water transportation improved only slightly. The rivers were difficult to navigate the year round. Not until 1830 was the Ohio really cleared to the city, which until then labored under a disadvantage with its downriver competitors.

Meanwhile the canal era had opened and the State of Pennsylvania embarked upon an ambitious and costly scheme to construct a series of locks over the Alleghenies that would permit the carriage of goods by water all the way to Pittsburgh. Work on the project began in 1826, but was not fully completed until eight years later. A series of inclined plane portage railroads carried the canal boats across the mountains. The barges then came by an aqueduct into a basin on the Allegheny and across the city through a tunnel to the Monongahela.

Although this enterprise was a triumph of engineering, it gave Pittsburgh no great advantage over its competitors

PITTSBURGH IN 1836: A CONTEMPORARY SKETCH OF SEVENTH STREET AND CHERRY ALLEY BY J. W. KERR.

MONONGAHELA BRIDGE.

THE FOLLOWING BY-LAWS, FOR THE GOVERNMENT OF THE BRIDGE, WERE ORDERED TO BE PUBLISHED.

1st.—If any person or persons shall wilfully ride or drive any horse, mule, or cattle, over the Monongahela Bridge, at a faster gait than a walk, he, she, or they, so offending, shall, each of them, for every such offence, forfeit and pay to the Corporation the sum of five dollars.

2nd.—If any person or persons shall wilfully drive or suffer to go on said Bridge, more than ten head of horses, mules, or cattle, at one time, every such person or persons, so offending, shall forfeit and pay to the Corporation the sum of five dollars.

3d.—If any person or persons shall wilfully deface, or cut, or otherwise injure any part of said Bridge, or write, or scribble on the same, such person or persons shall forfeit and pay to the Corporation the sum of ten dollars.

4th.—If any person or persons shall wilfully smoke Cigars or Pipes on or while crossing said Bridge, or take, or carry with him, her, or them, a torchlight, candle, or other light, otherwise than in a Lantern, he, she, or they, so offending, shall forfeit and pay to the Corporation, for every such offence, the sum of five dollars.

5th.—If any person or persons shall wilfully discharge a Gun, Pistol, or other fire-arms, whilst on any part of said Bridge, he, she, or they, so offending, shall forfeit and pay to the Corporation the sum of ten dollars.

6th.—That passengers attempting to evade paying toll, by passing in carriages to which they do not belong, shall be required to pay six and a fourth cents each.

RESOLVED, That each and every fine, forfeiture, and penalty, accruing for offences against any of the foregoing By-Laws, may be sued for and recovered, with costs of suit, before any Alderman of the city of Pittsburgh, or Justice of the Peace of the county of Allegheny, having jurisdiction for the recovery of debts, of the amounts therein stated.

Ordained and enacted as the By-Laws of the President and Managers of the Company for erecting a Bridge over the River Monongahela, opposite Pittsburgh, in the county of Allegheny, the first day of June, A. D. 1827.

IN TESTIMONY WHEREOF, The Seal of said Corporation was hereto affixed, by order of the Board, the same day and year.

JOHN THAW, Clerk.

REGULATIONS, issued in June 1827, for the use of the Monongahela Bridge.
For riding or driving "at a faster gait than a walk," or for willfully smoking "Cigars or Pipes on or while crossing" the bridge the offending person was fined five dollars.

for other canals out of Baltimore and New York and across Ohio, Indiana and Illinois kept opening up alternative routes. Ultimately, the railroads would supply the much-needed efficient connection with the East. Soon after the opening of the canal there were three short tracks that delivered goods around the city. The firm McClurg, Wade & Co. had built a locomotive, believed to be the first one constructed west of the Allegheny Mountains, in 1835. But it was not until 1851 that Pittsburgh had its first real railroad service when the Ohio and Pennsylvania Railroad completed a line running from Cleveland to Allegheny City.

In the late forties and early fifties, two railroads, the Pennsylvania and the Baltimore and Ohio, were in brisk competition to build a road to the Ohio. Both lines were completed about the same time. The Pennsylvania brought its first train to Pittsburgh in the fall of 1852, while the first train of the Baltimore and Ohio steamed into Wheeling six weeks later. In two more years the Pennsylvania finished its mountain division (replacing the Portage line), then the trains ran directly from Philadelphia to Pittsburgh.

Useful as these transportation developments were, they could not counteract a deeper force that shifted the center

A FRENCH NATURALIST SKETCHES PITTSBURGH IN 1825

Charles Alexandre Lesueur (1778-1846) was a member of the expedition which set out from Pittsburgh for New Harmony in Indiana on December 8, 1825. Robert Owen, the founder of the new Utopian colony, was on the boat with other distinguished scientists and educators, among them such lights as William McClure, Thomas Say, Gerard Troost, and Francis Wright.

During the trip Lesueur made sketches presenting a vivid record of the voyage. They are in the Museum of Natural History at Havre, France, as Lesueur was named the first director of the Museum.

DEPARTURE DAY of the expedition was December 8, 1825. Before the flatboat *The Philanthropist* with its 27 passengers—the largest scholarly assemblage ever to set out on the Ohio—left Pittsburgh for New Harmony in Indiana, Alexandre Lesueur made a sketch of the "Connection de l'Allegani avec Monongahela"—a charming and accurate representation of the Point.

right:

A MONTH LATER, on January 8, 1826, the expedition was still on its tedious journey down the ice-covered Ohio River. At one point, as Lesueur's drawing shows, a floating bridge was removed by workmen to clear the way for the boat's passage.

left:

MEETING A KEELBOAT. Lesueur sketched all that was worth recording on the way to Indiana and the happenings of a later exploring trip to the Missouri lead mines.

On the keelboat *The Philanthropist* encountered on the Ohio, three boatmen are pictured at the bow, while one is steering at the stern. The three passengers of the boat watch the proceedings with interest.

PITTSBURGH WATERFRONT, as drawn by Charles Alexandre Lesueur on December 8, 1825, the very day when *The* *Philanthropist* (in the background) left for New Harmony. The journey was sponsored by William McClure, the geologist

and patron of science and education, who became interested in the community which Robert Owen planned on the Wabash.

INSIDE THE BOAT OF KNOWLEDGE the scientists settle down to dinner. The food, which was cooked by the ladies of the expedition, is served on a long table in front of the sleeping bunks of the living-dining-bedroom of *The Philanthropist*.

The number of trunks filled with scientific equipment and other paraphernalia for the journey are stored underneath the bunks.

PURCHASES OF PITTSBURGHERS IN 1837—ENTRIES IN JOHN MOFFET'S DAY BOOK.

of internal trade westward. As the population of the interior grew and moved ever further toward the Mississippi, other cities—Cincinnati, Louisville, and St. Louis—took over the business of outfitting the farmers and exchanging their products for the manufactured goods of the East.

By 1830, however, the foundation of Pittsburgh's economy no longer rested on commerce. The steady growth of manufacturing had given the city a new role in the productive system of the nation. Michel Chevalier, who visited the place in 1835, wrote: "Nowhere in the world is everybody so regularly and continually busy . . . there is no interruption of business for six days in the week, except during the three meals, the longest of which occupies hardly ten minutes."

The transportation barriers that blocked the development of trade helped the growth of industry. The high cost of moving manufactured goods from the East offered some local merchants the opportunity to produce them on the spot and thus to profit from the economy of location. A shortage of labor was the only drawback, but the steady flow of immigration was to remedy even that.

To compensate for the relative scarcity of labor, Pittsburgh had the inestimable advantage of close proximity to resources that would have high strategic value in the developments of the future. Abundant stocks of timber offered a great reserve of wood for building and for fuel. A fertile backcountry assured its residents of adequate supplies of food. Inexhaustible beds of coal in the immediate vicinity gave the city all the fuel it needed for the expansion of its iron and glass manufactories. And in the nearby counties of Fayette, Westmoreland, and Somerset were abundant veins of iron ore, to be worked up in the furnaces and factories of the city. These resources offered a solid basis for future growth.

Already in 1817, Pittsburgh boasted of four glass factories, three breweries, two potteries, a grist mill, a steam engine factory, a slitting and nail mill, cotton and woolen factories, and four printing offices. Barges, flatboats and keelboats were built on the banks of the river, rope and rigging and other products were manufactured in the city proper. With the coming of the steam engine, larger yards and more ambitious enterprises undertook to construct the new vessels. Between 1812 and 1826, forty-eight steamships were built in Pittsburgh; and in the next four years alone, fully the same number. Though the output declined thereafter, while it lasted it created a significant demand for the engines and equipment needed in the ships.

At the beginning of the nineteenth century the iron industry started to take shape, at first in the rural hinterland, later in the nearby suburbs, stimulated by the low cost of iron ore and coal. Foundries turned out iron bars, nails, and all kinds of farm implements. Later, such firms manufactured engines and other iron products.

The first rolling mill powered by a steam engine of seventy horsepower was established in Pittsburgh by Christopher Cowan in 1812; from then on the number of steam mills increased rapidly. By 1830 Pittsburgh was carrying forward every branch of iron manufacturing by steam. Charles Dickens, who visited the city in the first spring days of 1842, noted: "Pittsburgh is like Birmingham in England, at least its townspeople say so. . . . It certainly has a great quantity of smoke hanging over it, and is famous for its iron works."

The Mexican War furthered the production of iron products; it turned Pittsburgh into a vital manufacturing place for guns, weapons, and ammunition. And by 1860 steelmaking already had sturdy roots in the city, enough to indicate the character of its future development.

Glass was another product difficult to carry across the mountains. Those who undertook to make it on the spot therefore had a natural protective advantage. In 1815, five firms were producing glass to a value of $235,000. The output increased steadily thereafter; in 1850 it was valued at more than a million dollars.

The rise of population in the interior rapidly expanded the markets for these goods and in addition created a place for other products in which transportation costs were not so critical. The Phoenix Cotton factory, using the labor of women, thrived as did a number of other textile, clothing, flour, brass, tin, and copper factories. Among these miscellaneous enterprises, not the least were those devoted to converting the corn and rye of the neighboring countryside into the whiskey which blended for its consumers "the mildness of milk" with "the vivacity of champagne" and, stealing "gently upon the senses, like music upon the soul," animated "the intellect without ever collapsing an idea." In all, 20,500 laborers in the 1191 workshops of Allegheny County by 1860 produced manufactured goods to the value of $26,563,000.

The trade of the city now turned about the import of the raw materials, to keep the factories going and the labor force supplied, and the distribution of their finished products. At first by wagon, then by river and canal boat, and finally by railroad, immense stores of coal, iron, corn, meat, cotton, and tobacco came into the city while finished metals, glass, cloth, and liquor moved out of it. The Monongahela Navigation Company was a monument to the new type of trade; its works, opened in 1841, permitted the cheap and efficient

(turn to page 101)

CHARACTERISTIC NEWSPAPER ADVERTISEMENTS in *The Pittsburgh Gazette* of 1834. David Parsons and William Inskeep ask for the return of runaway slaves; Hammond Marshall found a silver watch; Thomas Quart announces that his wife Sarah Anne has left his bed and board, thus will not pay her debts.

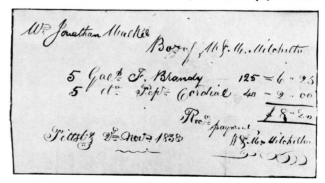

A RECEIPT FOR LIQUOR in November 1838 shows that five gallons of brandy cost no more than $6.25—what happy times!

A TRAVEL ADVERTISEMENT FROM 1837

BY WATER AND RAIL TO PITTSBURGH.

The Pennsylvania Canal was built during the period of rapid expansion in the country's transportation system. The western section, from Pittsburgh to Johnstown, was completed in 1830; the Juniata division was finished in 1832; the Philadelphia Columbia Railroad and the Allegheny Portage Railroad were completed in 1834.

The line was 395 miles long; building cost came to $25,000,000. Unfortunately, it never paid its way and was finally sold to the Pennsylvania Railroad in 1857 for $7,500,000.

To reach Pittsburgh the canal was carried over the Allegheny River through a 1100-foot long aqueduct entering the city near the present Pennsylvania Railroad Bridge.

As turnpikes had given way to canals, the waterways gave way to railroads. America was speedily constructing links between the extremities of the country.

Diorama by L. Evans Purcell.

THE TERMINUS OF THE CANAL IN PITTSBURGH, today the site of the Pennsylvania Station. From here the canal crossed the Allegheny and ran along the Kiskiminetas and Conemaugh rivers to Johnstown, where passengers changed to the Portage Railroad. On the inclined planes of the mountains the cars were pulled up and let down by stationary steam engines, while on the level stretches they were pulled by horses.

At Hollidaysburg the travelers had to change into a boat which took them on the Juniata and Susquehanna to Columbia, from where a railroad car took them to Philadelphia. The journey from Pittsburgh to Philadelphia lasted three and one half days.

THE CANAL AQUEDUCT AT JOHNSTOWN near the site of the present railroad station. Charles Dickens, who traveled from Harrisburg to Pittsburgh on the line in 1842, reported that the inside of the barge was like a caravan at a fair, "the gentlemen being accommodated, as the spectators usually are, in one of those locomotive museums of penny wonders; and the ladies being partitioned off by a red curtain, after the manner of the dwarfs and giants in the same establishments."

The English writer was embarrassed "to have to duck nimbly every five minutes whenever the man at the helm cried 'Bridge!' and . . . when the cry was 'Low Bridge,' to lie down nearly flat."

IN 1839 THE CANAL BOATS HAD TO BE PULLED UP THE INCLINES OF THE MOUNTAINS IN SECTIONS.

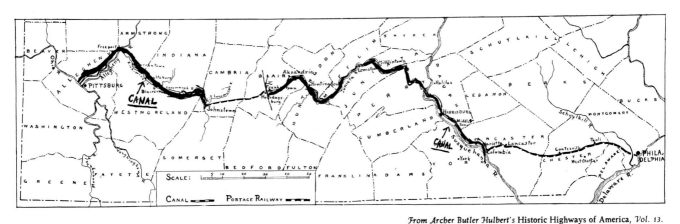

A MAP OF THE CANAL. Philip H. Nicklin, who made a canal trip in 1835 on the packet *Cincinnati*, noted that the boat "crossed the Allegheny through an aqueduct which carries the canal over that river to the northern bank of the Kiskinimetas," and later in the day "we passed over a beautiful stone aqueduct which leads the canal into the mouth of a large tunnel eight hundred feet long."

When the packet arrived at Johnstown the passengers changed to cars on the Portage Railroad. "As soon as we arrived at the foot of plane No. 1," wrote Nicklin, "the horses were unhitched and the cars were fastened to the rope which passes up the middle of one trace and down the middle of the other. The stationary steam engine at the head of the plane was started and the cars moved majestically up the steep and long acclivity. . . ."

MAKING IRON was the principal industry in Pittsburgh. In 1839, when this engraving appeared in *The Young Tradesman—The Iron Maker*, the city produced $4,946,400 worth of iron. The second largest Pittsburgh industry was textiles, which produced goods of only about one tenth the value of the products of the iron foundries and mills. By the middle of the century, Pittsburgh's iron was valued at about $6,500,000 and more than 5500 laborers were employed in the enterprises.

PITTSBURGH IN 1832: the Branch Bank of the United States as painted by Russell Smith.

This—the first bank west of the Allegheny Mountains—was organized in 1802 as a branch of the Bank of Pennsylvania. In 1817 it merged with the Bank of the United States and became "The Office of Discounts and Deposits of the U. S."

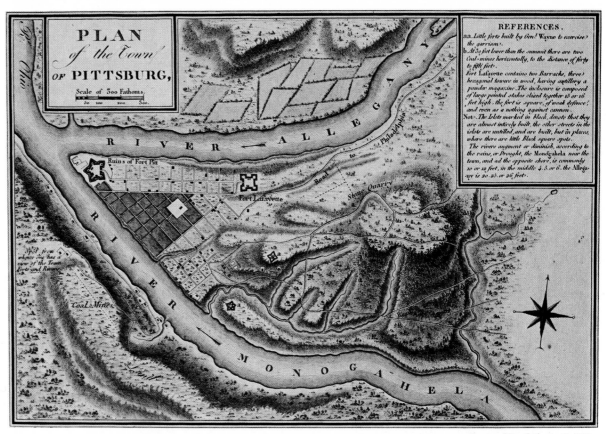

THIS PLAN OF PITTSBURGH WAS MADE IN 1826. IT IS BEAUTIFULLY DRAWN AND COLORED.

AN 1835 VIEW OF THE MONONGAHELA WHARF, PAINTED BY LEANDER D. McCANDLESS.

Courtesy J. Mellon & Sons.

THE MARKET PLACE, with the Courthouse on the left, was on the Diamond, where Market crossed Diamond Alley. The buildings were first occupied in 1794, and were torn down in the year of 1852.

The above lithograph by Otto Krebs was copied from a sketch made by the artist J. P. Robitser for the *Pittsburgh Directory* in 1859.

With Indian troubles a memory, Pittsburgh in 1800 was an established town of 1565 souls, the hub of an important agricultural area. The fertile soil of Western Pennsylvania enabled the settlers to produce a surplus crop and the practical place for exchange or shipment was Pittsburgh. Produce could easily be transported down the Allegheny River from northwestern Pennsylvania, and on the Monongahela from the southern part of the state and northern Virginia. Boats sailed down the Ohio and farther down the Mississippi.

Because of its favorable location Pittsburgh provided goods for the settlers who were on the way to the West. In 1794 alone, 13,000 emigrants passed through, and large numbers were yet to come. The Army expeditions to the Northeast and the Southwest helped business, using the city for the acquisition of supplies.

Pittsburgh, however, was not content to be only a middleman for the farmers. The 300 miles of overland transportation taxed the frontier's surplus too heavily to make the essential exchange with the East profitable. Thus at an early date Pittsburghers looked upon manufacturing as the solution to their economic problems. The natural advantages of the city were a fundamental help—there were large iron deposits and a rich supply of coal in the neighboring area. These resources were vital for the city's development.

From the date of the earliest estimates iron was Pittsburgh's leading manufacture —in 1803 the city's iron goods were worth $56,548. Next came textiles valued at $46,825 and boatbuilding estimated at $40,000. The increase of iron production was phenomenal. In 1810 it jumped to $94,890, in 1815 to $764,200. Though recovery was slow after the 1817 depression, by 1826 iron manufactures had risen to $1,155,094.

Population rose steadily—4768 in 1810, 7248 in 1820, 12,568 in 1830—as the city clamored for the internal improvements which in a few decades were to change the nature of its commerce and shift its ties from the Mississippi and New Orleans to the East.

Pittsburgh, the Gateway to the West, the Birmingham of America, was a fast-growing city, and nowhere could this be better observed than at its market place.

WESTERN UNIVERSITY of Pennsylvania, facing Third Street between Smithfield and Cherry Alley, was built in 1830. Three years later Russell Smith made this painting of the building which perished with many others in the great fire of 1845.

GARRISON IN LAWRENCEVILLE—AS PAINTED BY AN UNKNOWN ARTIST.

FIRST PRESBYTERIAN CHURCH. A colored lithograph of the second church building, erected in 1802 around the log cabin in which Presbyterians had worshipped since 1787. The congregation built three churches. The first one between Wood and Smithfield in 1787; the second in 1805, the third in 1853, and the fourth in 1905 facing Sixth Avenue.

Courtesy Mrs. Barron P. McCune.

THE MONONGAHELA BRIDGE AFTER IT HAD BEEN DAMAGED BY THE FRESHET IN THE YEAR OF 1832.

BIRMINGHAM
FROM THE
MOUTH OF
SUKE'S RUN

as it looked to the
painter in the year 1840.

Courtesy Mrs. David Bennett Hough.

SALT WORKS ON SAW MILL RUN: A painting by Russell Smith, dated 1832-34. In the early days of the city, the selling of salt was a lucrative business. One well on the south side of the Monongahela produced 15 barrels daily.

OLDEST HOUSE AT THE FOOT OF COAL HILL opposite Market Street, once the poorhouse of Pittsburgh. The artist, Russell Smith, one of the first to record what the city looked like, was 21 when he made this painting.

THE OLD BLOCKHOUSE when it was the residence of Isaac Craig. It was here that Neville B. Craig was born. The picture, a lovely and romantic representation of yesteryear was painted by Smith some time between 1832 and 1834.

THE AQUEDUCT as Russell Smith painted it in 1832. Completed in 1829, it carried the Pennsylvania Canal over the Allegheny near where the Pennsylvania Railroad bridge now stands. The boats were pulled across by horses.

THE AQUEDUCT OVER THE CONEMAUGH RIVER. In 1835 Philip H. Nicklin traveled over the Pennsylvania Canal, and wrote of the aqueduct and 800-foot tunnel: "you seem to be rushing against the steep side of the mountain, and then to your great astonishment you perceive an enormous archway which passes through the mountain's base."

A PERFORMANCE AT OLD DRURY. The theater on the south side of Fifth, between Wood and Smithfield, was opened on September 2, 1833 with *Busy Body* and *Of Age Tomorrow.* It was one of the most elegant in the West. The interior had two tiers of rose-colored boxes and 1200 seats covered with crimson studded brass nails.

BEWARE

Whereas, It has become a habit with idle and unruly boys and men to congregate upon the Canal and Foot Bridges of the city, where the passage is narrow and easily obstructed, and in the Market Houses after market hours, and at the Doors of the Churches, much to the annoyance of all well-disposed and peaceable citizens but more especially to females.   Therefore,

1. *Be it ordained and enacted by the Select and Common Councils of the City of Allegheny, and it is hereby enacted by the authority of the same,* That it shall hereafter be unlawful for any Persons to stand or loiter upon any of the Canal or Foot Bridges of the City, or on the Streets leading to the same within twenty feet thereof, or to stand or loiter in either of the Market Houses, except during market hours, and then not in the night time, or on any street of the city, at the door of any church or other place of public assembly.

2.   Any persons offending against any of the provisions of this Ordinance, shall for every such offence upon conviction thereof before the Mayor or any Alderman of the city, pay a fine of not less than *One*, or more than *Five Dollars*, for the use of the City, and the costs of prosecution.

G. E. WARNER, Pres't C. C.

H. J. Lemon, Cl'k C. C.

J. PAINTER, Pres't pro tem. S. C.

J. J. Carpenter, clerk S. C.

Courtesy Carnegie Free Library of Allegheny.

THE FEMALES were annoyed by the congregation of "idle and unruly boys and men" in the city's public places, announced the president of the Common Council and the president *pro tem.* of the Select Council. Therefore, according to this city ordinance of 1845, it was "unlawful for any Persons to stand or loiter upon any of the Canal or Foot Bridges . . . in either of the Market Houses . . . or on any street of the city, at the door of any church or other place of public assembly."

transfer of coal to the factories of Pittsburgh. Meanwhile, a growing and prosperous corps of middlemen handled the exchange; and banks and insurance companies provided the financial resources to facilitate it.

An expanding economy was given to speculation and therefore was particularly susceptible to depressions. The panics of 1819, 1837, and 1857 hit the city with particular severity. Business slackened and factories closed; and workingmen and merchants alike felt the impact of the hardships. But these were signs of growing pains. They did not long interrupt Pittsburgh's prosperity.

The thriving business life of the town depended upon and encouraged an expanding population. By 1815 it had almost 6000 inhabitants; it was far the largest urban place west of the mountains. In 1830 the city boasted 12,500 souls with some 10,000 more in the adjacent outskirts but was outdistanced by Cincinnati. In 1860 the population nearly reached the 50,000 mark, with about 100,000 more in the suburbs of Allegheny County.

This growth was largely the product of migration. A steady influx of newcomers enabled Pittsburgh to expand and to supply the hands needed for its trade and manufactures. The newcomers came not only from the eastern seaboard but from all the countries of Europe. The famine of Ireland in 1846 and the revolutions in Europe in 1848 forced many old-world citizens to search for a better life in the New World. At the opening of the Civil War more than one third of Pittsburgh's residents were European immigrants; the largest contingents among them came from Ireland and Germany, followed by Englishmen, Scotsmen, and Frenchmen.

In the fluid society of the rapidly expanding city, questions of national origin receded to the background. Each individual stood on his own feet, whether in the iron foundry or glass mill, on the river boats or the taverns where the wagoners bunked, or in the markets and shops where the merchants did business. Fortunes were too quickly made and lost for men to put much stock in antecedents. In any case everyone was more or less a newcomer in this melting pot. There was a brief period of anti-Catholic agitation by the Know-Nothings in the fifties when the rabble-rouser, Joe Barker, was elected mayor. But otherwise, all these ethnic groups managed to live in harmony with one another.

It was more difficult to cope with the physical problems of urban growth than with the problems that immigration brought about. To provide space for expanding economic activities and also to house the population which grew at so rapid a rate was in itself a continuing burden. Laid out in a checkerboard grid after the model of Philadelphia, the city was hemmed in on the north, south, and west by rivers and on the east by the steep heights on Grant's Hill. It could spread only along the flats that bordered the Allegheny and Monongahela rivers. Yet, the people came and their numbers increased; the population pushed steadily onwards gathering around the factories of the suburbs—the cotton and iron mills in the North Liberties (Bayardstown and Lawrenceville), the brewery in Kensington, the glass works in Birmingham and Sidneyville, and other enterprises in Allegheny City and Hayti.

Efficient communications with these places were essential. The early ferries soon proved incapable of carrying the traffic that poured back and forth across the rivers. In 1819 bridges across the Monongahela and the Allegheny were opened, to be supplemented by a steam ferry in 1831; and the first link in a street railway system appeared in 1859.

In the city proper, the press of the increased number of residents left little public or open space and created serious problems of overcrowding. Public improvements were not

easily planned or executed; they never are. The smaller markets were overshadowed by the imposing City Hall and Market Hall (erected in 1852). But other less profitable facilities did not expand as rapidly as the demand for them.

For a long time, Pittsburghers remained dependent upon wells for water. The first water works, served from a reservoir on Grant's Hill, was built in 1828 and extended in 1844. However, the water supply did not altogether meet the needs of the city. Up to the Civil War and even after that the slum districts had no adequate sewage disposal facilities. The streets were muddy, dirty, and poorly illuminated, although gas lights came along in 1837. Though there had been a paid watch, the town continued to depend upon volunteer fire fighters, spurred on by premiums awarded to the first company to go into operation.

The city was swept by a great holocaust in 1845 when some one thousand buildings and fifty-six acres were devastated. Many of the structures could have been saved if only there had been enough water. But the firefighters, when they attached their hoses, found only "a weak, sickly stream of muddy water." Thus, block after block became prey of the flames.

Catastrophies and epidemics came as season followed season. Nineteenth-century cities suffered from frequent attacks of disease. Cholera struck several times during these decades, yet public health provisions remained primitive. Mercy Hospital, the first in Pittsburgh, had not been opened until 1847 and the Board of Health was first organized in 1852. Burials continued to be made inside the city until 1844 when the Allegheny Cemetery Association for the first time provided space in the country.

The physical conditions of urban life in Pittsburgh thus presented an imposing challenge to the people who were attempting to build a communal life there.

As numbers grew and frontier conditions receded the differences among the residents of the town became in-

Courtesy J. Mellon & Sons.

PITTSBURGH IN 1840: a contemporary colored engraving after a drawing by Lehman by W. and A. K. Johnston, published in Edinburgh, Scotland.

At this time Pittsburgh had 21,115 inhabitants and was recovering from the depression which followed the panic of 1837. Iron was the backbone of economic life, with production valued at nearly $5,000,000.

There were some 50 churches, and the free public schools, in their fifth year of operation, were taking over a greater share of the educational task.

The city had gas lighting, a water system, and a volunteer fire department. At night one could hear the tired voice of the night watchman, alert for thieves and fire.

creasingly important. Economic and ethnic distinctions set the lines within which the population organized itself. "We have our castes of society, graduated and divided with as much regard to rank and dignity as the most scrupulous Hindoos maintain," noted the 1826 Pittsburgh Directory fondly. By then old-timers were already nostalgic for the good old days when "all was peaceful heartfelt felicity."

At the peak of the social hierarchy were the merchants, bankers, brokers, and underwriters, who formed a business community engaged in buying and selling, in importing and exporting merchandise. Some of them started out as partners or factors of great business houses in Baltimore or Philadelphia, then with their own capital established themselves on their own. Others began as petty shopkeepers, then raised themselves by thrift, ingenuity, and the willingness to take risks.

Of necessity all these men had to be speculators. In the rapidly changing economy, only those thrived who were willing to try new possibilities. Many plunged in land, in the stocks of new corporations, or in manufacturing. They did so not because they were reckless gamblers but because they knew that they had to take risks to come ahead in this bustling city.

The willingness to venture and to work were their basic traits. It made sense to take chances when one had faith in the future and devoted every energy to attaining success. There was neither time nor temptation for unprofitable distractions, except now and then for a ball when a distinguished visitor came to town, as the Marquis of Lafayette did in 1825.

But such indulgences were rare. The great men of the day who came for a visit, a Henry Clay, a Zachary Taylor, or a Daniel Webster, were feasted and acclaimed, but once they left town there was little excitement until the arrival of another celebrity.

Life in Pittsburgh was mainly work, with little enjoyment to break the monotony of the everyday existence.

The overriding faith in work and in the certainty of its rewards owed much to the Calvinism of the city's heritage. A substantial proportion of Pittsburgh's successful families were of Scottish, Scotch-Irish, or New England descent and, by virtue of their religious training, animated with the conviction that earnest labor was a duty that would earn them divine favor.

Such mercantile families dominated the economic life of the city and were influential also in its politics. With their wives they played a prominent role in every cultural, social, and philanthropic activity. Confident, self-made men, proud of their fashionable houses, they set the tone for the rest of the community and were models for the emulation of the scores of petty shopkeepers and the hundreds of clerks and salesmen who kept their books and were dependent upon them for a livelihood.

Allied to the merchants were a growing body of professional men. A handful of doctors made their appearance in the city early in the century; by 1830, there were more

A MENU OF THE TESTIMONIAL DINNER given in the Exchange Hotel for William W. Irwin, the former mayor of Pittsburgh to celebrate his appointment as minister to Denmark.

THE ROMANCE OF THE CENTURY

MARY GROGHAN AND CAPTAIN SCHENLEY.

Mary Croghan was the granddaughter of James O'Hara, the wealthy capitalist of early Pittsburgh. Her mother married William Croghan of Kentucky, but died in 1828 only a year after Mary's birth, leaving her huge estate in trust for her daughter.

Mary was not yet 15 when she was sent to a fashionable boarding school at Staten Island in New York. And there the troubles started. The school was run by a Mrs. McLeod, and Mrs. McLeod had a twice widowed brother-in-law, a dashing soldier of 43—Captain Edward Wyndham Harrington Schenley.

The two met, fell in love, and eloped.

If a man without means marries a wealthy girl the gossip is ready-made. Thus, when Captain Schenley, nearly three times the age of Mary Croghan, married her, tongues wagged from Pittsburgh to Dutch Guiana and back again to Victorian London. It was an event worth talking about.

After Mary's father learned of his daughter's marriage, he asked the Pennsylvania Legislature to pass a law whereby all of Mary's trust funds should be held by him—and this was done.

Historians have had little good to say for Captain Schenley. They called him a ne'er-do-well and a fortune hunter, they maligned him, spread poisonous tales about him. But if one looks at his relationship with his wife he appears in a favorable light.

He had married his young bride in February 1842. Soon after the wedding he took her to Dutch Guiana where he was a commissioner in the slave trade. After three years in South America they left for England. But in 1848, when Mary was expecting her first child, they came to Pittsburgh. She was then 21 and demanded her rightful estate. Receiving part of her inheritance, she and her husband returned to England, where they settled down for a long and happy married life.

In the marriage which lasted for 36 years, Mary bore her husband three sons and six daughters. Schenley died in 1878, in his 79th year.

Soon after her husband's death Mary won her battle in the Pennsylvania courts and was given the right to control her own property. She had no desire to live in her native city, but preferred to stay in England where she brought up her children. When she died in 1903 her Pittsburgh real estate holdings amounted to more than $50,000,000. It took another half a century to sell such large holdings without undermining the market.

Thus, Pittsburgh's greatest early fortune went abroad. But before it went Mary Schenley made large donations to the city—in 1889 she gave 300 acres in Oakland for a park. And she presented the Blockhouse, the city's oldest building, to the Daughters of the American Revolution as a memorial of less peaceful days.

than twenty of them and the Pittsburgh Medical Society was nine years old. At that date almost two score lawyers were practicing in the town along with a smaller number of teachers and ministers. Respectability, some degree of education, and good incomes gave these men prestige in the community; and their ranks continued to expand with the growth of Pittsburgh.

The professionals too were swayed by the ideals of material achievement that permeated the city and were likely to take fliers in speculative ventures when they had the opportunity to do so. Thomas Mellon, for instance, came to Pittsburgh as a barefoot boy in 1823. He studied at Western University, practiced law and invested shrewdly in real estate and business to found the family fortune. Such professional men were therefore more likely to follow than to lead the merchants who exemplified the success to which all aspired.

A comfortable way of life separated the traders and professionals from the rest of the population. Below these two well-to-do groups were a substantial variety of artisans and craftsmen—carpenters, tailors, blacksmiths, bootmakers, and the like. These were men with skill in a trade, generally self-employed and independent, and frequently property owners in their own right. A growing economy in which labor was short put a high value on their services, so that they were better off than their counterparts in the East or in Europe. Travelers were impressed with their high standard of living. They noted that they had all kinds of food which their European counterparts could hardly dream of and they had turkeys, beef, butter, and of course plenty of whiskey and cigars.

Yet the artisans were unstable and discontented, for their situation was precarious. Rising prices found them helpless and they often suffered from depreciation of the currency. More important, as the town grew, as large-scale industry appeared, and as transportation improved, they lost control of the local market. Thus they felt themselves isolated while the merchants and other great enterprisers prospered. In 1819, some of them organized the Pittsburgh Manufacturing Company, which briefly acted as a cooperative warehousing and marketing organization. Craft organizations also attempted to protect the artisans' position by regulating hours and rates of pay. In 1836, fourteen such groups created a federation, the Pittsburgh Central Labor Union, to further their common interests. In 1849, some 23 organizations joined in the Iron City Industrial Congress. But the weakness of such efforts ultimately led the mechanics to seek redress in politics, although without much success. Complaints against the merchants' greed and against oppression by the factory owners continued to be sounded throughout the period and, from time to time, led to visionary schemes for improving the conditions of the workingmen.

No clear line separated the artisans from the miscellaneous laborers who worked as operatives in the mills. The latter were wage earners and lacked the independence of

(turn to page 107)

Pennsylvania Forge.

EVERSON & CO.,

MANUFACTURERS OF ALL KINDS OF
HAMMERED IRON, WROUGHT IRON SHAFTS AND CRANKS,

PISTON RODS,
CRANKS FOR LOCOMOTIVES,
WRISTS, LEVERS, LINKS,
PITMAN JAWS.

CAPSTAN SPINDLES,
FURNACE RINGERS,
VICE MOULDS,
LADLE MOULDS, AXLES, &c.

AND ALL SIZES OF
ANCHORS AND CHAIN CABLES.
☞ *All Work Warranted, both as to Material and Workmanship.* ☜
JOSHUA HANNA, No. 31, Water st., Agent.

WILLIAM A. HILL & CO.
EXCHANGE BROKERS,

Since the Fire,

Are located on Fifth Street, immediately opposite the Exchange Bank, where they are generally prepared to buy and sell Gold, Silver, and Bank Notes, on the most favorable terms. Sight exchange on Philadelphia, Baltimore, New York, Boston and Cincinnati constantly for sale.

☞ Wm. A. Hill & Co. expect to occupy the old stand No. 66 Wood street, three doors above Fourth, as soon as the house is finished, which will he by the 1st of September 1845.

June 3, 1845.

From The Great Fire at Pittsburgh (*1845*).

A PITTSBURGH IRON MANUFACTURER OFFERS HIS WARES IN 1845, SHORTLY AFTER THE GREAT FIRE.

W. & D. RINEHART,

MANUFACTURERS AND DEALERS IN ALL KINDS OF TOBACCO, SNUFF AND SEGARS, AT NO. 33 HAND STREET, PITTSBURGH.

Have always on hand an assortment of every article in their line, "Aromatic Stag" Fives, Twelves, Sixteens, Balt. Plug, Va. Twist, Cavendish, and Ladies' Twist Tobacco. Principes, La Normas, Regalias, Castellos, Cazadores, Werners, Ugues, Cubreys, Half Spanish, Melees and Common Segars. Copenhagen, Am. Gen., Rappee, Maccaboy and Scotch Snuffs. Pipes, Snuff boxes, &c. &c.,

From The Great Fire at Pittsburgh (*1845*).

BUSINESS CARD OF W. & D. RINEHART, THE PITTSBURGH TOBACCO MANUFACTURERS AND DEALERS IN 1845.

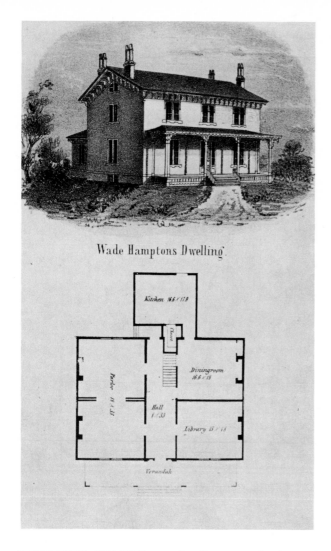

Wade Hamptons Dwelling.

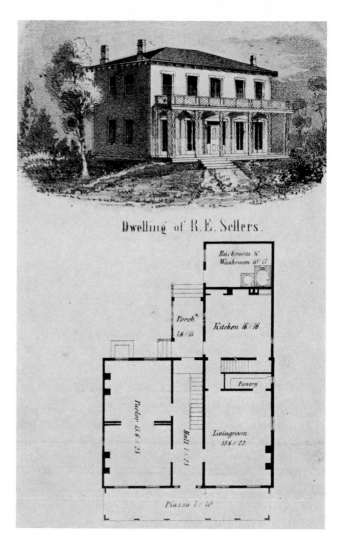

Dwelling of R. E. Sellers.

EVERGREEN HAMLET was the first community home development in suburban Pittsburgh. It was founded by the lawyer William M. Shinn, who in 1851 bought 85 acres of land and with five of his friends drew up *The Constitution of Evergreen Hamlet*, with the aim of securing for the members of the association and their families "the advantages and comforts of the country at a moderate cost, without doing violence to the social habits incident to city life."

Shinn's partners in the undertaking were Wade Hampton, who had a dry-goods business on Wood Street, was part owner of a wholesale clothing warehouse, and later became postmaster of Pittsburgh; Robert Emory Sellers, whose store sold drugs, oils, varnishes, paints, and dyes; William A. Hill, a broker with offices at 98 Wood Street; William B. Scaife,

THE FIRST
COMMUNITY HOUSING
PROJECT
IN PITTSBURGH

A CONTEMPORARY REPRESENTATION
of Pittsburgh's first suburban housing project.

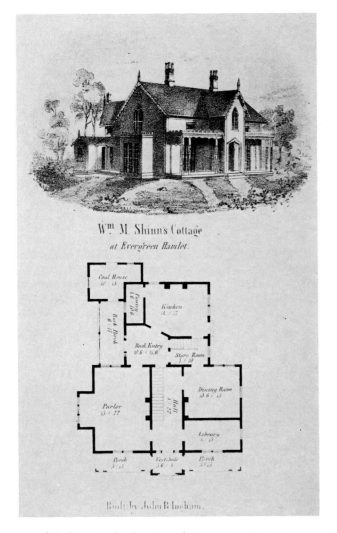

Wᵐ M. Shinn's Cottage
at Evergreen Hamlet.

Built by John Bingham.

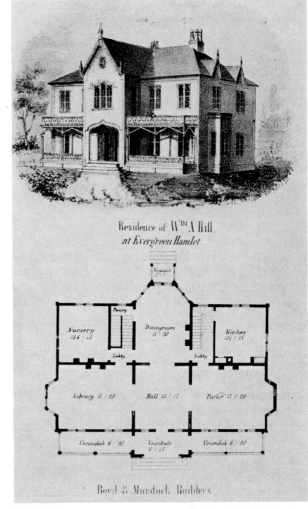

Residence of Wᵐ A Hill
at Evergreen Hamlet

Boyd & Murdock, Builders

Courtesy Charles C. Arensberg.

son of Jeffery Scaife, founder of Pittsburgh's oldest manufacturing firm, who operated the business from 1833 until his death in 1876; and John A. Wilson, who was bought out by Hampton in 1859.

The founders of Evergreen Hamlet envisioned recruiting only 16 families—they believed that would be all "that is required for the support of a suitable school, and form a sufficient neighborhood, to exclude all fear of that loneliness which so many persons dread in country life."

But alas, the plan did not work. By 1866 only four of the 16 houses had been built, and the association was dissolved.

The four houses still stand today. The Wade Hampton house belongs to Bernard J. Kelly, the William A. Hill house to Dr. Harrison Davies, the R. E. Sellers house to John A. Grove, Jr., the William M. Shinn cottage to Dr. Chester Beall.

the mechanics. Discontent led them also to strike as did the cotton mill laborers in 1841 and the iron mill hands in 1849.

Labor's condition was poor; a workman was lucky if he made a dollar a day. Those who could manage it left their jobs, looking for an easier life in the Far West. The Pittsburgh *Post* editorialized:

And what is Pittsburgh? Ask the hundreds and thousands of her citizens who are flocking off to California where there are no factories —no improvements. They will answer, "We are going to a place where we hope capital cannot oppress us. At the risk of our lives we will not be enslaved by the money power." This is their significant and withering reply. Now, what do we propose? Simply and undeniably this: To introduce some reforms here as will prevent this necessity which drives away to distant lands our very best, most useful and industrious citizens. We appeal to every honest and thinking man if it is fair that we should be hunted down, as we have been, by any class of people for this.

But though the lot of the workingmen was not an easy one, even the unskilled laborers in the factories could hope to rise in status in a community which suffered from a perennial shortage of manpower. All such settled breadwinners were above all anxious to improve themselves and to help their children on to better places in society.

Therein lay a sharp distinction between them and the casual, transient laborers who drifted through the city in large numbers. In the early decades of the century, Pittsburgh was compelled to accommodate a colorful lot of wagoners and rivermen who handled its commerce and who were as strenuous in their intervals of relaxation as they were in driving their teams across the mountains or in guiding their vessels down stream. Later, there appeared the railroad, canal, and steamboat crews, along with the construction gangs recruited in town. These transients merged with a resident population of unskilled labor that grew steadily in size throughout the entire period.

A significant number of free Negroes also had no fixed place in the community. Slavery had gradually disappeared. The city held but eight bondsmen in 1830, although the number of free persons of color had increased to 453 by that year. The Census of 1860 found fully 2725 in the City and its vicinity. Generally the Negroes were occupied in unskilled labor and in the service trades.

All these formed a troublesome group without fixed homes or roots in the city. They were mostly single men who lacked the capacity for settling down. Given to violence, they hung about in the less respectable neighborhoods and were responsible for serious problems. Drunkenness was the least of their vices. In 1819 the Grand Jury pointed out that there were fully thirty unlicensed dram shops and the number undoubtedly increased thereafter. The same Grand Jury also complained that "women of pleasure" swarmed in the city; and frequent prize fights were centers of disorder. To cope with such problems the beginnings of a professional police force were established

in 1836. But lawlessness remained general and was often uncontrollable in some parts of Pittsburgh, a condition to which the respectable elements preferred to close their eyes except when it affected them, as in the wave of arson in 1851.

This highly diverse population found it difficult to develop a sense of community. Drawn from many different parts of the country, and indeed of the world, they were united by few inherited ties. Set off by social and economic distinctions, enjoying or suffering from rapid fluctuations of fortune, the men and women of the city had to create all its institutions afresh. That they succeeded as well as they did was a testament to their capacity for autonomous action.

Pittsburghers learned early that they could not depend for everything upon their government. They found it difficult to secure an appropriate municipal organization, and they were usually on the minority side in both the state and the nation.

Though Pittsburgh had become a city, it remained under

(turn to page 117)

THE STEAMER of the Pittsburgh Fire Department with the Eagle Company's horse-drawn engines.

The chief engineer of the fire department for the past 20 years was William Eichbaum, Jr. (left inset).

The designer of the steam engine which was developed by Pittsburgh's oldest fire company was James Nelson (right inset). The first test of the engine was made at nightfall, as the men of the Eagle were not certain that the new contraption would work. "Better try it out in secret," said the firemen, "and don't let others know. If it doesn't work people would laugh."

PITTSBURGH IN THE YEAR 1840. A LITHOGRAPH PRINTED IN NUREMBERG, GERMANY BY C. BERG.

BEFORE THE FIRE. A PAINTING MADE IN THE EARLY MONTHS OF 1845 BY GEORGE BREED.

THE BURNING OF PITTSBURGH as painted by William Coventry Wall (1810-86) two days after the devastation.

The holocaust began around noon on April 10, 1845 in the icehouse of Colonel William Diehl at Ferry Street near the southeast corner of Second Avenue. It was believed that it started after an Irishwoman in a woodshed adjoining Colonel Diehl's residence lit a fire for her laundry. If this was so, the laundry was the most expensive one the world ever saw.

Before the Irishwoman's water was even boiling, the flames engulfed the shanty and, fanned by a high wind, spread to the adjoining house. Soon the bells of the Third Presbyterian Church sounded the alarm, but by then the breezes had already taken the flames eastward and building after building was crackling and burning.

"A pretty strong wind was blowing from the west," wrote Attorney Robert McKnight in his diary that night, "and some alarm existed as to the spread of the flames. I mounted an engine and labored with might and main but unfortunately the supply of water failed." There was confusion everywhere, noted the diarist, "drays, carts, furniture, houses & men . . . were running in all directions."

From Ferry and Second the flames crossed the street and burned part of the block. The fire moved across the square which was bounded by Ferry, Third, Market, and Second Streets and it also caused havoc at another block bounded by Ferry, Second, Market, and Front Streets. After the flames devastated Market they moved southeastward down to Water Street and northeastward from Third to Fourth.

Businessmen inside the fire area worked in a frantic effort to move their stock of goods out of the stores and to places of safety. Those who were able carted their belongings to the bank of the Monongahela, which "became piled up with an enormous and indescribable mass of matter."

At last, when the flames burned themselves out, the area between Ferry Street, Diamond Alley, and Water Street on the Monongahela side as far as the present Tenth Street Bridge was devastated. More than 50 acres had become prey of the flames. Some estimates of the loss ran as high as nine million dollars.

The Monongahela House, the covered Monongahela Bridge, the Customhouse, and Western University were among the 1200 landmarks that were destroyed in the conflagration.

The Pittsburgh Gazette's reporter wrote: "Nothing was spared—very little saved. The progress of the fire as it lanced and leaped with its forked tongue from house to house, from block to block, and from square to square was awfully magnificent."

Painted specially for this book by Harry W. Scheuch.

CHOLERA EPIDEMICS kept Pittsburgh in fear. Coal fires and pitch pots were lit in the streets, expecting that the flames would kill the cause of the disease. Hundreds perished in 1832, 1833, 1834, 1849, 1850, 1854, and 1855.

THE BURNT OUT CITY:
A Contemporary painting by William C. Wall.

DICKENS IN PITTSBURGH. Charles Dickens came to the city on March 20, 1842. In his *American Notes* the English writer observed that after his boat passed through a long aqueduct across the Allegheny River "we emerged upon that ugly confusion of the backs of buildings and crazy galleries and stairs, which always abuts on water, whether it be river, sea, canal or ditch; and were in Pittsburgh."

Although this is a somewhat imaginary painting, the details of it are correct. The footbridge over the canal ran at Liberty, opposite Washington Street. Fowler Exchange at Eleventh and Penn Street corner is on the right; the Railroad Hotel on Penn Street is in the center; Washington Hotel, here called the Canal Hotel, is on the left.

Painted specially for this book by E. J. Oleniacz.

Painted specially for this book by Ruth M. Covert.

KIER'S LAMP. In 1850 Samuel M. Kier (1813-74), the well-known Pittsburgh merchant and canalboat operator, began experimenting with crude oil, which he intended to use as an illuminant. The hitch was that the oil, when used in the existing whale oil and camphene lamps, not only had an unpleasant smoke, but also smelled to high heaven.

The undismayed Kier kept on with his experiments. He refined the oil by distillation, and finally, with a five-barrel still, he developed a fairly clear oil. However, the difficulty of the smell remained.

When, after a protracted period of trial and error, Kier succeeded in eliminating the smell and using his refined oil in the camphene lamps, the demand for his product soared; his refined oil was popular not only because it was serviceable, but also because it was far cheaper than all other illuminants.

Before long Kier produced the lamp he had envisioned all along —a four-pronged burner lamp in which the oil burned steadily without smoke and odor—the world's first petroleum oil lamp.

PITTSBURGH IN 1849. A colored lithograph by Tappan and Bradford after a contemporary drawing by B. F. Smith, Jr., printed on the press of C. Berg. At this time the city's population was about 45,000 and manufactures were approaching $50,000,000 per year. Commerce was still conducted mainly on the three rivers and the Pennsylvania Canal, but the age of the fast moving railroad was already foreseen.

Painted specially for this book by Roy Hilton.

MONONGAHELA WHARF was a place of immense activity. It was here that the singer Jenny Lind was welcomed on April 25, 1851, when she came to Pittsburgh. In 1845 a total of 27,257,870 pounds of freight arrived over the Monongahela, not counting sand, lumber, bricks, and coal, while 12,961,959 pounds were carried eastward.

Painted specially for this book by Dr. W. E. Brown.

PASSAVANT HOSPITAL, the oldest Protestant hospital in the city, was established in 1849 under the name Pittsburgh Infirmary and chartered by the state in the next year. Cre- ated through the efforts of the Lutheran Reverend William A. Passavant and his wife, the institution's first permanent building was erected at Roberts and Reed Streets in 1851.

PITTSBURGH PIETY, one of the outstanding paintings of David G. Blythe, shows the interior of the First Presbyterian Church.

In the early years of the city the churches grew slowly, but by 1842 the Pittsburgh directory enumerated 55 church buildings.

Courtesy Richard K. Mellon.

Painted specially for this book by Idabelle Kleinhans

THE RAILROAD ERA BEGINS. On December 10, 1851, the Pennsylvania Railroad began business in the city of Pittsburgh with a rail line extending as far as Turtle Creek. At that point passengers were transferred to a stagecoach which bridged a 28-mile gap in the connection. At last the dream of traveling in comfort to Philadelphia was a reality.

below:

BEITLER'S TAVERN on the south side of Greensburg Pike (now Penn Avenue near Shady) in East Liberty was a popular meeting place for Pittsburgh youth. In summer one rode there on horseback, in winter one went on a sleigh. Joseph R. Woodwell, father of the artist Johanna K. W. Hailman, painted this a few years before the Civil War.

Courtesy Historical Society of Western Pennsylvania.

PITTSBURGH POST OFFICE, the master-piece of David G. Blythe (1815-65), one of the city's great painters.

Blythe came to Pittsburgh when he was 16 to become an apprentice in Joseph Woodwell's woodcarving and furniture business. Besides his work, he drew and he painted and he made friends with the owner of the art store, J. J. Gillespie, a friendship which lasted until the end of his life and had great influence on him.

For a time Blythe earned his living as a house painter; then he joined the Navy and sailed the seas. But wherever he went he painted, it was the only thing he really cared about. He died in 1865 of pneumonia brought on by malnutrition.

the strict oversight of the state. The governor appointed the recorder and the twelve aldermen, from among whom the select and common councils chose the mayor. Property qualifications for voting and holding office limited the popular role even in the election of the councilmen. Although the merchants were in control there was little they could do, for the municipality suffered from low income and restricted powers. Heavy municipal investments in railroad bonds later made these limitations all the more irksome.

In the 1830s the mayor became elective, property qualifications disappeared, and the Northern Liberties were incorporated in the city. But the state legislature remained jealous of the power it would delegate.

Efforts to effect a union with the Allegheny City across the river, logical as that step was, were again and again frustrated.

The more general political interests of Pittsburghers centered on the internal improvements and the protective tariffs on which they thought the prosperity of their trade and industry depended. Even the Workingmans Party of the 1830s here took that stand, although it also sought free public education and the abolition of imprisonment for debt. Yet on both the tariff and internal improvements, Pittsburghers were generally outvoted in the state and nation; and not until the appearance of the Republican Party, which held its first national convention in the city in 1856, did they find an effective instrument to support the policies they favored.

As a result, the people of the city learned, for better or worse, that they had to perform many communal functions for themselves by cooperative voluntary effort without the aid of the government. These were pragmatic rather than dogmatic decisions. The needs existed and had to be met one way or another, through the municipality or independently, by transplanting old institutions or by creating new ones.

Religious concerns were almost as old as the community itself; and they were satisfied through a multitude of churches that reflected the city's diverse population. Each group that arrived in the city sought at once to create places of worship like those they had left behind in Philadelphia or New England or across the ocean. Already in 1815, of the eight churches in town, two were Presbyterian

Courtesy Mr. R. Lucien Patton.

PITTSBURGH HORSE MARKET at St. Clair (the present Sixth Street) and Duquesne Way as painted by David G. Blythe about 1860. The church is probably the Christ Methodist Church at the corner of Penn and Eighth Streets, but it may be the Second Presbyterian Church which stood at Seventh and Penn and had towers similar to the one in the painting.

while the Episcopalians, Catholics, Seceders, Covenanters, Methodists, and German Lutherans had one each. As time went on the number and variety grew. There were enough Catholics in the city to justify its elevation into a see, with its own bishop, in 1843; and the first Jewish congregation appeared in 1853. A good deal of energy went into buildings. Each sect harnessed the enthusiasm of its communicants to make as impressive a showing as possible, as the Catholics did when their new cathedral was consecrated in 1855.

Around the churches there sprang up a host of benevolent and philanthropic organizations. Some of these cut across denominational lines as did the Pittsburgh Moral Society, organized to improve the moral tone of the community. Others expressed the needs of a particular ethnic group, as did the Catholic orphanage. Still others were generated by intergroup rivalry; when the Catholics opened Mercy Hospital, the Lutherans hastened to build Passavant Hospital (1849) and other Protestants the Western Pennsylvania Hospital (1853). Again, some organizations devoted themselves to furthering one of the numerous reforms, such as temperance or abolition that grew in importance in the thirties and forties.

Finally, there were a multiude of fraternal associations like the Masons, devoted primarily to good fellowship. Not least among these were the voluntary fire and militia companies. However, the Duquesne Grays and the Pittsburgh Blues learned in 1847 that there was more to soldiering than marching and conviviality. Drawn into service during the Mexican War, they served gallantly at the taking of Vera Cruz and the defense of Pueblo.

It was more difficult to make provision for the educational needs of the city because there were no appropriate models to be imitated. All over the country school systems were in process of transition; and a young community was hard put to define its own needs or to know how to go about meeting them. At the start it was still the function of each family to provide for the upbringing of its children, either in the home or through tutors or private schools. Only the more advanced levels of learning seemed to call for organized social effort.

This was the reason that communal attention, for a long time, was primarily devoted to the support of the Pittsburgh Academy, and Western University. Neither institution thrived. The university burned down several times and even in the middle of the nineteenth century graduated but a handful of students.

Other provisions for education on a more or less advanced level also appeared from time to time, under the auspices of private groups. The Presbyterians established in 1825 the Western Theological Seminary in Allegheny. A half-dozen young ladies' boarding schools and female colleges appeared in the twenties and thirties. Duff's Mercantile College opened its doors in 1840, the Iron City Commercial College in 1855, and a manual training school for Negro children in 1849. The Catholic parochial school

went into operation in the year of 1844.

Elementary instruction, however, was at first available only in such private schools as Brevost's. Unfortunately the high cost of tuition limited the number of students; in 1816 less than one-quarter of the children of school age were in attendance. The remainder received only such attention as could be given in Sunday schools.

The Adelphi Free School in 1816 and the Union Society in 1818 were established to make some provision for the children of the poor; neither proved effective. For a few years after the War of 1812 there were hopes that the Lancastrian system, by which the pupils, in effect, taught themselves, might lower costs enough to permit all to attend. But the genuine expansion of opportunities did not come until 1834, when a state law provided for the creation of municipal public school systems with state aid. Pittsburgh opened two common schools a year later and the number grew steadily thereafter. A public high school began instruction on a higher level in 1855. In 1860, 118 teachers instructed more than 7000 pupils in the city's school district.

That the start was slow was not surprising in view of the fact that the prominent eastern cities, like New York and Philadelphia, were only then beginning to create their own systems of public education. Pittsburghers were eager for improvement; but it took them, like other Americans, time to learn how.

All those who left the settled places to make new homes at the edge of the wilderness labored under the anxiety lest they and their children revert to a primitive style of life. There was a danger, the Pittsburgh *Mercury* explained in 1813, that frontier conditions might "retard the progress of the human mind, and the liberal culture of science and literature."

Such formal institutions as churches and schools were one line of defense against that threat. But as the city acquired stability and some of its residents began to enjoy wealth and leisure, they sought spontaneously to develop a wide range of cultural activities. The Quintilian Society arranged discussions of literature and science and the Franklin Society sponsored debates. An Historical Society made an appearance in 1834 and an Institute of Arts and Sciences, in 1838. The Permanent Library had 500 volumes in 1816. In 1850 Colonel James Anderson threw open his own collection of books to young men who desired to pursue their reading; among the boys who used his books was Andrew Carnegie, who would never forget their value to him. Some decades later, when his money helped to create the first public library in Allegheny, a monument in front of the building memorialized the book-loving colonel.

The culture of the city also had lighter forms. Early in the century groups of amateurs and itinerant professional companies began to bring the drama to Pittsburgh. At first the theater was housed on the top floor of the courthouse, but in 1833 the Old Drury opened its doors. In many less imposing places of entertainment, casual singers and min-

(turn to page 122)

KIER FINDS OIL. Samuel M. Kier was an amazing personality of early America, a man with an original, inventive, and curious mind. His father was in the salt-producing business when young Kier began a career as a merchant in Pittsburgh. The firm—Hewitt & Kier—failed with many others in the depression of 1837, but a year later the young man organized a new firm—Kier, Royer & Company. This company operated boats plying the Pennsylvania Canal and the idea turned out to be a successful one. The "Mechanic's Line" was a booming business for many years.

In 1847, after Royer left the firm, Kier took in as partner Benjamin Franklin Jones, the iron manufacturer, and the two men started their lucrative connections with the railroads. The boats of their "Independent Line" were amphibious contraptions, pulled through the canal sections and hauled over the railroad.

It was about this time that Kier's father encountered difficulties with his salt wells at Tarentum. The cause of his trouble was oil, which flowed from the wells. Kier, who was financially involved in his father's undertaking, was conversant with the fact that oil could be used as a panacea for human ills. Thus he bottled, advertised, and distributed it, and sold it in medicine road shows.

When a market was established for "Kier's Rock Oil" the product was sent directly to druggists with Kier advertising it as "A REMEDY OF WONDERFUL EFFICACY" which the public would enjoy. He asserted that "The lame, through its instrumentality, were made to walk—the blind, to see. Those who had suffered for years under the torturing pains of RHEUMATISM, GOUT and NEURALGIA, were restored to health and usefulness" by "THE MOST WONDERFUL REMEDY EVER DISCOVERED." He had "no doubt that in another year it will stand at the head of the list of valuable remedies." It was "put up as it flows from the bosom of the earth, without anything being added to or taken from it."

The unfortunate thing was that there was more oil than the druggists were able to sell. So Kier began his attempts to use the superfluous fluid for illumination—a most successful step in his career.

In his later years he pioneered the manufacture of firebrick, establishing four works in Western Pennsylvania. He also owned a pottery and was engaged in coal mining and steel manufacturing.

But what kept his name alive were his successful experiments in oil refining. He was America's first oil refiner, the man whose clean burning fluid kept thousands of lamps in thousands of homes alight.

PETROLEUM, OR ROCK OIL.

A NATURAL REMEDY!

PROCURED FROM A WELL IN ALLEGHENY COUNTY, PA.

Four hundred feet below the Earth's Surface!

PUT UP AND SOLD BY

SAMUEL M. KIER,

CANAL BASIN, SEVENTH STREET, PITTSBURGH, PA.

The healthful balm from Nature's secret spring,
The bloom of health, and life, to man will bring;
As from her depths the magic liquid flows,
To calm our sufferings, and assuage our woes.

CAUTION.—As many persons are now going about and vending an article of a spurious character, calling it Petroleum, or Rock Oil, we would caution the public against all preparations bearing that name not having the name of S. M. Kier written on the label of the bottle.

PETROLEUM.—It is necessary, upon the introduction of a new medicine to the notice of the public, that something should be said in relation to its powers in healing disease, and the manner in which it acts. Man's organization is a complicated one; and to understand the functions of each organ, requires the study of years. But to understand that certain remedies produce certain impressions upon these organs, may be learned by experience in a short time. It is by observation in watching the effects of various medicines, that we are enabled to increase the number of curative agents; and when we have discovered a new medicine and attested its merits, it is our duty to bring it before the public, so that the benefits to be derived from it may be more generally diffused, but have no right to hold back a remedy whose powers are calculated to remove pain and to alleviate human suffering and disease. THE PETROLEUM HAS BEEN FULLY TESTED! About one year ago, it was placed before the public as A REMEDY OF WONDERFUL EFFICACY. Every one not acquainted with its virtues, doubted its healing properties. The cry of humbug was raised against it. It had some friends;—those that were cured through its wonderful agency. These spoke out in its favor. The lame, through its instrumentality, were made to walk—the blind, to see. Those who had suffered for years under the torturing pains of RHEUMATISM, GOUT and NEURALGIA, were restored to health and usefulness. Several who were blind have been made to see, the evidence of which will be placed before you. If you still have doubts, go and ask those who have been cured! Some of them live in our midst, and can answer for themselves. In writing about a medicine, we are aware that we should write TRUTH—that we should make no statements that cannot be proved. We have the witnesses—crowds of them, who will testify in terms stronger than we can write them to the efficacy of this Remedy, who will testify that the PETROLEUM has done for them what no medicine ever could before—cases that were pronounced hopeless, and beyond the reach of remedial means—cases abandoned by Physicians of unquestioned celebrity, have been made to exclaim, "THIS IS THE MOST WONDERFUL REMEDY EVER DISCOVERED!" We will lay before you the certificates of some of the most remarkable cases; to give them all, would require more space than would be allowed by this circular. Since the introduction of the Petroleum, about one year ago, many Physicians have been convinced of its efficacy, and now recommend it in their practice; and we have no doubt that in another year it will stand at the head of the list of valuable Remedies. If the Physicians do not recommend it, the people will have it of themselves—for its transcendent power to heal, will and must become known and appreciated—when the voices of the cured speak out; when the cures themselves stand out in bold relief, and when he who for years has suffered with the tortures and pangs of an immedicable lesion, that has been shortening his days, and hastening him "to the narrow house appointed for all the living," when he speaks out in its praise, who will doubt it! THE PETROLEUM IS A NATURAL REMEDY—it is put up as it flows from the bosom of the earth, without anything being added to or taken from it.

Courtesy Pennsylvania Historical and Museum Collection, Harrisburg.

KIER'S CIRCULAR LAUDING THE CURATIVE POWERS OF PETROLEUM.

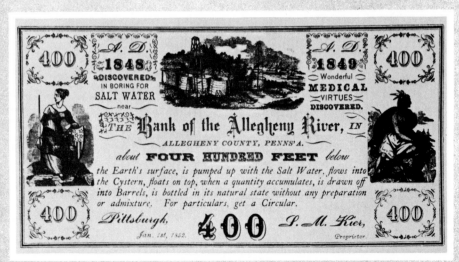

AN ADVERTISEMENT BY S. M. KIER, WHICH HE ISSUED IN THE YEAR OF 1852

PITTSBURGH IN THE NEWS.

Self-portrait.

JANE GREY SWISSHELM, journalist, abolitionist, fighter for woman's rights, was born in Pittsburgh in 1815. She taught school before she was 15. In 1847 she started the *Pittsburgh Saturday Visiter* (sic), writing it in a vigorous and sarcastic style. She served as a nurse during the Civil War, then returned to Pittsburgh and remained until her death in 1884.

After a daguerreotype.

JOE BARKER, a colorful street preacher, was arrested in 1849 when he was involved in a riot while delivering one of his many tirades against Catholicism. He was thrown into jail and while in prison he was elected as mayor of the city. After serving for one year he was defeated for re-election and sank into obscurity. He died in 1862 when run over by a train.

From Gleason's Pictorial Drawing-Room Companion, *June 14, 1851.*

BURNING OF ST. PAUL'S Cathedral at Grant Street and Fifth Avenue on May 6, 1851. The church was dedicated in 1833 and stood on a mound of earth about 20 feet high after streets on Grant's Hill had been graded for the second time in 1847.

From Gleason's Pictorial Drawing-Room Companion, *April 30, 1853.*

THE MANUFACTURING CITY with some 50,000 inhabitants was described in great detail in *Gleason's Pictorial* on April 30, 1853. The article gave not only the past history of Pittsburgh, but also a glowing account of its contemporary activities.

From Ballou's Pictorial Drawing-Room Companion, *April 14, 1855.*

THE SMOKING CHIMNEYS—a drawing of Pittsburgh which appeared in *Ballou's Pictorial* on April 14, 1855. Pittsburgh had begun to provoke interest all over the country. Newspapermen and artists were sent to the city to report on its progress.

A HISTORIC EVENT. On December 10, 1852, a wood-burning locomotive of the Pennsylvania Railroad arrived in Pittsburgh with four cars, making the first all-rail trip from Philadelphia to Pittsburgh.

Two years later, after a tunnel had been built, *The Pittsburgh Gazette* jubilantly reported that the journey between the two Pennsylvania cities could be made in no more than 15 hours. Such speed, wrote the *Gazette*, "ought to satisfy the fastest of this fast generation." It did, for a while.

STEPHEN COLLINS FOSTER (1826-64) was "the creator of the first distinctively American musical idiom, the singer of the commonplace, the elemental, and the democratic." His songs have simple themes; they are about love, home, friendship, loyalty. They could not be mistaken, they are as American as apple pie.

Born in Pittsburgh on the Fourth of July in 1826 as the ninth child of a well-to-do family, Stephen Foster showed early signs of his musical talent. Before he was 21 his songs were known all over the country. During his life he wrote more than 200 songs, many of them as popular today as they were when they first came out.

Songs like "Oh! Susannah," "My Old Kentucky Home," "Jeanie with the Light Brown Hair," "Old Folks at Home," "Old Black Joe," "We Are Coming Father Abraham, One Hundred Thousand Strong," are part of the American heritage, they became the songs of the nation. Some of the lyrics to them were written by

strels held forth, among them Nelson Kneass who set "Ben Bolt" to music that the whole nation learned to sing. Meanwhile a sprinkling of "professors" were teaching ambitious youngsters music and dancing, and a few artists were painting the portraits of the well-to-do citizens.

The most important cultural media were the newspapers, cheap enough to reach almost every element in the population and sensitive to the interests and tastes of their readers. The *Gazette* was almost thirty years old in 1815; and it began to appear as a daily in 1833. It soon acquired vigorous rivals as the number and variety of journals grew.

In 1842 there were six dailies and twelve weeklies, three of them published in German. Among the more important new publications were the *Post*, established in 1842, and, four years later, the *Dispatch*, the first penny paper in the city. The function of these newspapers was by no means confined to recording the news. Their advertisements provided a means of communication for business, and their columns were open to all kinds of political and literary opinions. And if the prose and poetry lacked polish or permanent value, it was none the less important that the people of the city should have available this means of

Courtesy Fletcher Hodges, Jr., The Foster Hall Collection.

George Cooper (on the right above).

Though Foster was successful, his earnings remained small. Royalty statements (above) from Firth, Pond & Company, the firm which published his songs, show that between 1849 and 1860 he received $15,000 in royalties, an average of less than $1400 per year.

Financial troubles bore upon him heavily and his situation became worse after his parents died in 1855. Foster grew despondent, and sought solace in alcohol.

His wife, Jane Denny McDowell, the daughter of a Pittsburgh doctor, took work as a telegraph operator for the Pennsylvania Railroad. She supported and cared for their daughter, but the composer was much too proud to accept her help.

Broken in health, a lonely man, he died on January 13, 1864, in New York's Bellevue Hospital. In his pocket were thirty-eight cents and a jotting on a scrap of paper—"Dear Friends and Gentle Hearts."

expression. And they used it with great vigor.

Within this raw and growing community, a variety of types could each seek its own cultural goals. For some, old models still had a clear validity and had only to be imitated and preserved. Henry Marie Brackenridge, thus, started with the example of his father, who had gained a literary reputation for himself and for Pittsburgh before the end of the eighteenth century. The son received a classical education, practiced law with distinction, and was active in every movement to bring education, gentility, and polish to the city. His *Recollections of Persons and Places* was

a charming and amusing memoir, gentlemanly in tone.

Other natives of the City also looked back, but with a greater sensitivity to the nature of the place in which they lived. Though Stephen C. Foster was born in 1826 when the old inland trade had lost much of its vitality, the awareness of the river and of the country through which it flowed, and of the people who worked along its shores, crept imperishably into his tunes.

And still others were catching a glimpse of the future. Andrew Carnegie, who came to Pittsburgh in 1848 at the age of thirteen to begin as a bobbin boy in the cotton mill

(turn to page 126)

123

From Ballou's Pictorial Drawing-Room Companion, February 21, 1857.
THE COURTHOUSE ON GRANT'S HILL.

The new pictorial magazines, *Harper's Weekly* and *Ballou's Pictorial*, which came into being in the years before the Civil War, began to publish illustrations of the rapidly growing city. America was curious to see what Pittsburgh looked like. Artists from Boston and New York came and made drawings of the streets

LAFAYETTE HALL, at Wood Street below Fourth Avenue, where on Washington's Birthday in 1856 the first Republican National Convention was held. Some 500 delegates, repre-

From Ballou's Pictorial Drawing-Room Companion, February 21, 1857.
THE GERMAN CATHOLIC CHURCH IN ALLEGHENY CITY.

Courtesy Union National Bank.
THE UNION NATIONAL BANK.

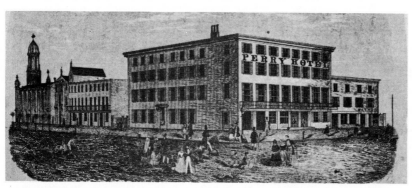

From a contemporary letterhead.
PERRY HOTEL, CORNER OF HANCOCK STREET AND DUQUESNE WAY.

PITTSBURGH LOOKED
OF THE FIFTIES

and the buildings; these drawings served as models for the woodcuts of the weeklies.

The writers whose articles accompanied the illustrations asserted that Pittsburgh's importance was rapidly gaining and predicted that before too long the Pittsburgh area would be the leading industrial community in the nation.

From Ballou's Pictorial Drawing-Room Companion, February 21, 1857.
THE CUSTOMHOUSE.

Courtesy Library of Congress.

senting 24 states and two territories, assembled to perfect their national organization and provide for a convention at Philadelphia to select candidates for President and Vice-President.

From Harper's Weekly December 4, 1858.

THE DUQUESNE DEPOT of the Pennsylvania Railroad was erected near the spot where Fort Duquesne stood when the French were in command at the Point. In November 1858 Pittsburghers —as this contemporary Harper's Weekly sketch shows—celebrated the hundredth anniversary of their city's foundation.

From Ballou's Pictorial, February 21, 1857.
THE FIRST PRESBYTERIAN CHURCH.

From Ballou's Pictorial Drawing-Room Companion, February 21, 1857.
MONONGAHELA BRIDGE BETWEEN BIRMINGHAM AND PITTSBURGH.

the career that led him into railroading and steel and a millionaire's fortune, never ceased to be moved by the impressions of his early years in the city. On the one hand he felt the zeal for material achievement, for the thrill of building and earning large amounts of money in an ever-expanding economy. On the other hand, he gradually became aware that this alone did not make a civilization, that libraries and universities and enlightened philanthropy were the ultimate marks of a community's advance out of the wilderness.

Pittsburgh, like Carnegie, would move into the era of the Civil War with a determination to go forward along both fronts; to expand its economy and yet to make greater provision for the cultural and social needs of its people. The city was ready for the great conflict that erupted in the spring of 1861; anti-slavery sentiment had long been strong in the city and was exacerbated by a series of fugitive slave cases in the fifties. But it was not quite prepared for some of the consequences of the war through which it would move to a new stage of industrial development and come to confront still graver problems of social order.

By 1860, the Iron City had come a long way. Tremendous gains in wealth and population had enabled it to outgrow its frontier past. But enormous challenges still remained to tax the ingenuity and enterprise of its citizens. The Civil War was to be a dividing point between old and new, between the Pittsburgh that was and the manufacturing and steel working center of the land that it was to become.

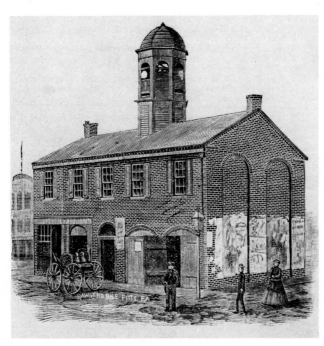

From Centennial History of Allegheny County (1888).
THE OLD TOWN HALL IN ALLEGHENY CITY.

THE CITY IN 1859—a lithograph "drawn from nature" by the artist William Schuchman. The picture was printed in Pittsburgh and copyrighted in the same year.

EW OF PITTSBURGH, PA.

At that time the city had about 10,000 houses and a population (including Allegheny) of almost 125,000. There were about 100 different industries and some 300 wholesale and retail outlets, not counting the drugstores and the groceries. The list of the manufacturing establishments was led by iron and metal working, and by the glass industry, producing the best flint glass in America.

From the collection of Stefan Lorant.

ROYALTY IN PITTSBURGH. On October 1, 1860, the Prince of Wales (later Edward VII) visited the city and received a warm welcome. He was accompanied by the Duke of Newcastle, Lord Lyons, the English ambassador (second from the Prince's right), Lord Bruce, the Earl of Germains, Lord Henchonbrook, Sir Henry Holland, and others.

This picture was taken by Mathew B. Brady, the famous Civil War photographer, in Washington shortly before the party set out for Pittsburgh and Canada.

At his arrival in Pittsburgh the Prince was welcomed at the Fort Wayne depot by Mayor George Wilson and escorted by the Duquesne Greys to the Monongahela House where he stayed overnight. The streets of the city were ablaze with light and were decorated with the flags of the two countries. All over town the bands played "God Save the Queen" in honor of Queen Victoria, the mother of the Prince.

Mayor George Wilson recalled four decades later in an article for the *Gazette* (January 22, 1901) that the manner of the Prince was "easy and dignified." His face did not "indicate a great amount of intellectuality nor the want of it. His features were good, with a little cast of German in them, and his person was graceful." Everyone was charmed by him.

Edward was delighted with his visit, which included a drive to the top of Coal Hill for a good view of Pittsburgh and tours through some of the busy factories.

Chapter 4

THE CIVIL WAR
AND ITS AFTERMATH

by J. Cutler Andrews

BY 1860 PITTSBURGH had become a place of considerable distinction, if not of renown; a steady stream of visitors came annually from abroad to marvel at this latest wonder of the West. She was not yet a metropolis; with her 50,000 inhabitants, she was the sixteenth city of the country. Even nearby Allegheny was half as big as her sister, and perhaps a score of river towns might reasonably be expected, in the foreseeable future, to rival and even to surpass the city at the headwaters of the Ohio. But Pittsburgh still commanded the magnificent river highway to the West; she was still the entrepôt through which commerce between the Ohio Valley and the ports on Chesapeake Bay logically had to pass, whether by rail or by water. And geography made Pittsburgh a railroad center as inevitably as it had made her an inland port. The Pennsylvania reached her in 1852; by 1880 she was served by no less than fourteen separate lines.

As a center of commerce Pittsburgh had already felt the irresistible impulse to become a center of civilization as well. The Monongahela House, the town's leading hotel, was constructed in the early forties. This magnificent edifice was destroyed by fire in 1845 and completely rebuilt —a monument to the persistence with which the inhabitants of Pittsburgh hankered after the refinements of civilized society. There were seventeen other hotels, some of which paled only in comparison with the largest of them. Among the city's fourteen banks, the Bank of Pittsburgh,

with capital assets of more than $1,000,000, occupied the same position as the Monongahela House among hotels. And John Roebling's Sixth Street suspension bridge, which replaced an old covered bridge that in times gone by had served as a place of promenade for belles and beaux, was generally regarded as the finest in the world, utilizing recent techniques in bridgebuilding; it made Roebling's own bridge at Smithfield Street on the Monongahela, built fifteen years earlier, seem quaint and archaic, a survival of some primitive epoch. The city was making improvements in feverish haste; "every day," said Washington Roebling, the architect's son and assistant, "somebody commences to tear down an old house and put up a new one with an iron front." Pittsburgh had succumbed to progress.

Nor, in all this fever of building, were the spiritual needs neglected. There were more churches than banks, and some of them rivalled the banks for architectural splendor; St. Paul's, at Fifth and Grant, was said to be second in size only to St. Patrick's Cathedral in New York. Pittsburgh had twenty-six rolling mills and twenty-three glassworks, yet its skyline was dominated, not by the grim smokestacks of a later day, but by the 163-foot steeple of the Third Presbyterian Church at Third and Ferry streets.

Steamboats came and went incessantly, and the waterfront presented a scene of bustling activity. Life in Pittsburgh, one editor wrote in 1860, "is of a social, genial cast, the stiffness and formality of larger cities not being felt in our more hospitable community. Our people resemble, in

(turn to page 131)

129

Painted specially for this book by Dorothy Jane Adams.

LINCOLN IN PITTSBURGH. In the evening of February 14, 1861, Abraham Lincoln came to Pittsburgh.

Next morning, in a drizzling rain, the President-elect spoke from the balcony of the Monongahela House, addressing a crowd under a sea of umbrellas. Concerning the actions of the South Lincoln said: "There is no crisis, excepting such a one as may be gotten up at any time by designing politicians."

After his speech Lincoln left for Washington. Before him were years of trial, years of war, years of tragedy and agony. Never again was he to return to Pittsburgh.

Courtesy Carnegie Library.

BOMBARDMENT OF FORT SUMTER. At 4:30 in the morning on April 12, 1861, the Confederate shore batteries at Charleston Harbor opened fire against Fort Sumter. Thus the war between the States began. The shelling continued for a day and a half; then the exhausted defenders surrendered. On Sunday, April 14, the Confederate flag flew over Fort Sumter.

some respects, more those of a borough than a city. . . ." The town which had already undergone so many transformations was destined to be made over yet again. That final change, a speedy change of great magnitude, was the work of two profound upheavals: the Industrial Revolution and the Civil War.

At ten o'clock on the evening of Friday, April 11, 1861, the Western Union instruments at Wood and Third streets laboriously spelled out a fateful message: that morning, the Confederates had opened fire on Fort Sumter in Charleston Harbor. "The War Has Commenced," the *Gazette* announced next morning. Flags appeared everywhere—on public buildings, stores, offices, private homes. A great mass meeting was held in City Hall, adopting solemn declarations of loyalty in support of the war. A Committee of Public Safety under eighty-two-year-old Judge William Wilkins, came into being; many prominent Pittsburghers served under him. Thomas M. Howe, the copper and iron tycoon; James P. Barr, editor of the Pittsburgh *Post*; William F. Johnston, George H. Thurston, and John

(turn to page 133)

"THE FIGHT HAS COMMENCED," wired the correspondent of the Associated Press from Charleston. "This is all I can say at present." Pittsburgh prepared for the war, enlisting its resources.

131

PITTSBURGH FACTORIES SUPPLIED ARMS FOR THE UNION.

From Harper's Weekly, March 30, 1861.

THE BIGGEST GUN in the world—the 15-inch Columbiad—was cast in Pittsburgh by Knapp, Rudd Company, later the Fort Pitt Foundry, under the direction of Captain Thomas Jackson Rodman (1815-71) of the U.S. Army Ordnance Corps.

Rodman, who for a while was the head of the Allegheny Arsenal, conceived improved methods for making guns; he cast a gun with the core hollow so that it could be cooled with water or with cold air. His experiments proved so successful that the War Department authorized the making of a 15-inch smooth bore gun.

The total length of the gun was 190 inches; it was loaded with 35 pounds of large grained powder, which projected shells of 305 and 335 pounds in weight. The gun's range at maximum elevation was four miles.

GUNS PRODUCED IN PITTSBURGH

Contemporary daguerreotype, probably by D. M Coates of Pittsburgh.

AT FORT PITT FOUNDRY enormous guns were cast for the Union.

The contemporary daguerreotype shows the casting of a 20-inch Floyd gun, named after the former Secretary of War; the same daguerreotype was used for an engraving which *Frank Leslie's Illustrated Newspaper* printed on February 25, 1860.

132

From the collection of Stefan Lorant.

FOR THE USE OF UNION TROOPS WERE DISPATCHED TO THE BATTLEFIELDS AS FAST AS THEY LEFT THE FOUNDRIES.

E. Parke, were all members of the Committee. The war was not only popular, it was respectable.

Even before the war the city was staunchly Republican. Abraham Lincoln had polled a record-breaking majority of 10,000 in Allegheny County, and Republicans jokingly referred to the county as "the State of Allegheny."

In December 1860, a large assemblage gathered to protest the shipment of a hundred big guns to military posts in the Southern states—an occasion commemorated by a plaque, still to be seen, on the Allegheny County Court House. And when President-elect Lincoln stopped over-

night in Pittsburgh on his way to Washington, he was accorded the greatest demonstration of enthusiasm that any of the old citizens could recall.

The popularity of the Union cause was attested convincingly enough by the enlistment figures. Allegheny County contributed 24,000 men, mostly volunteers, to the Union forces. Men departed for the front almost daily. A Pittsburgh woman remembered from her childhood seeing them bumping along Penn Avenue in mule-drawn cars, clad in "baggy trousers" and accompanied by their hoop-skirted ladies; she remembered also the tearful farewells

(turn to page 137)

133

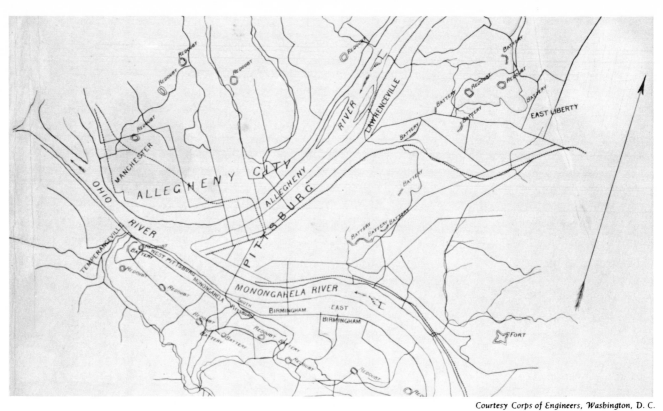

THE DEFENSES OF PITTSBURGH IN JULY 1863—A CONTEMPORARY SKETCH BY THE CORPS OF ENGINEERS.

THE LATEST PARIS FASHIONS, AS PICTURED IN THE *ILLUSTRATED LONDON NEWS*, NOVEMBER 1861.

From The Inside History of the Carnegie Steel Company by James Howard Bridge.

THE NAME OF CARNEGIE (1835-1919) is forever linked with that of Pittsburgh. In this 1862 photograph, the twenty-seven-year-old Andrew Carnegie (on the left) poses with George E. Lauder and Thomas N. Miller. Lauder was his uncle; it was he who imbued the young man with the love of poetry. Miller, the purchasing agent of the Ohio and Pennsylvania Railroad and a partner in the Pittsburgh iron forge of the Kloman brothers, was a key figure in the foundation of Carnegie's fortune.

Carnegie's career is like a Horatio Alger story. He came with his family from Scotland to Pittsburgh in 1848, when he was a boy of thirteen. At first he worked in a cotton factory as a bobbin boy at $1.20 per week. A year later he was a messenger in the telegraph office, for double his previous salary. On November 2, 1849, the *Gazette* printed a story—the first time Carnegie's name appeared in a newspaper —that a young messenger boy "had found in the street a draft for five hundred dollars and, like an honest little fellow, promptly made known the fact and deposited the paper in good hands, where it awaits identification."

In the telegraph office Carnegie met with Thomas A. Scott, the superintendent of the western division of the Pennsylvania Railroad, who was impressed and made him his private secretary with a monthly salary of $35. "I couldn't imagine what I could ever do with so much money", exclaimed the young man.

He read assiduously, borrowing books from Colonel James Anderson's personal library, an experience which he never forgot. (Today a statue of James Anderson stands outside the North Carnegie Library.)

From 1853 up to the end of the Civil War he was employed by the Pennsylvania Railroad. After he left this job he devoted his energies to the iron enterprises which he had acquired through his friendship with Miller. Bridge building, locomotive building, iron rails and steel were further steps in his career, as he accumulated one of the largest fortunes in America.

Courtesy Mrs. Agnes L. Starrett, University of Pittsburgh.

WAITING FOR THE WAR NEWS. During the Civil War people of the city met at the *Pittsburgh Dispatch* to learn the latest bulletins from the battlefields.

This photograph was taken on June 9, 1862, a week after the bloody fight at Fair Oaks in which 6000 Union men lost their lives. It was in this battle that General Joseph E. Johnston, the Confederate commander, was wounded and relinquished command to General Robert E. Lee.

Three weeks later Lee started his attack on the Union Forces. The Battle of the Seven Days ended with a victory for the Confederates; General George B. McClellan's attempt to conquer Richmond had failed; the Peninsular Campaign was over. Ahead lay the battles of Antietam in September and Fredericksburg in December. Not until Gettysburg and Vicksburg in the next year did the tide turn for the Union.

THE CIVIL WAR TOOK THE LIVES OF MANY PITTSBURGH CITIZENS FIGHTING FOR THE UNION.

at the railroad depot, where the soldiers waited in cattle cars to be hauled off to battle.

But the city's contribution to the war could not be measured in manpower alone. The war was a conflict of economies as well as of armies, and in such a conflict Pittsburgh was suited by nature to play a central role. Charles Knap's Fort Pitt Cannon Foundry, located at 28th Street in Allegheny, became to the Union what the Tredegar Iron-Works were to the Confederacy. It furnished to the army almost 3000 cannon, ranging from the twenty-inch columbiad to the six-pounder field piece, and 10,000,000 pounds of shot and shell. Emerson, lecturing in Pittsburgh in 1863, watched the casting of a fifteen-inch cannon and marveled at the "sublime in mechanics."

Production of iron and steel mounted steadily. The market for it seemed boundless and was protected from foreign competition by the raids of Confederate cruisers on Northern commerce. As the price of steel, and that of the ironclad ships and locomotives which were made from it, rose, the commerce of Pittsburgh thrived.

Among businessmen there were individual inconveniences, and some real hardship, particularly after the outbreak of the war when the trade with the South was interrupted, and when Pittsburgh merchants were not able to collect debts owed them by their Southern customers. Some merchants kept on sending goods along the old routes of trade, as if nothing had happened, but the results of these early experiments were discouraging.

From the collection of Stefan Lorant.

PITTSBURGH GUNS MANNED THE *MONITOR*, THE UNION'S FIRST IRONCLAD VESSEL.

"The experience of B. Corey & Company, a firm in which Judge Mellon, father of Andrew Mellon, was the leading stockholder, was instructive. Early in the war the company dispatched a fleet of barges to New Orleans, loaded with coal. Soon after the ships passed Vicksburg, the Confederates occupied the city and cut off communication with the lower Mississippi. Nothing was heard of the fleet for more than a year; it was assumed that the rebels had confiscated the coal and taken the crew prisoners. After the fall of New Orleans in the spring of 1862, however, B. Corey & Company received word that the barges were safely anchored in the river above the city. The company's agents had resourcefully protected the cargo from confiscation by manifesting a warm sympathy for the Confederate cause; they took pains to appear at parades, and even made contributions to the war chest. Such conduct did not, of course, suggest disloyalty to those raised in the spirit of American enterprise—and what Pittsburgher was not? The

men were heartily welcomed upon their return. The coal, however, did not fare so well. Having escaped the Confederates, it fell into the hands of General Ben Butler, "the beast of New Orleans," who bought it and then balked at paying the full price. In the end Judge Mellon and his associates collected the money only through court action.

The torrent of Pittsburgh's wartime prosperity was fed by the streams of soldiers who regularly passed through the city. Troops from all over western Pennsylvania assembled at Camp Wilkins on the County Fair Ground and at other training camps around Pittsburgh. War-weary veterans and green recruits alike availed themselves prodigiously of the city's facilities for amusement; on one occasion the city fathers had to call out an extra police force and order all taverns closed for two days to prevent drunken brawls among the 3000 troops stranded in the city.

The needs of the army fostered in Pittsburghers both a

(turn to page 140)

THE FT. PITT WORKS FROM THE RIVER—PITTSBURGH, PA.

FINISHING TRUNIONS.

ON ITS WAY TO BE BORED.

CASTING BIG GUN.

THE FIRST MONITOR GUN.

SECTION
PIT, FLASK, MOLD,
CORE-BARREL,
& GITER-PIPE.

SCALE OF FEET

From Harper's Weekly, August 23, 1862.

MAKING GUNS FOR THE NEW MONITORS. In the summer of 1862 Harper's Weekly sent Theodore R. Davies, one of its best artists, to Pittsburgh to report on the activities of the Fort Pitt Foundry. This was the result.

THE SUBSISTENCE COMMITTEE of Pittsburgh, to which many of the leading citizens belonged, served over 400,000 meals in the City Hall to soldiers who passed through Pittsburgh. It also provided hospital care for a time, but early in 1863 this responsibility was assumed by the United States Christian Commission.

lofty patriotism and a zeal for profits. Of the former impulse there were many gratifying examples. At the outset, before the organization of regular relief activities, B. F. Jones of Jones & Laughlin took the lead in furnishing crackers, apples, and cheese to the soldiers, gratis. In August 1861 the Pittsburgh Subsistence Committee, assisted by women volunteers, took over the job of supplying food and other comforts to soldiers passing through the city. Meanwhile the families of local volunteers were assisted by the relief committee of the Committee of Public Safety, headed by the prominent glass manufacturer Thomas Bakewell. The United States Sanitary Commission had a Pittsburgh branch, in which the philanthropist Felix R. Brunot distinguished himself; on a mission to the battlefield in 1862 he was captured and confined for several months in a Confederate prison. One of his special projects was the Pittsburgh Sanitary Fair, held on the Allegheny Commons in June 1864, which raised a higher per capita sum for war work than any other fair in the country.

Less generous instincts were also in abundant evidence. Workers, feeling the pinch of high prices, demanded higher wages; employers in some instances failed to see the merit of their claims; strikes, many of them violent, were the inevitable result. The struggle between the miners

THE SANITARY FAIR in June 1864 raised over $300,000 for medical supplies. Its organizer was Felix R. Brunot, a civil engineer who during the war was the mainspring of Pittsburgh's relief activities. He often led parties of doctors and nurses far into the battle lines, and in 1862 was captured with a field hospital and confined to Libby Prison in Richmond, Virginia.

and the operators in the coal fields was particularly bitter. The war bred intolerance as well as liberality, and proscription and patriotism often went hand in hand; the president of the Pittsburgh Female College was scurrilously attacked by the press for his crime of having voted for the Democratic candidate for governor.

Rumors circulated wildly, and sent people into a panic. In May 1862 word arrived that "the Rebels had blown up the *Merrimac*, Norfolk was taken, and the War was nearly over." In June 1863 news of Lee's invasion of Pennsylvania gave rise to a pervasive fear that Pittsburgh was the object of his march. "Report says Rebels coming on us with 18,000 cavalry under that Villain Stuart—the Rebel Thief—Lord Thou Art Our Shield," noted the industrialist William B. Scaife in his diary. Mills and factories closed; and thousands of men took up pick and shovel to construct emergency defenses. By the time it became evident that the defenses were not needed, twelve miles of entrenchments and twenty bristling forts crowned Bloomfield and Stanton Heights, Mount Washington, and Herron Hill. A few weeks later the approach of Morgan's raiders from the direction of Ohio led a number of families to bury their silver. And when workmen began digging trenches and earthworks near Judge Mellon's house, the

(turn to page 144)

PITTSBURGH HOMES

Courtesy Carnegie Library.

HOMEWOOD — the residence of Judge William Wilkins (1779-1865), was built in 1835, razed in 1924.

Judge William Wilkins was the son of John Wilkins, who moved to Pittsburgh in 1786. William attended Dickinson College in Carlisle, Pennsylvania, read law with Judge Watt, and was admitted to the bar in 1801.

He was the first president of the Pittsburgh Manufacturing Company, which began a banking and insurance business in 1812 and in 1814 became the Bank of Pittsburgh. When in 1816 the city was incorporated, Wilkins became the first president of the Common Council. In 1820 he was appointed president judge of the Fifth Judicial District of Pennsylvania; in 1824 he became judge of the United States District Court for Western Pennsylvania.

In 1831 Judge Wilkins was elected to the United States Senate, where he served until 1834 when he was named Minister to Russia by President Jackson. As Pennsylvania's favorite son for the Vice-Presidency in 1832 he received the state's vote in the Democratic convention.

In 1842 he was elected as a Democrat to the U.S. House of Representatives; two years later President Tyler made him his Secretary of War.

In 1855 he became a state senator; in 1862 a major general of the Pennsylvania Home Guards. He died at Homewood in 1865, at the age of 85.

WILLIAM G. JOHNSTON'S HOME William G. Johnston (1828-1913), the printer and bookseller, was one of the city's prominent citizens. His great-grandfather was Samuel Johnston, a surgeon in the Revolutionary Army. His grandfather, John, was the fourth postmaster of Pittsburgh and a trustee of the city's First Presbyterian Church. His father, Samuel, was a partner in one of Pittsburgh's earliest printing firms, a successor of the bookstore founded by John C. Gilkinson in 1798 which during the next decades changed its name a number of times. Under Zadok

Courtesy of Carnegie Library.

STORE OF WILLIAM L. DENISON ON FRANKSTOWN AND PENN AVENUE.

ON FIFTH AVENUE EAST OF HIGHLAND, ONE OF THE SHOW PLACES OF THE POST CIVIL WAR PERIOD

Cramer's ownership it was known as the Sign of the Franklin Head; in 1810 it became Cramer, Spear and Eichbaum, in 1818 Eichbaum and Johnston, and in 1824 Johnston and Stockton.

When William G. Johnston became 21 in 1849 the country was agog with the California Gold Rush. Young Johnston organized a party of Pittsburghers and off they went for the Sacramento River. What fun they had he recounted in a book—one of the best narratives to be written of those enthusiastic days.

In 1857 Johnston founded the printing and bookbinding firm of William G. Johnston Company. He also held offices in a number of other companies. He was president of the Duquesne National Bank, the Pittsburgh Steel Casting Company, the Citizen's Insurance Company, the Hainsworth Steel Company, the Atlantic and Pacific Telegraph Company, the Mercantile Telegraph Company, and the Woodruff Sleeping Car Company.

He was married three times. His first wife was Sarah Stewart from one of Pittsburgh's old families; she was the hostess of the Fifth Avenue mansion. After the death of his first wife, in 1889 Johnston married Charlotte Winslow, a Watertown, New York, girl, and when she died, Julia Ely, also of Watertown, became the third Mrs. Johnston.

Though in his declining years Johnston moved to Watertown, New York, his name, as the head of Pittsburgh's oldest printing establishment, lives on in his native city. The firm William G. Johnston Company is still in business to this day.

143

NOTABLE EVENTS

THE CONVENTION of the Soldiers and Sailors was held in the City Hall of Pittsburgh in September 26, 1866. The Convention passed a resolution upholding the 15th Amendment and denouncing President Johnson's Reconstruction policies. The assembled delegates declared "that the action of the present Congress in passing the pending Constitutional Amendment is wise, prudent, and just. . . . It righteously excludes from places of honor and trust the chief conspirators, guiltiest revels, whose purjured crimes have drenched the land in fraternal blood. . . ." Waving the bloody shirt was popular in the North for years.

From Harper's Weekly, October 12, 1866.

THE SCULL RACE between James Hamill of Pittsburgh and Walter Brown of Portland brought 15,000 Pittsburghers to the river bank to watch the event in the rain on May 21, 1867. The five-mile race with a purse of $1000 was to decide the championship of the United States. Brown won in 47 minutes, although Hamill charged that he was fouled.

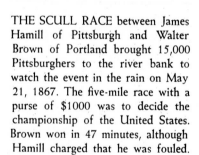

From Harper's Weekly, June 8, 1867.

family housekeeper gave an unloaded shotgun to the Judge's eight-year-old son, Andrew, and posted him at the orchard fence, not to fend off the Confederate raiders, but to protect the Mellon cherry trees against forays by the laborers.

Through all these vicissitudes business went on, not as usual, but in a perfect frenzy. The stalls of hucksters encroached on the traffic areas along Market Street and had to be driven back by city ordinance. Prices rose steadily. Money had never been so abundant; at the same time it had never been so scarce, because so greatly in demand. Greenbacks and national bank notes brought no more than temporary relief, and the difficulty of obtaining small change caused some firms to circulate fractional paper

currency called "shin plasters." Neither the scarcity of money nor the uncertainty of wartime conditions, however, retarded the amazing growth of business. If the war added to the risks, the risks in turn added to the profits.

The end of the hostilities, notwithstanding the material advantages which it had incidentally brought to the city, was celebrated in tumultuous fashion. Cannon boomed; mill sirens shrieked; fire engines clattered down the streets. Crowds on Fifth Avenue sang war songs and revival hymns as they dodged fireworks and falling rockets. The festivities came to an abrupt halt when news of Lincoln's assassination reached Pittsburgh. Overnight the city went into mourning. Newspapers appeared in black-bordered editions. The mills shut down and memorial

AFTER THE WAR

THE PRESBYTERIANS UNITE. Since 1837 the Presbyterian churches had been divided into two groups— the Old School and the New School Assemblies. After more than three decades the two sections were at last ready to heal the schism.

The deliberations were held in separate buildings, the Old School advocates meeting in the First, the New School in the Third Presbyterian Church. The meetings voted for union. Thus the Old School, with its 142 presbyteries, 2737 churches, 2330 ministers, and 252,555 communicants joined the New School, with its 113 presbyteries, 1500 churches, 1800 ministers, and 184,687 communicants.

From Harper's Weekly, December 4, 1869.

From Harper's Weekly, December 4, 1869.

CONSUMMATION OF UNION of the two religious groups in the Third Presbyterian Church on November 12, 1869. The two assemblies formed a procession, the two moderators leading, arm in arm, and each Old School delegate walking in like manner with a delegate of the New School. The procession, numbering about a thousand, moved down Wood Street, Fifth Avenue, Smithfield Street, and Sixth Avenue to the Third Church.

Harper's Weekly considered the ceremony the "greatest and most sublime spectacle ever witnessed in the ecclesiastical history of America."

services were conducted in every church of the city. Then in a somewhat more sober mood, Pittsburgh went back to work.

The war, with its tremendous demands on Pittsburgh's productive capacity, was the first of the two great upheavals which helped to transform the city from a river town into an industrial colossus. The other was the industrial revolution itself. By 1880, Pittsburgh produced one twelfth of the pig iron and one fourth of the rolled iron in the country, and her sixteen enormous steelworks manufactured two thirds of all the crucible steel.

With the advent of industrialism, the manufacture of iron and steel assumed great importance. Fundamental changes in the technique of producing it led to the central-ization of the industry at Pittsburgh. Before 1840 most American iron was smelted from charcoal rather than from coke. Since both timber and iron deposits were widely scattered throughout the country, the geography of the iron industry was determined, not by the location of raw materials, but by such considerations as access to markets and availability of a labor supply. After 1840 new techniques for smelting iron were introduced, techniques which utilized coke rather than charcoal. Bituminous coal —anthracite was not used in this process until a later day —was localized in a few great deposits, with the greatest deposits around Pittsburgh. With the manufacture of iron gravitating to the coal-producing regions, Pittsburgh rose rapidly to a commanding position.

A PANORAMIC VIEW OF THE CITIES OF PITTSBURGH, ALLEGHENY, AND BIRMINGHAM. THIS SUPERB

Another innovation, the Bessemer process for manufacturing steel, strengthened the city's hold on the iron and steel industry, for the Bessemer process required types of iron ore which were found most abundantly in the West, especially in the region around Lake Superior. Pittsburgh had not only easy access to this supply, but her command of coal resources gave her the advantage over cities still further west, like St. Louis, which at this time might have emerged as her rivals. Ultimately it was the coal fields of western Pennsylvania which determined the outcome of the struggle for steel.

In 1865, Pittsburgh blast furnaces produced about two fifths of the country's iron. At that time the value of their output was five times greater than that of Pittsburgh steel.

Courtesy Carnegie Library

THE NEGLEY HOMESTEAD AT NEGLEY AND STANTON.

From Sipes The Pennsylvania Railroad (1875).

IDYLLIC PROSPECT PARK IN ALLEGHENY CITY.

146

LITHOGRAPH WAS MADE BY OTTO KREBS IN THE YEAR OF 1871. IT SOLD BY THE THOUSANDS.

In 1870 the American Iron Works of the Messrs. Jones and Laughlin covered twenty acres on the banks of the Monongahela, with a coal mine at its back door, an iron mine on Lake Superior, and a payroll of 2500 employees. But twenty years later Jones and Laughlin had converted to Bessemer steel.

Andrew Carnegie, fresh from triumphs in the railroad, sleeping car, oil, and iron business, first saw the Bessemer process demonstrated in England. Hurrying home, he told his partners: "The day of iron is past! Steel is king!" Organizing a new partnership, Carnegie built a Bessemer plant at Braddock and named the mills after his largest prospective customer, the president of the Pennsylvania Railroad, J. Edgar Thomson. In four years Carnegie

THE EXHIBITION BUILDINGS FACING THE RIVER.

THE NORTH COMMONS OF ALLEGHENY IN 1868.

147

Brothers & Company produced 10,000 tons of steel a month and cleared $1,625,000 a year. "When was there ever such a business?" asked Carnegie. To his managers' report that they had produced more steel than in the previous week, Carnegie replied, "Congratulations! Why not do it every week?" And when they telegraphed, "Lucy Furnace No. 8 broke all records today," he shot back, "What were the other ten furnaces doing?" In 1881, Carnegie and his partners incorporated themselves at a capital of $5,000,000.

In 1883 they acquired the immense Homestead plant; within two years the purchase price was written off from the profits.

The rise of iron and steel gave a tremendous impetus to the coal industry. In coal, Captain W. Seward B. Hays occupied for a time the position held by Carnegie in steel. Powerfully built, with sharp eye and rugged jaw, Hays commanded an imperial domain and was known in Pittsburgh by an appropriately regal designation; he was the "Coal King." A self-made man, he had started out in life as the proprietor of a flatboat built by himself. During the Civil War he not only sold coal to the Union armies but delivered it by barge to the front, a perilous undertaking in Southern waters.

The glass industry took root in Pittsburgh long before the Civil War; during the war, like everything else, it underwent a spectacular expansion. By 1870 the sixty-eight glass factories in Pittsburgh produced half of the nation's total. And if Pittsburgh glass makers had not yet devised a champagne bottle as strong and as pleasing as those imported from France, they produced more of them.

While some of the industries had a foothold in Pitts-

(turn to page 150)

From Frank Leslie's Illustrated Newspaper, October 12, 1872.

THE PRESIDENTIAL CAMPAIGN OF 1872. Horace Greeley, the flamboyant editor of the New York *Tribune* was the presidential candidate of the Democrats and the Liberal Republicans opposing Ulysses S. Grant's re-election. He campaigned vigorously; attacking the President and his corrupt administration.

In Pittsburgh, Greeley addressed a large meeting from the balcony of the St. Charles Hotel. But it was to no avail. Grant won the election. Greeley died before the electoral votes were cast.

THE WATERFRONT OF PITTSBURGH—the landing place of the boats along the Monongahela River as it was sketched by the

From Every Saturday, March 25, 1871.

eminent artist and illustrator J. P. Davis.

The wharf remained a beehive of activity even after the coming of the railroads. It was a fascinating place to watch, with many boats bringing in and dispatching passengers and freight.

A VIEW OF THE BUSY TRIANGLE IN THE EARLY SEVENTIES, AS IT WAS SEEN FROM THE TOP OF COAL HILL

burgh before the war, others were of more recent origin. The city was the first great center of oil refining, leading all other places in 1867. Natural gas was another; the firms of Graff, Bennett & Company and Spang, Chalfant & Company were among the first to apply natural gas to manufacturing. And in two other fields, food processing and railroad cars, Pittsburgh made distinctive contributions to the development of modern America.

One of the most dramatic of these success stories, in an age when success seemed to be the rule rather than the

exception, began in 1869, when Henry John Heinz, son of a brickmaker, began to cultivate horse-radish on a tiny plot in Sharpsburg. With the backing of his family he began to sell his produce on a modest scale. Saving every penny he made, he soon built up a considerable business; and in time he was able to offer a complete line of processed foods. In 1875, however, his customary prudence temporarily deserted him, and in an extravagant mood he offered to buy up the entire output of a 600-acre vegetable farm in Illinois. A bountiful growing season proved

(turn to page 152)

From William B. Sipes, **The Pennsylvania Railroad** (1875).

THE UNION DEPOT BUILDING, erected in 1857, was one of the landmarks of Pittsburgh. It stood for only 20 years; then the mob burned it to the ground during the Railroad Riots of 1877.

From William B. Sipes, **The Pennsylvania Railroad** (1875).
BY THE ARTIST FRED B. SCHELL.

FIFTH AVENUE AT SIXTH STREET was one of the most fashionable thoroughfares of the city. Ladies came here to shop for the latest clothing and furnishings; elegant equipages brought the heads of the flourishing enterprises to their offices.

From William B. Sipes, **The Pennsylvania Railroad** (1875).

From History of Allegheny County (1876).

PITTSBURGH RESIDENCES after the Civil War were sumptuous affairs. This gingerbread palace at Penn Avenue was the home of D. O'Neill, publisher of the *Daily Dispatch*, the first penny newspaper west of the Alleghenies. O'Neill took control of the ailing *Dispatch* in 1865 and made a success of it. Circulation was 14,000, allowing its owner to live in style.

his undoing, and after stretching his credit to the limit to pay for the quantities of cucumbers and cabbages that poured relentlessly in upon him, he was forced into bankruptcy. Two months later he started again; and soon his food products became a household word all over the world.

The year after Heinz first went into business the Westinghouse Air Brake Company began operations in a factory occupying two city lots at the corner of Liberty Avenue and Twenty-fifth Street. George Westinghouse came to Pittsburgh from Schenectady, where he had already perfected the air brake. He hit upon the original idea for his invention after reading of Italian experiments in drilling with compressed air. Applying the same principle to railroad cars, he devised a brake which was successfully tested in April 1868 on the Pennsylvania Railroad near Pittsburgh. It was so effective that visiting officials were sent flying from their seats when engineer Dan Tate applied the new brake to avoid hitting a drayman. From then on, the "Armstrong brake," as the old hand brake was jocularly known among railroad men, became a thing of the past, and another new industry had sprung up in Pittsburgh.

Progress, indeed, was the order of the day. In 1870 the first power elevator was installed in the dry goods firm of Arbuthnot & Shannon. Merchants, who formerly delivered parcels to their customers in wheelbarrows, began to use handsome horse-drawn wagons instead. And in 1877 the telephone came into use among the city's businessmen. Telephones, however, were not available for private use until some years later, and even then the service was subject to constant criticism as "a fraud and a humbug." Complaining to the telephone company became so popular a diversion that critics had to rise early in the

OPULENCE, comfort, spaciousness were the attributes of the homes of wealthy Pittsburghers in the seventies. John Moorhead, one of the city's first art connoisseurs (who actually bought paintings for pleasure), resided in this house in Oakland which formerly belonged to William Eichbaum. According to legend Oakland was named after the German Eichbaum.

morning and stand in line for hours outside the office of T. B. A. David, president of the company. During the 1890s the chief of the Pennsylvania Railroad freight department became so infuriated with the treatment he had received from one of the telephone operators that he stormed into the general manager's office and demanded immediate satisfaction. The manager promised to discharge the guilty party, and the operator was sent for. She proved to be unexpectedly young and pretty. The railroad man eyed her uneasily, hesitated, flushed, and then blurted out: "Mr. Metzger, this is all a mistake, and I want to apologize to you and especially to this young lady." So saying, he retreated from the office. In a few minutes, however, he reappeared, once again in anger. "Metzger," he bellowed, "I don't believe that was my operator. I think you just keep that girl to receive the many complaints you get. You're a swindler and a cheat. You and your telephone can go to blazes!"

Progress was not achieved without a price. If communication became easier, owing to the introduction of the telephone, it also became more uncertain; the more one came to depend on a machine, the greater the inconvenience when the machine broke down. On a much larger scale, the industrialized economy was itself such a machine, on which millions of men had unwittingly become dependent; and this vast and intricate mechanism, like the telephone, was subject to periodic breakdowns in which businessmen lost their businesses and workers their jobs. These crises showed that the other side of progress, as Henry George was later to point out, was poverty; they cruelly revealed the extent of man's dependence on the very machinery he had built in order to render himself independent of his environment. In such emergencies man had little choice except to find safety in numbers: capital-

(turn to page 155)

THE BANKS

IN THE 1870s

In 1876, the centennial year of America's Independence, Pittsburgh and Allegheny had 87 banking institutions. Seventy-one of them were located in Pittsburgh. Of this number, 27 were national banks, six were private banks, while the others were organized under the state laws.

The Pittsburgh Clearing-House Association included 16 national banks, the Bank of Pittsburgh, and the private banking house of N. Holmes & Sons. Their total capital was over $10,000,000.

In the main, these banks supplied the need of Pittsburgh and Allegheny manufacturing interests, which had an estimated requirement of $100,000,000 in capital.

THE FIRST NATIONAL BANK was incorporated in 1863. Ten years later the annual deposits amounted to roughly two millions. Today, the Pittsburgh National Bank, the descendant of the First National, is the second largest bank in the city.

From History of Allegheny County (1876).

FRANKLIN SAVINGS BANK, located in Allegheny City, was one of the solid establishments serving that community.

DOLLAR SAVINGS BANK on Fourth Avenue was incorporated in 1855, as The Pittsburgh Dollar Savings Institution.

GERMANIA SAVINGS BANK at Wood Street and Diamond Alley was incorporated in 1870 with $150,000 capital.

EXCHANGE NATIONAL BANK at Fifth Street near Wood was chartered with a capital of $1,000,000, in the year of 1836.

From History of Allegheny County (1876).

MERCHANTS AND MANUFACTURERS NATIONAL BANK on Fourth Avenue was incorporated in 1833 with a capital of $600,000. In 1864 it became a national bank with its capital raised to $800,000. First located on Second Street, it occupied the above structure in April 1870. In 1876 the bank's deposits were a fraction less than $1,000,000.

ists in pools, traffic agreements, and monopolies; laborers in unions. To those who were neither capitalists nor laborers and who cherished a tradition of individualism, both forms of combination appeared to undermine the very basis of society; but of the two, organizations of labor usually occasioned greater alarm.

Labor unionism in Pittsburgh dated back at least to the 1830s. Pittsburgh had eight trade unions in 1835 and twenty-three by 1850. However, many of these unions became defunct during the period of hard times produced by the money panic of 1857. Those that survived the panic for the most part remained inactive. It was under these unpromising circumstances that in 1858 the iron puddlers organized as the Sons of Vulcan. In 1862 they formed a national union headed by one Miles Humphrey, subsequently fire chief of Pittsburgh. In 1865 they won a bitterly contested eight-month strike against attempted wage reductions, a victory which led to the establishment of a wage scale based on the selling price of bar iron, the first such arrangement in the iron industry.

These were balmy days for labor. Although hours were long, wages—at least of skilled workers—were relatively high. One observer, comparing Pittsburgh with English cities, saw no evidence there of "the infernal feeling that appears to exist in Sheffield and Birmingham between employers and employed"; another described the workmen in Pittsburgh as quite as independent and almost as prosperous as their employers.

Not until the hard times following the Panic of 1873 did industrial conflict become acute. During the dark and dreary winter of 1874-75 the ironworkers went out on strike. Although the strike was vigorously opposed by the employers, who had the support of the public, the workers won their demands. Their success not only led to the founding, in 1876, of the Amalgamated Association of Iron, Steel, and Tin Workers, but encouraged laborers in

THE INEXHAUSTIBLE OPPORTUNITIES LURED MASSES OF IMMIGRANTS TO PITTSBURGH TO SEEK WORK IN
THE MINES AND IN THE MILLS

other industries to imitate their example. These efforts led finally to the great railroad strike of 1877.

In June 1877 the Pennsylvania Railroad reduced all wages 10 per cent and ordered, moreover, that beginning July 19 all freight trains between Pittsburgh and Derry were to be run as "double-headers," meaning that two trains, with two engines, would be run by one crew. In justification of this unusual step Thomas Scott, president of the Pennsylvania, cited similar economy measures taken by other roads.

On the morning of July 19 the first two double-headers left the Pennsylvania yards without interference. The crew

of the 9:40 train, however, refused, on their own initiative, to take her out. The crews of incoming freight trains promptly joined the strikers. The railroad authorities, following a custom already sanctioned by usage, applied to Mayor Charles McCarthy for police "protection," but found him unco-operative. Probably he sympathized with the strikers, although it is possible that he simply had no policemen to spare, since the thrifty councilmen had in the previous year cut the police force in half and virtually abolished the day police.

At midnight, the sheriff of Allegheny County wired to Harrisburg for troops. With the governor out of the state,

(turn to page 158)

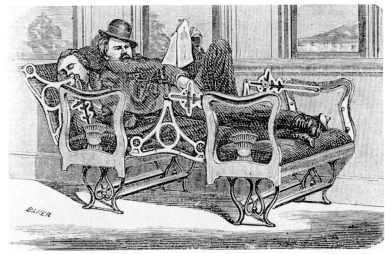

From Pacific Rural Press, *February 4, 1871.*

ON THE WAY to the new life, immigrants relax in the newly patented railroad seats. Long-distance travel had become a pleasant, comfortable experience.

Engraving by A. B. Houghton,
courtesy The Metropolitan Museum of Art.

THE BEST-KNOWN BARBER in the city was "Dr. General" Jackson, a colorful character who like to entertain his customers with tales of his imaginary exploits. Sure he was in Mexico, sure he fought in the Civil War. In parades the "General" usually rode a white charger, to the great amusement of the citizens.

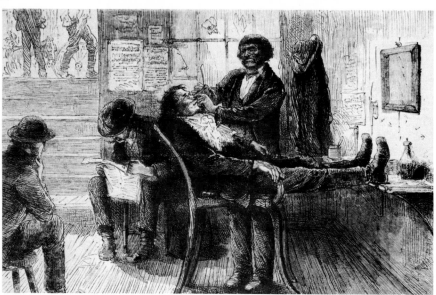

From Every Saturday, *March 25, 1871.*

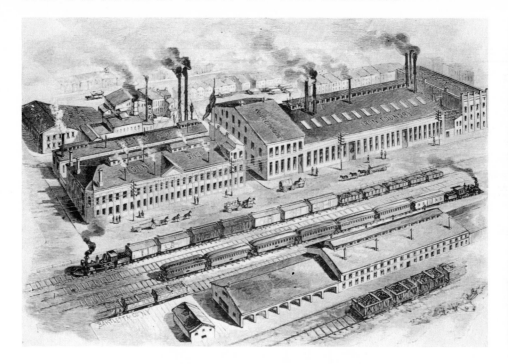

THE WESTINGHOUSE MACHINE COMPANY.

THE H. C. FRICK

THE WESTINGHOUSE AIR BRAKE COMPANY.

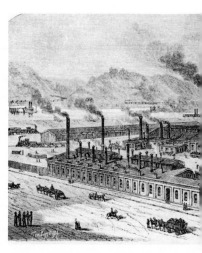

A VIEW OF THE PITTSBURGH

the adjutant-general ordered three Pittsburgh regiments of state militia to the scene. These troops, however, had no stomach for the work they were called upon to perform; most of them sided with the strikers. The authorities appealed for more loyal troops; 650 men, recruited, this time, in Philadelphia, were sent out by the obliging officials in Harrisburg. The new militiamen reached Pittsburgh at noon on Saturday, July 21.

By that time a large mob, in which the criminal element probably outnumbered the strikers, had assembled in the railroad yards. When the militia tried to clear the tracks at the Twenty-eighth Street crossing, firing broke out. About twenty people, mostly innocent bystanders, were killed, and a number of others wounded. At dusk the troops retired to a roundhouse for sustenance and sleep.

But the troubles had just begun. Breaking into nearby shops, the mob seized guns and ammunition and proceeded to give the beleaguered militiamen a wild night. They made repeated efforts to set fire to the roundhouse. At daybreak the garrison beat a retreat, subjected to a sniping fire by the rioters, who pursued them all the way across the Allegheny River. With the troops in full rout, looting and burning broke out all over the city and continued throughout the day. The mob destroyed 1600 railroad cars and 126 locomotives and burned sixteen buildings, including the Union Depot, the grain elevator, and several machine shops and roundhouses. At noon a group of citizens met at City Hall and sent a delegation headed by Bishop Tuigg to urge the rioters to desist. After another meeting late that afternoon the mayor recruited a

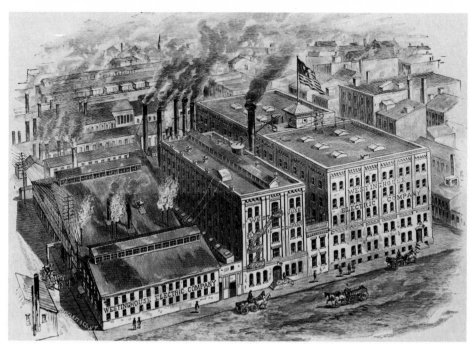

From a Spanish book Notas Interesantes Acerca de Pittsburg (1889)

COKE COMPANY.

WESTINGHOUSE ELECTRIC COMPANY.

LOCOMOTIVE AND CAR WORKS.

CRESCENT GLASSWORKS—THOMAS EVANS COMPANY.

force of 500 citizen-policemen.

Gradually the riot burned itself out. By Monday the city was quiet. The next day the governor arrived with federal and state troops, who remained in the city until railroad traffic was resumed on July 30. In the end Allegheny County reimbursed the Pennsylvania Railroad and various private claimants to the tune of $2,750,000. As for the strikers, they went back to work without having won any of the objectives for which they had been striking.

The violence of the strike set back the cause of unionism in Pittsburgh many years. Although it succeeded in unionizing every iron mill in Allegheny County during the 1880's, the Amalgamated Iron and Steel Workers remained the only union of any strength in the city.

Efforts to unionize the coal industry met with little but

failure. The Miners National Association, headed by George Archibald of Pittsburgh, went into eclipse during the depression, and the Knights of Labor, who tried during the winter of 1875-76 to organize the western Pennsylvania fields, fared no better. The miners at first showed some interest in the Knights, but when it became evident that the new organization had no magic formula for raising wages, they fell away from it as eagerly as they had joined. Pittsburgh remained, until the advent of the AFL, a haven of the open shop.

This arrangement, as might have been expected, was closely guarded by the city's business interests, and the preservation of it was one of the implicit objectives of the Pittsburgh Chamber of Commerce, organized in 1874 under the presidency of Thomas M. Howe for the purpose

From Every Saturday, March 18, 1871.

PITTSBURGH INDUSTRIES. In 1870 there were 33 rolling mills in Allegheny County which produced forged and rolled iron valued at $20,101,664, employed 7076 hands, and paid $4,502,463 in wages. At the same time $3,485,413 worth of cast steel was produced by six concerns in the county which employed 1009 hands and paid $753,841 in wages.

By the end of the decade the city of Pittsburgh alone was producing iron and steel valued at $35,490,634 in 39 establishments which paid wages of $8,072,110. Pittsburgh was firmly established as the nation's leading producer of iron and steel.

of "protecting, fostering and developing the commercial, manufacturing and business interests of Allegheny County by joint and concerted action." For the most part the city continued to be governed, often by the same men who sat on the Chamber of Commerce, in complete accord with these principles. As businessmen wanted to be left alone, there seemed no need to bring the machinery of the city government up to date, and thus Pittsburgh continued to function under a mayor and a bicameral city council— a system soon to be abandoned by other cities for more streamlined models. Still, few improvements were made in some departments. The police were given uniforms and a minimum wage of two dollars a day; a professional fire department was established in 1870. For the support of the fire department a tax of 3½ mills was at first levied on the receipts of all fire, marine, and life insurance companies doing business in the city, but this practice was shortly discontinued on request of the parties affected; thereafter fighting fires came to be looked upon as a public service rather than a special favor to the insurance companies, and the fire department was supported out of the city's general tax revenue.

Other problems were met in the same leisurely fashion. Between 1871 and 1878 the city constructed a new water works system, enabling water to be obtained from the Highland and Herron Hill reservoirs, but since the water supply was still unfiltered, the improvement was more apparent than real. Horsecar railways, introduced shortly before the Civil War, were the chief means of surface transportation; after 1870 a system of inclined railways, designed by the Prussian engineer John H. G. Endres and made possible by the development of the steel cable, pro-

Drawing by J. P. Davis from Every Saturday, *March 18, 1871.*

BLAST FURNACE in two views; on the left the top of the furnace, on the right the bottom.

The first furnace in Pittsburgh for the manufacture of iron was built by George Anshutz in 1793 at Shadyside, but when the venture proved unprofitable it was given up. Although Pittsburgh remained a center of the manufacture of iron, the second effort to reduce the ore locally was not made until 1859. Rapid development followed. By 1874 there were 11 blast furnaces in the city, producing 144,000 tons of metal. At the end of the seventies, 15 furnaces turned out 300,000 tons of iron.

vided transportation to Mount Washington and Mount Oliver. On the river below the Point, passengers still had to cross by means of ferries, and winter ice, summer sand bars, and slow-moving strings of coal barges made ferry travel both hazardous and tedious. As for public parks and playgrounds, the city refused to act at all, in spite of the example of Allegheny, which between 1868 and 1877 laid out a magnificent park on the Commons; there were no parks in Pittsburgh until after 1880.

In spite of so much inactivity the city's total expenditures continued to rise. Pittsburgh spent between five and six times as much money in 1880 as it had in 1865. Some of these mounting expenditures reflected a growth in population; Pittsburgh grew from 50,000 people in 1860 to 156,000 in 1880, a threefold increase; the population of the whole metropolitan area grew from 178,000 in 1860 to about 250,000 twenty years later. Such growth was the result not only of immigration and of a natural increase but of the annexation of outlying towns—of the East End (Oakland, East Liberty, and Lawrenceville) in 1867 and of the South Side boroughs on the left bank of the Monongahela in 1872. Owing to these acquisitions the area of the city increased more than fifteen times between 1866 and 1872.

But the threefold growth did not explain the five- or sixfold increase in the cost of governing it. The difference, since there was so little to show for it, had to be set down to the inefficiency with which American cities were customarily governed in the Gilded Age. Not only was the form of government in itself cumbersome, but the motives of the governors were sometimes open to question. City government, in Pittsburgh as elsewhere, was not an art,

Drawing by C. S. Reinhart in Harper's Weekly, February 18, 1871.

MELTING STEEL. Seven large steel works in Pittsburgh made 30,000 tons of steel in 1870. Five years later the Edgar Thomson Steel Works began to use the Bessemer converter under the supervision of ironmaster Bill Jones, heralding the era of steel. Within a decade Pittsburgh's steel production was valued at $18,300,000, capital had increased to $12,000,000. The industry employed 8100 workers.

GLASS was produced in great quantities during the seventies.

The first glasswork in Pittsburgh was established in 1797 by Isaac Craig and James O'Hara. Ten years later the Robert and Ensel

Sketch by J. Becker from Frank Leslie's Illustrated, March 25, 1871.

COAL. The coal production of the Pittsburgh area grew by leaps and bounds during the seventies—in a decade and a half an increase of 300 per cent brought annual output to $13,000,000, 20 per cent of the national total.

About one third of the coal mined in the area was turned into coke for use in the city's steel mills, and the remainder was used as a fuel or for the manufacture of gas.

COKE. The excellent coking coal near Pittsburgh, particularly at Connellsville, was an important element in the area's development as the nation's iron and steel capital.

By the end of the seventies the County's

still less a public service, but a business—a business, moreover, conducted not for the benefit of the public but for the servants of the public, whose interests did not always coincide with those of their constituents. The reverse, in fact, was usually true, for the same officials who were so niggardly in appropriating money for the support of the police or the upkeep of the streets dispensed funds among themselves with a lavish hand. The needs of politics were urgent and unceasing; a politician had to reward his friends; he had to maintain party solidarity; he had periodically to replenish the campaign chest. As a man of some importance, he had to live on a scale appropriate to his dignity. And if he had to dig deeply into the public treasury in order to fulfill these obligations, he could comport his conscience, if he had any, with the knowledge that he was only following the accepted practice of the day. There was nothing unusual about graft, except that it flourished so openly and aroused so little indignation. And whether one approved or condemned or simply ignored it, there was no denying that it added to the expense of running the city.

The glacial pace of civil improvement was in striking contrast to the phenomenal development of private enterprise, and reflected the general acceptance of the business

wing by C. S. Reinhart in Harper's Weekly, February 18, 1871.

glassworks was founded; in 1808 this business was purchased by Bakewell and Page and became the first successful flint-glass factory.

In 1870 Allegheny County had 32 glassworks whose products were worth $5,832,492.

LARGE MACHINERY. The mammoth shears which the Atlas Iron Works at Pittsburgh turned out were the largest of their kind at the time, capable of cutting through a bar five inches in diameter "as if

From Frank Leslie's Illustrated, September 4, 1875.

it was a straw."

By the end of the seventies, the city's foundries and machine shops made $5,530,309 worth of products. In another decade the value of this output had doubled.

Fred B. Schell in Sipes, The Pennsylvania Railroad (1875).

production exceeded all states except Pennsylvania, Ohio, and West Virginia.

Coke manufactured in the Pittsburgh area was also transported west and used to smelt most of the metals of the Rocky Mountains.

OIL. Following Edwin L. Drake's oil strike in 1859, petroleum was transported in barrels to Pittsburgh over Oil Creek and the Allegheny. During dry seasons artificial freshets were required to float the barges

Drawing by Fred B. Schell from Frank Leslie's Illustrated, January 28, 1865.

down Oil Creek. Such "flood days" were great attractions along the stream.

In early 1871, there were 60 petroleum refineries located in the city of Pittsburgh, with a capacity of 36,000 barrels per day.

ethic. The men who set the tone of Pittsburgh society were men for whom business was a religion on the altar of which comfort, tranquility, and even public order had sometimes to be sacrificed. One visitor left a collective portrait of these men:

"The masters of Pittsburgh are mostly of the Scotch-Irish race, . . . keen and steady in the prosecution of their affairs, indifferent to pleasure, singularly devoid of the usual vanities and ostentations, proud to possess a solid and spacious factory, and to live in an insignificant house. There are no men of leisure in the town . . ." Without leisure, there was no need of playgrounds and parks.

For the same reason society, as that term was understood in London and Paris, was almost unknown in Pittsburgh. Among the very rich, the forms associated with a more leisurely way of life were beginning to be imported, but without much of the spirit. It became unfashionable to call on one's friends without first leaving one's card, to seat husbands and wives together at large dinners, or to do any of a hundred things which in a simpler society had once been done without thinking. The very rich went to balls at which they danced the polka, the waltz, and the mazurka; they posed for portraits in studied manner; they attended parties at which

Drawing by J. P. Davis from Every Saturday, *March 18, 1871.*

A PITTSBURGH GLASSWORK in 1870. Although its expansion was not as dramatic as the metal industry's, glass maintained third place among Pittsburgh enterprises, trailing iron and steel and foundry and machine shop products.

At the end of the seventies Pittsburgh's 46 glassworks were employing 5796 persons and producing glass valued at $5,231,971. In ten more years the industry's output was worth $6,176,076, produced on a capital of $7,439,619.

The glass products included flint and lime glassware, window glass, and more than 85,000,000 bottles and vials annually.

charades and private theatricals spiced the entertainment; but there was little in the nature of these diversions, aside from their size, to distinguish them from those of less fortunate members of society. There was little music, except in church; little art; and nothing which could qualify as a literary salon. Valiant efforts were periodically made to supply these deficiencies. The Germans in the city went in for choral singing; the Mozart Club, a choral society founded late in the 70s, numbered at one time 200 singers, but failed to create interest in the oratorio as an art form. The Art Society, founded in 1873, occasionally brought exhibitions of paintings. Plays and musicals were performed at Library Hall. The Pittsburgh Opera House opened in 1871, and the Mercantile Library was founded in the same year.

Characteristically, however, Pittsburghers preferred more utilitarian forms of culture. The Allegheny Observatory, for instance, was a great success; founded through the generosity of William Thaw and directed by Professor Samuel Pierpont Langley, it justified its existence by distributing astronomical time to cities and railroads by what was known as the "Allegheny system." The city supported ten daily newspapers in 1880—more than any other city of its size. And if journalism and science, particularly applied science, were generally preferred to art, lectures were considered more edifying than plays or concerts, and the more uplifting the discourse, the more greatly to be admired; the sermon was still the most popular of all oratorical forms. Mark Twain spoke to an audience of 1500 in November 1868. Charles Sumner addressed a gathering of Pittsburgh intelligentsia in 1870 on "The Duel between France and Prussia with Its Lessons to Civilization." "Sunset" Cox, who might be considered the Will Rogers of his day, drew large crowds; so did

BORING FOR OIL. Success in selling petroleum as an illuminant led to efforts climaxed by Edwin L. Drake's well at Titusville. There followed an oil boom in Western Pennsylvania. The beam on the derrick, attached to a steam engine, furnished the power which caused the up and down movement by the string of tools.

BURNING GAS. Those who drilled for petroleum often found natural gas. Its quantity made it cheap, and wells which took fire were allowed to burn with no effort to save the gas. By the 1880's, however, the economy, ease of transportation, and cleanliness of the gas led to its increasing utilization as a fuel in place of coal.

the eminent divine, T. DeWitt Talmage. But attendance at church, for the majority, remained the leading intellectual pursuit, and a minister like the Reverend William Paxton, whose congregation at the First Presbyterian Church included some of the city's leading industrialists, enjoyed a respect which in a later day would be reserved for baseball players and movie stars.

The undiminished influence of organized religion, especially Presbyterianism, was reflected in the city's strict Sabbatarianism—the mills closed on Saturday afternoon and remained closed until Monday morning—and in the observance of a moral code which emphasized the frailty and corruptibility of the flesh. The young were carefully sheltered from crime and scandal; the novelist Margaret Deland remembered when she was sixteen having been told by her mother, "My dear, the papers are printing something about a trial that is going on in Brook-

lyn. It isn't a pleasant story, and you wouldn't be interested in it; so you are not to read it. If you happen to see the word 'Beecher' just skip it."

It was not that Pittsburghers were a narrow, unsmiling people who disapproved, on principle, of frivolity. They approved of frivolity so long as it was frankly frivolous and laid no claim to be taken seriously. Hence the popularity of such songs as "The Man on the Flying Trapeze" and "Dad's a Millionaire" and of the musical theater, which drew large Saturday audiences of workmen who regarded with fine contempt the admonitory signs posted by the management: "Hats Off," "No Hallooing or Whistling Allowed," "Applaud with Your Hands," "Order Must Be Observed." The popularity of boating on the river and of professional baseball, which came to Pittsburgh in 1877, reflected the same impulse. But for the refinements associated with a more advanced stage of

(turn to page 167)

165

From Every Saturday, *March* 17, 1871.

A FAMILY COAL MINE—AS SKETCHED IN THE PITTSBURGH AREA BY ARTIST H. FENN.

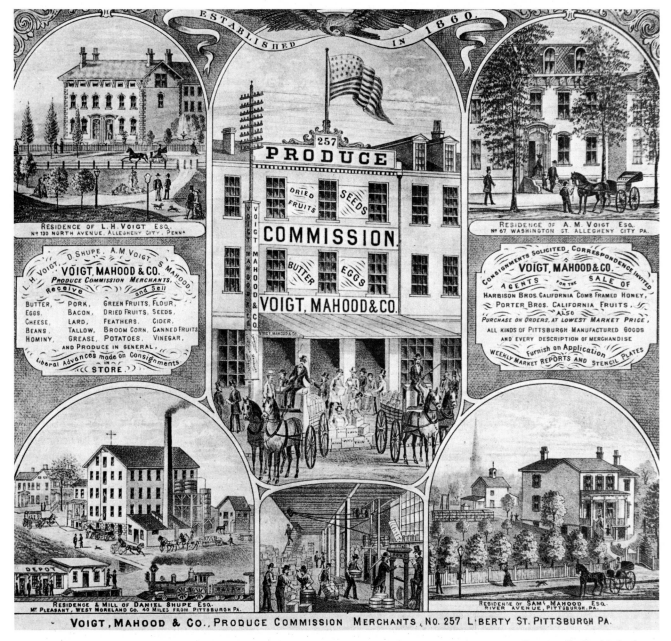

From the collection of Stefan Lorant.

ADVERTISEMENT FOR A PRODUCE COMMISSION MERCHANT FIRM AT 257 LIBERTY STREET.

civilization, for art and letters, Pittsburghers cared very little; these pursuits could not be dismissed as diversions and therefore competed for attention with the all-absorbing business of getting a living.

Nothing better reflected the aspirations of the people which craved wealth and power while lacking the taste of a more mature society than architectural styles. In an earlier period the fashionable streets had been graced by restrained and modest houses in the federal style. The expansion of industry in the Triangle, however, precipitated a flight to the suburbs, and the fashionable center of gravity shifted from Penn Avenue near the Point to Allegheny City, Herron Hill, and parts of the East End. In 1868 a visitor saw "villages . . . springing up as far as

twenty miles away to which the business men repair, when, in consequence of having inhaled the smoke all day, they feel able to bear the common country atmosphere through the night." Ridge Avenue in Allegheny City now became the "Park Avenue of Pittsburgh," and simplicity in architecture gave way to Gothic splendor. The mansions of the *nouveaux-riches* towered three and four stories above the ground, their outlines ornamented with a mélange of cupolas, turrets, mansard roofs, and heavy scrolls, their entrances guarded by fierce lions and gargoyles. Furnished with thick carpets of a dismal hue, horsehair furniture, massive center tables adorned with fantastic carvings, and an abundance of funereal urns, they seemed to have been designed to repel the invasion of light; in conception and execution they resembled not so much houses as fortresses or sealed tombs.

Yet there was appropriateness in an architecture which ran to the somber, for the whole city, during these years, was except on rare days blanketed by a dense layer of smoke from the mills; it was in this period that Pittsburgh got its reputation as "the blackest, dirtiest, grimiest city in the United States," as J. Ernest Wright has characterized it. Trollope, stopping at Pittsburgh on his way west in 1862, called it "the blackest place . . . I ever saw." At his hotel, he complained, everything was black

not black to the eye, for the eye teaches itself to discriminate colours even when loaded with dirt, but black to the touch. On coming out of a tub of water my foot took an impress from the carpet exactly as it would have done had I trod barefooted on a path laid with soot. I thought that I was turning negro upwards, till I put my wet hand upon the carpet, and found that the result was the same. And yet the carpet was green to the eye—a dull, dingy green, but still green.

The biographer James Parton, writing six years later, found that "every street appears to end in a huge, black cloud." By day, he exclaimed, Pittsburgh was "smoke, smoke, smoke—everywhere smoke"; by night it was "Hell with the lid taken off." This last phrase stuck; Pittsburghers themselves repeated it with a trace of pride, and years later Lincoln Steffens used it as the title of his

(turn to page 174)

THE CHUBBY FISHING CLUB of old Allegheny, an organization of businessmen, at its annual McKees Rocks outing in 1876.

Fishing was a favorite pastime of Americans. There were fishing clubs in the country ever since devoted anglers got together in Philadelphia and formed the "Colony of Schuykill" in 1732. However, these clubs did not become popular until the 1870's, when anglers' associations, sportsmen's clubs—like the Chubby

below:

A PITTSBURGH FAMILY. The family of Jacob and Catherine Biers Hill, who lived on River Avenue near Chestnut Street in old Allegheny.

The Hills had seven daughters and one son, but seemingly the son did not rate for the photograph. Amanda and Cornelia, the two girls at the right, were the first telephone operators in the city.

Courtesy Bell Telephone Company.

168

Photograph by Frank E. Bingaman.

Fishing Club—appeared in several parts of the country.

In the front row: C. Steffen, John Dippel, William Gerber, F. Thomas, Jake Dippel, unidentified, John Gass, Jr., and Sam Gass.

In the second row: unidentified, Charles Gass, John Gass, Sr., Henry Dippel, Henry Gerber, Charles Geyer, J. Beckert, Louis Geyer.

In the top row: A. L. Heddaeus, unidentified, Charles Rado, Albert Schwerd, Mike Geyer, Sr., Gustave Gerber, J. Haudenshield.

There is also a boy in the picture, but we have no record of whose son or grandson he was. His face shows satisfaction to be photographed in such a distinguished group. One day he will proudly tell his grandchildren. "I was the youngest of them all."

THE RAILROAD RIOTS. For two days in July 1877—on the 21st and the 22nd—Pittsburgh was controlled, so *Harper's Weekly* reported, "by a howling mob, whose deeds of violence were written in fire and blood." And Thomas A. Scott, President of the Pennsylvania Railroad, noted that the city was "such a scene of riot, arson and bloodshed as can never be erased from the memory of its people."

The upheaval began a week earlier in Baltimore, where the firemen and brakemen of the Baltimore & Ohio Railroad refused to accept a renewed ten per cent reduction on their wages. They felt betrayed by the management; they felt that there was no justification for the cut in their wages, no justification for the institution of new schedules which aimed at the reduction of the working force. From Maryland the strike spread rapidly to West Virginia and all the way along the lines to Illinois. Trains were stopped, wires west of Martinsburg were cut.

On the morning of the 19th the Pennsylvania Railroad freightmen struck at Pittsburgh; employees abandoned their trains, took control of the switches, stopped any movement of freight. By midnight 1500 cars were standing on sidings.

Next day the state adjutant general, acting in the absence of Governor John F. Hartranft, called out a force of 1000 militiamen from Philadelphia to move to Pittsburgh and disperse the strikers.

As the militia arrived they were greeted with a fusilade of stones. There was a melee; the soldiers opened fire, killing 20, wounding many more.

An eyewitness reported: "The news of the slaughter of the mob spread through the city like wild-fire, and produced the most intense excitement. The streets were rapidly crowded." Enraged rolling mill hands and workmen filled the streets. They broke into the Great Western Gun-Works, carrying away 200 rifles. From the South Side came 1000 mill hands who marched out to Twenty-eighth Street.

The hostile mob forced the militia to withdraw, the soldiers taking shelter in the Roundhouse at Twenty-eighth and Liberty streets. And while the troops inside the building considered themselves safe, outside their refuge the excitement of the people swelled.

By midnight there were 20,000 men on the scene, a quarter of them armed. They besieged the Roundhouse and opened a brisk fire upon it. Finding that the soldiers could not be dislodged, they resolved to burn them out. An oil train was fired and run down the track against the sand-house, a large structure near the Roundhouse. The building went up in flame; the smoke of the burning oil suffocated the soldiers inside, but they held on to their quarters for the entire night.

At seven o'clock the militia abandoned the Roundhouse and as the troops marched out they were attacked by the rioters. Twenty more dead and a number of wounded littered the pavement.

The air of lawlessness hovered over the city. The demonstrators lit freight cars, applied the torch to the machine shops and railroad offices. Along the tracks men and women were pillaging the freight.

As Bishop Tuigg walked the streets and prayed for the dying militiamen and workers, Pittsburgh was in the grip of the mob.

From Frank Leslie's Illustrated Newspaper, *August 4, 1877.*

Drawing by Fred B. Schell in Harper's Weekly, August 11, 1877.

THE BURNING OF THE DEPOT. While the people of Pittsburgh fought with the militia, a fire had taken hold among the hundreds of freight cars and locomotives in the Union Depot's yard between Washington and 33rd Street. The Union Depot and Hotel went up in flames, as did the Adams Express Building and the grain elevator. Though the total damage was around $5,000,000, the county commissioners were able to settle all claims for $2,772,349.53, of which sum $1,600,000 was paid to the Pennsylvania Railroad.

During the two-day rioting, hundreds were wounded and many lost their lives.

Sketched by M. B. Leisser and J. W. Alexander in Harper's Weekly, August 11, 1877.

THE CONFLAGRATION. In the foreground a burning freight train of the Pennsylvania Railroad, on the right the grain elevator of the Pittsburgh-Birmingham Passenger Railway is engulfed in flames. The mob, enraged by the behavior of the Philadelphia militia, looted stores for guns and foodstuffs, destroyed buildings and railroad stock; 1383 freight cars, 104 locomotives, 66 passenger coaches were burned. Men, women, and children were engaged in the work of pillage, and everything portable, of any value, was seized as fast as it was thrown from the railroad cars, carried away, and secreted.

171

From The History of the Great Riots by E. W. Martin (1877).

FREIGHT CARS WERE LOOTED AND BURNED.

From Frank Leslie's Illustrated, August 18, 1877.

STOLEN GOODS ARE RECOVERED BY THE POLICE.

From the collection of Stefan Lorant.

THE DESTROYED CAR SHOPS of the Pennsylvania Railroad, which the rioters burned on July 22. Two days later volunteer citizens' patrols appeared on the streets of Pittsburgh and gradually order was restored. Still the strike went on for another week. Not until August 1 did the troops ordered out by Governor John F. Hartranft succeed in breaking the strike.

From the collection of Stefan Lorant

AFTER THE STORM. America had suffered its first general strike movement, railway centers from New York to California had been hit, pitched battles had been fought, over 100 workmen had lost their lives, property worth millions had been destroyed, thousands of militia had been called out, federal troops had been used for the first time to put down a strike.

The Pittsburgh rioting had been more violent and destructive than anything the country had ever seen. The strikers had enjoyed the sympathy of a large part of the population, and suppression was therefore more difficult. Many believed the city being discriminated against in freight rates and suffered other disadvantages due to the company's policies. Professor N. J. Ware wrote that the Pittsburgh violence was not properly a strike, but a "revolt of the community against the Pennsylvania Railroad."

The most eloquent summary of the riots was made by Professor Henry David. "A storm had shaken the nation," wrote he, "and had blown over. What remained of it, other than some prickly problems to plague the community's conscience? Trial and punishment for strikers, praise from pulpit and press for their employers; misreading of the past, fear of the future; pride of victory, anguish of defeat; defiance of public authority, public power in the pocket of private interest; full consideration for the rights of property; . . . indifference to the needs of human beings."

173

exposé of the shame of Pittsburgh. Perhaps because they brought them such distinction, the people of Pittsburgh resented neither the smoke nor the steel mills from whence it emanated, and a visitor from Boston in 1871 found them "from high to low, without exception, the best-natured people I ever went among."

These good-natured people were still, in 1880, predominantly of English descent—a fact which doubtless contributed to their good humor, for it saved them from the problems created by a large alien population. A third of the population was foreign-born, with immigrants coming mainly from Scotland, Wales, Ireland, Germany, and England itself—from cultural backgrounds, in other words, not radically different from that of the native Pittsburghers. In 1880 the first immigrants from the Slavic countries were only beginning to arrive; in time they would transform the population and arouse anxieties as to the permanence of the "Anglo-Saxon" heritage. But these anxieties lay in the future.

Life remained, outwardly at least, placid and serene. The surface of national politics was unruffled by serious difference of opinion between the two major parties; in 1880 Pittsburgh indulged in lively speculation over whether General Hancock, a Pennsylvanian and hence a favorite son, would defeat James Garfield and end a period of Republican rule, but the election aroused no emotions more profound than those attending a sporting match. Sports, indeed, at times crowded politics from the news; in the same year respectable opinion was outraged by a "brutal" 66-round prize fight staged near McKeesport, and the Pittsburgh *Post* noted with approval

Contemporary stereographs by S. V. Albee.

WHEN CALM RETURNED: The devastation of railroad equipment, cars and locomotives, opposite 14th Street.

WHAT REMAINED OF THE DEPOT.

right:
THE RUINS OF UPPER ROUNDHOUSE.

174

that the mayor had forbidden their scheduled second fight. Thomas Edison's experiments with electricity commanded increasing attention; the press regularly rang with appeals on behalf of the starving Irish; the South Side suffered an epidemic of typhoid; carpenters in Allegheny struck for $2.50 a day. *Ten Nights in a Bar Room* and *Uncle Tom's Cabin* were performed.

The mood of the city was confident and complacent. Nor could anyone have said that either its pride in its accomplishments or its faith in the future was misplaced. The citizens of Pittsburgh had in twenty years laid the steel foundations of America's industrial empire; they had completely changed the face of the city; they had trebled its population and expanded its area fifteen times. As a result of their efforts, Pittsburgh stood as a monument to the matchless energy and ingenuity which Americans rightfully regarded as their characteristic virtues. If it lacked things now recognized as essential to a great city—efficient government, a filtered water supply, a system of parks and playgrounds, a permanent art collection, a symphony orchestra—it was not because the people of Pittsburgh were innately insensitive to such refinements but because the pace of their material advancement left them no leisure for anything else. They had devoted themslves to the pursuit of wealth with a single-mindedness which precluded pursuit of anything else, but even those who looked with misgivings on the pursuit of wealth as an end in itself could not doubt that it would ultimately justify itself. Was not wealth itself the indispensable condition of culture? Could poets exist without patrons?

Contemporary stereographs by S. V. Albee.

OPPOSITE 13TH STREET: This was the picture of the damaged track on July 24, after order was finally restored.

THE SCENE OPPOSITE 16TH STREET.

left:
DEBRIS OF RAILS AND EQUIPMENT.

175

From Harper's Weekly, *August 18, 1877.*

"THE FRENZY, AND WHAT CAME OF IT,"

read the caption under this drawing by E. A. Abbey for *Harper's Weekly.*

But the editors failed to mention that railway workers earned no more than $5 or $6 a week; not enough to feed themselves and their families. They also omitted the fact that the strike occurred because the railroads decided to reduce the workers' wages by another ten per cent and had announced their intention to run "double-headers"—freight trains made up of two locomotives and 34 cars instead of one locomotive and 17 cars—which not only meant doubling the work load for the same wages, but also meant layoffs for almost half of the railroadmen.

And the editors of *Harper's Weekly* were silent about the fact that while the major railroad companies were ready to reduce the workers' wages, dividends on their watered stock remained as high as before.

Chapter 5

THE HEARTH OF THE NATION

by Sylvester K. Stevens

THE COMING of the railroads radically changed the life of every American. With goods transported on rails, the manufacture and sale of industrial products had ceased to be confined to local areas; business now operated on a national scale. To buy a kettle or a plowshare one no longer went to the local blacksmith, who fashioned the implements and utensils on his forge, but walked into the nearest store, where goods manufactured in other regions could be purchased.

The expansion of the country proceeded at such a furious pace that within the span of a single generation America became an industrial state, the mightiest on earth. This transformation, in the words of Burton Hendrick, was "fitly typified in the evolution of the independent oil driller of Western Pennsylvania into the Standard Oil Company, and of the ancient open air forge on the banks of the Allegheny into the United States Steel Corporation."

Within a short time the value of industrial production outstripped that of the agricultural output, and with this the Jeffersonian dream of a rural America vanished. "The hither edge of the land"—a phrase of the historian Frederick Jackson Turner—disappeared too; the penetration of railroads into the West obliterated the frontier and its historic influence.

For the building of railroads, of cities, of factories, America needed iron and it needed steel. And as Pittsburgh was the center of iron and steel production, the city became the hearth of the nation.

> I'm Pittsburgh, the city of iron and steel,
> The city of crucible forge and mill;
> The mines of the world my treasury is;
> The forces of earth is slave to my will

wrote George H. Thurston in 1886, and the clatter and hammer of the mills along the rivers echoed the rhymes of his *Song of Pittsburgh*. During the day the smoke from the blazing furnaces blackened the skies; at night their flames painted the firmament fiery red, with lights sparkling on the hills like a thousand little stars.

Visitors were invariably impressed by the drama of iron and steel making. In 1871 a reporter from *Harper's Weekly* noted "the dense volumes of black smoke pouring from the hundreds of furnaces, the copious showers of soot, the constant rumbling of ponderous machinery, the clatter of wagons laden with iron." A decade later another traveler spoke with admiration of how "the fiery lights stream forth, looking angrily and fiercely up toward the heavens." And an observer in the nineties spoke of the changing scene in the mills:

Bessemer converters dazzle the eye with their leaping flames. Steel ingots at white heat, weighing thousands of pounds, are carried from place to place and tossed about like toys. Electric cranes pick up steel rails or fifty foot girders as jauntily as if their tons were ounces.

Though the city was smoky and dirty and its streets were crooked and poorly paved, it had a beauty of its own. The smokestacks against the red sky, the curving rivers with their steel-girdered bridges conjured a romantic picture. It was the landscape of a workshop, the greatest in the world, a workshop which supplied the railroads with rails, bridges and locomotives, shipyards with steel plates, factories with heavy machinery, telephone, telegraph and electric companies with wires, and which also furnished the tools and implements, the hardware and much of the farm and industrial machinery that went into the growth of the West.

If one speaks of Pittsburgh one thinks of it as a steel city. But Pittsburgh was never all steel. Its glass manufacturing predated the iron and steel mills, as did the production of wooden kegs and barrels. Its factories made turbines, generators and every kind of electrical equipment; they turned out packaged food, aluminum utensils, cork products and even fine carriages—Phaetons, Sulkies, Victorias, Rockaways—built by the firm of L. Glesenkamp on Penn Avenue.

A few figures illustrate the city's ascent to industrial dominance. At the opening of the Civil War the steel output of the entire country was no more than about eleven thousand tons; twenty years later one single plant in Pittsburgh was producing that amount within a single month. In 1870 less than 30,500 tons of Bessemer steel rails had been made in the United States, in 1880 over 850,000 tons, in 1890 nearly 1,900,000, with Pittsburgh contributing a large percentage.

In the brief span from 1880, when the Edgar Thomson Works went into operation, to the close of the century, the Pittsburgh area became the largest steel producer in the country. The output of the Carnegie steel mills alone increased from 600,000 tons in 1888 to 2,000,000 tons in 1897 and to 4,000,000 tons in 1900, only a million tons less than the entire steel production of England. By 1900 the Pittsburgh district supplied half of the nation's open hearth steel, two-fifths of all its steel and more than half of its coke. What this meant in dollars and cents is revealed in the profits of the Carnegie enterprises: in 25 years—from 1875 to 1900—the company's net profit was estimated at 133 million dollars, and that without an income tax!

This was the era of the businessmen, of the bankers and the millionaires; Mark Twain named it "the gilded age." The nation's wealth was controlled by a handful of individuals who, with vigor and imagination, built up

(turn to page 180)

Courtesy Dr. George Lipman.

Courtesy Adolphe Menjou.

PITTSBURGHERS AS THEY LOOKED IN THE EIGHTIES:

FROM THE FAMILY ALBUM OF DR. GEORGE LIPMAN.   THE MOTHER OF MOVIE ACTOR ADOLPHE MENJOU.

PITTSBURGHERS AS THEY LOOKED IN THE EIGHTIES:

AN IRISH IMMIGRANT FAMILY.

MEN ABOUT TOWN in the eighties. On this photograph the late Dr. Thomas Arbuthnot was able to identify, besides himself, the following friends: Theodore Cook, Wilson S. Arbuthnot, J. D. Hailman (center) and Charles McClintock.

production and organized output. They introduced new methods and new techniques, developed new materials, created cheaper goods and in the process converted America into a highly organized industrial state.

No other city had as many outstanding industrial leaders as Pittsburgh. The scene was dominated by Andrew Carnegie, the canny Scotsman who started out with the railroads and who became cognizant of their need for iron and steel. Because of this knowledge he was able to organize his enterprises in an efficient way, and because of such market orientation steel production could be integrated into a coherent system.

In 1901 Carnegie sold out his holdings to the Morgan interest. The price was the largest ever paid—$492,000,-000 in bonds and preferred and common stock, with Carnegie and his partners sharing the proceeds. As the great Pierpont Morgan sealed the deal with a handshake, he said: "I want to congratulate you on being the richest man in the world!" And Carnegie, who began his career on a $1.20 weekly salary, felt like a little boy who had fi-

nally been let out of school! "I am the happiest man in the world. I have unloaded this burden on your back and I am off to Europe to play," he told Morgan, and was off to the Riviera.

Though Carnegie's stature could not be matched by them, the achievements of the other Pittsburgh entrepreneurs were no less impressive. George Westinghouse—whom Carnegie called "a fine fellow and a great genius, but a poor businessman"—perfected the airbrake and made railway travel and transportation safe; he also proved the practicality of the alternating current system, and, by bringing electricity—light and labor-saving devices—into the homes of the land, he revolutionized American life. Captain Alfred Hunt, foreseeing the potentialities of cheap aluminum, helped the young inventor Charles Hall to develop his new process. Hunt and his associates secured the financial assistance of the Mellon brothers, Andrew and Richard, who also invested in coke ovens, oil and numerous other enterprises that turned Pittsburgh into the greatest production center of the land. Henry J.

1 - B.G. Wells
2 - W.H. Singer Jr.
3 - Professor Mitchell
4 - E.S. Mullins
5 - E.S. Craig
6 - F.W. Albree
7 - J. Vernen Scaife
8 - Robt. W. Flenniken
9 - W.W. Blair
10 - Wilson McCandless

STUDENTS in Dr. William Ralston Crabbe's tutoring school, which in 1882 was conducted in the stable of Calvin Wells at Allegheny. J. Verner Scaife (not Vernen as written on the picture) became the father of industrialist Alan M. Scaife.

Heinz, understanding the need for package food, expanded his factories for prepared food when the rise of the cities opened up new markets for such merchandise. Henry C. Frick, realizing the importance of coal and coke for iron and steel, purchased vast areas of coal land and organized coal production. Henry W. Oliver built a transportation system that brought much-needed iron ore from the Great Lakes to the Pittsburgh mills. And there was a host of others—William Thaw, who made a fortune in freight transportation; Dr. David Hostetter, who built a trunk line that brought oil to the city; Jacob J. Vandergrift, who laid the first natural gas line; Alexander M. Byers, who produced wrought iron and galvanized pipe; John and Harvey Flagler, who turned out light and seamless tubing. The list of Pittsburgh entrepreneurs is a long one.

Professors R. B. Nye and J. E. Morpurgo, in their history of the United States, suggest that the main purpose of these men was "to make money and anyone who was in the way had to perish." This is only part of the story. While it is true that these entrepreneurs amassed millions for themselves, in doing so they also remade the country and raised the living standard of every American.

Holding the power over production and men, daring and resourceful, ruthless and autocratic, they brooked no interference with their work.

"Carnegie had no business ethics to hamper him," said William C. Clyde, the president of Carnegie Steel, in a speech some four decades later. " Might was right. There was no Sherman Law, there was no Interstate Commerce or Federal Trade Commission . . . and no Clayton Act . . . There was no such thing as 'government by commission' in those days. Had Mr. Carnegie to encounter these 'brakes on business,' I am inclined to believe he would have had many tumbles."

The stupendous fortunes that these captains of industry amassed enabled them to live like oriental potentates. Their palaces, whether in New York, in Pittsburgh, or at other places, were filled with masterpieces of art. (Some of these collections grew into magnificent museums. The National Gallery in Washington, built with the donations

(turn to page 184)

181

ACTIVITIES FOR MEN.

Courtesy Jerry Rice.

THE AMATEUR CHAMPIONS of Western Pennsylvania—the McKeesport Star Baseball Club in 1884. First row: G. W. Rees, third base; J. Gibbons, second base; H. S. Hodge, first base. Center: W. Meigs, catcher; H. Snyder, catcher; F. Torreyson, manager; G. Keenan, pitcher; H. Jones, pitcher. Standing: W. Matthews, short stop; J. Dersam, right fielder; T. Torreyson, left field; and F. Ditmer, center field.

below:

THE OFFICIAL DIVAN of the Syria Temple. Front row: James Kerr, Jr., D. F. Collingwood, Benjamin Darlington, John Hazzard. Center: William S. Brown, A. B. Wigley, Geter C. Shidle, T. J. Hudson, A. V. Holmes. Standing: G. P. Balmain, J. D. Kramer, W. Ramsey, J. C. Bartlett, A. B. Davitt, G. C. Johnston, H. H. Arnold.

Courtesy Robert F. Hickman.

PHOTOMONTAGE OF THE GERMAN
Of Pittsburgh singing groups the Teutonia Mannerchor is perhaps the eldest. Founded in 1854, at present it has a male chorus of 60 and a female chorus of 45.

TEUTONIA MEN'S CHOIR OF ALLEGHENY CITY MADE IN THE YEAR OF 1883. THE CHOIR WAS FOUNDED IN 1854.

Other old German choirs, like the Schwaebischer Saengerbund founded in 1862, the Eintracht Singing and Musical Society, founded in 1866, the Bloomfield Liedertafel, founded in 1885, are still performing today, as are the singing groups of the various nationalities, like the Russian Orthodox Male Chorus and the St. Nicholas Serbian Orthodox Male Chorus.

Group singing is popular in the city. The concerts of the Bach and the Mendelssohn choruses draw large audiences.

183

of Andrew W. Mellon, houses the art objects of the financier, while the Frick Museum in New York, the former home of the coal baron, is the repository of paintings by Rubens, Rembrandt, Goya, El Greco, Franz Hals and other great masters that Frick collected during his lifetime. On a more modest scale the pictures of Alexander M. Byers form the nucleus of Pittsburgh's Carnegie Museum.)

They lived in an age of unrestrained Mammon worship, in which material prosperity was looked upon as the yardstick of achievement. Those who became rich were considered successes; those who remained poor were regarded as failures. The chief aim of American life seemed to be to increase production and to make money. Nonmaterial affairs—intellectual, scientific, artistic achievements—counted little.

Philosophers, writers, and even the churches gave encouragement to the race for material success. Social Darwinism was the fashion of the day. Herbert Spencer in England and his disciples in America, by adapting Darwin's biological theories to the social scene, maintained that life was lived in a jungle and was governed by jungle laws. There was nothing moral or immoral about it; in the struggle for existence the fit survived and the weak perished. The rich man grew rich because he was able; the poor man remained poor because he lacked ability.

The capacity to make money was the main proof of one's superiority. Private competition—with everyone looking after his own interest—produced the greatest amount of good; competitive ruthlessness was justified as it led toward perfection. Spencer, a thorough exponent of the laissez-faire theory of government, defined the ground rules for the human struggle and was acclaimed by the business community. Impressed by his philosophy, Carnegie sought him out and became his lifelong friend.

For William Graham Sumner of Yale the millionaire was "the finest flower of competitive society." (Henry Adams and others questioned whether men like Jim Fisk, Diamond Jim Brady or "Bet-you-a-million" Gates were really "the finest flowers of competitive society." Did they become rich because they were able, or did they make their millions because they violated fair competition, transgressed laws and disregarded the rights of their fellow men?)

Literature, not to be outdone by philosophy, sounded similar themes. The most prolific writer of this period, Horatio Alger, Jr., penned his "rags to riches" story no less than 109 times, reassuring his readers that the great American dream—to become rich—could be realized if one was able and would work hard for it. That this was the story Americans wanted to hear was proven by the stupendous success of Alger's books; between the Civil

(turn to page 186)

THE BEGINNINGS OF THE TELEPHONE.

Courtesy Bell Telephone Company.

INTRODUCING THE TELEPHONE. In June 1877, Gardiner Greene Hubbard came to Pittsburgh to demonstrate to Thomas B. A. David, the head of the Central District and Printing Telegraph Company, the new telephone. At the Monongahela House the two men talked through the magneto line. David was impressed.

Courtesy Bell Telephone Company.

THE FIRST PUBLIC ANNOUNCEMENT for the "speaking telephone" in Pittsburgh was made in January 1878. It emphasized that "NO SKILL WHATEVER is required in the use of the instrument." Telephones were not sold, but were rented to prospective customers in sets. The rent for the two sets was $50 annually.

EARLY WORRIES. Thomas Augustus Watson, one of the business partners in the Bell Telephone Company, came to see Thomas B. A. David in Pittsburgh to convince him that the Bell instrument was better than the Edison-developed Western Union Telephone.

Watson, a friend of Alexander Graham Bell, recorded in his notebook the highlights of his visit on March 6, 1878:

"Arrived in Pittsburg this noon. Called on Mr. David, was rec'd cordially.

"He says he has no complaint from anyone in regard to the working of insts. People are poor and business is very dull and he has not made as good a showing as he otherwise would. He is exceedingly anxious that we compromise with the W. U. [Western Union], he says he fears that we will not and that the result will be that either our party or the other will break and sell insts. and thereby ruin the whole thing. He is very strongly in favor of our policy of leasing and not selling under any circumstances. He says that no lines ever should be sold and that the final result will be that all lines that have been sold will come back into our hands on acc't of the necessary repairs.

"He is going to Washington to talk to Mr. Hubbard and will try to be there Saturday.

"He took me to see one of his lines and it certainly works well although the induction is very loud. As Mr. David is thoroughly posted my work with him was very easy and consisted only in explaining District circuit social lines and the necessity for readjusting all insts. he had working which later he promised to do. [In this, Watson is referring to the social use of the telephone, a distant possibility. Up till that time the instrument was only used for business purposes, not for private conversation.]

Courtesy John J. Hughes, Bell Telephone Company.

"Mr. D. controls the G [old] & S [tock] and Dist [rict] Tel [egraph] Co. in this city and if we retain him I don't see how the W. U. can get any foothold at all.

"He had a set of Phelps make . . . which he said he was testing and did not like."

NIGHT TELEPHONE OPERATOR. In the eighties the management of the telephone company thought it hazardous to employ women in the office after nightfall, thus all night operators were men. George O. Johnston was the night operator on the switchboard of the Bellefield Central Office of the Central District and Printing Telegraph Company for the Schenley area.

War and the turn of the century they sold well over two hundred million copies. And Orison Swett Marden's *Pushing to the Front*, which suggested that the most important ingredient of success was the will to succeed, went through two hundred and fifty editions.

The churches too, suffering a decadence in this period, embraced the "cult of success." Calvinism was no longer revelant. It was success that was to serve God and man. The wealthy were chosen by God to be stewards of His wealth; the power to make money was a gift of God. The Baptist minister Russell Conwell, who gave his "Acres of Diamonds" lecture about six thousand times, orated that to make money honestly was both a Christian obligation and a form of preaching the Gospel. And as everybody had the opportunity to get rich, one should not sympathize with the poor, who remained poor only because of lack of ability.

The whole structure of public life reflected the spirit of an era in which the making of money was considered the supreme virtue of human existence. Congress was reckless, bombastic, demagogic; Congressmen were involved in schemes and entangled in scandals. In the Senate big business domination was prevalent, with senators docilely voting for the interest of the large enterprises and being generously rewarded for their services. A Keppler cartoon of the era shows the trust as huge human-faced moneybags towering over the confused and submissive representatives of the people. The "People's Entrance" in the background is locked from the inside, and a sign nearby reads: "This is a Senate of the monopolists, by the monopolists and for the monopolists." In another cartoon Pennsylvania Senator Matthew Quay is auctioning off the Presidential Chair to the "money kings"—among them Rockefeller, Huntington, Jay Gould, Wanamaker and the rest.

The Presidency, from General Grant's election in 1868 until the inauguration of Woodrow Wilson in 1913, rested in Republican hands (with the exception of the two single terms of Grover Cleveland). But curiously enough, in this "typically Republican era" between 1874 and 1894

NAME.	BUSINESS.	PLACE.
* Reymer Bros.	Candy Manufacturers,	Liberty and 5th Sts.
* Reymer Bros. ✠	Retail Stores,	No. 124 Wood St.
* Robinson, Rea & Co.,	Engine Builders, &c.	South Side.
* Robinson, Rea & Co.,	Office.	Second Av. and Smithfield.
Riverside Prison, ✠		Woods Run.
* Standard Nut Co.,	Nut Manufacturers,	South Side.
* Singer, Nimick & Co., ✠	Springs and Axle Mfrs.	No. 83 Water St.
* Singer, Nimick & Co., ✠	Mill.	West Pittsburgh.
* Spang, Chalfant & Co., ✠	Iron Manufacturers,	70 Sandusky St., Alleghy.
* Spang, Chalfant & Co., ✠	Mill.	Pine Creek.
* Stewart, D. A., ✠	Pres't Locomotive Wks.	10 Sixth Street.
* Standard Oil Co., ✠	Refiners,	7th St. and Duquesne way.
* Smith, Sutton & Co., ✠	Steel Manufacturers,	Manchester.
* Speer, A. & Sons, ✠	Plow Manufacturers,	Duquesne Way & Cecil ay.
* Scaife, W. B. & Son, ✠	Iron Bridges, Roofing,	No. 119 First avenue.
* Stoner & McClure, ✠	Sawmill,	27th and Railroad streets.
* Standard Refinery, No. 1,		Standard Station.
* Standard Refinery, No. 2,		42nd St. and A. V. R. R.
Semple Wm., ✠	Dry Goods,	Federal St., Allegheny.
Semple Wm., ✠	Residence,	Irwin Avenue, Allegheny.
* Totten & Co., ✠	Foundry,	24th and Railroad streets.
* United Pipe Line Co.,	Oil Transporters,	Vesta Station.
* Vesta Oil Works,		Vesta Station.
* Verona Tool Works,		Verona Station.
* Voight, Mahood & Co. ✠	Produce Dealers,	No. 257 Liberty Street.
* Wood, W. D. & Co., ✠	Sheet Iron Works,	McKeesport, Pa.
* Wood, W. D. & Co., ✠	Office.	No. 111 Water Street.
* Wightman, Thos. & Co., ✠	Glass Manufacturers,	No. 43 Wood St
* Wightman, Thos. & Co., ✠	Works	West Pittsburgh.
* Wightman, Thos. & Co., ✠	Works	Temperanceville, Pa.
* Wilcox, Shinkle & Miller, ✠	Founders & Machinists,	39 Water Street.
* Wilson, Snyder & Co., ✠	Brass Founders,	52 Water Street.
* Weyman & Bro., ✠	Tobacco Manufacturers,	Smithfield & Diamond Sts.
* Weyman & Bro., ✠	do.	Liberty and Diamond Sts.
* Wells, C. F. & Co., ✠	White Lead Manufrs.	River Avenue, Allegheny.
* Waring, E. J. & Co.,	Refiners,	Bennett's Station.
* West Penn'a R. R.,	Freight Depot,	Allegheny City
* Wilson, Walker & Co.,	Iron Manufacturers,	28th St. and A. V. R. R.
Western Penitentiary, ✠		Allegheny City.
* Woodwell Joseph & Co., ✠	Hardware,	Wood and Second Ave.
* Young, J. B. & Co.		Phoenix Roll Foundry, 42nd St. and A. V. R. R.
* Zug & Co., ✠	Iron Manufacturers,	13th and Etna streets.

All communications, respecting interruptions to lines, &c., should be directed to T. B. A. David. Communications by mail should be by Postal Card.

ADDITIONAL NAMES.

NAME.	BUSINESS.	PLACE.
Hartley Bros	Leather Beltings	No 8t Smithfield St
Geo Sleys Co	Druggists	Cor Wood & 1st ave
Fr J Heinz ✠	Pickling House	195 - 1st Ave.
W E Schmertz ✠	Boot & Shoe	43 - 5th ave
" ✠	Shoe Shop	Western Penitentiary
Phillips Nimick &t ✠	Slip Mill	South Side
Pgh Gas Co ✠	Office	6th ave
" ✠	Gas Works	5th "
Westinghouse Air B Co	Brake Mfrs	25th & Liberty St
Peter Conley ✠	Boiler Mfrs	55 - Water St
W A Nimick ✠		
Pgh Transfer Co ✠		182 - 2nd ave
Lindsay & McCutchn	Iron Mfrs	98 - Rebecca st Allegheny
Logan Gregg &	Hardware	52 - Wood st
Bailey Farrell &t ✠	Water Gas &c Supplies	161 - Smithfield St
Max Schamberg ✠	Foreign Steam Agency	131 - "
Chamber of Commerce ✠		89 - Wood st
Kay McKnight &t ✠	Supplies	80 - Water st
Jn G Hatoy ✠	Iron Mcht	114 - " "
Jos Horne & Co ✠	Wholesale Dry Goods	Market St
" " " ✠	Retail	Penn ave
Brindley Hardware ✠	Hardware	48 - 7th ave
Eagle File Works		"
Iron City Bellows Co		"
J R McClurg & Co	Cracker Home	187 Federal St Allegheny

Courtesy Bell Telephone Company.

THE CITY'S FIRST PHONE BOOK, issued in the summer of 1878, had 12 pages. On four of them were printed the names of the subscribers. And following — on a page and a quarter — were handwritten names, among them H. J. Heinz Pickling House and Joseph Horne and Company, wholesale dry goods. The subscribers had no numbers, calls were made by name.

the Republicans did not control Congress (except for one term in 1889-91). Only after 1896—and for a span of sixteen years under the Presidencies of McKinley, Theodore Roosevelt and Taft—did the GOP achieve political supremacy, controlling both the Presidency and Congress.

The expansion of the country and its industrialization proceeded fast. Under Benjamin Harrison's Presidency the Federal Budget reached a billion dollars. "But this is a billion-dollar country," exclaimed Thomas Reed, the Speaker of the House. Such rapid growth changed every aspect of life. Factories grew so large that management and labor could no longer maintain personal relationship with each other. Before the Civil War, there was hardly a place which employed more than one to two hundred people; Andrew Carnegie knew every one of the men in his Keystone bridge building company by his first name. But by the eighties, when some steel mills employed ten to twenty thousand workers, this was no longer possible. How could a manager of Homestead or Braddock personally know such a large number of men?

The new production methods, too, caused changes. As the manufacture of goods was mechanized, skilled labor became superfluous, craftsmanship obsolete. Artisans were no longer necessary. By 1900 more than half of Pittsburgh's steel workers were unskilled.

The factories, the mills and the mines were in need of cheap, unskilled labor. Searching for it, agents of Carnegie and Frick combed the villages of the Old World, luring the peasants of Hungary, Slovakia and Poland to the mines and mills of Pittsburgh. Those who responded signed contracts (not until 1885 did Congress outlaw the contract labor system) that secured them passage. Carnegie placed a value of $1500 on each adult because "in former days an efficient slave sold for this sum."

Thus, the tide of immigration swelled. While in the four decades before the Civil War—between 1820 and 1860—only five million immigrants came, between 1870 and 1900 their numbers rose to well over twelve million.

Pittsburgh grew into a classic "melting pot." In the twenty years between 1880 and 1900 its foreign-born

SMITHFIELD STREET, LOOKING TOWARD LIBERTY.

LIBERTY AVENUE.

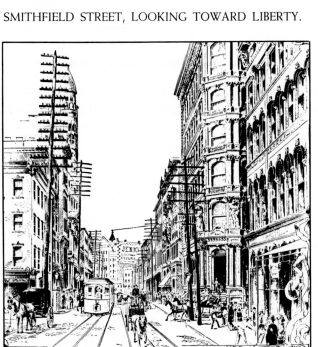

FIFTH AVENUE, LOOKING TOWARD LIBERTY AVENUE.

WOOD STREET, LOOKING TOWARD FIFTH AVENUE.

population doubled. The majority of the newcomers were no longer Anglo-Saxons; they no longer came from Ireland, Scandinavia and Germany as in the past, but from Poland, Hungary, Slovakia, Italy, and other European countries. (Between 1881 and 1900 immigrants from Great Britain dwindled from 81,736 to 12,509, those from Ireland from 72,342 to 35,730, those from Scandinavia from 81,582 to 31,151, those from Germany from 210,485 to a trickling 18,507.) And while in 1881 only 5614 immigrants came from Poland, 5,041 from the Baltic States and 15,401 from Italy, by 1900 the numbers of nationals from Poland and Austria-Hungary increased to 114,847, from Russia and the Baltic States to 90,787, from Italy to 100,135.

The influx of so many newcomers was reflected in the value of Pittsburgh's real estate. In 1860, when Allegheny County's population numbered 335,869 (including 156,389 Pittsburghers), the value of the city's real estate amounted to $100,000,000; by 1900, when the county's

PENN AVENUE, LOOKING TOWARD SIXTH STREET.

NINTH STREET, LOOKING TOWARD LIBERTY AVENUE.

FIFTH AVENUE.

From Industries and Wealth of Pittsburgh and Environs *(1890)*.

CORNER OF WOOD STREET AND LIBERTY AVENUE.

population climbed to 775,058 (including Pittsburgh's 321,616), the city's real estate rose to $321,700,000.

For Pittsburgh the immigrants posed thorny problems. The city's ailments were not different from those of other cities where industrialism took root. There was lack of housing for such large numbers of newcomers, not enough schools for their children, not enough funds for increased sanitation, fire and police protection, nor had the city fathers resources on hand for additional health and recre-

ational facilities. They seemed helpless against the recurring epidemics and against the spreading typhoid fever. (Not until 1896 did a commission recommend the filtration of the water, a measure which finally arrested the disease.)

Crowded in tenement houses without proper sanitation facilities, the immigrants started their life at the bottom of the ladder. The wooden shanties at the Point and on the hill, at Skunk Hollow or Painter's Row were

(turn to page 191

189

FIFTH AND GRANT, looking toward the south. On the right is
the Old Courthouse which burned down on May 8, 1882. On the
left, next to Samway's laundry, is the alderman's office. The large
picture (on the right) gives the opposite view of the same corner.

FEDERAL STREET IN ALLEGHENY, as it looked in 1885.
The vacant lot behind the Old Market building is the site where
the Carnegie Free Library of Allegheny was to be erected.
The library was completed and opened to the public in 1890.

FIFTH AND GRANT.
(See captions under top left picture)

left:

LIBERTY AVENUE, looking west
from Union Depot. The Eagle and
McCoy (the former Ruth House) Hotels are on the right, while the Globe
Hotel is beyond the footbridge in the
center. The trains of the Pennsylvania Railroad passed in the middle of
the street on their way to the yards.

Photograph by Frank E. Bingaman.

crammed with humanity; a single room housed a dozen or more people.

They were eyed with suspicion by those who were living in the city before. The "natives" regarded the newcomers, with their alien habits and customs, as intruders; they lived in filthy houses, were involved in labor unrest, and were not able to speak the language.

And the immigrants were equally suspicious. Coming from countries where they lived under autocratic rulers, they could not comprehend democracy and found it hard to understand the constantly changing tempo of American life. As the unpleasantness between natives and newcomers mounted, name calling, bickering and fighting became an everyday occurrence.

The influx of foreigners presented fertile ground for a political machine. Strangers in an alien country, the immigrants turned to the political organization, a friend in need. If a man was looking for a job or ran into difficulty

(turn to page 193)

THE MOORHEAD RESIDENCE, the home of General James K. Moorhead, at 113 Center Avenue. Elizabeth Moorhead, who was born in the house described it in her nostalgic *Whirling Spindle*.

Mary Moorhead, the general's daughter inherited the building, named it Bethany Home and used it as shelter for people who desired to study the Bible and live a quiet, religious life. Bethany Home was demolished to make room for the annex of the Irene Kaufmann Settlement.

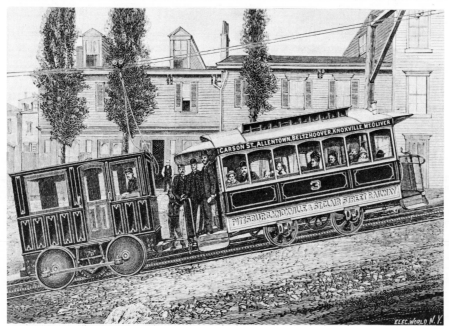

AN EARLY CABLE CAR of the Pittsburgh, Knoxville, and St. Clair Street Railway, which in 1888 operated the first electric streetcar in the city. The line traveled from Carson Street to Allentown, Beltzhoover, Knoxville, and Mount Oliver.

The cog wheel and the rack seen in the center of the track were safety precautions.

HORSE CAR ON SOHO HILL, on upper Fifth Avenue. From the East End to downtown Pittsburgh one travelled for almost two full hours. It was not until 1889 that the horse-drawn carriages were replaced by cable cars, cutting the running time in half though the cables were difficult to maintain in a city of steep ascents and sharp turns. Still, it took another seven years before the Fifth Avenue cars were substituted by the new efficient trolleys, that were driven by electricity.

with the police, it was the organization which helped him. For this a vote on election day was small reward indeed.

But political bosses would not have emerged solely on the backs of immigrants; they needed other support. And such support they received from the businessmen, who wanted franchises for public utilities, for gas and water, for street railways, who wanted building contracts and asked for other favors. For this they gave the nod to the existence of the political machine.

Two men ruled the city—Christopher Magee and William Flinn. Magee went after the franchises of public transportation; he built and ran railways, while Flinn wanted public contracts for his firm, Booth & Flinn, for the repair of streets, the laying out of new roads, the erection of public buildings. The two complemented each other perfectly. They operated within the law.

Magee's idea, according to Lincoln Steffens, who in *The Shame of the Cities*, described his operations, was not to corrupt the city government, but to be it; not to hire votes in council, but to own councilmen; and so, having seized control of his organization, he nominated cheap or dependent men for the select and common councils. Relatives and friends were his first recourse, then came bartenders, saloon-keepers, liquor dealers, and others allied to the vices, who were subject to police regulation and dependent in a business way upon the maladministration of the law. For the rest he preferred men who had no visible means of support, and to maintain them he used the usual means—patronage. And to make his dependents secure he took over the county government.

And how Flinn operated one could see from the following example: the stones for public buildings were specified so that only his quarry could supply them; asphalt for the streets had to be of a quality that only his firm possessed. In one instance, the specification for the new Public Safety Building was for "Ligonier Blocks," but when another firm offered to furnish the blocks at a cheaper price, the specifications were altered "that the Ligonier Block shall be of a bluish tint rather than a grey variety" so that Flinn, who had the bluish-tint stone, should not lose out.

QUIET AND UNHURRIED: AN 1887 VIEW OF WEST OHIO STREET IN ALLEGHENY.

IN 1881 GROUND WAS EXCA-

ON JANUARY 9, 1889, A SEVERE STORM DEVASTATED BUILDINGS ON WOOD STREET.

IN 1885 THE DAVIS ISLAND DA-

Magee and Flinn, expert manipulators of the graft, had their fingers in every pie. To reward and please their smaller supporters they allowed them a share of the "take" from vice. It worked this way: Houses of prostitution were rented by the real estate agent of the ward syndicates for a legitimate fee. But the women who rented them were obliged to buy the furniture from "the official furniture men," who charged many times more than the pieces would have cost elsewhere. Beer and liquor had to be bought from "the official liquor commissioner," with a 100% markup; clothes, hats, shoes or jewelry had to be purchased from those businessmen who belonged to the

/ATED FOR THE POST OFFICE.

AN 1889 VIEW OF THE MONONGAHELA HOUSE, THE CITY'S FOREMOST HOSTELRY.

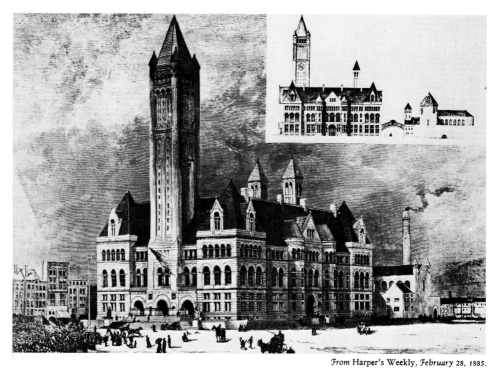

NEAR PITTSBURGH WAS OPENED.

IN 1888 THE NEW COUNTY BUILDINGS WERE GIVEN OVER TO THE PUBLIC.

ring. It was a safe and eminently satisfactory system to everyone.

There were many men in Pittsburgh, who would not submit to corruption and who were fighting the machine with determination. One was David Bruce, who in 1886 tried to bring about a new city charter. Another was

Oliver McClintock, a merchant, who in a rare civic wrath contested some of the contracts awarded by the machine and revealed graft in street paving and other services. He photographed Flinn's pavements at places where they were torn up to show that "large stones, as they were excavated from sewer trenches, brick bats and the debris of old coal-

195

tar sidewalks were promiscuously dumped in to make foundations, with the result of an uneven settling of the foundation, and the sunken and worn places so conspicuous everewhere in the pavements of the East End." McClintock maintained that "out of the entire amount of asphalt pavements laid during these nine years [succeeding the adoption of the Charter of 1887] represented by 193 contracts, and costing $3,551,131, only nine street blocks paved in 1896, and costing $33,400 were not laid by this firm." [Booth & Flinn]

In time the dissatisfied got together in the Pittsburgh Municipal League, which tried to institute reforms and to bring about better government. In 1896 the reformers nearly succeeded in ousting the ring. George W. Guthrie, their candidate for mayor, lost out only because the entrenched rulers of Pittsburgh stuffed the ballot boxes. It was not until after Magee died in 1901 that the machine disintegrated.

Life in Pittsburgh moved on with jolts and jerks. The rapid expansion of industrialism, like all innovations, could not be accomplished on an even keel. Good times were followed by bad, prosperous years by years of hardship. Depressions were recurring regularly—they came in 1873, in 1884, and again in 1893. At that time, wrote Professors Morison and Commager in *The Growth of the American Republic* "everything seemed to conspire to

41 Fifth Avenue.
Pittsburgh, Pa.

Courtesy Mary McSwigan.

A PITTSBURGH DARLING in 1888 solemnly strikes a pose for the photographer, giving her undivided attention to the birdie.

convince the people that democracy was a failure."

Prices and wages hit rock-bottom and there seemed to be no market for anything. Half a million laborers struck against conditions which they thought intolerable, and most of the strikes were dismal failures. Ragged and hungry bands of unemployed swarmed over the countryside, the fires from their hobo camps flickering a message of warning and despair to the affrighted townsfolk.

The disastrous winter of 1893-94 saw want and misery. The city spent $133,678 on relief. Private citizens contributed another $250,000, with Andrew Carnegie giving half of the sum, but all this money was not enough to alleviate the want of the needy. It took a long time before the city overcame that winter of hardship.

The gulf between the classes widened; there was steady conflict between capital and labor. Coxey's army passed through the city, swelled by scores of unemployed steelworkers from Homestead. The Populists were gaining strength by advocating federal ownership of railroads and telegraph lines, nationalization of banks, currency inflation through silver coinage, and a cancellation of unused railroad grants. These were years of turmoil. Everybody offered suggestions how to eliminate extreme poverty in

Courtesy George E. Shellaby.

THE ANGEL SODALITY from St. Mary's Church is memorialized on this tinplate photograph taken in the late eighties.

Drawing by Charles Graham in Harper's Weekly, *April 10, 1886.*

MAKING BESSEMER STEEL. A scene in a Pittsburgh steel mill with the converter at work. Henry Bessemer, an English ironmaster, patented a method in 1855 whereby carbon and other impurities were removed from the molten pig iron. The process of Bessemer, soon to be used by all the large mills, made steel manufacturing not only cheaper but more efficient. It heralded the era of steel in the United States—the era of unlimited opportunities, of tremendous industrial expansion.

the midst of material plenty. Reformers fought for the freer and more individualistic life that vanished with industrialism.

The appearance of the city changed rapidly. The growing industries hastened expansion. Boroughs of its suburbs and neighboring communities—South Pittsburgh, Monongahela, Allentown, St. Clair, Lawrenceville, Temperanceville, Birmingham, Sligo, Mount Washington, West Pittsburgh and Ormsby—were annexed in 1872.

Streets were lighted with gas (the first important natural gas well was drilled at Murraysville in 1874); horse-drawn trolleys carried traffic from one end of the city to the other. (In 1889 the Fifth Avenue horse cars were replaced by cable cars; electric trolleys came in 1896.) By 1880 the Allegheny County Light Company supplied electric current, and electric lamps, many of them manufactured by Westinghouse, were installed in the better restaurants and stores.

Large edifices—skyscrapers—made their appearance. The new office building of the Carnegie Steel Company was 15 stories high, and to dramatize the use of steel the structure was left uncovered for a full year.

The appearance of the factories and steel mills changed as well. In the last years of the century, especially between 1896 and 1900, the dismantling of the pear-shaped Bessemer converters went on. Mills became equipped with open-hearth furnaces. Within a short time the Bessemer process became a memory of the past. The steel industry modernized itself with great speed.

Pittsburgh was now not only a great production center

(turn to page 202)

Courtesy United States Steel Corporation.

ISABELLA FURNACE, named after Mrs. Isabella Herron, the sister of a member of Spang, Chalfant & Company, was 75 feet high, with 25 feet diameter of bosh. This furnace went into blast in the early summer of 1872 and produced 50 tons of pig iron a day.

Courtesy Pittsburgh Plate Glass Company.

THE GLASS PLANTS of the New York City Plate Glass Company were located in Creighton on the Allegheny 20 miles above Pittsburgh. They became part of the giant Pittsburgh Plate Glass Company when that trust came into being in the year of 1895.

Courtesy H. J. Heinz Company.

HENRY J. HEINZ, PRESIDENT OF THE GREAT FOOD CONCERN, TAKES SON HOWARD FOR AN OUTING IN 1880.

THE EDGAR THOMSON STEEL WORKS and blast furnaces as they looked in 1890. Founded in 1873 by Andrew Carnegie and a number of his associates, it was managed with immense success by Captain "Bill" Jones, without doubt the best steelman of his age.

LUCY FURNACE, named after Lucy, the wife of Thomas M. Carnegie, went into blast about the same time as the Isabella, competing fiercely with it. By the end of 1872, the furnace produced an average of 500 tons a week, which was a record for the times.

THE FIRST ALUMINUM PLANT of the Pittsburgh Reduction Company on Smallman Street. Here, on Thanksgiving Day of 1888, the first cheap aluminum using the process of the twenty-four-year-old inventor Charles Martin Hall was produced.

THE INTERIOR OF THE FIRST ALUMINUM PLANT with the electrolytic cells or pot line for making aluminum. At the beginning production averaged about 50 pounds a day. At that time the price of aluminum was two dollars for the pound.

THE BEGINNINGS OF A GIANT ENTERPRISE: THE AMERICAN IRON WORKS OF JONES & LAUGHLIN IN 1880.

THE MAN WHO LOVED THE STARS.

JOHN ALFRED BRASHEAR (1840-1920), a descendant of French Huguenots, attended public school in Brownsville, and studied for one semester at Duff's Mercantile College in Pittsburgh. No desire to become a bookkeeper, he went from job to job; from grocery store clerk to engine pattern maker. During the Civil War he earned his living by working in a steel mill. He married Phoebe Stewart, with whose family he boarded, and the young couple lived with Brashear's maternal grandfather, Nathanial Smith. Later, when Brashear's pay was raised from the weekly $10 to $25, he and his wife moved back to the South Side. Having no children of their own, they adopted a girl, then a boy.

Brashear, who in the meanwhile became a master millwright, bought some land on the cliff behind Twenty-Second Street in Birmingham and built a house on it with a workshop in the back.

Ever since his childhood days, Brashear was drawn to the stars. His desire was to make a lens and build a telescope so he would not have to study them with the naked eye. For two years, following 1872, he and his wife toiled every evening after he returned from his work, on a five-inch lens but when the lens was finished it slipped out of his fingers and broke. Undismayed, the couple began to make another one. After another year of arduous work, the new telescope was ready. It was mounted in the hallway of the Brashear home with its tube pointing out of the high bedroom window. A German neighbor who came to peep through the instrument cried out: "Mein Gott! We have them same stars in Germany."

Brashear was then 35. At the urging of Dr. Langley of the Allegheny Observatory, he left the mill and started on a lens ordered by his friend. Gradually he established an instrument shop that was to take his fame to all corners of the earth. He built telescopes and spectroscopes for observatories; his delicate measuring instruments helped widen the knowledge of mankind. And though Brashear became world famous, with friends among the great, to Pittsburghers, he always remained unassuming "Uncle John."

THE MAN WHO PIONEERED AVIATION.

SAMUEL PIERPONT LANGLEY (1834-1906) was born in Massachusetts, went to school in Boston, but had no college education. A thorough student of astronomy and physics, he was named Director of the Allegheny Observatory and professor of physics and astronomy in the Western University of Pennsylvania (the present University of Pittsburgh) in 1866, a post he held for twenty years. At the observatory, realizing the difficulties of the railroads that ran on different kinds of local time, Langley devised a method of regulating railroad time from the Observatory clock. The Pennsylvania Railroad made a contract with the Observatory for the standard time, delivered by telegraph, and paid for the service a handsome sum that for many years constituted the Observatory's main revenue.

Langley's studies in solar heat, lunar temperature, and drawings of sun spots were all pioneered in Pittsburgh. One of his foremost scientific achievement was the invention of the bolometer in 1878, an electrical thermometer that measured the distribution of heat in the spectrum of the sun.

Not long before Langley left the Allegheny Observatory for Washington, where he became the Secretary of the Smithsonian Institution, he experimented with a heavier-than-air machine. Studying the birds in flight, he built wings from paper and bamboo, threw them into the air and observed the results. He then constructed a "whirling table" which enabled him to measure the lifting power of the wings. His papers, "Experiments in Aerodynamics" (1891), and "The Internal Work of the Wind" (1893), were closely studied by all those who experimented with flying. In Washington, Langley built power-driven models (one of them had a 14-foot span) which flew as far as 4200 feet, but the launching of his large flying machine was unsuccessful and he was ridiculed by the press and the public. Nevertheless, the achievements of his models were "the first sustained free flights of power-propelled heavier-than-air machines ever made," clearing the path for the experiments of the Wright Brothers.

THE POLITICAL BOSSES.

Courtesy Carnegie Library.

CHRISTOPHER LYMAN MAGEE

(1848-1901), who together with William Flinn dominated Pittsburgh's political life with hardly a break from 1882 to 1899, began his career as a clerk in the comptroller's office when he was 16. In 1869 he was made cashier of the city treasury, and in 1871, at the age of 23 he was elected treasurer of the city. Within four years the city's debt was reduced from 15 to 8 million dollars. At the end of his term he resigned from his job; his ambition was to control the politics of Pittsburgh and Allegheny County. He journeyed to Philadelphia to study the methods of the political ring there, and when the Tweed ring in New York was broken he looked into the mistakes that led Tammany into the disaster. Returning to Pittsburgh, he said to a friend that a political ring could be made as safe as a bank.

Lincoln Steffens characterized the two Pittsburgh bosses in this memorable passage: "Magee wanted power, Flinn wealth. Each got both these things; but Magee spent his wealth for more power, and Flinn spent his power for more wealth. Magee was the sower, Flinn the reaper. In dealing with men they came to be necessary to each other, these two. Magee attracted followers, Flinn employed them. The men Magee won Flinn compelled to obey, and those he lost Magee won back . . .

"Molasses and vinegar, diplomacy and force, mind and will, they were well mated. But Magee was the genius. It was Magee that laid plans they worked out together."

He was twice elected to the state senate, was the agent of the Pennsylvania Railroad in Allegheny County and later in the entire state of Pennsylvania. He owned the Duquesne Traction Company, the most valuable transportation line of the city, made a fortune in natural gas, was proprietor of the Pittsburgh *Times,* held directorships in several banks and insurance companies, had his fingers in many pies.

Photograph by Frank E. Bingaman.

WILLIAM FLINN (1851-1924) was born in Manchester, England. His parents brought him to Pittsburgh before he was one year old.

He was elected to the State House of Representatives (1877), and to the State Senate (1890); was a frequent delegate to the Republican National Convention (1884-1912); was chairman of the county Republican Committee, and the avowed political boss of Pittsburgh.

His firm, Booth & Flinn, Ltd., received many public contracts for parks, buildings, and repavement of streets. The color of the stone in Flinn's quarries was specified for public buildings; the kind of asphalt he owned was specified for paving the public roads.

A CELEBRATION IN 1888. The occasion: the opening of the Cyclorama showing the great Civil War Battle of Gettysburg.

The Place: Federal Street in Allegheny in front of the half-finished Carnegie Free Library and the Allegheny Market House.

It was the twenty-fifth anniversary of the Battle of Gettysburg and the people of Pittsburgh and Allegheny flocked to see the giant pictorial presentation of that tragic battle, which was fought in the State of Pennsylvania the first three days of July 1863.

In the center of this contemporary snapshot, one can observe, between the uncompleted Carnegie library building and the Old Market House, a 100-foot-high light tower. Four carbon arc lights were mounted on the top of the tower, brought from Detroit in order to illuminate the streets of Allegheny. But alas, in spite of all efforts, the lights did not work. One could throw the switch, one could bang the coverings, one could adjust the arcs—they only flickered, then went out. So there was nothing they could do but give up.

but one of the capitals of American big business. In 1880 the Pittsburgh Clearing House reported $786,694,231 clearings, which rose to $1,615,641,592 in 1900. What it lacked was culture. Even its most ardent admirers admitted it. "Business was the chief concern of the majority and it promoted a solid, orthodox, materialistic attitude to life," noted Elizabeth Moorhead when she reminisced about the eighties. It was a workshop and cared little about anything else.

The life of the Pittsburgher was mainly work. The steel hand, at his post twelve hours or more a day, enduring the heat and noise of the mill, was too exhausted to do anything in the evening but fall into bed. He was too tired to read a book, and performances in the Grand Opera House, the Academy of Music, or in the theatres, like the Alvin, the Bijoux or the Duquesne, were outside his reach. Lectures were of interest only to those who spoke and understood English and who had the education to follow the discourse of the speaker. Thus, if the worker wanted to relax, he sought out the bars and saloons where he could bury his troubles in drink. There were saloons in profusion; Pittsburgh was always a "drinkingest town."

And though the lack of cultural life was bemoaned, these were the decades of the city's intellectual awakening. It was in these years that libraries, art and science museums were built; it was in these years that the great

PITTSBURGH CORRESPONDENTS pose on June 2, 1889, in Johnstown, where they reported on the flood (on the right) which took the lives of 3000 people.

In the group are J. Hampton Moore, who later became a congressman and mayor of Philadelphia; James Francis Burke, later a congressman; Alexander P. Moore; Charles Edward Russell, Parker Walters; A. S. McSwigan; J. B. Johnston; John B. Reynolds; S. F. Kerr; W. S. Power; Jack Murray; John B. Curley; Samuel Andrews; Alfred R. Cratty; Charles Vaughan; Bent Moore; Harry McCormick; and George Thornburg. All the men—save Hampton Moore and John B. Curley—were reporters representing Pittsburgh newspapers.

Carnegie Technical Schools, the present Carnegie Institute of Technology, came into being.

In 1890 Andrew Carnegie offered a million dollars for the erection of a library building. (He had in 1886 already donated a library to the city of Allegheny, the first of the 1946 free libraries erected in the country. When it opened in 1895, Carnegie, at the suggestion of William J. Holland, then Chancellor of the University, enlarged his donation, giving additional funds for a museum and art gallery, technical school and other departments. Before all his cultural projects were completed, the steelman's contributions had reached the staggering total of $36,000,000.

The little Scotchman was inordinately proud of his achievements. He wrote to William Gladstone, Queen Victoria's celebrated Prime Minister:

Pittsburgh is the smokiest place in the world; your Sheffield is clean in comparison. It has never been anything but a center of materialism: has never had a fine hall for music, nor a museum, nor an art gallery, nor public library, and yet the result proves that there has been lying dormant the capacity to enjoy all of these.

By 1896 the Pittsburgh Orchestra, under the baton of Frederick Archer, had begun regular concerts in the library building's music hall. In November of that year, the same building saw the first International Art Exhibition, an event that has been regularly repeated until the present.

These decades also saw the founding of learned societies—the Historical Society in 1879, the Botanical Society in 1886, the Academy of Science and Art in 1890.

Other millionaires of the city awakened to their social responsibilities and made sizeable contributions for the improvements of Pittsburgh's cultural life. William Thaw, Henry C. Frick supported the Allegheny Observatory, founded in 1860; Henry Phipps gave a Conservatory to the city in 1893; Christopher L. Magee and his partners in the Fort Pitt Traction Company built a zoo in Highland Park, stocked it with animals and presented it to the people of Pittsburgh in 1898.

Social conscience stirred the middle class too. Women entered the political arena, battling for reforms. Settlement houses, like Jane Addams' Hull House in Chicago, became a cultural and inspirational center for the humanitarian movement. In Pittsburgh, Kate McKnight, a pioneer for social improvements, founded the Civic Club in 1895, which fought for children's playgrounds, for a child labor association, for juvenile courts, for a hospital of contagious disease, and other worthy causes.

The Social Gospel Movement attempted to put the teaching of Christ to work in everyday life. It had many adherents in the city. The Rev. George Hodges of Calvary Episcopal Church founded Kingsley House in 1894, dedicating it to social work with the poor. He and Father Sheedy of St. Mary's Roman Catholic Church worked assiduously to build a bridge between the East End, where the wealthy lived, and the Point, the home of the poor. Dr. Hodges organized free Sunday afternoon concerts for workers at Exposition Hall; he also set up a day nursery for children of working mothers, which Mrs. Henry C. Frick financed. There is a story that one day when Mrs. Frick was to visit the place and not all the beds were filled, Dr. Hodges and his helpers scurried into the homes of

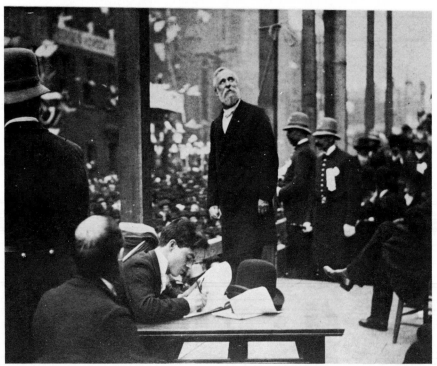

From the collection of Stefan Lorant.

RUTHERFORD B. HAYES, President of the United States from 1877 to 1881, visited Pittsburgh on September 24, 1888, to dedicate the Allegheny County Courthouse. The busy young man taking notes in the foreground is James Francis Burke, who later became Congressman from Pennsylvania (1905-15) and who was an influential figure in Republican National Conventions from 1892 on.

Photograph by Frank E. Bingaman.

THE AMERICUS REPUBLICAN CLUB, organized in Pittsburgh in 1884, usually traveled to Washington to attend presidential inaugurations. In 1885 and 1893 the men marched somewhat reluctantly in the parades for the Democratic President Gro-ver Cleveland, but in all the others they cheered heartily for a Republican winner—whether it was Benjamin Harrison, Theodore Roosevelt, or William Howard Taft.

This group picture of the organization was taken in the capital city. In the front row of the photograph one recognizes John B. Barlow (fourth from left), David W. Collingwood, General A. J. Logan, Dr. W. H. English, Captain John A. Reed, A. J. Roenigk, W. S. Colville, George S. Houghton, H. D. W. English, Harry S. Paul.

the neighborhood to borrow babies for the beds.

If one looks at this era one is bewildered by its vast extremes and contradictions. On the one side the worship of material values, vulgarity, crudeness and graft; on the other side the planting of libraries, museums and schools. On the one side man treating his fellow men harshly and without compassion, on the other side man raising the standard of living, making goods and services that for-merly were luxuries available to everyone. On the one side the entrepreneurs—haughty, imperious, arrogant—on the other side labor—overworked, underpaid, rebel-lious. In *The Age of Big Business* Burton Hendrick gives an apt single-sentence definition of the times: "It was an era of ruthlessness, of personal selfishness, of corruption, of disregard of private rights, of contempt for laws and legislature, yet of vast and beneficial achievement."

A FIRE COMPANY IN 1888—and what a company it was. There they pose, with all their machinery, before their home on Seventh Avenue.

The men, from left to right: John Herr, John Cul-hane, John Groetzinger, Thomas Fierst, Patrick Graham, Charles Woods, William Guntz, William McKelvey, Dan Barker, James Young, and Thomas Pritchard. Standing in the center is Chief John Steel.

Chapter 6

PROBLEMS OF LABOR

by Henry David

MORE GOODS and greater wealth are the obvious fruits of industrialization. Less immediately and readily visible are the changes it sets in motion in the very social fabric of a community. The Pittsburgh district, like other American communities which underwent the process, experienced alterations in its power structure, social relationships, values, living habits, and in still other respects. An observer described Pittsburgh as a community of violent contrasts: "First Prince, then Pauper; overwork, then underwork; high wages, no wages; millionaire, immigrant; militant unions, masterful employers; marvellous business organization, amazing social disorganization." The city and its industrial satellites had, of course, become acutely vulnerable to fluctuations in the economic climate. In good years, there was a sense of buoyant optimism and headlong rush. In bad years, the air of despair was as oppressive as the pall of smoke which blanketed the district when the furnaces and mills were going full blast. Charitable organizations and civic relief committees could do relatively little to minimize the price in human suffering exacted by severe unemployment during depression years.

In no aspect of the Pittsburgh district's life were many of the social and economic implications of industrialization more clearly manifested than in relations between workers and employers. Not only were most workers subject to the virtually absolute power of their employers late in the nineteenth century, but many of them had a constant struggle to make ends meet, and a significant minority lived in the shadow of poverty. However, there were working-class families which owned their own homes and lived in modest comfort. Moreover, many more did not view themselves as badly off, and, by contemporary standards, managed to maintain an adequate physical existence. It is revealing that British immigrants working in the iron and steel mills were earning more than they would have in England, but they also complained that they were compelled to work much harder in the United States. In his study, *British Immigrants in Industrial America*, Rowland Tappan Berthoff reports one immigrant as declaring, "I am quite a different man here; I can do more work; I feel that I have it in me, but . . . I shall be done in ten years."

The workman was at the crest of his life when he was thirty; by the time he reached thirty-five his strength began to decline. A fifty-year-old worker was a rarity; most of the workers died earlier.

Iron masters, big businessmen, and financiers amassed vast fortunes, and it seemed that as the rich grew richer, the poor remained poor. A Carnegie made millions from his mills. In the closing years of the 1890s, the profits of Carnegie Steel soared to new heights: $11.5 million in 1898 and $21 million in 1899. And in the single year of 1900, Carnegie's personal profit from his enterprises were reported to come to no less than $25 million. In the same year the average hourly wage of the unskilled millhand was 15 cents.

In spite the efforts of a handful of "militant unions," it was the "masterful employer" who dominated the Pittsburgh scene, and his characteristic posture toward his employees—like that of his counterpart elsewhere in the United States—was shaped essentially by narrow and shortsighted considerations of labor costs. He wanted to pay his workers as little as possible and get as much as

(turn to page 209)

208

he could out of them. Their safety and health were at best of minor concern to him. The determination of wages, hours, and working conditions was his affair.

In iron and steel, the characteristic mill owner would not, if he could avoid it, bargain with a union of his employees, which he regarded as an encroachment on his prerogatives. Only when he had no alternative, or when he found it a means of keeping his competitors in line, was he willing to entertain the thought of signing a trade agreement. The union was his natural enemy, and for him membership in the union was an adequate cause for discharging the employee. There were some employers, however, who seemed disposed to tolerate the existence of small, local unions at the plant level—Andrew Carnegie was among them—as long as they were not affiliated with national organizations, did not infringe upon management's province, and did not resort to the strike.

Only the highly skilled workers could use their strategic position in the manufacturing process to limit the power of their employers through either collective or individual bargaining. In iron and steel, however, technological advances served to undermine their relatively advantageous position even before 1890, and the rapid improvements which came in the last decade of the century further reduced their strategic importance. Vulnerable to unemployment, occupational accident and disease, and ill health, workers had to meet the frequently heavy costs imposed by these industrial hazards out of their own limited resources.

Between the highly skilled and the unskilled workers in the iron and steel industry, for example, there were striking differences in economic status, organization, and, consequently, industrial power. When it was at the peak of its strength in 1890 and 1891, the Amalgamated Association of Iron and Steel Workers of America represented the quite remarkable gains in union recognition and collective bargaining which skilled workers had been able to secure. In order to protect the relatively high earnings and other advantages which its members enjoyed, the Amalgamated Association sought to limit output, but did not resist the introduction of improved technology— because wages were based on tonnage rates—and opposed reductions in the length of the workday and the work week for many occupations. Furthermore, it did not admit all categories of semi-skilled workers to mem-

THE FACE OF LABOR. Iron carriers at the Eliza Blast Furnace photographed in 1880. They worked in 12-hour shifts, earning on the average two dollars a day. Most of them were young; many of the mills would not take men who were older than 40.

Courtesy E. E. Moore, U.S. Steel Corporation

THE HOMESTEAD STEEL WORKS, ten miles east of Pittsburgh, one of the largest steel-producing companies in the world, gave employment to 30,000 men. In 1892 the plant's wage contract with the Amalgamated Association of Iron and Steel Workers of America expired. Henry Clay Frick, who managed the works for the Carnegie interests, asked the eight lodges of the Amalgamated Association to submit a new wage scale.

In a conference on June 23 between management and steel workers, three issues were discussed—the minimum selling price of steel, upon which the quarterly sliding scale was to be based; the termination date of the new contract; and the tonnage rates for the open-hearth plants and 32-inch and 119-inch mills, which was to affect immediately the wages of some 325 workers.

Frick was ready to break the union. He hired 300 Pinkerton guards "for service at a Homestead mill as a measure of precaution against interference with our plan to start operation of the works on July 6, 1892." With this the troubles began.

bership until 1897 and continued to exclude common laborers until 1911.

The history of the Pittsburgh area is studded with labor disputes—many of them bitterly contested and of long duration—over questions of wages, hours, working conditions, and union recognition. The first "turnout," (the contemporary name for strike), is reported to have taken place as early as 1799, when shoemakers in Allegheny County stopped work in order to secure higher wages. The shoemakers went on strike again in 1804 when the masters raised the weekly boarding fee of the apprentices from $1.50 to $2.25. In the aftermath of the War of 1812, when prices skyrocketed, the journeymen shoemakers—known as cordwainers—who had organized a permanent trade union in Pittsburgh in 1809, called a strike, asking for a raise to be able to meet the increased cost of living. The masters not only refused to entertain the demand, but members of the society were brought to trial for conspiracy in two cases in 1814 and 1815. In the second trial the attempt by the cordwainers "society" to raise wages and establish a closed shop was held by the court to be unlawful and "prejudicial to the community," because it was a conspiracy "to compel an employer to hire a certain description of persons" and "to compel men to work at certain prices." This was not exceptional, for until the 1840s, courts in the United States, on the basis of the English common law doctrines of conspiracy, frequently held that it was illegal for workers to combine to fix the price of their labor. (It took almost a hundred years before the Supreme Court affirmed in the National Labor Relations Act of 1937 that an employer is not allowed to prevent his workers from organizing or to refuse to bargain with them collectively.)

A variety of craft workers were involved in industrial disputes during the following decades. Pittsburgh carpenters struck in 1829, and shoemakers walked out in 1835. Boilers in the rolling mills lost their strike against wage cuts in 1842, but won another three years later.

The early strikes were relatively peaceful. But after the steady growth and expansion of industries in the forties and fifties, the conflicts between employers and workers became sharper. Labor was suffering under adverse conditions. Working hours were long, eleven hours on the average during the winter months and about fourteen hours during the summer. Store clerks had to stay on their jobs twelve to eighteen hours daily with ten-minute breaks for meals.

Wages were painfully low. Girls in the cotton factories made $2.50 for a full week's work, and the pay for men in the steel mills, working six and even seven days, was between $9 and $14. There were a number of strikes by workers in iron and coal before the Civil War, in order to remedy low wages and wage cuts. The first serious attempt to form a union of the iron workers occurred after the Panic of 1857, when wage reductions prompted a group of puddlers organize themselves into a union, calling themselves the "Sons of Vulcan." After the outbreak of the Civil War, they reorganized themselves into the "Grand Vulcan." In 1862 this union became a national organization under the name "National Forge." Growth was slow. By 1868 the Forge had only 600 members; by 1873 the number grew to 3331 in eighty-three lodges.

In 1859 the bituminous coal miners in the Monongahela Valley were in a bitter struggle to secure scales at the pits for weighing their output. They were on strike again in 1864, and once more the next year.

A lockout by employers of puddlers who had demanded a wage increase in 1865 was settled by arbitration, marking the first time in the history of the country that a labor dispute was resolved in that manner.

Labor disputes and strikes after the Civil War became frequent. Two of the greatest ones—the Railroad Strike of 1877 and the Homestead Strike of 1892—transcended state boundaries. Their importance was nationwide, and they produced wide-ranging economic and political repercussions. Both strikes were marked by violence; both raised specters of rebellion; both received international attention.

The railroad strike was precipitated by severe wage cuts, but behind that conflict there was also a history of miserable conditions and the ruthless use of power. Before the upheaval ended in August, the country had experienced its first general strike movement; railway centers from New York to California had been hit; pitched battles had been fought; over one hundred workmen had lost their lives; property worth millions had been destroyed; thousands of militia had been called out; federal troops had been used for the first time during peace to put down a strike; and Pittsburgh had been terrorized by rioting more violent and destructive than any since the Civil War draft riots in New York City.

The strike shook the nation like a raging storm and left in its wake a preview of the issues vividly posed by the Homestead riots. This conflict, which pitted a powerful and disciplined union against a giant combination, could have occurred only in the Pittsburgh area. It was the fruit, bitter and incredible, of circumstances, personalities, and problems shaped by the newly grown, but massive, iron and steel industry.

With some justice one historian spoke of the Homestead Strike as a "titanic struggle, which, marked . . . with all the ferocity of a civil war, caused a shudder to run through the civilized world." One suspects that a producer of grade-B thrillers would turn it down as the subject for a film, on the score that much of it would be too improbable for even the most gullible movie-goer. For a faithful screen treatment would have to depict an amphibious landing operation attempted by two boats carrying armed Pinkerton guards resisted by armed strikers in a day-long engagement, in which cannon, dynamite, and burning oil were used, 300 Pinkertons compelled to walk the gauntlet between ranks of infuriated strikers and their families, the calling out of every regiment of Pennsylvania militia, a young anarchist's attempt to assassinate the head of the Carnegie Steel Company, Ltd.; a militiaman being strung up by the thumbs as punishment

Harper's Weekly, July 18, 1892.

THE BATTLE OF THE BARGES. As the two barges towed by the steamer *Little Bill*, with the 300 armed Pinkertons, reached Homestead at four o'clock in the morning on July 6, the striking steelworkers were ready for them.

They fired at the barges with small cannons, they hurled dynamite sticks against them, they poured oil in the river and lit it, they shot at the Pinkertons with revolvers and rifles, they threw stones. The battle went on the whole day. The Pinkertons

were unable to land. At four in the afternoon, they were exhausted, ready to give up. They were allowed to land, surrender their arms, and assured that they could leave the place in peace. As they came ashore, the strikers set the barges on fire.

for applauding this act; the arrest on charges of murder and riot of almost 170 strikers; the indictment of thirty-three strike leaders for treason against the State of Pennsylvania; the poisoning of strikebreakers.

Homestead, located about a mile below Braddock's Crossing on the Monongahela, was a town of 600 in 1879, when the Bessemer steel plant, which determined its future destiny, was built there. In 1892, its population rose to about 8000, and a third of that number were working in the mills. It had the vitality of all steel towns, and also their characteristic ugly drabness and squalor. Hamlin Garland later spoke of its "horrible" streets, "poor" buildings, "soot and dirt." Its saloons were many, and its club- and reading-rooms few. Charles B. Spahr, who visited Homestead after the strike, described it as "an unattractive town," but pointed out that its "private houses—except the shanties on the company grounds occupied by the strike-breakers in 1892—were much better than those of the mining towns, and the schools were in the happiest possible contrast. The buildings were good and the teachers competent."

Long hours of exhausting labor defined the lives of its steel workers, and all of them knew that mill accidents were frequent and could reduce a man and his family to grim poverty, to say nothing of killing him.

The workers in the mills during this period were mainly Irish and Anglo-Saxon origin. The great migration that was to fill the Pittsburgh area with a multitude of southern and eastern Europeans had not yet reached its full strength. But within a decade the largest contingents in the mills were the *Hunkies*—a descriptive term that included not only Hungarians, but Slavs, Croats, Greeks, Poles, and other nationalities as well.

"They were pouring in by thousands," reflected the steelman in Marcia Davenport's novel, *The Valley of Decision*, "almost swamping the market at slow times, helping to turn out phenomenal quantities of steel when business swung upwards, their sweated wages undercutting the hard-fought scale of the Amalgamated and all the old-established Irish and Scotch and native men. They held no skilled jobs."

In Europe these people had earned what amounted in the New World to about twenty-five cents a day; in the Pittsburgh mills their wage was fifteen cents for the hour. Thus they made in a day seven times as much as formerly in their old country. It was natural that they were content with what they believed was a large income.

The Irish and the Scottish, who held the skilled posts in the mills, gradually gave up their jobs, not because of the newcomers, but because of the hard conditions. They worked a daily twelve-hour shift, often seven days a week without any rest. Thus, as they were able to make a better living by taking jobs in other industries, there was no reason for them to stay in the steel mills, even though their wages were satisfactory. (A heater made on the average $5.65 a day, and a roller—the best paid man of the

entire working force—could earn as much as $11 a day.)

The great grievance of the steel hands was that work was never steady. The average working days in the year amounted to no more than 270. For two or three months every year the men were idle and without pay.

On the whole, the accepted regular working day was twelve hours. In 1886—six years before the Homestead strike—Andrew Carnegie wrote in *The Forum*:

At present every ton of pig iron made in the world, except at two establishments [meaning the Lucy and Isabella furnaces in Pittsburgh, owned by the Carnegie Company], is made by men working in double shifts of twelve hours each, having neither Sunday nor holiday the year round. Every two weeks the men change to the night shift by working twenty-four hours consecutively.

A steelworker exclaimed: "Home is just the place where I eat and sleep. I live in the mills." His night shift often lasted as long as fourteen hours, depending upon the arrangements he had made with his buddy.

If working conditions were poor, living conditions were not much better. The lucky worker who lived with his family in a comfortable and cleanly furnished company house with running water but no bathroom paid a rent of $11 a month, to which he had to add $1.50 for utilities.

Some families made the supreme effort of buying a house. The company made loans to them, as their settling down meant the stabilization of the working force. But the majority of the steel hands lived in rickety shanties, ramshackle cottages, filthy, overcrowded tenements with primitive sanitation and toilet facilities. Single men stayed in crowded lodging houses, some of which had as many as twenty boarders.

As the unskilled worker's average pay was about twelve to fifteen dollars a week, he was not able to save; he needed every penny for rent, food, fuel, clothing, and other necessities. If some money happened to be left over, it was usually spent in the saloons. Drinking was considered a remedy for cutting the grime and dust from the throat.

To improve their lot, skilled workers in iron and steel had finally fashioned a strong union in 1876 out of several existing organizations—the Amalgamated Association of Iron and Steel Workers of America. At its peak on the eve of the Homestead Strike, it had almost 300 lodges and dues-paying membership of over 24,000. At that time, the organized labor movement in the United States numbered about 400,000. The Amalgamated accounted for almost one tenth of the membership in the American Federation of Labor, was one of its larger affiliates, and had organized about a fourth of the skilled workers in the industry. It had won recognition from many employers, had developed a system of wage conferences with the manufacturers, and had negotiated elaborate collective agreements, which some employers viewed with favor as a stabilizing factor in a competitive and rapidly changing industry. A successful strike in 1889 by Amalgamated lodges in the steel plant at

Homestead had won an advantageous three-year contract.

Andrew Carnegie had been an important iron producer before he took part in founding the Edgar Thomson Steel Company, the Pittsburgh district's first Bessemer steel plant. This was only one step in a series of expansions, acquisitions (the Homestead mill was picked up in 1883), and company reorganizations which culminated, in July 1892, in Carnegie Steel Company, Ltd. This enormous industrial combination—then the largest steel company in the world—in the form of a limited partnership was capitalized at $25 million, and gave employment to over 30,000 workers. It was also the biggest coke producer in the country. It embraced, in addition to coal, coke, and iron ore properties, the Edgar Thomson Works at Braddock, the Duquesne Steel Works, the Homestead Steel Works, the Beaver Fall Mills; and, in Pittsburgh proper, the Lucy Furnaces, the Keystone Bridge Company, and the Upper and Lower Union Mills.

Carnegie held majority control in the new company— 55.3 per cent—but its direction lay in the hands of the forty-one-year-old Henry Clay Frick, who controlled four-fifths of the coal business in the Connellsville district and whose remarkable managerial capacities were repeatedly demonstrated both before and after his association with Carnegie. In its first year, Carnegie steel, in spite of the six-month strike at Homestead and work stoppages in other plants, produced 877,602 tons of steel, accounting for one fifth of the entire steel output in the United States. Profits for the year amounted to $4 million.

A new wage scale and other issues formed the basis for extended negotiations between the Amalgamated Association of Iron and Steel Workers and the management of the Homestead works, but the clash between the two actually turned on the question of union recognition. Carnegie wanted the plant to go non-union when the existing contract expired on June 30, 1892. Homestead was the only one of the three major steel works owned by Carnegie that was unionized. Carnegie had publicly praised the dignity and significance of manual labor, and he had urged that workers should be given a larger share of the wealth they helped produce. He represented himself as a friend of labor and of collective bargaining. He assailed strikebreaking as sinful, and even declared that the Decalogue might be improved by adding to it, "Thou Shalt Not Take Thy Neighbor's Job!" Yet he never displayed any sympathy with effective unions in big mills.

Two months before the contract between the Homestead plant and the Amalgamated was to expire, Carnegie drafted a notice addressed to the workers of Homestead which he submitted to Frick. This notice argued that the formulation of Carnegie Steel compelled its management to pursue a uniform policy toward union recognition. "As the vast majority of our employees are Non-Union," it read, "the firm has decided that the minority must give way to the majority. These works will necessarily be Non-Union after the expiration of the present agreement."

Frick was not overtly committed to this policy, but he was prepared to risk a showdown with the union.

Writing from Scotland, Carnegie pressed Frick to resist union recognition even at the price of a strike. The building of a three-mile fence topped by barbed wire around the Homestead plant and his inquiry about the availability of Pinkerton men for guard duty in the event of a strike early indicated his readiness to resist the Amalgamated's pressure for a new, long-term contract. Frick was accused of deliberately precipitating the upheaval while Carnegie, away at Europe, was looked upon as a friend of labor.

In his prose poem on Homestead, Haniel Long had Henry Phipps remark: "We his partners were of the opinion that the welfare of the company required he should not be in this country at this time. We knew of his extreme disposition to always grant the demands of labor, and all rejoiced we were permitted to manage the affair in our way." Frick later told a Senate investigating committee that, "We wanted men with whom we could deal individually. We did not propose to deal with the Amalgamated Association."

The last conference between management and the union ended in a stalemate in June 23. In this conference three main issues were discussed, (1) the minimum selling price of steel for determining the quarterly sliding scale; (2) the termination date of the new contract; and (3) the tonnage rates for the open-hearth plants, and 32-inch and 119-inch mills, which would immediately affect the wages of 325 workers. The conference produced no positive results and two days later the union was informed that no more meetings would be held. At the same time, Frick placed an order for 300 Pinkerton guards to be delivered with "absolute secrecy" to Homestead. On June 28, the armor

Drawing by Charles Mente in "Harper's Weekly", July 16, 1892.

AS THE SURRENDERED PINKERTON MEN marched between the lines of the enraged strikers and their families the excitement of the workers mounted; the pledge to allow the Pinkertons to move away in peace was forgotten; the strikers threw themselves on the surrendered men and let their anger flow.

plate mill in the open-hearth department was shut down and 800 men were locked out. The Amalagamated lodges responded by calling a mass meeting, and the 3000 workers who attended made it clear that they were ready for a strike. The conduct of the walkout was made the responsibility of an advisory committee headed by Hugh O'Donnell, and precautions were promptly taken to prevent the importation of strikebreakers. It was remarkable that the entire force acted with such unanimity in defense of the union, when only 325 men were directly involved in the dispute over the contract. By the end of June, the entire labor force at Homestead was discharged. By July 2, everyone was paid off but promptly invited to sign individual contracts as a condition for being rehired. No one accepted the offer, and, even after the strike had dragged on for two months, only 300 men had capitulated and returned to work.

On July 6, the strikers discovered that two barges carrying the detested Pinkerton agents were being towed up the Monongahela to Homestead. A furious battle ensued when the Pinkertons attempted to land, and a truce was arranged by the union leaders to permit them to come ashore in safety and be escorted out of Homestead. The truce was violated by enraged strikers and their wives, who administered a brutal beating to the Pinkertons. Ten strikers and three Pinkertons lost their lives during the day, and many were wounded by gunfire or otherwise injured.

The dramatic and violent events of July 6 thrust the strike upon the attention of the nation. Other developments fixed it there. On the order of Governor Robert E. Pattison, who had not responded to earlier pleas for help, the entire militia force of the state—8000 officers and men—began to march on Homestead. Troops occupied the town on July 12, and the last of them did not leave until October 13. Sympathy strikes broke out in other Carnegie Steel plants. The use of Pinkerton and other private police became the subject of debate and committee hearings in both houses of the Congress.

The responsible press attacked Frick for hiring Pinkertons to subdue the workers. The Chicago *Globe* said that the Pinkertons were no better than hired assassins who were "not entitled to the privileges of civilized warfare". And the Pittsburgh *Leader* declared that Carnegie's sense of social responsibility, expressed in his *Forum* articles, was "extinct as a dodo." The Populist platform of 1892—it was a presidential election year—spoke of the "hireling standing army, unrecognized by our laws, which has been established to shoot down workers."

And Frick told an interviewer of the Pittsburgh *Post* a day after the battle: "I can say with greatest emphasis that under no circumstances will we have any further dealings with the Amalgamated Association as an organization. This is final."

On July 23, Alexander Berkman, a twenty-five-year-old revolutionary anarchist, a disciple of Emma Goldman,

moved by the strikers' heroism and the theory of propaganda by deed, attempted to assassinate Frick.

Meanwhile the strikers stood firm. They received support, and contributions of money and food from workers and others throughout the country, who were touched by their courage and offended by the conduct of Frick and Carnegie. Leaders of the Social Gospel Movement in the Protestant churches tried to clarify the issues involved. Voices were heard in Congress defending the strikers and condemning the arbitrary power of capital and the employment of private police. True, the cries were louder that the lawless acts of the strikers on July 6 struck at the very pillars of the nation and demanded the severest punishment. As the strike dragged on, the workers' hopes for victory diminished. On November 20, the strike collapsed.

Haniel Long put the blame on Carnegie:

Ben Butler wanted Carnegie extradited for murder.
General Grosvenor called him the archsnake of this age.
A London paper said: "Here we have this Scotch-Yankee plutocrat meandering through Scotland in a four-in-hand opening public libraries, while the wretched workmen who supply him with ways and means for his self-glorification are starving in Pittsburgh."
A St. Louis paper said: "Say what you will of Frick, he is a brave man. Say what you will of Carnegie, he is a coward. And gods and men hate cowards."

The fighting at Homestead made Americans realize that there was a serious industrial problem which cried for solution. Homestead illuminated economic, social, political, and ethical issues which could no longer be hidden. Its immediate effect upon the larger labor movement was to give it a sense of unity around a common cause that it had never quite attained before. Its impact upon unionism in iron and steel, however, was almost catastrophic. The failure of the workers at Homestead virtually broke the back of unionism in the steel industry. The Amalgamated lost 5000 members by the close of 1892 and another 7000 next year. Determined anti-unionism distinguished the industry, and while the Amalgamated maintained some strength among iron workers, the strike that it called against the greatest industrial combination of the day, the United States Steel Corporation, in 1901 was a fiasco. Eight years later it lost a fourteen-month struggle against the same foe, and was driven from its plants. Not until 1919 was there a vigorous organizing and strike movement in the industry.

In Homestead itself, unionism, for practical purposes, had been interdicted. After the strike, reported Charles B. Spahr in *America's Working People*, "It was not the lowering of wages that caused the most bitter complaints among the men. Their wages, even when lowered, were not low, and most of them realized it. Their real grievances were the long hours, the Sunday labor, the strain under which they were compelled to work, and above all—or rather at the basis of all—the want of freedom to organize. Nobody in Homestead dared openly to join a trade union. The president [of Carnegie Steel] said, without reserve, that he would discharge any man for this offence, and the men all

Drawing by W. P. Snyder in Harper's Weekly, July 16, 1892.

THE MOB SCENE AT HOMESTEAD AFTER THE PINKERTONS GAVE UP

understood that this was the foundation principle of the present order. . . . The Union movement, to all appearances, was dead except in the hopes of the workmen."

Not until the great steel strike of 1919 was a public labor meeting permitted in Homestead, and another seventeen years went by before another labor gathering was held. This second meeting in 1936 marked not only the memory of the strikers who had died forty-four years earlier, but also the new union drive in steel. And the chairman of the gathering offered a prayer for the success of the militant effort to organize the industry: "Let the blood of those labor pioneers who were massacred here be the seed of the new organization in 1936, may the souls of the martyrs rest in peace."

The failure of the Homestead strike alone, however, does not explain the virtual collapse of unionism in iron and steel between the close of the nineteenth century and

the 1930's. Other developments followed on its heels which served to weaken unionism in the industry and crown with success the repressive labor policies of management. The long depression which followed the panic of 1893 meant a flooded labor market in which the unemployed competed for a reduced number of jobs and which undercut the ground from attempts to bargain collectively. Continuing improvements in technology made possible the utilization of unskilled workers who comprised three fifths of the work force in steel by the opening of the twentieth century. The flood of immigrants provided abundant supplies of relatively cheap labor from central and eastern Europe whose differences in language and religion, combined with national and ethnic rivalries, were obstacles to organization.

Moreover, through the formation of the United States Steel Corporation in 1901, the economic power which shaped and dominated the anti-union policies of the industry was concentrated in one firm. Thus, John A Fitch could write in *The Steelworkers*:

> That there has come about a reversal in relations between employer and employe in the steel industry is apparent. Before 1901 there was a national union which dealt with individual employers. Now here is one great corporation whose negative action, at least, practically fixes standards for the whole industry. This national corporation deals not even with local associations; it deals with individual workmen. In former years the Amalgamated Association had some advantage over employers because the latter were not organized... Now,... there is practically no bar to the domination of the employers ... today conditions are practically uniform in all steel mills, under the absolute and unregulated control of the employers.

This finding was reconfirmed a decade later by the Commission of Inquiry of the Interchurch World Movement in its *Report on the Steel Strike of 1919*. "Whatever the [U.S.] Steel Corporation does," concluded the Commission, "the rest of the industry will ultimately do; whatever modifications of policy fail to take place in the industry fail because of the opposition of the Steel Corporation."

It is not surprising that between the Homestead strike and 1907–8, the tonnage rates and, in some cases, the daily earnings of skilled workers declined, in spite of a longer working day. While the wages of unskilled laborers increased over that decade and a half, they did not go up enough to keep pace with rising living costs. Working conditions appear to have worsened during this period, and an investigator for the Russell Sage Foundation reported:

> The common laborer in and around the mills works seventy-two hours a week. The unit of wages is an hour rate for day labor and a Slav is willing to take the longer hours (twelve hours a day for men who work fourteen and sixteen in the fatherland) with extra work on Sundays, especially in connection with clearing the yards and repairing. Possibly sixty to seventy per cent of the laborers in the mills come out Sundays... the mechanics and other laborers on occasions work thirty-six hours in order that the plant may start on time... Many work in intense heat, the din of machinery and the noise of escaping steam. The congested condition of most of the plants in Pittsburgh adds to the physical discomforts for an out-of-doors people; while their ignorance of language and of modern machinery increases the risk. How many of the Slavs, Lithuanians and Italians are injured in Pittsburgh in one year is not known. No reliable statistics are compiled. In their absence people guess.... When I mentioned a plant that had a bad reputation to a priest, he said, "Oh, that is a slaughter-house; they kill them there every day." I quote him not for accuracy, but to show how the rumors circulate and are real to the people themselves.

What industrialization meant in broad terms to the working people and their lives in the Pittsburgh district was thus summed up in *The Pittsburgh Survey*, when the field work for this important study ended in 1908:

I. An altogether incredible amount of overwork by everybody, reaching its extreme in the twelve-hour shift for seven days in the week in the steel mills and the railway switchyards.

II. Low wages for the great majority of the laborers employed by the mills, not lower than in other large cities, but low compared with prices,—so low as to be inadequate to the maintenance of a normal American standard of living; wages adjusted to the single man in the lodging house, not to the responsible head of a family.

III. Still lower wages for women, who receive, for example, in one of the metal trades, in which the proportion of women is great enough

to be menacing, one-half as much as unorganized men in the same shops and one-third as much as the men in the union.

IV. An absentee capitalism, with bad effects strikingly analogous to those of absentee landlordism ...

V. A continuous inflow of immigrants with low standards, attracted by a wage which is high by the standards of southeastern Europe ...

VI. The destruction of family life, not in any imaginary or mystical sense, but by the demands of the day's work, and by the very demonstrable and material method of typhoid fever and industrial accidents; both preventable, but costing in single years in Pittsburgh considerably more than a thousand lives, and irretrievably shattering nearly as many homes.

VII. Archaic social institutions such as the aldermanic court, the ward school district, the family garbage disposal, and the unregenerate charitable institution, still surviving after the conditions to which they were adapted have disappeared.

VIII. The contrast ... between the prosperity, on the one hand, of the most prosperous of all the communities of our western civilization, with its vast natural resources, the generous fostering of government, the human energy, the technical development, the gigantic tonnage of the mines and mills, the enormous capital of which the bank balances afford an indication; and, on the other hand, the neglect of life, of health, of physical vigor, even of the industrial efficiency, of the individual. Certainly no community before in America or Europe has ever had such a surplus, and never before has a great community applied what it had so meagerly to the rational purposes of human life. Not by gifts of libraries, galleries, technical schools, and parks, but by the cessation of toil one day in seven and sixteen hours in the twenty-four, by the increase of wages, by the sparing of lives, by the prevention of accidents, and by raising the standards of domestic life, should the surplus come back to the people of the community in which it is created.

At the time of the strike in 1892, Homestead symbolized for the nation the vast industrial power newly located in the Pittsburgh area. The fashioning of the Pittsburgh industrial complex represented a remarkable achievement. True, nature was munificent with its gifts. It offered rich stores of bituminous coal, limestone, clay, shale, oil, and natural gas. Three rivers and their tributaries facilitated cheap transportation and made iron ore readily accessible. The Monongahela River carried the tonnage of a major seaport—over 3½ million tons in 1885 and almost 12 million thirty years later. Other key factors were important in the process of rapid industrialization: a vast and growing national market; a network of railroads; capital available for investment; advances in scientific and technological knowledge; favorable governmental policies; native and immigrant labor willing to work in mine, mill, and factory.

But no less important was the group of individuals with great gifts for organizing and utilizing men, money, materials, and machines for the purposes of production. Pittsburgh's industrial growth bears the marks of their entrepreneurial qualities. They were resourceful, inventive, skillful. They shared a buoyant optimism. They seemed moved by a singleness of purpose that made them, in the eyes of some contemporaries, ruthless. They hungered after wealth, and they drove themselves and others hard to attain it.

They fashioned the Pittsburgh district, just as their fellow industrialists, financiers, and businessmen were remaking not only the economy of the nation but also the very texture of its life and its power and prestige in the world.

Stereoscope in the collection of Stefan Lorant.

THE STRIKEBREAKERS with whom the Carnegie company operated the Homestead mill after the militia restored order were housed and fed within the plant; they were living there as actual prisoners, shunned by their fellow workers, despised by the community. Only later, after the sheriff had built an adequate force of deputies and violence had subsided, did they venture out of the walls of the plant.

Stereoscope in the collection of Stefan Lorant.

"POTTERSVILLE," the housing of the strikebreakers inside the plant, was constantly besieged by angry strikers and their families.

Drawing by J. de Thulstrup in Harper's Weekly, August 6, 1892.

RESTORING ORDER. The Eighteenth Regiment arrived on July 12. The militia did not leave Homestead until October 13.

217

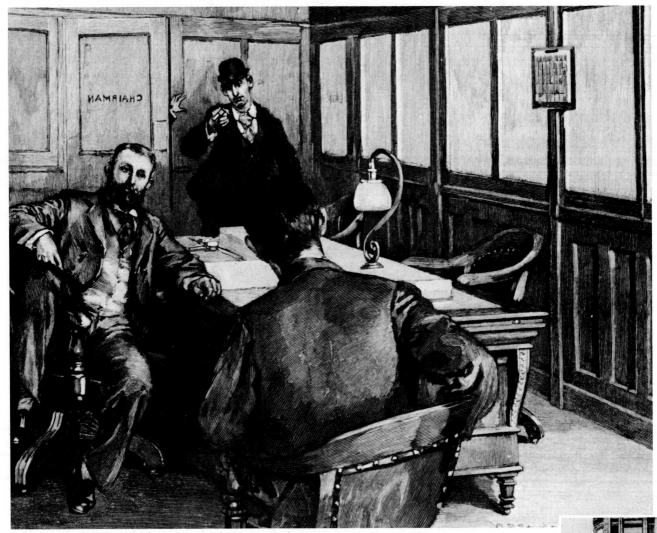

Drawn by W. P. Snyder for Harper's Weekly, *August 6, 1892.*

THE MAN WHO GOT INTO THE ACT. On July 23, 1892, the Russian-born anarchist Alexander Berkman entered Henry Clay Frick's office, hoisted his revolver and attempted to assassinate the head of the Carnegie enterprises.

Berkman had no connection with the strikers at Homestead, he did not even live in the Pittsburgh area. But moved by the strikers' determination he decided to apply the anarchist doctrine of "propaganda of the deed" and kill Frick whom he considered the cause of all the troubles.

In Haniel Long's prose poem Berkman says after entering the office of Frick:

"I find myself facing a blackbearded figure at a table in the back of the room. 'Frick,' I begin. The look of terror on his face strikes me speechless. I am at his head. He averts his face. The high-ceilinged room reverberates. I hear a sharp piercing cry and see Frick on his knees, his head against the arm of his chair. 'Dead?' I wonder. I must make sure. I crawl in the direction of the voice, dragging struggling men with me—get the dagger from my pocket —repeatedly strike with it—my arms are pulled and twisted and I am lifted bodily. My eyes meet Frick's. He stands in front of me, supported. His face is ashen grey; the black beard is streaked with red, blood is oozing from his neck. A strange feeling as of shame comes over me; but the next moment I am filled with anger at this sentiment so unworthy of a revolutionist."

Berkman's first bullet caused no damage. John G. A. Leishman, the vice-chairman of the company, threw himself at the would-be assassin and while they struggled the intruder fired again; this time the lead hit Frick in the neck. At last Berkman was overpowered.

The wounded Frick stayed in his office, resuming his work. "In the ambulance to his home in Homewood that evening," so Long continues his poem, "he dictated these words for the newspapers: 'I do not think I shall die; but whether I do or not, the company will pursue the same policy and it will win.'

"He did not die, but his baby boy, Henry Clay Frick junior, born the day of the Homestead battle, died twenty-eight days later."

Berkman was sentenced to twenty-two years, of which he served fourteen in the Western Penitentiary of Pennsylvania. After his release he played a vital role in the anarchist movement, violently opposing the entry of the United States into the first World War. Because of his activities he was arrested in the summer of 1917 and sent to prison for two years. On December 21, 1919 he was to be deported to Russia. While he was waiting for his deportation, Frick died on Dec. 2. Berkman commented wryly: "Well, anyhow he left the country before I did."

It was here on the first floor of the *Chronicle-Telegraph* building that anarchist Alexander Berkman tried to assassinate Frick.

Chapter 7

THE ENTREPRENEURS

by John Morton Blum

THE MEN who built the enterprises on which Pittsburgh thrived operated on a massive scale. The big businesses they founded and managed earned huge profits that provided the bases for great wealth, for lordly mansions, for ranging collections of exquisite art, for vast philanthropies, and for enormous reputations. Achievements of those dimensions clothed the protagonists of Pittsburgh's industries, like their counterparts elsewhere in the United States, in Olympian garments. They reigned, in the folklore of their own and later days, sometimes as wizards of frenzied finance or barons of corporate larceny, as often as the lords of creation, the emperors of American success. The dimension of the rhetoric fit the scale of the Pittsburgh experience, but it sometimes also obscured the enterprisers' actual qualities of person and mind and the strategies and structures of their accomplishments.

The titans of the folklore were in myriad ways like other men. They had their vanities, made their mistakes, suffered their doubts and failures, and their joys and triumphs, too. None was a magician, unless labor, perseverance, intuition, and pride—taken together—constitute magic. Taken together, and applied to the development of the American economy during the decades following the Civil War, those qualities did set the Pittsburgh venturers apart from ordinary men.

In that time the builders of great businesses relied in large degree on certain common insights and techniques. They shared, to begin with, an ebullient faith in the potentialities of the national market. The urban and industrial boom of the period, the ongoing growth and increasing concentration of the population created unprecedented demands for capital and consumer goods, demands whose supply in turn created further wants and means for satisfying them. Concurrently, the localisms of the economy were fading away. The completion and subsequent elaboration of the national railway network, in themselves a major source of demand, knit the country into the richest free-trade area in the world. Companion developments in communication, in the machinery for the rapid and comprehensive spread of information and ideas permitted the nation-wide dissemination of standard measures of quality and criteria of material aspiration and taste. Those entrepreneurs who recognized the scope of the market so created and so endowed, those who resolved to reach it with their products had made their first march along the road to business glory.

The march was quickened and extended by the exploitation of opportunities inherent in a burgeoning technology. The scientific advances of the previous century, continuing still, established the foundations for magnificent applications of pure knowledge to practical uses. The ensuing rush of innovations in industrial processes and equipment turned the calendar onto an age of unparalleled inventiveness and, for the daring who invested in invention, of unsurpassed profits.

The very pace of technological change, assuring the fast obsolescence of expensive plant and machinery, imposed on industry extraordinary and unavoidable expenses. To meet those costs and others and, more important, to stretch out across the national market, business units had to become big. The deliberate and bold recourse to size was in itself a major innovation, a compelling characteristic of great new enterprises. Size demanded of its masters

THE CITY IN THE NINETIES.

THE GOOD OLD DAYS when one could pose for the photographer in the middle of Penn Avenue. If the fellow at the streetcar was tired he stopped his horse and sat on the stairs of his vehicle and took it easy for a while. He felt that he

not only vision but also a capacity for organization and for selecting able associates and subordinates. Those qualities, too, the entrepreneurs shared.

They also perceived the advantages of consolidation. Competition among large business units fraught with heavy, constant costs led to disastrous instabilities of price and profit that threatened the solvency of a firm as well as the resources of its investors and the livelihood of its employees. Such competition magnified the insecurities of the business cycle. Several times during the thirty years before 1900 the cycle rose while venturers built new facilities and then dropped alarmingly when the resulting capacity produced more than the economy could for the while consume. For solving the problem of the busi-

ness cycle the men of the time knew no answer save resignation, but they did understand the shattering debilitation of unchecked competition, the wearing experience of "work by day and worry by night." Accordingly, the successful—audacious competitors when they had to be—were also, because of their worries, audacious organizers who combined under unitary control large segments of previously competitive industries. To those combinations they often added functional units that brought within one management the successive processes of extraction, transportation, manufacture, and distribution, with consequent gains in efficiency and profit. Some of the most arresting of those consolidations of wealth and power were in Pittsburgh, whose entrepreneurs, in the manner of

didn't miss a thing, and probably he didn't. The picture was taken from the corner of Penn and Frankstown Avenues looking in the direction of Negley Avenue and Blackhorse Hill. Liberty Hall and East Liberty Presbyterian Church on the left.

their type, either singly or in groups had the nerve and grasp for organization that supplemented their heightened sensitivities for the market and technology of their era.

Of those men, the most celebrated was Andrew Carnegie, steel master extraordinary—in the rhetoric of the day, King of the Vulcans. Born in Scotland in 1835, the son of a handloom weaver, Carnegie spent his boyhood in an impoverished home marked by its zealous commitment to learning and to those aspirations embedded in romantic poetry and the doctrines of liberal politics. Carnegie came with his parents in 1848 to a Scottish community in Allegheny, where he found employment as a bobbin boy and later an engine tender in a cotton factory. At fourteen, as a telegraph boy in Pittsburgh, he taught himself to dis-

tinguish transmitted letters by sound—then an unusual talent—and earned promotion to an operator's job. He met Thomas A. Scott, soon to become president of the Pennsylvania Railroad, who hired him as his personal secretary. During a dozen years with that road, Carnegie achieved the position of superintendent of the Pittsburgh division, and along the line introduced the use of sleeping cars and bought a one-eighth interest in the company holding patents for their manufacture. Personal energy, a shrewd bet on the salability of comfort to travelers, and astute ventures in the oil and iron business were paying their happy dividends before the young man was thirty.

At that age he left railroading to devote most of his time to iron, already the foremost object of his enterprising

221

THE CITY IN THE NINETIES.

THE SMITHFIELD STREET BRIDGE AT RUSH HOUR.

PENN AVENUE LOOKING EAST.

PEACEFUL SIXTH STREET AS IT LOOKED FROM DUQUESNE WAY.

YELLOW ROW AT SECOND AVENUE,

imagination. The iron industry was booming, spurred alike by the transitory demands of the Civil War and the growing needs of the railways which consumed about half the products of the finishing mills. In 1865 Carnegie organized the Keystone Bridge Company, a grander successor to Piper and Shiffler, a concern in which he already had an interest. J. L. Piper had whetted his enthusiasm for the business of replacing wooden with iron railway bridges, and to their new firm Piper contributed a sure craftmanship while Carnegie provided a vision of magnitude and a deluge of orders. An incomparable salesman—his Bobbie Burns burr and Scotch stories the hallmarks of a manner that beguiled the railroad men he had to convince —Carnegie was also bringing a volume business to the Superior Rail Mill and the Pittsburgh Locomotive Works and, partly through their orders, to the Union Iron Mills. In those three companies he was both the indispensable salesman and the most influential partner and manager.

The help he needed Carnegie found in Pittsburgh, in technicians like Piper and in partners like Henry Phipps. In its youth, Union Mills failed to command the confidence of the city's bankers. Phipps, the company's bookkeeper, a pale and gentle man, rarely venturesome but always calculating, obtained the credit necessary for the firm's survival. "What we chiefly admired about Henry Phipps," one banker later recalled, "was the way he could keep a check in the air for several days." Then one day, as Phipps remembered, "I noticed a change in our fortunes. Instead

SHADY AVENUE AT RIGHT.   THIS IS MARKET STREET, PHOTOGRAPHED FROM FOURTH AVENUE.

Contemporary photographs from the collection of Stefan Lorant.

ONE OF THE CITY'S WORST SLUMS.   FIFTH AVENUE AT LIBERTY HAD PLENTY OF CABLE TRACKS.

of my going to the banks, the banks were coming to me. I knew then that we had arrived."

Carnegie, the head conductor, reached that conclusion in 1868. "Thirty-three," he then wrote in a memorandum to himself,

and an income of $50,000 per annum! . . . Beyond this never earn . . . Settle in Oxford and get a thorough education . . . Settle then in London and purchase a controlling interest in some newspaper or live review, . . . taking a part in public matters, especially those connected with education and improvement of the poorer classes. . . . Whatever I engage in I must push inordinately. . . . To continue much longer overwhelmed by business cares and with most of my thoughts wholly upon the way to make more money in the shortest time, must degrade me beyond hope of permanent recovery. I will resign business at thirty-five.

The statement was significant not for its prediction but

for its revelations. Money in itself, while gratifying, was not enough for Carnegie, whose self-esteem and sense of social obligation together demanded the satisfactions of a gentleman's calling and a gentleman's life of service. These were the compulsions that in time bought castles in Scotland and gave fortunes for public libraries, for the pursuit of art and learning, and for the quest for permanent world peace. Carnegie knew he was a driven man who felt the weight of business worries and the fears of business failure and yet had the strength and courage to transcend them. He did not see, or perhaps would not admit, that his need to push inordinately expressed itself most naturally in business.

Not several years but several decades from retirement,

THE CITY IN THE NINETIES.

SEVENTH STREET BRIDGE

THE POST OFFICE

From Harper's Weekly June 14, 1890.
MAKING UP A TOW by searchlight—a drawing made by Charles Graham in 1890.

THE MECHANICAL HALL OF THE EXPOSITION BUILDINGS.

Carnegie by 1873 had set out on what he later recommended as the best course to success, the policy of "putting all his eggs in one basket, and then watching the basket." His basket was steel, then replacing and surpassing iron in the American market. While in England, Carnegie had met Sir Henry Bessemer, the inventor of the special furnace, or converter, which made steel by forcing a purifying blast of air through molten cast iron. The fulcrum of Great Britain's temporary supremacy in steel production, the Bessemer process had had only limited use in the United States even though Bessemer steel was ideally suited for rolling rails. Impressed somewhat belatedly by Sir Henry and by the American sponsors of his technique,

Carnegie and several of his partners erected a major steel works on Braddock's Field, the famous battleground on the Monongahela River some twelve miles from Pittsburgh. Among the partners were Henry Phipps, who was to remain associated with Carnegie's ensuing ventures, and J. Edgar Thomson, a temporary colleague who, as chief of the Pennsylvania Railroad, was an important investor and customer. The works, which bore Thomson's name, were located to take maximum advantage of the competition for traffic among Ohio River barges, the Pennsylvania, and the Baltimore and Ohio Railroad. Those roads abetted the growth of the new concern by their rivalry in rendering it favors in return for its business. The

MOUNT WASHINGTON INCLINE

TEARING UP FIFTH AVENUE

THE MONONGAHELA WATERFRONT ON A SUNDAY AFTERNOON.

From the collection of Stefan Lorant.
HORSE CARS AT NORTH AVENUE
ran between Pleasant Valley and City Hall.

group was to profit also from a series of protective tariff schedules that warded off the threat of British imports.

Carnegie, then and later the heaviest investor in his steel enterprise, exercised his characteristic acumen in judging men. To design the Monongahela works he selected Alexander L. Holley, the American champion and engineering genius of the Bessemer process. To supervise the plant, Carnegie, on Holley's recommendation, enlisted Captain William R. Jones, a colorful and gifted steel master. "Captain Bill," unlike his fellow executives, declined Carnegie's offer of partial remuneration in securities of the company. He preferred "one hell of a salary," and he got it—$25,000 a year—the sum, as Carnegie noted, then paid the Presi-

dent of the United States. Jones was worth it. Half a century ahead of other steel superintendents, he worked his men an efficient eight instead of an exhausting twelve hours a day. Something of a hero to them, he was also the supreme authority on the roaring furnaces they tended, the incomparable diagnostician of the normal and the idiosyncratic behavior of the machinery of steel. His prodigies helped to account for the growth in workers' productivity in the United States, which sped ahead of productivity in England. His achievements caught even the curious fancy, and won the admiring handshake, of Herbert Spencer, the British social philosopher whose doctrines intoxicated Carnegie (so much so that King Andrew had his autobiog-

THE CITY IN THE NINETIES.

TWENTY-TWO HORSES pulled this cumbersome memorial stone to Homewood Cemetery, where it was erected on the lot of industrialist Henry Clay Frick.

THE SKYLINE OF PITTSBURGH, a photograph taken in 1896 from Allegheny City. The billboard

THE MAIL CARRIER in the nineties was a familiar figure on the city's streets. Michael Thornton (left) delivered the mail in this elegant one horsepower equipage.

UNDERTAKING and EMBALMING was William Semmelrock's business on the South Side.

raphy partially ghostwritten by Spencer's amanuensis). In 1889 Jones organized hundreds of his men in a small army to fight the devastating flood at Johnstown. Later that year "Captain Bill" arrived to examine a furnace with a "hang"—a block in the flow of molten metal—just as it exploded, throwing him off his feet, scalding him, fracturing his skull, and thus ending his life precisely where he had lived it, in the slag pit. Carnegie missed him, but he had within his organization a talented replacement, Charles M. Schwab, who would one day win a wizard's reputation of his own.

By 1889 the Carnegie group had acquired the Homestead works, a competitor of the Thomson plant. He had also moved toward the integration of his steel holdings. The dominant producer of rails, rolled from the steel his company made, he had reached out to obtain supplies of coke, the fuel he needed for his ravenous furnaces. To that purpose, Carnegie had bought into the company of Henry Clay Frick, an entrepreneur of triumphant temperament and talent. Frick, whose grandfather Abraham was Old Overholt himself, in 1871 at the age of twenty-one, assisted by a judicious loan from Judge Thomas Mellon,

of the Exposition Baseball Park (in the right foreground) advertises Scotch Hop Ale for five cents.

THE BLOCKHOUSE at the Point, over a century old, shows neglect, decay and dilapidation. Theodore F. Brown took this poignant photograph in the early nineties.

He also operated a livery stable at his Carson Street place, next to Mrs. Schlicker's store.

THIS IS GRANT STREET, looking toward the Monongahela from Fifth Avenue. Though the photograph was taken at noon, only two people stroll on the sidewalk.

formed a company to purchase coal lands in the rich Connellsville area near Pittsburgh and to build ovens to bake coal into coke. Two years later, when the panic of 1873 crushed his rivals, Frick confidently bought them out with more money borrowed from the Mellons. Continuing to expand, within two decades he owned some 60 per cent of the coal acreage in the region and produced some 80 per cent of the coke.

The "Coke King" was, in the phrase of his sympathetic biographer, THE MAN for whom Carnegie and his associates had been looking as the manager of their vast prop-

erties, a role Frick assumed in 1889. Almost at once he acquired for the organization its important local competitor, the Duquesne Steel Company, another neighbor on the Monongahela. The several steelworks were then consolidated into the Carnegie Steel Company, a partnership in which Frick shared, and the various mills were connected with each other and with the railroad trunk lines entering the city by the construction of the Carnegie-owned Union Railway. Frick also, overcoming Carnegie's initial objections, arranged for long leases on ore lands in the wonderful Mesabi Range of Minnesota. The original development of that extraordinary resource had been in large part the enterprise of Henry William Oliver, a Pittsburgh ironmaster of remarkable talent and insight. Of Scottish-Irish ancestry, Oliver, like Carnegie, had at one time been a telegraph messenger boy. In 1893 he founded a firm to manufacture nuts and bolts. That business expanded quickly as Oliver and his brother, George, a successful lawyer and politician as well as an executive, undertook sundry activities in the ferrous industries, among them ventures in steel and tin plate, steel wire, and pressed steel cars. In 1892 Oliver had learned of the discovery near Duluth of enormous deposits of iron ore that could be scooped up from the ground by a steam shovel. He immediately leased huge annual tonnages for the Oliver Iron Mining Company, which Frick recognized as a significant adjunct to the Carnegie holdings.

Carnegie, by threatening to build a road of his own, held down rail rates from the mines to Lake Superior. Frick masterminded the establishment of a fleet of ore carriers on the Great Lakes, and the acquisition and construction of the units that formed the Pittsburgh, Bessemer and Lake Erie, the company's efficient railway that moved iron ore from the lake shore to the furnaces on the Monongahela. In the organization of that unit, Henry W. Oliver was again involved. The completed, integrated enterprise, as one engineering journal noted, was "so situated as to be absolutely in control of the market, and make the price of steel what it will."

The price of steel, while low enough to permit the satisfaction of the enormous demands of an expanding industrialism, was also sufficient to yield staggering profits for Carnegie, Frick, and their partners. The two crucial protagonists, ever respectful of each other, felt no mutual affection and some mutual jealousy. Reciprocal misunderstandings during the Homestead strike and about policy toward the railroads attenuated the bonds of their alliance.

THE MONONGAHELA WHARF IN 1890 was still an important center of commerce even though the railroads had linked Pittsburgh to the industrial complex of the North and Midwest.

Pittsburgh's commerce was soundly based upon its productive factories. It was the nation's leading producer of iron and steel; its output in 1890 was valued at $49,718,729.

The city stood seventh in the nation in foundry and machine shop products, of which 75 concerns produced $10,706,616 worth of finished goods.

The glass industry retained third place in its contribution to Pittsburgh's productivity, but was closely pressed in 1890 by three concerns which produced iron and steel wrought pipe valued at $5,992,395.

All in all, Pittsburgh's gross product totaled $126,859,657, making the city the tenth largest producer in the country. To bring about this impressive feat 56,438 workers were employed, earning $33,898,152 in yearly wages.

The Monongahela still carried a great deal of manufactured products to other parts of the country. The river continued to play a significant role in the support of Pittsburgh's booming industries.

From the collection of Stefan Lorant.

ANDREW CARNEGIE (1835-1919), whose enterprises grew with the growth of America, came into the right business at the right time. He was a superb salesman, able and charming, with an uncanny touch for selecting the right subordinates. A brooder and thinker, he was a disciple of the philosopher Herbert Spencer. His admirer, Richard Watson Gilder, described him as "a tremendous personality—dramatic, willful, generous, whimsical, at times almost cruel in pressing his own conviction upon others, and then again tender, affectionate, emotional, always imaginative, unusual and wide-visioned in his views . . . He is inconsistent in many ways, but with a passion for lofty views; the brotherhood of man, peace among nations, religious purity . . ."

While his mother was alive, Carnegie remained a bachelor, but after her death —in 1887—the 52-year-old man married Louise Whitfield.

In the article "Wealth", later known as "The Gospel of Wealth" Carnegie advanced the view that a man who dies rich dies disgraced.

After he had sold out his interest in 1901, Carnegie continued to give away his fortune for philanthropic purposes. During his lifetime he distributed three hundred fifty million dollars and left a substantial amount for further distribution.

It collapsed in 1899 when Frick refused Carnegie's demands for further concessions in the price of coke. Thereafter the two went their separate ways, each soon involved less in getting than in spending his kingly fortune.

They ruled their wealth in different ways, both magnificently. Less articulate than Carnegie, far less philanthropic, Frick was no less compulsive or august. The King of Coke became the emperor of American collectors whose New York mansion, a palace in itself, contained a lavish selection of Europe's greatest art. Still Frick retained the Connellsville spirit of his youth. Once, after spending $400,000 for a Velasquez painting, he learned to his shock that Philip IV of Spain had originally paid the artist a paltry $600. Frick found quick solace. That sum, he reckoned, at 6 per cent interest compounded semi-annually for two centuries and a half, came to a figure that proved he had obtained the masterpiece for much less than nothing.

Integration of a kind, a merging of the magisterial present and the princely past, imbued the Frick mansion on those afternoons when its master, high on a Renaissance

HENRY CLAY FRICK (1849-1919), a superb business organizer, a genius in management, a man of ideas and imagination, with hardly any formal education he had to earn his living from an early age. While keeping books in the distillery of his grandfather Overholt, he started to operate coke-ovens in the surrounding coal district. During the panic of 1873, he increased his holdings, buying coal lands for a pittance. By the time he was 30 he was a millionaire. In 1881, he married the daughter of Asa P. Childs of Pittsburgh with whom he is photographed above.

The mills of Andrew Carnegie were Frick's largest customers and Carnegie invested in Frick's firms; in 1889 Frick became the chairman of Carnegie Brothers. Thus, at 41, Frick was the head of the world's greatest steel and coke operation, employing 30,000 men. In later years, Carnegie and Frick became enemies.

After the formation of the United States Steel Corporation, in which he played an influential part, Frick retreated to his fabulous New York mansion, living with the superb art treasures that he accumulated.

In his will he left the building and its treasures to the public with an endowment of fifteen million dollars. His daughter Helen still looks after this most beautiful small museum in the world—the Frick Museum on New York's Fifth Avenue.

throne, Van Dyck and Rembrandt near his side, perused the *Saturday Evening Post* while his obedient organist rendered "Silver Threads among the Gold."

Frick, who on the one hand had demanded elegance in his boyhood boots as well as in his adult nostalgia, on the other hand subscribed to the dictum that held hard work and frugal living to pave the path to riches. Indeed all the Pittsburgh entrepreneurs, during the years they built their fortunes, were dedicated to the prudential virtue and their vigorous practice. Diligence, perseverance, temperateness, and self-improvement together fashioned character, the only basis for a business loan or trust. Ultimate success, in this view, depended, especially for the honest poor, on the presence of character; failure invariably revealed its absence. Carnegie called himself a "firm believer in the doctrine that people deserving necessary assistance . . . usually receive it. . . . Those who show willingness to help themselves need not fear about obtaining the help of others."

That was the doctrine, too, of Thomas Mellon, whose bank risked investments in Pittsburgh industries at

(turn to second column on next page)

THE GREAT ENTREPRENEURS.

HENRY JOHN HEINZ (1844-1919), the founder of Pittsburgh's food-packing industry, came from German stock. As a boy he helped his father tend the four-acre garden that provided support for the family. In 1869, the year he married Sallie Sloan Young, 25-year-old Henry J. Heinz entered into partnership with L. C. Noble to process horse-radish. When the business went into bankruptcy Heinz began afresh; with great unbending energy he built up the H. J. Heinz Company of "57 varieties".

GEORGE WESTINGHOUSE (1846-1914), one of ten children of an agricultural manufacturer in New York state, began work in his father's shop after he was mustered out of the Union army. Within a few months, he had obtained his first patent for a rotary steam engine and another one for a device that made it possible to get derailed cars back on the rails. These patents were followed by numerous others. Westinghouse, who in the meantime moved to Pittsburgh, was not yet 23 when he received a patent for an air-brake on April 13, 1869. The Westinghouse Air Brake Company that came into being shortly thereafter was located at the corner of Liberty Avenue and 25th Street. During the succeeding years the inventor steadily improved on his invention, making railway travel safe.

In the eighties, the company bought signal and interlocking switch patents which together with Westinghouse's inventions developed into a complete signal system. His introduction of alternating current for electric power transmission revolutionized life in America. In 1886, the Westinghouse Electric Company was formed; in 1893, it contracted to light the Chicago World's Fair. In the panic year of 1907, the firm was thrown into receivership; Westinghouse lost control of the business which until his death he tried to regain.

critical junctures in their growth. The largely self-taught son, born in 1813, of an Ulster farmer who immigrated to Pennsylvania, Mellon, like Carnegie, delighted in the poetry of Robert Burns and in the autobiography of Benjamin Franklin with its "wider view of life." As a young man, Mellon, by his own account "earnest, cautious and painstaking," husbanded his means "with a view to independence." He "never neglected" his "private affairs" which "increased through the accumulation of money and property" until they drew him in 1870 from bar and bench to finance, and thence to eminence. The first over-

Painting by Theobald Chartran.

THOMAS MELLON (1813-1908), came to Pittsburgh from Ireland when he was five years old. After his graduation from the Western University of Pennsylvania, he began a successful law practice. In 1859, he was elected judge of the common pleas court of Allegheny County, a post he held for ten years. In January 1870, he established a private banking house on Smithfield Street—T. Mellon & Sons. The firm handled real estate operations; extended credit to men like Andrew Carnegie and gave a $10,000 loan to Henry C. Frick in 1871.

Mellon's hero was Benjamin Franklin. As a child he read Franklin's autobiography and was deeply impressed by it. "For so poor and friendless a boy to be able to become a merchant or a professional man had before seemed an impossibility," wrote Mellon reviewing his life, "but here was Franklin, poorer than myself, who by industry, thrift and frugality had become learned and wise, and elevated to wealth and fame." Mellon regarded the reading of Franklin's autobiography as the turning point of his life.

In 1843, Thomas Mellon married Sarah Jane Negley, who came from one of the city's oldest families. They had eight children, Thomas Alexander, James Ross, Andrew William, Richard Beatty, George Negley, Sarah Emma, Annie Rebecca and Samuel Selwyn.

lord of one of the most powerful banking and industrial dynasties in the United States, Mellon sponsored his sons in their initial ventures in real estate, advised them during the Civil War against the "folly of soldiering," and cultivated their "comprehension to understand and will to execute." Earlier, in the spirit implicit in that advice, Thomas Mellon had made a "transaction" of his deliberate courtship. "There was no love-making," he later recalled. "Had I been rejected, I would have left neither sad nor depressed nor greatly disappointed, only annoyed at the loss of time."

(turn to second column on next page)

Photograph by Histed, courtesy Richard K. Mellon.

BROTHER AND SISTER. Mrs. Richard B. Mellon, mother of Richard King Mellon, and her brother Robert Burns King.

Their father was Alexander King (1816-90), who came to Pittsburgh from Ireland in 1856 and became an importer and manufacturer. Here he married Eliza Jane Smith of Cincinnati, and when she died he married her sister. He had four children with his second wife, three boys and a girl. The girl, Jennie, became the wife of Richard B. Mellon, younger brother of Andrew.

Painting by Oswald Birley in the National Gallery of Art, Washington.

ANDREW W. MELLON (1855-1937) was the sixth of Thomas and Sarah Jane Negley Mellon's eight children. Educated in Pittsburgh public schools and in the Western University of Pennsylvania, he entered his father's bank in 1874. A financial genius, he left his mark on Pittsburgh by helping the development of its major industries. He supplied capital that allowed Charles M. Hall and associates to develop the electrolytic manufacture of aluminum; the small firm eventually grew into the mighty Aluminum Company of America. He was associated with the development of Carborundum Company and of McClintock-Marshall, the construction company that built the Panama Canal locks and the George Washington Bridge in New York. He also played a vital role in the foundation of the Gulf Oil Corporation, was organizer of the Union Steel Company, of the Standard Steel Car Company and the New York Shipbuilding Company, and converted the small business of Heinrich Koppers into the successful giant Koppers Gas & Coke Company.

At one time Andrew Mellon was an officer or director of more than sixty corporations. But his chief interest remained T. Mellon & Sons, which was incorporated in 1902 as the Mellon National Bank. In 1920, President Harding appointed him Secretary of the Treasury, a post he retained under President Coolidge and President Hoover. In 1932, Mellon resigned to become American ambassador to Great Britain. On the eve of his seventy-eighth birthday, he bade goodbye to London, returned to Pittsburgh, and resumed his activities at his bank.

In the words of historian Allan Nevins: "Mellon had unquestionably been one of the major figures in the industrial and financial development of the trans-Allegheny region and the most powerful personage of the Harding-Coolidge regimes. His resourcefulness, shrewdness, and foresight had fostered numerous enterprises that others neglected . . . His veiled and reticent personality cloaked an essentially simple, thoughtful and just nature. With the misfortune of excessive wealth he coped as conscientiously and efficiently as his training and tradition permitted."

His sons, following his example, wasted not, and neither did they want. Richard excelled as a banker and business manager. His brother Andrew, equally proficient in those roles, quietly accumulated a fortune rivaled only by those of John D. Rockefeller and Henry Ford. That fortune grew, in the words of a director of the Mellon bank, as "a sort of revolving fund for the promotion of enterprises." Much of it lay in the Mellon National Bank and the Union Trust Company and Union Savings Bank, all established by the brothers. Among the enterprises they promoted during a spectacularly profitable half century were Alcoa, Gulf Oil, and the Koppers Company, as well as various other ventures in steel and railroading and chemicals. Andrew Mellon, by design inconspicuous, achieved national attention only in 1921 when Warren Harding appointed him Secretary of the Treasury, a position Mellon embraced with exactly the efficiencies and attitudes he had earlier brought to his business responsibilities and continuously gave to his momentous collection of art—the core, thanks to his generosity, of the National Gallery in Washington.

Richard and Andrew Mellon fully satisfied their father's expectations. It was, after all, determination that Thomas Mellon trusted, not accident. "Poverty," he wrote as he reviewed his own career, "may be a misfortune to the weaklings who are without courage or ability to overcome it, but it is a blessing to young men of ordinary force of character: it protects them from excesses, withholds unwise pleasures and indulgences, teaches the value of time and of wealth, and the necessity of well doing to better their condition."

Their personal condition, men famous for that stamp believed, was the condition of their calling—or, in a favorite phrase of one of them, Henry J. Heinz, "quality is to a product what character is to a man." The eldest of eight children of a German immigrant, Heinz grew up in Sharpsburg, six miles from Pittsburgh, and attended a Lutheran school there until his confirmation at age thirteen. Five years earlier, in 1852, he had begun to sell the surplus from the family vegetable garden. By the time he was sixteen, the products of his intensive cultivation, in which several women employees assisted, filled three wagonloads a week. In 1869 Heinz and L. C. Noble, his partner in a brick business, formed a new firm to process and sell horse-radish, which had traditionally been packed in green glass bottles that concealed the turnip filler. Now Heinz grated and packed his unadulterated horse-radish in clear and revealing bottles. He started with three quarters of an acre under cultivation and with grating, packing, and sales operations all snugly grouped in the basement of his father's farmhouse. Expanding sales of horse-radish and other products, including celery sauce and pickles, led the partners within a few years to plant some 125 acres of vegetables, soon thereafter to lease business and warehouse space first in Pittsburgh and then in St. Louis and Chicago, and in 1875 to contract for the full crop of 600 acres in Illinois. But the bumper crop of that year inundated the firm. Unable to get credit from banks overcome by the reverberations of the recent panic, Heinz and Noble went into bankruptcy.

Heinz was determined to start again, as he did in 1876, as the manager of F. and J. Heinz, a partnership of his brother, wife, and mother. Though the new firm was small, Heinz had already exhibited the inspiration as well as the courage for success. The food business had been largely local, even domestic. Sensing the possibilities of the markets of the growing cities speckled across the whole country, Heinz realized that commercially produced food could sell to millions of customers if they trusted its quality and recognized its brand. Quality depended, he knew, on the integrity and efficiency of each step in the process— on growing superior crops from selected seeds and by tested methods, on quick and sanitary packaging that protected flavor and nutrition, on distribution from plant to warehouse to store to customer at a controlled pace that precluded deterioration. He was one of the first to promote agricultural science, the special concern of his cousin Frederick, and food technology, the province of his brother John. Together they applied "a research viewpoint . . . to all phases of the company's activities." Further, like Carnegie, Henry Heinz understood the importance of location. He placed his plants with their kitchens close to the fields but close also to urban markets. He profited from the easy availability in Pittsburgh, the center of his enterprise, of glass and steel, the basic ingredients for making the improved bottles and cans his firm developed.

As the Heinz company flourished, reorganized in 1888 as H. J. Heinz and incorporated in 1905, as the number of its plants rose, it also followed the path toward integration that Heinz marked. It acquired thousands of acres of cropland, seed farms, receiving stations, warehouses, bottle, box and can factories, railroad cars, and branch sales offices. It also acquired the reputation for quality foods that Heinz had sought, a deserved reputation later re-enforced by the company's co-operation with the Department of Agriculture in the campaign for pure food and drugs. And Heinz, again like Carnegie a master salesman, provided the company with a special stamp of recognition. He had been "casting about for some word or phrase that would aptly convey a true idea of our line of goods" when one day in 1896, aboard an elevated train in New York, he noticed the sign of a concern that advertised twelve styles of shoes. His own company had varieties rather than styles of products. "Counting up how many we had," he later recalled, "I counted well beyond 57, but '57' kept coming back into my mind. 'Seven, seven'—there are so many illustrations of the psychological influences of that figure . . . that '58 varieties' or '59 varieties' did not appeal at all." He got off the train, went at once to a lithographer, and designed the streetcar placard that started the "57 varieties" toward the van of telling trademarks. A splendid intuition had Henry Heinz, who was also a man of re-

Courtesy Library of Congress.

RICHARD BEATTY MELLON (1858-1933), a younger brother of Andrew, began his business career in earnest at 19, when he and his brothers constructed the Ligonier Valley Railroad from Latrobe to Ligonier; he became president and manager of the railroad. In 1883, he accompanied his brother George, who went West for his health. In Bismarck, North Dakota, the two young men opened the "Mellon Brothers Bank," but when George died three years later Richard returned to Pittsburgh and entered the family's banking firm. After his elder brother was appointed Secretary of the Treasury, Richard became president of T. Mellon & Sons, a post he held until his death.

A director of a number of banks and corporations, R. B. Mellon was first president of Alcoa. Together with his brother Andrew, he was instrumental in the establishment of the Mellon Institute of Industrial Research in 1913, an organization that was founded to narrow the gap between science and industry. He was a trustee of the University of Pittsburgh, also of Carnegie Tech and the Children's Hospital of Pittsburgh.

In 1897, he married Jennie King, the daughter of a wealthy glass manufacturer. They had two children: Sarah Cordelia and Richard King Mellon, the present head of the Mellon enterprises.

markable warmth and decency. He preached to his employees the importance of saving as a factor in encouraging self-restraint; he bargained joyfully with the sharp dealers from whom he bought the jades and crystals and especially the ivory carvings that he collected passionately; he made his firm one of the few giants in the huge and immensely competitive food industry; and for sufficient reasons embedded in his career, he maintained that "it is

(turn to page 238)

235

Courtesy Library of Congress.

HENRY PHIPPS (1839-1930) was Carnegie's business associate right from the beginning. In 1867, Phipps, Carnegie and others formed the Union Iron Mills. Phipps was an eagle-eyed manager, watching over accounts, costs, and production methods, suggesting improvements and economies. His reputation for close trading was legendary. A man who sold scrap iron to him said: "Divil a cint was left to a harrd wurrking man after a thrade with Harry Phipps, bad cess to him!"

Courtesy U. S. Steel Corporation.

CAPTAIN "BILL" JONES (1839-1889) worked in iron mills from childhood. Passing through every branch of iron and steel manufacture, he had intimate knowledge of everything inside the works. He was a superb organizer, a skillful handler of men, fertile in invention. With unbounded energy and a will to outproduce everyone else, he made the United States supreme in steel production. He died in an explosion at the Edgar Thomson Works, whose superintendent he was for sixteen years.

Courtesy U. S. Steel Corporation.

CHARLES M. SCHWAB (1862-1939) was a grocery clerk at Braddock when Captain "Bill" Jones gave him a job at the Edgar Thomson Works. At the age of 19 he became assistant manager, and when Jones died in 1889 Schwab followed him as general superintendent. By 1897 he was president of the Carnegie Steel Company. In 1901, he played a vital part in the sale of the Carnegie properties to the Morgan interests. Leaving his job he bought and reorganized Bethlehem Steel.

Courtesy Carnegie Library.

JACOB J. VANDERGRIFT (1827-1899), who began as a river captain, built oil pipe lines from the wells to the shipping terminals, thus greatly reducing the cost of transportation. With John Pitcairn and others, he also built the Imperial Refinery and laid the first natural gas line. In 1877, he and others formed the United Pipe Lines. He founded the Pittsburgh Petroleum Exchange, the Seaboard National Bank in N. Y., the Apollo Iron and Steel Co., and the model town of Vandergrift.

Courtesy Library of Congress.

HENRY W. OLIVER (1840-1904) a childhood friend of Thomas Carnegie, made several fortunes in iron and steel. In 1892, he formed a company to operate the Mesabi mountain mine in Minnesota to provide a cheap and steady supply of high-grade ore for his Bessemer furnaces. His work marked the beginning of the great Mesabi ore traffic to Pittsburgh's steel mills. Oliver joined forces with the Carnegie interests; in 1901 he sold out his holdings for seventeen million dollars.

Courtesy Carnegie Library.

WILLIAM THAW (1818-1889) together with Thomas S. Clarke, his brother-in-law, operated several steamboat lines, notably the Pittsburgh and Cincinnati Packet Line. In 1857, the partners took charge of the freight business west of Pittsburgh. Thaw was responsible for devising the first through freight system. From 1881 to 1889 he was a director of the Pennsylvania Railroad. He tried to make Pittsburgh an educational center and supported the Western University of Pennsylvania.

ALUMINUM.

CHARLES MARTIN HALL

(1863-1914), who in February, 1886 made his first aluminum in a wood-shed at Oberlin, Ohio, by dissolving aluminum oxide with cryolite and passing an electric current through it. The importance of this discovery was that aluminum could be produced cheaply. He came to Pittsburgh, where Alfred E. Hunt and his friends financed his further experiments.

At his death Hall, who had never been married, left a fortune which was estimated at 30 million dollars.

ARTHUR VINING DAVIS

(1866-1962), the son of a Massachusetts Congregational minister, graduated from Amherst College and took his first job with the Pittsburgh Reduction Company at $14 a week. In 1888, he helped Charles M. Hall pour the first commercial aluminum ingot and the two young men became life-long friends. After Captain Hunt died in 1899, Davis became general manager of the company. In 1910, he was named president of Alcoa, a post he held until 1928, when he was elected chairman of the board. Davis lived to a ripe old age of 95, making several fortunes during his lifetime. His holdings at his death were over three hundred fifty million dollars.

TWO ALUMINUM PIONEERS: Captain Alfred Ephraim Hunt (1855-99), organizer and first president of the Pittsburgh Reduction Company which grew into the giant Aluminum Company of America, and his son, Roy A. Hunt, who became president of the company in 1928, as they looked in 1898.

Alfred E. Hunt, a graduate of the Massachusetts Institute of Technology, had a metallurgical laboratory and consulting service in Pittsburgh when a friend of young Charles M. Hall came to him with the proposition to invest money in a pilot plant to test the commercial feasibility of Hall's laboratory experiments. Hunt was impressed, and with some of his friends he formed a company. Hall arrived in Pittsburgh, and within weeks he produced his first aluminum ingot. On December 9, 1888 the inventor wrote to his sister Julia: "Everybody is convinced of the success of the scheme — although we are not making sixty pounds a day right along as calculated."

Captain Hunt of Battery B, Pennsylvania National Guard, died of an illness which he contracted in the Spanish-American War.

237

Courtesy L. Robertson.

AT J. G. BENNETT & COMPANY at 447 Wood Street one could purchase headgears of all descriptions—hats, caps, everything.

Courtesy Paul J. Bergman.

H. & C. F. AHLERS, custom tailors, the parent firm of Ahlers and Bergman was founded in 1854. At the entrance is Henry Ahlers.

neither capital nor labor that brings success, but management, because management can attract capital, and capital can employ labor."

So it was in the case of the first commercially useful process for making aluminum, invented by Charles M. Hall, whose "first knowledge of chemistry was gained from reading a book" which his "father had studied in the forties." His father, a Congregational minister, and his mother, ambitious for her children, moved to Oberlin, Ohio, in order to facilitate the education of their serious-minded sons and daughters. At Oberlin College young Charles, while enrolled in a liberal arts curriculum, responded most powerfully to the teachings of his Yale-trained chemistry professor, F. F. Jewett. Hall, according to one of his sisters, had been fascinated since boyhood by the problem of making aluminum. Jewett furthered that interest. "Speaking to my students," he later wrote, "I said that if anyone should invent a process by which aluminum could be made on a commercial scale not only would he be a benefactor to the world but he would also be able to lay up for himself a great fortune. Turning to a classmate, Charles Hall said, 'I'm going for that metal.'"

Just out of college, the twenty-two-year-old inventor in 1885 set to work—aided by an ebullient spirit, his sister Julia, and equipment borrowed from Jewett—in a "summer kitchen" and "winter woodshed" of the family home.

In less than a year he succeeded where giants of chemistry had failed. Using an old clay crucible lined with carbon, he passed electric current for several hours through aluminum oxide dissolved in melted cryolite. In the cooled mass he found shining buttons of aluminum. He applied for a patent for his process in 1886 and the next year went to work with an electric smelting company in Lockport, New York, which took an option on his patent but gave it up in 1888. A Frenchman, Paul L. T. Héroult, had filed a similar patent claim, and later the Lockport company tried to establish its hold on the process, but Hall, whose discovery predated Héroult's by two months, received the American patent in 1889 and, after considerable litigation, won judicial confirmation of his rights in 1893.

Hall had always recognized the industrial importance of aluminum. Victory in the patent fight, he realized, would provide a monopoly within the United States on a potentially huge enterprise. But the promise of aluminum, which hinged also on imaginative marketing, was not so obvious to those whom Hall first approached for indispensable financial backing. A chemical concern in Cleveland and a group of investors in Boston turned him down. His patent was still not secure when in 1888 a Lockport friend, Romaine C. Cole, introduced him to a Pittsburgh metallurgist and engineer, Alfred E. Hunt, who brought Hall's inventiveness to commercial fruition.

Hunt, eight years older than Hall, had graduated in 1876 from the Massachusetts Institute of Technology and immediately joined a steel company for which he helped to build the second open-hearth furnace in the United States. In 1881 he became superintendent for Park Brothers and Company in Pittsburgh, and two years later, with George H. Clapp, he established a metallurgical laboratory and consulting service for steel mills in the area. Gripped by Hall's invention, Hunt undertook to organize the Pittsburgh Reduction Company, originally capitalized at $20,000, to control the patent and erect a pilot plant to make aluminum. The first venturers were young men, all under thirty-five, among them three steel company executives of whom one was from the Carnegie group. A further capital issue in 1888 brought to the enterprise Judge Mellon's sons, Andrew and Richard, who continued to contribute timely loans and constructive faith and direction to the development of the concern—by the end of the century they had acquired a thousand shares of its stock.

In the pilot plant Hall went to work twelve hours of each twenty-four, beleaguered by the technological uncertainties of his raw process and by the ineptitudes of his inexperienced employees. Soon he wrote his sister, "Captain Hunt got Davis to take my place when we work nights. He is a boy from Boston and fresh from Amherst College. He has a good deal of ability as well as grit to stand it working all night in the dirt and soot and worse." Arthur Vining Davis, that diminutive but determined Amherst boy, was earning fourteen dollars a week in the service of producing what was then regarded "as a more or less mystical substance." He and Hall on Thanksgiving Day, 1888, gave up their holiday meal in order to pour their first commercial aluminum. They met continuing difficulties in trying to achieve the anticipated quota of sixty pounds a day, but by 1890 they were up to 475 pounds. In 1891 the company moved to a new plant at Kensington (soon New Kensington) on the Allegheny River, where production rose quickly to 1000 pounds a day. In still newer plants it reached 8000 pounds by 1897. The price of aluminum, $2 a pound in large lots in 1888, fell to $1.50 in 1891, to 75¢ in 1893, to 30¢ before the century ended. Hall's process had demonstrated its worth.

Yet for years the Pittsburgh Reduction Company had to borrow to meet its payrolls. On January 1, 1897, its cash statement, as Hunt wrote Andrew Mellon, "showed an excess of available assets over real liabilities of $2,014.69.

Courtesy Fred Maeder.

J. F. MAEDER'S tailoring establishment, where the well-dressed Pittsburgher might have gone to purchase his suit was located on Fifth Avenue at the corner of Cherry Alley.

At the right of store one can barely see St. Paul's Cathedral, at the left are the offices of the *Pittsburgh Leader*, one of the city's several enterprising newspapers.

THOSE WHO HAD ARRIVED: Prominent Pittsburgh businessmen in 1892, who for decades had met regularly at the Duquesne Club to partake of a weekly luncheon. Sitting: S. Schoyer, Jr., Campbell B. Herron, B. F. Jones, Sr., John W. Chalfant, and Max K. Moorhead. Standing: John H. Ricketson, A. E. W. Painter, General Charles L. Fitzhugh, U.S. Supreme Court Justice George Shiras, Jr., Albert H. Childs, Major Frank H. Phipps (the commander of the Allegheny Arsenal—a guest of the group), and Charles N. Spang. Henry W. Oliver, also a member, was not present when the photograph was taken.

In the ready assets are $70,000 of bonds unsold and $142,521.69 worth of metal in store." The faith in aluminum of Hunt and Hall, of the Mellons and Davis, whose stock holdings were growing, would pay its prodigious dividends only if and when they found customers with broad uses for the metal. In the early days, as Hunt observed, "practically no one wanted 1000 pounds." Smaller quantities were bought by local steel companies that fed aluminum into the hot steel in an open hearth to take up oxygen and thus prevent "blow holes" in the ingots. Hunt published technical articles suggesting other uses and, with Davis, opened new markets for products which the company discovered in some instances it had to make itself. Davis borrowed a molder to cast an aluminum teakettle in order to persuade a utensil manufacturer to use the metal for that purpose. The manufacturer instead ordered 2000 kettles from the Pittsburgh Reduction Company which had then to add a fabricating unit to its New Kensington Works.

Similarly, when brass mills declined to roll aluminum, Hunt started the "development of our rolling mills, forging plant and foundry in the making of aluminum into all shapes in which brass is shipped and sold." So, too, the company created subsidiaries to make wire and seals for canning jars. The Aluminum Cooking Utensil Company, one subsidiary, expanded its sales by employing college students as door-to-door canvassers, effective salesmen of the precursors to the famous Wear-Ever brand. More mature salesmen found the Navy a customer for aluminum superstructures for men-of-war, and the Army for aluminum canteens, one of which Theodore Roosevelt carried in Cuba.

During the 1890s the trend toward verticalization in fabricating operations had its counterpart in production itself. "If it be true," Hunt wrote Hall in 1897, "as I understand from you, that we can make as much aluminum per unit of horsepower from bauxite (of which we can

THOSE WHO WERE COMING: Immigrants from the Old World heading for Pittsburgh arrived in New York by the thousands; they carry their earthly belongings on their backs as they walk across Brooklyn Bridge.

In 1890 the total population of Pittsburgh was 238,617. Of this number, no less than 73,154 were foreign born, about one third of the total. The mills and the mines needed workers; there was a dearth of labor. Shipload after shipload of men, recruited by agents of the companies, came from Slovakia and Hungary, from Poland and Greece, from Italy and Ireland.

obtain large quantities) as from pure aluminum, then it would seem that this is the field which is now ripest for us to investigate for increasing the economy of manufacturing." Accordingly, and with the predicted gains, the Pittsburgh Reduction Company bought into and ultimately wholly owned the Georgia Bauxite and Mining Company. Later it acquired its own steamship company. Meanwhile it had installed its own direct-current generators at a new reduction plant, above Niagara Falls, that utilized the cheap alternating current delivered by the Westinghouse Company. These new efficiencies assured advancing profits from an expanding business that was fully protected from domestic competition by the company's patents. The company gained also from an agreement of 1897 by which it held a large fraction of the British market in return for its guarantee to deliver 500 tons of aluminum for two years at the low price of one shilling a pound.

The various constituents of the Pittsburgh Reduction Company were consolidated within one new holding company and under one general management in 1907 with the incorporation of the Aluminum Company of America. Alcoa took over at the threshold of the aviation age which was to generate, as were other changes, demands for aluminum in excess even of the spirited forecasts of the adventurers of 1888 and 1889. Those entrepreneurs laid the foundations of expectation and policy on which the aluminum industry thrived. So did they. Though Hunt died in 1899 of a bad heart weakened by malaria which he contracted in Puerto Rico while in command of a volunteer regiment during the Spanish War, his son Roy became in time one of the great managers of Alcoa. As for Hall, one third of his $30,000,000 bachelor's estate went in 1914 to Oberlin College, to which he had earlier given the best of his excellent collection of rugs, paintings, and Chinese porcelains. Davis, who lived until 1962, was asked shortly

241

Courtesy Jones & Laughlin Steel Corporation.

AN OFFICE IN 1895. The Jones & Laughlin general office was a pleasant place to work, even if one had to dress up to the hilt. In the picture J. Cad Thompson, F. A. Ogden, T. Sprone Trumbull, E. K. Barker, and Thomas M. Jones, Jr.

HENRY A. LAUGHLIN IN HIS OFFICE.

before his death whether he was the second or third richest man in the world. "Fifth," he said, walking briskly away.

Aluminum was a Pittsburgh product, as one Alcoa engineer put it, because Pittsburgh was "primarily interested in men . . . and it was Pittsburgh that listened to an Ohio college boy with his vision of possibilities of a new and light metal. Not only did it listen, but it gave substantial assistance . . . nurtured by Pittsburgh capital and fostered by Pittsburgh control."

Pittsburgh also listened to Westinghouse when he dreamed of stopping a train with air, and with that dream set forth upon explorations of technological continents then still dark. George Westinghouse was born in Central Bridge, New York, the eighth of ten children of a small manufacturer of farm and mill machinery. A tinkerer in his boyhood, he was also a romantic young patriot who at fourteen ran off to join the Union Army. Brought home by his father who permitted him to enlist two years later, he served first in the infantry and cavalry and then as an engineering officer in the navy. Three

MEETING OF THE MANAGER in Jones & Laughlin's general office at Try Street and Third Avenue. The men, from left to right: W. C. Moreland, Irvin B. Laughlin,

B. F. Jones, Jr., Willis King, Charles C. Briggs, Roland Gerry, and W. W. Willock.

months at Union College persuaded him he preferred the practical labor of his father's shop. "My earliest capital," Westinghouse recalled, "was the experience and skill acquired from the opportunity given me, when I was young, to work with all kinds of machinery, coupled later with lessons in that discipline to which a soldier is required to submit, and the acquirement of a spirit of readiness to carry out the instructions of superiors."

Instructed also by the needs of the railroads, Westinghouse at twenty-one organized a partnership in Schenectady, New York, to market two of his first inventions, one a device to replace derailed cars on their tracks, the other an improved steel frog that permitted wheels on one rail of a track to cross an intersecting track. Appropriately, on a train in 1867 he met his future wife. The next year he moved his firm to Pittsburgh, where he could have his products manufactured more cheaply. He was already at work on a straight air brake for trains. Though the New York Central and the Erie Railroad refused to give that

idea a trial, Ralph Baggaley, a Pittsburgh foundry manager, helped to finance the construction of a pilot unit which, in its first application in 1869, prevented a collision between a train and a wagon at Second Avenue in the city. Baggaley and some Pittsburgh railroad men then joined the inventor in the formation of the Westinghouse Air Brake Company, which controlled the series of patents through which he improved the brake.

Before Westinghouse's air brake, the difficulty in stopping trains had seriously limited their weight and speed. Gradually he dispelled that limitation. His initial mechanism operated the brakes on all the cars in the train by air that was compressed at the engine and sent backward through an air line. Accordingly the cars at the front stopped sooner than those at the rear, which tended to jerk and swing. He eliminated the resulting hazards after 1887 by perfecting the automatic air brake. It operated through an air-pressure reservoir in each car. The air in the line was held at constant pressure until the engineer

(turn to page 246)

From the collection of Stefan Lorant.

THE COMPOSER OF "THE ROSARY," Ethelbert Nevin, next to Stephen Foster the best-known composer of the city, was born at Edgeworth near Pittsburgh in 1862 and died thirty-nine years later in New Haven, Connecticut. His mother was an accomplished musician and it is said that the first grand piano which was carted over the Allegheny Mountains belonged to her. From his early childhood Nevin studied music, at first in Pittsburgh, then in Dresden, Boston, Berlin, and Paris.

Besides playing the piano and giving concerts, he turned into an accomplished composer. His pieces had grace and melodic charm, they were simple and spontaneous; his music reflected rather light than shadow, rather joy than sorrow. "Narcissus," from his *Water Scenes,* "May in Tuscany," "A Day in Venice," were widely played and sung. But his most famous composition, a song which sold more than two and one half million copies, was "The Rosary," which Nevin composed in 1898. The text of the song was sent to him by his childhood friend Elizabeth Dickson (shown in this early tintype with Nevin). She had read the verse in a publication, liked it, and mailed it to Nevin who set it to music.

Courtesy Edgar A. Roth.

left:

A BEVY OF BEAUTIES, photographed on the wooded campus of the Pennsylvania College for Women in Pittsburgh's East End.

reduced it by opening a valve, whereupon the reservoirs in the cars set the brakes simultaneously throughout the length of the train. The three-way cock which served as the valve in this system was a patented Westinghouse invention, as were other constituents, including the hose couplings for the air lines which sealed automatically when the couplings were disconnected. Westinghouse designed his various improvements in order to permit the railroads to adopt them successively without abandoning equipment already purchased from his company. He also made his apparatus interchangeable so that cars of different roads could be joined in one train. This policy, which prevented unnecessary obsolescence, kept the market content and active.

While developing his business in England, Westinghouse was impressed by British signaling and switching equipment, which was markedly superior to American gear. In 1881 he bought control of two American firms which he merged to form the Union Switch and Signal Company in Pittsburgh. Adding inventions of his own to patents he had purchased, he produced various automatic devices in which he combined a force he had mastered—compressed air—with a force then emerging from its industrial infancy, electricity. His technological and business success in his new venture, supplementing as it did the accomplishments of his brake company, gave him the means, the organization, and the reputation necessary for promoting his interest in electrical manufacturing.

(turn to page 248)

below:

A FASHIONABLE PRIVATE SCHOOL in the nineties was the Alinda Private School on North Craig and Fifth Avenue. Standing at the fence with his elegant cap is attorney Miles H. Jones, the boy sitting on the left is attorney Oliver W. Brown.

Courtesy Mrs. Miles H. Jones.

ONE OF THE CHILDREN is the past governor of Pennsylvania—David Lawrence. He stands on the right before his

DUQUESNE

Courtesy Robert A. Foley.

elder sister, just behind the woman facing the camera. The young David was a pupil in the Duquesne Public School on Second Avenue and Liberty Street. Each year the whole school dressed up in its best Sunday clothes and departed for Aliquippa where a picnic was held. But first they posed for a photograph—the faculty on the balcony over the entrance, the pupils below them.

THE WOMAN'S CLUB of Pittsburgh was the first federated club in Pennsylvania and the second in the entire General Federation of Woman's Clubs.

In 1867 Charles Dickens told a gathering of New York's literary women about the work of the women's societies in England. The correspondent of the Pittsburgh *Post*—Mrs. Helen P. Jenkins—was among Dickens' audience, and impressed by the English writer's exhortation, she invited a few Pittsburgh women for a "Blue Stocking Tea" at her home in Allegheny. Thus the Club came into being.

In the photograph taken in the early 1890s one can see Mrs. C. I. Wade who wrote for newspapers under her pen name Bessie Bramble, Miss Lyde Armstrong, Mrs. Joseph Hanna, Mrs. James Prentice, Mrs. Elizabeth German, Mrs. Sarah Rosenstock, Mrs. Martha Taylor, Mrs. C. C. Huff, Mrs. Henry J. Bailey (center), Mrs. Louisa C. McCullough, Mrs. Martha Archer (mother of organist Harry Archer), Mrs. Isaac Wade and Mrs. Charles Wade (sister-in-law and daughter-in-law of Mrs. C. I. Wade), and Tillie Orr Hays.

To that end his experience with natural gas also contributed. The abundance of natural gas in Pittsburgh had had little commercial significance because of the dangers in handling it. The very high pressure at the wells, which baffled others, provided, for the system which Westinghouse contrived, the force he sought for moving the gas rapidly and inexpensively through narrow pipes for long distances. To reduce the pressure so that gas could be delivered safely, he widened the pipes in successive stages near the point of consumption. For many profitable years, his company then distributed that fuel to Pittsburgh factories and households. Perhaps more important, the basic conception of high pressure for transmission converted to low pressure for consumption was analogous to the conception which Westinghouse applied to the distribution of electricity. There he obtained inexpensive and high transmission voltage by his innovative recourse to alternating instead of direct current, and he safely and efficiently reduced voltage at the point of consumption by his adoption of the transformer.

Westinghouse's genius lay in combining the units that were to revolutionize the transmission of electricity. His instinct for combination also spurred his later promotion of his system. He first entered the electrical business in 1884 when he employed an electrical engineer, William Stanley, in the Union Switch and Signal Company for the purpose of developing an incandescent-electric lighting system founded on Stanley's patents for a self-regulating direct-current dynamo and an incandescent lamp with a carbonized-silk element. In 1885 Westinghouse read about

THE PIRATES IN 1893, when they occupied second place in the twelve-team league. 1. Denny Lyons, 2. Elmer Smith, 3. Louie Bierbauer, over whom the Pirates received their name (Bierbauer, whom the Philadelphia Phillies neglected to reserve, was signed by the Pittsburgh Nationals whereupon the American Association charged the Pittsburgh club with piracy. Later a board of arbitration awarded Bierbauer to Pittsburgh), 4. Red Ehret, 5. Joe Sugden, 6. Jake Beckley, 7. George Van Haltren, 8. Frank Killen, 9. Connie Mack, who became Pirate manager in 1894, 10. Jack Glassock, 11. Addison Gumbert, 12. Pat Donovan, 13. Bill Terry, 14. Manager Albert Buckenberger, 15. Colcolough, 16. Diggy Miller, 17. Jake Stenzel.

an alternating-current system on display in London that used transformers to reduce a high transmission value to one low enough to operate a lamp. He instructed a subordinate then in Europe to obtain opinions about the patents of the French inventors of the transformer, and he purchased a British-made alternator and assigned Stanley and others to study alternating current and its problems. These decisions overruled the advice of most of his own experts. "The opposition was far greater than I had thought possible," one of them later recalled. ". . . It was only Mr. George Westinghouse's personal will that put it through."

As modified by Westinghouse, the European system for the first time linked transformers in parallel (rather than in series) for the primary objective of reducing voltage between transmission and consumption circuits. In that way, as Westinghouse alone realized, he could have an economical distribution system superior to the direct-current systems then known in the United States, and based on the use of transformers and a.c. generators designed and produced by his company. Rapid progress toward that goal persuaded him in 1886 to incorporate the electrical department of the Union Switch and Signal Company as a separate concern, the Westinghouse Electric Company, with an initial capital stock of $1,000,000, most of it his own. The company sold its first commercially successful system that year and almost at once received orders for twenty-five more. In 1888 the company's chief engineer invented a meter, suitable for commercial production, for measuring the consumption of alternating

(turn to page 251)

THE GRAND ARMY OF THE REPUBLIC PARADES DOWN FIFTH AVENUE AT LIBERTY IN 1893.

THE PRESIDENT IN PITTSBURGH. In May 1899 President William McKinley came to the city to greet the 10th Regiment as it returned from the Spanish war. He rode through Oakland's Forbes Street in an open carriage pulled by four white chargers, and surrounded by secret service men. Two years later in September 1901 McKinley was felled by an assassin's bullet.

current. Equally important, Westinghouse hired a brilliant young Hungarian, Nikola Tesla, who had patented an a.c. motor, and financed Tesla's improvement of that device. The delivery of alternating current, so much cheaper over long distances than was direct current, to an industrially useful motor opened vistas even brighter than those of the incandescent lamp.

From the first, the Westinghouse Electric Company faced rough competition from the Edison Electric Light Company, founded in 1878, and its successors, the Edison General Electric Company, 1898, and the General Electric Company, 1892. The fame of Thomas Alva Edison as an inventor in the field of electricity was without equal in the United States. Further, his companies had controlling patents for the best type of incandescent lamp and had constructed and installed many impressive direct-current systems for generating and transmitting electricity for illumination. Where power had to be sent over only short distances those systems were for some years as effi-

(turn to page 253)

THE WAR IS OVER. Soldiers of the Spanish-American War were welcomed with cheers in Oakland on their return from the Philippines. In the background is the new Schenley Hotel.

251

VIEWS OF PITTSBURGH taken by Peter Krumel in the latter part of the eighteen nineties. Krumel, one of the city's early photographers, used an 8 x 10 camera with glass plates. His photographs of the growing metropolis have exceptionally sharp details.

THE POINT IN THE LATE NINETIES

A MASTER

LENSMAN

PICTURES

HIS CITY

252

Courtesy Pittsburgh Press.

AS SEEN BY PETER KRUMEL, ONE OF THE OUTSTANDING EARLY PHOTOGRAPHERS OF THE CITY.

cient or more efficient than their alternating current rivals.

Westinghouse had therefore somehow to excite an interest in his innovation. He scored a first triumph by winning the contract for lighting the Chicago World's Fair of 1893. Edison, confident that the courts would sustain his patent monopoly on his lamp, submitted a high bid, over $1,000,000. Westinghouse, who bid $399,000, surprised his competitor by devising a lamp that used a two-part globe and thus did not infringe upon the Edison patented one-piece globe. Though inferior, the Westinghouse lamp,

powered by alternating current, worked admirably at the fair and undersold its superior competitor on the commercial market. When in 1894 Edison's Canadian patent expired, various firms began to manufacture lamps with a one-piece globe, and a price war broke out in the industry.

By 1896 several improvement patents vital for making high-quality lamps gave Westinghouse new advantages. The two large firms then settled the contest by an agreement, which several smaller companies also entered. It guaranteed a royalty to Westinghouse of one third of a cent on all lamps produced, and in return Westinghouse in effect contracted "to . . . maintain the established prices of the General Electric Company." That concern kept prices low enough to discourage newcomers from attempting to gain the share of market of either of the big manufacturers. It was not patent control but the intercorporate agreement, and especially the ensuing policy of low pricing—a policy based on efficient production for a growing national market—that assured G.E. and Westinghouse continuing dominance of the lamp industry.

The two giants had meanwhile fought bitterly over the market for generators and distributing systems. Here the Edison interests, wedded to direct current, set out to prove that alternating current was inefficient, unreliable, and unsafe. The increasing efficiency of the Westinghouse installation drove the Edison firm to concentrate on the alleged dangers of a.c., which was described, sometimes by Edison himself, as a "horrible menace," a vehicle of "instant and painless death." The latter claim drew heavily on the adoption by New York State of alternating current for the electrocution of criminals. Understandably agitated, Westinghouse in 1888 thought it a "matter of very serious consideration as to whether or not we could not proceed against the directors of the Edison Company . . . for conspiracy . . . for their recklessness, and, you might say, criminal course." But instead Westinghouse joined the battle of words, writing articles on the technological advantages of a.c. and spurring his colleagues to attacks on the Edison interests as the "electricity trust." In the end, alternating current won on its merits. Though Edison thought his rival a "man . . . gone crazy," the General Electric Company at the time of its formation included one unit engaged in the business of making and selling a.c. equipment, which eventually became the means of generating 95 per cent of the nation's electrical energy.

In the judgment of Harold Passer, the ablest student of electrical manufacturers, Westinghouse was "an independent thinker who had the courage to act on his beliefs no matter how strong the opposition." He was a master at contriving systems or combinations in business as well as in invention. He suffered severely from the temporary financial difficulties of his electrical company in 1907, difficulties that forced him out of its control, but in the years before his death in 1914 he brought the integrity and stamina of his person to his role as trustee in the reorganization of the shaky Equitable Life Assurance Society. Nikola Tesla remembered him most for his vitality, for "the tremendous potential energy of the man . . . the latent force . . . powerful frame . . . a rare example of health and strength. Like a lion in a forest, he breathed deep and with delight the smoky air of his factories. . . . He was transformed into a giant when confronted with difficulties." And as a giant he helped to transform America during the wonderful dawn of the electrical age.

It was by then high noon in the growth of Pittsburgh and of steel, the city's staff and stay. Like all industries,

the steel industry stumbled through the depression that followed the panic of 1893. Like the others, steel entered a new period of boom in 1897. Investment, employment, and prices were again rising, and William McKinley, safely victorious over Bryan, offered from the White House a dinner pail full of permissiveness for enterprise and its agents. The experience of the depression, moreover, by whetting the ordinary yearnings of businessmen for stability and certainty, had provoked new interest in industrial combinations designed to restrain competition or to enhance efficiency and profits. The promotion of such consolidations caught the fancy of men, some wise and some foolish, who sought personal wealth from the boons available to successful architects of mergers. In steel they built their grandest edifice.

Carnegie and his associates had, of course, provided a glowing example of the benefits of consolidation. Notable for its efficiency and power, the Carnegie Steel Company manufactured chiefly semi-finished steel and such heavy products as rails, plates, structural steel, and bridge materials. At the century's end, reorganized as the Carnegie Company of New Jersey, it produced some 18 per cent of American ingots which it sold largely to makers of wire, nails, tubes, sheet, and tin plate. It had strong competitors. J. Pierpont Morgan, the Jupiter of American finance, presided in 1898 over the consolidation of the Federal Steel Company which was integrated in the Carnegie model and manufactured the same kind of products, including 15 per cent of the nation's ingots. Some of those were consumed by other Morgan properties, like the American Steel and Wire Company, consolidated and incorporated in 1898, the National Tube Company, 1898, and the American Bridge Company, 1900 —all founded for the purpose, among others, of restraining competition in their separate fields. Other mergers created the American Tin Plate Company in 1898, the American Steel Hoop Company in 1899, and the American Sheet Steel Company and the Shelby Steel Tube Company in 1900. All but the last of these represented the promoting efforts of Judge William H. Moore and his brother James, who, in contrast to Morgan, tended to build their corporate structures on rather flimsy foundations. In that manner in 1899 they also put together the National Steel Company, a concern directly competitive with Carnegie and Federal, and the supplier of some 12 per cent of the country's ingots. Largely as a result of the power of the many new consolidations, the prices of steel and steel products moved perceptibly upward between 1898 and 1900.

Yet all was not stable in the trade, for the original promoters of the "wire trust" had still unrealized designs. They were a strange brace. One, Judge Elbert H. Gary, was a shrewd negotiator and administrator with the appearance and manner of "a Methodist bishop—benign, suave, cordial, and earnest." Even J. P. Morgan trusted him. The other, John W. Gates, was, in the phrase of his

(turn to page 256)

THE HOME OF A SOUTH SIDE FAMILY WITH EVERYBODY ON DECK, AS PHOTOGRAPHED BY PETER KRUMEL.

secretary, "a great boy with an extraordinary money sense annexed." A notorious plunger, "Bet-a-Million" Gates was rumored to have spent one afternoon aboard a train wagering with a friend on the race of raindrops from top to bottom of their windowpane, at a thousand dollars a match. Though suspicious of Gates, Morgan had to accept his place in the entente established by his participation in the forming of the "wire trust" and by his closeness to Gary whom Jupiter designated president of Federal Steel. And it was Gates who fired the first shot in the skirmish that threatened to set off a steel war.

Gates envisaged vast profits, some from promotion, some from efficiencies, in the possibilities of an integrated super-combination to contain units not only for finishing but also for producing steel, and even for mining iron ore. Such a combination would be free of the need to buy semi-finished steel from Carnegie, whose earnings Gates coveted. Audaciously he informed the Carnegie Company that American Steel and Wire would cancel its contracts for crude steel and henceforth make its own. Shortly Carnegie Company received the same warning from American Bridge, where surely the Morgan influence was somehow at work, and from the three properties of the brothers Moore.

Carnegie was in Scotland when he learned of these challenges. He accepted the battle offered him. "Urge prompt action essential," he cabled his associates; "crisis has arrived, only one policy open: start at once hoop, rod, wire, nail mills; no halfway about last two. Extend coal and coke roads; announce these; also tubes . . . have no fear as to the results; victory certain." Now even Morgan trembled, for Carnegie could win the war. His closely held company had the cash, the credit, and the organization to outproduce and undersell its brash rivals. Outmaneuvering them, too, Carnegie opened negotiations for building a railway to break the monopoly of the Pennsylvania on traffic between Pittsburgh and the seaboard. "Carnegie," Morgan complained, "is going to demoralize railroads just as he has demoralized steel."

On December 12, 1900, Morgan heard the dulcet voice of prosperous peace. That night Charles Schwab, after a dinner at the University Club in New York, described the glorious future open to steel if a fully integrated, efficient, super-consolidation could arise to bring discipline to the industry. "In intimate conversation" after that speech, Morgan drew Schwab out. Days later the financier enlisted Gates to entice Schwab back to New York, where the three men talked through the night. Schwab returned to Pittsburgh with Morgan's offer to buy out Carnegie, who quickly set his terms: for every $1000 of bonds in the Carnegie Company, the new super-corporation was to exchange $1000 of its securities; for every $1000 of stock in the Carnegie Company, $1500 of those securities; Carnegie himself was to get payment only in bonds, worth some $225,639,000. This would make him a creditor without responsibility for management and

(turn to page 258)

FROM THE PHOTOGRAPH ALBUM OF THE HOWE FAMILY

DINING ROOM AT "GREYSTONE."

THE FRONT PARLOR AT "GREYSTONE."

THE MUSIC ROOM AT "GREYSTONE."

A CEREMONIOUS DEPARTURE: FARE-THEE-WELL, FARE-THEE-WELL, AND DON'T FORGET TO WRITE.

The two Howe girls bid good-by to their mother on the entrance porch of "Greystone," the spacious home of the family. Left to right: Mrs. George Wilkins Guthrie, the former Florence Julia Howe; Mrs. Thomas Marshall Howe, the mother of the girls; Miss Ella Howe, who later became Mrs. Francis Bailey Nimick; Miss Mary Brown, and Miss Alice Bryan Howe. It was an emotional farewell. Where did the two girls travel? Who knows? They might have gone as far as downtown Pittsburgh.

LIFE OF A PITTSBURGH LADY

K. P. DUTY. Florence Brown and Ella Howe seem to enjoy the peeling of potatoes; but Mrs. George W. Guthrie has had enough.

CORRESPONDENCE. Alice Bryan Howe stayed hours at her desk writing letters—the telephone was not yet used for social calls.

SIESTA. Jennie and Ella Howe are having a quiet time relaxing in the hammock. Jennie catches up on her sleep, Ella reads her mail.

thus permit the retirement he had contemplated so long. So informed, Morgan said at once, "I accept." Several weeks later, when the two principals met, Morgan congratulated Carnegie "on being the richest man in the world."

Still further weeks remained before Morgan completed his work. Gates tried in vain to squeeze more from him than he would exchange for securities of American Steel and Wire. The Rockefellers set and received an astronomical price for their Lake Superior Consolidated Iron Mines, which held the largest ore deposits in the Mesabi Range. In March 1901 the job was done, and Morgan announced the organization of the United States Steel Corporation. Schwab served as the first president of the giant merger that brought together the Carnegie, Morgan, and Moore properties, as well as some others within a few years, all in all, about 60 per cent of the nation's steel industry, capitalized at a record figure of $1,402,846,817.

Much of that sum represented not tangible property but a confidence in the earning capacity of the first billion-dollar corporation. Earnings during the next decade repaid that confidence. There was still competition in steel —indeed, the United States Steel Corporation gradually lost some of its share of market to competitors like Bethlehem, which Schwab organized as a fully integrated concern after he left the Morgan-made colossus. U. S. Steel made its profits during the first decades of the twentieth century, largely as Schwab had predicted and Carnegie had demonstrated it could, by efficiencies in production for an expanding market to which it sold vigorously, fairly, and without coercion.

In retirement and on his own, King Andrew also remained vigorous, dedicated at last to his good works and to building foundations to pursue them, especially, as he had written in 1868, "those concerned with education and improvement of the poorer classes." Just as he had in many respects set a model for Pittsburgh's ablest entrepreneurs, so did he now set an example for the wisest and most beneficent (though by no means a majority) of the nation's multimillionaires. What he conceived to be the "duty of the man of wealth" became in time, partly, to be sure, under the prodding of federal tax laws, the privilege of those richest men—the Rockefellers, Guggenheims, Fords, and Mellons, among others—who, absorbing his lesson, came "to consider all surplus revenues . . . as trust funds . . . to administer in the manner . . . best calculated to provide the most beneficial results for the community." Philanthropy on Carnegie's imperial scale left a mark upon America that princely ostentation never equalled.

But the largest mark was made by industry itself, by the strategies and structures and achievements of the businesses that made kinetic the potential energies of the continent. In that process, the entrepreneurs of Pittsburgh, whatever their foibles and their faults, performed Olympian parts.

COURTSHIP TIME.
The William St. C. D. Corcorans.

MARRIED LIFE.
The William St. C. D. Corcorans.

Dinner.

Saturday, December 25, '97.

Blue Points   Celery

Giblet a l'Anglaise   Haute Sauterne

Consomme Printaniere Royale   Sweet Cider

Boiled Kennebec Salmon a la Trianon

Fillet of Striped Bass a la Joinville

Duchesse Potatoes

Olives   Lettuce   Young Onions   Salted Almonds

Young Capon, Supreme Sauce   Asparagus, Butter Sauce

Ribs of Prime Beef au Jus, St. Julienne   Turkey Chestnut Dressing, Cranberry Sauce

Sweet Corn

Suckling Pig, Apple Sauce   Sweet Potato Chips

Breast of Pheasant a la Victoria

Sweetbreads Glace a la Financiere, Green Peas

Stewed Terrapin in Casses a la Maryland

Imperial Punch

Canvas Back Duck. Currant Jelly   Fried Hominy

Boiled and Mashed Potatoes   Spinach with Egg   Cauliflower Hollandaise

Chicken Salad

English Plum Pudding, Hard and Brandy Sauce

Mince Pie   Pumpkin Pie

Fruit Jelly   Assorted Cakes

Ice Cream in Forms   French Confections

Selected Fruit   Mint Wafers

Mixed Nuts, Raisins and Figs

Roquefort, Swiss and Neufchatel Cheese

Toasted Crackers

Coffee   Tea   Buttermilk

Courtesy Mary McSwigan.

CHRISTMAS MENU at the Monongahela House in 1897. Now that the depression years were gone, Pittsburghers—all those who could afford it—enjoyed the pleasures of life. Business was excellent; steel, iron, glass, and coal were doing fine. In the election the year before the hard-money idea prevailed—William Jennings Bryan and the Populists were defeated; the Democratic plank to coin silver in the ratio of 16 to 1 was voted down. The country was content with William McKinley and the full dinner pail.

As Pittsburghers celebrated Christmas in 1897 they looked toward a rosy future. In the last two decades the city's working population increased well over 100 per cent. One-fourth of the steel, one-sixth of the world's pig iron came from Pennsylvania, much of it from Pittsburgh. Some of the city's furnaces produced 800 tons of steel a day—a capacity not matched anywhere else.

Prosperity was in the skies. A few more months and Theodore Roosevelt, with his Rough Riders, stormed San Juan Hill. And when the war was over, Cuba was free; Hawaii, the Philippines, and Puerto Rico became dependencies. The United States, and Pittsburgh, were truly on the march.

Chapter 8

THE MUCKRAKING ERA

by Gerald W. Johnson

THE HISTORY of Pittsburgh between the turn of the century and the First World War may fairly be described as a period of thunder on the left. It was the time when astute publishers, S. S. McClure in the van, discovered that a magazine, to be marketable, need not restrict its color to the pastel prose of the Rev. Dr. Henry Van Dyke and the equally pallid verse of Mr. Richard Watson Gilder. The raw, primary hues of the literature of protest would build circulation, and once the discovery was made it was exploited to the limit; the magazines became lurid in a way that Mr. Hearst's and Mr. Pulitzer's newspapers never had because the monthly publications dealt not with sex and mayhem, but with political, economic, and sociological malefactors.

Lincoln Steffens was operating on the cities, David Graham Phillips on politics, Ida Tarbell on big business, each at the head of a legion of writers only less—sometimes no less—spectacular; and these groups, which radicals called allies, and reactionaries accomplices, largely dominated the field of public discussion.

"Muckrakers!" snorted John Bunyan's assiduous student, Theodore Roosevelt, President of the United States. The reference was to Bunyan's allegory of the man behind and above whom stood a celestial being proffering a golden crown which the man did not see, because he would not raise his eyes from the muck he was raking together on the ground. The epithet, like many of Roosevelt the First's, was venomous and vivid, therefore adhesive. Perhaps the President's disgust was based on dislike of the writers' thematic material, or perhaps on their ability to outshout stentorian T. R., who had small affection for voices louder than his own; regardless of its

origin, the term has survived into our own day and has been extended from a class to a period grown familiar to us as the muckraking era.

The allegory, to be sure, is truncated. We can see the man and the muck clearly enough, but the celestial being and the crown are hard to descry in the murk of that decade and a half. Cynics aver that they existed only in the politician's imagination, but in the perspective of half a century it is possible to believe that the muckrakers were in fact overlooking a good thing, although not the things that Theodore Roosevelt would have pointed out as good. They were intent upon arousing moral indignation, a force too erratic to be of great efficacy, but their work resulted in familiarizing a large public with certain political and economic realities, and that was a release of power.

In 1903 Lincoln Steffens described Pittsburgh physically as "Hell with the lid off," politically as "Hell with the lid on." But by the time Steffens published his findings, the heyday of the Magee-Flinn ring had already passed. Magee had died in 1901, and the Pittsburgh reform elements were on the march.

Civic-minded citizens of both parties formed the Municipal League, asking for honest and good government. The quarrel between William Flinn and Senator Matthew Quay, the head of the Republican forces in Pennsylvania, helped the efforts of the reformers. Quay guided a bill through the Legislature which was to change the city charter. On March 7, 1901, "An Act for the Government of Cities of the Second Class" became law. This law became popularly known as the Ripper Act, because it empowered the Governor to remove or "rip out" recorders (another

(turn to page 264)

TRINITY CHURCH ON SIXTH AVENUE NEAR WOOD STREET IN 1901.

OLD PENNSYLVANIA RAILROAD DEPOT ON FEDERAL STREET IN 1906.

PITTSBURGH SKYLINE FROM ACROSS THE MONONGAHELA IN 1902.

THE CITY
AT THE TURN
OF THE CENTURY.

262

THE POINT IN THE EARLY YEARS OF THE TWENTIETH CENTURY—A DRAMATIC PICTURE OF THE TWO RIVERS.

The suspension Point Bridge in the foreground was built in the year when Pittsburgh celebrated the first centennial of the country's independence. The bridge lasted for half a century—it was torn down in 1927.

The large structures on the Allegheny side are the buildings of the Pittsburgh Exposition. They were destroyed—save the Machinery Hall—in the great fire of 1900, but were soon rebuilt.

Looking at this contemporary photograph it is difficult not to be impressed by the vast transformation which took place within the span of only two generations. Were it not for the rivers and the marked geographical position of the city one would have difficulty to recognize that this cluster of buildings once adorned the Golden Triangle.

The tracks and warehouses are gone. In their stead are modern office buildings, a luxurious hotel, and a park.

People like to talk of the good old days. But if these were—as far as appearance is concerned—the good old days, we can rejoice that the new ones are even better.

263

name for mayor). Soon after the bill was enacted, Governor Stone "ripped" out of office Mayor William Diehl and appointed in his stead Major A. M. Brown as the first recorder of Pittsburgh. But when Major Brown showed independent traits, he too was "ripped out" and replaced by another Brown––J. O. Brown, who formerly had belonged to the Magee-Flinn ring. The citizens of Pittsburgh were enraged when they learned that the ring had raised a substantial fund for the Governor, obviously to reward him for his services. They founded the Citizens' Party and in the 1902 election put up candidates in opposition to the members of the ring. In the election the reform candidates were eminently successful; they won the office of the comptroller and took half of the council seats. However, their victory was not a lasting one.

A new political potentate, Thomas Bigelow, emerged on the scene. Joining forces with Quay, he began where Flinn and Magee left off. The old ring was smashed, but there was Bigelow to be boss of the new ring. In the spring of 1903 his candidate, William B. Hays (after the recordership had been abolished), became mayor. Those who asked for better government kept on with their fight; they rallied behind the Democrat, George W. Guthrie, whose father had been mayor of the city before the Civil War, and elected him to the mayoralty in 1906. Guthrie held office for three years, and, though his performance was good and honest, he was not able to assert his control on the council, an unwieldy body in which all the forty-five wards of Pittsburgh were represented. This situation got worse when the cities of Pittsburgh and Allegheny merged in 1907; the additional councilmen, each of them looking after the interest of his own ward (and some of them after their own interests) made a smooth administration all but impossible.

After Guthrie came William Magee, a nephew of Chris, who according to the local historian, George Swetnam, "set off a new rush of city buildings, with the lion's share of the contracts going once more to the firm of Booth and Flinn." Under him graft flourished once again. Council members were bribed for voting away valuable franchises. A. Leo Weil and other prominent Pittsburghers organized the Voters' Civic League, which presented damaging evidence against the corruption of councilmen to the grand jury. Over a hundred persons—councilmen, businessmen, bankers—were involved in the wholesale exposures; sixty of the indicted pleaded *nolo contendere*; in the end a number of them were sentenced to jail or penitentiary.

This sordid affair brought about the most important municipal reform of the period—the passage of an act by the State Legislature in June 1911 that set the mayor's term at four years and abolished the two-chamber council. The act provided for a single-chamber council composed

(turn to page 266)

LIBERTY AVENUE IN 1900 had all kinds of vehicles scurrying around. There were horse-drawn drays, equipages, and even locomotive-drawn trains. The railroad tracks were firmly embedded in the center—not until 1905 were they removed.

IT WAS A BUSY CITY—traffic on the main avenues passed in a steady flow, the multitude of horse-drawn vehicles carried produce and people, there was a feverish activity everywhere; people scurried and hurried, they were busy making money.

It seemed that in the early years of the century the traffic in Pittsburgh was less regulated than it is now. If one looks at this 1906 photograph of Liberty Avenue toward east, one sees horses moving in all directions. On the whole the traffic flowed on the left of the street, but observe the scene and see how many drivers disregarded the rule. They drove as the spirit moved them, the street was their kingdom, nobody was to interfere in their free movement. They parked their carriages whether they happened to be on the left side or on the right. Nobody cared. And there was no policeman to give a ticket.

265

of nine members, all of them elected at large. Thus, each councilman represented and was responsible for the whole community and not only one ward.

Though the political corruption in Pittsburgh was admittedly one of the most shameful chapters in the city's history—there was graft that the ring members received for granting contracts and franchises; there was a well-organized syndicate that exacted large sums of money through vice—it may be plausibly argued that this sooty chapter in the Pittsburgh story was historically necessary. The fact that it was duplicated in the development of every other big city sustains the argument. But if the experience was necessary, so were muckraking and the muckrakers. The mere titles of some of the popular successes of those days—*The Shame of the Cities, The Treason of the Senate, Frenzied Finance*—are enough to inspire in a more tolerant, or perhaps merely suaver, generation a touch of disdain of the raw emotionalism they reflect. We hold in low esteem fellows who operate with a meat ax instead of a scalpel.

True enough. But it is also true that just at this time—in 1902, to be exact—George F. Baer, the head of the Pennsylvania Railroad, gained unenviable fame through a letter which contained the often-quoted passage:

The rights and interests of the laboring man will be protected and cared for—not by labor agitators, but by the Christian men to whom God in His infinite wisdom has given the control of the property interests of the country.

Upon complacence so ineffable could any implement short of a meat ax produce the slightest effect? The butcher boys at any rate did produce an effect. Its magnitude is attested by a message received by Upton Sinclair, in some respects the greatest of the muckrakers, after publication of his book on the meat packers, *The Jungle.* Theodore Roosevelt wrote to a friend: "Tell Sinclair to go home and let me run the country for a while."

On the other hand, the fury of the muckrakers was often misdirected. In so far as it was leveled against conditions then existing it was, if anything not vehement enough, but it was off the beam when it attributed those conditions solely, or even largely, to the moral turpitude of the ruling class. Of some villainy they were certainly guilty, but less than the furious reformers pretended. Among them were honest people who eventually acknowledged the fact; Steffens and Tarbell, for instance, in later life realized that they had personalized guilt beyond the measure justified by the facts, by attributing to individuals faults that were inherent in the system dominant at the time. Steffens admitted that city officials are frequently trapped into crookedness. Tarbell became a friend and sincere admirer of the original Rockefeller.

The Ironmasters of Pittsburgh and their allies in other industries and in finance come under the same rule. A few of them, it cannot be denied, had the ethics of Captain Kidd and the esthetics of an orangoutang, but in the main they were quite ordinary types, exceptionally energetic,

(turn to page 268)

THE MEAL OF MILLIONAIRES. THE BANQUET AT
On the evening of January 9, 1901, 89 officials of the Carnegie Steel Company, among them Charles M. Schwab, Lawrence C. Phipps, S. L. Schoonmaker, Charles L. Taylor, William Singer,

THE SCHENLEY HOTEL CELEBRATING THE FORMATION OF THE UNITED STATES STEEL CORPORATION.
Alexander Peacock, Daniel Clemson, Thomas Morrison—to name only a few—celebrated the founding of the nation's first billion-dollar corporation. Andrew Carnegie, who, together with his partners received about half a billion dollars worth of bonds and preferred and common stock, was absent but sent his best wishes, predicting the company's future would "eclipse its past."

THE HOMES OF THE MILLIONAIRES.

"BEECHWOOD," THE RESIDENCE OF W. N. FREW.

"EBONHURST," THE HOME OF DAVID P. BLACK.

"CLAYTON," THE RESIDENCE OF HENRY CLAY FRICK.

THE RESIDENCE OF D. M. CLEMSON ON FIFTH.

RESIDENCE OF HENRY C. BAIR ON NORTH HIGHLAND.

"SOLITUDE," THE HOME OF GEORGE WESTINGHOUSE.

certainly, but not exceptional either for greed or for brutality. Their failure was lack of perception of the realities of their own situation.

The labors of scholars in later days have clarified our understanding of the process of capital accumulation. We know now that the rapid industrialization of a nation is not to be accomplished without stresses, some of which are sure to inflict formidable pain on a large number of people. Machines cost money, much money. Hence rapid industrialization necessarily involves immense expenditures, and expenditures on that scale presuppose an immense accumulation of capital. If the necessary capital is not in hand, there are only three ways of obtaining it— by borrowing it, stealing it, or sweating it out of the people, first of all out of the labor force.

In the case of the United States, industrialized, in the

268

"GRANDVIEW," RESIDENCE OF LAWRENCE C. PHIPPS.

"RHU-NA-CRAIG," RESIDENCE OF THOMAS MORRISON.

RESIDENCE OF JOHN EATON ON BIDWELL STREET.

"LYNDHURST," THE RESIDENCE OF MRS. WILLIAM THAW.

RESIDENCE OF WALLACE H. ROWE, MOREWOOD AVENUE.

Photographs taken for **Palmer's Pittsburgh** *(1905).*

HOME OF A. A. FRAUENHEIM AT BEACON AND MURDOCH.

generation after the Civil War with speed hitherto un-precedented, the method of theft was impractical because the contiguous territory, in Canada and Mexico, was less advanced industrially than our own. We borrowed great sums. As late at 1914, when many of the loans had been repaid, American investments of Great Britain alone amounted to from four to six billions, and we had bor-rowed from many other countries. But at that, borrowing

alone could not maintain the pace at which our economy was advancing, so taking it out of the hides of the workers was the sole remaining recourse. And we took it.

Thus baldly stated the process seems to be so monstrous as to render it incredible that civilized men tolerated it. But it was not so baldly stated, or at least so understood. Dimly and uncertainly, but definitely, American public opinion between 1865 and 1900 comprehended, or rather

Photograph by R. W. Johnston.

HOW PITTSBURGHERS LIVED: THE LIVING ROOM OF THE PEACOCK'S MANSION ON HIGHLAND AVENUE.

Courtesy Art Commission Survey.

HOW PITTSBURGHERS LIVED: the back porch and the privy of a poor family in one of the slum districts of the city.

felt without fully understanding, that an enormous undertaking was in process, and if it called for enormous exertion on the part of everyone engaged, well, what else could you expect? Public sympathy with labor, therefore, tended to be sporadic, usually confined to individual instances of peculiarly outrageous exploitation.

By the turn of the century, though, public sympathy with labor was becoming generalized and formidable. The muckrakers were its literary expression, while its political manifestation took the form of a variegated and shifting series of adventures loosely summed up under the name of Populism. Today, with the inestimable advantage of hindsight, we know that what had happened was that industrialization was "over the hump," which is to say that industry, taken in the large, had begun to make profits equal to or in excess of the capital requirements of the expanding economy. Thus the process of sweating labor,

(turn to page 272)

Art Commission Survey.

BUT ALL WAS NOT WELL in the city. There was plenty of bad housing, slums, dirt and squalor, billboards, bad wiring, poor pavement, and rows and rows of mutilated trees, their destruction caused by horses. What to do about it? How to solve the problems of the rapidly growing metropolis? An Art Commission was appointed to make a survey in the second decade of the century; it collected data, made recommendations to remedy the situation, but the Pittsburghers were not yet ready. Much water had to flow under the bridges, smoke had to become much denser, the floods more destructive, before the people of Pittsburgh realized that they must act. They behaved as others in similar situations; they postponed decisions, and they acted only when conditions grew so bad that they were forced to attempt to do something about them.

271

at one time a grim necessity, had become needless and therefore outrageous.

The inevitable result of the sweated labor system was to convert Pittsburgh for a time into a lifelike imitation of hell as visualized by the Reverend Jonathan Edwards. There is no need to take the muckrakers' word for it. Startled by their rhetoric, the Russell Sage Foundation sent into the city its own observers, in no way dependent upon the ten-cent magazines for their income and with no reason to report anything but cold fact. Nevertheless, their objective survey, issued by the Foundation in six imposing tomes, contains passages hardly less lurid than the most startling pages of *McClure's, Everybody's* or *Cosmopolitan.*

The English philosopher, Herbert Spencer, after a visit to the town, voiced the opinion that a month in Pittsburgh would justify anyone in committing suicide. It was a false generalization, of course, but it had a substratum of truth firm enough to give it wide currency. Pittsburgh in these years was rough and unlovely, but Pittsburgh was a big city—553,905 population in 1910 (which at this time already included the population of Allegheny, incorporated three years before)—and any generalizations about a big city can be supported by citation of selected facts.

At this same time sumptuous residences sprang up, monumental business structures were erected (the Keystone Bank Building in 1902, the Farmers Bank Building in 1903, the Diamond National Bank Building in 1905, the Commonwealth Building in 1906, the Benedum-Trees Building in 1906, the Union National Bank Building in 1907, the Century Building in 1907, the Henry W. Oliver Building in 1910, the Bell Telephone Building in 1911, the Jenkins Arcade in 1911, to mention only a few), theatres and hotels came into being (the Nixon Theatre in 1903, the Hotel Fort Pitt in 1906), the magnificent gothic St. Paul's Cathedral was built at a cost of about $900,000 (it was consecrated on October 24, 1906), ornate railroad stations (Wabash Terminal in 1905), institutions of learning (Carnegie Technical Schools, buildings of the University of Pittsburgh in Oakland, the magnificent Mellon Institute for Industrial Research) sprang up—not to speak of the numerous bridges and parks that appeared in the city with mushroom-like speed and profusion.

If residence there was enough to justify suicide, as one viewed certain aspects of the city, as one viewed others it was justification for aspiring to rival Methuselah. In sum, Pittsburgh was vibrantly, furiously alive, which is tantamount to saying that it was filled with contradictions. The city was moving with the times. In 1909 the first taxicab

CHRISTMAS RUSH AT THE CORNER OF SMITHFIELD and Fifth Avenue in the second decade of the century. There were already motor cars on the streets, but the most common means of transportation were trolleys and horse-drawn vehicles. On the right Kaufmann's Store, across from it the Park Building.

SALVATION ARMY
XMAS BASKET DINNERS TO POOR FAMILIES
GENERAL RELIEF DURING WINTER
PLEASE HELP — THANK YOU

273

Courtesy Marie McSwigan.

AN OUTING OF PITTSBURGH MEN. On the right of the front seat is editor A. S. McSwigan. The others are well-to-do businessmen on their way to enjoy a ride.

Courtesy Albert D. Liefeld.

THE SHADYSIDE ACADEMY CLUB as it posed in the summer of 1900. When the boys strummed their guitars, mandolins, and banjos, and maidens swooned like willow trees in the breeze.

From The Library, April 21, 1900.

OPENING NIGHT at the Grau Opera was one of the city's fashionable occasions. This illustration of the event appeared in *The Library*, a Pittsburgh weekly.

Burg and Hager Hotel Saloon, Courtesy Jones & Laughlin.

THERE WERE SALOONS where worries ebbed away. Even if one complained all the time, while there was beer in the tap and someone to talk to life was bearable.

Photograph by Frank E. Bingaman in the Carnegie Library.

THE NATIONAL LEAGUE CHAMPIONS OF 1902, the Pittsburgh Pirates. They also won the pennant in 1901 and 1903. Back row: Zimmer, Sebring, Phillipe, Thompson, Leever, Phelps; center row, Chesbro, Bransfield, Manager Fred Clarke, President Barney Dreyfuss, Honus Wagner, Clarence Beaumont, Smith; front row, Conroy, Tommy Leach, Claude Ritchey, McLaughlin.

Courtesy Mrs. Richard S. Large.

TO SHOP IN PITTSBURGH was an experience. This snapshot from the early 1900s shows the family of Samuel P. Large on their journey home from the city.

company came into being with a fleet of eighteen automobiles. In the same year the Pittsburgh Pirates defeated the Detroit Tigers at Forbes Field in the seventh, decisive game of the World Series and became the champion team of America.

But, even with all its other activities, the dominant phenomenon of the city's life was the steel industry with its attendant satellites—smelters, coke ovens, coal yards, limestone dumps, and many other chemical and metallurgical facilities. Steel recorded phenomenal progress during this period. Though there were many areas in the city which cried for radical improvement and change, the production of steel was not one of them. The output of steel ingots and castings in the district rose from 10 million

TURN OF THE CENTURY.

Courtesy Carnegie Library.

THE FIRST CLASS in Margaret Morrison Carnegie School for Women, a part of Carnegie Technical Schools. This Charter Class of 1909 had 70 students on entrance of which 43 Seniors graduated.

Photograph by Frank E. Bingaman in the Carnegie Library.

THE PITTSBURGH PIRATES IN TRAINING IN 1902. This picture was taken in Thomasville, Georgia. Back row: Fred Ely, Sam Leever, Fred Clarke, Unknown, Jimmie Williams, Tom McCreery, Jouett Meekin; center: Tommy Leach, Tom O'Brien, Walter Woods, Pop Shriver, Clarence Beaumont, Jack Chesbro; front: Jess Tannehil, Claude Ritchey, F. Dillon, Latimer, Flaherty.

tons at the opening of the century to double that figure in 1905 and to 31 million tons in 1913. (The national figures were 23,276,000 tons in 1901, 42,678,000 tons in 1914, and in the war year of 1917 no less than 53,914,000 tons.) Rolling mill output increased threefold—from 12.4 million tons in 1901 to 20 million in 1907 and to 25 million in 1913. The country's production of pig iron was 23,961,000 tons in 1901 of which amount about one-fourth came from Pittsburgh mills; in 1917 the furnaces of America created 51,368,000 tons of pig iron. But the most succinct illustration for the growth of the city are the figures for the river and rail tonnage. In 1900 they amounted to 65,818,631; in 1910 they rose to 167,733,268, more than two and a half times as much.

From The Library, June 23, 1900.

THE RIGHTEOUS LADIES of the D.A.R. who had a strong opinion on all matters and a professed knowledge of how to uphold morals, visit Mrs. McCandless.

From The Library, June 23, 1900.

CONVENTIONS were usually jolly affairs. An exception might have been these homeopaths in August 1900, but perhaps it was the camera which froze them stiff.

Courtesy Carnegie Library.

UNCLE JOHN at play. The scientist, John Alfred Brashear (see page 178), was a warmhearted humanitarian, with a rare understanding and love for people.

From The Library, June 30, 1900.

A LOVELY AFTERNOON at Oakwood, but the two girls in the foreground are not enjoying it. They keep their umbrella within easy reach — just in case.

The other Pittsburgh industries prospered equally well; some of them, like the glass and electric industries, became gigantic enterprises, but in general they all more or less subserved steel. Thus, in a very real sense, the steelworkers were Pittsburgh, and their lives might reasonably be held to typify the city's life.

It was brutish. That is putting it bluntly, but it is as true as it is blunt. To this day, under the best conditions that modern technology has been able to devise, steelmaking is no kid-glove job; it involves very high temperatures and very great pressure, both capable of destroying human life. Survival among them depends upon strength, skill, and never-flagging alertness. This is valid even today, after safety devices and regulations have been vastly improved. What it must have been like before these were introduced almost persuades one that Spencer might have said that residence in Pittsburgh *was* suicide, sometimes long-drawn-out, but often brutally swift.

It is unnecessary to resort to the purple prose of the muckrakers of the time to find documentary evidence of the conditions that provoked the philosopher's statement. The sober language of the Russell Sage Foundation Survey is sufficient. They conscientiously sought facts, not literary effects, yet the sociologists who wrote the volumes were occasionally shaken out of their scientific detachment by their discoveries.

A curious feature of the report on *The Steelworkers*, written by John A. Fitch, is that famine, usually the most conspicuous factor in studies of the sub-cellars of the social structure, played a relatively small part in this one. Except when disturbances of some kind—strikes, lockouts, financial juggling, or economic depression—halted or slowed down operations, the steelworkers ate pretty well. They had to. It is not physically possible for a man to wrestle immense weights of red-hot metal twelve hours a day, seven days a week, without being well-nourished.

Misery in Pittsburgh in those years was of a different type. Its most active toxin was the cold brutality of irresponsible power. The pride of the steel industry at the moment was its modernization of the process of steelmaking by the introduction of automatic machinery. From the standpoint of the second half of the twentieth century, it was pretty crude stuff, but in those days it was the very last word. The propagandists of the industry never tired

(turn to page 280)

A LONG REMEMBERED CONCERT. In March 1904 the Pittsburgh Symphony gave a celebrated concert. The conductor was Victor Herbert, who was to resign shortly thereafter. Richard Strauss, too, conducted a composition of his own, but in this photograph he modestly took a place behind the contrabass. The composer of *Der Rosenkavalier* is first from the right, last row.

277

Courtesy Carnegie Institute of Technology.

GROUND BREAKING for Industries Hall, the first building of Carnegie Technical Schools. The photograph, showing Mrs. Andrew A. Hamerschlag, and her husband (standing behind her), the School's first Director, was taken on April 3, 1905.

THE BEGINNINGS OF CARNEGIE TECH.

MACHINE DRAWING CLASS of 1906 at the School of Apprentices and Journeymen, which grew into the College of Industries in 1921, and in 1934 to the College of Engineering.

right:

CORNERSTONE CEREMONIES, on April 25, 1912 for the School of Applied Design, College of Fine Arts was a gala affair.

A STUDENT'S ROOM AT CARNEGIE TECH IN 1911.

A. A. HAMERSCHLAG WITH CHARLES M. SCHWAB.

THE FIRST CLASS OF THE CARNEGIE TECHNICAL SCHOOLS, AS IT WAS PHOTOGRAPHED IN THE YEAR 1905.

THE HEINZ HOME was moved from its original Sharpsburg location to the site of the Heinz's works in Allegheny. A barge carried the house in the spring of 1904 and residents by the hundreds lined the river bank to watch the fascinating spectacle.

LUNCH HOUR at the H. J. Heinz Company at the turn of the century. An orphenium, the forerunner of the player piano provided music during the meal for the neatly dressed girls.

of boasting of its wonders—traveling cranes that could toss five-ton ingots about as if they weighed no more than tennis balls, ladles the size of boxcarts that could tip molten metal into molds with the delicate precision of a woman watering plants in a flower box, giant hammers powerful enough to flatten an ingot, yet so accurately adjusted that they could crack the crystal of a watch without damage to the works.

They thought it was wonderful, and they were right. Yet they ignored the fact that in the pioneer stages of automation its first effect is not to lessen, but to heighten, the strain on the workmen. In an earlier day, when steelmaking was still largely a handicraft, journeymen and apprentices could be driven no faster than the ironmaster could drive them, and they were nearly, often quite, as good men as he was. The mill hand who could work the boss down was a proud man, and very certainly on the way to becoming a boss himself.

But after the coming of automation the utmost hope of

the workman was barely to keep up with the machine, which nobody could beat. The old folk song of John Henry, the steel-drivin' man, and the steam hammer is, like most genuine myths, a fictional presentation of historical fact. John Henry, according to the myth, actually beat the steam hammer in a steel-driving contest, but in the moment of victory he dropped dead.

The power-driven machinery required in the steel industry is enormously expensive, and interest on the investment continues to run whether the machinery runs or stands idle. It is therefore essential to keep it in continuous operation, and since the human working force cannot operate continuously, it was necessary to divide it into shifts. The obvious pattern of organization comprised two—a day shift and a night shift. This logic of the clock seemed to early employers no doubt as much a part of the order of nature as the courses of the sun and stars. To question it was sheer perversity, for years were to pass before "practical" businessmen grasped the pre-eminently practical fact that working twelve hours a day at a handicraft or on a farm is widely different from working twelve hours a

day in a steel mill. In the eighties, Captain Bill Jones had explained that the reason for the great output in the Edgar Thomson Works was that he "discovered it was entirely out of the question to expect human flesh and blood to labor incessantly for twelve hours, and therefore it was decided to put on three turns, reducing the hours of labor to eight."

But after the Homestead Strike in 1892 the mills had returned to the 12-hour day, which in general remained in force until the days of the first World War. The monstrous twenty-four hour shift, when the day force and the night force exchanged places every two weeks, was the natural result of unimaginative planning.

A dry recital of the facts, without any assistance from rhetorical flourishes, is sufficiently horrifying to the modern age. Men worked close enough to them to reach with tongs masses of molten or red-hot metal weighing many tons, at a date when air-conditioning was unheard of, and when ventilating systems, if they existed at all, were primitive. The flooring on which they stood was of steel plates, so heated by the metal passing over them that shoes had

Photograph by Norman M. Jeannero.

MAY DAY AT THE PENNSYLVANIA COLLEGE FOR WOMEN WAS A FESTIVE AND LIGHTHEARTED OCCASION.

to have thick wooden soles to prevent blistering the feet. This had to be endured for twelve hours a day for twelve days and for twenty-four hours on the thirteenth shift, after which the workers would have twenty-four hours off. A man could spend a full day with his family only once every two weeks.

Not only were the steelworkers subjected to infernal heat, especially in midsummer, but the noise attending most of the operations was almost unbearable. Some impairment of hearing was so common among the employees of the industry as to be accepted almost as a normal condition. It was suspected, even then, that the effect might not be confined to the auditory nerves but could result in some impairment of the whole nervous system—a suspicion that the development of neurological science in the subsequent years has amply confirmed.

Nor was the lethal potential of dust, especially dust composed of particles of finely divided stone and metal, more than half understood in those days. Silicosis, as an occupa-

tional disease of miners, was recognized, but it was an exceptionally advanced doctor who appreciated, before the First World War, the effect on the respiratory system of constant inhalation of tiny fragments of steel. *Mycobacterium tuberculosis* was charged with many a death whose primary cause was metallic, not bacterial.

The hazard of fatal accident was too patent to be overlooked. When by some mischance a ladle of molten steel spilled its contents not into but over the edge of the mold and fourteen men were incinerated, there was no possibility of dissociating the danger from the job.

There are no reliable statistics about the fatalities in the Pittsburgh steel mills. William Hard, one of the muckrakers, made the educated guess in his article, *Making Steel and Killing Men*, which appeared in *Everybody's* magazine in November 1907, that during the year of 1906 at one steel mill (the south Chicago plant of the United States Steel Corporation) 46 workers were killed, 368 disabled permanently and 184 disabled temporarily. And the pro-

(turn to page 284)

IN 1905, MARKETING ON THE MONONGAHELA RIVER WHARF WAS DONE IN A LEISURELY MANNER.

THE SCANDAL OF THE DECADE.

Photograph by Sarony.

EVELYN NESBIT, a stunning chorus girl and artist's model, was married to Harry Kendall Thaw in the parsonage of the Third Presbyterian Church in Pittsburgh.

The 34-year-old Thaw was one of the ten children of William Thaw, the Pittsburgh transportation millionaire.

It was freely gossiped that Evelyn had been an intimate of Stanford White, the celebrated architect, also of John Barrymore, the celebrated actor.

On June 25, 1906, Harry Thaw and his wife attended the opening of *Mamelle Champagne* in New York's Madison Square Garden theatre, built by Stanford White. When Thaw discovered that the architect was in the audience too, he left his table, took out his revolver and shot White, killing him instantly.

To the policeman, who took him into custody Thaw said: "He deserved it. I can prove it. He ruined my wife and then deserted the girl."

The trial that followed was a sensational one. It was the first time that sex was discussed in an open court.

Thaw's doting mother engaged the lawyer Delphin Michael Delmas of San Francisco, "the Napoleon of the Western Bar" for a reported fee of $100,000 to defend her son. Delmas tried to prove that Thaw was insane when he committed the crime and offered clinical evidence to that effect. Dr. Britton D. Evans of the Morris Plains, N. J. Mental Hospital testified that Thaw was "a person of unsound mind who suffered delusions and exaggerated personal importance", and who shot White while he had "a brain storm or mental explosion." The phrase caught on; "brainstorm" became part of our language.

However, Thaw issued a statement from the tombs: "I am not crazy. I was not crazy when I shot Stanford White. I'm glad I did it. I was justified when I shot him."

On the stand Evelyn, dressed in girlish innocence, related that she was told by a man that Thaw "had put a girl in a bathtub and then poured scalding water on her" and she told of another person who informed her that Thaw "took morphine and that he was crazy and that he was in the habit of taking girls and tying them to bedposts and beating them." But she investigated these stories and found no truth in them.

Thaw's defense was successful. The jury was not able to reach a verdict. In the second trial that followed, Thaw was found not guilty because of insanity, and was ordered to the institution for the Criminal Insane at Mattawan. From there he divorced Evelyn.

Five years later Thaw escaped from the institution, motored to Canada, but was returned to the United States, where in a new trial in 1915 he was declared sane and acquitted of all charges.

Pittsburgh welcomed him on his return. A crowd of 1,000 escorted him to his mother's home.

During the following years, Thaw was in the limelight on and off. A suit charging him with the whipping of a young boy in a Philadelphia hotel room was settled out of court.

He died in Miami in 1947 at the age of 76.

Courtesy Library of Congress.

HARRY K. THAW (right), the killer of Stanford White, whom Cleveland Amory in his book *Who Killed Society?* called "a sadistic pervert who became insanely jealous over the fact that someone else once had been intimate with his girl . . . and with whom he enjoyed an almost incredibly unnatural relationship."

PITTSBURGH FACES IN 1910. Five friends of long standing pose for the pho-tographers. In the front row: J. Denniston Lyon and Harry Darlington. Standing: Richard B. Mellon, father of Richard K. Mellon; Samuel Felton; Senator Newbury.

fessors Cochran and Miller, in their treatise, *The Age of Enterprise*, state that, "in 1913 deaths from industrial accidents totalled 25,000, and injuries nearly 1,000,000." Whether the figures are exact, no one could say, but they are not far from the truth.

In his article Hard gives a dramatic description of a steel-mill accident. He writes:

On the twelfth of last December, Newton Allen, up in the cage of his 100-ton electric crane, was requested by a ladleman from below to pick up a pot and carry it to another part of the floor. This pot was filled with the hot slag that is the refuse left over when the pure steel has been run off.

Newton Allen let down the hooks of his crane. The ladleman attached those hooks to the pot. Newton Allen started down the floor. Just as he started, one of the hooks slipped. There was no shock or jar. Newton Allen was warned of danger only by the fumes that rose toward him. He at once reversed his lever, and, when his crane had carried him to a place of safety, descended and hurried back to the scene of the accident. He saw a man lying on his face. He heard him screaming. He saw that he was being roasted by the slag that had poured out of the pot. He ran up to him and turned him over.

"At that time," said Newton Allen in his testimony before the jury, "I did not know it was my brother. It was not till I turned him over that I recognized him. Then I saw it was my brother Ora. I asked him if he was burned bad. He said no, not to be afraid—he was not burned as bad as I thought."

Three days later Ora died in the hospital of the Illinois Steel Company. He had told his brother he wasn't "burned bad," but Ira Miltimore, the doctor who attended him, testified that his death was due to a "third-degree burn of the face, neck, arms, forearms, hands, back, right leg, right thigh, and left foot." A third-degree burn is the last degree there is. There is no fourth degree.

But why did the hook on that slag pot slip.

Because it was attached merely to the rim of the pot, and not to the lugs. That pot had no lugs. It ought to have had them. Lugs are pieces of metal that project from the rim of the pot, like ears. They are put there for the express purpose of providing a proper and secure hold for the hooks. But they had broken off in some previous accident and they had not been replaced. . . .

The jury brought the following verdict:

"We, the jury, believe that slag pots should not be handled without their lugs, and we recommend that the lugs be replaced before the pots are used in the future."

(turn to page 286)

GENTLEMEN—And who is the dapper young man in the center with the soft hat and the dashing handkerchief in the breast pocket? It is no other than David Lawrence, the former governor of the state of Pennsylvania, posing for this group photograph outside the headquarters of the P. F. Toole Athletic Club at Fourth Avenue and Ferry Street.

In the first row: unidentified, Frank Connors, Carl Fisher, John O'Connell, Joseph Keisel, and Martin Riley.

Second row: Joseph Flaherty, James Conley, Herbert Flaherty, Thomas S. O'Connor, John O. Flaherty, Harry Earle, David L. Lawrence, Michael McNally, Ray Earle, Peter Tanney, Thomas Nester, Peter McLaughlin, and Thomas Joyce.

Third row: Thomas Gilmore, William Joyce, Joseph Connelly, Albert Neeland, Harold Snyder, and Hugo Montgomery.

LADIES—a faculty group of the Duquesne School photographed at their reunion on June 6, 1905.

Standing, left to right: Professor M. J. McMahon, Mrs. Robert A. Foley, Edna Keyser, Jane Bryce, Anna Powers, Elizabeth Langan. Seated: Kate Schumaker, Bella Moffat, Mary Eaton, Amanda McKinley, Virginia Hunter, Mary Mullin

THE RED LION HOTEL WHERE THE FULTON BUILDING IS TO-DAY.

EXPOSITION HALL ON DUQUES.

COLFAX SCHOOL NO. 5 POSES FOR THE PHOTOGRAPHER IN 1905.

LATEST FASHIONS DISPLAYED BY THE

But the life of Ora Allen was wiped out, and his family was left penniless. His widow was not entitled to damages because the law of that time recognized the doctrine of contributory negligence.

If an error of the crane operator caused the ladle to tip over, no damages could be collected from the company. The slow growth rate of a sense of social responsibility accounts for many of the abuses of the system, but not for this. The desperate and too-long-successful efforts of

employers to retain this legalistic savagery cannot be explained away on the ground of ignorance of its essential injustice. The ugly motive was greed, and nothing else. As the rate of accidents mounted, the federal government and many of the states hastened legislation for compensation. By 1912, thirteen states had passed Workmen's Compensation laws, and by 1917 forty states had enacted such regulations.

From the moment her husband took a job in the steel

Courtesy Carnegie Library.

AY, NOT FAR FROM THE POINT.

Photograph by Pittsburgh Art Commission.

THE ELEGANT DISPLAY WINDOW OF C. REIZENSTEIN SONS STORE.

Photograph by Pittsburgh Art Commission.

CITY'S JOSEPH HORNE COMPANY.

Courtesy Carnegie Library.

THE ELEVEN MAN JURY OF THE ASSOCIATED ARTISTS SHOW IN 1910.

industry, the wife was, in important respects, widowed. After his twelve-hour shift, her husband came home too utterly spent to have much energy left for domestic problems, far too fatigued to give intelligent supervision to the training and education of his children. This left the woman to struggle with the task alone, and unless she was endowed with great strength of character as well as of body it meant that the children were too much left to their own devices. Inevitably juvenile delinquency flourished and

bodily health was impaired. A grimly eloquent passage from the *Homestead* volume of the Russell Sage Foundation Survey reads:

One third of all who die in Pittsburgh die without having anything to say about it. That is, they die under five years of age. One fourth of all who die, die without having anything to say about anything. That is, they die under one year of age. Most of these deaths are preventable, being the outcome of conditions which, humanly speaking, have no right to exist.

The conditions were impure milk and housing unfit for

human habitation. In 1906 there were 5730 cases of typhoid fever in the city, a disease transmitted by impure water and filth.

This forced the city government to erect filtration plants that were to purify the water. A number of such plants were built between the years of 1905 and 1914 (the Pittsburgh filtration plant on the north bank of the Allegheny east of Aspinwall started operation in 1905; it delivered the first filtered water on December 18, 1907. By October 1908, Pittsburgh's entire water supply was filtered. By February 1908, the South Side received its first filtered water; by March 1914, the North Side.

"Why did the people stand for such conditions?" The answer to that is short, simple, and savage. These weren't people, these were a labor force. The tender-minded may interject, "You mean they were *regarded* as a labor force." But no. They *were* a labor force. Man is a social animal, and the social is an elemental constituent of his humanity, which comes into existence contingently upon its recognition, partly by himself, but mostly by his fellow men. When society unanimously and for a long time treats a man as less than human, he becomes so. Witness the American slave, the Russian serf, the Anglo-Saxon esne, and so on back to Cheops' pyramid builders. You find it always the case that reduction to a chattel eliminates from the genus homo an indispensable component of humanity.

Among the steelworkers there was at this period a group that retained its full humanity and demonstrated it from time to time with a ferocity that brought out goose flesh upon occupants of palatial homes and lordly offices. These people were native Americans or Irishmen, with a sprink-

(turn to page 290)

Photograph by R. W. Johnston.

WINTERS WERE HEAVY AND LONG. If one had a sled one had fun. This photograph of Woodland Road was made in 1905.

DARK DAYS were common in Pittsburgh. Whether winter or summer, more often than not, the sky was pitch dark, with the sun hiding behind the smog. In winter the air was chilly and the dampness penetrated to the marrow of one's bones. One coughed and sneezed and read advertisements of the latest remedies.

This scene was taken near the depot of the Pennsylvania Railroad on a wintry morning in 1906. The men are probably walking toward their offices, they are more comfortable when in company. They could talk about the weather and they could talk about the never ceasing, never boring, never slackening subject of Theodore Roosevelt. What will the President do to the railroads? And what will be his next move against the trusts?

On the right of the picture is the horse-drawn hotel bus, which takes the new arrivals toward a warm meal and a friendly room Smog, grime, snow! When, oh when, will the sun come out again?

MEETING OF PITTSBURGH AND ALLEGHENY COUNCILS. In December 1907, when the two cities were united, the common councils of Pittsburgh and Allegheny, numbering 100 men, met in an organization session. The city's population became 521,000, sixth largest in the nation.

right:

AFTER PITTSBURGH AND ALLEGHENY MERGED the two mayors —Charles Kirschler of Allegheny and George W. Guthrie of Pittsburgh —sealed the consolidation with a handshake before the governing bodies.

ling of Scots, Englishmen, and Welshmen—that is, natives of the British Isles—speaking English. But these, except for the raw apprentices, were almost invariably straw bosses or highly skilled workmen—puddlers, machinists, and the like—distinct from the mass of the labor force that consisted of recent immigrants, predominantly Slavic, with some intermixture of Italians and other Mediterraneans. The skilled workmen—the puddlers for a conspicuous example—did not, because they would not, endure conditions to which the others submitted meekly. They organized early, fought wickedly, proved themselves dangerous, and commanded a reluctant but genuine respect.

They enjoyed the inestimable advantage of command of the language of their employers. They could communicate with the high brass. They could make their grievances comprehensible, thereby giving their demands some color

of reason, which probably had more to do than their belligerence with establishing their superior status.

The newly arrived immigrant, on the other hand, a stranger alike to the language and to the customs of this country, had no recourse but to accept what he was offered, at least until he could find his feet in the new environment. If it killed him, what of it? There were thousands and hundreds of thousands of his like crowding in behind him. He was expendable—and was expended, ruthlessly. (Immigration between 1900 and 1914 multiplied threefold. In 1900 the number of immigrants that came to the United States was 448,572; in 1912 this figure jumped to 1,218,480, of which a sizable number gravitated to the Pittsburgh area.)

This recital gives the system prevailing in Pittsburgh— and not in Pittsburgh only, but throughout American

Photograph by Frank E. Bingaman in the Carnegie Library.

THE VICE-PRESIDENT lays the corner-stone to the building of the School of Mines, the first one on the new University of Pittsburgh campus. It was one of the main events in the city's sesquicentennial activities in 1908. Theodore Roosevelt's Vice-President, Charles W. Fairbanks, officiated, and a group of distinguished citizens and students watched the proceeding.

The picture above and others in this chapter were taken by Frank E. Bingaman (1875-1948). He began taking news photographs in 1904 and kept at it until his death in 1948. He worked for the Gazette-Times and for the Chronicle-Telegraph which in the year 1927 became the Sun-Telegraph.

heavy industry—the look of something dreamed up by a demonic mind, obsessed with hatred of the human race, so that one is tempted to wonder what manner of men these employers could have been.

It is an illusion. There was nothing about them setting them conspicuously apart from their contemporary successors, except the conditions under which they lived and worked. If at times they seem to have been wicked and stupid, well, aren't we all? Convincing evidence that they were exceptionally wicked, or exceptionally stupid, is not to be found; they were exceptionally powerful, that is all, and their exceptional power was due to circumstances over which they had little or no control.

For one thing, it is notoriously true that dealing with the abject brings out the worst qualities latent in any human personality, and the immigrants flooding into this

(turn to page 295)

Courtesy Richard K. Mellon.

THE MELLONS SEND GREETINGS. A card prepared for the 95th birthday celebration of Thomas Mellon, February 3, 1908.

GROUNDBREAKING for the Twentieth Century Club in the summer of 1910. Miss Ann Phillips poses for the photographer while Bishop Cortlandt Whitehead holds an umbrella over her.

UNVEILING THE CHRISTOPHER L. MAGEE MONUMENT in front of Carnegie Library, on Independence Day in 1908. Christopher Lyman Magee who in the late seventies allied himself with William Flinn (seated on the left in the first row),

OAKLAND IN 1900. AT LEFT IS THE CARNEGIE INSTITUTE, AT RIGHT THE SCHENLEY HOTEL OPENED THE YEAR

Photograph by Frank E. Bingaman in the Carnegie Library.

and became one of the most influential political figures in the city. He controlled Allegheny County politics from 1882 until 1899 and fought Senator Matthew Quay in a bitter battle.

He was a handsome, dashing and magnetic man. He made money with ease. He owned considerable real estate, was director in 15 banks and published the *Pittsburgh Times*. At his death his estate was in excess of $4,000,000, most of which went to Elizabeth Steel Magee Hospital — a lasting monument to his mother.

Courtesy Jones & Laughlin Steel Corporation

FORE. IN BACKGROUND SCHENLEY PARK.

Photograph by Frank E. Bingaman in the Carnegie Library.

THE SOLEMN MOMENT. The widow of Christopher L. Magee pulls the cord during the ceremonies to unveil the memorial for her late husband. To her right: Mrs. Augustus St. Gaudens, widow of the celebrated creator of the monument, Mrs. Warrington Warrick, and Mrs. James Neal, who were sisters of Mrs. Magee.

PITTSBURGH CELEBRATES ITS 150TH BIRTHDAY.

THE VICE-PRESIDENT, Charles W. Fairbanks, representing President Theodore Roosevelt, drove in a parade through the city with Mayor George W. Guthrie.

THE STAR-SPANGLED BANNER is raised by Miss Mary Brunot Roberts over the remains of Fort Pitt on September 28, 1908, in a sesquicentennial observance.

D.A.R. PRESIDENT Edith Darlington Ammon, one of the most prominent Pittsburgh women, took part in the Blockhouse sesquicentennial ceremonies at the Point.

JAMES S. SHERMAN, the next Vice-President, came for the celebration. With him are W. S. Brown, William Graham, Dave Collingwod, Jim Watson, Lee Smith.

From The Story of the Sesqui-Centennial Celebration of Pittsburgh *(1910)*

HAPPY ANNIVERSARY. During summer and early fall of 1908 the city celebrated its 150th birthday. There was a sesquicentennial pageant on the Monongahela, seen by 300,000 citizens who lined the banks from Smithfield to the Point.

Photograph by Frank E. Bingaman in the Carnegie Library.

"I CHRISTEN THEE *NEW ORLEANS,*" announced Alice Longworth, the daughter of T. R. and a descendant of Nich- olas Roosevelt who built and launched in Pittsburgh in 1811 the *New Orleans,* the first steamboat to travel western waters.

Photograph by R. W. Johnston.

THE PARADE OF THE POLICEMEN, held on October 1, 1908, in celebration of the great event. Superintendent Thom- as A. McQuaide led the men in a march through the streets of the city and Pitts- burghers applauded the demonstration.

Photograph by Frank E. Bingaman in the Carnegie Library.

SOON-TO-BE-PRESIDENT WILLIAM HOWARD TAFT RECEIVES A VOCIFEROUS GREETING AT THE MONONGAHELA WHARF.

country in the century's early years were among the most abject creatures upon the face of the earth. Many of them fled from conditions worse than those in the steel mills. Here at least they could eat, while at home hunger had been their constant familiar, and the oppression they suffered here was in some ways lighter than that behind them.

Nor was the illusion of their separateness monopolized by their employers. The investigators who made the Sage Foundation Survey were carefully selected for their freedom from prejudice and preconceived opinion, yet they constantly betray their naive astonishment at discovering how often these bohunks, polacks, guineas, and spics, when approached in a comradely, equalitarian fashion, turned out to be kindly, generous, often merry, and altogether amiable people. The investigators could not refrain from recording their surprise at finding in Przbylsky and Schiavone the same basic qualities they expected to find in Perkins and O'Mara, Gwynn and MacPhail. Why, then, expect the general run of employers to be more perceptive than men chosen for that very quality?

Nevertheless, the somber fact remains that in these years life in Pittsburgh for the bulk of the workers in its dominant industry was harsh, very harsh. Economics, a science powerful at explication after the event, is ready with an answer. The labor force in Pittsburgh was being mishandled, not maliciously, but through ignorance of economic reality.

Correct handling of a labor force, say economists, results in the greatest attainable production at the lowest attainable unit cost, this leading to the largest attainable profit. The greatest attainable production is possible only with the most efficient labor force, and misery is productive of inefficiency—psychic, no less than physical, misery.

This truth was beginning to percolate into the thinking of the more intelligent industrialists by the end of the century's first decade and was proved conclusively in 1914 when the outbreak of war in Europe suddenly cut off the supply of expendable labor and at the same time made the demand for steel insatiable. Automation alone could not keep pace with the demand. It became imperatively necessary to correct the mishandling and abusing of the labor force, and as soon as brains were applied to the problem, working conditions began to improve. The worst abuses disappeared years before collective bargaining was

THE PITTSBURGH PIRATES.

Photograph by Frank E. Bingaman in the Carnegie Library.
THE "FLYING DUTCHMAN" IN ACTION: HONUS WAGNER, the all-time great Pittsburgh Pirate shortstop, lopes and slides across home plate. Wagner led the National League in batting eight times (in 1900, 1903–4, 1906–9, 1911) and made 3430 base hits during his career. When he retired his lifetime batting average was an outstanding .329.

established as a legal right of employees in all industry.

Yet there is force in the argument that the old industrial system had actually received its mortal wound six months before the shot at Sarajevo killed not only the Austrian archduke, but old-style imperialism as well. If there had been no war the old system would have died of the wound it received on the day that Henry Ford, of Detroit, proclaimed a minimum wage of $5 for an eight-hour day in his automobile plant. The seriousness of this wound was not perceived for some time—not, in fact, until Ford, instead of going bankrupt, prospered beyond all precedent under the new system. In the business world there is no arguing against methods which yield fabulous returns. Ford's first billion pragmatically established the truth of

Ford's theory, and business—slowly and reluctantly, but inevitably—had to acknowledge it.

Because the war was so much more spectacular, it is generally accepted as the end of this era in Pittsburgh's history. However, it may be plausibly contended that the end really came not on June 28, in Herzegovina, but on January 5, 1914, in Detroit.

Whatever the date, it affects Pittsburgh only as the history of Pittsburgh is an integral part of the history of American industry. In the city's own story this era furnishes a chapter that, while in general it parallels the larger national history, is yet filled with particulars that are distinctly individual and, far from being invariably gloomy, are sometimes hilarious, frequently inspiring, occasionally

Photograph by Frank E. Bingaman in the Carnegie Library.

"WELL DONE" OF THE PRESIDENT. President William Howard Taft happily applauds a "two-bagger" by Honus Wagner at the old Exposition Park. The date is May 29, 1909. But however hard the President rooted for the home team, the Pirates lost 8 to 3 to the Chicago Cubs.

To the right of the President are Philander C. Knox, Secretary of State; President Hadley of Yale, and Charles P. Taft, half-brother of the President, who owned part of the Chicago Cubs. Behind Taft, the uniformed man is his trusted military aide Archie Butt, who met his end on the *Titanic* disaster three years later in 1912.

startling, and always fascinating.

The formation of the United States Steel Corporation created some three dozen millionaires overnight. They were associates of Carnegie; they worked for him for years; they spent most of their lives in the mills. Stewart Holbrook, in his *Age of the Moguls*, writes that when these men became millionaires:

Some of them still smelled a bit of burning coke, and a Penn Avenue barber in Pittsburgh reported that the first shampoo one of these newly rich men ever had brought out two ounces of fine Mesabi ore and a scattering of slag and cinders.

Before long the epithet, "Pittsburgh millionaires," became a derisive designation. The image of a Pittsburgh millionaire was that of a nouveau riche with low tastes and ostentatious habits, vulgar and uneducated, coarse and without refinements, freewheeling and free spending.

They built atrocious-looking homes with rows of rooms filled to the brim with gaudy furniture, giant vases, and all sorts of bric-a-brac. When Alexander Peacock, the former sales manager of Carnegie and now the squire of "Rowanlea"—the elephantine mansion on Highland Avenue—heard that one of his former colleagues had bought two gold-plated pianos, not to be outdone he installed four, although no one in his family played the instrument.

The new millionaires spent their money with careless abandon. They cruised about the country in their glittering private trains; they took suites on ocean liners to Europe and made the Grand Tour with their families; they

(turn to page 301)

297

THE STREETS OF THE CITY.

From the collection of Stefan Lorant.

A 1903 STEREOSCOPE depicting Wood Street on a busy morning. On the right the Charles Hotel. Views like this impressed the country; so this was how the steel city looked when the sun was not hiding behind the clouds.

WINDY DAY DOWNTOWN, IN 1910 —

Photograph by Frank E. Bingaman.

AT THE CORNER OF FIFTH AVENUE AND WOOD STREET. PITTSBURGHERS ARE HOLDING ON TO THEIR HATS.

Pittsburgh Art Commission.

PARKING was already a problem in 1910. On Fourth Avenue the horse-drawn carriages blocked the way. Curbstone parking was a nuisance, but what was the alternative? No one knew.

Photograph by Frank E. Bingaman.

SUNNY DAY in 1910. The Easter Parade before Carnegie Music Hall in Oakland.

Photograph by Frank E. Bingaman in the Carnegie Library.

FIRST MUNICIPAL BAND CONCERT in Schenley Park was given on July 2, 1911. From left to right are John D. Dailey, secretary to the mayor, Mayor William A. Magee, Joseph Armstrong, and John M. Morin with his three children.

A FAMOUS COUPLE. Lillian Russell, whose name evoked flutters in many a man's heart, married Pittsburgh newspaperman Alexander P. Moore on June 12, 1912, and settled down in the city. Moore, a native Pittsburgher, was at times part owner of the *Pittsburgh Telegraph* and the *Pittsburgh Chronicle-Telegraph*, and had been editor of the *Pittsburgh Press*. From 1904 on he was chief editor of the *Pittsburgh Leader*. He also owned the *New York Daily Mirror* and the *Boston Advertiser*. Between 1923 and 1925 he served as Ambassador to Spain, and 1928 to 1930, the year of his death, he was U.S. Ambassador to Peru.

WHERE THE FUTURE IS SEALED. The license bureau in 1910 with two young couples waiting for their papers. But what is the odd gentleman leaning on the desk doing there? Perhaps he is a friend of the prospective bridegroom, or a brother of the bride who came to see that everything should be done just right.

Photograph by Frank E. Bingaman in the Carnegie Library.

Or he might be just a frightened bachelor who came to the place to see what it looked like and whether it would hurt when he at last made the final decision.

commissioned artists to paint portraits of themselves, their wives, and their children; they bought paintings by the yard and sculptures by the ton, jewelry and antiques, homes and boats in Newport and Florida.

They acquired such prodigious wealth that they were hard-put to count their money. A steward of the Duquesne Club remembered how one of these new millionaires covered page after page of the Club's stationery with figures. "I am trying," he said as he poured down his sixth drink, "to find out whether I am worth six million or if it is eight million."

Their wives, anxious to be admitted to society, dressed in expensive furs and Paris gowns, entertained lavishly, and were on the lookout for titled Europeans who eventually would become the husbands of their daughters, making the Pittsburgh maidens baronesses, princesses, or duchesses.

The behavior of this class, their marriages and divorces appeared on the front pages of all the newspapers in the country. One of the most notorious news stories was that of Harry Kendall Thaw, the son of William Kendall Thaw, the Pittsburgh railroad and coal magnate. When the elder Thaw died he left a measly $200 monthly allowance to his son until the time he could be trusted to take his $12 million share of the $40 million estate. But Harry's doting mother raised this allowance to a yearly $80,000.

In 1905 Thaw married the chorus girl, Evelyn Nesbit, whom Irvin S. Cobb described as "the most exquisitely lovely human being I ever looked at—the slim, quick grace of a faun, a head that sat on her faultless throat as a lily on its stem, eyes that were the color of blue-brown pansies and the size of half dollars, a mouth of rumpled rose petals."

Before her marriage Evelyn was often seen in the company of the celebrated architect, Stanford White, with whom she traveled to Europe and with whom she was once ejected from a New York hotel. She was also known to be a close friend of actor John Barrymore.

(turn to page 304)

A PITTSBURGH VIEW IN 1908: THE 500 BLOCK ON SMITHFIELD STREET, NOW THE SITE OF THE OLIVER

Pittsburgh Art Commission.

TRAFFIC DOWNTOWN had its problems in 1910 just as in later years. At times Liberty Avenue and Market Street were so congested that the police had to come out and unsnarl the vehicles.

Photograph by Frank E. Bingaman.

ANOTHER VIEW OF THE CITY. Grant Street at the corner of Sixth Avenue in 1913. At the site of the parking lot the Union Trust Building was built in 1916, while the adjoining lot became the site of the William Penn Hotel.

Courtesy T. Mellon & Sons.

BUILDING WHICH WAS ERECTED IN THE YEAR OF 1910.

Photograph by Frank E. Bingaman in the Carnegie Library.

"DOUBLE X" ORTON, one of the city's most colorful characters, sold cough drops which he fabricated himself. On one occasion he was persuaded to be a candidate for sheriff — "Double X" Orton lost—his friends had given him the double cross.

Photograph by Frank E. Bingaman in the Carnegie Library.

THANKSGIVING DAY INSPECTION. Top-hatted Mayor George W. Guthrie, who served from 1906 until 1909, and Superintendent of Public Safety Edward G. Lang make the annual inspection. It was a great event for the police force, with drills and exercises, and a great event for the citizens of Pittsburgh who came out to watch the colorful ceremonies.

During the seventies and eighties of the last century it became fashionable to spell Pittsburgh without the final "h". In 1894 the U. S. Geographic Board of Names listed the city as Pittsburg, omitting the "h". This roused the ire of those inhabitants who could not think of their city as Pittsburg

On June 25, 1906, Harry Thaw went with his wife to the opening performance of *Mamzelle Champagne* in the theater of New York's Madison Square Garden, a building designed by Stanford White. The architect happened to be watching the show as well. Thaw seeing him, left his table, casually walked over to White and shot him. As he moved away from the body, he told the policeman, "He deserved it. . . . He ruined my wife and then deserted the girl."

The trial that followed was the most sensational ever held in an American court; it brought to light the illicit sexual relations of men and women, a topic that under the blanket of Victorian morality was taboo, not to be talked about in public.

Thaw's mother retained Delphin Michael Delmas of San Francisco, "the Napoleon of the Western Bar," to defend her son, paying him a fee of $100,000. Delmas was the most successful criminal lawyer of his time; he

(turn to page 306)

Photograph by Frank E. Bingaman in the Carnegie Library.

SWEARING IN of William A. Magee as mayor on April 5, 1909. Ceremonies were held in the old City Hall on Smithfield Street. Magee followed George W. Guthrie from 1909 to 1914, who presided over a growing city of well over a half a million people.

THE FIRST SMALL COUNCIL of nine citizens was installed in 1911 after the State Legislature abolished the old ward Common and Select Councils.

Seated, from left to right: W. A. Hoeveler, Enoch Rauh, E. V. Babcock, and John M. Goehring. Standing, David P. Black, Dr. J. P. Kerr, A. J. Kelly, Jr., Dr. S. S. Woodburn and William G. Wilkins.

without the "h". Their battle for restoration of the letter succeeded in 1911 when Senator George T. Oliver (1848-1919), the newspaper publisher, ap- *pealed and won against the "h"-less decision. Once more, and now forever, the city was proudly spelled Pittsburgh—to the glory of the Scots.*

SWEARING IN of Joseph G. Armstrong as mayor of Pittsburgh took place on January 5, 1914, with Justice Robert S. Frazer officiating. It was a solemn ceremony. To the judge's left is Councilman John M. Goehring. Mayor Armstrong served for four years.

SWEARING IN of E. V. Babcock as mayor on January 7, 1918. From left to right: George Boxheimer, clerk; Judge John D. Shafer; Dr. J. P. Kerr; Mayor Babcock; Enoch Rauh; John S. Herron; Eddie Martin, city clerk; Robert Clark, leaning over book.

NEGLECT AND DECAY.

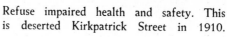

UNPAVED STREETS grew into quagmires when the rain came; they were hardly usable.

Refuse impaired health and safety. This is deserted Kirkpatrick Street in 1910.

OVERHEAD WIRES caused everlasting hazards. It looked as if the city had been

BILLBOARDS marred the landscape. The dilapidated buildings were not cared for, the ugly

empty spaces were hidden with advertisements. This is a section of Fifth Avenue near Brady.

SQUALOR, depredation, no pride in one's possessions, small consideration for

won nineteen acquittals in nineteen murder cases. Mrs. Thaw also bought—for a reported $50,000—the bundle of letters written by Stanford White to Evelyn, that were in the hands of Evelyn's mother, a Mrs. Holman of Pittsburgh. And Mrs. Thaw—so the rumor went—paid Evelyn $200,000 to take the stand on Harry's behalf and exonerate him of his crime.

Evelyn did all that was expected of her. In her plain navy-blue suit with a shirt waist and a schoolboy's stiff collar tied with a black bow, she looked the picture of innocence. She told the court that she loved Thaw and she testified that all the rumors about him—like the one about the girl that he put "in a bathtub and then poured scalding water on her" or the other that he "took morphine and that he was crazy and that he was in the habit of taking girls and tying them to bedposts and beating them" were untrue. Evelyn's testimony impressed the court; there was not a dry eye when she finished.

The defense did its best to blacken the character of White, recounting his dubious relationships with young

wired together. Bricks were broken off on the pavement. This is Carson Street.

TREES WERE DESTROYED, their limbs butchered to make way for wires. Who cared

for the preservation of nature? Who cared for beauty? Gradually the city grew into a jungle.

Pittsburgh Art Commission.

others. Refuse and what was no longer needed was thrown in the back yard.

IN INCLEMENT WEATHER poles holding the electric and telephone wires broke down,

creating a menace to human life. It was a disgrace. But nothing could be done about it.

girls; it also offered clinical evidence that Thaw was insane when he committed the act. Dr. Britton D. Evans of the mental hospital at Morris Plains, New Jersey, testified that the defendant was "a person of unsound mind who suffered the delusions of exaggerated personal importance." And coining a phrase which is still with us, he said that Thaw had shot White in the midst of a "brain storm."

While Delmas tried to free his man by pleading insanity, Thaw would not hear of such defense. He kept on saying that he had the right to do what he did. "I am not crazy," he told newspapermen. "I was justified when I shot him. I was never insane."

The trial resulted in a hung jury. In the second trial, a year later, Thaw was found not guilty but was ordered to be sent to the asylum for the criminally insane. Five years later he escaped from the asylum, went to Canada, was brought back to the states and stood trial once more. In the trial the court declared him sane and acquitted him of all charges. Thaw was now a free man. He returned to his home town, and Pittsburgh gave him a hero's welcome;

(turn to page 310)

THE REMOVAL OF THE HUMP.

Courtesy Mrs. McCullough.

THIS WAS THE THIRD ATTEMPT. In 1836 and also in 1849 the city had done some grading in this area.

Pittsburgh Art Commission.

EXCAVATIONS ran as deep as 16 feet. This picture shows progress on Diamond by August 23, 1913.

Courtesy Mrs. McCullough.

IT COST $800,000 to cut the ground and another $2,500,000 was paid for resulting property damages.

Courtesy Mrs. McCullough.

IN 1912 work was begun to remove the hump which dominated the Triangle between Diamond and Sixth.

Photograph by Frank E. Bingaman in the Carnegie Library.

THE DEEPEST CUT, and perhaps the most difficult one, was an excavation of 16.3 feet at Wylie not far from the Courthouse.

Courtesy J. F. Maeder.

SIDEWALK SUPERINTENDENTS are watching the grading of the streets. This picture of the work was made October 5, 1912.

AFTER THE HUMP WAS REMOVED, other corrections could be made in the streets of downtown Pittsburgh. Between 1912 and 1914 Oliver Ave. was levelled. The drawn in line compares the street level before the digging with the result.

AFTER THE HUMP WAS REMOVED, and all the paving was completed and all other beautifying was done, this was the appearance of Fifth Ave. and Grant St. It was a far easier climb for all concerned—men, trolleys, and automobiles.

Photograph by Frank E. Bingaman in the Carnegie Library.

THE FOUNDER. On November 15, 1900 Andrew Carnegie offered a million dollar endowment to the city for a technical school. This was the beginning of the *Carnegie Technical Schools*, renamed in 1912 as *Carnegie Institute of Technology.* It had a school of Science and Technology, of Fine and Applied Arts, a school for Apprentices and Journeymen, and a school for Women.

On his last visit to the campus in 1914 Carnegie mixed with trustees, students and employees. Here he shakes hands with John A. Whyte of the machine shop, while James Scaife and Ross Polis look on.

Photograph by Frank E. Bingaman in the Carnegie Library.

THE LAST VISIT IN PITTSBURGH. Andrew Carnegie and his wife bid good-by on October 30, 1914. He died in 1919.

thousands escorted him in a noisy parade to his mother's home. (Two years later he was back in the limelight for the kidnaping and brutal whipping of a nineteen-year-old boy in a hotel room.)

Pittsburgh balanced this racy scandal with what Macaulay might have called one of its "periodic fits of morality." It was in 1907, the year of the Thaw trial, that the William E. Corey divorce case, *et seq.,* resulted in the resignation of the second president of the United States Steel Corporation. The first president of the company, Charles M. Schwab, so the story went, had been eased out because J. P. Morgan disapproved of his gambling at the Riviera. Anyhow, that is how the press reported his reasons for leaving U. S. Steel. According to the press reports, Schwab asked Morgan whether his gambling was thought detrimental to the company and whether Morgan was disturbed by it: "I didn't do anything to be ashamed

HUNGER WAS A PART OF LIFE. In February 1915 long lines of men stood patiently in the breadlines in the center of Pittsburgh, waiting for their rations. Though in Europe the war was already a year old, America did not yet feel its impact on her commerce and her industries. There was widespread hunger and misery for the workers and for their families.

of. I didn't do anything behind closed doors," he said, to which Morgan replied that, after all, "That is what doors are made for."

In reality Schwab left United States Steel not so much because of his gambling, but because his authority had been curtailed while he sojourned in Monte Carlo. He demanded a free hand in running the company's affairs and threatened that if he could not be the sole master he would leave the corporation. Morgan held that U. S. Steel was in size and complexity not unlike the United States Government—both had to be governed through checks and balances—so Schwab bought into Bethlehem Steel, reorganized and expanded it, and built it up to a giant enterprise.

Corey, his successor, had come up the hard way, from the ranks of the actual steelworkers to ownership of his own plant, then of a flock of plants, for which he received a vast price when U. S. Steel was formed. Suddenly coming into great wealth, he decided to build a magnificent home in New York and resolved to adorn it with an appropriately decorative wife. The chatelaine of his choice was Mabelle Gilman, a reigning beauty of the stage, but her installation had to be prefaced by disposal of the wife he had acquired while he was still a workman. This seems to have been arranged without difficulty; the wife was at least acquiescent, and suspicion lingers that riddance of William was to her more of a relief than a disaster.

After all these years, though, the point of interest is not how either the wife or the bride-elect took it, but how the directors of United States Steel took it. Adhering, for the most part, to a markedly puritanical form of Protestantism, they regarded legal dissolution of the marriage tie, no matter how amicably arranged, as far more subversive of public morals than keeping a mistress. Step by step, they

(turn to page 314)

THE SMOKY CITY as it looked before the First World War. The photograph was taken around 1913 looking toward Downtown. On the hilltop is Duquesne University.

GAZETTE SQUARE in the summer of 1914, taken from Bigelow Boulevard and Strawberry Way. What a peaceful scene! The countries in Europe were already at war.

OAKLAND as it looked in 1915. In the foreground on the left are Fifth Avenue and Bigelow Boulevard. The landscape was still open, there was plenty of room for building.

THE ERA OF THE MOTOR CAR. By 1915 it seemed evident that automobiles

THE TIN LIZZIES BECAME

In the summer of 1903 the first Ford was bought by Dr. E. Pfenning of Chicago. Fifteen months later the last of the 1700 Model A's was sold. Ford developed

Pittsburgh Art Commission

were here to stay. They cluttered up the streets and were parked wherever the driver could find a free place. Half a century later the same problem is still with us—we have still not been able to find a solution to the stifling parking situation.

PART OF THE LANDSCAPE, CHANGING THE APPEARANCE OF AMERICA.

model after model, designating them with the letters of the alphabet up to the letter "T". The failure of the $2,500 Model "K" and the success of the $500 Model "N" convinced the company that the future belonged to the cheap car.

Model T was launched in 1908, and by the time is was outmoded in 1927 not less than fifteen million of the "tin lizzies," had been sold. The little car had revolutionized the life in America. It bridged distances, it knitted the country together.

313

POLITICAL VISITS.

Photograph by Frank E. Bingaman in the Carnegie Library.

THEODORE ROOSEVELT often came to Pittsburgh. He liked the city. He came to expound his ideas before he became President "in his own right," and he came to arouse the citizenry to his Progressive ideas when he fought Taft and Wilson in the Bull Moose campaign of 1912. And when he came he was assured of a tumultuous ovation from a Republican town.

Photograph by Frank E. Bingaman in the Carnegie Library.

WILLIAM JENNINGS BRYAN, the Great Commoner who had been the presidential candidate of the Democrats in 1896, 1900, and again in 1908, visited Pittsburgh again in 1912 when he campaigned for Woodrow Wilson and the Democratic ticket.

fought a rear-guard action, first against the divorce, then against immediate remarriage, then against marriage to an actress, and as a last stand against any publicity.

They lost on all counts. Corey's nuptials could be called shrinkingly modest only if compared with three steam calliopes and a Shriners' band. The stage-set was the Hotel Gotham in New York, and the press was generously supplied with details by the bridegroom—such items as that the wedding breakfast cost $5000, the flowers $6000, that the bride's wedding gift was a French château, price $200,000, that another $200,000 had been set aside to cover the expenses of the honeymoon, which, with various accessories, ran the total bill to a cool half million.

Naturally not all Pittsburgh marriages ended like those of Thaw and Corey. But decent marriages cause no excitement in the press; they stir no ripples. Therefore one should not forget to salute the many thousands of contented Pittsburgh couples who loved and respected each

PRESIDENT WOODROW WILSON last was in Pittsburgh during his 1916 campaign for re-election. He came with his second wife, whom he had married the year before. Next to Mrs. Wilson is Joseph F. Guffey, who later became a U. S. Senator, and Noble Matthews, then superintendent of police. The redcap was calm; he had seen Presidents before.

other and who enjoyed a good relationship, and raised admirable families. One such celebrated marriage was that of the beautiful Lillian Russell, America's beloved musical comedy star who, after being wedded three times before, at fifty-one decided to become the wife of Alexander Pollock Moore, the publisher of the Pittsburgh *Leader*. Though many prophesied a bad end to the union, the Moores settled down in their comfortable home to a happy married life that only ended with Lillian's death in 1922.

The massive achievements, the startling vulgarities, and the lusty buffooneries of the giants that were in those days, as well as their very considerable contribution toward the endowment of the arts and letters in America, are sufficiently treated elsewhere in this volume. Here it is enough to point to the radical change in their status that was inaugurated and largely accomplished between the beginning of the century and the First World War.

It was the era of the transformation of Pittsburgh's men

SENATOR BOIES PENROSE (the towering figure in the center), boss of the Pennsylvania Republican organization, came to Pittsburgh regularly. Shown with him are Senator George T. Oliver, Joe Armstrong, Marcus Aaron, and E. V. Babcock.

of property into men of wealth. There is a widespread delusion that the terms are synonymous—but it is a delusion. The classical example is the case of Andrew Carnegie, who, starting with nothing, became the very archetype, first of the man of property, then of the man of wealth. Incidentally, it was a status not to Carnegie's liking, and he spent the rest of his life getting rid of his money. It kept him about as busy as ever, for he found that dispensing money without running into waste is as difficult as accumulating it without running into criminality.

If the earlier Carnegie is the very model of the man of property in Pittsburgh, the complete man of wealth was the banker, Andrew William Mellon, although for a long time only a few realized it. In contrast to such contemporaries as the suave Carnegie, the bellicose Frick, Mellon was all but imperceptible. "Who's Mellon?" President-elect Harding is said to have asked when the Pittsburgher was recommended to him for the Secretaryship of the

Treasury; yet Andrew Mellon was the greatest man of wealth of them all. Son of a banker, he was bred to the manipulation of evidences of indebtedness, currency, notes, bonds, stocks, and other forms of securities—all, that is to say, claims to a share of production, but never property itself. That he wisely left to men who knew how to handle it.

The wizardry of Mellon was the facility with which he shifted his claims on production from fading to flowering industries. In his early years he bought shares in coke ovens, later shifting from coke to iron, from iron to steel, from steel to oil, from oil to aluminum, always coming in just before the industry reached its full flower. As a man of money, rather than a man of property, he accumulated a much greater fortune, but far less notoriety than his only serious rival, the original J. Pierpont Morgan—that is until Mellon tired of business and turned to public life, where he achieved the singular distinction of presiding over the

(turn to page 319)

Photograph by Frank E. Bingaman in the Carnegie Library.

OFF TO WAR. Pittsburgh boys are given a warm farewell as they depart for the camps "to make the world safe for democracy." They trained and made themselves ready for the fight. For many of them it was a disappointment; the war was over and the Kaiser was defeated before they could reach Europe.

About the time this photograph was taken in Pittsburgh, in Russia the Union of Soviet Socialist Republics was formed—a portentous event of the 20th century.

A LIBERTY PARADE, with Mrs. E. V. Babcock carrying the flag. She was always in the forefront of the patriotic effort. Behind her are Mrs. Christine Miller Clemson and Mrs. Nathaniel Spear.

Women worked hard in Pittsburgh to rouse the citizens to contribute to the war effort. Their organization was highly effective, their campaign most successful.

THE DIANTHEAN SORORITY, later πβφ, University of Pittsburgh. First row: Dorothy Stanley, Betty McCabe, and Jesse Flanagan. Center row: Beryl Amity Pope, Regina Brown, Helen Hunt, Marie McSwigan, Regina Sexton, and Carmelita Crowley Standing: Marian Parker, Emilie Solomon, Minnie Wehmeier.

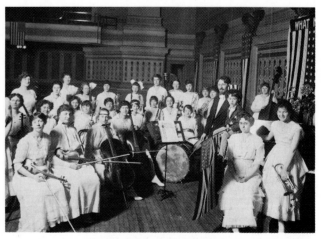

"HOME CONCERT" IN THE MEMORIAL HALL by a group of vocal and instrumental soloists under the direction of Albert D. Liefeld after their return from a cross country tour. It was a great affair, with all the musicians' families present in force. They loved what the young ladies did, even the trumpet solo.

THE GREAT WAR.

Courtesy Carnegie Library

THE FAREWELL SCENE OF THE 15TH ENGINEERS AT FORBES FIELD.

CHEERING THRONGS along Liberty Avenue welcome the 15th Engineers and 111th Infantry as they enjoy a triumphant

Photograph by Frank E. Bingaman in the Carnegie Library.

THE 15TH ENGINEERS, RETURNING FROM FRANCE AFTER THE WAR.

Photograph by Frank E. Bingaman in the Carnegie Library.

return through the streets of Pittsburgh.

A summary at the Armistice revealed that some 60,000 Allegheny County men had seen service in the war, and that 1527 had died or been killed in action. The city's steel and other industries had also been active just before and during the war. Government contracts executed in Pittsburgh totaled $215,405,000.

nation's fiscal policy at the time, following the panic of 1929, when money vanished with unprecedented speed, although property was not diminished.

The increasing dichotomy of property and wealth in this period was, of course, nothing peculiar to Pittsburgh. Under the name of "the managerial revolution," it has come to be accepted as one of the turning points in the economic history of the United States, not just of a single city. The particular interest of the Pittsburgh phase is that it demonstrated the process with extraordinary distinct-

ness, because the organization of United States Steel fixed it in point of time, and the astonishing efflorescence of the Pittsburgh millionaires made it imperishable in memory.

As a chapter of municipal history it is somewhat less than edifying, but it is not necessary to conclude on that dreary note. The cheerful reflection is that it was only a chapter, a phase through which the city and the nation passed into a new way of life, markedly different from the old way and one that, since it is hard to see how it can be worse, we are permitted to hope can only be better.

Photograph by Frank E. Bingaman in the Carnegie Library.

PITTSBURGH STEELWORKERS TAKE PART IN A GREAT LIBERTY BOND PARADE ON FIFTH AVENUE AT WOOD.

MORE THAN 30,000 PEOPLE listened as Theodore Roosevelt, making a tour in support of the war effort, addressed a huge rally in Pittsburgh on July 25, 1917

Chapter 9

BETWEEN TWO WARS

by Stefan Lorant

THE WAR IN EUROPE brought full employment and prosperity to Pittsburgh. Factories were humming, plants were operating around the clock. At day the pall of smoke blackened the sun; at night the glow from the mills painted the skies red. Pittsburgh worked as never before to produce the tools that were to bring victory.

By the fall of 1918 Germany was defeated. The Austro-Hungarian Empire in ruins, Russia ruled by a Communist government, newly formed independent countries taking their first unsteady steps—Europe presented a picture of chaos.

In the United States jubilation over the victory did not last long. President Wilson, battling for a treaty based on his Fourteen Points and anchored on a League of Nations, could not convince the European political leaders of the reasonableness of his suggestions. It was Georges Clemenceau and not Wilson who emerged as the maker of the new Europe. The proposals of the "Tiger of France" were based on unforgiving *realisme*, on vindictiveness and revenge. It was evident that the documents of Versailles and Trianon carried the germs of future disaster.

To Americans the disagreements of the quarrelling statesmen brought disillusionment. They had entered the war—"the war to end all wars," the war which was to "make the world safe for democracy"—with high ideals. They went into the battles to bring about a better world. And now that the war was over everything seemed to be as before; nothing had changed.

In Pittsburgh peace began badly. Before the year of 1918 was out, an influenza epidemic took the lives of

2052 people—525 more than the number of Allegheny County men killed in action.

The industrial change-over to peacetime conditions was not going smoothly; it led to production cutbacks, to men losing their jobs, to declining wages.

The labor force of the area was seething with dissatisfaction. In August, 1919, streetcar motormen and conductors struck for pay increases. In September steelworkers went on strike for union recognition and reduction of the 12 hour day. In November 42,000 miners in the district walked out, striking for shorter hours and higher wages.

Management and labor faced each other as enemies. President Wilson's attempt to prolong their wartime truce was not successful. As the leaders of industry persisted in retaining a free hand in their labor relations, strikes, lockouts, shootings and bombings—the full paraphernalia of industrial warfare—continued.

Why was it that management and labor were not able to establish a satisfactory relationship. Professors Miller and Cochran answer this question in *The Age of Enterprise* in this way: American workers thought in terms of democracy, of majority control, of representative government, which for them meant a voice in decisions involving their lives; management, on the other hand, led by independent and vigorous entrepreneurs striving to uphold the free enterprise tradition, was not willing to allow any interference with its right to make the decisions.

On one issue, however, management and labor were in accord: neither wanted the continuous influx of immigrants. With mechanization on the increase, factories were no longer dependent on large numbers of unskilled men, and labor, faced with a steadily declining job market, feared the competition of the foreign workers. Thus, when the year 1921 came along, Congress hastily adopted legislation halting immigration. No European country was allowed to send in any year more than 3% of its nationals resident here at the time of the 1910 census. Subsequent regulations in 1924 and in 1929 further reduced the quotas.

Pittsburgh was deeply affected by these restrictions. Before the war some two-thirds of the industrial working force was foreign-born. Now that the flow was stopped, few who lived in the city could hope to bring over members of their families and relatives. Gradually the language, the traditions and customs of the old country receded into the past. Gradually the old immigrants became Americanized. Their children learned English in their schools; they grew up as Americans. The "melting pot" fulfilled its task: it moulded people of different countries, of different nationalities, of different cultures into a single new nation.

Everywhere one looked in America the continuity of customs appeared to be broken; life was undergoing rapid and bewildering changes. People longed for the good old days, or, as the Republican candidate for the Presidency, Senator Warren Gamaliel Harding, phrased it, "to return to normalcy."

In the 1920 presidential election, the first one after the war, Pittsburghers as usual supported the Republican candidates. They gave Harding and Coolidge 138,908 votes, while the Democratic ticket—James M. Cox and his handsome young running mate, Franklin D. Roosevelt—received only 40,278. This was the first presidential election in which women were allowed to vote, the 19th Amendment having become part of the Constitution the previous year. (Within a short time the women of Pittsburgh were to occupy public offices. Mrs. Enoch Rauh, as a member of the Magee administration, headed the Department of Charities; Mrs. Minnie Penfield became the first woman to serve on a jury; Miss Sara Soffel was named as the first woman judge in Pennsylvania.) Mrs. Mary Roberts Rinehart, the novelist, exhorted the voters in her campaign speeches to vote Republican, which they would have done even without her exhortation.

The result of the election was given through the radio, an innovation for which Pittsburgh can take the credit.

The city was a pioneer in radio communication. Frank Conrad, the eminent Westinghouse engineer, installed a transmitter in his garage as far back as 1916 which was licensed as 8XK. After the end of the war, when amateurs were again allowed to operate, Conrad began to send out messages. One day when he felt tired he placed a microphone before his phonograph to spare his voice and he played some records. This was on October 17, 1919—the birth of the first musical broadcast. Urged by amateurs, Conrad began to send out gramophone music every Wednesday and Saturday evening for two full hours. He bor-

LIFE WAS NOT EASY. The city grew into a jungle. The skies were dark. Traffic was in a snarl. The days seemed like nights. White shirts turned into black in minutes. There was smoke and smog and grime. This photograph was taken at Liberty Avenue looking east from Fifth

Courtesy Joseph LaPointe.

at 14 minutes after four o'clock in the afternoon of February 13, 1925.

This day was not bleaker than others, the griminess of the scene was no more than usual. Pittsburghers became used to this drab existence, to a life without beauty, without joy, full of obstacles, hazards, and unpleasantness. Was it the purpose of human existence to live in such a way?

Many Pittsburghers took conditions for granted. It had always been this way. They said that this is how it was, they said that is how it is, and they said that is how it will be. But there were others who rebelled. They said the drab and intolerable conditions were man-made, thus they could be un-made by man. They held that intelligent planning and stringent laws of smoke control could change the situation and prevent further suffering.

DARKNESS AT NOON, BUT LIFE MUST GO ON, HOWEVER HEAVY THE SMOG, HOWEVER PERVADING THE FUMES.

A picture postcard
called HIGH NOON.

rowed records from a neighboring music store; in exchange he mentioned the store's name and thus instituted the world's first radio advertisement.

On election night—November 2, 1920—the returns were telephoned to Westinghouse Electric's station from the newspaper offices of the Pittsburgh *Post*, with publisher Arthur E. Braun and his editors manning the phones. These messages were sent out from the 100 watt KDKA transmitter in East Pittsburgh, with crystal set listeners in neighboring states as well as in the city picking them up. In movie houses the figures were transcribed on slides and projected to audiences. In the Edgewood Club a large horn was set up, magnifying the announcer's voice to a ballroom full of listeners. Between returns some singers, two banjoists and master of ceremonies A. S. Duncan provided "live" entertainment.

With the increase of sets a variety of programs was developed in Pittsburgh. Arthur E. Braun, the sprightly

(turn to page 327)

THREE O'CLOCK OF A DISMAL AFTERNOON.
A bleak scene on Wood Street in the winter of 1913.

DURING THE FIRST DECADES OF THE TWENTIETH CENTURY PITTSBURGH WAS THE MOST PICTURESQUE PLACE

There was an eternal mist, an everlasting fog in the air. The silhouettes of the buildings and those of the boats were soft, at times hardly visible, more felt than seen. The figures of humans as they walked through the streets seemed unreal, like in fairyland. The world was quiet, one could hardly hear the steps of the men who emerged from the fog, coming from nowhere and disappearing into nowhere. The city had about it a dreamlike quality—a phantastic and ro-

and alert septuagenarian, remembers those early days of broadcasting as if they were yesterday. "In our newspaper offices at Wood Street we installed a studio. We put up a partition, carted in a grand piano and a few chairs and that was it. Our performers were actors who played at the Alvin or the old Nixon Theatre. They came to the studio and performed without a fee. And when no visiting celebrities were around we put on some records. As time went on, we fixed up a larger room on the second floor of the building with acoustically treated walls and ceilings, and this served as the Pittsburgh *Post* studio of Station KDKA until 1927."

Under President Harding the country returned to peacetime conditions. "Normalcy" was restored; life was a bed of roses—for all those who had money. And for those who could not partake of the country's riches—so spokesmen of the government declared—there was an abundance of opportunity. Every man who had ability and who was willing to work could match his achievements with those of a Horatio Alger hero. And if he could not, the fault was his, not the government's.

*

Pittsburgh at the end of the war was not a beautiful place to look at. Its buildings spread out without planning, its streets were congested, its rivers polluted. Smoke and smog, the curse since earliest times, blackened the skies, the curtains and everything white. Flood waters inundated the streets at the Point at regular intervals.

In his *Prejudices*, Henry L. Mencken wrote about the appalling desolation of the Pittsburgh landscape:

> Here was the very heart of industrial America, the center of its most lucrative and characteristic activity, the boast and pride

THE SMOG HUNG OVER THE RIVERS AS AN IMPENETRABLE CURTAIN.

Courtesy Carnegie Library.

Photograph by Frank E. Bingaman.

ONG THE GREAT CITIES OF AMERICA.

mantic paradise for photographers and painters. It is strange that no more works of art were done during Pittsburgh's smoky decades—it is strange and it is a pity.

THE BUILDING BOOM.

of the richest and grandest nation ever seen on earth—and here was a scene so dreadfully hideous, so intolerably bleak and forlorn that it reduced the whole aspiration of man to a macabre and depressing joke. Here was wealth beyond computation, almost beyond imagination—and here were human habitations so abominable that they would have disgraced a race of alley cats.

I am not speaking of mere filth. One expects steel towns to be dirty. What I allude to is the unbroken and agonizing ugliness, the sheer revolting monstrousness, of every house in sight.

The 1920 census gave the city a population of 588,343, of which 120,266 were foreign-born. Two classes dominated the scene. On the top a small group of well-to-do industrialists, businessmen and financiers; at the bottom the large mass of industrial workers.

The Cathedral of Learning of the University of Pittsburgh, the world's tallest educational structure, was begun late in 1926.

Hotel Webster Hall, originally a men's club hotel, opened in 1926. It was built at a cost of $3,500,000. When the idea failed, Webster Hall became a commercial hotel.

The Gulf Building, with its 38 stories and an additional six story pyramid tower, was completed in the spring of 1932.

Koppers Building was ready for occupancy in 1929. It had 34 stories above the street and 3 more floors below the ground.

Chamber of Commerce Building erected by George T. Oliver was opened to the tenants in May 1917.

below:

The Mellon Bank, as the architect visualized it. The building was completed in 1923.

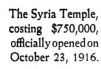

The Syria Temple, costing $750,000, officially opened on October 23, 1916.

The rich lived in ornate mansions that cost millions to build. For the panelling of the rooms woods were imported from Europe; marble for the hand-carved fireplaces came from Italy; tapestries and silks for the wall coverings brought from France.

A. M. Byers' homes had ninety rooms and 14 baths; the Fifth Avenue residence of R. B. Mellon had 65 rooms and 11 baths; Henry C. Frick's place at Penn and Homewood had 30 rooms. The house of Michael Benedum, "the great wildcatter," on Woodland Road (now belonging to Chatham College) abounded in marble pillars and statuary; its hall was panelled in oak, its dining and living room in red mahogany, its billiard room with limed oak. The McCook mansion had its own chapel, A. A. Frauenheim's residence its own ballroom. Many homes had bowling alleys.

And while the well-to-do enjoyed their splendid surroundings, the masses dwelt in overcrowded tenements or in simple houses without sanitary facilities. As late as 1934 three out of four houses on the lower North Side or in Woods Run had neither hot water nor bathrooms; nine out of ten were without furnace heat.

*

From earliest times Pittsburgh was a working town, a town of business, a town where money was made. A magazine author called it "an esthetic abortion, a municipal hovel, a mining town on a vast scale." For the short story writer O. Henry it was the "low-downdest" hole in the surface of the earth, with people who are "the most ignorant, ill-bred, contemptible, boorish, degraded, insulting, sordid, vile, foul-mouth, indecent, profane, drunken, dirty, mean, depraved." (But one must remember that O. Henry wrote this after he was released from prison, so he was probably not in the best of moods.)

In the city the rich worked as hard as the poor, the manager as long hours as his steel hand. Pittsburghers had little time for pleasures.

When the wealthy entertained in the twenties they did so in a formal way. Dinners, cotillions, coming-out parties were gala affairs. The scions of the established families—the Arbuthnots, Armstrongs, Bailies, Bakewells, Byers, Carnegies, Chalfants, Childs, Churches, Darlingtons, Dennys, Dilworths, Fricks, Heinzes, Hornes, Hostetters, Hunts, Joneses, Laughlins, Lockharts, Mellons, Moorheads, Morelands, McCandlesses, McClintics, McCooks, Nimicks, Olivers, Painters, Phippses, Reases, Robinsons, Scaifes, Schoonmakers, Sheas, Snyders, Thaws, Thompsons, Willocks—congregated at the exclusive Pittsburgh Club or in the Pittsburgh Golf Club.

The workers spent their leisure time in bars and saloons, at sports events or at the movies. The immigrants from foreign countries frequented their Nationality Halls. There was the National Slovak Society, the Greek Catholic Union, the Polish National Alliance; there were the German Turn and Gesangvereins. The Russian-Americans, the Serbian-Americans, the Hungarians, the Czechs, the Croats, the Slovenians, the Italians, all had their organizations, where they congregated, where they spoke in their

(turn to page 332)

THREE GENERATIONS. Henry J. with son Howard and grandson Henry John Heinz II in 1917.
Grandfather began the company in 1869. When he died in 1919 his son Howard became the head of the enterprise, which by then employed 6523. In 1941 Howard died and was succeeded by his son Henry J. II.

ARTISTS AND WRITERS
OF PITTSBURGH.

MARY R. RINEHART

(1876-1958), the author of mystery novels and plays, was born and educated in Pittsburgh. In 1896 she married Dr. Stanley M. Rinehart. Her first two novels, *The Circular Staircase* (1908) and *The Man in Lower Ten* (1909), were immediate successes and sold well for many years. She combined suspense, humor, and characterization with a style which was widely imitated. In 1920 she and Avery Hopwood wrote *The Bat*, a dramatic version of her first novel; it enjoyed a protracted run on Broadway.

GERTRUDE STEIN

(1874-1946), whose influence on the writers of the twenties, especially on Hemingway and Anderson, was marked, was a Pittsburgher by birth. Educated at Radcliffe College and Johns Hopkins, where she studied medicine, she settled in Paris in 1903. She counted among her friends Picasso, Matisse, Cocteau, and many of the artists and authors of the period. She wrote many stories, poems, a novel, art criticism, operas, plays and autobiographical works, including the *Autobiography of Alice B. Toklas* (1933).

MARY CASSATT (1845-1926), one of Pittsburgh's most outstanding painters, was born on the North Side, the daughter of a wealthy banker. During her childhood she lived in France, and when her family returned to America, she enrolled at the Pennsylvania Academy of Fine Arts.

In 1868, she was back in Paris where she established her permanent home. She made journeys to Italy, Spain, and Holland, studying the old masters. In Paris she joined a group of impressionists and became a friend and disciple of Degas, who said of her work: "I will not admit a woman can draw like that." The main theme of her paintings and prints was motherhood, showing mothers and children in their intimate moments.

Mary Cassatt was independently wealthy, and she occupied a leading position in Paris society. Half blind and an invalid, she died at her French chateau in 1926 shortly after her 81st birthday.

MARGARET W. DELAND

(1857-1945), poet, novelist, and author of short stories, was born at Allegheny and married L. F. Deland of Boston in 1880. Her first successful novel, *John Ward, Preacher*, a bestseller in 1888, reflected the liberal religious trends of the day. She was best known for studies of village life, her characters battling against heredity or religion. She wrote *Old Chester Tales* (1899), *Dr. Lavendar's People* (1904), and two autobiographies: *If This Be I As I Suppose It Be* in 1935, and *Golden Yesterdays* in 1941.

WILLA S. CATHER

(1876-1947), born in Winchester, Virginia, moved with her family to Nebraska and graduated from the University of Nebraska in 1895. She worked as telegraph editor and drama critic for the Pittsburgh *Daily Leader*. In 1901, she became head of the English Department at Allegheny High School. Her first book of poetry, *April Twilights*, appeared in 1903, her first stories, *The Troll Garden*, in 1905. In 1906 she joined *McClure's Magazine* in New York. Many of her stories were written in Pittsburgh

GEORGE S. KAUFMAN

(1889-1961), the playwright, was born in Pittsburgh. After trying law and different jobs, he became a newspaperman. He wrote a column for the *Washington Times* and became assistant drama critic on the New York *Times*. Most of his works he produced with collaborators—Marc Connelly, Edna Ferber, Morris Ryskind, Ira Gershwin, Katherine Dayton, Moss Hart, J. P. Marquand, Leueen McGrath.

His sardonic humor and witty remarks at the Algonquin Round Table were legendary.

MARC CONNELLY

(1890-   ) was born in McKeesport and went to school in Washington, Pa. Until 1915 he was a reporter and columnist on Pittsburgh newspapers. In that year he left for New York to see the production of a musical comedy for which he had written the lyrics. The following year his first play, *The Amber Princess,* was produced. In 1921, he began his collaboration with George S. Kaufman, creating a number of successful plays. His best known play, *The Green Pastures,* was awarded the Pulitzer Prize.

ROBINSON JEFFERS

(1887-1962), the poet, was born in Allegheny. He attended several colleges, including the University of Pittsburgh and Occidental College (A.B. 1905). He received a legacy in 1914 which allowed him to live independently; he built a house at Carmel, California, with his own hands, where he led a hermit-like existence. His first of numerous books of poetry was published in 1912. His powerfully realistic work, emphasized civilized man's divorce from nature, and was marked by a sense of tragedy.

HERVEY ALLEN

(1889-1949), Pittsburgh-born novelist, poet, biographer, attended U. S. Naval Academy of Annapolis and the University of Pittsburgh from which he graduated with honors in 1915. After the first World War, in which he was badly wounded, he did graduate work at Harvard, taught English at Charleston (S.C.) High School, taught at Columbia and Vassar. He was one of the original staff members of the *Saturday Review of Literature.* His *Anthony Adverse* published in 1933 was a sensational best-seller.

NELLIE BLY (1867-1922), as Elizabeth Cochrane called herself, took the name from Stephen Foster's "Nelly Bly, Nelly Bly! bring the broom along," began her journalistic career at the Pittsburgh *Dispatch.* She reported on factories and public institutions, wrote on the theater, on art, on society.

In 1887, she left Pittsburgh for New York where she established herself as the outstanding sob-sister of her generation. In 1890 the twenty-two-year-old Nellie Bly completed a trip around the world that lasted for 72 days, 6 hours, 10 minutes, and 11 seconds, a week less than the eighty-day journey of Jules Verne's fictional hero, Phileas Fogg. From then on Nellie Bly was a celebrity; her yearly earnings ran to $25,000.

She married Robert Seaman, a wealthy hardware manufacturer, who was forty-four years older than she. When he died Nellie took over the management of the business, with disastrous results.

As the outstanding reporter of her generation she sought truth; her work was influential in bringing about much-needed reforms.

EVENTS IN THE TWENTIES.

THE NEW COMMUNICATIONS. Will Rogers performed on the Pittsburgh radio station KDKA in 1922. On November 2, 1920 the station was the first which broadcasted the votes of the Presidential election.

Photograph by Frank E. Bingaman in the Carnegie Library.

THE FIRST AMERICAN SOLDIER killed in action in the First World War was the Pittsburgher, Private Thomas F. Enright. His body was returned to the city and was put to rest in an elaborate funeral in July 1921.

Photograph by Frank E. Bingaman in the Carnegie Library.

THE WIDOW OF THE PRESIDENT, Mrs. Woodrow Wilson, came to Pittsburgh on Armistice Day in 1927 for the dedication of a plaque in honor of her husband in the City-County Building. Wilson died in 1924.

native tongue and where they found the newspapers of the old country.

A number of these groups were active in the pursuit of national political aims. On April 3, 1917 at a hall at 97 South 18th Street (now honored with a Penn State marker) the great Polish pianist Ignace Jan Paderewski addressed the convention of Polish Falcons, thus beginning the movement to recruit a Polish army in America to fight with the Allies and to work for the creation of an independent Poland.

On May 30, 1918 the great Czech patriot Thomas G. Masaryk, then chairman of the Czecho-Slovak National Council in exile, spoke to a cheering crowd of 50,000 in the Exhibition Hall demanding the formation of an independent Czechoslovakia. On that day he signed an agreement with representatives of the Slovak and Czech organizations guaranteeing the autonomy of the Slovaks in the future State. When Masaryk became President of Czecho-Slovakia, he denied this, saying that it was only a "local understanding between the American Czechs and Slovaks." Whatever the truth, the "Pittsburgh Convention," as the meeting was called, had a vital influence on the birth of Czecho-Slovakia.

*

America emerged from the war as the mightiest power on earth—no longer a debtor but a creditor nation, with a production capacity second to none. The growing mechanization and electrification of the factories increased the amount of consumer goods. Automobiles came off the assembly line by the millions (by 1929 the country produced 5,358,000 units). Refrigerators, washing machines, electrical appliances, labor-saving devices raised the standard

Photograph by Frank E. Bingaman.

INAUGURATION of Charles H. Kline as Mayor of Pittsburgh on January 4, 1926. The oath to the new mayor is administered by Daniel Winters, the President of the Council, at high noon.

of living. A Model T cost $500, well within the purchasing power of the small wage earner. To own a car was no longer a luxury; with a car workers could move away from the clatter and noise of the mills—out to the open spaces, to the spreading suburbs.

As the twenties began, they promised to be years of prosperity, a promise more than fulfilled. They were the years of crazy living and crazy spending, years of the flappers, short skirts and bobbed hair, years of pole sitters, six day racers, goldfish swallowers, marathon dancers, years of the homemade whiskey, bootleggers and gangsters. It was "The Jazz Age," in which the restless search for pleasure seemed to be the paramount aim of life. It was the era of Edna St. Vincent Millay, Scott Fitzgerald, Sinclair Lewis—an era which burnt its candles at both ends, the era of *The Great Gatsby* and of *Babbitt*.

They were Republican years, the years of the businessmen, who dominated the American scene. They were the last unbridled years of laissez faire and of rugged individualism, which marked a dividing line between the economy of the past and that of the future. In these years production was high and rising. In these years the industrial apparatus of the country surpassed the combined output of England and Germany, two of the greatest industrial nations on earth. But most of all, these years are remembered as the years of prohibition and the years of speculation.

Prohibition was probably a greater nuisance in Pittsburgh than anywhere else. From earliest times the place was "the drinkingest town in the West," with more bars and saloons than any other American city of comparable size. A steelworker's second home was the saloon; it was

(turn to page 335)

Photograph by Frank E. Bingaman in the Carnegie Library.

THE NEW LIGHT HEAVYWEIGHT CHAMPION—Harry Greb, "The Pittsburgh Windmill," who defeated Gene Tunney at New York's Madison Square Garden in 1922 for the American title. Pittsburgh went wild when Greb returned to the city with the crown. A year later Tunney regained the championship, but within the same year Greb returned to the middleweight ranks and won the world title in that division. He lost it in 1926 and died nine months later while undergoing eye surgery.

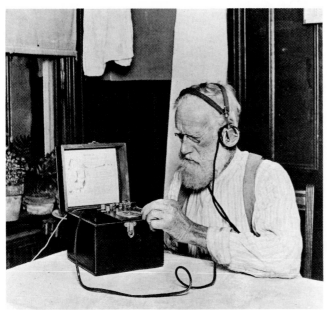

Courtesy KDKA Radio.

THE EARLY RADIO SETS. In 1921 rural listeners of KDKA tuned their crystal sets for farm news and for church services when weather conditions made the journey to church difficult.

FOR THREE DAYS IN OCTOBER 1929, THE CITY CELEBRATED HAPPILY THE CANALIZATION OF THE OHIO RIVER.

WORLD CHAMPIONS. In October 1925 Barney Dreyfuss's Pirates won the World Series for the second time. Although the Washington Senators went into the fifth game with a 3 to 1 lead, the Pirates took the next three games. In the rainy ninth inning of the seventh game, played at Forbes Field before 42,856 fans, Kiki Cuyler's double secured the four out of seven game victory for the Pirates. The city was seething with excitement. Stores closed; everybody celebrated the victory.

334

MARKING THE LIGHT'S GOLDEN JUBILEE IN 1929 PITTSBURGH TURNED INTO A VERITABLE FAIRYLAND.

there that he washed down the grime of the mill. Thus it was no surprise that a year after prohibition Pittsburgh was still regarded as "the wettest spot in the United States." Its five-hundred-odd drinking places became speakeasies and cabarets. Sixth Street turned into "the Great Wet Way" where whiskey was sold at $16 a quart, $150 a case, and where booze barons riding in flashy cars were pointed out as celebrities. Nightclubs like "The White Cat," "The Devil's Cave," "Little Harlem" were "playing" to standing room only.

On July 1, 1920, the first birthday of prohibition, the city's prohibition agent, J. W. Connors, promised that "before another anniversary . . . Pittsburgh and Western Pennsylvania will take on the semblance of a Sahara, and the whiskey dealer will gradually become extinct." Yet when that day came there were more whiskey-selling nightclubs in Pittsburgh than ever before.

Connors resigned and was replaced by John Exnicios,

LIBERTY BRIDGE, built at the cost of $3,400,000, was opened with the usual ceremonies on March 27, 1928. The bridge led into the $6,000,000 Liberty Tube, giving the residents of Pittsburgh direct access to the South Hills.

STEELWORKERS' ENGLISH CLASS began at the Lawrenceville Y.M.C.A. in 1913. On the left are printed phrases which begin with: "I awake from sleep. I open my eyes. I look for my watch." And they end: "I put on my vest and coat. I open the door of my bedroom. I go down stairs." The newcomers from Europe found it difficult to master the English language.

who promised "action within 48 hours." He shut off the liquor supply but was helpless against the trucks that brought beer into Pittsburgh and were guarded by city detectives. "If I get the men I've requested next week, I shall put the bootlegger out of business," orated Exnicios. But when Federal Government did not send requested re-inforcement agents, Exnicios bowed out, leaving Pittsburgh to three large bootlegging rings.

Under the new agent, Frederick C. Baird, who started out in 1922, ward politicians came to the fore, making their influence felt. Police and racketeers formed a liaison: bootleggers received protection, speakeasies and stills were allowed to function; for their services policemen received fat fees. In 1926, speaking before the Yale Alumni Associa-tion, Administrator Baird admitted that 10,000 stills were still operating in Allegheny County.

When Baird resigned he was replaced by John D. Pennington, under whom the raids on drinking places increased. The new enforcement agent padlocked open saloons and obtained convictions against speakeasies. In the year of 1928 alone the number of persons arrested for drunkenness in the city was 37,759. Still, people went on drinking.

Before the end of the decade Pittsburgh had a strong anti-prohibitionist movement. Led by Samuel Harden Church, the president of Carnegie Institute, the anti-prohibitionists fought valiantly against the law which was degrading the nation and which begat nothing but law-lessness. But it took a few more years before "the great social and economic experiment, noble in motive and far-reaching in purpose," as President Hoover put it, could be repealed. Not until 1933, the year Franklin D. Roosevelt was sworn into the Presidency, were beer and liquor sold openly in Pittsburgh again.

As to speculation, the other evil of the twenties, the fever in the city was not as high as in New York or in Chicago, but there were plenty of people in Pittsburgh who jeopardized their savings, mortgaged their future so they could speculate in stocks, in real estate, in buildings, in commodities, expecting that the prices would only go one way—up. John Kenneth Galbraith in his superb study *The Great Crash* makes this pertinent observation: "The striking thing about the stock market speculation of 1929 was not the massiveness of the participation. Rather it was the way it became central to the culture." The majority of American workers, farmers, employees, were

(turn to page 340)

Photograph by United Press International

A STRIKER IS ARRESTED, an everyday occurrence during the great steel strike of September 22, 1919, to January 7, 1920, for the unionization of the steel industry, during which the company police used clubs and fists freely. The bulk of the strikers were "new immigrants" from the eastern and southeastern part of Europe; they belonged to the unskilled class.

A PICTORIAL DOCUMENTATION of the State Constabulary's behavior.

Rudolph Dressel, the proprietor of a hotel in Homestead, asserted in his affidavit, printed in William Z. Foster's *The Great Steel Strike and its Lessons,* that on the 23rd day of September 1919, as he was standing in front of his place of business with a friend "the State Constabulary on duty . . . stopped directly in front of me and demanded that I move on. Before I had time to comply I was struck by the State Policeman." As proof that he was telling the truth, Mr. Dressel referred to the above photograph, in which the policeman's "threatening club is plainly seen descending toward me." The brutality of the police earned them the name "Cossacks." They broke up meetings, they beat up men, they demanded that in their assemblies the strikers speak only English, knowing well that most of them could not speak the language. Workers were arrested without provocation, fined summarily without being allowed to call witnesses in their defense. A news dispatch of September 26, 1919, revealed: "Horses of the Pennsylvania State Constabulary are trained not to turn aside . . . but to ride straight over any one against whom they were directed. Lizzie, a splendid black mare ridden by Trooper John A. Thorp, uses her teeth as well as her heels when in action. Her master will sometimes dismount, leaving Lizzie to hold a striker with her strong jaws, while he takes the pursuit of others on foot." The strike collapsed in January; the men failed to achieve their objective. The 12-hour day remained as did the low wages.

337

EDUCATORS.

JOHN G. BOWMAN (1877-1962), Chancellor of the University of Pittsburgh from 1921 to 1945. Under him the institution's enrollment increased from 2300 to 23,000. His supreme achievement was the building of the 42-story-high Cathedral of Learning, costing 32 million dollars. But he said: "I have never believed that a great building is great education. I would rather be known for having made headway in teaching good manners and a purpose in life than for having built *any* buildings."

ROBERT E. DOHERTY (1885-1950), President of the Carnegie Institute of Technology from 1936 to 1950, following A. A. Hamerschlag and Thomas S. Baker. He introduced the Carnegie Plan of Education. During his administration the enrollment of the institution increased from 2250 day and 308 evening students to 3400 day and 1465 evening students. In the year Dr. Doherty became president, Carnegie Tech gave only 27 graduate degrees; when he left in 1950 more than 200 were awarded.

WILLIAM J. HOLLAND (1848-1932), Chancellor of the University from 1891 to 1901, was pastor of the Bellefield Presbyterian Church for seventeen years (from 1874 to 1891). A versatile man, he was keenly interested in paleontology and entomology, especially lepidoptera (moths and butterflies). He was an accomplished artist, painting the illustrations for his books. After his resignation from the University, he remained director of the Carnegie Museum, a post he held 34 years.

SPORTSMEN.

BARNEY DREYFUSS (1848-1932) was born in Freiburg, Germany and came to America when he was 17 years old. In 1899 he bought the Pirates, merged it with members of his Louisville club, and led the new team on its meteoric rise. In the thirty-two years that Dreyfuss, a small man weighing only 125 pounds, owned the Pirates, the team won six National League pennants (in 1901, 1902, 1903, 1909, 1925 and 1927) and was World Series champion in 1909 and 1925.

JOHN PETER WAGNER (1874-1955), baseball's great shortstop (called "Honus," "Hans," or "The Flying Dutchman"), played 2785 games and hit over .300 in 17 successive seasons. His lifetime batting average was .329, his highest in 1900 at .381. His top salary never exceeded $10,000 "but," as he said, "there was no income tax then and a glass of beer cost a nickel." When he retired in 1917 he had scored more runs, made more hits and stolen more bases than anyone in his league.

JOHN B. SUTHERLAND (1889-1948) was born in Scotland and came to Pittsburgh in 1907. After Glenn H. ("Pop") Warner resigned in 1924, "Jock" Sutherland became coach of the University of Pittsburgh's football team. Under him Pitt won 111 games, tied 12 and lost 20.

In 1939 Sutherland resigned over a policy disagreement with Chancellor Bowman.

In 1946 he returned to the city as the coach of the Steelers, but his five year tenure was cut short by his tragic death.

FAMOUS

VISITORS.

EINSTEIN IN PITTSBURGH. In December 1934 the discoverer of the relativity theory came to the city to speak before the American Association for the Advancement of Science in the Carnegie Tech Theater on the "Equivalent of Mass and Energy". He was greeted by department store owner Edgar J. Kaufmann (on the right).

Edgar Kaufmann (1885-1955), a handsome, dashing and magnetic man and a lover of life, was one of the key figures in Pittsburgh's rebirth. His effervescent mind was constantly bubbling with new ideas for his department store and for his native city. He wanted to make Pittsburgh the best city in America. His manifold contributions helped to raise the area's cultural standards. His home "Falling Water" at Bear Run, built over a waterfall by Frank Lloyd Wright, was filled with exquisite paintings, and on the grounds and around the swimming pool were sculptures by Rodin, Lipschitz, Henry Moore and other celebrated artists. To provide enjoyment to Pittsburghers, Kaufmann financed the Light Opera Company, and he donated a million and a half dollars for the erection of a Civic Auditorium with a retractable roof. The bulk of his estate was left to his charitable fund to be used for cultural projects in his native city.

PRESIDENT CALVIN COOLIDGE came to Pittsburgh in October 1927 for the Carnegie Institute's Founder's Day Exercises. Samuel H. Church, the head of the Trustees, had told the students that the President would address them, so Coolidge said: "I shall not break Colonel Church's promise to you." That was all.

339

nowhere near the stock market.

In these years the industrial plants of the city became targets of the hysteria. During the summer of 1929 Westinghouse stock rose from 151 to 285, that of U. S. Steel from 165 to 258. On September 3, the last day of the bull market, U. S. Steel was sold for 262. (Three years later, in 1932, when the bottom of the depression was reached, the price of the same stock was 22. At that time Pittsburgh steel mills produced 1/10 of their capacity).

To a thoughtful observer—if there were any—it would have been apparent that the American economy was losing its vitality and elasticity. The country was no longer expanding as rapidly as in the past decades. In 1926 unemployment reached the half million mark; in 1929 it rose to 1,800,000.

Still, production, because of mechanization, modernization and electrification, was rising. The trouble was that not many had the means to buy the goods. With wages remaining low—the average factory worker in the twenties earned about $25 a week—six million families, amounting to one-fifth of the nation, made less than $1,000 a year. Thus, a vast segment of the population was not able to acquire more than the bare necessities of life. Agricultural overproduction, low farm prices without adequate margin for profit brought hardship to the farmers, cutting into their buying power.

Our chauvinistic trade policies, our poorly planned foreign investments, together with the speculative mania that gripped the country, augured ill for the future. It seemed obvious that disaster was bound to come. And when it came in the fall of 1929 the world of dreams collapsed; it ended with a bang, not with a whimper. The crazy, carefree days of the twenties had run their course; they were gone forever.

The depression that followed hit Pittsburgh harder than other areas where industries were less predominant. The factories of the city quickly cut back production, workers were dismissed overnight.

Those who kept their jobs were forced to take large cuts.

(turn to page 343)

THE SHEPHERD OF THE UNEMPLOYED, Father James R. Cox, addressed a large rally at Pitt Stadium on January 17,

THE "HUNGER CARAVAN" of the unemployed met in front of Father Cox's church to begin their long march to Washington.

IN THE NATION'S CAPITAL the marchers were halted by the police. But Father Cox went on and presented his petition.

1932 after he returned from Washington. In the Capital he had urged the President (above) to provide work and petitioned Congressmen to vote for immediate relief. Back in Pittsburgh he offered himself as the Jobless Party's presidential candidate.

THE LONG LINE of the unemployed Pittsburgh men on their way to the Capital. They came in all sizes and nationalities.

ON THEIR RETURN to Pittsburgh the "hunger marchers" were welcomed with a good, city-provided meal in Bohemian Hall.

THIS IS MY CITY. Luke Swank was one of the greatest photographers who came out of Pittsburgh. He did not romanticize, his sensitive eye focused his camera on reality. He had no desire to beautify, no desire to sentimentalize. His photographs of Pittsburgh, taken during the twenties, show the city as he saw it, grim, hard, cold, dirty, but also vibrant and dynamic.

Wages declined by 60%, salaries by 40%. The National Income toppled from 81 billion dollars in 1929 to 68 billion in 1930, to 53 billion in 1931 and to 41 billion in 1932.

Men in their prime wandered the streets in despair. Unemployed banded together and set off on "hunger marches." Father James Cox, pastor of old St. Patrick's Church, led 15,000 men from Pittsburgh to Washington. And when he returned he announced his candidacy for the Presidency on the Jobless Party ticket—but even that pronouncement did not seem to help the situation.

The traditional optimism of the American people yielded to dismal pessimism. Hopelessness took hold of their spirits. Gone was the exuberance, the belief in easy money and easy living. Life grew as dark as the skies over the city.

Two eminent chroniclers, both of them writing for the Pittsburgh *Press*, left a vivid description of depression days. One, Cyrus L. Sulzberger, came to the city from

(turn to page 348)

THE HABITAT OF HUMANS. A grim line of houses, one of Luke Swank's revealing photographic portraits of Pittsburgh.

LEGACY.
Photograph by Luke Swank.

THE CITY IN TRANSITION.

Photograph by Arthur Rothstein.

THE HILL IN THE 30'S.

SHANTIES IN

Photograph by John Vachon.

A DISMAL WINTER DAY.

PARKING ALONG

Photograph by Luke Swank.

THE HILL DISTRICT.

Photograph by Arthur Rothstein for the Farm Security Administration in 1936.

NEAR THE MONONGAHELA.

Photograph by Arthur Rothstein.

THE ALLEGHENY RIVER.

Photograph by John Vachon for the Farm Security Administration in 1936.

AFTER THE RAIN.

A PITTSBURGH PRIMITIVE.

PAINTER JOHN KANE AND HIS WIFE IN THE EARLY THIRTIES.

INDUSTRY'S INCREASE.

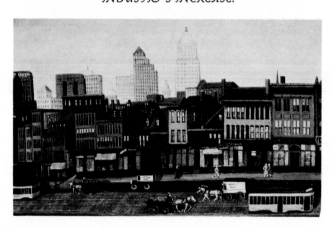

TWO OF KANE'S PAINTINGS: *Scene from My Studio* and *Frankstown Avenue Bridge*, illustrate the power of his work.

JOHN KANE was 67 when he became one of America's most significant painters. He had led a humble and unpretentious life. He was a worker, earning a meager living with the use of his two hands. At times he toiled in a coal mine, at other times at a steel mill. He was a street paver, a watchman at a railroad crossing, a construction-gang foreman, a munitions worker, a master carpenter, and a house painter. "I have done almost every kind of work a laboring man can do," he said. "I liked to work, and I did not care how hard it was. I liked to use my strong muscles."

Born in Scotland of Irish parents, one of seven children, he had scant education. He followed his stepfather and his brother to America in the eighties when he was 19 years old. His name was originally Cain, but when a bank clerk in Akron, Ohio, misspelled it in his bank book, Kane let it go. He "didn't like to make a point of it."

Kane's life is filled with dramatic incidents. At the age of 31, while crossing the tracks, he was knocked down by an engine. His left leg had to be cut off five inches below the knee.

His only son died two days after he was born. Kane took to drinking, left home for long periods. Once he was away for four years, his wife and two daughters did not know where he was.

He was footloose, irresponsible, and intemperate; gloried in working hard and fighting hard. In his young years his cronies in the Connellsville region gave him the name "Jack the Giant Killer." It was recalled that once he even fought with "Gentleman" Jim Corbett.

But he went to mass nearly every day of his life; he was a deeply religious man.

From his early youth he liked to draw and to paint. He painted the hills and rivers and valleys and he painted Pittsburgh. He said: "I paved its streets, made its steel, and painted its houses. It is my city; why shouldn't I paint it?"

For him painting was a vital part of life.

He based his canvases on the most minute observation. "I study it all out," he said to Marie McSwigan, who recorded Kane's life story in her sensitively written *Sky Hooks,* "I puzzle and figure and work . . . . By and by it comes to me . . . . I like to arrange things in a picture . . . . Sometimes, we can add something beautiful to a scene, or take away something that seems unreasonable."

He set his heart to exhibit one of his works at Carnegie Institute. Twice he tried, twice he was rejected; the third time he succeeded and his *Scene from the Scottish Highlands* was accepted by a jury of six painters. Though they felt the craftsmanship faulty, the freshness impressed them. This was Kane's first public recognition. He sold the canvas later for $50. (Today Kane paintings sell for a hundred times that figure.)

Kane was one of America's greatest primitive artists. He held: "Truth is love in thought. Beauty is love in expression. Art and painting are both of these."

Courtesy Marie McSwigan.

THE SOLITARY FUNERAL of a great painter. It was a rainy day, August 13, 1934, when six pallbearers, among them Jack Nash and John O'Connor, carried the coffin of John Kane. Behind them walked the painter's wife and his two daughters—no one else. The great artist had few friends—his last way was like the road of his entire life—a solitary one.

Courtesy East Liberty Presbyterian Church.

DEDICATION of the East Liberty Presbyterian Church on May 12, 1935. Banker Richard B. Mellon and his wife donated a sum of $4,000,000 for the building of the new church which was to be erected in memory of their respective parents. Wags in Pittsburgh nicknamed the church "the Mellon's fire escape."

Though the City Council voted emergency appropriations to help needy families, though the Mellons and other wealthy men donated hundreds of thousands of dollars to the Welfare Fund, though actors, like Phil Baker and Dick Powell, gave benefit performances, more stringent measures were needed to cope with the situation.

President Hoover still hoped that the "rugged individualism" of the American people could overcome the disaster. But with the economic structure of the country in shambles, it was beyond the strength of the individual to pull himself out of his miserable condition.

The philosophy of business held that the workers should save and be self-sufficient. But as wages were low and the cost of living high, saving was not possible. The welfare of society demanded a more even distribution of purchasing power; it cried for higher wages to absorb increased production. Unfortunately, business was slow to understand this. Businessmen clung to their acquisitive habits formed through the decades of scarcity. Instead of increasing the purchasing power of the masses, they reduced wages. Instead of enjoying the economy of abundance they reduced production. Instead of full employment jobs became scarce, with people starving, families despairing.

Suffering under the hardship of the depression years, in the 1932 presidential election Pittsburgh abandoned its long-time Republicanism. The people of the city rallied behind the Democrat Franklin D. Roosevelt, who offered them a helping hand and a New Deal. With banks closed, with millions out of work, the new government made a bold attempt to put the economy back on the rails.

The New Deal's priming of the pump brought employ-

(turn to page 357)

New York, dressed in poverty and walked the streets until he was as tired and hungry as the unemployed about whose plight he wrote. He registered at the Allegheny County Emergency Relief Bureau of Transients on Fernando Street and spent his days and nights with the destitutes. In five graphic articles he revealed their plight, giving an unforgettable picture of their life.

The articles written by Gilbert Love, Pittsburgh's outstanding newspaperman, were equally memorable. His reportage on the situation at Helping Hand, where 1800 men were staying in dire poverty, was a journalistic masterpiece. On October 24, 1935 Love wrote eloquently about the city's youngsters: "The children of the depression sit in schools these days with feet tucked back under their chairs, so schoolmates cannot see that their toes are sticking out of their ragged shoes." Still, Mayor McNair would not release the $40,000 that had been earmarked for helping the children because he was afraid that with the coming of winter the city would have to support 100,000 on relief, and he had no sufficient funds.

Courtesy Louis Americus.

END OF PROHIBITION. A month after Franklin D. Roosevelt's inauguration in 1933 beer drinking was legalized. The oyster bar of Louis Americus on the McMasters Way was quickly filled with thirsty Pittsburghers. In December of that year the Twenty-first Amendment repealed the "noble experiment."

THE CITY IN THE THIRTIES AS SEEN BY SAMUEL ROSENBERG.

GOSSIPS, FROM THE HILL LOOKING TOWARD OAKLAND, PAINTED IN 1938.

UPPER SOHO, FIRST EXHIBITED IN THE BUTLER ART INSTITUTE IN 1940.

GREENFIELD HILL, one of the outstanding paintings of Samuel Rosenberg. Done in 1932, the painting was widely exhibited. Its first presentation was in the Associated Artists Show of Pittsburgh in 1932. The same year it was shown in Washington's Corcoran Gallery, a year later in the Pennsylvania Academy of Fine Art, and in 1940 in the San Francisco Golden Gate International Show. It is possessed by the Carnegie Institute.

Courtesy Dr. and Mrs. John M. Johnston.

THE SUN SHINES IN THE CITY.

Courtesy Mrs. J. Kenneth Gardner

AUTUMN IN PITTSBURGH.

BIGELOW BOULEVARD under construction. A painting first exhibited in the Associated Artists Show, 1946.

MONDAY MORNING. Samuel Rosenberg painted this scene in 1935 and was awarded the Carnegie Institute Group Prize for that year.

FIFTH AVENUE GARDEN, a painting of Samuel Rosenberg made in 1938. This canvas is now owned by Dr. Percival Hunt, Pittsburgh, through whose courtesy it is reproduced here.

SAMUEL ROSENBERG (1896-1972), the most influential Pittsburgh artist, taught painting at the Carnegie Institute of Technology from 1925 till 1966. Between the years of 1937 and 1945 he also directed the art department of the Pennsylvania College for Women (the present Chatham College).

A much beloved and gentle man, he made Pittsburgh the focal point of his career. For half a century he exhibited with the Associated Artists.

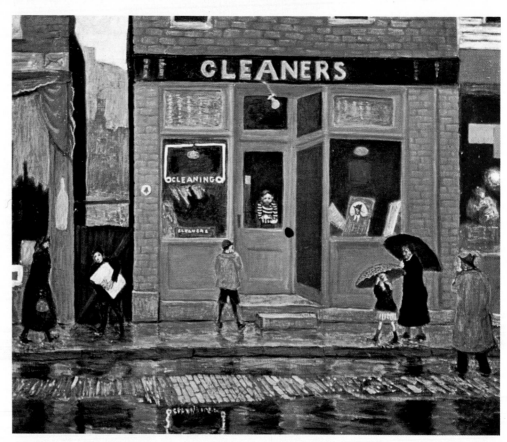

LOWER FIFTH AVENUE as it looked in 1936. It is an exceptionally vivid painting of a cleaning store, one of the delightful Pittsburgh scenes which Samuel Rosenberg enjoyed to paint.

CAMPAIGNING

FOR THE

PRESIDENCY.

FRANKLIN DELANO ROOSEVELT came to the city on his campaign tours in 1932, in 1936, and again in 1940.

It was in Pittsburgh in 1932 that Roosevelt promised a balanced budget. When four years later he told Sam Rosenman to prepare "a good and convincing explanation" of what he had meant in the 1932 speech, Rosenman replied: "Mr. President, the only thing you can say about that speech is to deny categorically that you ever made it." So Roosevelt forgot the explanation and talked about the Federal Budget in dollar and cents terms.

WENDELL WILLKIE, the presidential candidate of the Republicans, was jubilantly received in Pittsburgh in 1940, but when the election figures were counted, it was that "Old Campaigner" Roosevelt again. The country would not change the administration during a war, and that remained valid for 1944 too when FDR received the mandate of the country for the fourth time.

IN OCTOBER, 1940 President Roosevelt, after inspecting the district's flood control program came to the city, where he toured steel mills and armaments plants and dedicated the $13,800,000 Terrace Village, the nation's second largest housing project.

353

THE FLOOD OF 1936.

STREETS BECAME WATERWAYS as the flood engulfed many blocks in the Downtown section. Traffic came to a standstill. Vehicles disappeared from the city. Volunteers in boats cruised the streets to rescue those who were marooned.

THE FLOODED TRIANGLE. The scene as it looked from an aeroplane on March 20. Streets grew into canals, buildings were submerged. Life in Pittsburgh came to a virtual standstill. There was nothing to do but to wait until the waters receded.

ON ST. PATRICK'S DAY IN 1936 Pittsburgh suffered one of its most devastating floods. On Monday, March 16, the waters rose to 21.7 feet; two days later

Photograph by the Pittsburgh Sun-Telegraph.

they had risen to 46 feet.

The Triangle was inundated; power and telephone lines were blown down. Fires raged; there was a dearth of un- polluted water, there was a fear of epi- demic and of looting. The Downtown section was placed under martial law. The National Guard and the state police fought to keep order. When at the end of the week order was restored, many citi- zens had died, some 3000 had been in- jured, more than 100,000 had lost homes.

BROKEN AND HELPLESS SHANTY BOATS ON THE RAPIDLY RISING WATERS OF THE ALLEGHENY ON MARCH 17.

Photograph by the Pittsburgh Sun-Telegraph.

AN UNUSUAL SIGHT: STREETCARS ON PENN AVENUE, AT THE TIME WHEN THE FLOOD WAS AT ITS PEAK.

ment to the jobless masses of Pittsburgh. The WPA projects created jobs, even though many of them turned out to be temporary. There were research projects: compilation of physio-graphic data, the charting of maps needed by the Army Engineers for flood control studies, mine mapping, the making of bibliographies (one for the glass industry summarized articles on glass manufacture). There were recreational projects, statistical surveys, mural paintings, an educational program given in 208 centers, Negro work projects executed by the McClure Center in Homestead, sewing projects employing thousands of women. The WPA Symphony of "65 men and a girl" gave public concerts; writers assembled material about the city's history; thousands were trained by the Red Cross in first aid and home accident prevention methods; illiterates were taught to read and write in evening classes.

Yet with all the power of the government, recovery was slow. In 1934 one-third of Pittsburgh's employable population was still without work (of 544,187 employable persons 176,156 were seeking jobs). Not until the demands of the Second World War called for vastly increased production could the unemployment problem be solved.

*

"Pittsburgh has never been notable for culture," said Adolph Schmidt, the president of the A. W. Mellon Educational and Charitable Trust and a governor of T. Mellon & Sons, to a magazine writer, "and I am not inclined to insist that it has to keep up with other cities in this area if it is not disposed to do so. Pittsburgh has its own particular genius. It has made the country's steel and aluminum. It has its own directions."

The city's cultural ambassador is right on this point: culture was late in coming to Pittsburgh. One of the first

(turn to page 360)

Photograph by Frank E. Bingaman.

ENTRANCE TO THE JENKINS ARCADE BUILDING

Courtsey U. S. Steel Corporation.

ISABELLA FURNACE: WAVERLY OIL FIRE IN BACKGROUND

Courtesy Johnston and Johnston.

FIFTH AVENUE AND MARKET STREET ON MARCH 18, 1936.

THE BIG DAM HAS BROKEN! A dramatic photograph taken in Johnstown on March 17, 1936, shortly after an amateur radio operator announced on a national network that the Big Quemahoning Dam had burst.

The terror-stricken residents—recalling the disastrous flood of 1889—were running for their lives, scurrying for safety. The city was gripped by panic. As it turned out, the announcement was a false alarm. The Big Quemahoning Dam had not burst.

Still, that night the water rose to 18 feet in Johnstown's business district, swamping cars, vehicles and everything else in the streets. Over 15,000 residents were trapped in their homes. Newspaper reporters canoeing and wading through the city sent heart-rending stories to their home papers describing the plight of the people, the moaning and cries emanating from the dark houses. "Save me. Please God save me," rang out a woman's voice in the darkness, reported the man from the Pittsburgh *Sun-Telegraph*.

When the news from Johnstown reached Pittsburgh, apprehension spread throughout the city. People feared that the dam would break, the waters would rise higher, inundating more streets and more buildings. Already the whole Point area and its neighborhood was under water; office files, books, papers soaked in mud. The flood destroyed most of the photographic record which had been kept by the libraries of the Pittsburgh newspapers, representing the city's pictorial past. It destroyed property of great value.

It destroyed articles that could never be replaced; it destroyed historical documents.

Every hour brought new rumors, and every rumor warned of more trouble.

But the Quemahoning Dam held fast; Johnstown was saved from the worst; it suffered less damage than either Pittsburgh or Wheeling further down the river. After days of anxiety, the roaring waters in the Conemaugh River and Stony Creek subsided. Gradually the flood receded; Johnstown and Pittsburgh began to clean up the débris and start life afresh.

Photograph by the Pittsburgh Sun-Telegraph.

THOSE WHO COULD LAY HANDS ON A BOAT COULD MOVE ABOUT—OTHERS STAYED WHERE THEY WERE.

Photograph by the Pittsburgh Sun-Telegraph.

NOT UNLIKE THE GRAND CANAL IN VENICE.

effective steps toward it was the building of the Carnegie Institute in the late nineties. Andrew Carnegie always remembered Major Anderson, who allowed him to borrow books from his library when Carnegie was a penniless youngster. So he in turn wanted to make books available to young and old so they too could educate themselves. To further this purpose he built a library, a music hall, a natural history museum and an art gallery.

Unhappily, his good intention was marred by grave faults, hampering the effectiveness of the institution. Of the four units only one, the library, functioned smoothly; the others had difficulties right from the beginning. The Museum of Natural History had never enough operating funds; the beautiful music hall, in spite of its grandiose foyer, was much too small. The art museum, if properly administered, could have acquired the best contemporary

Photograph by the Pittsburgh Sun-Telegraph.

BY MONDAY, MARCH 23, THE WATERS AT LAST RECEDED AND PITTSBURGH EMERGED FROM THE FLOOD.

collection in the world. Carnegie's fundamental idea was sound: to hold an annual exhibition of paintings selected by an international jury and to make awards for the best works—expecting that the museum would buy the prize-winning canvases. All the great painters of the times submitted their work for the exhibitions—a Picasso, a Monet, a Matisse, a Roualt—but the museum committee rather bought conservative canvases than the unconventional art of the moderns. As a result, the museum's collection never amounted to much. Only lately, through the generosity and good offices of Sarah Mellon Scaife, has the museum received some notable paintings—a Renoir, an Il Perugino, a Vuillard, a Degas, a Gauguin, a Matisse, a Monet.

It may be that Carnegie's fundamental mistake was that he named the Institute after himself; because of it other art collectors were reluctant to make contributions. (Andrew W. Mellon's collection went to the National Gallery in Washington; Henry C. Frick established his own museum in New York.)

*

The career of Pittsburgh's colleges and universities was fraught with obstacles as well.

While the Rockefellers founded the University of Chicago, Eastman the University of Rochester, responsible capitalists of Cleveland the Western Reserve University, there was not enough support in Pittsburgh for its institutions of higher learning. Carnegie Tech did not develop as rapidly as M.I.T. or the California Institute of Technology. Pittsburgh was not supplied with the scientific and technical resources so necessary to the development of the area.

361

THE AFTERMATH OF THE FLOOD.

EMPLOYEES OF ROSENBAUM'S STORE CLEAN UP.

A FAMILY ATTEMPTS TO CLEAN UP ITS HOME.

TRUCKS HAUL AWAY DEBRIS IN OLIVER AVENUE

CLEAN-UP CREW EATS IN FIRST LUTHERAN CHURCH.

In 1921 the University of Pittsburgh had an enrollment of 2300 and was cramped for space. John G. Bowman, the new chancellor, startled the city with the proposal to build a 52 story skyscraper costing ten million dollars. The trustees opposed his plan, but in time Pittsburghers began to see the advantages of a university that was not the conventional cluster of buildings spread over an elm-shaped grassy campus but which rose boldly into the skies. Andrew W. Mellon donated the land, and gradually the building fund grew.

Of the projected fifty-two stories only forty-two were erected. When the edifice was completed, critics said that it resembled not a gothic cathedral, "but one built of bubble gum and stretched vertically out of all reasonable shape." Still, the Cathedral of Learning focused national attention on the University and on the city and became a landmark of Pittsburgh.

Music from the earliest times was practiced and enjoyed in the city. The German, Hungarian, Italian and other immigrants played their instruments, sang in their choirs, and gathered together to listen to music. The Symphony Orchestra came into being after the Carnegie Music Hall was completed but became defunct by 1910. In 1927 Edward Specter, the energetic director of the Symphony Society, revived the organization with the financial help of Mrs. Enoch Rauh and others. In the subsequent years, conductors of international renown—Otto Klemperer, Victor de Sabata, Fritz Reiner, and finally William Steinberg—moulded the musicians into one of the outstanding orchestras of the world.

Pittsburgh foundations, some of them established during this period, fostered the city's cultural aspirations. The Buhl Foundation, formed in 1927 with a $15,000,000 gift of the Buhl family, donated a planetarium which was

(turn to page 364)

REBUILDING THE BOULEVARD.

Courtesy Allegheny Conference.

BIGELOW BOULEVARD seemed in bad shape when the photograph was taken in the summer of 1936. The road had holes and patches, it was filled haphazardly with macadam, motorists referred to it as "no man's land." The Pittsburgh Motor Club urged the laying of a concrete surface. It was obvious that something had to be done about the heavily travelled road.

Courtesy Allegheny Conference.

AND SOMETHING WAS DONE ABOUT IT. The rebuilding of the Boulevard nears completion—a picture from November 1939 which shows Frank M. Roessing pointing to the new lights.

Courtesy Allegheny Conference.

READY FOR THE OPENING. Everything was spic and span when this photograph was taken on the morning of December 13, 1939, a few hours before the official opening of the Boulevard.

dedicated in the fall of 1939. Early in the thirties, in the depth of the depression, the foundation, which was then directed by Charles F. Lewis (who three decades later capped his distinguished career as president of the Western Pennsylvania Conservancy, creating park and recreational areas for the region), started a unique experiment. It built a community on Mount Washington with homes, gardens, shopping center, town hall, park, playgrounds. The 197 homes of Chatham Village, as the community housing development became known, were not for sale but for rent. The experiment demonstrated that a rental policy based on fairness and not on greed could be financially rewarding. Ever since, Chatham Village has flourished; it had a 100% occupancy, and it grew and expanded.

The A. W. Mellon Educational and Charitable Trust, created by Andrew Mellon in 1930, contributed large sums for the University of Pittsburgh, for the research activities of the Mellon Institute (which the Mellon brothers founded in 1913) and for numerous other cultural projects. By the sixties the amount distributed by the fund was well over a hundred million dollars.

*

Pittsburghers have always been too busy working to give much attention to their surroundings. While they grumbled about the bad housing conditions and complained about the poor transportation and about the eternal smoke and smog, they did little to remedy the abuses.

In 1917 Theodore Roosevelt orated before a Chamber of Commerce audience:

> There is no more typical American city than Pittsburgh. And Pittsburgh, by its Americanism, gives a lesson to the entire United States. Pittsburgh has not been built up by talking about it. Your tremendous concerns were built by men who actually did the work. You made Pittsburgh ace high when it could have been deuce high. There is not a Pittsburgh man who did not earn his success through his deeds.

Yet despite the ex-President's boasting words, the city was heading to decay. People felt that a town of steel mills and factories had to be dirty and its skies had to be dark. "A smoky Pittsburgh is a healthy Pittsburgh," went the saying. As long as the stacks emitted smoke, things were fine. "We didn't mind the smoke so much," says an old Pittsburgher recalling those days, "for it indicated production and it indicated prosperity."

Periodically, efforts were made to change the untenable conditions. One was in 1910 when the Pittsburgh Civic Improvement Commission under the leadership of Harry D. W. English instigated a series of studies. Three planning experts, Frederick Law Olmsted, Bion J. Arnold and

(turn to page 368)

THIS WAS PITTSBURGH—as Margaret Bourke-White saw it when she flew over the city in 1936 to photograph it for a new picture magazine which was launched in that year—*Life.*

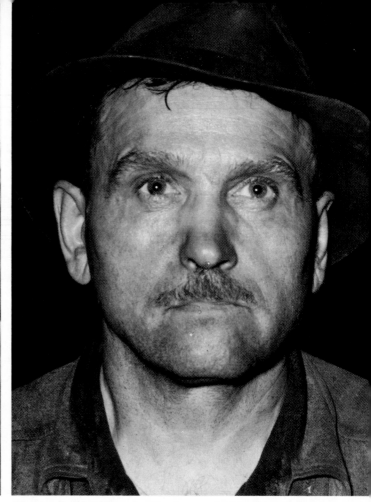

THE MEN WHO MADE PITTSBURGH. They came from all parts of the country and all parts of Europe. Among them were Englishmen, Irishmen, Germans, Italians, Hungarians, Poles, Estonians, Latvians, Czechs, Greeks, Armenians and Negroes.

They worked in the steel mills, they worked in the coal mines, and they worked in the factories. Their muscles made Pittsburgh the greatest industrial city of the world.

These portraits of Pittsburgh workers were taken by Arnold

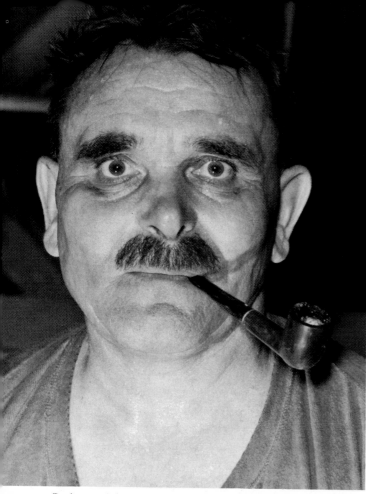

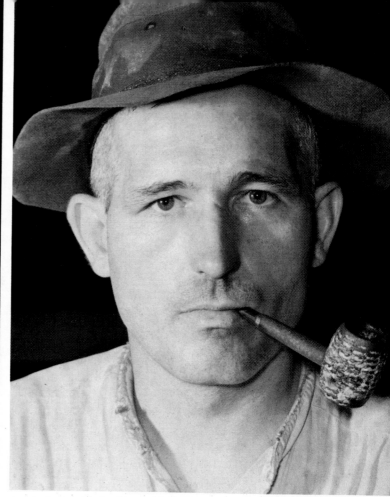

Rothstein, John Vachon and John Collier, who in 1936 came to the area and took photographs for the Farm Security Administration. They took hundreds of pictures, recording for posterity how the people and the city looked. A depression undertaking, their work is a historical document, that will serve later generations with a priceless pictorial record of the Thirties. Their photographs of Pittsburgh and of other parts of the country are now preserved in a row of file cabinets in the Library of Congress.

John R. Freeman, analyzed the city's problems and made the following recommendations:

1. A study of the district's steam railroad facilities to find an answer to the questions whether the facilities should be enlarged, extended or changed; whether the suburban divisions should be electrified; whether stations should be relocated.
2. Protection against the ever-recurring floods by controlling the rivers.
3. A study of the rapid transit system and suggestions for its improvement.
4. A better street system.
5. A clear policy for parks, playgrounds, squares and public buildings.
6. Sanitary and ample water supply.
7. A sewage system that would not pollute the rivers.
8. Public control over developments on private property, particularly the need for a new building code.
9. The organization of a bureau of smoke abatement control that would counsel and cooperate with factories to improve "the Pittsburgh atmosphere without hampering its industrial success."

This preliminary report was followed by more detailed studies. Frederick Law Olmsted in his *Pittsburgh Main Thoroughfares and the Down Town District* proposed three main remedies to cure the city's ills: 1) a comprehensive system knitting all sections of the civic industrial area together; 2) a group location of all public buildings; 3) the boring of a tunnel so that the South Hills could be opened up to relieve Pittsburgh's overcrowded housing conditions.

Olmsted's report set off a chain reaction. Planning-conscious citizens pressed for the creation of the Department of City Planning, and when the State Legislature passed the necessary law in 1911 Mayor Magee appointed a nine-member commission to man the new department. Unfortunately, by 1917 the department operated on a budget of only $100 for the year. However, the Citizens Committee for a City Plan, kept on its fight. In 1920 the organization was renamed the Municipal Planning Asso-

ONE OF THE GREAT EVENTS OF THE THIRTIES WAS THE

ciation with the aim to promote "orderly and efficient development of municipalities" and "scientific methods of city and municipal planning." It pressed the city fathers to increase the budget of the City Planning Commission to $30,000 and it pressed the commission to submit a zoning code. For the next three years a violent battle was fought between the pro- and anti-zoning factions in the city. Not until 1933 could the act be passed, the first realistic step toward an overall long-range plan.

Pittsburgh was sorely in need of such a zoning law. Because of the prevalence of hills, level lots were scarce, so houses were built on vertical box-like construction. The

Taken on October 11, 1936, by a Sun-Telegraph photographer.

IMPRESSIVE EUCHARISTIC CONGRESS AT PITT STADIUM, ATTENDED BY A HUNDRED THOUSAND CATHOLICS.

result was an uncharted, chaotic development, with industry and commerce gravitating to the flat land at the river banks and adjoining areas. Structures were built closely together and they were densely populated. Thus Pittsburgh became a town of dingy, narrow, two or three flight walkup houses on streets that offered little sunlight, few trees, no space for flowers or lawns. The hillsides were used as trash dumps. Junkyards moved into the heart of the residential areas. Even better neighborhoods were deteriorating into semi-slums. Although it was not expected that the zoning law would eliminate the errors of the past, it was hoped to prevent such mistakes in the future.

The Planning Association issued a number of studies, which contained suggestions for the improvement of streets, public transit, parks, playgrounds, railroads and waterways. The most notable report recommended the canalization of the Ohio, a river-rail terminal, greater use of wharves, a system of water storage, reservoirs for flood protection as advocated by the 1911 Flood Commission.

Still, nothing effective was done about flood control until the St. Patrick's Day catastrophe in 1936 dramatized conditions that should have been remedied long before.

On March 17, 1936 waters at the Point had risen to 36.4 feet. "Terror gripped Pittsburgh as the flood surged

U. S. DECLARES WAR!

1500 Die In Hawaii; Fleets Clash; Nazis Abandon Drive For Moscow

ONCE MORE — WAR. From its beginning, Pittsburghers participated in the wars of the nation. They fought in the Revolutionary War, in the War of 1812, in the War with Mexico, in the Civil War, in the Spanish-American War, in World War I and now again in World War II.

Man—master of the universe—who invented complex machines, bridged continents, soared the skies, found remedies against illness, produced goods in amazing quantities—seemed to accomplish everything except being able to settle his differences without recourse to arms.

Pittsburgh played a vital part in winning the wars. It produced the tools necessary for victory. Said Claire, the great granddaughter of steelmaster Scott in Marcia Davenport's novel *The Valley of Decision*: "This city and all its means is the last hope of civilization . . . This thing we're going through is the supreme convulsion of the mechanical age. Nothing will win for us except more machines and greater machines than anybody else can possibly produce." And Pittsburgh produced the machines, it produced the goods, it helped the nation to victory.

about office buildings downtown and around homes in the North Side," reported the Pittsburgh *Sun-Telegraph*. "Deaths mounted every hour. Houses were swept loose from their foundations. Power went off . . . Phone lines went down. Fires broke out all over the district . . . Boats cruised about streets rescuing marooned families . . . Six hundred guests were marooned in the Roosevelt Hotel as the flood swept up almost to Smithfield Street . . . State police and highway patrolmen were called in . . . and the National Guard was mobilized."

The flood made 135,000 homeless and caused an estimated damage of $150 to $200 million. Congress, prodded by Pittsburgh's Chamber of Commerce, at last acted upon a planned flood control program. The Flood Control Act set up funds for the control of the rivers. Nine flood control dams were to be built at the headwaters of the strategic rivers creating a permanent foundation for the control of the ever-recurring floods.

The other crucial problem of the city, smoke control, though not solved in this period, was constantly on the mind of the people. It was in these decades that the battle for an effective smoke control ordinance was fought. The efforts of Edward R. Weidlein and Harry B. Mellor of the Mellon Institute, the Institute's studies on smoke, the increasing fight of City Health Director Dr. I. Hope Alexander and the other crusaders for such legislation bore fruit. In October 1941, the City Council passed a Smoke Control Ordinance; the outbreak of the war necessitated the postponement of its enactment. But at last, Pittsburgh was ready to clear its skies; it was ready for a big change, ready for its Renaissance.

*

By the late thirties Europe was once more in a turmoil. In America the debate raged between the isolationists and the interventionists. In 1936 Russia and Germany had a dress rehearsal of their weapons in the Spanish Civil War. Benito Mussolini won an easy conquest—with the League of Nations impotently looking on — when his troops

THE ARMY NEEDED STEEL and Pittsburgh supplied it. The mills worked day and night to make goods and materiel for the fighting forces. This is Turtle Creek Valley with the Edgar Thomson mills and the East Pittsburgh Works of Westinghouse.

THE NAVY NEEDED SHIPS and Pittsburgh supplied them. The boatyards of the Dravo Corporation at Neville's Island where LST-750, financed by the people of Allegheny County, was launched on Memorial Day, 1944 built a large number of boats.

THE WAR IS OVER. On August 14, 1945 the welcome news came at last. World War II was won. Fifth Avenue was filled with a dancing crowd, with soldiers and sailors kissing the girls within reach. Pittsburgh celebrated happily.

marched into Abyssinia. Adolph Hitler, the megalomaniac corporal of the Master Race, led his goose-stepping troops first into the Rhineland, then into Czechoslovakia, and then to Danzig and Poland, igniting the holocaust of the Second World War.

In the 1940 election both Franklin Roosevelt and Wendell Willkie promised not to involve the country in a foreign war. The Japanese attack on Pearl Harbor made these promises no longer valid. By 1941 the country was once more at war. Once more Pittsburgh industry was on the front lines to supply the tools and weapons against the enemy. Once more Pittsburgh steel mills worked around the clock. From Pearl Harbor day until the end of the war in 1945 the area produced 95 million ingot tons of steel —steel that powered the drive of the armies in Europe and forged victory over Japan in the islands and seas of the Pacific. Once more Pittsburgh was on the march.

THE HEAD of the War Production Board, Donald M. Nelson, visited Pittsburgh on July 1, 1943 to inspect the Victory Valley plants. At the airport he was greeted by C.I.O. President Philip Murray (left) and Benjamin Fairless, President of U. S. Steel.

THIS WAS ROBERT MOSES' PROPOSAL FOR A NEW POINT PARK.

A $38,000,000 PLAN.

The renowned city planner of New York was asked to advise the Pittsburgh Regional Planning Association and to suggest ways of easing the flow of traffic. Moses agreed to act as "a diagnostician" and submitted a 26-page report, which was embellished by 23 illustrations. Later a number of his proposals were adopted by the city.

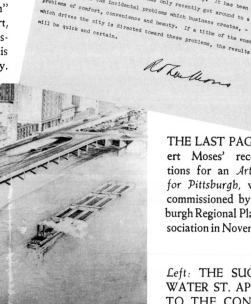

THE LAST PAGE of Robert Moses' recommendations for an *Arterial Plan for Pittsburgh*, which was commissioned by the Pittsburgh Regional Planning Association in November 1939.

Left: THE SUGGESTED WATER ST. APPROACH TO THE CONVERTED WABASH BRIDGE.

Chapter 10

REBIRTH

by David L. Lawrence
as told to John P. Robin and Stefan Lorant

THE PITTSBURGH RENAISSANCE was the title self-awarded to the city's enormous gathering of energy and leadership in the years that followed the Second World War and to the changes that came to the city.

Pittsburgh's great effort has been to remake itself, to change as fast as it could from the environment of the old nineteenth-century technology into the sleek new forms of the future. The city was racing time. It had no inclination to look back; it had no nostalgia for the past.

The city welcomed tomorrow, because yesterday was hard and unlovely. Pittsburgh erected buildings that glistened with stainless steel and aluminum; it had little time for the niceties of architectural criticism. It counted the gains and shrugged off the losses, not worshipping, not even respecting landmarks. The town took pleasure in the swing of the headache ball and the crash of falling brick. It tore down bridges without a second thought, and it regarded a tunnel through a mountain as the most natural kind of highway in the world.

Pittsburgh remembered some things well. It remembered when its air was so thick with soot and smog that the lights burned at high noon; it remembered the days when its rivers were polluted with the wastes of two million people and a hundred industries. It remembered a twelve-hour day in the steel mills, and it also remembered the times when there was no work, when the mills were operating at six per cent of capacity. It also remembered when its vaunted Golden Triangle was more grime than gold, when no building was erected in downtown Pittsburgh for twenty years.

When the war was over and the city contemplated its future, the people of Pittsburgh learned to their surprise that their city government could be a constructive force for the general welfare; that stories of municipal corruption were out of date, that corruption was at a minimum. The city and county government were executing great urban renewal programs, operating a huge airport at a profit, constructing parking facilities that paid their way.

Pittsburgh, after all the grim years, was proud and self-confident. It began to receive good notices in the national magazines and in the international press. Its leaders no longer got flustered when outsiders picked a sore point here or there within the city's improvement program.

There remained, however, one sure irritant. It was a reference to "The Smoky City." Pittsburgh's victory over air pollution was its great community triumph, and no Pittsburgher would be patient with those who had not learned that times had changed. There were many smoky cities in the United States still, but Pittsburgh was not one of them.

Attempting to chronicle the period of rebirth and renewal — to give proper perspective to each major achievement and to acknowledge the work of hundreds of individuals — would require a book, not a single chapter. Here in the short space allotted to the survey, only the peaks of accomplishment can be mentioned, with concentration on the early stages of the work and the people who played prominent parts in the development. Much noteworthy accomplishment and many imaginative plans remain to be discussed in another place. Dozens of citizens, from all walks of life, deserve attention and praise as equally indispensable and invaluable to the renaissance as those mentioned in this short survey.

Pittsburgh's success with smoke control has been the crucial element of its environmental revolution. The political and civic leadership which has carried out the imaginative and far-ranging program staked its future on the issue. It was clear that the economic revival of the city could not be accomplished if the very air above the city remained as reeking and black as generations of Pittsburghers had known it. The great concentrations of corporate administration and research, so vital to the modern Pittsburgh, would have moved elsewhere in the nation. The central business district would have decayed. Community morale and momentum would have been lost, and Pittsburgh would have become a community almost beyond hope of rescue.

The rescue, as it happened, was a close thing. Pittsburgh had lived with its smoke problem since the soldiery dug the first soft coal from Coal Hill (now Mount Washington) to keep them warm nights at the fort. In 1804 the burgess proposed a smoke-control ordinance related to the height of chimneys, and in the 1830s good citizens were meeting to discuss public action against smoke. Few people, through the years, thought that much could be accomplished, although the Mellon Institute for Industrial Research carried out important studies and the city created a bureau of smoke regulation in its health department. A folklore grew up that smoke was really a good thing: Soft coal was a cheap warm fuel, smoke at the mills meant prosperity, a little dirt never hurt anybody, the coal miners were Pittsburgh's good customers, the railroad engines were the life of the town. As late as 1939 City Council actually abolished the bureau of smoke regulation. The city to all appearances had quit a fight it had never really joined.

Two years later the City Council, with virtually the same membership, passed the ordinance which eventually brought effective smoke control to Pittsburgh. There were a series of reasons for the reversal. The 1940-41 heating season was an exceptionally black one because defense orders had carried the mills and railroads back to peak capacity. The city of St. Louis, historically as smog-choked as Pittsburgh, had found a simple and drastic

(turn to page 377)

Photograph by John Vachon in 1936.

FROM WORLD WAR II Pittsburgh emerged as a tired, run-down and overcrowded city. Its two basic problems — smoke and flood control — were unsolved. Other civic concerns like

"THE SMOKY CITY"
OF THE DEPRESSION ERA.

Photograph by Margaret Bourke-White in 1944, Courtesy Life Magazine.

housing, roads and transportation, were equally pressing.

"The decrepitude showed in its worn-out office buildings, its degraded housing, its traffic-choked streets, its sordid alleys, its polluted and uncontrolled rivers, and, above all, in the dense-choking smoke that covered the city and the river valleys . . ." Karl Schriftgiesser in the *Atlantic Monthly* of May, 1951.

Courtesy Allegheny Conference on Community Development.

BEFORE SMOKE CONTROL — A PHOTOGRAPH IN THE WINTER OF 1945 AT 9 O'CLOCK IN THE MORNING.

formula for the prevention of smoke. Three men in Pittsburgh had decided that the time for action had arrived. This was the first battle for smoke control, fought and won before the beginning of the Pittsburgh renaissance. The men who led the fight were an editor, a physician, and a city councilman. The editor was Edward T. Leech, who ran the Pittsburgh *Press* in the old slashing Scripps-Howard tradition. Leech used his paper like a war club. When he declared war on smoke, smoke was in trouble. The physician was I. Hope Alexander, the city's health director. Ike Alexander cultivated a lovable simplicity; actually, when his heart was in a public-health crusade, he was as artful as a fox. He told and retold the story of what smoke was doing to the lungs and health of Pittsburghers. The councilman was

Abraham L. Wolk, a gentle and voluble man, filled with evangelistic fervor for the good causes his good heart taught him to embrace.

The mayor of the city, Cornelius D. Scully, gave them his blessing. The City Council, led by Wolk, went to St. Louis to see, observe and learn. The St. Louis smoke-control man, Raymond Tucker, who later became his city's mayor, visited Pittsburgh. Pittsburgh doctors resolved, and women's clubs petitioned. The mayor appointed a citizens' commission to recommend an effective smoke-control law.

With Councilman Wolk in the chair, the commission held hearings, achieved unity, and prepared legislation. It adopted a report drafted by Gilbert Love, of the Pittsburgh *Press* staff, and John P. Robin, the mayor's secre-

(turn to page 380)

Courtesy Allegheny Conference.
ELEVEN O'CLOCK in the morning. This is Fifth Avenue on November 5, 1945 before smoke control took effect.

377

TWO LEADERS IN PITTSBURGH'S RENAISSANCE.

When Richard King Mellon and David L. Lawrence joined hands to clean up, rebuild and improve their city, the co-operation of the traditional rivals — the wealthy Republican industrialists and financiers with the Democratic city politicians — augured well for the future of Pittsburgh.

The Mellon prestige, money and pro-fessional competence, merging with Lawrence's political astuteness and the support of the rank and file Democrats and organized labor, accomplished what neither man could have done alone.

Lawrence banked his political future on smoke control; Mellon used his influence on business leaders to enlist their help in improving and rebuilding their city.

Together the two men achieved a minor miracle: the smog over the city vanished, modern buildings replaced slums, the ever-recurring floods were brought under control, new and vital roads, bridges and tunnels were built. Pittsburgh, formerly considered by many as the smokiest and ugliest city of America, became one of the sunniest and most beautiful in the nation.

Photographed specially for this book by W. Eugene Smith.

THE DEMOCRAT: DAVID L. LAWRENCE, (1889-1966), mayor of the city from 1946 to 1959 and governor of the Commonwealth from 1959 to 1963, was the undisputed leader of the Democratic Party in Pennsylvania. For more than half a century in political life, he was one of the main forces in the rebuilding of Pittsburgh. Born at the Point of Scotch-Irish ancestry, his political leadership was instrumental in accomplishing the great changes which transformed the city.

Photograph by Margaret Bourke-White, Courtesy Life Magazine.

THE REPUBLICAN: RICHARD KING MELLON (1899-1970), governor and President of T. Mellon & Sons, was the head of the Mellon interests that controlled Gulf Oil, Koppers and Alcoa and which had a dominant influence on many other corporations like U.S. Steel, Westinghouse Air Brake, Pennsylvania Railroad, Pittsburgh Plate Glass, Pittsburgh Consolidation Coal. A shy and retiring man, he offered leadership to all those who played a part in the rebuilding of Pittsburgh.

Photograph by Norman M. Jeannero.

ARTHUR VAN BUSKIRK, (1896–1972) governor of T. Mellon & Sons, board chairman of the Cleveland Federal Reserve Bank, a key figure in Pittsburgh's Renaissance, a spokesman for the Mellons. He, with a number of other civic minded citizens created the Allegheny Conference and planted the seeds that led to the development of Gateway Center. And it was he who, when the Equitable Life Assurance Society entered the project, came up with the suggestion to charge the company an annual toll of $50,000 for twenty years, enabling the Urban Redevelopment Authority to operate without public funds.

An eminent lawyer, educated at Yale and the University of Pennsylvania Law School, he first worked as secretary to Chief Justice Robert von Moschzisker, then joined the law firm Reed, Smith, Shaw & McClay, becoming a partner in 1934. In World War II he was deputy administrator of our Lend Lease program.

From the earliest days of the Allegheny Conference Van Buskirk was the anchor man of Richard K. Mellon. And while he believed that physical improvements were of immediate importance at the beginning of the city's renaissance ("There had to be something in sight, something people could see with their own eyes."), he knew that there also had to be a spiritual rejuvenation. Next to roads, bridges, tunnels, parks, new office buildings, the city must also have improved labor relations ("This is the field where we have fallen down . . . not just in Pittsburgh, but nationally too."), fresh educational facilities, more up-to-date governmental methods ("The structure of city government in metropolitan areas is antiquated and cumbersome."), and other achievements.

For him the triumph of Pittsburgh's rebuilding meant that "leaders of both industry and government have been able to work together for the good of the city, above either party or economic interest," and that "at the municipal level we have forged a new and stronger democracy of significance to the nation as a whole."

tary. The commission plan was essentially the St. Louis program, which insisted that all fuels capable of producing smoke be burned in mechanical equipment which prevents smoke—or that the fuels be inherently smokeless. There was a time phase in the application of the program, with domestic users coming last.

Council passed the new smoke-control ordinance by a vote of eight to one. The city's health department had a mandate for an intensive smoke-control program. The battle was concluded when Mayor Scully signed the ordinance. Actually it had not been much of a fight; people realized smoke control was a necessity.

The city was in the midst of a mayoralty campaign while the commission worked and while the ordinance was before Council, but no one attacked smoke control. Mayor Scully was re-elected by a narrow margin and the

WALLACE RICHARDS

(1904–1959), one of the prime movers behind Pittsburgh's redevelopment. Governor Lawrence said of him: "He had powers to dream and think up things that some of the more staid people couldn't grasp." And Park Martin described him: "He was a super salesman with a talent to influence the public and put over what he had in mind. A man of tremendous vitality."

Richards started out with the Indianapolis *News* as a reporter, soon to become that paper's art editor. After a two year stint in Europe he left the *News* and went to New York City, where he joined a theatrical publicity agency. In 1930 once

again he was in Europe; when he returned to America he supervised Indiana's exhibit at the Chicago World's Fair.

In his first governmental post—executive secretary of the Sub-Marginal Land Program—Richards was responsible for the redevelopment of areas damaged by drought and soil erosion. An ardent New Dealer, he joined the Resettlement Administration in 1935, supervising the planning and construction of Greenbelt in Maryland, one of the country's model planned communities.

The veteran city planner Frederick Bigger invited him to come to Pittsburgh as his assistant. Subsequently, Richards was named to the Parking Authority and

became civic advisor to Richard K. Mellon, who had great confidence in him.

Richards took part in the foundation of the Allegheny Conference, becoming the first secretary of the executive committee. There was hardly a highway or civic improvement project in the city with which he was not associated.

In the fall of 1948 he was appointed director of the Carnegie Museum.

A man of boundless inspiration and energy, he strained his resources to the limit. In January 1953 he suffered a heart attack. A subsequent fatal stroke ended his career. He lingered a few years and died at the University of Pittsburgh's Medical Center on January 25, 1959.

Democratic councilmen who voted for the ordinance won easily. The year was 1941; Pearl Harbor came upon the ctiy and the world a few weeks after election day, and the process of enforcement had to be postponed. The war and its economy made it advisable to change fuels, and the program remained in abeyance until 1946.

By then the Allegheny Conference on Community Development was formed and I had already been elected

Mayor. Dr. Edward R. Weidlein, president and director of the Mellon Institute, who was present at the early talks which led to the creation of the Conference told me what he remembered about them. And this is what he said: "It was sometime in the winter of 1943 that Richard King Mellon, Wallace Richards and I had a breakfast meeting in Washington. We talked about the future of Pittsburgh in the postwar years and came to the conclusion that un-

PROPAGANDA AGAINST SMOG. Pittsburgh ladies in 1946 do their shopping with masks over their faces as protection against the smoke pall that frequently blanketed the city. It is a propaganda photograph—it was staged by the Allegheny Conference to arouse support for smoke control legislation which went into effect on October 1, 1947.

THE AROUSED CITIZENS PAINTED SLOGANS on walls and vehicles. By 1946 they were ready to end the conditions which made the city the butt of jokes and a tragedy for residents.

less something was done Pittsburgh would become a dying city. Our discussions led to the thought of creating an organization which could do a job of research and study and evolve a community plan for improvements."

The talk with Mellon, then head of Army Emergency Relief in Washington, and subsequent ones with him assured the Pittsburgh "smoke-fighters" of his support. They returned to Pittsburgh and enlisted the aid of more men who were interested in doing something for the future. In Arthur Braun the group had the benefit of years of experience with planning; Edgar Kaufmann, the imaginative president of the department store, provided a link with the downtown merchants; J. Steele Gow, director of the Falk Foundation, always ready to assist with funds the city's social and educational institutions, offered practical suggestions. Other members of these early discussion groups were the industrialists William P. Witherow and Joseph Dilworth, Robert C. Downie, president of the

Photograph by Clyde Hare, March 1951.

THE MEN WHO LED THE FIGHT. The Allegheny Conference was in the forefront of the battle to clean up and rebuild the city. From l. to r.: Leland Hazard, Park Martin, Arthur Van Buskirk, Wallace Richards, William P. Snyder III, John Grove, Adolph Schmidt, Edward Weidlein, Lawrence Woods, A. H. Burchfield, George Lockhart and Leslie Reese.

Peoples First National Bank, Benjamin P. Fairless, president of U. S. Steel, James H. Hillman, head of Harmon Creek Coal Corporation, Charles J. Graham, president of the Pittsburgh and West Virginia Railroad, Louis W. Monteverde, real estate executive, Alan M. Scaife, president of the second oldest company of Pittsburgh, to mention a few other men of distinction — public officials, district congressmen, legislators — had joined them.

"We just talked aimlessly at the first meeting in May," recalled Dr. Weidlein. "Then in June, some of the people thought we should organize and have a little money. Several individuals and companies made appropriations— enough to get things started."

Thus on June 29, 1943 a luncheon meeting was held at the William Penn Hotel, attended by representatives of business, industry, civic groups and state, city, county and local governments. At this meeting the Allegheny Conference on Post-War Community Planning came into (turn to page 385)

Photograph by Clyde Hare, March 1951.

THE EXECUTIVE COMMITTEE of the Allegheny Conference listens to a presentation of Wallace Richards, one of the prime movers behind the civic spirit that created the new Pittsburgh.

383

IN THE CONFERENCE ROOM of the mayor Park H. Martin, executive director of the Allegheny Conference, reads a memorandum to prominent coal dealers on smoke control in October, 1947. Next to him is Sumner B. Ely, superintendent of the Bureau of Smoke Prevention. Mayor David L. Lawrence, who underwent an eye operation in August and wears a black patch over his eyes, is sitting in the foreground on the left. On his right, his secretary John P. Robin, and Councilman A. L. Wolk; on his left, David N. Kuhn, of the United Smoke Council. At the other side of the table the president and execu-

THE CITIZENRY IN ACTION. The people of Pittsburgh were determined to improve their city. In this photograph taken on November 15, 1945 a number of Pittsburgh's leading citizens inspect a model for the proposed Fort Pitt Park showing a suggested transformation of the 36.2 acre Point area. From left to right: H. J. Heinz II, the head of the Heinz Company, County Commissioner John J. Kane, Edgar J. Kaufmann, the head of the Kaufmann Department Store, City Councilman Frederic G. Weir, Mayor-elect David L. Lawrence, Mayor Cornelius D. Scully, Robert E. Doherty, President of

Photograph Pittsburgh Sun-Telegraph.

tive director of the Retail Merchants Association, J. Don Horner and Howard D. Gibbs, listen intently; next to them on the far right is the director of the Department of Public Health, Dr. I. Hope Alexander.

Photograph Pittsburgh Sun-Telegraph.

the Carnegie Institute of Technology, Arthur E. Braun, banker and publisher, Tom Killgallen, President of the City Council, and Park H. Martin, executive director of the Allegheny Conference.

being. Dr. Robert E. Doherty, president of the Carnegie Institute of Technology, was elected chairman, Dr. Weidlein vice-chairman and Wallace Richards secretary. Willard E. Hotchkiss, director of humanistic and social studies at Carnegie Tech, was named chairman of the basic study and planning committee.

On September 15 the sponsoring committee appointed nine groups to work with and under Dr. Hotchkiss' studying and planning committee. They were to consider: a land-use survey to cover the city and county; an analysis of zoning ordinances to improve and strengthen them; a study of existing housing conditions; a unified program of public and private improvements; a survey covering fields of economic, social, engineering, scientific, educational and other research; a campaign urging State and Federal governments to support regrowth and improvement of the area; coordination and integration of expansion of cultural activities of government, museums, schools and other facilities; wider dissemination of music and development of broader interests in visual arts and crafts.

By 1945 the group was on its way to fulfilling its aims as "a citizens organization concerned with the future of this region." The name of the organization had been reduced to the Allegheny Conference on Community Development. Its incorporators were Robert E. Doherty, Arthur E. Braun, L. W. Monteverde, J. Steele Gow, Alexander P. Reed, Edgar J. Kaufmann. The attorney of the organization was Charles F. C. Arensberg. Park H. Martin became executive director in February 1945 and before the year was out he and his staff offered a fairly comprehensive program which has been followed in substance ever since.

The chairman of the Allegheny County Board of Com-

Courtesy Pittsburgh Post-Gazette.

THE FIRE THAT HELPED THE CREATION OF GATEWAY CENTER: The Wabash Terminal was a sizeable obstacle to the Point's rebuilding. When the terminal was destroyed by fire on March 22, 1946 the green light was given for Gateway Center.

missioners and my close friend and political colleague was John J. Kane, who had brought imagination and forceful leadership to the Courthouse. He worked closely with the Conference from its very beginning and, as a matter of fact, took me to the very first meeting of its sponsors that I attended. His association with this group, indeed his unprecedented service to the community, earned him one of the highest places in the honor roll of the new Pittsburgh.

It was generally conceded in those early days that the rejuvenation and restoration of the city must begin with smoke and flood control.

No one in the city denied that smoke was one of the chief obstacles to Pittsburgh's progress. Young people needed by industries would not want to come there, large corporations were ready to leave. Yet for generations very little was done to eliminate the smoke. The reason for this was simple: Pittsburgh was a coal-producing center and a great number of people made their living by digging coal; large coal corporations had fortunes invested in their companies. Thus the interest of many was not to eliminate but rather to *make* smoke. Smoke was the symbol of prosperity, of moneymaking, of employment. It took courage and determination to tackle the problem.

We had been fortunate to receive the support of the officials of the Consolidation Coal Company on the one hand and the officers of the United Mine Workers Union on the other. They had joined forces to make the control of smoke a reality. Needless to say, this stand called for community dedication and just plain guts. Fortunately, the local head of the Mine Workers, Patrick T. Fagan, always had an abundance of these traits and he fought for the cause he considered to be right. Later on, he was elected to City Council and went on to be its president.

I became mayor in 1946. By then the smoke control ordinance had already been passed. But a provision in the ordinance stipulated that it was not to go into effect until after the war. The reason for it was that as steel and other material was channelled into our military establishment, there was not enough steel to make stokers, one of the chief implements to eliminate smoke. So the city fathers wrote a section into the ordinance saying that the regulations would not take effect until the war was over.

As no peace treaty had been signed, technically the war was not over yet. Now I—together with members of the City Council—declared that the war was over and we fixed a date for the ordinance to go into effect. Richard King Mellon and his associates in the Allegheny Conference gave their strong support. Without them I would not have been successful. I had not much influence with the Consolidation Coal Company, while Mr. Mellon's prestige with them was great. He was a sort of bell cow in Pittsburgh; as he moved, others moved with him.

The second battle for smoke control, which was soon joined, helped to cement our relationship; and we remained together on major public programs ever since. I had committed my administration to enforce the smoke-control ordinance at the earliest practical date. The due date for industry, commercial buildings, and railroads was October 1, 1946; the residential furnace, grate, and stove came under regulation one year later.

The Allegheny Conference supported these decisions and called for the extension of smoke control to the county government. It was obvious that air pollution would not respect the city limits.

The city enforcement program was not punitive. Arrests were kept to a minimum. But inspections, explanations, complaints, and troubles came in by the thousands. The smoke bureau had one of the hardest public-relations jobs in history. The coal industry had failed to provide sufficient smokeless fuel for the new Pittsburgh market; the

(turn to page 390)

AFTER THE SMOKE CONTROL ORDINANCES TOOK EFFECT.

Courtesy Allegheny Conference.

THE FIRST NATIONAL BANK BECOMES WHITE.

Courtesy Allegheny Conference.

THE FRICK BUILDING IS SHEDDING ITS GRIME.

THE CLEANING UP: WORKMEN ON THE PENNSYLVANIA RAILROAD STATION DURING THE SUMMER OF 1948.

AND WHEN THE SMOKE AND SMOG HAD GONE — AND THE STREETS, RIVERS AND HILLS OF THE CITY

Photographed specially for this book by W. Eugene Smith in 1955.

EMERGED — PITTSBURGH PRESENTED ITSELF AS ONE OF THE MOST BEAUTIFUL PLACES IN THE LAND.

improvised mixes of anthracite and bituminous were often inefficient, hard to start, and much overpriced. Stokers were expensive and subject to mechanical failure. Many a good Pittsburgh Democrat was far from pleased with his mayor, who had interfered with the supply of good soft coal, smoky perhaps, but full of heat and B.T.U.s per dollar. The program had its "bugs." It would have had the same bugs if the start had been deferred, so I resisted all pressure and temptation to ease up and take it slowly. The majority of Council stood with me. So did the Allegheny Conference, and the Pittsburgh *Press* and *Post-Gazette*.

The second battle for smoke control had some climactic engagements. I remember a dinner given by the Conference in the William Penn Hotel for the purpose of discussing the impending legislative program. After opinions were exchanged one member of the Republican delegation rose, and he said: "Well, if we do this and these things happen, the Mayor will get the credit for it." Others had similar views, so after they aired them I got up and told the meeting that, speaking for the City Administration and the Democratic Party, I was supporting the proposed laws with all my heart. "Now," I said, "speaking to you fellows as a politician, I'll be perfectly happy if you don't go along with this. But speaking as the Mayor of Pittsburgh, I plead with you to support it, because it is going to mean a lot to everybody around here, Democrats and Republicans alike. We must recapture a lot of the old-time zip that Pittsburgh had. As a politician, if you fellows oppose it, that will be grist to our mill. We are going to pass these bills anyway and I have the word of the governor that he's going to sign them. So you put yourself in just the position we want you to be. But as the Mayor of Pittsburgh, I urge and plead with you for your own sake and for your families and for your children and those who will come after you to support the legislation and help to rebuild and renew our city." It was in this spirit that we went to Harrisburg.

In Harrisburg, legislation to provide for county-wide smoke regulation was introduced in the 1947 session of the Pennsylvania Legislature. The bill passed the House of Representatives without difficulty, but ran into the redoubtable barriers of the Pennsylvania Railroad in the State Senate. When the amendment to the county ordinance which was to bring the railroads under the terms of the county smoke ordinance was up, a delegation from Allegheny County journeyed to Harrisburg for a hearing. Before we went, Park Martin talked in the Pittsburgh Chamber of Commerce board room with the railroad

NIGHT OVER THE MONONGAHELA. In the foreground the Pennsylvania and Lake Erie Railroad Station; in the background on the right the stacks of Jones & Laughlin. The band lit up on the other side of the river is the Boulevard of the Allies.

Photographed specially for this book by W. Eugene Smith in 1955.

WRITERS AND ARTISTS OF THE AREA.

WILLIAM POWELL of the movies, born here in 1892.

PERRY COMO, the singer, born in Canonsburg in 1912.

GLADYS SCHMITT, the novelist, born here in 1909.

RACHEL CARSON, biologist, was born in Springdale in 1907.

SARAH HENDERSON HAY, the poet, born here in 1906.

MARTHA GRAHAM, the dancer, born here in 1895.

ERROL GARNER, jazz pianist, born in Pittsburgh in 1921.

GENE KELLY, the actor and dancer, born here in 1912.

representatives and they promised him not to make opposition to the amendment. So after I had my say in the Harrisburg meeting Park Martin rose and stated that the amendment would be supported by all the railroads in Allegheny County and that they were willing to acquiesce to a law which would not exempt them from the smoke ordinance regulations. To the surprise of us all, Rufus Flynn, the assistant general manager of the Pennsylvania Railroad declared that he wanted to go on record as opposed to the amendment.

Wallace Richards was greatly upset; he dashed to the telephone and reported to Mellon in Pittsburgh what had taken place at the hearing. I understand that after this Mr. Mellon called the president of the Pennsylvania Railroad, who happened to be in Florida, and told him in no uncertain terms that the Pennsylvania Railroad must change its position. Benjamin Fairless too was on the phone talking to the heads of the railroad—so it was related to me—and told them how distressed he was by their position. He let them know that there were other railroads besides the Pennsylvania that would be only too happy to ship the products of the Mellon enterprises.

In the Pittsburgh *Press* Ed Leech ran a front page editorial: "A Hell of a Way to Run a Railroad." Public opinion was mobilized. Under pressure the railroads called off their lobby and ceased their opposition to the legislative proposals. The bill moved, unamended, through the Legislature and to the governor's desk. The victory was vital, because public acceptance of smoke control was dependent upon proof that it would apply with equal

(turn to page 397)

DEMOLITION AT THE POINT: A scene in 1950.

THE GATEWAY BUILDINGS EMERGE: A scene in 1956.

THE CITY OF BRIDGES. *Photograph by Stefan Lorant.*

Photograph by Stefan Lorant.

THE CITY OF STEPS.

Photograph by Stefan Lorant.

THE CITY OF A SKYSCRAPER UNIVERSITY.

THE MOODS OF PITTSBURGH: THE CITY AT SUNDOWN.

SPRING

HAS

COME.

THE MOODS OF PITTSBURGH: THE CITY IN THE EVENING.

VIEW

FROM

THE INCLINE.

STEELMAKING AT JONES & LAUGHLIN'S NO. 4 OPEN HEARTH SHOP IN PITTSBURGH.

SOUTH SIDE.

stringency to big business and the small householder. Of course—and I understood it clearly—the railroads had a great problem. They were hauling coal and they stood to lose large sums of money if the legislation were to pass. Still their civic patriotism prevailed and they gave way. It was the same with the coal companies, and also with the union representing men whose jobs might be put in jeopardy.

That was the very point of the most critical political test of the program to build a new Pittsburgh. One councilman, Edward J. Leonard, made a planned record of opposition to enforcement of the smoke-control law. He was the vocal defender of "the little Joes," who, he said, were paying the price of smoke control in extra expense and inconvenience while the railroads and big industries were allowed their own sweet time to install new equipment. He was the head of the Plasterers' Union, a power in the Building Trades and the AFL Pittsburgh Central Labor Union and chairman of the County Housing Authority.

Leonard wanted to become Mayor. But to win the office, he had to defeat me first in the primary. That was in 1949. So he went out campaigning and told the voters that I had become too friendly to the Mellon interests, too neutral in labor matters, and that I was pressing the smoke program on them and that it was going to be expensive. There was as usual in a political campaign a lot of gross misrepresentation and propaganda against the en-

Photographed specially for this book by W. Eugene Smith in 1955.

PITTSBURGH IS A CITY OF MANY RELIGIONS:
Ordination of priests in the Catholic Cathedral.

below: In the East Liberty Presbyterian Church.

Photographed specially for this book by W. Eugene Smith in 1955.
AT THE MEETING OF JEHOVAH'S WITNESSES.

397

IN THE CROATIAN CHURCH AT MILLVALE: The paintings are the work of the Yugoslav artist Maxo Vanka.

FIRST PRESBYTERIAN CHURCH ON 6th STREET. The photograph was taken during the Sunday morning service.

A DRAMATIC PHOTOGRAPH OF THE EXQUISITE CHOIR

forcement of the ordinance. In the poorer sections of the city the people believed that it was they who had to foot the bill for the changes, that it was they who would have to buy the non-smoke-producing fuels and the stokers and that this would cost them a great deal in expenditures. I had a hard time selling the idea that the enforcing of the ordinance would actually save them money because much of the soft coal went up in smoke before and smoke doesn't produce heat. They were reluctant to accept the fact that

Photographed specially for this book by W. Eugene Smith in 1955.

IN THE CENTRAL BAPTIST CHURCH AT HILL DISTRICT'S KIRKPATRICK STREET AND WYLIE AVENUE.

in reality they were getting less heat out of a bushel of coal than they should, whereas if they would buy other kinds of coal or get a stoker they would, in the long run, make substantial savings. One must remember that many of these people were in the lower income bracket; they bought coal off a truck a bushel at a time. Certain areas had no coal bins and thus coal could not be stocked up. These were the problems, stressed by Leonard. Campaigning chiefly against the smoke control enforcement,

he made an astonishingly hard campaign.

I won the primary by a vote of 77,000 to 50,000, but it was a close shave. Leonard carried many of the predominantly labor wards. If the organization had not worked at its best, and if I had not gone out and campaigned as in a general election, Leonard would have won and the political constellation which had developed the new Pittsburgh would never have become a reality.

This dramatic primary was the final climax for smoke

(turn to page 402)

399

Courtesy University of Pittsburgh.

UNIVERSITY OF PITTSBURGH IN 1955.

The Hunt Library, completed in 1961.

CARNEGIE TECH.

E. H. LITCHFIELD, born in 1914 was educated at the University of Michigan. He has been appointed Chancellor of the University in 1955.

JOHN C. WARNER, born in 1897. Educated at Indiana University he became president of Carnegie Institute of Technology in 1950.

THE UNIVERSITY OF PITTSBURGH dates to 1787 when the Pittsburgh Academy was incorporated. It was rechartered in 1819 as the Western University of Pennsylvania and received a grant of 40 acres in Old Allegheny, now the North Side. The school moved to Oakland in 1908 and became the University of Pittsburgh. In the early sixties the campus occupied some 110 acres and was the largest employer in the city.

The student body in 1964 was 15,000. To insure superior instruction the authorities decided to level off the rapidly growing enrollment. By the end of the sixties Pitt expected to stabilize the student body at 22,000 (with 11,470 full time and 10,260 part time students). By the following decade — the year 1980 — the number of faculty members was to reach 2,000.

CARNEGIE INSTITUTE OF TECHNOLOGY was founded in 1900 by Andrew Carnegie with an initial grant of one million dollars. Ground was broken in the spring of 1905 on the 32 acres adjoining Schenley Park. (In 1963 the campus covered 145 acres, including the Nuclear Research Center in Saxonburg.) The following spring Margaret Morrison Carnegie College opened its doors to women. The initial student body of 125 in 1905 grew to 3500 in 1963, of whom 700 were graduate students. 1500 more attended the evening and summer sessions. The seven major divisions of the Institute in the early sixties had a faculty of 400 full time and part time members.

In fifty-one years—through June, 1963—Carnegie Tech conferred 23,401 bachelors, 3617 masters and 870 doctors degrees.

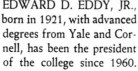

Courtesy Chatham College.
CHATHAM COLLEGE.

Photograph by W. Eugene Smith.
DUQUESNE UNIVERSITY IN 1955.

EDWARD D. EDDY, JR., born in 1921, with advanced degrees from Yale and Cornell, has been the president of the college since 1960.

HENRY J. McANULTY, born in 1915 in Pittsburgh, became ninth president of Duquesne in 1959 when he succeeded V. F. Gallagher.

CHATHAM COLLEGE, the fourth oldest women's college in the United States, was founded in 1869 at Shadyside under the name Pennsylvania Female College. In 1890 the institution's name was changed to Pennsylvania College for Women, and in 1955 it was changed again — to Chatham College, in honor of William Pitt, first Earl of Chatham.

By 1940 the enrollment doubled. Andrew W. Mellon's son Paul gave two buildings and his father's residence to the school.

In the early sixties about 2/3 of the students came from 38 states and foreign countries; 90% of the students resided on campus; 45% continued their education in graduate schools. The ratio of faculty to students was 1 to 12. Chatham maintained a cooperative program with Carnegie Institute of Technology.

DUQUESNE UNIVERSITY located in downtown Pittsburgh was founded in 1878 as the Pittsburgh Catholic College of the Holy Ghost. Its founders were Holy Ghost priests banished from Germany under Bismarck's Kulturkampf. In 1911 the school became the first Catholic institution of higher learning in Pennsylvania to achieve university status.

Duquesne is a coeducational institution which is open not only to Catholics, but to students of all races, creeds and denominations. From its original enrollment of 40 in the year of 1878 the University's student body has grown to 6632 students in 1963. This number included 1503 graduate students and 2859 women. The faculty of the University numbered 365. The 12.9 acre campus of the sixties has a potential growth to 36.9 acres.

MOUNT MERCY COLLEGE

Photographed by John L. Alexandrowicz.

SISTER THOMAS AQUINAS became president of Mount Mercy in 1963 after she had served for eleven years as the college's academic dean.

MOUNT MERCY COLLEGE, a four year college for women, opened in 1929 with 24 students. In 1963 the institution had a full time enrollment of over 600, and by 1980 it is expected to grow to 1500, of which 1000 will be attending on a full time basis. The college in the early sixties had some 140 faculty members, of whom about half were teaching full time.

When Our Lady of Mercy Academy, which along with the Sisters of Mercy Convent shared the 13-acre site with the college, moved to new quarters, Mount Mercy had a ready-made chance to expand. Until that time the limited and steeply sloping property at Oakland posed an almost insoluble problem for organic growth, and the lack of land available for building forced the college to occupy a tightly-knit, severely cramped campus.

control. The Republican candidate for mayor, Tice F. Ryan, made an unavailing effort to capture Leonard's primary vote by criticizing the program, and I was re-elected with a record-breaking majority of 56,000 votes.

Since that time, smoke control has had no political challenge. Its continuing problems have been administrative and technological, with time and industrial processes working on its side. The railroads introduced the smoke-less diesel engines for economic reasons of their own, but Pittsburgh's smoke-control law pushed them into assigning their new equipment to the area on a first-priority basis. The superior convenience of gas heat made it a natural substitute for coal in residential heating, and the rising cost of coal helped to equalize the expense. Smoke-and-air-pollution control has become a county function. The old soot and smoke are gone; some serious problems of fly ash from electric power plants, metallurgic dust from the steel mills, and fumes from the coke by-product plants remain to be completely solved. Pittsburgh has survived to see the smog capital of the world transferred to Los Angeles, and to see its air-pollution program televised by the B.B.C. as an example to Britons.

Statistics and the shirt collar both proved that Pittsburgh had become as clean as the average American city. The victory over smoke had been the signal for a concentrated attack on the entire range of community problems. It was Pittsburgh's breakthrough from the landing beaches; the other triumphs came in an accelerating rush.

The story is one of men and events, of a combination of circumstance, public temper, resourcefulness, intelligence, and vision. The men were there, and the time was ripe for their ideas.

During my thirteen-year mayoralty, Pennsylvania had four governors. Allegheny County had seven commissioners. Only one councilman still serves who was present when I took my first oath of office. The corporate executives who direct the larger companies are still another changing group. Great business names—Fairless, Somervell, Moreell, Swensrud, Robertson, Hood, Cresap—come and go in Pittsburgh as regularly as the passing seasons which bring them to board chairmanships and to retirement.

The future was to establish the working relationships between the Democratic administration and Richard Mellon, whose uncle was Secretary of the Treasury under Harding, Coolidge, and Hoover, and whose family was one of the main sources of the Republican Party's national financing.

I do not think I had met Mr. Mellon more than half a dozen times until then; I had no social contact with him. But we both had a common interest in the development of Pittsburgh and a sense of identification with the city of our birth. We have taken pride in the city's achievements and we are happy that the people acknowledged our efforts. Without the joining hands of the city's Democratic

(turn to page 406)

MEN BEHIND THE RENAISSANCE.

JOHN P. ROBIN,

Mayor Lawrence's civic adviser and political strategist, the early liaison man between the Democratic city administration and Republican industrialists whose cooperation made the rebuilding possible.

He laid the foundations for smoke control, public housing, expansion of park and recreation facilities. In 1948 he became director of the Urban Redevelopment Authority, in 1955 Secretary of Commerce of Pennsylvania. Since then he planned urban renewal projects in Philadelphia and later in Calcutta, India.

PARK H. MARTIN

(1888-1972), was executive director of the Allegheny Conference till 1958.

Educated at Carnegie Tech, he became Chief Engineer and Assistant Director in the County Department of Public Works in 1933. As director of the County Planning Department he planned the Greater Pittsburgh Airport and had a major hand in the building of the Penn-Lincoln Parkway. In 1959 he became Secretary of Highways, a post he held until 1963. He was consultant to engineering firms until his death.

FREDERICK BIGGER

(1881-1963), a pioneer city planner for more than half a century, directed his energies to making Pittsburgh into a better place to live.

Bigger started out in 1918 as executive secretary for the Citizens Committee for a City Plan, directing studies on playgrounds, street plans, transit problems, waterways, parks, etc. He was one of the early pathbreakers for Pittsburgh's renaissance, offering advice, devising plans and fighting for an improved highway system and better recreational facilities.

THEODORE L. HAZLETT, JR.,

(1918–1979), solicitor to the Allegheny Conference and general counsel of the Urban Redevelopment Authority graduated from Harvard Law School. A brilliant lawyer, for the past two decades he played a major part in every aspect of the city's renewal. As the legal architect of Pittsburgh's renaissance he wrote much of the legislation which comprised the "Pittsburgh Package," the series of laws passed by the Pennsylvania Legislature in 1947. He has participated in most of the litigation involving the civic programs.

EDWARD J. MAGEE,

executive director of the Allegheny Conference, who succeeded Park H. Martin.

Educated at Phillips Andover and Yale University, he began as a lumberman in the West. In the Air Corps, he was shot down over Germany and taken prisoner. When the war ended he joined the Scaife Company as manager of industrial relations; later he worked as an independent management consultant. Patient, energetic and resourceful, he had prime responsibility for the execution of Pittsburgh's multiple new civic projects.

JOHN J. GROVE,

assistant director of the Allegheny Conference since 1952, graduated from the University of Pittsburgh. After a successful career in publishing and public relations he became public relations director for the Allegheny Conference. Affable helpful and full of ideas, he endeared himself to the nation's press. It was he, together with Park Martin, who penned under the picture of Mr. Parkinson, "A great project needs a great builder," thus committing the Equitable president to Gateway Center.

MAYOR DAVID L. LAWRENCE

DEMOCRACY

URBAN REDEVELOPMENT PROBLEMS
Photographed specially for

ADOLPH W. SCHMIDT AND COUNCIL PRESIDENT TOM GALLAGHER.

LADIES IN THE AUDIENCE FOLLOW THE PROCEEDINGS.

below: THE ISSUE IS ARGUED

ADDRESSES THE MEETING.

IN ACTION.

UNDER DISCUSSION IN 1955.

this book by W. Eugene Smith.

COUNCILMEN BENNETT RODGERS, PAUL F. JONES AND A. L. WOLK

BEFORE THE COUNCIL.

below: A PLAN IS DISCUSSED BY KEENLY INTERESTED PARTICIPANTS.

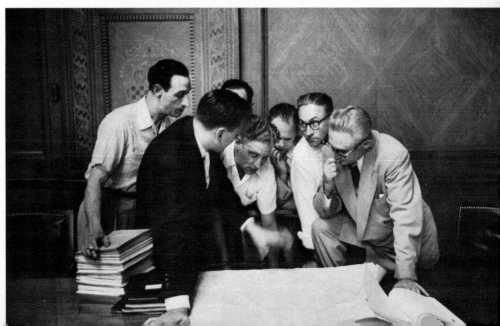

1906: The old Symphony, founded in 1895, with concert-master Luigi Von Kunits on the conductor's stand. In its fifteen year existence the orchestra had three conductors: Frederick Archer, the organist and music director of Carnegie Music Hall (1895-1898), Victor Herbert, the celebrated composer of operettas (1898-1904), and the German Emil Paur (1904-1910).

1935: The new Pittsburgh Symphony's string section rehearses. This orchestra was formed in 1927 with Elias Breeskin as its conductor and Edward Specter as its manager. In 1930 Breeskin was succeeded by conductor Antonio Modarelli. In the 1936-1937 season the Symphony began its series of radio concerts which were sponsored by the Pittsburgh Plate Glass Company.

BETWEEN 1938-1947 the Hungarian Fritz Reiner, one of the great conductors of the world, welded the orchestra into shape.

administration with the Mellon economic power, the revival of Pittsburgh could not have taken place.

Richard K. Mellon came back from the war about the same time as I had won my first election. His military assignments had been in Harrisburg and Washington, so that he had been accessible to the Pittsburgh civic workers participating in the formative period of the Allegheny Conference. He had an inherited responsibility for the Pittsburgh Regional Planning Association, which his father, Richard B. Mellon, helped to organize in 1918 to further such basic elements of community life as zoning and a city-planning department.

The executive of the Regional Planning Association, Wallace Richards, who had been brought to the city by Frederick Bigger, was responsible for many of the plans and concepts forming the foundation of Pittsburgh's renewal. Richards enlarged the scope of Mellon's interest in public problems, and became his close associate and civic advisor. He was an outstanding man, vigorous, enthusiastic, full of ideas; he became a sparkplug of the city's rebuilding program. I remember clearly how our first meeting came about. After I had decided to run for mayor I went to New York to see La Guardia, an old friend of mine, and ask his advice. When I told him of my decision, the Little Flower snapped: "You're a God-damned fool." I told him I didn't come to hear that but wanted some advice. He turned me over to Bob Moses, and it was in Moses' office on Long Island that one of his associates suggested that I meet with Wallace Richards. Soon thereafter in Pittsburgh we met and that was the beginning of friendship, a personal friendship as well as a business-governmental friendship that lasted until his untimely death.

Richards was not only a dreamer, but an activist; he had powers to dream and think up things that some of the more staid individuals couldn't grasp. And he was able to transpose these dreams into reality.

But back to the Mellons, whose interests are close to being the Pittsburgh economy. *Fortune* magazine has estimated the combined net worth of Richard K. Mellon and his sister, Mrs. Alan M. Scaife, and of Paul Mellon and his sister, Mrs. Ailsa Mellon Bruce, at three billion dollars. The Mellon influence controls the Mellon National Bank, which has more than two billion dollars in assets. The Mellon family has great weight in the affairs of Gulf Oil, with more than three billion in assets, and of Alcoa, which is another member of the corporate billion-dollar club. Mellon people sit on the boards of such giants as General Motors, Equitable Life, Westinghouse Electric, and Pittsburgh Plate Glass. They sit on such Pittsburgh-based companies as Koppers, Consolidation Coal, Westinghouse Air Brake, and Jones and Laughlin.

Mellon family names are recurrent on the boards of the University of Pittsburgh, Chatham College, Carnegie In-

left:
1952: The German William Steinberg, founder of the Israeli Symphony Orchestra, became conductor. The same year William McKelvey Martin succeeded Edward Specter as manager.

WORLD RENOWNED: The Orchestra under William Steinberg became one of the great symphony orchestras of the world.

In 1963 three foundations—the Howard Heinz, the Richard King Mellon, the A. W. Mellon, and Paul Mellon presented

the Symphony with an endowment fund of $5,000,000 of which more than half came from the Howard Heinz Foundation.

stitute of Technology, the Carnegie Museum. The influence is pervasive and persuasive, but the city has escaped the deadening stamp of the company-or family-controlled town. The family has been too restrained, the city is too big, the balance of forces is too delicate for that. The city has drawn enormous strength from the Mellons, and has kept its prideful independence in the process.

The Mellons are a quiet family. They make few public speeches and few ceremonial appearances. There are no Mellon committees issuing definitive reports on national defense or the national economy. Like so many men of great wealth, R. K. Mellon gives the impression of shyness—a shyness which seems to be lessening as his years of civic effort gain acceptance. He is not, for instance, a member of the executive committee of the Allegheny Conference, nor does he serve in any honorary public office. The extent of his commitment to the development

1951: The Italian Victor De Sabata conducted the highly successful opening concerts of the orchestra's 25th anniversary season in Syria Mosque, the home of the Symphony.

Photograph by Margaret Bourke-White, Courtesy Life Magazine.

DR. JONAS EDWARD SALK, the conqueror of polio, was associated with the University of Pittsburgh from 1947 on. It was there, in the Virus Research Laboratory of the institution he developed a vaccine preventative of poliomyelitis in 1954. He left the city in 1960 to head a new research institute in California.

below:

DR. BENJAMIN MACLANE SPOCK, whose *Common Sense Book of Baby and Child Care* became the bible of American mothers, was Professor of Child Development at the University of Pittsburgh from 1951 to 1955. In this picture he is in his outdoor waiting room at the Arsenal Health Center of the Pittsburgh Health Department, an institution affiliated with the University.

NICOLAI LOPATNIKOFF, the noted composer, was born in Russia in 1903. He began teaching at Carnegie Tech in 1945. After his retirement in 1969 he became Professor Emeritus at Carnegie—Mellon. He died on October 7, 1976.

right:

STEPHEN BORSODY, the Hungarian political scientist and author of *The Triumph of Tyranny*, is Professor of History at Chatham College.

THE CITY ALWAYS LURED GREAT TALENTS.

of Pittsburgh has become so great, however, that he does not hesitate to impress upon the federal administration the importance of a continued federal program for urban renewal or to tell the federal highway administrator of the importance to Pittsburgh of the Crosstown Boulevard.

General Richard K. Mellon has had some remarkable lieutenants. His Chief of Staff would be Arthur B. Van Buskirk; his liaison officer in the field was Wallace Richards. These two men, more than any others, understood both their mission and the mechanics of its execution. They sensed the necessity of uniting public and private action for Pittsburgh's advancement; they were bold, imaginative, and apt at their work. There was nothing of the organization man, none of the rigidities of corporate training, in either Van Buskirk or Richards. Because they had no built-in distrust of government, and because they sought accomplishments, not ideologies, they were successful negotiators between government and business. As Mellon spokesmen they had great inherent power; as brilliantly resourceful men they made a most successful use of that power in the transformation of Pittsburgh and Allegheny County.

Each man took a public office. Van Buskirk was the vice chairman of the Redevelopment Authority. Richards was

ARTHUR E. BRAUN, banker, publisher, editor, industrialist, was made an honorary Doctor of Laws from Chatham College in 1956. Dean Lucille Allen and Charles F. Lewis were present at the ceremonies.

left:
RICHARD K. MELLON with heads of Mellon Institute General Matthew Ridgway and Edward Weidlein.

Photograph by Margaret Bourke-White, Courtesy Life Magazine.
LELAND HAZARD, President of WQED, the first community-financed educational television station in the country. He resigned his vice-presidential post at Pittsburgh Plate Glass to become a professor at the Carnegie Institute of Technology.

the chairman of the Parking Authority. Each man had a civic assignment. Van Buskirk was president and chairman of the Allegheny Conference. Richards was the executive of the Regional Planning Association. The agencies in which the men played vital roles are together responsible for the physical rebuilding of Pittsburgh's business district.

Van Buskirk was by training a Philadelphia lawyer with all the suavity, subtlety, intelligence, and underlying strength of purpose associated with the breed. He is a master hand in a meeting, quick to summarize essentials, adept at the courteous trades and concessions which bring agreement among equals. Richards, in the period of his active life, was an exhilarating mixture of fire and fluff, a man who loved the new and the dramatic, always intrigued by the fantastic, and always ready to risk his career in a gambler's throw for the grand design against the merely practical. He had a wonderful contempt for the dollar values that meant so much to his business associates, and a constant impatience with the accepted rule book that meant so much to his planning associates. He planned by ear, eye, and instinct, not by formal training, and most of the time he planned well.

Point Park, Mellon Square, Gateway Center, the Penn-Lincoln Parkway, the city's public-parking program, and

(turn to page 411)

H. J. HEINZ II and G. DAVID THOMPSON, two of Pittsburgh's art patrons at the Carnegie International before the fourteen abstract paintings which they presented to the Museum's collection.

THE CARNEGIE LIBRARY.

"FREE TO THE PEOPLE" reads the inscription over the Library's entrance. The building, financed by Andrew Carnegie, was opened to the public in November, 1895.

In 1964, the library had two million books and 471 staff members. Its annual operating expense was $2,500,000.

AN ENTHRALLING TALE.

A LISTENER TO RECORDS.

Photographed specially for this book by W. Eugene Smith in 1955.

SELECTION OF THE RIGHT BOOK POSES A PROBLEM — FATHER'S ADVICE IS ALWAYS WELCOME.

DR. RALPH MUNN (1894-1975) was director of the Carnegie Library until 1964.

its many new office buildings are, of course, the work of many minds and hands. But without Van Buskirk and Richards, in their own persons and as Mellon spokesmen, it is difficult to see how these great projects could have come to pass. These men were ready to pioneer in municipal techniques which have since become commonplace— the use of public powers to clear blight, the use of public powers to provide parking spaces, the use of public and private funds to clear the way for open spaces in the congested city, the planning and construction of limited-access highways.

A Democratic city administration acting on its own to take by process of law the properties of one set of owners so that they could be redeveloped by another set (turn to page 417)

WORKING ON A PAPER.

A CONSULTATION.

LECTURE ON DINOSAURS. In the Carnegie Institute's Natural History Museum lectures are given to youngsters on dinosaurs and early man. Area school children participate in the nature contests sponsored by the Museum, which are held annually in May.

left: **The Carnegie Institute and Library Building in Oakland.**

DRAWING INSTRUCTION AT THE INSTITUTE. On Saturdays the Tam O'Shanters assemble for their drawing class. These 1000 fifth graders were chosen by their teacher from the schools of Allegheny County and the City of Pittsburgh. The eighth, ninth and tenth graders in the Palette groups sketch and paint and take instructions in creative art courses.

Photographed specially for this book by Don Bindyke.

GATEWAY CENTER ON A RAINY MORNING AND ON A WINTRY NIGHT IN THE EARLY SIXTIES.

THE POINT AS IT LOOKED IN THE WINTER OF 1963.

THE CIVIC AUDITORIUM DOMINATES THE LOWER HILL.

THE GOLDEN TRIANGLE IN 1964. Point State Park is in the stage of completion. The Point Bridge over the Monongahela (front) and the Manchester Bridge over the Allegheny will be demolished by 1966. This demolition would then enable the builders to finish the fountain at the Point.

The four buildings of the Gateway Center, erected by Equi-

Photographed specially for this book by Don Bindyke.

table Life Assurance Society, stand at the site which once was a blighted area. Gateway Towers (on the left), Pittsburgh's newest luxury apartment building, was completed in 1964. Next to it the glittering Hilton Hotel offers a magnificent view of the rivers and the hills. The State Office Building, the Bell Telephone Building and the originally beautiful IBM Building are the other highly interesting newcomers in the Gateway Center area.

Beyond them, in the center, the tall U.S. Steel-Mellon Building covers the Alcoa Structure. The large edifice on the left with the pyramidal top is the home of Gulf Oil. In the distance is the Civic Auditorium on the Hill (not visible). Beyond it in Oakland the Cathedral of Learning, the skyscraper of the University of Pittsburgh.

THE RESTAURANT WITH A VIEW: Le Mont Restaurant atop Mount Wash-

ington was established by the brothers Frank and James Blandi, who converted an

Photographed specially for this book by Don Bindyke.

old movie theatre on Grandview Avenue into a fabulously attractive showplace.

Courtesy Allegheny Conference.

FLOATING CONCERT AT THE POINT. In the evenings during the balmy summer months the American Wind Symphony Orchestra under the leadership of its founder-conductor Robert A. Boudreau plays to enthusiastic audiences. Their podium is on a converted barge in the shadow of Manchester Bridge.

THE THREE RIVER ARTS FESTIVAL started in 1960 and has been repeated each summer ever since. Its main features are an open-air exhibition of paintings, performances of plays and high school band concerts.

Courtesy Allegheny Conference.

416

Photographed specially for this book by W. Eugene Smith.

THE CATHEDRAL OF EARNING — AS JOKESTERS CALL THE MELLON NATIONAL BANK AND TRUST COMPANY.

of private owners would have been met in 1950 by out-raged screams from every defender of private enterprise. A Democratic city's petition for a public parking authority would have been condemned as socialism gone rampant by the overwhelmingly Republican Legislature which sat at Harrisburg in 1947. No one, however, could call the Mellons "socialists" and enemies of the profit motive; there was some headshaking, of course, and a feeling that the world was upside down, but the heresies were made ortho-dox by the character of their sponsors. My administration had no such qualms and was at ease in the use of its new tools of the trade of government.

The program for downtown Pittsburgh—the Golden Triangle of the city's professional publicity—began at the

Triangle's apex, the point of land where the Allegheny and the Monongahela meet to form the broad Ohio. As the original city grew from these Forks of the Ohio, so did its redevelopment move forward in the years of the renais-sance. The first project was Point Park. Men had talked of a park at the junction of the rivers for as many years as they had talked of smoke control. In 1806, Hugh Brack-enridge wrote that the "finest gardens in the known world may be formed" at the Point. Instead, the passing years turned the area into an ugly jumble of warehouses and railroad trackage, with a tiny reminder of its place in his-tory—the Blockhouse, an outlier of old Fort Pitt—buried in its midst.

All through the depression thirties, there were recurrent

(turn to page 419)

417

proposals for a historic park at the Point. Mayor Scully kept the idea alive by the appointment of a Point Park commission, which sponsored surveys and test borings, seeking the outlines of the fort's redoubts. The Regional Planning Association brought Robert Moses to Pittsburgh to make a plan. The "Moses Plan" called for a park at the Point. State Senator John M. Walker called for state appropriations for a historic park at the Point, to be the equivalent of the state's mall for Philadelphia's Independence Hall. Together with Pennsylvania's two senators, Joseph F. Guffey and Francis J. Myers, I went to Secretary Ickes' office to urge that the National Park Service make a national historic park at the junction of the rivers.

On October 26, 1945 during the last days of my first campaign, the Republican administration made the announcement that the Commonwealth would build Point Park and a limited-access highway (then called the Pitt Parkway) for nine very expensive miles from routes 22-30 to downtown Pittsburgh. The announcement was to embarrass me and make me lose the election. However I welcomed the news. I issued a statement praising the Republican governor and saying how wonderful I thought Governor Martin's plan was and what a great asset it would be to Pittsburgh. It was such commitments from the state that I and the Democratic city administration had been hoping for, working for, begging for, and when elected mayor I would be a hundred per cent in back of it.

Arthur Van Buskirk became chairman of a special Point Park committee of the Allegheny Conference. The state bought its first property in the park area on July 15, 1946,

Photograph by Samuel A. Musgrave.

MELLON SQUARE PARK, dedicated to the memory of Andrew W. and Richard B. Mellon, was built with funds supplied by three Mellon family foundations, costing over $4,500,000. Under the Park is a multi-level garage for 900 cars.

Photograph Pittsburgh Sun-Telegraph.

DEDICATION CEREMONIES on October 18, 1955. Front: Richard K. Mellon with Mayor David L. Lawrence and Leland Hazard. Behind them Adolph W. Schmidt, the President of the A. W. Mellon Educational and Charitable Trust.

MELLON SQUARE PARK.

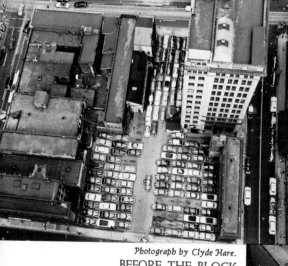

Photograph by Clyde Hare.
BEFORE THE BLOCK
BECAME MELLON PARK.

Photograph by Samuel A. Musgrave.
AND THIS IS HOW IT
LOOKED AFTERWARDS.

N OASIS IN THE HEART OF THE CITY.
Photograph by Margaret Bourke-White, Courtesy Life Magazine.

Photographed specially for this book by W. Eugene Smith.

SLUMS WAITING FOR CLEARING — THE HOUSES DIRTY AND DILAPIDATED, THE GARBAGE ON THE SIDEWALKS.

This bathroom has served 21 families.

less than nine months after Martin's announcement, and by the close of 1949 it had bought all the properties required for a total sum of $7,588,500. The thirty-six acres of the park were clear of structures by the fall of 1952, except for the historic Blockhouse, stoutly held as in the past by its D.A.R. defenders who had saved it from destruction many years before.

Pittsburgh has reacted with one voice whenever the progress of the park seems threatened or delayed. Successive state secretaries of Forests and Waters (who were charged with the park's development) and Highways (who were responsible for the highway interchanges in the park) have been under polite but unremitting pressure to get on with the work. Because development of the park has been contingent on the highway program, with its mounting costs and engineering complexities, the park itself has been more symbolic than real in the first years of its existence. Its outstanding feature, when completed, will be a huge fountain at the very tip of the peninsula, jetting a stream of water a hundred feet into the sky.

The Point Park and the Penn-Lincoln Parkway are public projects. Substantially they are simple in form. The public body decides what it wants, contracts to have it done, pays for it from taxes. The long period of develop-

(turn to page 422)

THE HILL DISTRICT.

Photographed specially for this book by W. Eugene Smith.
THE JUNKSHOP ON THE HILL—A SCENE IN THE FIFTIES.

Photograph by Don Bindyke, Courtesy Pittsburgh Post-Gazette.
THE HOME OF JOHN WILSON IN THE HILL DISTRICT.

CHILDREN OF THE AREA GREW UP ON THE SIDEWALKS.
Photographed specially for this book by W. Eugene Smith.

Photograph by Margaret Bourke-White, taken in 1956, Courtesy Life Magazine.

THE HILL AS IT WAS. Since this photograph ninety-five acres of the residential slums with homes of 1600 families were cleared by the Urban Redevelopment Authority. In the cleared area twenty acres have been reserved for the Civic Auditorium, and for parking, ten acres for the Arts Center, twelve acres for residential and twenty acres for commercial use.

ment, with the change of public administrators and the complexities of intergovernmental relationship, has marked them off from the ordinary public improvement, but they are in the accepted pattern of public responsibility.

Urban redevelopment is another story. It is a mingling of public and private investment. It cannot be executed by public power alone, unmixed with private negotiation and business judgment. It is relatively new, with the first redevelopment law in Pennsylvania dating to 1945 and the first in the national government passed as a 1949 statute. The redevelopment process is not quite slum clearance, although it is often so called in the newspapers and in politics. It is the removal of urban blight, the correction of obsolete and harmful land uses, a mechanism for accomplishing city planning.

Pittsburgh was one of the first cities in America to see

Photograph American Air Surveys, Inc.

THE HILL IN 1964. In the center the Civic Auditorium with its retractable roof (see architect's original model on right).

the process work. Van Buskirk and Richards were among the first Pittsburghers to see its opportunities. Their plans for Point Park brought them to a border area where blight still remained in downtown Pittsburgh; their practical sense brought them to the urban redevelopment law which Pennsylvania had enacted in 1945 as an exercise in post-war planning.

The redevelopment law was soon put to use in down-

(turn to page 425)

THE MOON
ABOVE
THE CITY

*Photographed specially for
this book by W. Eugene Smith.*

Photographed by Schrader Studio.

THE MAYOR OF THE CITY: JOSEPH M. BARR, a seventh generation American, was educated at the University of Pittsburgh. Starting his political career in 1936 as a secretary of the Allegheny County Democratic Committee, he rose fast. In 1940 he became the youngest state senator in the history of Pennsylvania. He sponsored much of the enabling legislation that made Pittsburgh's rebuilding possible. A respected and popular man he was elected mayor in 1959 by a resounding 54,000 majority.

left:
The mayor with John Mauro, the Urban Renewal Coordinator.

town Pittsburgh. Point Park would clear thirty-six acres of urban blight; its border areas comprised twenty-three acres of additional commercial wasteland, extending to Ferry and Stanwix Streets where Horne's Department Store held its ground like a beleagured frontier post against the inexorable spread of decay. The city had moved uptown; only a massive redevelopment could roll back the years and decades of misuse.

In the twenty-three acres of blight on Point Park's borders, there were twelve acres of station, warehouse, and trackage that belonged to the Pittsburgh & West Virginia Railway Co. These were the "Wabash" properties, memorials to Jay Gould's unsuccessful effort to buck the Pennsylvania in its own state. The Pittsburgh & West Vir-

ginia, a prosperous little coal carrier, had no use for the properties in its operations and dearly wished to find a buyer. The proposed redevelopment area also contained the properties of more than sixty other owners—a miscellany of wholesaling, printing shops, a run-down hotel, down-graded stores, and even a few rooming houses. The plant of the Pittsburgh *Press* was the only important building in the area which could not be swept out of the path of progress.

Except for the *Press*, there was little worth preserving in the area; yet, unless it could be assembled, cleared, and replanned as a whole, nothing good could be done with it. Only the public powers of condemnation contained in the redevelopment law made it possible to consider the assem-

Photographed specially for this book by Shrader Studio.

THE MUNICIPAL GOVERNMENT of Pittsburgh consists of a Mayor and a City Council of nine members. Members of the Council seated from l. to r.: Irma M. D'Asecnzo; Thomas J. Gallagher; Philip Baskin, James A. Jordon, Walter T. Kamyk, John G. Counahan, J. Craig Kuhn, Charles J. Leslie. Standing: Patrick T. Fagan, President; George Boxheimer, City Clerk.

Photographed specially for this book by Don Bindyke.

URBAN REDEVELOPMENT AUTHORITY IN 1955.
Seated, from l. to r.: J. Craig Kuhn; Henry L. Hillman, (Treasurer); David L. Lawrence, (Chairman); George W. Rooney, (Vice Chairman); John L. Propst. Standing from l. to r. William Farkas, Assistant Executive Director; Robert B. Pease, Executive Director; Theodore L. Hazlett, Jr., General Counsel.

blage of more than seventy parcels of Downtown real estate and to plan for a new and higher use by private investment. A March fire had helped the cause; it had swept the Wabash freight terminal and accomplished some major clearance of its own.

In my first year as Mayor, I had many vexing problems. A lingering labor-management dispute at the Duquesne Light Company, supplier of the city's electric power, brought strikes and threats of strike from February through October. We had weeks of dimouts, but the city took a firm position for the public interest and the crisis was overcome.

It was during these critical days that Wallace Richards and Arthur Van Buskirk came to City Hall to talk to me about Urban Redevelopment. They asked me to appoint a five-member authority, as provided in the state law, and to name myself as chairman.

When Van Buskirk suggested that I ought to be the chairman I said to him: "Arthur, you are putting me in a ridiculous position. I don't think there's a case in all the

MEN BEHIND THE REBUILDING. Seated, left to right: Merritt A. Neale, Executive Director, Public Parking Authority; Aldo Colautti, Executive Secretary to the Mayor; Sidney M. Ruffin, noted attorney; Calvin Hamilton, Executive Director, Department of City Planning; Frank Briggs, Vice President, Equitable Life Assurance Society and President of ACTION-Housing, Inc.; Howard B. Stewart, Director, Pennsylvania Economy League; Ronal Woods, Planning Director.

Photographed specially for this book by Shrader Studio.

Standing, left to right: Alfred Tronzo, Administrator, Public Housing Authority; Paul Cukas, Controller, Urban Redevelopment Authority; David Craig, City Solicitor; Bernard Loshbough, Executive Director of ACTION-Housing, Inc.

history of this country where any man ever appointed himself to a job. I just can't do that." But Van Buskirk insisted: "There's nothing wrong about that. We feel that we want the prestige of the Mayor's office involved in the Authority."

So after the newspapers began to urge me in their editorials to become the chairman I gave in and I think it's probably the only instance—I never heard of another one —where anybody appointed himself to an office. I also named Van Buskirk, Lester Perry, the retiring head of the Carnegie-Illinois Steel Corporation, and Edgar Kaufmann, the department store owner, as members of the Authority. They were all Republicans. William Alvah Stewart, then a City Councilman, was my fourth appointee and the only other Democrat on the Authority. For the first time in my public career I put myself knowingly in the minority with three Republicans and only two Democrats on the board. As it turned out the bipartisan approach was very effective because it took out of the minds of people that the

Photograph James Klingensmith, Courtesy Pittsburgh Post-Gazette.

THE UNITED STEELWORKERS OF AMERICA, based in Pittsburgh, was led during the fifties by the able and popular David J. McDonald, president (center), Howard R. Hague, vice-president (right) and I. W. Abel, secretary-treasurer.

Authority would be a place to be filled up with patronage jobs. And from that day to this in all the authorities there's never been a job given on the basis of sponsorship or as political patronage.

Thus, when we went before the board of the Equitable Life Assurance Society asking them to become a developer of the Point area, we went there with a constructive program. This was our first business—to redevelop the area in the neighborhood of the Point. In the summer of 1946 Van Buskirk, Wallace Richards, Park Martin and Charles J. Graham, president of the Pittsburgh and West Virginia, journeyed to New York in order to interest the Metropolitan Life Insurance Company to become a developer in that blighted area that later became the Gateway Center. The Metropolitan people refused. Park Martin recalls that as he and the others left the Metropolitan offices Charlie Graham suggested seeing Mr. Thomas J. Parkinson, President of the Equitable Life Assurance Society. "I know him; he and I are members of the Pennsylvania Society, and I am sure he would see us." So the three men jumped into a taxicab (Van Buskirk had another appointment to keep) and soon they were in the office of the president of Equitable. For a while Mr. Parkinson listened to their proposal silently; then said: "Well gentlemen, you'll have to answer two questions before I say anything more. What are you doing about smoke control in Pittsburgh and what are you doing about floods?" When the answer to these two key questions was satisfactory the negotiations began.

Meetings ranged from Pittsburgh to New York and back again. Equitable's real estate adviser, Robert W. Dowling rejected the area as one for apartment housing, which had been first proposed, but reported that Pitts-

Photograph by Margaret Bourke-White, Courtesy Life Magazine.
THE EXECUTIVE COMMITTEE IN 1956. Standing, from l. to r.: James F. Hillman, Lawrence C. Woods, Jr., John A. Mayer, John T. Ryan, Jr., Robert C. Downie, Adolph W. Schmidt, James M. Bovard, Carl B. Jansen, William H. Rea, A. H. Burchfield, George D. Lockhart, Sidney A. Swensrud, Park H. Martin. Sitting, from l. to r.: Leland Hazard, Edward R. Weidlein, Arthur B. Van Buskirk, William P. Snyder III, Clifford F. Hood, I. W. Wilson. The photograph was taken in The Duquesne Club.

THE EXECUTIVE COMMITTEE of the Allegheny Conference. *Seated, l. to r.:* Edward J. Hanley, Vice President of the Conference, and President, Allegheny Ludlum Steel Corporation; Edward J. Magee, Executive Director of the Conference; Leon Falk, Jr., Industrialist; John T. Ryan, Jr., Chairman of the Conference and President, Mine Safety Appliances Company; Carl B. Jansen, President of the Conference, and Chairman of Board, Dravo Corporation; Gwilym A. Price, Vice President of the Conference, and Chairman of Board, Westinghouse Electric Corporation; Leslie B. Worthington, President, United States Steel Corporation; John A. Mayer, Vice President of the Conference, and President, Mellon National Bank and Trust Company. *Standing, l. to r.:* John J. Grove, Assistant Director of the Conference; Frank L. Magee, Chairman, Executive Committee,

Photographed specially for this book on January 20, 1964.

Aluminum Company of America; Dr. Edward R. Weidlein, former Chairman, of the Conference, and retired President, Mellon Institute; George A. Shoemaker, President, Consolidation Coal Company; J. Stanley Purnell, Assistant to the President, T. Mellon and Sons; William H. Rea, President, Oliver Tyrone Corporation; David G. Hill, President, Pittsburgh Plate Glass Company; Henry L. Hillman, President, Pittsburgh Coke and Chemical Company; Arthur B. Van Buskirk, former Chairman of the Conference, and Vice President and Governor, T. Mellon and Sons; A. W. Schmidt, former Chairman of the Conference and President, The A. W. Mellon Educational and Charitable Trust; James M. Bovard, Secretary of the Conference and President, Carnegie Institute; Theodore L. Hazlett, Jr. Solicitor and Patrick J. Cusick, Jr., Assistant Director of the Conference.

Missing from the picture: Frank E. Agnew, Jr., Chairman of Board, Pittsburgh National Bank; Charles M. Beeghly, Chairman of Board, Jones & Laughlin Steel Corporation; E. Delwin Brockett, President, Gulf Oil Corporation; Robert C. Downie, former Chairman of the Conference; Aiken W. Fisher, Treasurer of the Conference, and President, Fisher Scientific Company; Philip A. Fleger, Chairman of Board and President, Duquesne Light Company; H. J. Heinz II, Vice President of the Conference, and Chairman of Board, H. J. Heinz Company; William P. Snyder III, former Chairman of the Conference, and President, The Shenango Furnace Company; James F. Hillman, former Chairman of the Conference, and President, Harmon Creek Coal Corporation.

The portraits on the wall: Andrew W. and Richard B. Mellon.

Photographed specially for this book by W. Eugene Smith in 1955.

PITTSBURGH LANDSCAPE AT DAWN: THE STEEPLY RISING STREETS, THE ROW OF HOUSES — A MEMORY.

burgh had an enormous potential demand for office space. Would that be all right with the Authority? It was, very much so. The city could sell the area to be assembled for its acquisition cost. Would that be all right with Equitable? It was about that time—we were having breakfast in Van Buskirk's rooms in the Ambassador Hotel on Park Avenue right by St. Bartholomew's Church —that Arthur said: "What about charging tolls to these companies? Do you realize we're giving them value and the prestige and the power of the act of assembly that gives the Authority the right of eminent domain. For a few minutes I did not grasp what he was talking about;

until then, I and probably the others as well had figured that we were going to operate these authorities on funds from the government. But it did not take us long to realize the importance of Van Buskirk's suggestion. We held on to it and it turned out to be a boon to the rebuilding of the city. It financed a large part of our overhead. Equitable paid the Authority a "toll charge" of $50,000 a year for twenty years—one million dollars.

Of course things did not go as smoothly as this narrative might imply. One crisis followed another. We were so enthusiastic with the toll idea that we raised the sum to two million, however as the negotiations proceeded we

Photographed specially for this book by W. Eugene Smith in 1955.

A GOOD CLEAN UP IS BADLY NEEDED: A SPRAWLING JUNKYARD ACROSS FROM THE GATEWAY BUILDINGS.

had to go back to the one million figure.

It was at this time that the United States Steel—Mellon Bank Building and the Alcoa Building were announced for Mellon Square uptown. The men of Equitable winced. Here they were, putting millions of dollars into redeveloping the Point area when large buildings were planned for the midtown area. But the business community gave prompt assurance that there were many other Pittsburgh companies that needed office space, and Dowling kept Parkinson's enthusiasm warm.

The Pennsylvania Legislature changed a restrictive law to permit insurance companies to invest in real estate in the Commonwealth. The City Planning Commission formally certified the area as ready for redevelopment under the terms of the law. A test case was initiated so that Pennsylvania's Supreme Court could pass on the legality of the proposal. The Authority employed an executive director, John P. Robin, who had been my executive secretary, a trusted friend and advisor, whose work and contributions no one values more highly than I, and a general counsel, Theodore L. Hazlett, Jr., a brilliant lawyer who with unflinching energy saw to it that the myriad of procedural necessities were accomplished.

Equitable would assume the redevelopment respon-

431

sibility and build three major buildings forthwith if Pittsburgh could assure the Society of long-term lessees for 60 per cent of the space. Van Buskirk took the lead in finding the prospects—Jones and Laughlin Steel, Westinghouse Electric, Peoples Natural Gas Company, National Supply Company, Pittsburgh Plate Glass. The lease negotiations were hard and businesslike, but everyone concerned knew that the objective was to find answers, not difficulties. Admiral Ben Moreell, of Jones and Laughlin, was chairman of the tenants' committee. He liked conclusions and he got one.

The companies were prepared to sign twenty-year leases for space in buildings which were not yet designed, let alone built, on sites which had not yet been acquired. The venture was equally bold on Equitable's part. The insurance company agreed to a redevelopment contract which made it a party to the condemnation and destruction of buildings whose owners were still protesting the Authority's right to do so in the federal courts. Owners of exist-

ing office buildings had sent the Society's directors pictures of the site under water in the 1936 flood, and the key directors of the Society had come to Pittsburgh to view the site on a day when the city was wrapped in a thick before-smoke-control smog. They took the Army engineers' flood-control program and the city's smoke-control program on faith. Their judgment of the Authority's integrity was so great that they underwrote *in toto* the cost of land acquisition, reserving only the right to agree to negotiated prices or to ask for condemnation.

City Council approved the redevelopment proposal unanimously. On February 14, 1950, all the documents were signed—redevelopment contract, the city's co-operation agreement, sales contracts for the old buildings of Jones & Laughlin and Peoples Gas, and the tenant leases. To those who were deep in the negotiations, St. Valentine's Day is a very happy anniversary.

Each return of the anniversary date has seen steady progress in the accomplishment of Gateway Center. Con-

(turn to page 435)

Photographed specially for this book by W. Eugene Smith in 1955.

THE BARGES ARE CARRYING COAL, THE RAILROADS TRANSPORTING PITTSBURGH GOODS TO ALL THE LAND.

OVER FIVE THOUSAND DIFFERENT PRODUCTS ARE MANUFACTURED IN THE PITTSBURGH AREA. THE ANNUAL

Within a hundred mile radius of the Golden Triangle are 7800 manufacturing plants. Steel and coal are the main products of the area. About 1/5 of America's steel making capacity is concentrated here; the annual bituminous coal output of Western Pennsylvania mines is 37 million tons.

The number of different goods produced in the district is

Photographed specially for this book by W. Eugene Smith in 1955.

VALUE OF EXPORTED GOODS EXCEEDS $350,000,000. estimated at 5650, made by over a quarter of a million workers. The yearly export of these goods runs to half a billion dollars; the annual bank clearings amount to more than $24 billion.

struction had started on three major buildings before the first year was out; by the third year the corporate executives and their supporting legions of lawyers, accountants, and secretaries were trooping into the new buildings. The Commonwealth of Pennsylvania chose a Gateway Center site for its western Pennsylvania headquarters building. Bell Telephone of Pennsylvania made the same decision. These structures have now been joined by the Pittsburgh Hilton, another Equitable office building, the unique IBM Building, and a towering apartment building constructed by Tishman Brothers. So we got the apartments, after all! The whole area, with its landscaping and plazas, has remained uncrowded and pleasant.

The Redevelopment Authority had a smashing and visible success. Concurrently it had cleared the way for major expansions of Jones and Laughlin's integrated steel plant in the South Side and Hazelwood sections of the city and executed with the University of Pittsburgh a redevelopment job in Oakland which provided a fine site for the university's new Graduate School of Public Health. The redevelopment process was now well understood in Pittsburgh; the city had the climate and the will to do much more.

Since those early days, the concept has spread to many other sections of the city—to the North Side, where Alcoa was sponsoring a spectacular residential and commercial neighborhood, to East Liberty, to other parts of Oakland, and to the Bluff. Besides the Alcoa project, the North Side also is the site for an extensive industrial

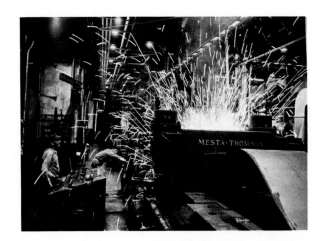

PITTSBURGH, THE MANUFACTURING GIANT OF THE SIXTIES.

U. S. Steel
The blast furnace "Dorothy" at the company's Duquesne works is Pittsburgh's largest.

H. J. HEINZ
the makers of Heinz "57 Varieties"; its food products are known throughout the world.

WESTINGHOUSE
Its East Pittsburgh plant makes electrical appliances and other Westinghouse products.

ALLEGHENY LUDLUM STEEL
one of the major producers of stainless steels, electrical steels and many other special metals.

GULF OIL
conducts its extensive research near Harmarsville, giving employment to over 1300 people.

PITTSBURGH STEEL
Its new $18 million Basic Oxygen Furnace Plant covers five acres near the Monongahela.

WESTINGHOUSE AIR BRAKE
Its many products range from molecular electronic devices to huge earth-moving machines.

KOPPERS COMPANY
operates a large chemical and plastics producing plant at nearby Kobuta in Beaver County.

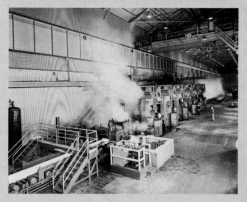

JONES & LAUGHLIN
One of the city's oldest steel producing companies with a large plant on the South Side.

renewal program and for the new Public Stadium, which will have the most dramatic and convenient location of any baseball-football facility in the world.

The most challenging project involved the Lower Hill district, which was an area of dense slum with the worst housing in the city. Now it's gone. The Redevelopment Authority bought a thousand pieces of real estate; some eight thousand people have found new homes—most of them better than they had known before.

The Crosstown Boulevard has a clear path across the area, from the Liberty Bridge approaches to Seventh Avenue; from Seventh Avenue, across Bigelow Boulevard and the Pennsylvania tracks; from the crossing of the railroad to a new crossing of the Allegheny and a great new highway along East Street. Redevelopers are constructing apartments where the slum rows stood. The Downtown business district will finally spread out Fifth Avenue, as people have been predicting for a generation, and the

DRAVO CORPORATION
Its Neville Island shipyards have launched more than 4500 naval and other vessels.

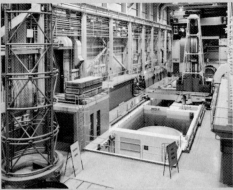

DUQUESNE LIGHT
This is the fuel canal room of its brand new atomic power plant at Shippingport.

PITTSBURGH PLATE GLASS
is heir to a great tradition; from earliest times the city has been manufacturing glass.

PITTSBURGH CHEMICAL
a primary producer of industrial chemicals, end-use chemical products and pipe coatings.

MESTA MACHINE
designs and builds steel plants. The picture shows shoe plates used building mill stands.

ALCOA
employing 42,000 people, continues to pioneer new uses and markets for aluminum.

MINE SAFETY APLIANCES
The company is the world's largest manufacturer of safety products for mines and all industry.

CONSOLIDATION COAL
which cleans and sizes bituminous coal to render it suitable for general distribution.

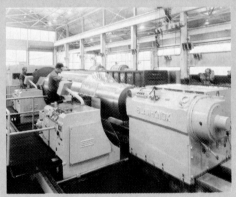

BLAW-KNOX
manufacturer of heavy steel mill rolls which are used in sheet production by rolling mills.

Golden Triangle and the university district in Oakland's civic center no longer seem so far apart.

There will be $12,000,000 in public funds and many millions in private money invested in the Lower Hill. It is a classic piece of slum clearance and urban redevelopment that has gone forward under four redevelopment authority directors—John P. Robin, Howard B. Stewart, Theodore L. Hazlett, Jr., and Robert B. Pease—and with a changing authority board, in which I am the only charter member.

The dominating architecture of the new Lower Hill is the Civic Arena, constructed and operated by the Public Auditorium Authority of Pittsburgh and Allegheny County; with its retractable roof, the structure cost twenty-two million dollars to build, of which the first million was given by the late Edgar J. Kaufmann. That the community was willing to spend so much money for recreation and amusement is as sharp a break with its past as pure air and clean rivers.

The Pittsburgh Parking Authority has built 5200 parking spaces in the Triangle. The Authority has procured the investment of $21,000,000 in Downtown parking facilities, not one cent of it from tax funds. It has been a pragmatic body, aware that there is no great measure of social significance in parking cars, untroubled by governmental theory, taking its fiscal opportunities where it finds them. It has financed some of its projects with revenue bonds and the city's pledge of parking-meter revenues; it has financed others by long-term leases in which department-store credit became the security for the Authority's bond issues. The Authority itself is a prosperous enterprise, with a good operating income from the royalties due it from its various leasing agreements. Without question, the parking program has helped to maintain the Golden Triangle as a shopping center against the formidable competition of suburban growth.

Once again, its success depended largely upon the willingness of leading citizens to give their time and their special talents to this public undertaking. As an example, Rufus Fitzgerald, who preceeded Edward Litchfield as Chancellor of the University of Pittsburgh, was the first chairman of the five-man board. Wallace Richards followed him and then George Main, vice president of

Westinghouse Electric, gave hundreds of hours to the chairmanship and he, in turn, has been succeeded by Judge Frederic G. Weir of the Court of Common Pleas.

The most spectacular project of the Authority was the underground garage under Mellon Square Park; it has also built six orthodox parking facilities which play their part in changing the physical and economic face of downtown Pittsburgh.

Mellon Square's existence reflects the decision of the United States Steel Corporation and the Aluminum Company of America to build new home offices in Pittsburgh. These buildings, each designed by Harrison and Abramowitz, flanked the square to be. They needed openness, a relief from congestion. The Mellon interests proposed that a whole city block be cleared for a new Downtown park; further, they offered to pay the cost. The city, it was understood, could lease the subsurface rights in the park for construction of a parking facility, if that should prove practical.

It all so proved. The city was happy to acquire the block with foundation funds; a by-product was the purchase of the Peoples Gas Building, leaving that company free to go to Gateway Center. Mitchell and Ritchey, Pittsburgh architects, did a rich and lovely park design. There had

Photographed specially for this book by W. Eugene Smith.

SUNDAY IN PITTSBURGH: AT THE STEELWORKERS' OUTING AND AT FOX CHAPEL CLUB.

ART AT HOME: Mr. and Mrs. Charles J. Rosenbloom in the living room of their Beechwood Boulevard home.

Photographed specially for this book by W. Eugene Smith in 1955.

Hanging on the walls are paintings by Lucas Cranach, Joshua Reynolds, Louis Forain, Thomas Lawrence.

been gloomy "expert" forebodings that a parking garage under the park could not pay out economically, but it did.

Without any cost to the taxpayers except the maintenance of the square, Pittsburgh has gained for its area of greatest need a truly splendid mid-city park and an essential parking facility. There was a mutter of complaint that valuable property was taken from the tax rolls to build Mellon Square Park; it subsided when it was shown that the gain in tax assessments from the new buildings bordering the park was six times as great as the tax loss.

The Allegheny Conference, with its admitted business orientation, has been a ready sponsor of public expenditures at every level of government. Organizations in which large taxpayers predominate are usually resistant to spending in the public economy; it has been otherwise in "renaissance" Pittsburgh. The business community, guided in large measure by the western division of the Pennsylvania Economy League, has been willing to face the compelling fact that the maintenance of progress in the private economy of the Pittsburgh area depends in large measure on necessary public improvements in the area's environment. The Conference was fortunate in its executive director,

Photographed by Margaret Bourke-White, Courtesy Life Magazine.

ART AT-HOME: Mr. and Mrs. H. J. Heinz II (the dancing couple in the foreground) in their Morewood Heights residence. Over the mantel a Modigliani painting — one of many priceless pictures in the Heinz collection.

Another large collection of modern paintings is gathered together by the eccentric steelman G. David Thompson in his Brownsville Road house. Mr. Thompson, for reasons only fathomed by him will not allow local photographers to memorialize his collection.

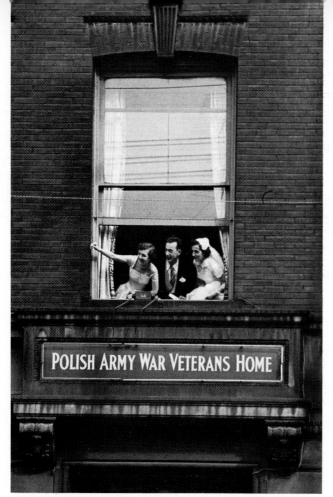

Photographed specially for this book by W. Eugene Smith in 1955.

THE MELTING POT.

Pittsburgh is the home of many nationalities. About 10% of the district's population is foreign-born; the number of second generation Americans is well over 400,000.

Park H. Martin. Martin, an engineer and planner, had a long experience in public responsibility before coming to the Conference job. He brought an intuitive sense of how fast a public official can move to the councils of the Conference; he realized that a civic organization cannot last very long if its projects result in an unusual number of political corpses. When he retired, he was succeeded by Edward Magee, whose dynamism has kept the Conference deeply involved in Pittsburgh's rebirth. Its position has also been helped by an excellent public relations posture, maintained by its associate director, John J. Grove.

The first presidents of the Conference were academicians Dr. Robert E. Doherty, president of the Carnegie Institute of Technology, and Dr. Edward R. Weidlein, president of the Mellon Institute for Industrial Research. Shy, retiring James F. Hillman, who built entirely on his own a coal empire of no small means, was next. Van Buskirk succeeded to be followed by Adolph Schmidt,

(turn to page 450)

Nationality Broadcasts

Saturday			
WPIT		German..	10:15-11:00 a. m.
German...	3:00- 4:00 p.m.	Jewish...	11:00-11:15 a. m.
WHOD		Croatian..	11:45-12:30 p. m.
Greek	10:30-11:15 p.m.	Slovak...	12:30- 1:00 p. m.
Polish...	11:15-12:15 p. m.	Polish...	1:00- 1:30 p. m.
Italian	12:15- 1:45 p. m.	Greek....	1:30- 4:30 p. m.
Croatian.	1:45- 2:00 p. m.	Italian...	3:00- 4:30 p. m.
WMCK		Lithuan'n	4:30- 5:00 p. m.
Croatian..	5:30- 5:45 p. m.	**WLOA**	
		Slovenian	12:00- 1:00 p. m.
Sunday		Yugoslav.	1:00- 1:30 p. m.
WPIT		Lithuan'n	1:30- 2:00 p. m.
Lithuan'n	12:30- 1:00 p. m.	Slovak...	2:00- 2:30 p. m.
Ukrainian	1:00- 1:30 p. m.	**WEDO**	
Serbian..	1:30- 1:45 p. m.	Polish...	12:05- 1:00 p. m.
Italian Hr.	4:00- 5:00 p. m.	Serbian..	2:05- 2:30 p. m.
WHOD		Italian...	2:30- 3:00 p. m.
Hungari'n	9:30-10:15 a. m.	Greek....	3:30- 5:30 p. m.
		WMCK	
		Italian...	12:15- 1:30 p. m.

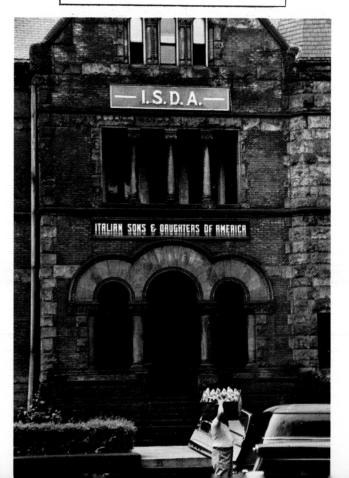

PRESIDENTIAL
CAMPAIGNS
IN
THE CITY.

1956: President Dwight D. Eisenhower acknowledges the ovation of the cheering multitude that came to greet him.

1956: Vice-President Richard Nixon is welcomed by his supporters at the Greater Pittsburgh Airport.

1960: Democratic presidential candidate John Fitzgerald Kennedy is acclaimed by a turnout of his fellow Democrats.

1956: Democratic presidential candidate Adlai Stevenson is welcomed at the airport by beaming Mayor David L. Lawrence.

THE ALCOA BUILDING is a prime example of aluminum in architectural use. Its 30 stories are sheathed in stamped aluminum panels; its window sashes and frames, heating and ventilating ducts, water piping and complete wiring system are made of aluminum. Architect: Harrison & Abramovitz; completed in 1951.

and Robert C. Downie. William Penn Snyder III, a manufacturing executive, has been the only top officer of the Conference who came from a background of direct business responsibility combined with inherited wealth. Recent leadership is being given by John T. Ryan, Jr. and Carl B. Jansen, both nationally known industrialists.

The Economy League, in spite of its penny-pinching title, has been a strong force for prudent public expenditure. Its direction came from Leslie J. Reese; its research came from David H. Kurtzman; Howard Stewart directed its staff. Their recommendations have gained business support for city and county bond issues totaling many millions of dollars. They have explained the need for the extension of government into new authorities and commissions. They have developed acceptance for the tax

increases, including Pittsburgh's earned income tax, necessary to meet inflationary costs and a higher level of public services. The League has had a large share of the mundane job of doing municipal housekeeping so that the highest officials could concentrate on their responsibilities to the improvement program.

The Conference and the League will make histories in themselves. The measure and the method of their co-operation with public agencies is one of the central themes of the Pittsburgh renaissance, as interesting and as important as the projects themselves. But the same history should be careful not to claim too much. Pittsburgh's public-housing program—one of the country's best—began in the New Deal thirties. The development of the Greater Pittsburgh Airport was pulled through by Commissioner Kane, with much headshaking in the civic agencies. The development of a treatment system to prevent pollution of the district's rivers did not have a high priority on the Conference agenda; John F. Laboon, supported in the event by the city government, pushed that program forward through the instrument of the Allegheny County Sanitary Authority. The flood-control program for the area was first announced by Franklin D. Roosevelt as he toured in the aftermath of the 1936 floods.

But there have been no unseemly credit squabbles about any of these things. The Conference and the League have cheerfully pitched in to make good programs become better ones. The airports, for instance, have an advisory board in which the League voice is heard. The Sanitary Authority was revised and strengthened according to an understanding reached by the mayor, the commissioners, and Conference. The flood-control program has been a continuous process of making both Democratic and Re-

(turn to page 445)

THE U. S. STEEL AND MELLON BUILDING has 41 stories. Its exterior is covered with stainless steel. Designed by architects Harrison & Abramovitz, it was completed in 1951.

SOME NEW BUILDINGS OF THE FIFTIES AND EARLY SIXTIES.

FOUR GATEWAY CENTER, the 22 floor building designed by Harrison & Abramovitz (the architects of U. S. Steel and Alcoa buildings), was completed in 1960.

GATEWAY TOWERS has 26 stories and 314 luxury apartments. The ninth and tallest building in the Gateway Center at the Point, it was completed in early 1964.

HILTON HOTEL at the Point is 22 stories high and cost $15,000,000 to build and furnish. The hotel, designed by architect William B. Tabler, opened in 1959.

BELL TELEPHONE's 12 story high building cost well over $8,500,000. It was designed by Press C. and William C. Dowler of Pittsburgh and was completed in 1957.

IBM, the unusual 13 story building with a structural steel framework on the outside. Designed by Curtis and Davis, New Orleans, it was completed in 1963.

STATE OFFICE BUILDING, 16 floors high, costing $10,000,000, designed by Altenhof & Brown and built by Tower, Levinson & Long, was completed in 1957.

MANOR BUILDING, the 13 story high structure west of 6th Avenue is owned by the Pennsylvania Railroad. The multimillion dollar building was completed in 1960.

WASHINGTON PLAZA APTS. on the Lower Hill, has 396 units. Designed by I. M. Pei & Associates and Deeter & Ritchey, it cost 10 million dollars to build.

PORTER BUILDING, an 18 story high, 8 million dollar edifice with aluminum exterior, is the work of the architects Harrison & Abramovitz. It was finished in 1958.

443

444

Courtesy American Air Surveys, Inc.

publican friends in Congress, a work of bipartisanship in which all have joined. There is a general understanding that the city's strength has come from its unity. So the unity persists.

There is also a general recognition that the work is far from over. It is agreed that the Golden Triangle has been rescued, that great corporate home offices and research installations have been secured to Pittsburgh for a generation, that air pollution is largely gone, and that stream pollution is going. There is agreement on slum clearance and its necessary public instruments. The parking program is well established. The first phase of the expressway program has been completed. The universities and colleges in the city have a new depth of public support. Pittsburgh is willing to give public funds to educational television, art, exhibits, symphony music, and summer musicals. Public health has immense prestige in the Pittsburgh district where Jonas Salk developed the polio vaccine, and where a Mellon foundation established a great new graduate school of public health.

Fortunately the community is not content. It sees its successes as a mandate to do more.

The area needs to hold the manufacturing jobs it has as technology changes, and to gain more as population rises. The result is a nonprofit Regional Industrial Development Corporation charged with the basic task of estimating and developing the district's economic potential.

The civic team has been concerned with the housing supply. Redevelopment quickly points out the need for new housing, so that slum residents will not be forced into still other slums. The result is another nonprofit corporation, Action-Housing, Inc., to work with private and public agencies in the cause of more and better housing.

There has been a growing realization that massive support and special attention must be given to public education, and Pittsburgh's schools, under a Board headed by William H. Rea, have received national praise for both their approach and their program. This job has just begun and this problem, like all the others, will require more

PITTSBURGH IN 1963: A photograph taken with a vertical aerial mapping camera with a six-inch distortion free lens. Comparing this view with the map of the city in 1795 (see page 62-63) one can see how Pittsburgh has grown.

On the upper part of the photograph flows the Allegheny. Its bridges from left to right are the Manchester, Fort Duquesne, Sixth Street, Seventh Street, Ninth Street, Pennsylvania Railroad and Sixteenth Street Bridges.

At the lower part is the Monongahela. Its bridges from left to right are the Point, Fort Pitt, Smithfield, Pennsylvania Railroad, Liberty, South Tenth Street, Brady Bridges.

In the center the cleared Hill district with Civic Auditorium.

LIFE IN PITTSBURGH: BAPTISM IN TRINITY CATHEDRAL.

SCHOOL YEARS:

AFTER THE WEDDING—PRESENTS HAVE TO BE EXCHANGED.

MARRIED BLISS:

money, more action, and more citizen concern before the goals of excellence become realities.

Like other urban areas, Pittsburgh has been plagued by inadequate and uncoordinated mass transit. Now the County Port Authority has the responsibility to unite the old systems and to provide modern methods and dependable service for residents throughout the county.

Pittsburgh has spread far beyond its corporate limits, yet the word metropolitan is still a term of political abuse in the suburbs. In spite of this the county government

has assumed complete county-wide responsibility for public health, air-pollution control, the care of the chronically ill, the development and operation of airports, and the development of an inland waterway port system. It is responsible for urban redevelopment and for public housing in much of the county. Sewage treatment is very near to being a county-wide function.

Up till now there has been no slackening of efforts. Joseph M. Barr, who was elected Mayor after I became Governor, has retained the City's advocacy of renewal

TELEVISION IN THE CLASSROOM.

COURTSHIP: A SCENE IN SCHENLEY PARK.

SHOPPING AT DOWNTOWN.

Photographed specially for this book by W. Eugene Smith in 1955.

DEATH: EDGAR J. KAUFMANN'S FUNERAL.

and he continues to be assisted, as I was, by a hard-working City Council and by a highly competent and dedicated staff of co-workers in his own office and in the various City agencies. The erosion of time has retired some men and sent others to new assignments. Some of the brightest spirits—Kaufmann, Somervell, Richards—are dead. Pittsburgh will need more than good will to keep its pace; it will need proficiency, imagination, a certain recklessness that shocks and stirs the hardheaded men of business and of politics. It is not enough to be industrious; there must

be a flair, a touch of genius. The community's test will be its ability to produce younger men, who can both lead and serve.

The area is full of portents of the future. The nation's first atomic generator throbs at Shippingport, only twenty miles away; the engines for the *Nautilus* were built at Bettis Field, less than ten miles from Allegheny County's Romanesque Courthouse. In Point Park, Pittsburghers are reconstructing a fragment of the past. In every other sense, in every other place, the city is building the future.

Chapter 11

LEVELLING OFF

by Stefan Lorant

THE VISITOR RETURNING to Pittsburgh after an absence of a decade asked the obvious question: What has happened while he was away? "Nothing," came the answer. "Nothing at all."

He was sitting with a friend at the window of Christopher's Restaurant up at Mount Washington, a luxurious place, incomparable in its decor, incomparable in the view from its large windows. Below them they could see — hardly more than a stone's throw away — the sprawling Ohio, formed by the confluence of the meandering Allegheny and the stately Monongahela, and embraced between the two, the Golden Triangle glistening in the setting sun.

The visitor asked: "Nothing new since I left in 1964?" And the friend replied somberly: "Nothing; nothing at all."

The visitor scanned the familiar landscape, his eyes resting on the buildings which were new to him, which were not there before. Pointing to the large doughnut-shaped structure on the other side of the river: "What about that?"

"Oh yes, the Stadium. It was finally built after much controversy and delay."

"And the building over there?"

"Oh yes, that is the Westinghouse Building, completed in 1970."

"And that gushing fountain down at the Point?"

"Oh, that was dedicated a few months ago."

"What about those towering skyscrapers in the downtown area?"

"You mean the U. S. Steel Building? The Pittsburgh National Bank? Equibank? They are new. The interior of Equibank is not even finished."

"And the vast dome beyond the U. S. Steel Building?"

"Oh, that is the retractable roof of the Civic Arena. I guess that was completed since you were here last."

"So something new has happened, some physical changes did take place after all," said the visitor with a smile.

"Well, if you look at it that way — yes."

This dialogue — which actually did take place — gives an insight into the thinking of Pittsburghers who had been used in the postwar years to instant transformation, to instant regeneration of their city. Now they feel let down if an area is no longer demolished overnight and if no new skyscrapers strut up on land formerly blighted by slums. In the years of the Renaissance things were happening every day — every minute. The air was cleared, the black grime of generations was scoured away, the rivers were harnessed, the shacks at the Point were razed to make room for the modernistic buildings of Gateway Center. Point Park emerged as dramatically as spring after a hard winter, Mellon Square Park was chiseled into the heart of downtown Pittsburgh, skyscrapers shot up like pole vaulters at the Olympics.

There was a will, there was excitement to build a new city — a city their grandfathers never dreamed possible. "If we could clear the smoke from the air, if we could make the sun visible, we can do anything" was the spirit. And they did. The grimy milltown was transformed into a sparkling metropolis.

Two men were principally responsible for the transformation: Richard K. Mellon, the banker, and David L. Lawrence, the Mayor. There were of course many

others: Wallace Richards, Arthur van Buskirk, Edgar J. Kaufmann, Jack Heinz, Park Martin, Theodore Hazlett, Jack Robin, Frederick Bigger, to name a few, but the partnership of Mellon and Lawrence was dramatic and visible. And unique. The élitist banker and the politician son of Irish immigrants — one exerting his influence on the business and financial community, the other holding an iron fist on the political machine — got to trust and respect each other, got to like each other. They shared a vision for their city — a vision they determined to make reality.

The first step was to clear the air. Then, after the passage of the smoke control ordinance, came the rebuilding of the blighted downtown. The great turning point came on Valentine's Day, 1950, when the contract for Gateway Center was signed. With that the physical reconstruction program began in earnest. Though there was immense work and planning before, the buildings of Gateway Center were a tangible symbol of the rebirth; they sparked many other projects. Civic pride was soaring.

DON'T LOOK NOW,
BUT THE MAYOR IS COMING!

THE MAYOR AND HIS ASSOCIATES BANTERING WITH *PITTSBURGH PRESS* REPORTER DAVID WARNER.

Mayor Flaherty is flanked by two of his assistants, James Kelly and David Welty. His genial Executive Secretary Bruce D. Campbell watches the scene with an amused look. City Treasurer Joseph W. Cosetti is partly visible on the right.

Photographed specially for this book by Joel Librizzi in 1975.

THE MAYOR OF PITTSBURGH, Peter Flaherty, who turned fifty on June 24, 1975 is a popular and charismatic personality. Born in Pittsburgh, he graduated from Allegheny High School. In World War II he served with the Air Force with a rank of Captain. After the war he completed his law studies at Notre Dame University, graduating in 1951, and subsequently started a law practice in the city. He became Assistant District Attorney, serving for five years. In 1966 he was chosen to the City Council, and in 1969 he was elected Mayor. Four years later, after he won both the Republican and Democratic nominations, he ran unopposed and won by a substantial majority.

He administers Pittsburgh on a businesslike basis. In 1974 the number of budgeted positions for employees of the city was cut from over 7200 in 1970 to 5400; tax burden was reduced, and wage taxes and other taxes, were eliminated. While his critics laud the Mayor's achievement in balancing budget and giving Pittsburgh an honest administration they berate him for not offering a more dramatic leadership, and not initiating more new projects.

About the same time the Jones & Laughlin Steel Corporation decided to go ahead with their expansion on the South Side, creating eleven new open hearth furnaces, and their expansion in the Hazelwood district. Civic leaders sighed with relief: the company had decided to keep its operations in Pittsburgh — a great contribution to the economic base of the city. Other plans followed in quick succession: the expansion of Children's Hospital, the construction of the Graduate School of Public Health at the University of Pittsburgh, the first federally-aided project at the Lower Hill, Washington Plaza, Chatham Center, Boy Scout Headquarters and a number of others.

The ball was rolling. After a short breathing spell another series of projects was initiated: Allegheny Center on the North Side, urban renewal in East Liberty, Homewood and Brushton. Robert Pease, the executive director of the Allegheny Conference on Community Development, remembers that when in 1967 he left the Redevel-

BUILDINGS OF THE LATE SIXTIES AND EARLY SEVENTIES.

U. S. STEEL BUILD-ING, designed by Harrison, Abramovitz and Abbe, is the tallest office building between New York and Chicago. Opened in 1970 it has 64 stories, is 841' tall with 11,000 windows.

1 OLIVER PLAZA, a 39 story office complex, was completed in 1968.

THE PITTSBURGH NATIONAL BANK, a 30 story building, has been in use since 1972.

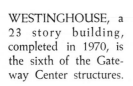

WESTINGHOUSE, a 23 story building, completed in 1970, is the sixth of the Gateway Center structures.

opment Authority "there might have been something like twenty-eight renewal projects under way, most of them in the neighborhoods — rehabilitation efforts, new housing efforts, public housing, subsidized projects and others. Some of these projects are still under way."

The achievements of those years were spectacular; they could be seen by the naked eye. As success breeds success, the people's confidence in their city's future grew. There was a vibrancy, an excitement in the air — an upsurge of civic enthusiasm. It was not unusual for those who could afford it, following Richard King Mellon's lead, to contribute vast sums of money to the rebuilding, to the universities, to cultural endeavors. Many millions were donated by private individuals and by family foundations to further the creation of the Civic Auditorium, the expansion of hospitals, new facilities in the colleges. The foundations particularly were in the forefront, granting funds to worthy projects with unprecedented generosity.

The heydays of the Pittsburgh Renaissance lasted all throughout the Lawrence administration, and, in a somewhat muted key, through the Barr administration. But feverish rejuvenation cannot last forever. In time the high cycle of creativity and productivity were bound to subside into a period of retrenchment, of mellowing, when the fields seemed to lie fallow as the harvester enjoyed the fruits of his rich harvest. The high cycle ran its course by the end of the sixties — about the time a new Mayor was elected to office.

For those who opposed the new man, Mayor Peter Flaherty became the scapegoat. For them it was he who put an end to the Renaissance; for them it was he who stopped the further rejuvenation of the city. Many voices uttered such sentiments. Edward J. Magee who followed Park H. Martin as executive director of the Allegheny Conference in 1958, told the visitor with much feeling: "A few months after Mayor Flaherty took office in 1970 everything was over; all progress came to a standstill. A great and powerful city came under the power of a nitwit." But the views of Magee, who locked horns with the Mayor on many issues, were not universally shared.

"I don't like the word stagnation," says veteran television newscaster Paul Long, the shrewd observer of the city for many decades. "It is not the right word; it doesn't describe what happened in the seventies, what happened since Flaherty became Mayor. I would rather say that we arrived at a period in which things were levelling off."

The visitor went to the Mayor and asked for his opinion about the charges, and Pete Flaherty spoke with candor: "This city is over two hundred years old. It is an active, vibrant, beautiful city, full of interesting people, full of activity that many cities wish they had. When people say stagnation, what do they mean? They use the word only as their opinion, but opinion is not a fact.

THE GOLDEN TRIANGLE IN 1975, AS PORTRAYED BY PILOT-PHOTOGRAPHER NORMAN SCHUMM

A CLOSE UP VIEW OF THE FOUNTAIN IN POINT STATE PARK.

FROM THE SKETCHBOOK OF ARTIST HENRY KOERNER.

SMITHFIELD STREET BRIDGE

BUILDING THE CIVIC ARENA

OUTSIDE FORBES FIELD

SCAIFE GALLERY AND SCULPTURE GARDEN

What are the specifics, I would like to know? What stagnation are they talking about? Our employment? Though the nation is in a recession, the city has a far better rate of employment than the national average. While the average unemployment rate in the nation is 9.4%, our rate in Pittsburgh is about 8.1% — large enough, but still a full 1.3% below the national average. Can one call that stagnation? If you walk through the city you will see buildings going up. Is that stagnation? Our neighborhoods have vastly improved. Go to see the institutions, go to see the old Carnegie Library on the North Side, the renovated building which is now the home of the public theatre and that of other performing groups. Is that stagnation? Go and look what we have here in 1975. Before my administration came in we had two senior citizens' centers; today we have eighteen. Is that stagnation? See the activities in the parks, with the many new programs. Is that stagnation? There are more recreational facilities in Pittsburgh then ever before. I don't think we have a stagnant city."

The visitor then asked his old friend Jack Robin, and that wise bird faced the issue in his usual straightforward manner: "We are in a period of economic decline," he said. "Yes, it may be called stagnation, or stagflation if you like the word better. We have lost the economic euphoria and we don't have a political euphoria. It is

CORNER OF FIFTH AND DIAMOND

ST. MARY'S CHURCH ON POLISH HILL

PIERS FOR BRADY STREET BRIDGE

PARK BUILDING AT FIFTH AND DIAMOND

true that during the Renaissance the city wasn't doing as well economically as the rest of the country, but we had a fervor which moved it forward. Now we have neither. Still, the Mayor did one important thing: he realized that there were fiscal limitations as to what the city could do and to which the people would consent, and thus he put a clamp on the growth of its establishment. He brought back a sense of discipline to the city government, he imposed fiscal restraints and obedience to order rather than to political decisions. One has to admit that he has run an honest and fairly efficient administration, but when money is cut and when payroll is reduced, the effect of such measures is bound to show. We experienced the

drop in public service; downtown turned shabby; the maintenance of the streets became terrible. Pittsburgh has the reputation of being the pothole capital of the world. The general upkeep, the small housekeeping details have slipped perceptibly.

"As to the Mayor, my impression of him is — and it may be wrong — that he is an unusual politician who is without any great zeal for a particular project or projects or group of public services. Most politicians identify themselves with some objective. Mayor Flaherty's principal objective has been to remain popular and to do this by controlling the city's expenditures and what it requires of the taxpayer or citizen."

(turn to page 458)

Photograph by Norman W. Schumm

DORMITORIES OF THE UNIVERSITY OF PITTSBURGH were officially named A, B and C buildings, but the imaginative students nicknamed them "Ajax," "Babo," and "Comet," because of their apparent similarity to scouring powder cans.

THE LIT-UP STADIUM DURING A NIGHT GAME

1970 JULY 16: A DRAMATIC PHOTOGRAPH OF

Photograph by A. Church

THE OPENING GAME AT THE THREE RIVERS STADIUM: THE PIRATES LOST THE GAME TO CINCINNATI 3-2.

Photographed specially for this book by Joel Librizzi in 1975.

A CHARMING SCENE OF A HAPPY PITTSBURGH FAMILY OUTSIDE A LIBERTY AVENUE SPECIALTY STORE.

ONE OF THE TEENAGERS' FAVORITE PASTIMES.

The visitor wondered whether such explanations were really valid. That the Renaissance ended simply because of a new Mayor and a new city administration doesn't seem to be convincing. By 1970 events and ideas came to the fore which radically changed the climate of thought not only in Pittsburgh but across the nation. Could it be that the Renaissance came to a halt because the public reacted against the élitist-controlled machines both in the political and economic spheres which, though efficient, were not loved? Could it be that the break came because of the country's reaction to the war in Vietnam and the disillusionment with those in authority? Or the race tensions which surfaced after the assassination of Martin Luther King, Jr.? Could it be that people were forced to alter their priorities, or that the Allegheny Conference got off the track?

The visitor pondered about these questions and also whether the passing of the men who were in the fore-front of the Renaissance made it inevitable that the pace

(turn to page 463)

Photographed specially for this book by Joel Librizzi

IN THE SHOPPING DISTRICT OF DOWNTOWN PITTSBURGH ON A VERY HOT SUMMER DAY IN JULY, 1975.

FAIRYLAND PITTSBURGH—A MOONLIGHT PHOTOGRAPH FROM 1975 WITH THE POINT PARK FOUNTAIN

THE UKRANIAN CATHOLIC CHURCH

HOUSES ON TROY HILL AT SUNDOWN

Photographed by Tom Hollyman, courtesy Town & Country

THE OLD POST OFFICE MUSEUM on the North Side was dedicated after its conversion in January, 1972. Its exhibits — artifacts, costume, furniture, business machines, models of early transportation — provide glimpses of the city's and county's past. Mrs. William Metcalf III, great-granddaughter of Henry W. Oliver, poses in the main hall of the museum to which she donated many family heirlooms.

Photographed specially for this book by Joel Librizzi

STEPHEN COLLINS FOSTER, a statue created in 1900 by Guiseppe Moretti and largely paid for by pennies collected by schoolchildren, originally stood in Highland Park. When vandals stole Foster's pencil and the banjo "Uncle Ned" was strumming, the sculpture was moved on the Fourth of July, 1938 to its location outside the library.

GIANT STATUES OUTSIDE CARNEGIE INSTITUTE: Astronomer and physicist Galileo Galilei and playwright William Shakespeare, both born in 1564. The sculptor: J. Massey Rhind.

slowed down. David Lawrence died in 1966, Richard King Mellon in 1970. It is often forgotten that the load of the Renaissance was carried by only a handful of individuals, and when these people were no longer around, things obviously began to lapse. Nobody was succeeding them, no one was in their place to carry the burden, nobody was on the stage who with fire, imagination and a sense of responsibility took command. To replace men takes time, and while time passes things bog down.

Then there is human nature. The fifth development project is never as interesting as the first one. People lose interest. Another new building, another project no longer excites them.

All these may be clues why the high cycle of achievements ran its course.

The visitor felt that it would be better to leave the question about the responsibility for the decline of Pittsburgh's Renaissance to the graduate students of the future, who in their annotated doctoral theses will shed light on the issue and give a definitive interpretation. Presently one is too near the issue, too involved with personalities, to distinguish the trees from the forest.

It became clear to the visitor — if it wasn't clear to him before — that it makes little sense trying to analyze events which only happened yesterday. Instant history is bunk. Only in retrospect can one hope to find the historical line, to sift the inconsequential from the important. Experiencing events while they unfold makes it difficult if not impossible to recognize their lasting significance. One sees pieces of a large puzzle — little bits of mosaic — but how they fit together, how they make a telling picture can only be evaluated after "all the evidence" is in, when one can judge the real importance of the events without being prejudiced by one's own likes or dislikes.

So the visitor was after the pieces which would one day form the mosaic. He was aware that he could only give an impression and not a definite picture of the city's history. He talked to many Pittsburghers — interviewing bankers, industrialists, politicians, city planners, artists and men and women on the street. He assembled a considerable number of facts, mirroring the views of the people and their reaction to events. His talks confirmed what he had already guessed: that there was no stagnation in the city, but rather that things had, for valid reasons, simmered down a bit. He wondered whether the simmering down might not result in the long run in a tastier, heartier flavor.

Indeed, it became obvious that the period of the first half of the seventies was a period of levelling off. Things happened no longer in a rash of excitement and creative upsurge but in a calmer way; projects were still in progress and accomplished, some with success, others with failure.

Frank N. Hawkins, Editor of the *Post-Gazette*, gave

Life-size statue of
H. J. HEINZ
sculptured by Emil Fuchs

LIVING STATUES AT POINT PARK

this assessment: "We are in a civic period akin to what in government would be known as an interregnum, a period in which the normal functions of government or control are suspended. This need not be wholly bad. Perhaps we have reached a point of maturity at which a breathing spell can be used advantageously to take stock of the civic larder and to determine how it should be replenished."

Still, the visible aspects of progress, such as the erection of structures went on. In the late sixties under the Barr administration and in the beginning of the seventies under the Flaherty administration building proceeded at a continuous rate. Of the skyscrapers, the U. S. Steel Building, the Pittsburgh National Bank, the Oliver Plaza, the Westinghouse Building went up; Equibank's new headquarters were pretty nearly complete in 1975.

In the cultural field the success was phenomenal. Through the generosity of Jack Heinz and his family, Heinz Hall for the Performing Arts came into being. Originally a plush movie house built in baroque and rococo splendor, the Penn Theatre was remade and refurbished into a magnificent concert hall, the home of the Pittsburgh Symphony Orchestra, of the Opera and the Civic Light Opera. Its acoustics, under the direction of the Austrian consultant Dr. Heinrich Keilholz, who designed some of the best European concert halls, are unsurpassed. The place had its opening in September, 1971.

THE CITY OF LOVERS. Such scenes in the downtown area are taken in stride. People don't bother looking at what goes on. Why should they? Everyone knows what it's all about.

But if the grandparents of the couples coming from Slovakia, Poland, Hungary, or Greece, from Italy, Germany, Ar-

Photographed specially for this book by Joel Librizzi in 1975.

menia or Lebanon could look at their offspring they would not believe their eyes. 1975 is not 1905 — times have changed and people have changed with them.

RESTAURANTS WITH A VIEW: NO CITY HAS AS MANY EATING PLACES WITH SUCH SUPERB VIEWS.

The Scaife Gallery, a magnificent addition to the Carnegie Museum in Oakland was headlined in *The New York Times* as "an unflawed Paradise." Built with donations of the Scaife family and named for Mrs. Alan M. Scaife who died in 1965, it was opened with fanfare at the end of October, 1974. The leading art critic John Russell called it "among the unquestioned successes of modern museum buildings." The front of it is a gigantic wall of glass, spectacularly hinged and bracketed, flanking the main staircase; through it one can see the sculpture court

THE VIEW FROM CHRISTOPHER'S on Grandview Avenue is breathtaking. One can see far up the Monongahela and the Allegheny Rivers and deep down the Ohio.

THE TOP OF THE TRIANGLE
on the 62nd floor of the U.S. Steel Building

THE CLIFFSIDE RESTAURANT ON GRANDVIEW AVENUE.

Photographed specially for this book by Stefan Lorant

THE LE MONT OFFERS A MAGNIFICENT PANORAMA OF THE THREE RIVERS AND THE GOLDEN TRIANGLE.

THE PRESS CLUB, the popular gathering place for the Fourth Estate in the Three Hundred Sixth Avenue Building is elegantly decorated. It serves fine food and offers dramatic vistas of the city and its surrounding hilly countryside.

467

FROM A PHOTOGRAPHER'S SKETCHBOOK

SMITHFIELD UNITED CHURCH

DOWNTOWN VISTA

PARKING LOT AT THE CIVIC ARENA

COAL BARGE ON THE RIVER

and the walls of the old Carnegie Museum Building. "Once inside the new wing," wrote Russell, "a diffused whiteness comes steadily, consistently, unaggressively from above. We don't see how it's done, but we can't help noticing that it suits Bonnard as well as Nicola d'Ancona, and Joan Miró as well as that local minor master, John Kane. Noting the superfine representation of the European decorative arts across the way, and looking at the paintings by Cézanne, Pissarro, Monet, Degas, Matisse, Bonnard and Vuillard which have been acquired since Mrs. Scaife got going in 1961, we say to ourselves, 'This is terrific! What a model to other cities! What's stopping them?' "

Heinz Hall and the Scaife Gallery were both opened

UNION TRUST BUILDING ON GRANT STREET

Photographed specially for this book by Joel Librizzi in 1975.

THE EQUIBANK (LEFT) GOES UP

VIEW FROM THE INCLINE

BUILDING NEVER CEASES IN PITTSBURGH

after the Renaissance period. They offer dramatic proofs that Pittsburgh is not stagnant.

And if more proof is needed about progress, the advances in the universities supply them.

The visitor found that in the past decade the colleges and universities of the city — from the giant multi-level University of Pittsburgh to the small, business-oriented Point Park College — had greatly changed, expanded and matured. The physical transformations at the campuses were eye-catching; everywhere new structures were completed or under construction.

By the middle of the seventies the University of Pittsburgh had fifteen schools and ten major centers; it employed 5400, of which 2000 were faculty members. In its

(turn to page 472)

469

Photograph by Toni Frissel, Courtesy Library of Congress.

PAUL MELLON, the son of Andrew Mellon, Secretary of the Treasury under three Presidents, who through the two Mellon family trusts, the Andrew W. Mellon Foundation of New York and the A. W. Mellon Educational and Charitable Trust of Pittsburgh gives sizeable donations to the city's cultural institutions. His wealth is estimated between $500 million and a billion.

Born when his father was 52 and five years old when his parents were divorced, he and his sister remained in Pittsburgh in the family mansion. When he was 12 he was sent to Choate in Connecticut, and from there to Yale and then to Cambridge, England. While at Cambridge he took up foxhunting, which became a lifelong passion. In 1946 his wife died and left him with two small children, Catherine and Timothy. Two years later he married Rachel Lambert Lloyd, an heiress to the Listerine fortune.

Art is Paul Mellon's second passion. The rooms of his Upperville, Virginia farmhouse are filled with paintings by the great French impressionists. In 1970 he donated a large Cézanne canvas which he bought for over a million dollars to the National Gallery in Washington. His collection of books (about 20,000 volumes) and of British art from Hogarth to Turner (about 1000 oils and 3000 watercolors and drawings) will eventually go to Yale.

In a graduation speech he summed up his philosophy: "To see, to hear, to smell, to taste, to feel — these are privileges all too often neglected, or even forgotten. . . . At least part of the purpose of life is enjoyment."

THE SONS OF RICHARD K. MELLON: SEWARD PROSSER AND RICHARD PROSSER. They are the heads of the Richard K. Mellon and Sons investment management firm, which represents the financial and philanthropic interests of General Mellon's immediate family.

Seward Prosser Mellon is directing the business and investment activities, while Richard P. Mellon, President and Trustee of the Richard King Mellon Foundation, looks after the philanthropic, civic and cultural matters. Both of them are keenly interested in the future of their city.

MR. & MRS. RICHARD MELLON SCAIFE
He is the publisher of the *Tribune-Review* of Greensburg and chairman of Carnegie Institute's art committee. She played an outstanding role in the planning and furnishing of the Sarah Scaife Gallery, the beautiful new art museum in Oakland.

Photograph by Norman W. Schumm

471

Photographed specially for this book by Joel Librizzi

ROBERT DICKEY III, Chairman and President of Dravo Corporation, the builder of vessels and barges. He graduated from Princeton University in 1939 with a B.S. in Mechanical Engineering and has served with Dravo ever since 1948. A leading figure in Pittsburgh, he was President of the Allegheny Conference from 1973 to November 1976.

main campus and in its four branch campuses — in Bradford, Greensburg, Johnstown and Titusville — it served 33,000 students.

While in the sixties the universities and colleges across the nation suffered from unrest, Pitt on the whole remained unscarred. The reason for it was mainly because of the constant dialogue between students, faculty and administrators, who felt a common commitment to their institutions. The financial troubles which gave nightmares to Chancellor Litchfield were mitigated when, during the interim administration of Chancellors Stanton Crawford and David Kurtzman, Pitt became State-related and entered into a private-public partnership for financial support.

In 1967 when Dr. Wesley Wentz Posvar became Pitt's 15th Chancellor, he adhered to a strict budget and demanded fiscal accountability from all departments. The major concerns of his administration have been threefold: broadening the curriculum in international affairs, in problems of urbanization, and in instituting meaningful academic reforms. The Center for International Affairs, founded the year after and the creation of programs in Asian, Latin American and Russian-East European Studies greatly enhanced the University's stature with

(turn to page 475)

Edgar B. SPEER, Chairman of U.S. Steel, before his company's new 64 story building in the early seventies.

Photographed by Tom Hollyman, courtesy Town & Country

HENRY LEA HILLMAN is one of the richest men in Pittsburgh. According to *Forbes Magazine*, he is "worth something like $300 million, most of which is in solid value, rather than in inflated stock-market paper."

Through the family investment company he controls and exerts influence over numerous great enterprises. He is director of ten major companies, among them National Steel, Cummins Engine, General Electric, and Chemical Bank, and through Pittsburgh Coke & Chemical he either owns or controls half a dozen fair-sized institutions. He is imaginative and resourceful. It is said that he

trebled the wealth he inherited.

He was educated at Shady Side Academy, Taft and Princeton, where he majored in geology. He joined Pittsburgh Coke and is its President. As President of the Allegheny Conference he instituted a program to improve relations between big business and the black community. He offered help to set up black businesses in the city. Because of his and his friends' efforts there is less racial tension in Pittsburgh than in most other places.

Photographed specially for this book by Joel Librizzi in 1975.

TASTING HIS PRODUCT.

Suave and debonair, Henry John Heinz II, Chairman of the Board of the H. J. Heinz Company is the grandson of H. J. Heinz, "the founder." The net sales of the company are about $1.5 billion yearly, net income in 1974 amounted to $64 million.

He attended Shady Side Academy and the prestigious Choate School in Connecticut. Following his graduation from Yale in 1931 he studied economics at Cambridge in England.

Joining the family business, he started out as a salesman, then left for Australia where he set up H. J. Heinz Co. Pty. Ltd. — which became the leading food processor on that continent.

After his father died in 1941 he became the President of the company; since 1959 he has been Chairman of the Board.

At home all over the world, an avid skier, a masterful executive, he is a philanthropist and a patron of the arts. A leader in the Pittsburgh renaissance; his benefactions to his city are manifold.

learned institutions around the world.

Chancellor Posvar, who was educated at Harvard, Oxford and West Point, realized that the University of the seventies had to address itself to pressing social questions as well as meeting the professional and vocational goals of students, without sacrificing the traditional research and scholarship which are the province of a great University. Thus Pitt, eschewing extreme innovations, has avoided being sucked into the vortex of trendism which disoriented many other institutions of higher learning during this period.

Spectacular buildings serving the needs of the University mushroomed. In 1971 the Michael L. Benedum Hall of Engineering — a $16 million concrete and lime-

(turn to page 477)

475

CURTIS E. JONES, President of the Mellon National Bank. He began his banking career with the Union Trust Company of Pittsburgh, and when that institution merged with the Mellon National Bank in 1946 he joined it.

JAMES H. HIGGINS, Chairman and Chief Executive Officer of the Mellon National Corporation since 1974. Born in Kansas City, he went to Groton and graduated from Yale University.

Photographed specially for this book by Joel Librizzi

MERLE ELLSWORTH GILLIAND is Chairman and Chief Executive Officer of the Pittsburgh National Bank. He earned his degree in business administration from Duquesne University in 1948, and after being instructor of accounting at the University for five years he joined Pittsburgh National Bank, where he had a meteoric rise: Executive Vice-President by 1965, President by 1967, President and Chief Executive Officer by 1970 and Chairman and Chief Executive Officer by 1972.

An elder of the Presbyterian Church, Gilliand serves as director of a long list of diverse organizations, among them the Pittsburgh Theological Seminary, the Pittsburgh Opera, the Urban Transit Council, Bell Telephone Company of Pennsylvania, and the Duquesne Club. He is president of the United Way of Allegheny County and trustee of the University of Pittsburgh, as well as being on the boards of various banks.

BANKERS

Photographed specially for this book by Joel Librizzi in 1975.

THE HEADS OF EQUIBANK:
M. A. Cancelliere (right), Chairman of the Board and Chief Executive Officer of Equibank Corporation, with William E. Bierer, the President and Chief Executive Officer of Equibank N. A.

The assets of the company are near the $2.5 billion mark, its net income in 1974 was in the neighborhood of $10 million.

Cancelliere, a native Pittsburgher, was raised in the Highland Park section.

After attending Shady Side Academy, he went to Brown University, where he graduated with a major in history.

In 1932, after the death of his father, "Cancy" returned home; he drove a truck, was part-time lifeguard, and finally landed the job of a clerk in the tax revision office.

Two years later in 1934 he married Helen Shaw, the daughter of the President of the First National Bank in Mc-Keesport. He joined the bank and

climbed the ladder. By 1952 he was the President of the bank, whose name was changed in 1956 to the Western Pennsylvania National Bank, and in 1973 to Equibank. In 1961 his wife died. Subsequently he married Mrs. Richard A. Gourley, now Mary Jane Cancelliere.

William E. Bierer was born in Uniontown. He earned a Bachelor's Degree in business administration from the University of Pittsburgh and a graduate degree in banking from Rutgers University.

stone building financed by the General State Authority and the Claude Worthington Benedum Foundation — was completed. It consolidated 2000 engineering students and their 140 teachers; as a result, the Engineering School's enrollment increased by 20%.

Perhaps the most dynamic change at Pitt was in its vast inter-related University Health Center, which has 6000 members on its payroll. The formation of this corporation, which affiliated Pitt's six schools of the health

RICHARD D. EDWARDS, President, and CHARLES D. MC CUNE, Chairman of the Board of the Union National Bank.

Photographed by Tom Hollyman, courtesy Town & Country

PITTSBURGH COUPLES: Leon Falk, Jr. and his wife, the former Loti Grunberg Gerard, whom he married in 1963. The Falk family fortune was founded on steel; they helped to set up Weirton Steel Company, which in time became National Steel Corporation.

Mr. Falk, a graduate of Philips Exeter Academy and Yale, has been a trustee of the University of Pittsburgh for the past 44 years and a board member of the University's Health Center since its inception. His interests, next to furthering medical research, encompass a wide range. Among his many accomplishments his influence on the development of the polled Hereford breed of cattle is significant.

Mrs. Falk, who is deeply involved with the cultural institutions of the city, is President of the Pittsburgh Ballet Theatre.

professions (The School of Medicine, the School of Dental Medicine, the School of Nursing, the School of Pharmacy, the School of Health-Related Professions, and the Graduate School of Public Health) with the six Oakland hospitals (Presbyterian-University Hospital, Magee-Women's Hospital, Children's Hospital, Montefiore Hospital, Eye and Ear Hospital, and Western Psychiatric Institute and Clinic) was facilitated by a $1 million grant from the Richard King Mellon Foundation in the early months of 1975. The appointment of Nathan

PITTSBURGH COUPLES: Joshua C. Whetzel, Jr. and his wife, the former Anne Farley Walton outside their Fox Chapel home. He is President of the Western Pennsylvania Conservancy, the state's largest private land conservation organization. She is President of Pittsburgh Civic Garden Center.

Photograph by Stefan Lorant

478

DUQUESNE INCLINE, a cable railway, was built in 1877.

Photo: Tom Hollyman, courtesy Town & Country

PERSONALITIES:

THEODORE L. HAZLETT, JR. (1918-1979) president of the A. W. Mellon Educational and Charitable Trust, and a great supporter of the area's cultural endeavors.

The Trust awarded grants to the International Poetry Center the Selma Burke Art Center, the Manchester Craftsmen's Guild, the Pittsburgh Film-Makers, the Marionette Theatre, the Arts and Crafts Center, the Ballet Theatre, the Oratorio Society, the Opera, the Symphony and other institutions.

ARTHUR HARRIS, the resourceful and imaginative President of the Tri-Rivers Improvement and Development Corporation. His aim is to restore the total potential of the rivers of Western Pennsylvania, to eliminate the clutter from the banks and make the rivers appear as they were before humanity polluted them.

J. Stark to administer this vast complex marked an attempt to coordinate the area's facilities for health education, health care delivery and medical research.

Within the walls of the center several significant scientific discoveries were achieved, attracting worldwide attention. In 1960 Dr. Klaus Hofmann made the first successful laboratory synthesis of the cortisone-producing hormone ACTH — a breakthrough in modern chemistry. Three years later an active enzyme was synthesized for the first time, ushering in synthetic insulin developed by Dr. Panayotis Katsoyannis.

In the School of Medicine, Dr. Ernst Knobil, with a $1 million federal subsidy, established a primate research center where primate reproductive and hormonal function were studied for clues on fertility control and other problems of human reproduction. Dr. Gerhard Werner, Dean of the School of Medicine, was and is engaged in research on the electrical patterns of the brain; in the Western Psychiatric Clinic researchers were conducting studies of the brain's activity in sleep, which led to discoveries about the nature of mental and emotional disorders. Pitt counts among the nation's top Comprehen-

ROBERT B. PEASE, executive director of the Allegheny Conference on Community Development, was formerly the head of the Urban Redevelopment Authority. During the past two decades he was involved in many of the city's projects which transformed Pittsburgh into a modern and attractive city.

480

sive Centers for the diagnosis and cure of Sickle Cell Anemia. It is also headquarters of the National Adjuvant Breast Project, which conducts research into breast cancer. The Department of Orthopedic Surgery was the first to prove that metal implants could be used in human bones, by successfully implanting in hip joints a metal piece called the "Pittsburgh Nail."

In 1974 the Magee-Women's Hospital of the University complex opened its computerized intensive-care unit to monitor high-risk infants and mothers during labor and delivery. A pioneer in the use of sonography in fetal diagnosis, the hospital was also credited with major discoveries in the care and prevention of RH disease in infants.

In the Children's Hospital the cleft palate center continued research with the physical and emotional problems of the common birth defect, while its Poison Control Center became the hub of a National Poison Control Network. This unique enterprise started when Dr. Richard W. Moriarty, who became its director, observed the frequent calls made to hospitals by parents whose small children had swallowed chemicals, medicines and

JUSTIN T. HORAN arrived in Pittsburgh in the spring of 1975 to become executive vice-president of the Greater Pittsburgh Chamber of Commerce, which has a membership of 1700. A 6 foot 2 inch, 230 pound New Englander, he is a jovial personality who works well with both the city administration and the Allegheny Conference. Some of his immediate aims are the building of a convention center, the development of the river fronts, and a World's Fair in 1984.

PAUL G. BENEDUM, a humanitarian and philanthropist, the head of the Benedum-Trees Oil Company and the Claude Worthington Benedum Foundation, is a trustee of numerous institutions, especially those concerned with character development of youth. Expansive and forthright, his friends are legion.

Photographed specially for this book by Norman W. Schumm

ADOLPH W. SCHMIDT, our Ambassador in Canada in 1969-1974, was one of the key men in Pittsburgh's renaissance. Educated at Mercersburg Academy, Princeton and Harvard Business School, he is actively involved with environmental problems, population control and foreign policy.

481

Photographs by Tom Hollyman, courtesy Town & Country

CYRUS COTTON HUNGERFORD is a Pittsburgh institution; no less. His editorial cartoons are a popular feature of the *Post-Gazette*, where they have appeared since 1927. He devised various cartoon characters, among them "Pa Pitt."

BROTHERS: Roy A. Hunt, Jr., vice-president of the Mellon Bank, N. A., and Alfred M. Hunt, vice-president and secretary of the Aluminum Company of America, are trustees of the Hunt Foundation.

other poisonous substances. Finding that most people had little knowledge about the ingredients of common liquids and powders and were usually ignorant of the antidotes, Dr. Moriarty set up a "hot line" for potential poisoning victims manned around the clock by experts who gave instructions how to deal with the emergencies. The "hot line" was tremendously effective — many children's lives were saved.

Moriarty wondered how to deter children from opening potentially dangerous jars or bottles, and found that because of its exploitation by television, comic books and movies, the familiar skull and crossbones symbol was no longer intimidating to youngsters; in fact, because of its association with pirates and buried treasure, it connoted excitement and adventure. So he searched for the effective symbol and — testing its efficacy with groups of children — found that the design showing a green-faced man sticking out his tongue with a disgusted grimace proved most repellent to them. In this way, "Mr. Yuk" was born. The Center has since pressed industry for more informative labelling on containers, and distributes

ARTHUR JOSEPH ROONEY, who was 75 on January 27, 1976, is the President of the Steelers. He is unique in two ways: as the best-liked club owner in pro football, and as perhaps the only man who made a fortune on the race track.

Photograph by Tom Hollyman, courtesy Town & Country

JAMES MELLON WALTON, the president of Carnegie Institute, which includes the Museums of Natural History and Art, is also president of the Board of Carnegie Library.

Born in Pittsburgh, the grandson of William Larimer Mellon, he was educated at St. Paul's School, Yale University, and Harvard Business School. Before he came to the Institute he was with Gulf Oil and served the company in several positions all around the globe, from Tokyo to Rome.

THE CITY OF FOUNTAINS:

THE MARY E. SCHENLEY MEMORIAL FOUNTAIN.

Photographed specially for this book by Joel Librizzi

THE MAJESTIC FOUNTAIN AT THE CONFLUENCE OF THE TWO RIVERS OFFERS A SPECTACULAR SIGHT.

the green "Mr. Yuk" stickers free of charge to anyone who requests them.

Next to Pitt the most prominent and best known educational institution in Pittsburgh is Carnegie-Mellon University. It became known by that name in 1967 when the old Carnegie Institute of Technology (Carnegie Tech) merged with the Mellon Institute, a leader in scientific research. In the middle of the seventies the University had over 3100 undergraduates and 1200 graduate students, who are taught by 450 faculty members. Since the merger substantial changes have taken place. The separate women's college was phased out and incorporated in the College of Humanities and Social Sciences. The School of Urban and Public Affairs and a graduate school for the study of city administration were established. A Science Hall with a huge computer laboratory and research facility was built, and an exciting new course of engineering study was begun.

Under Dr. Richard M. Cyert, who became President of Carnegie-Mellon in 1973 (following J. C. Warner and H. Guyford Stever), the enormous deficits of the institution turned into a modest surplus. Dr. Cyert is not

only an educator of repute, but an eminent administrator. He used the University's computer simulation program in quest of answers to economic questions vital to the running of the institution. One such question was how to predict the potential value of endowments over the long

FATHER AND SONS ENJOY THE WATER.

ALLEGHENY CENTER FOUNTAIN.

term; another one, to find the most advantageous way to invest annual operating funds in short term securities. It is because of his imaginative management that Carnegie-Mellon had fiscal stability at a time when other schools were foundering in debt.

The unique quality of Carnegie-Mellon is its emphasis on the practical, on demonstrated competence rather than purely academic mastery. Its curriculum accents preparation for professionalism, carefully concentrating its rich resources in a select number of academic and technical fields, which it cultivates assiduously. The University encourages the participation of practicing artists, historians, scholars, engineers, scientists, politicians and performers, who share their expertise with the students. The emphasis of these programs is on the interaction of the individual with society — on education as encounter.

The activities in the two leading Universities are mirrored by the academic achievements of the other institutions, the newest of which is the Community College of Allegheny County, which was founded in 1966 to provide two years of college study or continuing education at low cost. In less than a decade, new buildings have risen on three distinct campuses: Allegheny, Boyce and South. Together they served well over 25,000 students by the mid-seventies.

In addition to the 350 acres included in the general improvement program, all three campuses are extending their educational facilities into the community, giving instruction at industrial plants, churches, prisons, department stores and in vacant storefronts. Its student body is cosmopolitan and diverse; it includes not only college students, but workers and professionals seeking job retraining, older persons returning to school after raising families, rehabilitated prisoners, veterans, and those who want to learn a specific skill or foreign language.

In contrast to the bustling, pragmatic Community College, Duquesne University, one of the nation's foremost Catholic institutions of higher learning, a co-educational, church-related university conducted by the Holy Ghost Fathers, seems an island of tradition in a sea of educational waves and tides. Not that it has resisted change; it has grown with the times and has changed and improved its facilities dramatically and its offerings to young men and women of all races and creeds are manifold. In its eight schools Duquesne had an enrollment in the middle of the seventies of some 8400 students.

The Rev. Henry J. McAnulty, President of the University since 1959 describes the growth: "You who remember the campus of ten years ago and see what it is now, must observe that we have built a whole new university in less than 15 years. . . . We thought that it was better to go with Pittsburgh into a progressing future than to wither on the vine in a little college with a wall around it. So we joined the Renaissance, and with help from the Urban Renewal Authority, we became a whole new university." In his opinion, "it is in the best interests of society to support . . . at least a few independent colleges across the country which will keep us in focus and keep the total society aware of other individual and specialized needs. . . . We must encourage a diversity of insights and viewpoints." McAnulty believes that "In a democracy, with its systems of checks and balances, the independent Carnegie-Mellon and the Church-related Duquesne and the State-related Pitt and Penn State are all good for one another."

Certainly the women's colleges, which cherish their special role of providing modern education for women, would not disagree. Chatham College, founded in 1869, one of the oldest liberal arts colleges for women, has grown from its modest beginnings to a beautiful campus

(turn to page 492)

BOOKSELLERS.

AT JOSEPH HORNE'S DEPARTMENT STORE:
The bookbuyer is the popular Evelyn Schildhouse. Well-known and well-liked by the city's intellectual community, she has a keen mind. She knows books and knows how to sell them.

AT GIMBEL'S DEPARTMENT STORE:
The manager of the bookstore is Nan Hustead, who spent her entire life among books. A charming woman, she has a large following, with many friends among bookbuyers and authors.

"THERE IS NO FRIGATE LIKE A BOOK TO TAKE US LANDS AWAY" — *EMILY DICKINSON*

All photographs on these pages are by Joel Librizzi

AT THE UNIVERSITY OF PITTSBURGH BOOK CENTER:
Manager Mary Bonach with Fine Arts Buyer Russell Kierzkow-ski. The Center in Oakland is the mecca of university students and professors, who fill the aisles and browse among the titles.

AT KAUFMANN'S BOOK STORE:
The buyer of books is Fabienne L. Audette (in center) who with a number of efficient helpers, some of them selling books for decades in the store, look after the customers' needs and requests.

"PITTSBURGH GIRLS HAVE THE MOST BEAUTIFUL LEGS IN THE WORLD," SAYS A FRENCHMAN, SAYS AN

Photographed specially for this book by Joel Librizzi in 1975.

ITALIAN, SAYS A TURK, SAYS A GERMAN, SAYS A HUNGARIAN. NEVERTHELESS — IT IS THE TRUTH.

IF THESE PITTSBURGH GIRLS WOULD WALK IN PARIS ALL SIDEWALK CAFES WOULD BE FILLED BY MALES.

Photographed specially for this book by Joel Librizzi in 1975.

BUT ALAS, PARIS DOES NOT HAVE THE STEEP HILLS OF PITTSBURGH TO DEVELOP SHAPELY LEG MUSCLES.

NEWSPAPERS:

Photographed specially for this book by Joel Librizzi

THE *PITTSBURGH PRESS* TEAM: Editor John Troan with executive editor Leo Koeberlein in the city room.

The *Pittsburgh Press* belongs to the Scripps-Howard chain with an autonomous voice. It has 175 editorial em-

ployees. Its daily circulation is pretty near 300,000; its bulky Sunday edition appears in well-nigh 700,000 copies.

with 600 students. Originally called Pennsylvania Female College, then The Pennsylvania College for Women, it received its present name in 1955, in honor of William Pitt, first Earl of Chatham. Carlow College, founded in 1929 as Mount Mercy College, continues to provide a four-year college education for women, though men may matriculate. It has a student body of a thousand.

Of the smaller colleges in the city, Point Park College in the Golden Triangle has some 1300 students, and excellent departments of Journalism, Business Administration and Performing Arts; Robert Morris College with an enrollment of 3800 is a business oriented school; La Roche College on the North Hills, founded in 1963 by the Sisters of Divine Providence, became a co-educational

THE EDITOR OF THE *PITTSBURGH COURIER*, the weekly of the black community, is Hazel Garland. Her father was a coal miner and she was one of sixteen children. She has been with the *Courier*, which has a circulation of 50,000, since 1942.

THE *POST-GAZETTE* TEAM: Publisher William Block (center) with editor Frank Hawkins (right) and managing editor James E. Alexander in the city room of their paper. The Pittsburgh *Post-Gazette*, one of the country's oldest newspapers, has been published continuously since 1786. It has a staff of 100 editorial employees, and a circulation of 200,000.

Photographed specially for this book by Joel Librizzi in 1975.

college six years later. It has about six hundred students.

Thus, in the middle of the seventies more than 70,000 young men and women attended institutions of higher learning in the city. The day may not be far off when Pittsburgh will no longer be referred to as "the steel city," but as "the university town."

The progress of the universities is far from being the only success story in Pittsburgh. Another one is the preservation of land, of mountains and streams, clean, unspoiled, unpolluted. Environmental organizations — foremost among them the Western Pennsylvania Conservancy under the leadership of Joshua C. Whetzel — made significant strides to preserve some of the area's natural features. This is a vital undertaking when one

THE EDITOR OF THE *PITTSBURGH CATHOLIC*, one of the oldest continuously published Catholic weeklies in the country, founded in 1844, two years after the founding of the Pittsburgh Diocese, is Tom O'Neil. Its circulation is 100,000.

realizes that each and every day not less than 140,000 acres of land in the United States are being built up or paved over (yes, each and every day) — a frightening legacy for future generations.

There are several areas in western Pennsylvania with unique scenic, scientific, historical, educational or recreational value which the Conservancy was trying to save. During the middle of the seventies one of its objectives was the preservation of the Allegheny and Youghiogheny River corridors; another was to keep some of the lush Pennsylvania mountains in their natural state, foremost Laurel Hill.

Along the Allegheny, in the sixty-mile reach of river above Tionesta, the Conservancy acquired over 5000 acres of land (including two islands) which one day will become the Allegheny National Forest. In the early sixties the Ohiopyle State Park, a 40,000 tract of land across the southern tip of Laurel Hill, was formed.

The Conservancy expects to receive a sixty-mile long rail bed from the Western Maryland Railway for use as a hiking and biking trail, providing access to the gorge of the wild and scenic Youghiogheny and Casselman Rivers. Along the forest slope of Laurel Hill lie more than 120,000 acres of public and private lands which are managed so that their scenic integrity and the purity of their streams is preserved .

But the organization is not only after the big fish; it has made many small catches. Thus it acquired a one-acre site where the rare Fringed Gentian could be admired, a bog in Erie County where wild orchids grow in profusion, a 25-acre tract in Lancaster County which is a prime habitat of the endangered Muhlenberg's Turtle. It was in 1963 that the Conservancy received Fallingwater, the famed home of Edgar J. Kaufmann built by the celebrated architect Frank Lloyd Wright. The fabulous place at Bear Run is now the mecca of hundred thousands of visitors.

(turn to page 497)

CHANNEL 2, KDKA (CBS): MARIE TORRE, THE STAR
On the left behind the camera floor manager John Fabac gives

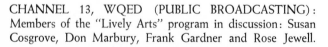

CHANNEL 13, WQED (PUBLIC BROADCASTING): Members of the "Lively Arts" program in discussion: Susan Cosgrove, Don Marbury, Frank Gardner and Rose Jewell.

CHANNEL 11, WIIC (NBC): The "Newswatch" team of the station: Wayne Van Dine, Adam Lynch, Ray Tannehill, Beverly Byer, and Dave Kelly after their report of the news.

Photographed specially for this book by Joel Librizzi in 1975.

INTERVIEWER AT KDKA QUESTIONS THE AUTHOR OF THIS BOOK ON HER POPULAR DAILY TALK SHOW.
instructions to technician Gene Turanchik. The Marie Torre Show is aired every weekday and is produced by Audrey Eisman.

CHANNEL 4, WTAE (ABC): The A. M. people: Lynn Hinds, Cathy Milton and Al McDowell listen to the instructions of floor director Amy Broz as they prepare for the show.

CHANNEL 4, WTAE (ABC): Action News: Paul Long (in center), one of the best newcasters in the country, with his associates Don Cannon, Joe De Nardo and Jack Fleming.

THERE ARE NOT MANY CITIES WHERE ONE CAN FISH DURING LUNCH HOURS.

A SUMMER DAY IN THE CITY — A TIME FOR LEISURE AND THE ENJOYMENT OF THE GOOD LIFE.

All the land the Conservancy acquires is held by it for eventual sale, usually at cost, to public agencies, so it can be maintained in a pristine, natural state. The philosophy of the organization, in the words of its President, is simple: "Leave some of our lovely western Pennsylvania the way God made it."

Whetzel acknowledges the necessity to develop housing, mining, roads and business, but holds that "they

Photographed specially for this book by Joel Librizzi in 1975.

STRANGE SIGHTS: REFLECTIONS OF GRANT STREET IN THE LARGE WINDOWS OF THE U.S. STEEL BUILDING.

SHE WAS ALWAYS DREAMING OF LARGE HATS.

should be channelled around those places which are significant for their natural beauty or scientific importance, biologically, geologically, or historically." His commitment is unwavering: "It is imperative that our nation's economic judgments must integrate the real value of intact ecosystems. Until man is able to demonstrate that he can do *without* natural systems, he should plan to keep the life support systems alive and healthy."

While the Conservancy concentrates in landforms, the objective of another successful environmental organization — the Three Rivers Improvement and Development Corporation — is to save the rivers and restore the riverfronts. TRIAD, as it became known under the energetic leadership of Arthur V. Harris, has a many-faceted program to clean up the rivers, to remove junk from the banks, to plant trees and vegetation along the shores, and to transform the reclaimed waterfront areas into parks and playgrounds. Among its many plans is the replacement of the stockyards on Herr's Island (not far

Photographed specially for this book by Joel Librizzi in 1975.

STRANGE SIGHTS: A SURREALISTIC PAINTING IN THE THREE RIVERS ART FESTIVAL AT GATEWAY CENTER.

from the Golden Triangle) with a recreational area. Instead of tearing out the old railroad tracks on the island, Triad proposes to install push-pull handcarts which children could propel along the network of unused rails. What fun it would be!

Triad's pollution abatement program aims to enlighten small businessmen how to stop pollution emanating from their plants. Its Industrial Preparedness Committee acts like a volunteer fire department in the event of an industrial spill on the river. If this happens, Triad musters out its pontoon boat, equipped with a 1000-foot-long floating boom and with it fences in the slick before it can spread along the surface and contaminate water for miles.

The History & Landmarks Foundation, another highly successful organization, saved a number of historic buildings, though some landmarks were destroyed before the Foundation came into being. Still, the city was able to keep some pleasant neighborhoods. Shadyside and Squirrel Hill still retain an unusually fine residential ambience.

NEVER MIND THE ADMONITION — KEEP MOVING.

The Corner Pulpit

Everybody thinks of changing humanity and nobody thinks of changing himself.

MOTHER AND CHILD.

MOTHER AND CHILD: enjoying a book on a bench outside Carnegie Library.

MOTHER AND CHILD: discussing a serious problem at Mellon Square Park.

Photographs taken specially for this book by Joel Librizzi

MOTHER AND CHILD: SHARING THE WONDERS OF ART MASTERPIECES IN THE SARAH SCAIFE GALLERY.

The Foundation was also successful in converting the Old Post Office Building in Allegheny into a museum, making it a showplace. In it a variety of fascinating exhibits picturing Pittsburgh's and the county's past are displayed.

Conservation of historic buildings and conservation of natural resources had caught up with demolition and rebuilding as objectives for planning and development.

It wasn't long before the visitor became aware that the Pittsburgh of the middle seventies was a very different place from the Pittsburgh of the earlier decade. The fever of the Renaissance years had broken; the excitement about achievement had become muted. The banker Cancelliere put it succinctly: "We are now in a transition period." One heard little about new projects, about rebuilding dilapidated neighborhoods, about putting up new skyscrapers. While a decade before the emphasis had been on the city's physical rejuvenation, by the seventies the main concern was for its social regeneration.

The change of climate became manifest when in 1968 the Allegheny Conference made its new policy formulation, radically shifting its priorities.

The Allegheny Conference on Community Development in Pittsburgh is a remarkable and unique organization. It was formed by civic-minded citizens in 1943. Leaders of industry, commerce, finance and big business,

Photograph by Tom Hollyman, courtesy Town & Country

IN THE LIBRARY ROOM OF THE DUQUESNE CLUB:
R. F. Barker, chairman of PPG Industries, Ralph Bailey, president of Consolidation Coal, R. E. Kirby, chairman of Westinghouse Electric, and Thomas Graham, president of J. & L. Steel.

got together in response to the multiple problems that were choking their city to death — smoke, floods, stream pollution, urban blight, old and inadequate housing, poor mass transportation, lack of recreational and cultural opportunities, the need for acute changes in the region's economy — and they decided to do something about it. The structure of the organization was simple: a sponsoring committee of some 150 men, who elected from their ranks fifteen to form an Executive Committee, the policy-making body.

One might ask: Why should these successful executives care about the lot of their brethren? Why should they give their time to improve conditions in the city? Were they doing it because they desired to do good, or were they doing it to reap personal benefits? It would be unnatural if some self-interest did not motivate their actions, though personal profit played no part. Happily, their self-interest coincided with the welfare of the city where they themselves lived and worked. They felt a civic responsibility for their home town where their forebears settled, the town where they had put down their roots.

They were also forced by circumstances to bring about drastic changes. From its outset the Conference spearheaded the projects of rebuilding and rejuvenation.

THE DUQUESNE CLUB, the exclusive men's club "for social enjoyment" in downtown Pittsburgh has been on the same spot at Sixth Avenue since 1888.

Gurdon F. Flagg, a Connecticut Yankee and an incomparable administrator, has been secretary of the Club since 1934. He also has been the President of the Pittsburgh Opera since 1952.

Photographed specially for this book with a candid camera by Joel Librizzi

ONE OF THE PRINCIPAL DINING ROOMS OF THE CLUB, WHERE PHOTOGRAPHY IS STRICTLY FORBIDDEN.

DUQUESNE CLUB.

TWO OF THE DUQUESNE CLUB'S 55 DINING ROOMS, WHICH ARE USED BY THE CLUB'S MANY MEMBERS.

HOW A STEELWORKER LIVES

CHARLES KOREY, a millwright helper at the Jones & Laughlin Steel Company where he worked for the past 11 years. Men like he earn the average of $10,000 to $12,000 a year. When the recession closed down mills on the South Side, Korey was temporarily laid off.

THE FAMILY HOME: The Koreys have four children, three boys and a girl. The eldest son, 25, is married. The second oldest

THE FAMILY PLAYS MONOPOLY in their attractively furnished dining room. 14 year old Richard, the youngest, is a 9th grade student; 22 year old Charles, Jr., works for the Department of Labor; beautiful Diane, 19, is employed by an engineering company.

THE CARPORT BEHIND THE HOUSE has room for Charles, Jr.'s and Diane's cars, while father's bigger car is locked in the gar-

The enlightened businessmen, financiers, corporate executives of Pittsburgh — the native aristocracy, the élite — realized that if they did not band together to clean the air, to harness the floodwaters, if they did not restore the dilapidated neighborhoods where their workers lived, if they did not change archaic social patterns, the city, the foundation of their own well-being, would rot away from under them and collapse. So they rolled up their sleeves, and, in typical Pittsburgh fashion, set to work.

By the late sixties most of the reconstruction plans,

Photographed specially for this book by Norman W. Schumm

graduated magna cum laude from the University of Pittsburgh and works for the government. The daughter is employed as well.

THE KITCHEN of the Korey home has all modern appliances. Mrs. Korey, an excellent cook and housekeeper, is of Lebanese extraction like her husband. Both of them came from old Lebanese families and speak their mother tongue with each other.

age. When Daniel, the eldest of the boys lived at home, he also had a car; thus the cars owned by the family totaled four.

A COOKOUT ON THE BACK LAWN. Father serves daughter Diane, while mother and the two boys wait their turn. There is also a vegetable garden which father and the boys tend. Usually after the cookout comes a spirited game of horseshoe pitching nearby.

most of the renaissance projects were completed. And hardly had the city risen from its ashes when the urban crisis in America exploded, with rioting and rebellion in Harlem, in Watts, in Newark, Detroit and elsewhere. Though the situation in Pittsburgh was less explosive, the grievances of black Americans were basically the same: lack of training and educational opportunities, poor housing conditions, lower salary levels than whites, higher unemployment and the pre-judgment that many were "unemployable."

505

Alarmed by the eruption of racial violence over the land, these men faced the problem squarely. On a cold winter evening in 1968 — the date was February 9 — eight corporate heads of Pittsburgh largest companies met with militant black leaders of the Hill district. Henry Hillman, who was with the group, remembers: "It was behind the bar at the Loendi Club in the Hill district. We took some three hours of abuse — but we listened patiently to their complaints and their demands. When the meeting was over both groups felt that we should work together and try to solve the problems. Other meetings followed — plans were evolved."

Their program aimed to alter the lot of the ill-fed, ill-clothed and ill-housed by offering them education and training, helping them find adequate housing, but foremost of all, seeing to it that the vast number of unemployed among them were given a chance to work. Their reasoning was simple: if a man can get education and training, he can find a job. If he has a job he can earn money to pay for adequate housing for his family and thus with a stake in the community, he becomes a participant, not a rebel. Therefore, plans were offered in three areas: education, employment, and housing.

The first step was to find jobs for the hard core of unemployed. 1500 companies were approached and asked for a pledge to reserve 10% of all the available jobs for them. The program worked. The corporate leaders cooperated, hiring unskilled men and training them on the job. Since its inception in 1968 more than 25,000 people obtained jobs this way.

Neighborhood organizations were helped with funds, giving people a chance to discover ways to help themselves and not to rely on welfare agencies or social work groups to tell them how to run their lives. Some of them were successful, others were not, but many groups survived. The Urban Youth Action Program provided opportunity for youngsters to work and earn

(turn to page 510)

RALPH C. JONES, President of the New World National Bank, a minority-controlled institution which opened its doors in March, 1975. The bank's 550 shareholders — mostly black — own 80,000 shares. Its main task next to the routine banking transactions — is giving advice to its customers how to buy major appliances, how to buy cars, how to budget money.

BLACK BUSINESSES

LARSTON CORRUGATED CARTON COMPANY: John E. Whitted, president, began the enterprise with seven employees; now there are thirty. Their annual billing is $3 million.

THOMPSON'S ELECTRIC COMPANY, which deals in wholesale lighting and electrical supplies, is a family business run by Taylor Thompson, along with his wife and children.

Photographed specially for this book by Joel Librizzi in 1975

WYLIE CENTRE INDUSTRIES, owned by Pittsburgh's United Black Front manufactures 600 different types of aluminum nails, tie wires for fences and several other products.

PRYOR FURS, INC., run by William Pryor at Centre Avenue, designs and makes fur garments — coats, hats, stoles, capes — from simple rabbit to luxurious sable for the area's women.

Photographed specially for this book by Joel Librizzi

BEETHOVEN'S MISSA SOLEMNIS in Heinz Hall as conducted by Donald Johanos and sung by Maralin Niska, Joanna Simon (in light dress), Seth Mc-Coy, Ara Berberian, and the Westminster Choir is sung to a full house.

HEINZ HALL, the stunning edifice for the Performing Arts in downtown Pittsburgh, was originally the Penn Theater — a plush movie house. In 1967 Henry J. Heinz II and the Howard Heinz Endowment acquired it, hired the architectural firm of Stotz, Hess, MacLachlan and Fosner. The $10 million restoration was completed in sixteen months and opened in 1971.

HENRY J. HEINZ II, his wife, and his aunt, Mrs. Clifford S. Heinz, in the marble vestibule of the Hall.

Photograph by Tom Hollyman, courtesy Town & Country

Photographed specially for this book by Joel Librizzi in 1975.

THE SARAH SCAIFE GALLERY one of the most beautiful art museums in the world, came into being with donations by the Sarah Scaife Foundation and the Scaife family. The building, costing $12.5 million opened its doors for its first exhibition in October, 1974. It was designed by the eminent New York architect Edward Larrabee Barnes.

money while going to school. Other organizations — particularly those dealing with the young — were assisted, helping with employment, education, and training.

One of the most successful efforts was the Minority Entrepreneur (ME) Program, which gave opportunity to black people to own and operate their businesses. Since its inception in 1968 up to the middle of the seventies a total of $15,700,000 loan and loan commit-

CONTEMPLATION OUTSIDE THE GALLERY: A student in a curiously identical pose with Aristide Maillol's "Night."

INSIDE AND OUTSIDE: A view of the Gallery's lobby and the yard at the entrance as seen through the large glass walls.

A GALLERY OF LIGHT. On the white walls and with natural lighting the pictures present themselves to their best advantage. The atmosphere of the museum is that of calm and serenity. A meditative and joyful feeling pervades the rooms. The building was erected in the memory of Mrs. Sarah Scaife, the sister of General Richard King Mellon.

ments had been made available to 645 entrepreneurs in cooperation with leading Pittsburgh banks and the Small Business Administration. There were some failures, but not more than the national average for new businesses.

And some of the enterprises are on the way to becoming large establishments. With these and other social programs, the conservation of human resources had become a major goal for Pittsburgh in the seventies.

A LECTURE ABOUT ART in one of the Gallery rooms in which a large figure by the sculptor Giacometti is on display.

"THE FREE EXCHANGE" — the $325,000 painting-sculpture by the contemporary French artist Jean Dubuffet in the lobby.

511

THE CITY PLAYERS under the jurisdiction of the Parks and Recreation Department, perform in the summer in the Allegheny Theatre; in the fall, in the parks and in the public schools.

THE INTERNATIONAL POETRY FORUM under the leadership of Samuel Hazo, brings poets and poetry to Pittsburgh audiences. Since 1966 more than two hundred poets have performed, among them the Russian Yevgeny Yevtushenko.

THE PITTSBURGH BALLET THEATRE was founded to develop a resident professional dance company in western Pennsylvania. Since its incorporation in 1969 it has given many performances and lecture demonstrations in the city.

PERFORMING ARTS.

The People's Renaissance was off to a flying start.

The visitor found more people in the streets, in the parks, in the museum, in the libraries, at concerts and theatres. This was not only because of the multiplying population. People had more time than ever before. The days of their grandfathers — when work went on for six days a week — had gone. Workers were usually through with their jobs by afternoon; they had their Saturdays and Sundays free, their holidays and vacations. What to do with all that leisure time? How to cope with it?

Pittsburgh met the challenge in a variety of ways. It

Photographed specially for this book by Joel Librizzi in 1975.

THE FOUNDERS OF THE PUBLIC THEATRE: Mrs. Joan Apt in her Woodland Road home discusses plans with Mrs. Margaret Rieck and Ben Shaktman, the theatre's general director.

The Pittsburgh Public Theatre began its opening season in the fall of 1975. From the outset it established a variety of programs, a training program, a high school program, a community arts program, and also was offering to talented young people master classes in theatrical performing techniques.

created beautiful parks — parks which were teeming with people. Art, music, theatre, ballet, libraries, museums offered meaningful experiences. The early years of the seventies saw the opening of Heinz Hall, the Scaife Gallery, the Frick Museum of Art with its collection of Italian Renaissance, French and Flemish masterpieces, the Old Post Office Museum on the North Side.

Music was played in profusion. Audiences flocked to the Symphony concerts, to the Chamber Music series and the Renaissance and Baroque series, to the Opera, to the Civic Light Opera, to the performances of the Pittsburgh Savoyards, and to the offerings of the three community choirs — the Bach, the Mendelssohn and the Oratorio. During the summer numerous concerts were given in the open. The American Wind Symphony Orchestra played on its barge on the Monogahela.

At Point Park the Royal Americans offered their colorful pageant recreating revolutionary history. In the spring Gateway Center had its mammoth annual open air art show, the Three Rivers Arts Festival. The Folk Festival presented folk music and dances by Pittsburgh's numerous ethnic groups.

513

NEW LIBRARIES

THE HILLMAN LIBRARY, of the University of Pittsburgh, opened in January, 1968. The Hillman family and the Hillman Foundation donated $3 million; the General State Authority appropriated another $8 million toward the building's construction. Before the building: Henry Lea Hillman and his beautiful wife, Elsie, chairman of the local Republican Party.

HUNT LIBRARY at Carnegie-Mellon was dedicated on October 10, 1961. Built mainly with the donations of Roy Alfred Hunt and his wife, the building, which was designed by the architects Lawrie & Green, cost $3.5 million. Among its 500,000 volumes are the four Shakespeare's Folios, willed to the institution by Charles J. Rosenbloom. The library also can claim the largest collection of botanical books in the world.

THE JENNIE KING MELLON LIBRARY at Chatham College, a $5 million building designed by the architects Philip Chu and B. K. Johnstone, was named after General Richard K. Mellon's mother, who was a member of the class of 1887. Dedicated in 1973, it has individual study carrels and seminar rooms. There are about 175,000 volumes on its shelves.

The International Poetry Forum offered poetry readings by famous poets as well as giving younger poets a chance to read their works before the packed houses the Forum has attracted since 1966.

Enthusiasm for the Pittsburgh Ballet Theatre mounted with each season, reaching a peak of anticipation in the fall of 1975 with the world premiere of the new ballet "Steel Concerto," set in a steel mill. The Pittsburgh Dance Council brought outstanding professional groups, supplementing the resident company's repertoire.

Curiously, despite its long tradition, serious theatre did not take hold in the city. But in the middle of the seventies, after William Ball with his repertory group moved to San Francisco, after the Pittsburgh Playhouse petered out, a new resident company under the direction of Ben Shaktman, the Pittsburgh Public Theatre, was formed. Also the Nixon Theatre on Liberty Avenue reopened its doors to touring productions, and Heinz Hall made preparations to bring successful Broadway shows to the city.

Sports events have ever been an integral part of Pittsburgh life. Ever since the time of Honus Wagner and before, Pittsburghers have been exuberant baseball fans. Thus when the Pirates won the World Series, an enthusiasm was unleashed which knew no bounds. The city has been in a perpetual Pirate Fever ever since, with children donning Pirate caps to hit balls in yards and parks, while summer baseball camps have become a venerated institution. "Glue Glove" Bill Mazeroski and the late Roberto Clemente, National League batting champion four times, were acclaimed as heroes and treated with a reverence reserved for saints.

The Steelers brought masses of football fans to the Stadium, hockey enthusiasts cheered the Penguins in the Civic Arena, and tennis fans applauded the colorful World Team Tennis champions, the Triangles.

And not only have spectator sports boomed, but all over the city the building of ice rinks, tennis courts, swimming pools and baseball diamonds has temporarily supplemented the construction of skyscrapers as the focus of Pittsburgh fervor. The Flaherty administration points with pride to the installation of the first night lighting for public tennis courts, and boasts of new million-dollar ice rinks in the parks.

The rivers provided recreation for many, with water skiers almost as numerous as coal barges, and with sailing and boating right off the Golden Triangle.

Thus Pittsburgh in the seventies offered a diversity of activities for spectators and participants alike to fill their leisure time with pleasure and relaxation, whether contemplating a Rembrandt canvas or splashing in one of the many fountains jetting in the city's parks and plazas.

The city has been fortunate to have a reservoir of great wealth on which to draw. What surprises outsiders is the extent to which wealthy men and women of

Photographed in the Hillman Library by Joel Librizzi

"I KNOW HOW BUSY YOU ARE IN YOUR LIBRARY, WHICH IS YOUR PARADISE." *Erasmus* (1466-1536)

Pittsburgh feel a sense of responsibility for their community. It seems natural to them to establish foundations and donate large sums of money to a variety of civic, cultural, medical, educational, social and experimental projects. There are about a dozen large, and some hundred and fifty or more smaller family foundations, all actively seeking projects to support or initiate.

The visitor pondered whether Pittsburgh millionaires were unique, and if so, what made them unique. Why were so many people with so much money so willing to give their support to foster art, research and other creative projects? The ordinary glib responses — for tax relief, for conscience-salving — did not give a clue to the explosion of civic-minded philanthropy which Pittsburgh had enjoyed for many past decades. What did explain it then? Is Pittsburgh really different from other cities in the land?

It is. *(turn to page 518)*

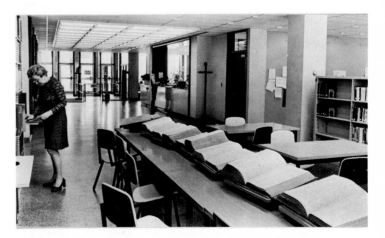

PEACEFUL MOMENT in the Hunt Library. One of its units is the famed Hunt Institute for Botanical Documentation, originally called the Rachel McMasters Miller Hunt Botanical Library, which was named after Mrs. Roy Alfred Hunt.

515

RICHARD M. NIXON, vice-president under President Eisenhower, throws out the first ball at an All Star game in Pittsburgh on July 7, 1959.

PRESIDENTS

COME AND GO.

JOHN F. KENNEDY campaigned in the city just a month before his election.

PRESIDENT LYNDON B. JOHNSON with a copy of the first edition of this book, presented to him by Governor David Lawrence (at the left) when he campaigned in the Civic Arena late in October, 1964. A short time later the President phoned Lawrence to complain: "That damn book you gave me — it kept me awake for two whole nights!" — a compliment if there ever was one.

PRESIDENT GERALD R. FORD arrived in Pittsburgh in September, 1974, not long after he gave a pardon to his predecessor, Richard M. Nixon.

"GOODBYE, MR. PRESIDENT! AND REMEMBER PITTSBURGH!" were the parting words of Mayor Flaherty to Ford as he left the city in 1974.

516

FILMING THE PAST: A scout outside the walls of the Fort which the French blew up in 1758. Behind the ancient walls Gateway Center offers an anachronistic backdrop.

Photographed specially for this book by Joel Librizzi

FILMING THE PAST: THE BATTLE FOR FORT PITT IN 1758 AS FILMMAKERS SAW IT IN THE YEAR 1975.

The city is unique because most of its people — rich and poor — have their roots there. The first generation of immigrants stayed on. They raised their families there, sent their children to school, and when the children left, they remained. Some of them amassed wealth. They cultivated the area's resources, and they became wise enough to wish to help others establish equally strong roots. Wealthy Pittsburghers give not only their money, but their time to serve causes in which they believe. They spend long hours organizing cultural events; they are on hand for community functions. They husbanded their resources, plowing the riches back into the soil, making Pittsburgh grow and flourish.

Instead of squandering their fortunes the wealthy families set up foundations to enrich the community and insure a vital future for their children and grandchildren. A sampling of the work of these big foundations indicates the extent to which their support is vital to the city.

In 1974 the Pittsburgh Foundation, administered the funds of 136 different trusts and distributed $1.3 million.

The A. W. Mellon Educational and Charitable Trust gave a million dollars during that same year, mainly for cultural, art and educational projects.

Grants from the Richard King Mellon Foundation dur-

BOB R. DORSEY, chairman of Gulf Oil, one of Pittsburgh's outstanding business executives, with his wife, the former Angelina Johnapelus.

LIVING HISTORY

Photographed specially for this book by Joel Librizzi in 1975.

GENERAL MATTHEW RIDGWAY, the distinguished military leader in World War II and former Chairman of the Board of Trustees of Mellon Institute of Industrial Research, briskly reviews young Royal Americans at Point Park.

ing 1974 amounted to $10 million, principally for medicine, education, social services, and cultural activities.

The Sarah Scaife Foundation's greatest expenditure during the year of 1974 was $1 million for the maintenance and operation of the Scaife Art Gallery; for its creation the Foundation had previously given $3,681,250.

The Hillman Foundation distributed $1.2 million, with the largest single commitment in 1974 going to the Carnegie Institute for the development and presentation of a mineral collection. *(turn to page 522)*

EIGHTEENTH CENTURY UNIFORMS IN MODERN SETTING.
The Royal Americans present their colorful pageant at the Point.

A TWO HUNDRED YEAR OLD CEREMONY

THE FOREFATHERS OF THESE
The Royal American Regiment — clad
in uniforms of the original 60th Regiment of Foot which had been organized

Photographed specially for this book by Joel Librizzi

YOUNG MEN DROVE THE FRENCH FORCES FROM THEIR FORT AT THE POINT. THE YEAR WAS 1758.

by Colonel Henry Bouquet in the year of 1756. The "new" Royal Americans — young men from Pittsburgh and its environs — recreate the pageantry of the 18th century at the very spot where the "old" Royal Americans fought under General Forbes and forced out the Frenchmen, paving the way for the foundation of the future city of Pittsburgh.

MARKET SQUARE: AN ELEGANTLY DRESSED COUPLE IS ON THE WAY TO THE SQUARE.

The Buhl Foundation concentrated on education and related areas of child development. The Maurice Falk Medical Fund distributed about $100,000 to such projects as drug rehabilitation, ambulance service training, the University Health Center. The C. W. Benedum Foundation. whose motto is "help people help themselves," disbursed close to $10 million. The Allegheny Foundation sponsored many youth camps and sports programs. The Carthage Foundation paid out $748,422 in

(turn to page 525)

THE OYSTER BAR, now a Historical Landmark, is on the site of the Bear Tavern, which opened its doors in 1827 under the Presidency of John Quincy Adams. The original Oyster House flourished on this same spot from 1871 until 1971.

Photographed specially for this book by Joel Librizzi in 1975.

MARKET SQUARE: WHERE ONE CAN DISCUSS THE EVENTS OF THE DAY — EVEN THOSE OF YESTERDAY.

OBSERVED AT THE SQUARE:

READY FOR HIS DATE. A FRIEND OF PIGEONS. LISTENING TO THE GAME.

OUTDOOR CONCERT BY AN ETHNIC GROUP

"LORD!
I wonder what fool it was that first invented kissing." Jonathan Swift (1667-1745)

Photographed specially for this book by Joel Librizzi

WHEN IT RAINS IT DOESN'T NECESSARILY POUR, BUT UMBRELLAS ARE HANDY TO KEEP ONESELF DRY.

COMMUNITY COLLEGE of Allegheny County, built on the former "Society Hill" on and near Ridge Avenue where 19th century millionaires like B. G. Jones, Jr. and Frederic T. Byers had their residences. Its bold design was done by architect Tasso Katselas, who came from Carnegie-Mellon. It was dedicated in 1973 and serves 5500 students.

grant monies, with the largest single gift going to the Carnegie-Mellon University Research and Teaching Center for the Study of Public Policy.

By highlighting the signal achievements, the visitor might give the impression that Pittsburgh is a utopia, that there were no failures. Far from it.

While things went well in economy, education, environment, and also to a certain extent in race relations, they went poorly in mass transit, in highway construction, in transportation. Pittsburgh failed in the continuing development of the downtown area; it failed in creating housing for the poor and for those of lower income.

The ever-recurring controversies which went on for years and which in one way or another were resolved in the middle of the seventies put a damper on the community spirit. The controversies about Skybus (a misnomer), about the East Street expressway, about the Convention Center and other matters not only slowed down their solution, but insured that they would become prohibitively costly — because of the inflationary spiral — if everyone finally did agree to do them. Time and

SOUTH CAMPUS at West Mifflin, another part of the institution which offers residents two years college at low cost.

BOYCE CAMPUS at Monroeville, the former East campus, opened in September, 1966. The College has 32,000 students.

FLETCHER L. BYROM
Chairman of Board
Koppers Company

D. M. RODERICK
President
U. S. Steel Corporation

W. H. KROME GEORGE
Chairman of Board
Aluminum Company of America

WILLIAM H. REA
Chairman of Board
Oliver-Tyrone Corporation

JOHN T. RYAN, JR.
Chairman of Board
Mine Safety Appliances

ROBINSON F. BARKER
Chairman of Board
PPG Industries

K. M. WEIS
President and Chief Executive
Mobay Chemical

ROBERT E. KIRBY
Chairman and Chief Executive
Westinghouse

ROBERT E. SEYMOUR
Chairman of Board
Consolidated Natural Gas

JOHN M. ARTHUR
Chairman and Chief Executive
Duquesne Light Company

STUART E. McMURRAY
President
People's Natural Gas

JOHN CORCORAN
Chairman of Board
Consolidation Coal

money were lost, and the squabbles sapped the energies of a people once buoyed up by constant doing and achieving. The spectacular public projects of the sixties were not sustained, and without them the creative ebullience was deflated. These were failures which cannot easily be corrected.

The visitor found a new phenomenon in the city — distrust and infighting between the city administration and the business, financial and corporate community. There was open hostility between City Hall and the Allegheny Conference. This was not so in the past, under Mayor Lawrence or Mayor Barr. They and the

Conference leaders worked closely together. However with the coming of Mayor Flaherty in 1970 this cooperation ended not with a whimper, but with a bang.

The new Mayor and his associates were suspicious of the Allegheny Conference's motives, and the leaders of the Conference were distrustful of him. "He has a bitter hatred for everything that happened in the past," one of the pillars of the Conference characterized the Mayor. And the Mayor's executive secretary responded: "The Conference is a special interest group which tries to influence and run the city government. They are not able to accept the change."

JAMES E. LEE
President
Gulf Oil Corporation

ROSCOE G. HAYNIE
Chairman and Chief Executive
Jones & Laughlin

ROBERT J. BUCKLEY
President and Chief Executive
Allegheny-Ludlum

CHARLES F. HAUCK
President
Blaw-Knox Foundry

BENJAMIN R. FISHER
Chairman of Board
Fisher Scientific Company

JAMES W. WILCOCK
Chairman and President
Joy Manufacturing Company

WILLARD F. ROCKWELL
Chairman of Board
Rockwell International

JOSEPH M. KATZ
Chairman and President
Papercraft Corporation

AARON P. LEVINSON
Chairman of Board
Levinson Steel Company

ROBERT E. LAUTERBACH
Chairman and President
Wheeling-Pittsburgh Steel

GEORGE A. STINSON
Chairman and President
National Steel

T. M. EVANS
Chairman of Board
H. K. Porter Company

Obviously there seemed to be a lack of communication between the two groups. City government and community leaders hardly talked to each other. Even in the middle of the seventies when the animosity between them was cooling and reason was gradually returning, there was only spare contact between them. The visitor found that some of the Mayor's closest associates had never met the editors and publishers of Pittsburgh two major newspapers, though their offices were only a few blocks away.

Asking the Mayor about this brought the answer: "As good as the Renaissance of Pittsburgh was in the forties or fifties, we can't go back to that. Some critics bemoan the fact that the old days are gone — the days when Dave Lawrence and Richard King Mellon decided what was best for the city. Well, that was true twenty years ago, but today there is no David Lawrence, there is no Richard King Mellon. I am the Mayor, and I have to deal with many problems that David Lawrence did not have to deal with. Twenty years ago the Mayor could walk across the street to Mr. Mellon, and the two determined what should be done. Today such a thing is no longer possible. The Mayor has to confer with all groups of people, people in the neighborhoods, businessmen

and merchants. He has to talk to many different groups and hear them out, and if he doesn't, they will come anyway and talk to him. When Dave Lawrence was Mayor he only saw whom he wanted to see. The political element was a big thing to him. Today, it is an entirely different ball game. One can't go back to the good old days and determine single-handed what should happen in Pittsburgh. One has to recognize that the situation has changed and that people have changed as well."

Flaherty's critics have no basic disagreement with that. They too understand that the ball game of the seventies is different from the ball game of the fifties and sixties. Says Robert Pease of the Conference: "It is true that Mayor Flaherty isn't doing the things David Lawrence did, but by the same token he is not living when Lawrence lived — that was twenty years ago." And he elaborated: "The city has reached a point where it has gone through a tremendous expansion that was costly. Now we have inflation and a recession. Some-

THE CHURCH DIRECTORY in the lobbies of Pittsburgh hotels give the list of services by numerous denominations.

AFTER THE SUNDAY SERVICE: at the First Presbyterian Church. Minister John A. Huffman, Jr. is at the door.

AFTER THE SUNDAY SERVICE: at Trinity Cathedral on Sixth Avenue Canon Allen M. Miller greets the parishioners.

one has to go through the dark tunnel to straighten things out. The Mayor is doing just that. And while he walks through that dark tunnel he makes people angry; but that cannnot be helped.

"No one likes to be fired, and the Mayor fired out of necessity a number of city employees; he had to tighten the purse strings. Still, I believe that history will find Pete Flaherty made a vital contribution to the city.

"Furthermore — and I am not hesitant to say this — he is intelligent, and he has organized an honest administration. He surrounded himself with excellent men. Joe Cosetti, the Treasurer, is extremely able, as is Ralph Lynch, who was City Solicitor until recently. Bob Paternoster, the head of Planning, is first rate. Bruce Campbell is a very bright fellow. He can be tough, but he is in a job where he has to be tough."

So the visitor found that there was no real animosity between the opposing factions. They berated each other from a distance instead of facing each other in person and thrashing out their differences. (turn to page 532)

Photographed specially for this book by Joel Librizzi in 1975.

PITTSBURGH IS A RELIGIOUS CITY, predominantly because those who migrated there — even in the second and third generations — are still holding fast to the beliefs of their forebears and remain devoted to the religion of their parents.

on the right: AT "LITTLE SISTERS OF THE POOR."

529

MELLON SQUARE PARK IS AN OASIS AMID THE CITY'S BUSTLE, A SANCTUARY FROM THE NOISE AND HURRY —

Photographed specially for this book by Joel Librizzi in 1975.

A LOVELY SPOT NESTLED BETWEEN THE SKYSCRAPERS OF DOWNTOWN, A PLACE TO RELAX AND MEDITATE

PITTSBURGH, THE MANUFACTURING GIANT OF THE SEVENTIES.

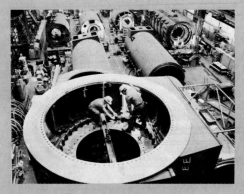

WESTINGHOUSE ELECTRIC
Dwarfed by the giant turbines, workers adjust its mechanisms in the east Pittsburgh plant.

ROCKWELL INTERNATIONAL
a Pittsburgh-based multi-industry, makes aerospace, automotive and electronic products.

U. S. STEEL
A "hot" saw shoots sparks as it slices a glowing structural beam at the Homestead works.

GULF RESEARCH AND DEVELOPMENT
Engineers at the Harmarville center carefully monitor the catalytic coal liquefaction process.

MOBAY CHEMICAL CORPORATION
operatives guide a slab stock of flexible urethane foam; it may become a mattress or chaise.

ALCOA TECHNICAL CENTER
Researching the use of aluminum for auto bodies, an engineer checks his spot-welding.

H. J. HEINZ COMPANY
Chefs in the company's kitchen tend the huge, shiny cooking vats as the many soups simmer.

MINE SAFETY APPLIANCES
manufactures safety equipment for protection of workers' health and quality of environment.

PPG INDUSTRIES
Fiberglass modules which may be the prototype for future homes are among its innovations.

The critics admitted that governing the city was more complicated in the seventies than it had been in the fifties. Before proceeding with projects one had to have environmental impact statements; one had to hold participatory planning and design hearings. In almost every major undertaking four governments were involved: city, county, state and federal. To keep things moving had become far more difficult.

Their criticism boiled down to these fundamental points: the city administration stopped things too abruptly. With the projects halted, the good technical staff was lost; able men moved away. The slowdown on projects led to loss in time and momentum which could never be completely recouped, loss of stimulus and cooperation from the governmental bodies which hastened loss of private participation, and finally, the loss of a challenging working place which lured the best quality of professionals.

DUQUESNE LIGHT
constructs the Beaver Valley Power Station with two 856,000 kilowatt nuclear generating units.

KOPPERS COMPANY
An eerie light suffuses the intricate structure of the Bridgeville, Pennsylvania chemical plant.

PAPERCRAFT CORPORATION
one of the world's leading manufacturers of gift wraps, ribbons, bows and greeting cards.

JONES & LAUGHLIN
The new 56 oven coke battery at Aliquippa equipped with the latest air pollution controls.

DRAVO CORPORATION
a diversified engineering, construction and manufacturing firm with many undertakings.

JOY MANUFACTURING COMPANY
Continuous mining machines are produced for the coal industry at Joy's Franklin plant.

FISHER SCIENTIFIC COMPANY
makes apparatus used in medical and industrial research, quality control and education.

PENN CENTRAL PROJECT
The Pittsburgh Consolidation, a 150 mile rail system, is controlled by a central computer.

RIDC INDUSTRIAL PARK
contains 70 different companies. The 600 acre park is a prototype for land use planning.

But in the opinion of Merle Gilliand, president of the Pittsburgh National Bank, "The Mayor is all right. He promised a balanced budget without a deficit and he kept his word. But he has also learned that he had to work with people, with all the people, which includes businessmen and corporation as well."

So the storm which brewed between the two groups for years might turn out to have been a tempest in a teapot after all.

After many months of looking for pieces of the mosaic which one day might form a picture of Pittsburgh's history in the sixties and seventies, after walking through its streets, watching and listening, talking and rubbing elbows with the people, searching in the libraries and universities, the visitor felt a fresh and acute kinship with the people, and a renewed, deeper love for their city.

Photographed specially for this book by Joel Librizzi in 1975.

LUNCH HOUR AT THE HEALTH SPA, THE MECCA FOR THOSE WITH EXPANDED GIRTH AND FLABBY MUSCLES.

LUNCH HOUR IN THE PARK NEAR THE RIVER.

Pittsburgh was as vibrant and exciting as ever, and as comfortable as an old slipper.

Here old and new flowed together. The customs of the old world nested with the ideas of the new. They formed that new kind of man whom Crèvecoeur said was "neither an European nor the descendant of an European," but "whose labours and posterity will one day cause great changes in the world." They formed the American.

Pittsburgh and its history are the capsule history of America, the saga of its cities. It is the familiar story: fighting for the land, clearing the wilderness, working, toiling, struggling, putting down roots, inventing, producing, consuming, despoiling, then rebuilding, regenerating, and renewing.

The visitor was taken by it all over again.

Saying goodbye to his friends, he was asked: "What do you *really* think of our city after all is said and done?"

The visitor's answer came fast and without hesitation: "I'll buy it!"

Photographed specially for this book by Joel Librizzi

THE SELMA BURKE ART CENTER'S DIRECTOR, Walter B. Sims, a designer and illustrator, poses before an exhibit in his gallery.

The principal reason for the creation of the Center was the growing artistic dynamism of the black community. Classes in drawing and painting, ceramics, sculpture, weaving, photography, modern dance, television production, puppet crafts are offered for $1 for children and $2 for adults per class.

The Selma Burke Art Center was named after its founder, the distinguished black sculptor, Selma Burke, the widow of the Jamaica-born poet Claude McKay.

THE MANCHESTER CRAFTSMEN'S GUILD on the Northside is a privately supported arts and crafts workshop which teaches ceramics to young people between the ages of nine and twenty-five. Founded by William E. Strickland, Jr. and helped by the Episcopal Diocese of Pittsburgh, its aim is to foster the artistic aspirations of the minority youth.

PITTSBURGH YOUNGSTERS GREATLY ENJOY A PERFORMANCE OF THE LOVELACE MARIONETTE THEATRE.

THE FOUNDER OF THE MARIONETTE THEATRE AND SOME OF HER ACTORS.

Margo Lovelace is producer-director of the unique little theatre in Ellsworth Avenue which offers marionette and puppet pro- ductions. Advised by the Marionette Theatre Art Council, the institution is supported with grants from Pittsburgh foundations.

Chapter 12

THE CITY OF CHAMPIONS

by Stefan Lorant

"... and then in the year of 1979, both the Steelers and the Pirates reached the top. The Steelers won the Super Bowl, the Pirates won the World Series—Pittsburgh became "The City of Champions."

"Grandpa, this sounds like a fairy tale. Surely it was not so simple."

"No my son, it was not simple at all; the road to the Championship both for the Steelers and the Pirates was not easy. The Steelers were not able to win a league championship ever since Art Rooney bought the team in 1933, which he did with some $2,500 he won at the race track. Not until Chuck Noll joined the team as head coach in 1969 did things really begin to happen to them. Since 1974 on they won the Division Title each and every year.

"Do tell me grandpa, against whom did they play and what was the score?"

"It is all here in my little black book my son and I will read it to you. In 1975 in Super Bowl IX they defeated the Minnesota Vikings 16–6; in 1976 Super Bowl X they licked the Dallas Cowboys 21–17; in 1979 in Super Bowl XIII they won again over the Dallas Cowboys, 35–31. And in the 1980 Super Bowl XIV—and what an exciting game it was—they defeated the Los Angeles Rams, 31–19."

"Grandpa, you are a fund of knowledge; you know everything. Tell me more about the Steelers."

"Well my son, their history is fascinating. I lived through it and I remember it well. It was in 1895, long before your time, that a professional football team was put together in Greensburg by a fellow named Lloyd Heff. Others sprouted up, and Pittsburgh became 'the cradle of professional football.' Anyhow, that is what that great sportswriter Bob Smith says.

"In 1902, not long after President McKinley's assassination, when Theodore Roosevelt was President, the Pittsburgh Pros beat Connie Mack's Athletics for the Championship, but it took seventy-three more years, almost three quarters of a century before a Pittsburgh team—in 1975—could win the World Championship."

"How did Mr. Rooney get involved with the Steelers, Grandpa?"

"That is a good question, my son—Art, like his brother Jim, was a football player from way back; it was in 1933, the same year Hitler came to power in Germany, the very year Franklin D. Roosevelt started his first presidential term here, that Art Rooney applied for a franchise in the National Football League and bought the team. They were then called the Pirates—not until 1941 did they adopt the name Steelers, so that people would know that they came from the steel city 'Pittsburgh.' The team was popular, the fans came by the thousands to watch them—but as to winning—well they just couldn't do it.

"Art said more in desperation than as a joke: 'We've got new players, new uniforms, and a new coach (Joe Bach), but they look like the same old Pirates to me.'

"After Boston thrashed them 30 to 0, a disaster, John McNally, the legendary 'Johnny Blood' became their coach. Under his guidance the team won 4 games in 1937 and lost 7; the following year in 1938 they won 2 and lost 9. They were no great shakes. It was in that year Art Rooney hired 'Whizzer' White for the terrific salary of

THE MANAGER OF
THE PIRATES

CHUCK TANNER succeeded Danny Murtaugh as the manager of the Pirates in 1976. Three years later—in 1979—he led the team to 98 winning games.

Under him the Pirates won the 1979 World Series.

$15,000. But Whizzer's heart was not really in the game, all he wanted to do was to become a lawyer. He used the money he got from Rooney to pay for his studies. And do you know what happened to him? You won't believe it. He became a Justice on the Supreme Court—no ball-fumbling there."

"The year of 1942—we were in the war—the Steelers had their first good season; they won seven games and lost only 4. In 1946, the year after the end of the war, Rooney hired as coach 'Jock' Sutherland, under whom they almost won the Championship in 1947.

"A year later, in 1948 Sutherland died of a brain tumor. Coaches came and went. The Steelers lost and lost and lost.

"At last, Charles Henry Noll became their coach on January 27, 1969, a red letter day for the team. From then on they were on the upgrade.

"Noll, the Steeler's 16th coach, demanded discipline; no fooling around, no horse playing, less beer drinking. He made up his mind to build a championship team for Pittsburgh; he wanted victories, and he got them.

"Fate helped him too, and he had luck. In the 1970

THE PIRATES IN ACTION

Photograph by U.P.I. taken on October 14, 1979

SHORTSTOP TIM FOLEY AGAINST THE BALTIMORE ORIOLES. THE PIRATES WON THE GAME BY 7 TO 1.

collegiate draft, the first player he selected was a fellow named Terry Bradshaw.

"Under Noll the Steelers have been in the playoffs for eight straight years and they have won the Super Bowl four times in six years—quite a record, don't you think my son? After waiting patiently for four decades, Art Rooney finally had his championship team.

"That is their story in a nutshell, but of course there is much more to it, much more."

*

"Now Grandpa, and what about our other Champions —The Pirates."

"They, too had an interesting story. Pittsburgh was a baseball city ever since the Army men who returned from the Civil War began to start swinging bats and driving baseballs through its soot-laden atmosphere.

"The National League was born in 1876, in our Centennial year. In that year the Pittsburgh team, calling themselves the Alleghenies, downed the Xanthas, 7 to 3. Then followed dark years, with defeat after defeat. In 1882 the Allegheny Club became the charter member of the second major league, the American Association. They won 39 games and lost 39.

"I often wondered how they got their name—why they are called 'Pirates.'

"I will tell you my son; it is a strange story. It happened because of the baseball war between the National League and the American Association. The National League was the big league, charging 50 cents admission, while the American Association charged only two-bits: 25 cents. In 1887 the ballplayers of the National League formed a union, known as the Brotherhood; they asked for bigger shares of the profits to enhance their meager salaries.

"A new League came into being, the Players League, and many of the National League and the American Association joined it.

"Two of the players who changed their affiliations were Louis Bierbauer, a second baseman, and Harry Stovey, a base-stealing outfielder. As their names did not appear on the American Association's reserve list for 1891, Pittsburgh signed Bierbauer, and Boston signed Stovey. The Association cried murder. It said that the names of the players were not printed on the list because of an error and demanded their return. But the President of the Pitts-

(turn to page 542)

Photograph by U.P.I. taken on October 12, 1979

CATCHER STEVE NICOSIA MAKES THE TAG AGAINST KEN SINGLETON OF THE BALTIMORE ORIOLES.

Photograph by U.P.I. taken on January 6, 1980

STALLWORTH TAKES A PASS FROM BRADSHAW IN THE A.F.C. CHAMPIONSHIP GAME AGAINST THE OILERS.

Photograph by U.P.I. taken on January 7, 1979

RIC MOSER recovers a fumble by Houston Oiler Johnny Dirden in the title game between Steelers and Houston Oilers.

Photograph by U.P.I. taken on January 21, 1979

RON JOHNSON snatches the ball, dropped by the Dallas Cowboys. The Steelers won their third Championship by 35–31.

Photograph by U.P.I. taken on January 6, 1980

TERRY BRADSHAW RUNS FOR A GAIN IN THE LAST QUARTER OF THE GAME AGAINST THE HOUSTON OILERS.

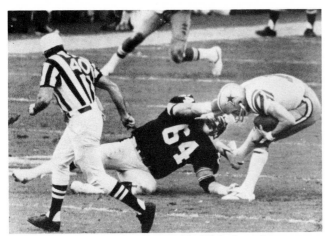

Photograph by U.P.I. taken on January 21, 1979

STEVE FURNESS sacks Cowboys quarterback Roger Staubach in the first quarter of the game, which was played in Miami, Fla.

Photograph by U.P.I. taken on January 21, 1979

FRANCO HARRIS goes over for a touchdown in the championship game; Oiler Gregg Bingham is unable to stop him.

Photograph by U.P.I. on January 20, 1980

LYNN SWANN CATCHES Terry Bradshaw's pass in the third quarter of the Super Bowl XIV game against the L.A. Rams.

THE COACH OF
THE STEELERS

CHUCK NOLL became the head coach of the Steelers in 1969. Since 1972, the first of eight straight playoff seasons Noll's record was 88–27–1.

Under his guidance the Steelers won four Super Bowl trophies—in 1975, in 1976, in 1979, and in 1980.

burgh Club, Palmer O'Neil refused to release Bierbauer. Thus the matter came before a board of arbitration where the spokesman for the American Association orated: 'The action of the Pittsburgh Club in signing Bierbauer was piratical.' The word 'piratical' stuck—and the Pittsburgh Club became the Pirates."

"And how did the Club fare with Bierbauer?"

"Not too good my son. In 1891 the team won 32 games and lost 33. The National League and American Association merged into a twelve-club circuit, and the Pirates were reorganized under Al Buckenberger as manager. The League announced that the top salary for any player would be no more than $2,400.

"Pittsburgh's fortunes soared during the six seasons in the National League. Though the Pirates did not win the pennant, in 1893 they finished second behind the strong Boston team. The following year, catcher Connie Mack (whose real name was Cornelius McGillicuddy), became manager of the club. He was followed two years later by Patsy Donovan, the hard-hitting rightfielder. But whatever the changes were, there was no improvement in the team's scores. Pittsburgh was in eighth place in the twelve-club league with 72 victories and 76 defeats.

"In 1900 Barney Dreyfuss, a 34-year-old German

Photograph by U.P.I. on January 20, 1980

TERRY BRADSHAW SIGNALS VIC-
TORY against the Los Angeles Rams in
the 1980 Super Bowl XIV Championship
at the Rose Bowl in Pasadena. Franco
Harris (on the left), who scored a second
touchdown against the Rams, goes after
the ball. The Steelers won their unprecedented fourth Super Bowl Championship,
defeating the Los Angeles Rams by 31-19.

immigrant, who owned the Louisville ball club, had a
stroke of bad luck. His ball park burned down. About the
same time the owners of the Pirates—Captain Kerr and
Philip Austin—decided to sell their club; they were tired
of losing money.

"Barney was interested. He acquired half interest in the
Pirates, and was made President.

"He brought a number of his Louisville ballplayers
to Pittsburgh, among them two of baseball's immortals:
John Peter Wagner (Honus Wagner "The Flying Dutchman") and Frederick Clifford Clarke. With them the
team became rejuvenated. They won pennants in 1901,

1902, 1903 and again in 1909, but never the title. And
Dreyfuss made money, a lot of it. Grandstand prices were
raised to a dollar; bleachers sold for two-bits.

"The eight game series in 1903 between the Pittsburgh
Pirates and the Boston Pilgrims which Dreyfuss arranged
drew over 100,000 fans; the gate receipt amounted to
$55,000, an enormous sum in those days.

"Dreyfuss generously donated his entire share to his
players, even though they lost the series.

" 'They've won three pennants for me and they stuck
by me during the American League raids. I'm glad to do
it,' he said.

"In 1909 Barney Dreyfuss bought some land in Oakland through the good offices of Andrew Carnegie, and built on it Forbes Field, which became the home of the Pirates for over half a century. Forbes Field opened on June 30, 1909 before a crowd of 30,338 (that was the official figure).

"In that year the Pirates won the World Championship, and Mayor Magee proclaimed Oct. 18 a general holiday in honor of the new champions and Pittsburgh celebrated as never before.

"Then came the slump which lasted for a decade and a half. Not until 1925 did the Pirates win the World Series again in an uphill victory against the Washington Senators. Each member of the team received a $5,332 bonus.

"Another 35 years passed before they became World Champions again.

"In the World Series of 1927, the Yankees, 110 game winners in the American League, defeated the Pirates in four straight games. Pittsburgh fans were mourning.

"In 1931, four days before Barney's 65th birthday, his son Sam died. The heartbroken father called in his son-in-law Bill Benswanger to manage the club.

"The grief-stricken Dreyfuss had no will to live. He died a year later, in February 1932—and Benswanger became the President of the Club. Benswanger made Pie Traynor manager, who stayed in this position until the end of the 1939 season.

"In 1946 the Dreyfuss family sold the Club to a consortium of four men: John Galbreath, a Columbus realtor, Bing Crosby, the crooner, Frank McKinney, an Indianapolis banker and Tom Johnson, vice-president of the Standard Steel Spring Company. With them a new era began.

"In 1955 Joe L. Brown became general manager; he rebuilt the team and five years later in 1960 they won the World Championship. Bill Mazeroski's homer in the ninth inning clinched the victory. But it took another ten years before the Pirates could win a divisional title, and the World Championship in 1971.

"The Pirates won the series, with Roberto Clemente's performance a legend. He had two home runs in the series, and he hit .414. A year later he made his 3000th hit at Three Rivers Stadium, just before his death in an airplane accident.

"After the 1976 season coach Danny Murtaugh, who managed the Pirates on four different occasions, and led

(turn to page 549)

Photographed specially for this book in 1980 by Joel Librizzi

ART ROONEY WHO HAS OWNED THE STEELERS SINCE 1933 IN THE SCOUTING ROOM AT THE STADIUM.

All the names of all the players in every team in the National Football League are listed on the board, also their height, their weight, their college affiliation, and other pertinent data. The list is constantly updated, noting all the changes.

ARTHUR J. ROONEY,
father of 5, grandfather of 34.

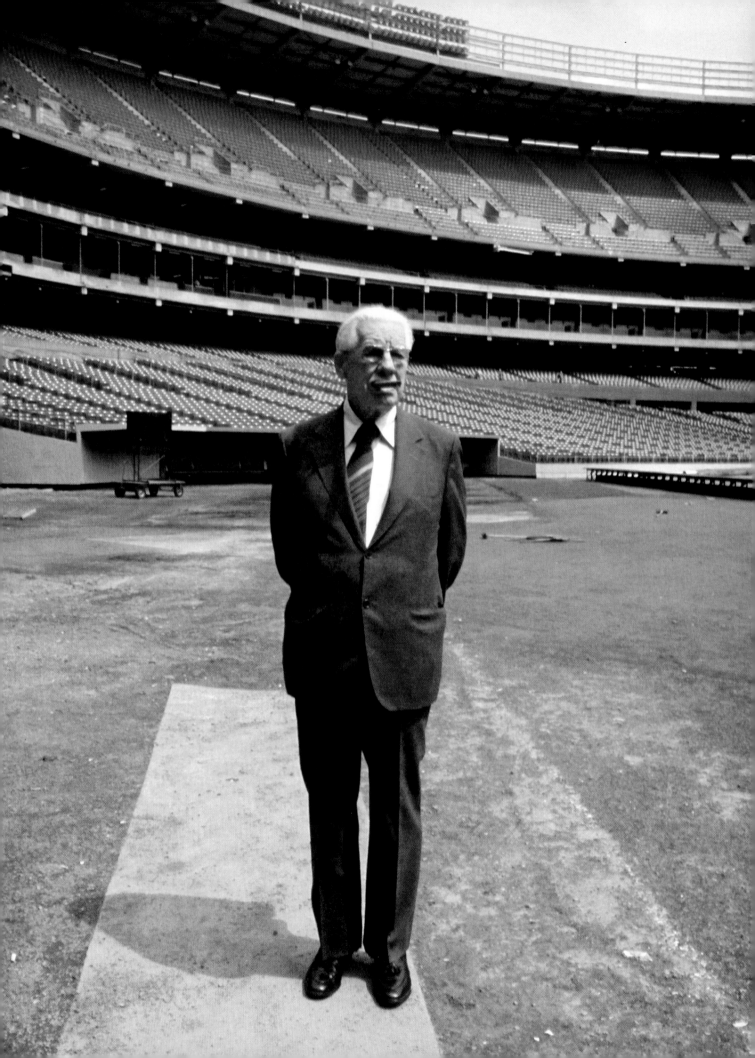

THE STEELERS IN 1979.

First row: Field Manager Jack Hart, Craig Colquitt (5), Matt Bahr (9), Terry Bradshaw (12), Mike Kruczek (15), Cliff Stoudt (18), Rocky Bleier (20), Mike Wagner (23), J. T. Thomas (24), Greg Hawthorne (27), Equipment manager Tony Parisi.

Second row: Head coach Chuck Noll, Ron Johnson (29), Larry Anderson (30), Donnie Shell (31), Franco Harris (32), Anthony Anderson (33), Sidney Thornton (38), Rick Moser (39), Mel Blount (47), Dwayne Woodruff (49), Loren Toews (51), Assistant Head Coach George Perles.

Third row: Offensive Backfield Coach Dick Hoak, Mike Webster (52), Dennis Winston (53), Zack Valentine (54), Jon Kolb (55), Robin Cole (56), Sam Davis (57), Jack Lambert

(58), Jack Ham (59), Willy Fry (60), Thom Dornbrook (63), Defensive Coordinator Robert Widenhofer.

Fourth row: Administrative Assistant Paul Uram, Steve Furness (64), Tom Beasley (65), Ted Peterson (66), Gary Dunn (67), L. C. Greenwood (68), Fred Anderson (69), Gerry Mullins (72), Joe Greene (75), John Banaszak (76), Defensive Backfield Coach Dick Walker.

Fifth row: Offensive Line Coach Rollie Dotsch, Trainer Ralph Berlin, Assistant Trainer Robert Milie, Steve Courson (77), Dwight White (78), Larry Brown (79), John Stallworth (82), Theo Bell (83), Randy Grossman (84), Jim Smith (86), Lynn Swann (88), Bennie Cunningham (89), Receiver Coach Tom Moore.

The picture was taken in Pittsburgh's Three Rivers Stadium.

SOME OF THE PIRATES FAVORITE PLAYERS

PHIL GARNER

KENT TEKULVE

DAVE PARKER

WILLIE STARGELL

the team to four Eastern Division titles and two World Series victories, retired for the fourth and final time. Three months later he died. Chuck Tanner from Oakland replaced Murtaugh. He was traded for catcher Manny Sanguillen and $100,000 in cash. Under him, the Pirates won the World Series in 1979."

"Grandpa, how do you know all this; how do you know all the facts?"

"Well my son, I can read. I have read Robert Smith's and Frederick Lieb's histories, Lou Sahadi's, Jim O'Brien's, Marty Wolfson's and Pat Livingston's books and a number of other volumes, and I got the facts from them."

"And what about the other sport teams in the city, the other Champions, the other outstanding athletes of Pittsburgh?"

"Yes, they should be remembered too. Talking of football, one cannot omit Pitt, the University of Pittsburgh's great football team, which in 1978 and 1979, under coach Jackie Sherrill, put together back-to-back 5–0 home records. The team won in 1974 the Sun Bowl, beating Kansas 38–19; in 1977 it won the Sugar Bowl, defeating Georgia 27–3; in 1979 it won the Fiesta Bowl, winning over Arizona 16–10. During the seventies the Pitt Stadium in Oakland had been renovated; it is now the finest football field in the country.

"The superb basketball teams of the city should not be forgotten either. Duquesne University has a great basketball tradition. In the sixties it was a winning team. In the first four years of the seventies they won 17, 21, 20 and 16 games respectively. But in the 1978–1979 season their record was only 13–13. However, their new coach Mike Rice, who succeeded John Cinicola in 1978, has great hopes for their future.

"The Panthers, the basketball team of the University of Pittsburgh, played unevenly in the seventies. In one year they won 25 games, while in another year they won only 5. Since 1979 their head coach has been Roy Chipman, who succeeded Buzz Ridl and Tim Grgvorich.

"The team of Carnegie-Mellon under the coaching of Dave Maloney finished 6–14 in 1975—but has done much better since then. In 1977 they won the Championship of the President's Athletic Conference.

"The basketball teams of Robert Morris, Point Park College and Allegheny Community College are greatly improving as the years go by.

STEVE NICOSIA

THE OWNER OF THE PIRATES

Courtesy John W. Galbreath

JOHN W. GALBREATH

bought the ballclub a year after the war—in 1946—together with Bing Crosby, Tom Johnson and Frank Mc-Kinney, for $2.5 million. After McKinney sold his shares, and Crosby died, Galbreath, with about 70%, and Johnson, with about 30% became the sole owners of the Pirates, the team that has won them three World Series.

The photograph shows the 81-year-old Galbreath with the 1979 Championship trophy.

THE PIRATES IN 1979

FIRST ROW, LEFT TO RIGHT: Steve Nicosia (16), Bat-boy Steve Hallahan, Batboy Steve Graff, Phil Garner (3) and Ed Ott (14).

SECOND ROW, LEFT TO RIGHT: Ed Whitson (31), Trainer Tony Bartirome, Coach Al Monchak (42), Coach Harvey Haddix, Manager Chuck Tanner (7), Coach Bob Skinner (48), Coach Joe Lonnett (32), Jim Rooker (19) and Enrique Romo (15).

THIRD ROW, LEFT TO RIGHT: Grant Jackson (23), Rennie Stennett (6), Matt Alexander (36), Manny Sanguillen (35), Tim Foli (19), John Milner (34), Mike Easler, Dale Berra (4), Lee Lacy (17), Rick Rhoden and Traveling Secretary Charles Muse.

BACK ROW, LEFT TO RIGHT: Bill Robinson (28), Bert Blyleven (22), Omar Moreno (18), Dave Parker (39), John Candelaria (95), Jim Bibby (26), Kent Tekulve (27), Willie Stargell (8), Bruce Kison (25) and Don Robinson (43).

Courtesy Pittsburgh Pirates

"The Penguins, the hockey team of Pittsburgh, play to sellout crowds in the Civic Arena. Their owner Edward J. de Bartolo has big plans for them.

"And there are many individual athletes whose achievements are acknowledged all over the country. Danny Seemiller is rated as one of the best table tennis players in America; Bruno Sammartino as an outstanding wrestler. And there are many, many more. Pittsburgh is not only the Champion City of the Steelers and the Pirates but a Champion City for other sports and athletes as well.

"One more question, Grandpa: Why do history books fail to mention sports?"

"Perhaps, because historians are old-fashioned people. They are like elephants in the circus, holding onto the tails of each other while walking in a circle."

"Is that why Uncle Jack called the championships of the Pirates and the Steelers 'ephemeral'? And is that why Uncle Felix berated my dad for allotting a whole chapter in his book to the World Champions?"

"POPS"

Willie Stargell, the head of the "fam-a-lee" was born in 1940, joined the Pirates in 1962. "Captain Willie" led his team to a World Series victory in 1979. His best seasons were in 1971 and in 1973. In 1971 he led the league with 48 homers, drove in 125 runs and hit .295; in 1973 he had 44 homers and hit .299.

Photograph by U.P.J. on October 17, 1979

THE JUBILANT PIRATES LEAVING THE FIELD AFTER WINNING THE 1979 WORLD SERIES.

Chapter 13

RENAISSANCE II

by Stefan Lorant

PITTSBURGH MOVED into the eighties with a buoyant spirit. The years of austerity, the years of stagnation were over. The future looked bright; there was a sense of excitement in the air.

Under the Flaherty administration, the accent was on saving, on retrenchment. It was a leveling-off period. By the beginning of the eighties the city was on the move again.

Mayor Flaherty resigned in April 1977 to become deputy attorney general in the Carter administration and was succeeded by Richard Caliguiri.

The new mayor's first aim was to repair the rift between the public and private sector. Flaherty's "doing alone" policy antagonized the business community; businessmen felt they were left on the sidelines by the city government. Not much love was lost between City Hall and the Allegheny Conference. Because of the distrust between the two sectors, it was hard to reach a consensus on any project. Caliguiri realized that without the cooperation of the corporate and financial business leaders, Pittsburgh's future looked bleak indeed.

"I have tried to establish partnership with the private sector" he said, "and I have attempted to make the people once more interested in the continuing rebuilding and improving of their city." In this he was eminently successful. By the eighties business and government were working partners again.

Early in his term Caliguiri presented a comprehensive program for Pittsburgh's future. He called it Renaissance II. It was to be the continuation of the first Renaissance, the era which began in the late forties and continued through the fifties. People remembered that period

mainly because of two major changes in the environment: 1) the elimination of smoke and the harnessing of the rivers (smoke and flood control); and 2) the rebuilding and rejuvenation of the Golden Triangle.

After those great projects were realized, the excitement simmered down. Pittsburgh grew tired; the steam went out of it. Many of the key figures who instigated the first Renaissance—David L. Lawrence, Richard K. Mellon, Edgar Kaufmann, Arthur Van Buskirk—were dead —and the new men who followed them lacked their spirit.

It took two decades and more before the exuberant spirit of the fifties returned. By 1980, Pittsburghers were once more full of plans, anxious to make things happen.

Says Paul Long, the popular newscaster: "Pittsburgh is off and running." Comments Herbert Berger, the genial President of Creamer Advertising Agency: "The city has moxie . . . it also has the money and the horsepower." Exclaims John P. Robin, Chairman of the Urban Redevelopment Authority: "Pittsburgh is one of the most fortunate cities on the Eastern seaboard, it is definitely on the move again."

Such optimism is infectious, such spirit is catching.

In 1980 Renaissance II was clearly on the march. Announcement followed announcement about projected new office buildings in the downtown area.

The corporations were badly in need of additional space. The Building Owners and Manager's Association reported that 99.3% of the downtown offices were occupied. There was no space for expansion. The city government became concerned that some of the corporations might leave to set up offices elsewhere.

Then came the news and it came with a bang. Not one, not two, but five huge office buildings were to be constructed in downtown, adding 4 million square feet of office space to the existing 20 million. It was estimated that the cost of the developments in the Golden Triangle alone during the first half of the eighties would come to a billion dollars.

The five office buildings were soon under construction. Builders were busily at work on the Dravo Building at Grant Street, on PPG Headquarters near Market Square, on Riverfront Center at Stanwix Street and Fort Pitt Boulevard, on Oxford Center at Grant and Smithfield, on 2 Chatham Center in the upper Triangle.

The Dravo Building, a 54-story skyscraper constructed by the U.S. Steel Realty Development Division on a five-and-a-half acre site, will dramatically affect both the skyline and ambience of Grant Street. It will be one of the most prominent manifestations of Renaissance II. Its main tenant is the Dravo Corporation with 15,000 employees and a billion dollars in annual revenue.

The eight-sided edifice will rise 725½ feet above Grant Street, providing 1,700,000 square feet of office and commercial space. A garage on two lower levels will accommodate parking space for 3,000 cars.

Designed by Weldon Becket and Associates, the project entails the first and most significant move by the private sector to carry out the development which has been tried unsuccessfully for many years by an intergovernmental and public-private partnership.

The tower will complement the other structures on Grant Street—the Romanesque County Courthouse, the Gothic Union Trust Building, the William Penn Hotel, the U.S. Steel headquarters, the Gulf Oil Building, the Koppers Tower. It will cost well over $100 million.

The other large office complex in construction is the headquarters of PPG Industries (the former Pittsburgh Plate and Glass Company) in the Market Square area. The 40-story reflective glass tower will have a million square feet of office space, while in the surrounding buildings there will be about 600,000 more square feet.

Designed by the architectural firm of Philip Johnson and John Burgee, the building will have a crenelated roofline of small tower peaks and indented walls reminiscent of the British Parliament in London. The walls will be right-angled to "re-reflect themselves." Because of the modification of glass-cladding, it will glitter with the passage of the sun.

After the announcement of the PPG project a controversy developed over the building site. The city, in an effort to help PPG Industries to put up its edifice, condemned the area under the eminent domain code and declared it "blighted." The owners of five small businesses opposed the landtaking procedure. Their protest delayed construction by well over a year.

They could not understand why they should be driven from their premises. They argued that the city had no right to their buildings and joined together in protest.

Ned and Paul Cass of the Cass Plumbing & Heating Company, William Jacobowitz of Federal Paint & Hardware, Louise Kerner of Frank H. Kerner Catholic Book Store, Robert Ginsburg of Market Rug Company, and the Troiani brothers, owners of several parking lots, engaged lawyer Thomas J. Dempsey and brought suits against the city, against the Urban Redevelopment Authority and against PPG. The legal battle lasted for 15 months. It was a thrilling David-Goliath fight—five small

JOHN P. ROBIN, who as a young man served under Mayor Lawrence on the Urban Redevelopment Authority, became the Authority's Director in 1948.

In 1955 he left Pittsburgh to work on urban projects in Philadelphia, in India and Africa. Since his return in 1970 he served as program advisor of the Allegheny Conference and Chairman of the Urban Redevelopment Authority.

Photograph specially taken for this book in 1980 by Joel Librizzi

THE MAYOR OF THE CITY: RICHARD S. CALIGUIRI IN 1980.

He succeeded Peter F. Flaherty in the spring of 1977 when Flaherty became U.S. Deputy Attorney General in Washington. In the general election later that year Caliguiri was elected to a full four year term as Mayor.

He labeled his program "Renaissance II" asking for "the improvement of the quality of life in the neighborhoods, and improvement of the business and economic climate by encouraging private investment and development, to provide new job opportunities and expand the city's tax base."

His proposals received wide support. By 1980 five major office buildings in downtown were in construction, which will add 4 million square feet of office space in the Golden Triangle.

Caliguiri, a popular mayor, is a low-key politician. In a schoolboy essay a youngster wrote of him: "I remember everything on that city's mayor except who his name."

merchants against a giant corporation. And while it lasted there could be no groundbreaking.

At last, in the summer of 1980, a settlement was effected. Its terms: PPG Industries agreed to erect for the five businesses not far from their present location a brand-new two-story building square by square. In exchange for this the merchants would give up their land and buildings to PPG. The Troianis, who owned land, on which they operated their five parking lots, were to receive some $2 million in cash and the right to lease a

555

THOMAS C. GRAHAM, since 1974 president and chief executive officer of Jones & Laughlin Steel Corporation, the nation's third largest steel producer. J&L has large integrated steel plants in Pittsburgh and in other places in the east and midwest. With total employment of 38,000 the company has a yearly raw steel production capability of about 9.3 million tons of finished steel products. Its sales in 1979 totaled $4.1 billion.

ROBERT J. BUCKLEY is Chairman, President and Chief Executive Officer of Allegheny Ludlum Industries—a vast multi-national multi-product specialty manufacturing company.

Allegheny Ludlum Industries is a diversified company with more than 40,000 employees at 180 locations in the U.S. and abroad. Its annual sales top 1.5 billion dollars. In the first six months of 1980 the company's earnings were over $40 million.

ANTHONY O'REILLY
President and Chief Executive officer of the H. J. Heinz Company since 1979.

HOWARD M. LOVE
President and Chief Executive officer of National Steel Corporation since 1980.

parking space in the new complex.

With the lawsuit dropped (PPG assuming all legal costs), the $100 million project could finally proceed.

The third office building to go up in downtown, called Riverfront Center, is a 20-story tower at the corner of Stanwix Street and Fort Pitt Boulevard. The 364,000 square foot structure, designed by the architectural firm Skidmore, Owings, and Merrill, is to be built by the Oliver Tyrone Corporation in partnership with the Hartford, Connecticut, based Aetna Life Casualty.

One Oxford Center, the fourth new commercial building in downtown, will have 41 floors of offices, five floors of retail space and a parking garage for 900 cars. It was designed by Hellmuth, Obata & Kassabaum, the architects of Washington's Air and Space Museum, and is a joint venture of the Oxford Development Company

JERRY MCAFEE, Chairman and Chief Executive Officer of Gulf Oil Corporation since 1976. Gulf Oil is the nation's seventh largest petroleum producer and fifth largest gasoline marketer, with assets of more than $17 billion, gross operating revenues of nearly $26 billion, and a total worldwide employment of 58,000. The company's facilities worldwide process on the average about 1.7 million barrels of oil every single day.

DAVID M. RODERICK is the 10th board chairman of United States Steel, the 14th largest U. S. corporation according to *Fortune* magazine. U. S. Steel's activities have steadily diversified throughout its history. Today, its 171,000 employees are engaged in five major lines of business, including: steel manufacturing, chemicals, resource development, fabricating and engineering, and domestic transportation and utilities.

and the Edward J. De Bartolo Company of Youngstown. Mellon Banks headed a consortium providing $92 million toward its cost.

The fifth office building in construction is a 16-story tower—2 Chatham Center—in the upper Triangle. Financed by the Prudential Insurance Company, it will contain 18,200 square feet of new office space and complement its sister building, 1 Chatham Center.

The construction of the five buildings is visible proof that Caliguiri's Renaissance II was not an empty slogan. Their completion will change the appearance of downtown and will encourage private developers to pursue new projects. They will show that Pittsburghers have faith in their city, faith in its future.

The physical transformation of downtown will be further enhanced when the Convention Center and the

STANTON WILLIAMS
Chairman of the board of directors and Chief Executive officer of PPG since 1979.

ROBERT ANDERSON
Chairman and Chief Executive officer of Rockwell International Corporation.

Heinz Hall Plaza will be opened.

The David L. Lawrence Convention Center at Park Avenue and Tenth Street cannot be considered a Renaissance II project. It had been discussed for many years, its construction went on for many more.

It will have an exhibit capacity of 135,000 square feet and could accommodate 12,000 people, with a main hall as large as two football fields put together, big enough for any convention. The $30 million structure was designed by Celli-Flynn Associates.

At the adjacent site, on the land owned by the Urban Redevelopment Authority, a new hotel will rise; its estimated cost is $125,800,000. Called Vista International Pittsburgh it will be operated by Hilton International. The 615 room hotel will have 500,000 square feet for offices.

The center and the hotel will be a catalyst for restoration, reconstruction and renewal of the entire area.

Heinz Hall Plaza—the new public park in downtown

(turn to page 562)

SMALL:
TARASI & TIGHE practice in a picturesque house off Grant Street.

LAW FIRMS IN THE CITY:

Photographed specially for this book by Alan Sperling in September 1980

LARGE:

REED SMITH SHAW & McCLAY, Pittsburgh's largest and most prestigious law firm was founded in 1877.

In 1980, one hundred and three years after its founding the firm had 74 partners, including those in Washington, Philadelphia and Harrisburg.

In the photograph taken especially for this book 39 of the partners are shown.

From left to right, seated around the table: J. L. Smith, Jr., C. E. Glock, Jr., E. K. Trent, R. J. Dodds, Jr., E. W. Marsh, D. McNeil Olds, G. J. Helwig, W. T. McGough.

From left to right standing: H. H. Weil, G. C. Paris, J. McN. Cramer, B. S. McMillin, T. Todd, R. T. Wentley, S. F. Zimmerman, L. A. Rau, R. G. Lovett

(back), J. H. Hill, J. H. Hardie, W. P. DeForest, W. E. Miller, Jr., R. J. Dodds III, E. W. Seifert, J. Van Buskirk, W. J. Smith, A. N. Farley, D. I. Booker, P. Denby, J. H. McConomy, E. P. Reif, R. W. Hartland, A. T. Stein, J. H. Demmler, R. C. Wiegand, J. Q. Harty, W. P. Hackney, E. R. Dell, D. C. Auten, J. S. McLaughlin.

MEDIUM:

Photographed specially for this book in 1980 by Joel Librizzi

MEYER, DARRAGH, BUCKLER, BEBENEK & ECK is one of the city's medium-sized law firms. It was founded in 1913.

The partners shown in the photograph seated left to right: W. Pietragallo, R. J. Mills, J. E. Kunz, K. Darragh, H. J. Zimmer, J. E. Hall.

Standing from l. to r.: R. H. Conaway, P. B. Hart, A. J. Banyas, III, R. A. Nedwick, S. D. Hirschberg, G. I. Buckler, J. A. Mollica, Jr., D. H. Patterson, A. J. Murphy, Jr., T. J. Ward.

Not present when picture was taken: D. W. Bebenek, C. A. Eck, T. A. Lazaroff, F. C. Trenor, II, J. Bosick, L. B. Loughren.

Photographed specially for this book in 1980 by Joel Librizzi

THOMAS J. SMITH,

Chairman and Chief Executive Officer since 1978 of Ketchum MacLeod & Grove, Pittsburgh's largest advertising agency.

In his business dealings, Smith adheres to a four-point philosophy: 1. involvement, 2. disciplined marketing 3. idea generation and 4. accountability.

Ketchum MacLeod & Grave's yearly billing in the U.S. and overseas is in excess of $70 million.

HERBERT F. BURGER,

President and General Manager of Creamer Inc. The agency has been in Pittsburgh for 25 years and serves such clients as Alcoa (aluminum), Stouffers (frozen foods), Ryan Homes (homebuilding), Penn's Southwest (regional development), Equibank (banking), Joy Manufacturing (mining equipment). Creamer is a major producer of television commercials and has 94 professional people on staff. Its Pittsburgh office bills $40 million.

THE KETCHUM MANAGEMENT TEAM: from l. to r.: John Mather, marketing and research director; Ray Werner, creative director; Herb Gordon, operations director; (Mather, Werner and Gordon are also senior vice-presidents of Ketchum.) Thomas J. Smith, Chairman and Les Gallagher, President of the firm.

THE CREAMER TEAM: from l. to r.: Albert H. Kiefer, Associate Creative Director; James M. Nellis, Public Relations; President Herbert F. Burger, Richard J. Weber, Group Manager; William E. Sprague, Executive Vice President; Allan Linderman, Media Director; John Waldron, Creative Director of Creamer.

Photographs by Norman W. Schumm

A 1980 PORTFOLIO OF SEVEN COLOR PHOTOGRAPHS BY NORMAN W. SCHUMM

561

—is also in its final stage of construction. Before the first Renaissance, the only open spaces in downtown Pittsburgh were the parking lots for cars. In the ensuing years, Point Lake Park and Mellon Square were created, Market Square was rejuvenated and reborn, and now Heinz Hall Plaza, a public park extension of Heinz Hall for the Performing Arts, will bring the number of parks in downtown to four.

Two of the principal aims of Renaissance II are the expansion of the core of the city and the improvement and revaluation of the neighborhoods.

Says John Robin about the first aim:

"Pittsburgh in the eighties is overcoming the constraints of its urban geography: the steep hills, the broad rivers, the narrow flatlands. For the first time in the city's history there is an opportunity to treat Central Pittsburgh—the heartland of the urban region—as an integrated whole." This means that the Triangle, no longer a separate entity, could be meshed with its adjacent areas —it could expand to the South Side and the lower North Side, to Mt. Washington, to the Hill District, the Strip and even as far as Oakland.

Says Mayor Caliguiri about the second aim:

"The keystone to Renaissance II lies in the neighborhoods. The first thing I wanted to do was to get the neighborhoods improved. To improve the quality of its streets, of its bridges, of its sewer lines, of its water lines, all of which were getting old and dilapidated. Thus I devised a program to solve these problems."

But back to the first point—the expansion of the core of the city. Says Mayor Caliguiri: "What we are trying to do is to give the Triangle some more rooom to breathe, open it up a little, to brighten up the dark areas and finally, to use all of the area."

With the restoration at Station Square, a $30 million project, Renaissance II jumped over the river, bringing the renewal program to the South Side. The old Pitts-

Color photographs taken for this book in 1980 by Norman Schumm

burgh and Lake Erie railroad station was converted into a spectacular restaurant.

In a relatively short time the project grew into a lucrative commercial venture; its Freight House Shopping Mall, a conglomerate of boutiques, specialty shops and restaurants, were fully rented and flourishing. The construction of the Sheraton Motor Inn in the area is in its final stage of completion.

Station Square turned out to be just as successful as Faneuil Hall Market in Boston and Ghirardelli Square in San Francisco.

As to bringing Renaissance II to the North Shore, there are plans under way to expand the Triangle over the Allegheny River, to redevelop the 116 acres between the Three Rivers Stadium and the Heinz Company plant, which at present is an urban desert, sterile in terms of tax yield and employment. Its redevelopment had been discussed for decades, but nothing came out of it; all the plans were shelved. But by the eighties new plans were considered for a number of high-rise, high income housing, also for condominiums and marinas.

Once the development is completed, the link between Allegheny Center and the Triangle will be established. The renewal of the area will probably lead to the renewal of the entire North Side, where—according to the 1977 Allegheny Conference Report—"the Manchester area is being renewed through an assisted program of historic restoration, and where the Mexican War Streets and Allegheny West are prime examples of the growing trend toward neighborhood conservation by private and personal investment."

As to the problems of the neighborhoods, housing is the most pressing. Funds are appropriated for new constructions to foster residential and commercial development. It was found that rather than tear down old houses, it made more sense to renovate them. Many of the buildings erected a century ago were built well, with good material, on solid foundations. Thus, low-interest loans were offered to those who promised to renovate their homes. "We've gone through at least two $20-million bond loans for this program and we're ready to embark upon another one" says the mayor. Low-interest mortgages were given to people who would buy old houses elsewhere in the city and rehabilitate them.

*

But Renaissance II is more than brick and mortar; it goes well beyond buildings. It is a comprehensive philosophical concept. It is a program for a new kind of environment. Building, construction and renovation are only one phase of it. The other is the preservation and beautification of the area's natural features. There are plans afoot to beautify the riverfront—on both shores of the Allegheny—with new walks, jogging ways, marinas. The reconstruction will extend from Clemente Park to Herrs Island and from Point State Park to the 31st Street bridge.

(turn to page 570)

THE PITTSBURGH BALLET THEATRE

Photos: Gustavo Lago

A FOOTBALL PLAYER AMONG THE BALLERINAS OF THE FUTURE

The School of the Ballet Theatre, which opened in the fall of 1979, is visited by football star Lynn Swann. The 200 students of the school, from eighth year up, study and train under the guidance of professional dancers.

Photographed by Norman W. Schumm

SCENES FROM THE BALLET THEATRE REPERTOIRE. ON THE LEFT: *CELEBRATION*, ON THE RIGHT *MOBILE*.

PITT STADIUM
IN 1980.

The Pennsylvania legislature has already appropriated $4.5 million for the project; funds are in hand for the acquisition of Nine Mile Island, Twelve Mile Island, Fourteen Mile Island and some of Herrs Island.

*

The Western Pennsylvania Conservancy, the leading environmental organization in the area, is instrumental to preserve much of the area's natural features. Since its inception it acquired 80,000 acres of land, then transferred it to federal, state and local public agencies.

The Conservancy's largest acquisition, the 12,670-acre Cherry Run project in Centre and Clinton Counties is a habitat for white-tailed deer, wild turkey, black bear and other forest wild life. It will become a permanent gameland under the auspices of the Pennsylvania Game Commission, providing watershed protection for five mountain streams, among them Cherry Run, the "Wilderness Trout Stream."

To protect the scenic shoreline and islands along the Allegheny River is another aim of the Conservancy. Most of the 7,000 acres of land which it bought was sold to the Allegheny National Forest. Another acquisition, the 26 miles of abandoned railroad right-of-way in Fayette County, will be made into a hiking and biking trail. Not many people are familiar with this wildland that winds along the Youghiogheny River beneath 900-foot bluffs from Confluence through Ohiopyle to Bruner Run.

Money for the above projects came from Pittsburgh foundations. Since the land was almost sold at cost the funds keep rolling over.

Among the Conservancy's smaller acquisitions are the 3,500 acre-Bear Run Nature Reserve, the 90 acres of Beechwood Farms Nature Reserve, the 310 Jennings Nature Reserve, the 300-acre Wildflower Reserve, the 30 acres of 14 Mile Island, the 220 acres of Pine Swamp, the 100 acres of Wolf Creek Narrows, one of the loveliest natural areas with hemlock-ravine and beech-maple forests.

*

Pittsburgh learned a great deal from its first Renaissance. Some of the buildings which went up during that period were of undistinguished design. Renaissance II has

(turn to page 574)

DEPARTMENT STORES

GIMBELS' Chief Executive is Harvey Sanford, with a long career in retailing.

The Gimbels store in Pittsburgh—part of a 38-store chain—is a subsidiary of

Brown & Williamson Industries, which is owned by British American Tobacco Co.

JOSEPH HORNE's President Joseph Vales was born in Spain and is a graduate of New York's Columbia University. Horne belongs to one of the largest department chains in the country, specializing in fine quality merchandise.

KAUFMANN'S President and Chief Executive Officer is William T. Tobin, a graduate of Lawrenceville School and Yale University. Founded by the Kaufmann Brothers in 1870, the firm now has nine branch stores in the Pittsburgh area.

THE MINISKIRT OF THE SEVENTIES (see pages 488–491) IS SUPERSEDED BY THE SPLIT SKIRT OF THE EIGHTIES.

Photographed specially for this book in the summer of 1980 by Joel Librizzi

THOUGH FASHION TRENDS HAVE CHANGED, THE WOMEN OF PITTSBURGH REMAIN AS BEAUTIFUL AS EVER.

a greater sensitivity to architectural quality and the amenities of urbanism.

*

Renaissance II attempts to enter all aspects of human endeavor.

In the past Pittsburgh was regarded as a city of steel, a city of coal, a city of glass, a city of corporations, a city of the Mellons', of the Heinz's, of the Hillman's. Not many realize that Pittsburgh is also a city of culture, a city of vital research for the country, a city of universities, a city of music and art. A few facts might prove the point. In 1980 the enrollment at the University of Pittsburgh was 34,010; Carnegie-Mellon had 5,644 students; Duquesne University, 6,766, Chatham College, 636; the Allegheny Community College, 16,124.

Pittsburgh has a vigorous art life with many artists, painters and sculptors creating in its confines. The Scaife Gallery—perhaps the most beautiful modern gallery in the world—is teeming with visitors, young and old, admiring the exhibitions.

(turn to page 578)

A SUMMER MORNING IN 1980 at the corner of Smithfield and Fifth Avenue. Much has been changed since a photographer

Photographed specially for this book in 1980 by Joel Librizzi

took the picture in the 1920's from almost the same spot (see page 273), but much has remained the same. The clock before Kaufmann's is still at the same place, and people are still busily shopping. But there are no more horse-drawn carriages.

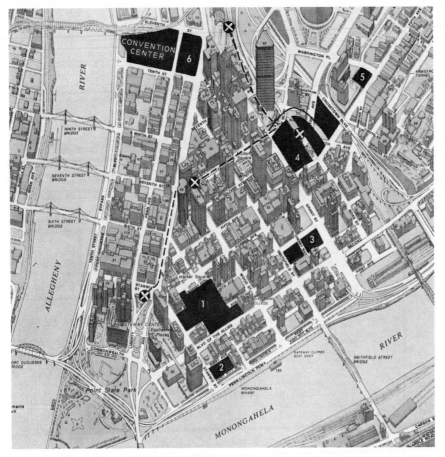

THE SITES: #1. P.P.G. Headquarters; #2. Riverfront Center; #3. One Oxford Center; #4. Dravo Headquarters; #5. Two Chatham Center; #6. Convention Hotel.

THE

BUILDING BOOM

IN THE

EIGHTIES

ONE OXFORD CENTRE (#3) a 46-story structure, designed by Hellmuth, Obata & Kassabaum, expected to be ready for occupancy in the spring of 1982.

RIVERFRONT CENTER (#2) a 20-story building, designed by Skidmore Owings & Merrill, is built by Oliver Tyrone Corporation and Aetna Life.

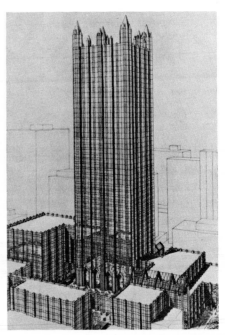

P.P.G. INDUSTRIES 40-story building (#1) designed by Johnson/Burgee, a $100 million complex on a five acre site next to Market Square in downtown.

Courtesy: United States Steel

THE CHANGING CITY. The Dravo Building (#4) to be built by U.S. Steel will rise on the site where the Carlton House stood before. It will be a 54-story high skyscraper with 1,700,000 square feet of office and commercial space. The building was designed by Welton Becket Associates and is expected to be ready for occupancy by the year of 1983.

Courtesy: Prudential Insurance Company

2 CHATHAM CENTER (#5) a 16-story office tower, is to be built by the Prudential Insurance Company. The architects are Burt Hill Kosar Rittlemann and Associates and Langdon & Wilson.

Courtesy: Urban Redevelopment Authority

THE HOTEL NEXT TO THE CONVENTION HALL (#6) will be called Vista International Pittsburgh. The architects of the 615 room hostelry are Burt Hill Kosar Rittlemann Associates, the Architects Collaborative and Urban Design Associates.

577

Photographed specially for this book in 1980 by Joel Librizzi

SUMMER IN PITTSBURGH: A BAND GIVES A LUNCHEON CONCERT IN THE PLAZA OF GATEWAY CENTER.

The symphony draws capacity audiences. Under André Previn, the former Hollywood composer and pianist, and principal conductor of the London Symphony Orchestra, the orchestra regained its former glory. Once more it is regarded as one of the leading orchestras in the world. Its tours in the United States and in Europe are highly successful. Its television show, "Previn and' the Pittsburgh," is very popular. Its records sell exceedingly well.

"If anything is wrong here, it's that the sport teams are the pride of Pittsburgh and not the orchestra," complained Previn in a lighthearted way to *Newsweek*. "But you can't send the football team to Vienna."

Yet, Pittsburghers are proud of their orchestra. And they are proud of their Ballet Theatre, a classical ballet company with 38 dancers under the artistic leadership of Patrick Frantz, a former principal dancer at the Paris Opera. Founded in 1969, it gives 32 performances a year in Heinz Hall, 60 performances on tour, and 70 lecture

GREENERY ON THE WALL.

Photograph by Norman Schumm, taken in August 1980

SUMMER IN PITTSBURGH: THE THREE RIVER REGATTA, A SPECTACULAR TWO DAY EVENT.

demonstrations. It also performs in hospitals, nursing homes, in school auditoriums and parks.

Its repertoire has a wide range—in the 1980–1981 season its main attractions were *Swan Lake, Romeo and Juliet, Les Sylphides, Giselle, Petrouchka, Sleeping Beauty, Nutcracker Suite,* and *La Ventana, Barre Inn the Tavern, Harp Concerto Pas de Deux.*

The Ballet Theatre's guiding spirit is Mrs. Leon Falk, who with unfailing energy and enthusiasm keeps the company going, confident of its future. The budget figures give an idea of the scope of the organization. In the 1980–1981 season, total operating expenses were projected to be $1,778,032, with an earned income of $1,204,700. Mrs. Falk expects that the more than half a million deficit will be made up by contributions from corporations, foundations and those in the city who love ballet. "Now that we have survived our first decade, I do not believe that Pittsburgh will let us down," she says.

The Arts and Crafts Center, founded in 1944 and

PIGEONS AT MARKET SQUARE.

579

located in the former mansions on Fifth Avenue, is perhaps the most comprehensive community cultural center in the land. It arranges monthly exhibitions for some of its 1,700 artist members and in its Mart it sells handmade jewelry, enameled ware, ceramics, glass, weavings, embroidery, worked metal, wood and plastics, prints, paintings and drawings, photographs and sculptures, all created by the artists of the area. Its four-semester school has an annual enrollment of 4,500. There are classes and workshops in the arts, crafts, and dance, it offers classes in ceramics, Raku, calligraphy, chair caning, ballet, drawing and painting, quilting, weaving, jewelry design, etching, silk screen printmaking, sculpturing in clay, metal

and wood, stained glass, photography and woodworking.

The Arts and Crafts Center acts as an umbrella for a number of participating art organizations, like the Amateur Artists Association, Associated Artists of Pittsburgh, the Pittsburgh Parent Group, the Photo Imagers, the Pittsburgh Society of Artists, the Pittsburgh Water Color Society, the Society of Sculptors, and the Weaver's Guild. This unique organization teaches art, it induces people to appreciate art and it involves them in art projects.

*

Now a word about the theatre, the weakest link in Pittsburgh's art life. The city was never a theatre town,

THE NINETEEN NATIONALITY ROOMS IN THE UNIVERSITY OF PITTSBURGH ARE

RUSSIAN, Design Andrey Avinoff

ENGLISH, Design Albert Klimcheck

FRENCH, Design Jacques Carlu

GREEK, Design John Travlos

LITHUANIAN, Design Antanas Gudaitis

HUNGARIAN, Design Dénes Györgyi

ROMANIAN, Design N. Ghica-Budesti

SCOTTISH, Design Reginald Fairlié

SWEDISH, Design Carl Milles

even though many well-known playwrights and actors were born there. In the past, the shows from Broadway were imported and were presented in the old Nixon Theatre. Those days are gone. The Nixon Theatre fell to the wrecker and became a parking lot; the Pittsburgh Playhouse in Oakland declared bankruptcy in 1973, then it opened again.

Though in general Pittsburghers favor musicals, and light plays, there is a variety of theatre offerings, commercial and experimental alike.

The only professional residential Equity company in the city which made great strides since its founding in 1975 is the Pittsburgh Public Theatre, which under the

(turn to page 585)

DESIGNATED "HISTORIC LANDMARKS."

The EARLY AMERICAN Room was designed by Theodore Bowman

Color photographs © Herbert K. Barnett

GERMAN, Design Frank Linder

CZECHOSLOVAK, Design Bohumil Sláma

ITALIAN, Design Ezio Cerpi

IRISH, Design Harold Leask

NORWEGIAN, Design George Eliassen

POLISH, Design A. Szyszki-Bohuz

YUGOSLAV, Design Vojta Branis

CHINESE, Design Teng Kwei

SYRIA-LEBANON, Designer not known

LORI HORNELL excels in architectural weaving and tapestry. She is an artist in fiber, a weaver and a colorist in fabric. "I design and build a feeling that has dimension, color and motion" she says. Her innovative creations decorate a number of Pittsburgh's commercial buildings and are in many private collections in the city and all across the county.

left:
HENRY KOERNER a charming, outrageous, outspoken Viennese, says what comes into his mind. During the fifties and sixties he painted dozens of covers for TIME magazine. His credo: "I simply paint in each picture always the same story—the relationship of man to woman, man to man, man to his surroundings, man to himself."

When asked about the title of the painting he answered: "GETHSEMANE (the scene of the agony and arrest of Jesus)." Did he paint it in his studio? "I do not have a stupid studio. The whole world is my studio."

right:
IRENE PASINSKI, an industrial designer and aluminium plexi-glass sculptor, is one of Pittsburgh's innovative artists.

Photographs specially made for this book in 1980 by Joel Librizzi

DOUGLAS PICKERING is professor of Art and Design at Carnegie-Mellon University since 1960. A versatile artist, he works in many mediums. His 28 foot tall marble and stainless steel sculpture "Pittsburgh Reflections" decorates Century III Mall in West Mifflin. "It is meant to be seen," says Pickering "as something bright and beautiful."

583

Photographed specially for this book in 1980 by Joel Librizzi

GRAFFITI OF A LOVE-STRICKEN SWAIN ON THE WALL OF A DOWNTOWN BUILDING

imaginative leadership of Ben Shaktman give performances of the classics and of contemporary plays. Among
the plays in the 1980/1981 season is Shakespeare's *The
Two Gentlemen of Verona*, Arthur Miller's *Death of a
Salesman*, Berthold Brecht's *Galileo*. Unfortunately, the
scaffold-seated Allegheny Theatre where the company
performs, is not the best place for serious plays. Yet, the
company is a great success; its subscriptions have grown
within five years to 10,000.

The Civic Light Opera have its staunch supporters;
Pittsburghers who flock to operettas. When the Broad-

way musical *Chorus Line* came to town, it played to
capacity audiences for a long time.

The 4000 seat Stanley Theatre opened its doors to
Broadway musicals; its "Annie" will be followed by "The
King and I." Heinz Hall too has its popular Broadway
season.

Of the smaller local groups, the City Theatre Company
leads the way. It shares the Allegheny Theatre with the
Pittsburgh Public Theatre; it also gives performances in
schools, universities, senior citizen centers and other
places.

Photo: Joel Librizzi
SUNDAY BRUNCH
in Grand Concourse,
the restaurant in the
renovated Pittsburgh & Lake
Erie Railroad Station.

585

IN THE PRESBYTERIAN CHURCH at Sixth Avenue, guest minister Bruce W. Thielemann delivers the Sunday sermon, substituting for the vacationing senior Pastor Ernest J. Lewis.

place where they perform; and there is the *Pittsburgh Savoyards*, true to their Gilbert and Sullivan tradition. So the theatre in Pittsburgh, both commercial and experimental is alive and kicking.

*

Renaissance II is developing in time of national economic stress. It offers Pittsburgh a golden opportunity to improve upon its economic stability in the eighties.

But not everyone is enthusiastic about Renaissance II. Some of its critics point out that it takes little count of the poor, of the blacks, and of the workers who lost or will lose their jobs. They say that the economic developments help only the big corporations, that it is an elitist program, that it wants to reshape Pittsburgh into a

Of the experimental theater groups, the Pittsburgh Laboratory Theatre is the most prominent. It acquired the Lion Walk Performing Arts Center on Baum Boulevard and it expects to share its stage with other experimental groups like the Metro, the Allegheny Repertory Company, the Theatre Express.

And there are a host of other companies, operating under catching names.

There is a group called *The Fine Line*, there is another group called the *Iron Clad Agreement*, there is *The 99 Cent Floating Theatre* of the University of Pittsburgh students, there is *The Pennsylvania Repertory Theatre*, formed by teachers and students of the Allegheny Country Community College, there is the *Mattress Factory* on the North Side which took its name from the

AT SAINT PAUL CATHEDRAL, during a Sunday Mass that was conducted during the absence of Bishop Vincent M. Leonard by John E. Kozar, the associate Pastor of the Church.

city of the well-to-do. To a newspaper interviewer Mayor Caliguiri has said: "We don't need 700,000 residents in Pittsburgh, as we had in 1970. I'd rather have less people with high incomes than more people with relatively low earning and spending power."

Is the Mayor's statement a portent for the future? Will Pittsburgh become, by the end of the century, a city of the rich?

*

While Renaissance II is successful in several different areas, in others it is lagging.

Transportation facilities are still not what they should be. Though progress has been made during the past years, it is not enough. Only the South Busway has been

Photographs taken specially for this book in the summer of 1980 by Joel Librizzi

AT RODEF SHALOM TEMPLE, the home of the oldest Jewish congregation in the city, the regular services are usually held by Rabbi Walter Jacob, who succeeded Rabbi Salomon B. Freehof.

IN TRINITY CATHEDRAL, the city's oldest Episcopal Church, the Reverend George L. W. Werner conducts a service in August while Bishop Robert B. Appleyard is on vacation.

completed; the East Busway is still under construction. When finished, it will be the first exclusive travel artery for buses in the country, providing express bus service to and from Shadyside, East Liberty, Homewood, Wilkinsburg, Swissvale and Edgewood. It is not expected to be ready till 1982.

The vehicles for the Light Rail Transit System will not run on the crowded downtown streets, but will move to the Triangle in a subway corridor from Grant Street to Gateway Center. The subway will be built under Sixth Avenue. Underground stations are planned at Penn-Central Station, at Grant Street, Wood Street, and Gateway Center. $600 million will be spent on the PAT program.

Other negative aspects: Housing for the less affluent

The painted bodies receive final inspection in the paint department before they begin their trip along the mile-and-a-half long line.

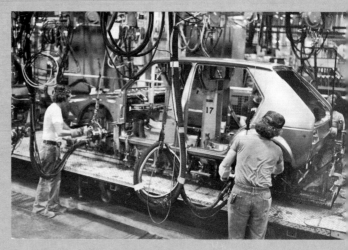

Twenty-three body shells on the oval-shaped framing line are in stages of production at any one time in this portion of the plant.

The crews of the paint department spray all the inner parts of the completed body which the automatic equipment cannot reach.

Special welding is accomplished on the trunnion line. The body shells rotate 90 degrees to either side, so welding can be done easier.

and the poor is a continuous problem. The housing industry is in a serious depression and many projects had to be postponed.

The maintenance of streets and bridges, though better than before, is still far from perfect. The potholes in the streets infuriate drivers; bridges are frequently closed down.

Says the 1979 report of the Allegheny Conference:

"A standard fault of public ownership—the failure to apply preventive maintenance—is showing itself at the Three Rivers Stadium, the Civic Arena, Mellon Square, the older garages of the Public Parking Authority and in the bridges which are so important to the Pittsburgh urban region."

However, progress has been made and the authorities are aware of the faults and are determined to correct them.

Another serious problem which needs solving is the high unemployment rate among the young people, particularly among black youth.

When asked about the future, Robert Pease, Executive Director of the Allegheny Conference, mused, "I can list at random some of the problems which we have to tackle in the eighties: building housing in the downtown area, enticing people to move back and live in the heart of the city; to improve on air and water pollution; to beautify the surroundings; to create green strips along the waterfront; to ease transportation by expanding the Rapid

With doors in place, the front fender is mounted in the body shop. The plant employs 5500 people, its weekly payroll is $2 million.

Gasoline and Diesel engines, completed at VW Westmoreland, are installed on a special system for an 18-minute operational test.

Each instrument panel of the Volkswagen Rabbit is carefully checked for proper performance before it is installed in the vehicle.

The completed cars reach the end of the final assembly line. They are now ready for delivery to the dealers by rail cars or carriers.

Transit System; to offer more cultural activities; to find job opportunities for young blacks."

Justin Horan, the head of the Chamber of Commerce, cites the following as aims of Renaissance II: 1) to erect necessary buildings; 2) to improve the housing situation; 3) to create jobs; 4) to expand transportation; 5) to develop the city's economy.

Businessmen, corporations, executives, bankers and blue collar workers almost unanimously echo the statements of Pease and Horan. They agree on the issues. They are upbeat about their city, they feel positive about it.

The improvements in Pittsburgh are evident. The physical transformation of the place is spectacular. By the end of the eighties, the city will look vastly different. After the buildings are completed, 30,000 more people will be working in downtown; 30,000 more customers will shop in the stores. And as Pittsburgh's per capita income—$16,200 in 1978—ranks fifth among the nation's cities, this new working force will have money to spend. Downtown Pittsburgh will be booming.

During the seventies some 100,000 people moved out of Pittsburgh. Now some of them are coming back. "The people are regaining their confidence in the city. They realize that it is the place to live, to work and play," says the mayor. The exuberant feeling of the first Renaissance is back. Pittsburgh is once more on the march. Its future looks golden.

THE MEN OF PITTSBURGH ARE IMMACULATELY DRESSED, EVEN ON THE HOTTEST SUMMER DAY THEY

Photographed specially for this book in the summer of 1980 by Joel Librizzi

WEAR A VEST AND A TIE.—DOWNTOWN EXECUTIVES ARE CONSCIOUS OF CHANGES IN FASHION

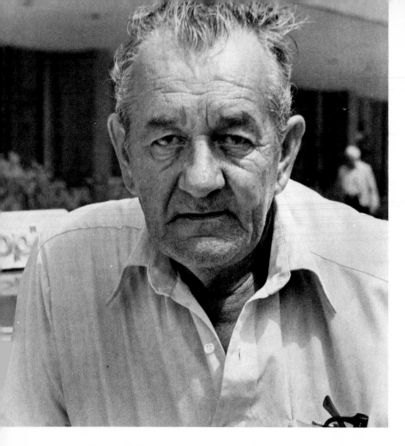

CALVIN HALL, 55, a cab driver of four years and a look-alike of President Johnson, comes from German stock. Previously he worked as a carpenter. Married, with three children.

WILLIAM KOONTZ, 34, of Croatian descent, graduated from a technical school. Before he drove cabs he did data-processing (running computers). Married, with two children.

CAB DRIVERS IN THE CITY

HARRY FORBE, 46, of Scotch-Irish-German descent, has been driving cabs for five years. A bachelor, he held several jobs, including that of a YMCA locker room attendant.

BEVERLY HODGES-KLINE, 33, of English stock, completed two years at the Community College studying psychology. A former restaurant manager. Married, with two children.

Chapter 14

THE GREAT TRANSITION IN THE EIGHTIES

by Stefan Lorant

THE CRASH came not with a bang, but a whimper. Dark clouds covered the economic horizon. In the early years of the eighties the heavy metal industry collapsed; and with that, the optimism of the seventies receded into the past. The future looked no longer rosy. Steel works after steel works cut back their production, laying off thousands of workers. In 1981 the Jones & Laughlin mill, for 122 years a landmark of the city, stopped making steel altogether. By 1983 the Pittsburgh area was in a severe recession.

Between 1981 and 1983 Pittsburgh and its surrounding area lost over 100,000 manufacturing jobs. Employment of steelworkers in the mills, once 140,000, dropped to 14,000. Unemployment rose to 16%.

In the past, Pittsburgh and its neighborhoods made 40 million tons of steel yearly, equal to the combined output of Germany and Japan during World War II. By 1987 they made only 5 million tons. The "steel capital of the world," "the forge of the universe," was no longer pouring steel. By 1987 not a single ton of heavy steel was made within the city's limits. Steelworkers were without hope for new jobs.

"Everybody blamed everybody else for the demise of the steel industry" wrote Roy McHugh, columnist of *The Pittsburgh Press*. "Management talked about unfair competition from abroad and the government indifference to it and about the high cost of American labor, in part caused by rigid union rules. Labor pointed at the chief executive officers, who diversified instead of modernizing. They bought up oil companies, chemical companies and shopping centers, but neglected to re-invest in the latest efficient steelmaking equipment."

In 1984 and in a follow-up in 1985 the *California Newsreel Company* in San Francisco filmed a documentary in which management, labor, academicians and stock market analysts gave their views of the situation.

Here are a few quotes from that film:

Says a steelworker: "The steel industry . . . never did anything to rebuild the place . . . They just didn't care."

Says Ron Weisen, President of the Steelworkers Union, Local 1397: "They were supposed to spend the money for a lot of modernization . . . I haven't seen it yet . . . They never put no money into our plants. We're still the most profitable steel industry in the world. We made 6.7 percent return on our dollar, where Japan only made 1.6. But when you can make 23 percent in real estate, chemicals, transportation, now probably Marathon Oil, naturally you're going to get out of the steel industry. But we say they have a moral obligation to the goddamn steelworkers. They made their money off the steelworkers' back."

Says Robert Hayes, Professor at Harvard Business School: "American companies in this industry didn't compete like companies, they competed like banks, that they were just essentially interested in buying and selling companies, not interested in producing and selling products."

THE MEN WHO PLANNED THE FUTURE

Photographed by Stefan Lorant in 1987

JOHN P. ROBIN, Chairman of the Urban Redevelopment Authority. He was Mayor Lawrence's civic advisor and political strategist (see about him on pages 403 and 555) and Director of the Authority from 1948 to 1954. In January, 1988 the 75 year old Robin was appointed to the Chairmanship of the organization's Transit Board.

Photographed by Norman W. Schumm

JAY ALDRIDGE, President of Penn's Southwest Association, an organization whose aim is to attract new companies to Pittsburgh.

see more opportunities in tax dodges, in mergers, than they do in the painfully slow process of developing new products, new ways of actually producing goods."

Says David Roderick, the Chief Executive Officer of U. S. Steel: "Many people don't fully appreciate that the primary role and the duty I think of management really is to make money. And in our case, our primary objective is not to make steel, it's to make steel profitably."

Says David Healy, a Wall Street analyst: "When you're comparing a five percent return in the steel business with

Says the Narrator of the film: "Some business analysts argue that such projects indicate a fundamental reorientation of American corporations, from manufacturing enterprises to financial conglomerates. These critics charge that American managers have become paper entrepreneurs. In 1982 alone, U. S. corporations spent more money buying each other than in net new manufacturing investments, more money suing each other than in basic research."

Says Robert Lekachman, Professor at the City University of New York: "American businesses have turned away from making useful products and useful services to essentially focusing on very short-term financial results. They

(turn to top of column)

perhaps fourteen percent that you could earn by investing in the average manufacturing company in the United States it just doesn't make sense to pour money into the steel business."

Says a steelworker: "When Ronald Reagan got elected president, U. S. Steel told him, 'Hey look, we're in trouble, we need money, we need capital to modernize our mills. Once we modernize our mills, we'll be competitive.' Reagan passed the Economic Recovery Tax Act which saved U. S. Steel an annual increase in their capital of one-half billion dollars. All of this was done under the auspices that this money would go into modernization. And what did U. S. Steel do? They bought Marathon Oil."

HIS LAST INTERVIEW. Richard S. Caliguiri, three times Mayor of Pittsburgh, was the principal leader of Renaissance II. On October 2, 1987 he acknowledged that he was suffering from a rare and incurable disease: Amyloidosis. He died seven months later, on May 6, 1988—fifty-six years old. Not long before his death he was inter-

Photograph by Stefan Lorant during the interview

viewed by Stefan Lorant to whom he talked about his hopes and aspirations for the future of Pittsburgh. What the Mayor said is recorded in the text of this chapter.

Monsignor Charles Owen Rice offered this prayer in 1982: "Almighty and most merciful God, I ask you to bless and assist our country and the industry in this area. We find that that in which we trusted is failing. We trusted in the smartness of our industrial leaders. We trusted in the great corporations. We trusted in money. We trusted in the power of steel. We couldn't imagine that there could ever be a day that they'd be closing steel mills and that they wouldn't need steel."

The steel controversy was summed up in five points by lawyer William Pietragallo III:

1. Reluctance of the steel companies to rejuvenate their outmoded equipment and change their old technology.

ROBERT B. PEASE. The imaginative Executive Director of the Allegheny Conference since 1968.

A MONONGAHELA VALLEY STILL LIFE AS DEPICTED BY THE GREAT ARTIST PHOTOGRAPHER PAMELA Z. BRYAN.

THE DEAD STACKS OF HOMESTEAD:

A 1985 photograph by Pamela Z. Bryan.

2. High cost of labor.

3. Dumping of cheap foreign steel on the American market. Germany, Japan, Thailand could sell their steel cheaper because of their more efficient equipment and because of their lower labor cost.

4. Higher profits by other divisions of the companies. U. S. Steel made much more profit in real estate and ceramics than in the production of steel.

5. Diminishing demand for steel. Manufacturers were using less steel in their products.

And there were no doubt many other reasons, some big, others small. One of the big reasons which should be emphasized was the diminishing profit picture in steel production. In the last quarter of 1979 U. S. Steel lost $293 million, the largest loss in its history and in 1986, (the year when its name was changed to USX) the company lost $1.83 billion. Not only steel was doing poorly;

Photographed by Pamela Z. Bryan

THE END OF AN ERA: "ANN" THE JONES & LAUGHLIN FURNACE BEFORE ITS DEMOLITION.

Photographed specially for this book in 1987 by Norman W. Schumm

THE CITY IN TRANSITION: AN AERIAL VIEW OF POINT STATE PARK IN THE SUMMER 1987

The walls of Fort Duquesne, the fort which the French built in 1754 are outlined on the lawn. The rivers are buzzing with pleasure boats. It is not commonly known that the County of Allegheny has the highest pleasure boat registration in the nation.

other companies and distributors in the city were losing money too. In 1987 Allegheny International lost $140 million, Dravo lost $26 million, Mellon Bank lost $844 million.

And while unemployment was at a record high, while a severe depression wracked Pittsburgh—the building boom of Renaissance II went on. In the Triangle, high-rise buildings sprouted into the sky, dramatically changing the city's skyline, the second time in two decades.

In 1982 the 46-story One Oxford Centre was completed; in 1984 the PPG Place, the impressive glass tower modelled after the British Parliament in London was ready

Photographed specially for this book in 1987 by Norman W. Schumm

THE CITY IN TRANSITION: PITTSBURGH IS NO LONGER THE STEEL CAPITAL OF THE WORLD

For one hundred and twenty-two years a fifty acre lot on Second Avenue was the home of the Jones & Laughlin Steelmills. In 1981 steel production at the mills stopped abruptly and in 1986 the ground was broken for a High Technology Industrial Park.

for occupation. (That same year the 64-story high U. S. Steel building was sold to a Connecticut partnership for $292.2 million, while the De Bartolo Corporation bought the Union Trust Building, which after its renovation became Two Mellon Bank Center.)

Early July in 1985 the new subway was opened, one of the signal successes of Renaissance II. A ride in it from Gateway Center to the U. S. Steel building on Grant Street was free.

In that same year the 54-story high One Mellon Bank Center and the Liberty Center—with the 27-story high Federated Investors Tower and the 615-room Vista International Hotel—were finished and by 1988 the Fifth Avenue Place, built on the site of the Jenkins arcade was ready for occupancy.

These, and the other new buildings brought new life to the businesses in downtown. They revitalized the city's economy.

Still, the growth has not been a panacea, wrote Lindsey Garson in *The New York Times* in 1987. "It has bypassed the region's legion of laid-off steelworkers, leaving nearby communities boarded-up remnants of another era. Unemployment has dropped to about 8 percent, from a high of 15.9 percent in January 1983. But many black neighborhoods are still virtually untouched by the growing prosperity."

And in his review on the Revivals of American Cities in *The Boston Globe* in 1988, Jonathan Kaufmann observed:

"The collapse of the steel industry in the late 1970's with waves of layoffs should have meant the death of the city. Instead of it Pittsburgh was transformed from an old-style blue collar town into a new-style city pinning its future on medicine, education, high technology and corporate headquarters."

Pittsburgh became a service town of white collar workers, "an internationally renowned center for health care, a national power in the computer programming industry and a leader in the nascent robotics field." The quote is from *The New York Times*.

In the nineteen sixties the ratio between white and blue collar workers in the area was one to one, but in the late eighties that ratio changed to five to one.

"It was a painful shift from heavy industry to service industry, medicine, high technology and higher education" said Jay Aldridge, President of Penn's Southwest Association. "More than half of Pittsburgh's work force

THE NEW SUBWAY

Photographed specially for this book in 1987 by Norman W. Schumm

THE HALF A BILLION DOLLAR SUBWAY SYSTEM WAS BUILT IN THE EARLY EIGHTIES

Colorful murals—no advertisements—embellish the walls of the stations. A ride from the Point to the Mellon Building in Grant Street is free.

was engaged in the production or provision of goods and services that did not exist a decade before."

"Pittsburgh used to be known for its brawn; now it is for its brain" declared Doreen Boyce, Director of the Buhl Foundation.

*

The transformation of the city in the eighties was incredible. Pittsburghers called it "miraculous."

The steel mills were gradually replaced by the mushrooming High Tech companies. By the late eighties the

number of these new companies grew to 500, providing jobs to some 40,000 people. High Tech was the hope of the future. Predicted Richard M. Cyert, President of Carnegie Mellon University: "It will change our lives the way automobiles did."

Most of the new High Tech companies were small, only 13% of them employed 100 or more people. Their annual sales were mostly under $1 million.

Said Timothy Parks, Executive Director of the High Technology Council, the umbrella organization founded

(turn to page 604)

601

Specially photographed for this book in 1987 by Norman W. Schumm

SQUARE DANCING OUTSIDE THE PPG PLACE IN DOWNTOWN PITTSBURGH

The glass tower was modeled after that of the English Parliament in London. The dancers move before the decorative column, which Peter Leo, the Columnist of the *Pittsburgh Post-Gazette*, nicknamed "The Tomb of the Unknown Bowler."

THE PPG PLACE,
designed by the architects Philip Johnson
and John Burgee was completed in 1984.

603

THE FIVE STORY HIGH ATRIUM inside the building offers 50,000 square feet retail space for specialty stores and boutiques.

ONE OXFORD CENTRE

THE 46 STORY STRUCTURE, the third highest building in the city was designed by Hellmuth, Obata & Kassabaum. Tenants began to move into the edifice in the Spring of 1982.

THE ELEGANT STORES in the Atrium like Gucci, Polo/Ralph, Lauren, Ann Taylor, Hardy & Hayes, Lugene Opticians, Molly Moses, and others, are admired by shoppers and tourists alike.

in 1981, with the aim to expand Pittsburgh's high technology base and encourage individual entrepreneurs:

"Many of these companies were formed by the faculty members and students of the two big universities in the city. The founders were young and agile, they constituted a significant brainpower."

*

In this period, in the late eighties the Allegheny Conference came under heavy criticism. *The Pittsburgh Press* in its November 1987 survey on the Conference, implied

Photographed specially for this book by Norman W. Schumm

EDWARD J. LEWIS, the creator of One Oxford Centre, the 46 story high glass and aluminum tower, is the most successful real estate developer in the Golden Triangle. A man of vision, he admires and pursues quality. The office space in his building had by 1987 a 96% occupancy rate.

Lewis, who is the driving force behind Oxford Development Company, was born in 1937. He began his career as a lawyer then joined his father's real estate firm, which built two of Pittsburgh's largest Sub-urban Malls (Monroeville Mall and South Hills Village).

To the question "Why did you invest in the Golden Triangle?" his answer came fast: "Because I have faith in the city and its downtown business district."

that the failure of the *Strategy* plan highlighted the decline of the organization itself.

The unfortunate remark of David Bergholtz, the Conference's Assistant Executive Director, naming the institution "the old boy network in its most classic sense" was not conducive to calming the ruffled waters.

The critics carped that the Conference was no longer effective. They recalled the organization's leadership in the past on smoke and flood control, they remembered that the Conference was the dominant force in the creation of Point State Park and the building of Gateway Center, but they were blind to the facts that since the forties and fifties, times had changed, and people with it. By the eighties most of the men who were instrumental in the reshaping of Pittsburgh were dead. The new men, the new managers, the new chief executives had other worries than spending sleepless nights over the fate of the city.

Wrote *The Pittsburgh Press* in November 1987: "With corporate raiders roaming the land, with foreign competi-

(Turn to page 610)

THE NEW AND THE OLD

MELLON AND U.S. STEEL BUILDING

MELLON SQUARE AND SURROUNDINGS

EAST VALLEY EXPRESSWAY

POST OFFICE AND GULF BUILDINGS

Photographed specially for this book in the Summer of 1987 by Norman W. Schumm

FIFTH AVENUE PLACE AND CNG TOWER

ONE OXFORD CENTRE NEXT TO GRANT BLDG

NATIONAL STEEL AND WESTINGHOUSE

STATION SQUARE AREA

Following spread:
THE CITY BEAUTIFUL
The Golden Triangle with its impressive new
skyline as it looked in the Summer of 1987.

tors snatching the market share, the Chief Executive Officers are so busy running their companies, that they simply have less time to spend on civic affairs than their predecessors who reigned in a calmer, fatter economy."

Wrote the *Pittsburgh Post-Gazette* in February 1988:

"Since the mills closed, some local corporations have left, shrunk or been reconstructed. New Chief Executive officers have come in, and others have turned their attention to the more demanding task of running their companies in a time of corporate takeovers."

Some of the new men were timid, some of them were ineffectual, some of them lacked the qualities of their predecessors. Though the Conference could not operate the same way as it did half a century before, it still had clout, it still had at its helm Robert Pease, it still attracted the best brains in the community.

It is true that on some issues it took a hesitant stand. It was reluctant to develop plans for the rejuvenation

Photographed specially for this book in 1987 by Norman W. Schumm

HOWARD M. LOVE

Chairman and Chief Executive Officer of the National Intergroup, says this about the city: "It is an exciting place and one that responds to challenges by rolling up its sleeves and calling on its citizenry to look beyond their immediate responsibilities and work toward the betterment of all of its citizens."

THOMAS H. O'BRIEN

President and Chief Executive Officer of PNC Financial Corporation says this about the future of Pittsburgh.

"We are going through a major transition, changing from heavy to light industry and to technology. We are making great strides in research, innovations in medicine, in development of robots. We are moving forward; we have not lost our momentum."

ANTHONY J. A. BRYAN

The retired Chief Executive of the Copperweld Corporation

Photographed specially for this book by Norman W. Schumm

ANTHONY J. F. O'REILLY

Chairman and Chief Executive Officer of the H. J. Heinz Company, one of the most successful business executives in the country. Between the year 1979, when he became Chief Executive of Heinz, and 1987 he tripled his company's profits. *Business Week* in its October, 1987 issue on the 1,000 leading CEO's described his achievement this way: "Aggressive marketing, greater foreign sales, fanatical attention to costs. He never thinks small. Insists on keeping record of double-digit profit increases." Under his guidance the sales of Heinz rose to 4.6 billion dollars, profit to $338 millions.

Asked about his impressions of his adopted city Dr. O'Reilley (he has a Ph.D.) replied: "Pittsburgh is the most international village in America; stimulating, accessible, warm and friendly. It is a modern equivalent of Rousseau's Greek City State—a very civilized place to live."

of the Monongahela Valley, it did not go into battle for strengthening the neighborhoods, it did not present effective suggestions for affordable housing.

Douglas Danforth, at that time still the Chief Executive Officer of Westinghouse and President of the Conference answered the critic in one terse sentence: "The Confer-

ence can't perform miracles; it can't transform an area by waving a wand."

In another much publicized issue to keep the Pirates baseball team in the city, Danforth followed the Mayor's lead, as did David Roderick of U. S. Steel, but other corporate leaders were not too enthusiastic.

FEDERATED INVESTORS

HENRY J. GAILLIOT, Senior Vice President and Chief Investment Officer of Federated Research Corporation, the money management arm of *Federated Investors* in the company's Trading Room, where well over a trillion dollars of trades are executed during a year.

THE FEDERATED INVESTORS TOWER, completed in 1986, is the main 27 story high building in the $300 million Liberty Center Complex. Its neighbor is the 600 room Vista International Hotel and a four story podium which houses restaurants and shops.

In 1985 the Pirates were 23 games behind. "Given a choice of watching them or having a root canal operation, it was a toss-up" quipped Carl Barger, who later became the Pirates President. As the ball club was losing $7 million a year the Galbreath family decided to sell it.

In *Business Week* Michael Schroeder wrote: "By the tail end of the 1985 season, Pittsburgh's Mayor . . . and a group of never-say-die corporate chieftans went to bat to keep the 98-year-old franchise in town. The city raised $20 million through bond issue. Executives from 10 of the city's corporations, including Westinghouse, USX, PPG, Alcoa, and PNC Financial, had their companies chip in $2 million apiece, another $2 million each from three private investors brought the total to $46 million, of which $21.5 million went to buy out the Galbreaths and minority holders. The rest went for working capital."

Danforth, the prime mover behind the plan, contributed

the know-how. Asked about it in 1988 he said: "In typical Pittsburgh fashion, we were able to put together a coalition of corporate and private investors, together with the city, to purchase and operate the franchise here. Fortunately things have gone extremely well under the new ownership in that fans are returning to the games and we are operating in a sound financial way."

Mayor Caliguiri was content—the Pirates remained in Pittsburgh. "Alone we could not do it", remembered the Mayor. "We needed the help of private individuals, and we needed the help of the big companies. And thank God, we got it."

*

On a quiet morning in 1987 Mayor Caliguiri spoke feelingly about his hopes and aspirations for the future of his beloved city.

"The steel industry is down" he mused, "it is down

Photographed specially for this book by Norman W. Schumm

JOHN F. DONAHUE, Co-Founder and the President of *Federated Investors*, Pittsburgh's largest investment management firm, comes from an old Pittsburgh family. His maternal great-great-grandfather, Charles O'Donnell, arrived in the city under Monroe's Presidency in 1818, and moved with his family into the Blockhouse at the Point.

"Jack", as everybody calls him, was born in the East End and went to Central Catholic High School from where he graduated in 1942. After a stint in the Army Air Corps he entered the United States Military Academy at West Point, graduating in 1946.

In 1955, together with his former schoolmate, Richard B. Fischer, he founded *Feder-* *ated Investors, Inc.* The firm prospered. Ten years later its assets rose to $200 million and by 1975 to $750 million. From then on the sky was the limit. By the end of 1977 its assets under management topped the $1 billion mark; by 1987 the firm was one of the largest money managers in the country, with assets over 40 billion dollars.

not only here but all across the land. It might come back, and I hope it will, but in the meantime we must attempt to find avenues to revitalize our economy. We must create more opportunities for those who live here. The future, as I see it, is in High Technology, it is in our educational and health institutions, in our research and development. Our efforts in High Tech already created 40,000 new jobs."

(turn to page 616)

HOWARD W. HANNA III, the head of Pittsburgh's largest real estate company, which was founded by his parents, Howard and Anne Hanna in 1957. Thirty years later, in 1987 it had 20 offices with 625 active agents. The total volume of sales of the firm in 1987 was $1,240,000,000.00—a remarkable achievement.

Hanna is married and the father of five children. His two sisters, Helen Carson and Annie serve as officers of the company.

VINCENT A. SARNI, Chairman of the Board of P.P.G. Industries says: "After some difficulties in the early eighties, when we had to adjust ourselves to global competition, we succeeded to turn the corner. The best part of the future is in front of us."

Photographs taken specially for this book in 1987 by Norman W. Schumm

DOUGLAS D. DANFORTH who retired as Chairman of the Westinghouse Electric corporation at the end of 1987 is one of the most respected and influential Pittsburghers. A director of many of the city's corporations and financial institutions, he is also chairman of the board of trustees of Carnegie Mellon University, and Chairman and Chief Executive officer of the Pirates.

Asked about his thoughts on Pittsburgh's future, Mr. Danforth said: "We must continue to establish an overall climate that will attract medium and small foreign and domestic companies to the city. We have had considerable success in this regard with unemployment at or near the national average. We also must continue to improve our primary and secondary education to assure a well-educated work force in the service and industrial sector. Private and public sectors must work together to improve our area's attractiveness for those who live and work there. If we do that, our future looks promising."

LEADERS OF HIGH TECHNOLOGY COMPANIES IN THE EIGHTIES

DONALD H. JONES
Founder and President
International Cybernetic Corp.
(Founded 1982, employs 105)

DAVID M. SPITZER
President and CEO
Actronics, Inc.
(Founded 1981, employs 30)

JOHN D. FOLLEY, JR.
Chairman
Applied Science Associates, Inc.
(Founded 1961, employs 140)

ROMESH T. WADHWANI
Chairman and CEO
American Cimflex
(Founded 1979, employs 370)

DENNIS YABLONSKY
President and CEO
Carnegie Group, Inc.
(Founded 1983, employs 150)

C. BRETT HARRISON
President
Extrel Corporation
(Founded 1964, employs 62)

GLEN F. CHATFIELD
President
Duquesne Systems, Inc.
(Founded 1970, employs 250)

PAUL POTTGEN
President
Med-Chek Laboratories, Inc.
(Founded 1977, employs 300)

GERALD E. McGINNIS
President
Respironics, Inc.
(Founded 1976, employs 185)

PETER C. ROSSIN
Chairman
Dynamet Incorporated
(Founded 1967, employs 205)

JOHN F. HARTNETT
President
Molytek, Inc.
(Founded 1977, employs 70)

EUGENE R. YOST
President
Black Box Corporation
(Founded 1977, employs 450)

Reminiscing about the past, the Mayor said: "After I took over the office in 1977 I went out knocking on doors of the private sector and succeeded to establish a better relationship between City Hall and the business community. The responses were encouraging. One, the proposal "Strategy for Growth"—instigated in 1984 by the Allegheny Conference and prepared by 206 volunteers offered a blueprint for Pittsburgh's future. Its basic assumption was that the economic environment would keep on

TIMOTHY PARKS, the agile, indefatigable and imaginative Executive Director of the *High Technology Council*, which represents over 600 High Tech Firms in the Pittsburgh area alone.

ROBERT G. MAZUR
Chairman and President
Solid State Measurements, Inc.
(Founded 1970, employs 40)

JACK ROSEMAN
Former President of *On-Line Systems*
Founder of *Actronics, Inc.* in 1981

JAY S. TROUTMAN
President
Aptech Computer Systems, Inc.
(Founded 1965, employs 60)

M. S. HEILMAN, M.D.
Chairman
Vascor, Inc. and *Lifecor, Inc.*
(Founded 1986, employs 10)

THOMAS H. WITMER
President and CEO
Medrad, Inc.
(Founded 1964, employs 306)

WILLIAM A. WULF
Founder
Tartan Laboratories, Inc.
(Founded 1981, employs 52)

GIORGIO CORALUPPI
President and CEO
Compunetics, Inc.
(Founded 1968, employs 140)

ALI R. KUTAY
President
Formative Technologies, Inc.
(Founded 1983, employs 50)

ROBERT THOMPSON, JR.
President and CEO
Redshaw Incorporated
(Founded 1976, employs 300)

IRENE SKOLNICK
President
Dymax Corporation
(Founded 1980, employs 20)

JAMES D. GAY
President
Expert Technologies, Inc.
(Founded 1985, employs 13)

SANDRA H. ROSEN
President
Micro Training Specialists Co.
(Founded 1983, employs 11)

changing and that the regional economy had to diversify to be healthy."

"Strategy" was a joint effort by the city and county governments, together with the heads of our great universities and with the Conference, to reshape the economy of the area.

"In two hefty volumes the task force of 'Strategy 21' mapped out a variety of plans, which would bring 36,000 new jobs by the end of the century. One of the strategy's

JAMES COLKER, the former head of *Contraves Goerz Corporation*, now Managing General Partner of the *CEO Venture Fund*, was co-founder of the Council and is its first President.

Photographed specially for this book in 1987 by Norman W. Schumm

RICHARD M. CYERT, President of Carnegie-Mellon University since 1972. He married Margaret Shadick in 1946. Mrs. Cyert's great interest is Child Care to which she volunteers her services. The Cyerts have three married daughters.

main suggestions was the construction of the new midfield terminal at the Airport, a proposal which now is translated into reality.

"However, in recent years the criticism of 'Strategy' mounted. Some thought it a flop, others believed its proposals were too unrealistic. Obviously not everything that the task force proposed could be accomplished, still most of its suggestions had validity and were helpful.

"The loss of 100,000 jobs was a traumatic experience. It really hit us hard. We knew something was coming, we expected some kind of stagnation in steel production, but the force of it was far bigger than we thought. Doubters predicted that the city could not survive the shutting of the mills. But unemployment dropped from the 16%

Photographed specially for this book in 1987 by Norman W. Schumm

WESLEY W. POSVAR became the 15th Chancellor of the University of Pittsburgh in 1967. His wife, the former Mildred Miller, is an internationally known opera and concert artist. The Posvars are the parents of a son and two daughters.

high in the early years of the eighties to 6% in 1987."

"We turned into a service and retailing center, a center for health care, a city of transplants, a city of High Technology, a city of Robotics, of computer programming. We became a world major research center, the third largest in the nation with some 25,000 scientists and technicians doing research at 170 places and laboratories. We are spending over a billion dollars on R & D — research and development. These efforts will reinvigorate our economy picture, breathe new life in the old industries."

"Well—I don't want to sound as if everything we touched was a success," said the Mayor, "No! Ranaissance II had its ups and downs, its successes and its failures. Our successes: the renovation of Station Square, the revi-

(turn to page 622)

THE WEISES, Konrad Weiss, born in Germany came to the U.S. in 1971 and became an American citizen in 1985. For twelve years he was Chief Executive Officer of Mobay Chemical Corporation. Since 1986 he has been President of Bayer, U.S.A. Inc.

His wife Gisela, serves as a "docent" at the Carnegie Museum.

Photographs taken in 1987 specially for this book by Norman W. Schumm

THE FELLHEIMERS: Alan S. Fellheimer, the head of Equimark, Pittsburgh's third largest commercial bank, is an accomplished musician. On February 7, 1988, a day after his 45th birthday, he conducted the Pittsburgh Symphony in Sousa's *Stars and Stripes Forever*. His wife, Judy, the Bank's Executive Vice President, bought him this chance at the Symphony Ball's auction, and he loved it.

THE CAMPBELLS: Lawyer Bruce Campbell served in the Flaherty Administration, then became U.S. Associate Deputy Attorney General. In 1986 representing the city's School Board he negotiated with the Teachers' Union a two year extension of the teacher's contract. His wife, Gail, is teaching Chemistry and Physics.

The Campbells are the parents of three children.

Photograph taken specially for this book by Norman W. Schumm

THE HILLMANS: Henry Lee Hillman, the richest man in Pittsburgh, inherited from his father in 1959 the family's business, which he, through The Hillman Company, diversified into an extensive and financial power. In 1987 Forbes Magazine listed his net worth as more than a billion dollars.

The Hillmans are the parents of four children and they have seven grandchildren.

THE PIETRAGALLOS: Lawyer William Pietragallo II started his own law firm while still in his thirties, which, among other prominent clients, represents Japanese auto manufacturers. His wife, Helena, is active in public affairs.

The Pietragallos are the parents of two children.

talization of our neighborhoods, the building of the subway. Our failures: the Convention Center that turned out to be far too small and not too attractive, and . . ." the Mayor broke off in the middle of the sentence; "but why give ammunition to my enemies."

Then he went on:

"I wish I could have achieved more. What I tried to do was to galvanize the community, to set policy and attitude, to be a cheerleader, to rehabilitate our neighborhood, to lure people back to the city, to create jobs."

And he ended his reverie: "I am very impatient—I realize that we have not done enough, that we must create more opportunities for the people who live here."

It was perhaps his last interview. A few months later, on May 6, 1988 he died. What a great man he was, what a lovely human being.

*

In the transition period the heads of the two great Universities—Dr. Richard M. Cyert of Carnegie Mellon and Dr. Wesley W. Posvar of the University of Pittsburgh—came to the fore. They had helped to form business–municipal coalitions to confront urban fiscal problems.

Dr. Cyert responded to questions about his and his University's efforts during that time: "We had to be here," he said. "We could not stay away, we could not retreat in an ivory tower, we had to participate. We offered changes, we offered suggestions."

Photograph taken specially for this book by Norman W. Schumm

ELSIE HILLMAN, the wife of Henry Lee Hillman, in the living room of her Morewood Heights home. An oversized replica of a gorilla rests on the sofa to the delight of her seven grandchildren.

Born in Pittsburgh in 1925, educated in Ellis School and Westminster Choir College, she married Henry Lee Hillman in 1945 when she was twenty years old.

Photographed specially for this book by Norman W. Schumm

ONE OF THE CITY'S BEST-LIKED WOMEN: Elsie Hillman got into politics in 1952 as a volunteer for Eisenhower. In 1967 she was elected County Chairman of the Republican Party; 1974, was awarded with a "Distinguished Republican" citation; 1975, appointed to her party's National Committee; 1983, Victor International named her as "Woman of the Year."

WEST END

NORTHSIDE

MOUNT WASHINGTON

DORMONT

"We had close connections with many of the newly formed High Tech companies, which began operating in Pittsburgh. They were managed by young executives, many of them former teachers or graduates from Carnegie Mellon. Their firms created new jobs for 40,000 people.

"In those critical years we were able to raise funds from government and corporations for the establishment of a number of new projects. In 1980 we inaugurated

BLOOMFIELD

WEST END

EAST LIBERTY

POLISH HILL

Photographed specially for this book in 1987 by Norman W. Schumm

the Robotics Institute for the study and development of usable robots to be used in manufacturing and health care, robots for the automotive industry, robots for the disabled. I believe that the Institute is the best in the country—it employs some 200 scientists and engineers.

"In 1984 we created the Software Engineering Institute for which we received a $103 million grant from the Department of Defense and which had the support of

FOUNDATION HEADS

Photographed specially for this book in 1987 by Norman W. Schumm

GREGORY D. CURTIS, President of the Laurel Foundation and chief operating officer of numerous charitable trusts, oversees the distribution of an estimated $10,000,000 in charitable grants per year. Curtis, the youngest Foundation head in the city is a Harvard Law School graduate and a poet of distinction. He was the recipient of the American Poet's Prize in 1968.

the National Science Foundation, and other corporations and universities.

"In 1982 Carnegie Mellon together with the University of Pittsburgh concluded an agreement with IBM for our experimental computer center. In 1986 the supercomputer consortium of Carnegie Mellon, Westinghouse and other universities received a Gray X-MP/48 supercomputer capable of performing 840 million operations per second. It is one of the largest, fastest and most advanced supercomputers in the nation. It will revolutionize higher education. We have gone beyond MIT and Stanford in computer science. And we have played our part in numerous other

DOREEN E. BOYCE, Director of The Buhl Foundation. Since 1927 the foundation has distributed over 35 million dollars.

BENEDUM CENTER FOR THE NEW PERFORMING ARTS

The $42 million restoration and expansion of the Stanley Theater, the former plush movie house, was accomplished between the years 1984 and 1987. Master

Craftsmen restored the old auditorium with its decorative murals and elaborate plaster work to its old glory.

The place—the new home of the city's

Ballet Theatre, its Opera, its Civic Light Opera, and its Dance Council—was opened to the public on September 25, 1987 with a star-studded gala performance.

PITTSBURGH
THEOLOGICAL SEMINARY:

CARNEGIE SAMUEL CALIAN,
(born 1933) is President of the
Theological Seminary since 1981.
In 1988 the enrollment in the
Seminary was 343 students. They
were taught by 21 full-time and
12 adjunct faculty members.

ROBERT MORRIS COLLEGE:

CHARLES L. SEWALL, (born
1920) is the first and only President of Robert Morris College,
which was founded in 1967. In its
two campuses 5,400 students are
taught by 150 faculty members.

JOHN E. MURRAY, JR., (born 1932) became Duquesne's first
lay President in July 1988. The eight schools of the institution
have an enrollment of 4300 undergraduate and 2300 graduate
students. They are taught by a full-time faculty of 271.

projects which we are developing in partnership with the University of Pittsburgh."

"Computer is the essence of the future" concluded Dr. Cyert—"to understand Pittsburgh, one must understand computer science."

Dr. Posvar, President of the University of Pittsburgh responded to the questions about his and his University's part in the transition period in this way:

"Since 1981 American corporations have been encouraged through research and development tax credits to support basic research in universities and other institutions. These credits, embodied in the Economic Recovery Tax Act, have impressively increased R & D spending by more than $10 billion, benefiting new growth technologies as well as basic domestic industries."

"We had the great good luck to receive as a gift from the Chevron Corporation their Pittsburgh Applied Research Center in Harmarville, that included more than $40 million worth of specialized analytical lab equipment. The facilities belonged to Gulf Oil, but after Chevron acquired that company, it did not have use for it—because it had its own research center in California. So it was donated to us."

"With the $40 million grant from the National Science Foundation we established together with Carnegie Mellon University and Westinghouse the most powerful super-

PRESIDENTS

COMMUNITY COLLEGE OF ALLEGHENY COUNTY.

JOHN W. KRAFT (born 1928), President of the college which has enrollment of 93,000.

In the year of 1987 the Community College had 19,397 full time students, while the full time teaching faculty numbered 370.

POINT PARK COLLEGE:

J. MATTHEW SIMON, (born 1941) President of the College since 1986. Some 2,600 students are enrolled at the Institution which has a 76 full-time faculty.

REBECCA STAFFORD, (born 1936), a Harvard graduate became President of Chatham College in 1983. There are 640 women enrolled in the college, which has a teaching staff of 64.

computing center in the nation."

"Also, together with Carnegie Mellon we are transforming the 48-acre former site of J & L's Hot Strip mill on the banks of the Monongahela into a center of post industrial technology. When the High Technology Park will be completed—presumably in 1995—we assume it will create 1600 permanent and 4400 related jobs."

"And there are a number of other projects which have helped and which are still helpful to weather the difficult transition period."

"On November 1, 1985 the University adopted the system, an optic-fiber communication network that transports voice (telephone), date (computers) and video (tele-

vision)" wrote Robert G. Alberts, "which will constitute the basis for global information society."

"We hope to turn Mon Valley in Biotech Valley."

"In 1981 we recruited Dr. Thomas Starzl, under whose pioneering work Pittsburgh became a world center for organ transplants. More organ transplants are done here than in any other city in the world. Up till now, in the Presbytarian-University Hospital alone over 2000 of these special operations were performed."

*

In the late eighties the city's eighty schools had an enrollment of 40,000 pupils, 52.2% of them black and 46.4% white. The decade before, in the seventies, black

(turn to page 632)

TELEVISION PERSONALITIES
YVONNE ZANOS (WTAE, Channel 4)

CATHY MILTON (WTAE , Channel 4)

DELLA CREWS (WPXI, Channel 11)

PATTY BURNS (KDKA, Channel 2)

A HEART BY-PASS OPERATION PERFORMED BY DR. BARTLEY GRIFFITH

Photographed specially for this book in 1987 by Norman W. Schumm

DR. BARTLEY P. GRIFFITH, the heart surgeon, has been Assistant Professor of Surgery at the University of Pittsburgh since 1981.

Between 1983 and 1988 Dr. Griffith and his team at the city's Presbyterian and Children's Hospitals performed a total of 604 heart bypass operations, 447 open heart surgery, 119 heart transplants and 38 combination of heart and lung transplant operations.

students performance scores were 30 percent lower than those of white students. High school dropout rose to 35%. In 1980, Dr. Richard C. Wallace, Jr. was appointed superintendent of schools.

Under his administration, the quality of education lessened the gap between black and white student achievement. High school dropout in 1986 was down to 21%. Dr. Wallace upgraded classroom instruction through elementary and secondary teacher centers; the supervising roles of principals were improved. A program of educational reform was instituted. One was MAP (Monitoring Achievement in Pittsburgh), which linked instruction in the basic skills to systematic testing and planning. Another was PRISM (Pittsburgh's Research-based Instructional Model), a program of retraining teachers and principals. But his most successful achievement was the teacher center at Schenley High School, where all high school teachers must go for retraining. It was a rewarding experiment, the first of its kind. About it Dr. Stevens commented: "We have created such a powerful group of professionals at Schenley they think they can do anything anywhere, and they can."

*

In 1984, at the height of the recession a statistical guidebook published by the Rand McNally Company tagged Pittsburgh as "the most livable city." The people at the Chamber of Commerce went bonkers and mounted a massive campaign with banners, posters and full page ads in newspapers and magazines. As if Pittsburghers needed to be told what a good place their city was.

Other publications and organizations followed suit in

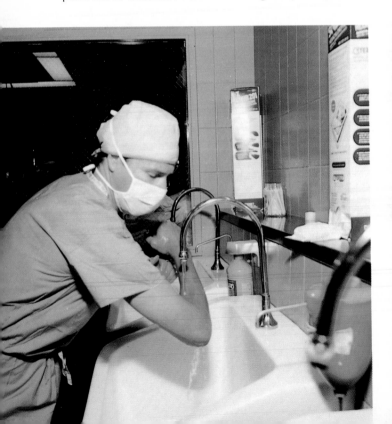

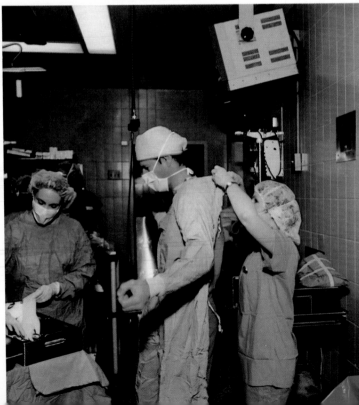

AND HIS TEAM AT THE PRESBYTARIAN UNIVERSITY HOSPITAL IN 1987.

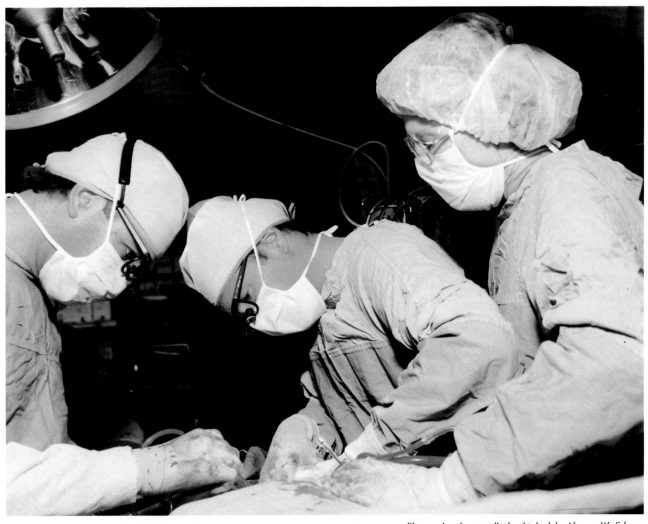

Photographs taken specially for this book by Norman W. Schumm

DR. BARTLEY GRIFFITH AND HIS ASSISTANTS DURING A HEART TRANSPLANT OPERATION

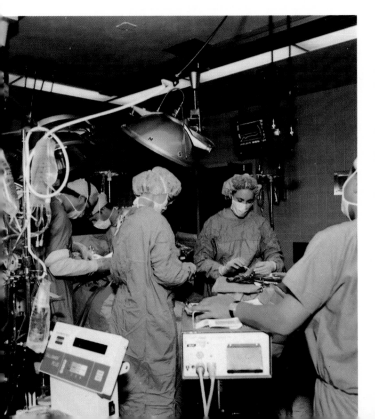

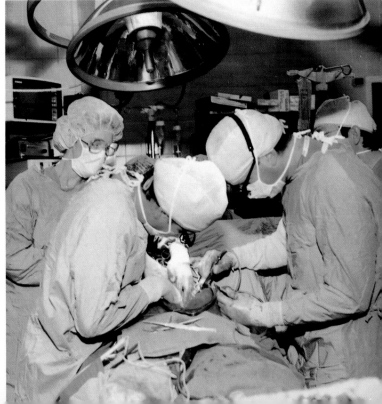

ROBOTIC INSTITUTE

Photographs by Mary Jo Dowling of the Robotics Institute

the praise of the city. *Fortune* magazine declared that Pittsburgh was "the most conducive city for marriage" while researchers in Oregon stated that it had "the healthiest climate of all American cities."

Regardless of all this ballyhoo the fact remained that in the opening years of the eighties some 100,000 jobs were lost in the area, most of them in manufacturing, and that in the last half of the seventies and the early eighties more than 60,000 residents left the area to find employment elsewhere.

Still life went on as usual. The Pirates and the Steelers drew large crowds into the Stadium. The Three Rivers Regatta grew into one of the most popular events in the city. The race began at Herr's Island, while the finishing line was at the Point. The contestants were cheered by a crowd of 100,000 spectators.

In September 1986, in the tenth annual marathon race, 12,000 runners participated.

Pittsburgh was always a good city for sports. Sports events, boxing, hockey, tennis, enjoyed great popularity. But most of Pittsburgh's sport fans were not aware of one "sport" in which they were leading. It is the "sport" of marbles. Ten Pittsburgh boys and seven Pittsburgh

At the beginning of the eighties Carnegie Mellon University started its Robotic Institute. Soon the Institute made robots which simplified the manufacturing of goods and improved health care.

The Terregator is a driverless, outdoor vehicle, used in autonomous navigation research.

The Direct Drive Robot eliminates transmission mechanism and increases accuracy.

The Flexible Manufacturing Lab focuses on automating small, mixed batch manufacturing.

The Intelligent Sensors Laboratory develops sensors and emphasizes new technologies.

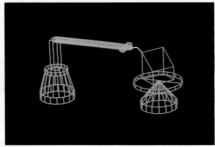

The Welding Laboratory developed a computer system which generates welding programs.

The Remote Work Vehicle, a electrohydraulic system for radiological decontamination.

UNEMPLOYED

Photographs by Norman W. Schumm

PAUL FABANICH, 35, single. He worked for the American Rolling Mill as a pipefitter for 6 years, from 1979 to 1985.

After he lost his job he became a student at the Pittsburgh Aviation Mechanic School from where he hopes to graduate in 1988.

THOMAS M. BLATNICK, 50 is married and has two children. He was employed at Wheeling Pittsburgh Steel for 23 years, from 1963 to 1986. After he was laid off he enrolled at the Institute of Aeronautics, from where he hopes to graduate in 1989.

TED SUNDBERG, 57 years old is married and the father of four children. He has worked as a millwright for 39½ years at National Tube Works in McKeesport. Unemployed for two years he was reinstated on January 1, 1988 at the successor of the Tube Works.

FRANK FREDRICK, 49 years old, is married, and has four children. Worked for 21 years at Homestead Steel in the electrical maintenance department. Out of work for over two years, he was rehired in January 1988 by the Cornelius Architectural Products, Inc.

girls won national championships in it. "It is a game that is geared to kids only, one in which you are not only washed up at 15, but not even allowed to compete" wrote the Smithsonian Magazine in 1988.

*

Some statistical figures taken at random highlight the history of the transition decade.

Pittsburgh is the home of 15 of the 500 largest corporations in the country, right behind New York and Chicago.

There are 29 colleges and universities in the area. The city itself has within its limits nine higher educational institutions: Carlow College, Carnegie Mellon University, Chatham College, Duquesne University, La Roche College, Pittsburgh Theological Seminary, Point Park College, Robert Morris College, The University of Pittsburgh. The Community College of Allegheny is not far off.

And there are some 50 technical and vocational schools. in the city and its neighborhood.

The University of Pittsburgh had an enrollment of 18,000 full-time and 10,000 part-time students. They receive instruction from a 2,450 full-time and 650 part-time faculty.

Photographed specially for this book in 1987 by Norman W. Schumm

DURING THE EIGHTIES Rock Clubs—the gathering place of the young people—blossomed out in the city. Graffiti, in a former warehouse on Baum Boulevard, owned by Tony di Nardo, was regularly filled to the rafters. And there were others, most of them having fanciful names like Electric Banana, Cahots, Decade, Shadyside Balcony, Confetti, Upstage, Kicks.

ANNA KAZALAS, 21
Travel Consultant at
Ponzio International Travel

DENA HORNACK, 27
Therapeutic Recreation
Specialist in South Hills

ANDREA PERRY, 31
Volunteers as Program Coordinator
at *The Carnegie* in Oakland

SUSAN HARRIS, 30
Works in the Office of
P.P.G. Industries

Carnegie Mellon University has a 6,916 student enrollment (undergraduates and graduates) and a 517 faculty.

In the area 200 art groups and 50 classical music groups gave regular performances in 1988.

The average household income in the area is about $30,000—in some neighborhoods even $35,000.

The area has 49 hospitals—which take care of 750,000 patients yearly. Fees for the semi-private rooms in the hospitals range from $325 at Western Pennsylvania Hospital to $380 in Montefiore Hospital. The cost of an average

room in the Children's Hospital is $550.

Since the early eighties some 3000 transplants were performed in the Pennsylvania University Hospital alone.

In April 1987 Andrew Schneider and Mary Pat Flaherty wrote in *The Pittsburgh Press* a series of articles which won them the Pulitzer Prize for investigative reporting, that the price of a kidney—a 5 ounce organ—was seven times higher than the same amount of gold.

It was rather money than medicine that set the path of kidneys from the donors to recipients. The rich got

BOBBIE MICOCHIN, 32
Administrative Secretary at
P.P.G. Industries

LORA FULTON, 21
Secretary for *Monroe Systems*
for Business

SHELLY L. BOEHM, 23
Law Secretary at
Harrington and Schweers

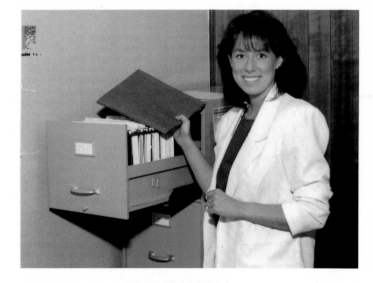

HEATHER McMINN, 22
Sales Representative at
Monroe Systems for Business

the kidneys and the livers and the poor had to wait.

The reporters stated that one could buy kidneys in Korea for $3200, in Mexico for $2500, in Japan for $5000, in Germany and the U.S. for $10,000 to $40,000.

*

What will the future hold for the city? Will Pittsburgh be able to solve its problems? Could new life be infused into the Monongahela Valley, could the neighborhoods be strengthened, could affordable housing be built?

"People are impatient" said Robert Pease the Director of the Allegheny Conference. "Those who lived through the years of Renaissance I are disappointed at the slower pace things are moving in the eighties. They want a faster change, they want to make Pittsburgh a better place to live in a hurry. They ask for the creation of jobs, they demand a sound economic base. But all these cannot be achieved overnight. We must have patience. There is no quick fix."

Quick fix, or no quick fix, Pittsburgh will make it. It always did.

TWO HUNDRED YEARS
OF PITTSBURGH'S HISTORY

A chronology of events compiled
by
Mel Seidenberg, Lois Mulkearn and James W. Hess

No chronology can ever be complete. There always remains the question: are the entries that are included the really representative ones, and those that were left out of lesser significance? The compilers tried their best to give a fair representation of the main events during the first two centuries of Pittsburgh's history. Their arduous job took more than two years to accomplish. Every item has been carefully checked and compared with contemporary records. The entries which, because of space limitation had to be left out, would fill another hundred pages.

That there will be omissions, that there will be mistakes, I am aware. My hope is that these few dozen pages serve as a framework on which future historians can build a more elaborate edifice. Thus I regard this chronology only as a beginning for a fuller work. I trust that it will be carried on and completed by others. S.L.

1717 Michael Bezallion, Pennsylvania fur trader, passed the future site of Pittsburgh en route from the Illinois country to Philadelphia, where he made a report of the trip.
White traders began to establish trading posts in the territory of the Ohio, Allegheny, and Monongahela valleys. The largest settlement was Logstown (now Ambridge), about four miles north of the fork of the Ohio.

1748 Conrad Weiser (1696-1760), the German, who for thirty years was prominent in Pennsylvania's negotiations with the Indians, was the guest of the Delaware Indian Chief Shannopin at the mouth of Two Mile Run (the present Lawrenceville section of Pittsburgh).

1749 *August 7:* Céloron de Blainville (1693-1759), with 43 French soldiers, 180 Canadians, and a band of Indians, floated past the site of Pittsburgh, once more claiming possession of the Ohio Valley for King Louis XV of France. Chaplain Father Bonnecamps kept a journal and made a map of the trip.

1751 *May:* Philippe Thomas Joncaire, with a troop of Indians, passed by en route to Logstown to establish a French trading house there.

1752 *May 28-30:* Joshua Fry, James Patton, and Lunsford Lomax, Virginia agents chosen to treat with the In-

IN THE BEGINNING
was the wilderness, with rivers and trees, with flowers and birds, deer and rabbits. William Libby's drawing, made specially for this book, sketches the landscape as it appeared before the English and the French came to the forks of the mighty Ohio River.

dians at Logstown, held a conference with Chief Shannopin.

1753 *November 23:* The 21-year old Major George Washington (1732-99), emissary from Virginia's Governor Robert Dinwiddie to the French commandant at Fort LeBoeuf on French Creek (now Waterford, Pa.), observed the land at the junction of the Allegheny and Monongahela rivers (where Pittsburgh is today) and described it as "extremely well situated for a Fort; as it has the absolute Command of both Rivers. The Land at the Point is 20 or 25 Feet above the common

Surface of the Water; and a considerable Bottom of flat, well timbered Land all around it very convenient for Building."
December 30-31, night: George Washington and his guide, Christopher Gist, were stranded on Garrison Island in the Allegheny River after their raft had been dashed to pieces by floating ice.

1754 *February 17:* William Trent (1715-87), the Indian trader, came to the forks. When the militiamen whom he had enlisted in the Monongahela Valley arrived, Trent began to build a fort and named it Fort Prince George.
April 13: Ensign Edward Ward, temporarily in charge of Fort Prince George, learned that French troops were on the march against him.
April 17: When the French force of about 500 men, under Commandant Pierre de Contrécoeur, arrived at the forks, Ensign Ward and his 41 men had to surrender their building. The French began to build a large fort on the spot and named it Fort Duquesne, after the Marquis de Duquesne (1700-78), governor general of New France from 1752 to 1755.
July 4: The French subdued Colonel Washington at Fort Necessity.
July 28: The Scotsman Robert Stobo, a friend of Governor Dinwiddie, was

FIRST CHRISTIAN WORSHIP
At the site of Fort Duquesne, Denys Baron, a Recollect, offered the first Christian service in Pittsburgh on April 17, 1754. The painting of the scene is by Charles Hargens.

one of two hostages taken to Fort Duquesne after the battle at Fort Necessity. During his imprisonment he sent out letters and a sketch of the fort to the English.

1755 *May 24:* The French commandant announced that Fort Duquesne was completed.

July 9: A British expedition under General Edward Braddock, marching to attack Fort Duquesne, was defeated not far from the fort by an army of French and Indian warriors. Some of the English captives were burned alive by the Indians.

1756 *Spring:* Fort Duquesne was damaged by a flood.

1758 *August 30:* The French commandant at Fort Duquesne learned that a British force led by General John Forbes was at Loyalhanna (the present Ligonier) and was planning to advance against the fort.

September 14: Major James Grant, with Forbes's army, received permission to attack Fort Duquesne. He led his force of 800 into disaster; one third of his men were killed.

November 24: General Forbes's army took possession of the remnants of Fort Duquesne, which the French had burned and evacuated earlier in the day.

November 25: The English flag flew over the ruins of the demolished Fort Duquesne.

November 26: Five thousand soldiers knelt near the fort in observance of Thanksgiving.

November 29: A detachment of soldiers who had been with Major Grant on his fateful attack in September, buried the bodies of their dead comrades.

Novemebr 29: A detachment of sol-day the camp at Fort Duquesne was referred to as Fort Argyle.

December 1: General Forbes formally named the camp Pittsburgh. On January 21 the following year, writing from Philadelphia, the general told William Pitt, the English prime minister, that he had "used the freedom of giving your name to Fort Duquesne, as . . . it was in some measure the being activated by your spirits that now makes us Masters of the place."

December 4-5: Indian chiefs, at a conference in the fort, promised peace to Colonel Henry Bouquet (1719-65), the Swiss soldier who accompanied General Forbes. They also promised the return of all English captives.

1759 *January 9:* Temporary barracks, about a thousand feet from the site of Fort Duquesne, had been built; General Forbes authorized a payment of £124/13/2 for the work.

September 3: The building of a permanent fort—Fort Pitt—had begun under the direction of a new commanding officer, General John Stanwix, and engineer Harry Gordon.

October 24–26: General Stanwix made a treaty of peace and friendship with the Indians.

October 29: Adam Stephen, a lieutenant colonel in the Virginia regiment who survived Grant's defeat, complained that the Pennsylvania Indian traders were taking over the lucrative fur trade and that the Indians had brought 20 tons of skins and furs to Fort Pitt in the previous three months.

1760 *July:* Colonel James Burd counted the population of Pittsburgh; he found that 149 people, besides the soldiers, were living there.

August 12: General Robert Monckton, in command at Fort Pitt, reaffirmed Stanwix's treaty with the Indians.

James Boggs, Allegheny's first white settler, built his cabin.

1761 *Spring:* Lieutenant Bernard Ratzer drew up a plan for the British military reservation which included 40 acres of vegetable and flower gardens and the "King's Orchard" of apple and pear trees in the area between Fort Pitt and the Allegheny River.

April 14: According to a count ordered by Colonel Bouquet, Pittsburgh's population consisted of 163 men, 45 women, and 25 children, who lived in 160 houses outside the fort.

October 12: George Croghan, an Irishman who came to America in 1741, was the most prominent of the Pennsylvania traders. As Indian agent at Fort Pitt, he noted that the Indians had returned 338 white captives to the fort since June 1759.

Winter: Fort Pitt, surrounded by moats drawing water from the Allegheny River, was completed. Its cost was estimated between £60,000 and £100,000.

1762 *January 9:* The Allegheny, Monongahela, and Ohio rivers, reaching a stage of 39.2 feet at the Point, badly damaged the fort. All but 13 barrels of powder were destroyed.

May 2: The Indian Chief Delaware George a faithful friend of the British, was buried with full military honors on the north side of the Allegheny River opposite Fort Pitt.

1763 *March 9:* When the rivers rose to 41 feet at the Point, Fort Pitt was inundated by six inches of water.

May 30: Pontiac's uprising against the whites brought all the inhabitants from the outside within the confines of Fort Pitt. Most of the surrounding homes were demolished.

June 3: Those houses which had not been destroyed were burned by the Indians.

August 11: Colonel Bouquet's army defeated the Indians at the Battle of Bushy Run on August 5 and 6, thus the siege of Fort Pitt had come to an end. The people, who had taken shelter in the fort, returned to the places where they once lived and set out to build new cabins.

1764 *October 3:* Bouquet's army forced the Delaware and Shawnee Indians to fulfill their agreement and bring all their English captives to the fort.

November 15: The Indians brought 60 captives to Fort Pitt.

Colonel Bouquet's Redoubt — the Blockhouse, which is still in existence —was built outside the walls of the fort, midway between the Ohio and Monongahela bastions.

John Campbell made a plan for the town, consisting of four blocks between Water and Second streets and Ferry and Market Streets, with an alley, Chancery Lane, between Ferry and Market.

Richard and William Butler's log cabins were the first to be completed after the lifting of the siege.

1766 *Spring:* Baynton, Wharton, and Morgan, the well-known Philadelphia trading firm, erected a storehouse, the first shingle-roofed building in Pittsburgh.

1768 *April and May:* Conferences between the Indians and the British were held at Fort Pitt; 1103 male Indians came with their retinue of wives and children.

THE MARCH OF BRADDOCK IN 1755
The British expedition under General Edward Braddock, trying to take Fort Duquesne, ended in failure. The engraving is by H. B. Hill, Jr., after a drawing by A. B. Frost.

1769 The Penn's Pittsburgh Manor, some of it within the present Golden Triangle area, was surveyed and found to include 5766 acres.

1770 *October:* George Washington arrived for a visit in Pittsburgh. He noted in his diary: "We lodged in what is called the Town, distant about 300 yards from the Fort, at one Mr. Semples, who keeps a very good house of entertainment."

1772 *October 12:* Captain Charles Edmonstone of the Eighteenth Royal Regiment, in command at Fort Pitt, sold the installation to William Thompson and Alexander Ross for 50 pounds New York currency. Thus ended the Crown's jurisdiction over the military reservation and fort at Pittsburgh.

1773 John Ormsby was granted the right to keep the first licensed ferry across the Monongahela River.
Pennsylvania obtained permission from Great Britain to garrison militia at Fort Pitt.

1774 *January 6:* The unsettled boundary between Pennsylvania and Virginia became hotly contested when Dr. John Connolly posted a proclamation on the walls of Fort Pitt to announce his appointment by Lord Dunmore, governor of the southern colony, as "Captain, Commandant of the Militia of Pittsburgh and its Dependencies." He ordered the people to assemble as a militia on January 25.
January 24: Pennsylvania challenged Virginia's claim to Pittsburgh by arresting Dr. Connolly and removing him to Hannastown to stand trial.
February 2: By promising to return in April for trial, Dr. Connolly persuaded the sheriff of Westmoreland County to release him. He then obtained a commission as justice of the peace from the court of Augusta County, Virginia, which was held to include Pittsburgh, and returned to the forks, took possession of Fort Pitt, and organized his militia.
April 25: Governor Dunmore ordered all the inhabitants "to pay their quit-rents and all public dues" to officers appointed by him.

EARLY COAL MINING

In the eighteenth century barges moved with the current carrying the coal. At the destination they would be broken up and sold for wood. Frank Mélega portrayed the scene.

1775 *February 21:* Dr. Connolly changed the name of Fort Pitt to Fort Dunmore. The Augusta County Court, which had been adjourned from Staunton, Virginia, on December 6, 1774, was organized at the Fort.
February 23: Jacob Bausman was licensed by the Virginia Court to keep a ferry over the Monongahela at the foot of Wood Street where John Ormsby had his establishment for the previous two years.
Spring: Governor Dunmore advised Dr. Connolly to disband his militia and devote himself to winning the support of the Indians for the British cause.
May 16: In a convention held at Pittsburgh, frontiersmen of the territory set up a Committee of Safety, approved the action of the colonies in their revolt against the Crown, and resolved that it was the "indispensable duty of every American" to resist tyranny.
July 25: Dr. Connolly left for Virginia; Pennsylvania authority prevailed generally in the Pittsburgh area.
August 25: A band of "patriots" burned the tea stock of the merchants Joseph Symonds and John Campbell.
August: John Neville (1731–1803), with 100 militia, took possession of the fort.
October 7: By the Treaty of Pittsburgh, the chiefs of the Indian tribes in the area pledged friendship and neutrality in the conflict between Great Britain and her colonies.

1776 *October:* By a Second Treaty of Pittsburgh, the Indians confirmed their agreement of the year before.

1777 *June 1:* Fort Pitt, once again bearing its proud name, became a United States fort when Brigadier General Edward Hand took it over from Captain John Neville.
August 20: The Virginia Court moved out of the fort.

1778 *June:* David Rogers, with about 40 men, left Fort Pitt to bring a much-needed cargo of ammunition from New Orleans. His return was intercepted.

1779 *August 11:* Colonel Daniel Brodhead left Fort Pitt with 600 men to destroy the Seneca Indian villages along the upper Allegheny River.

1781 *Early:* Hugh Henry Brackenridge arrived from Philadelphia to practice law. He soon became an important civic and political leader in western Pennsylvania.

1782 The German Evangelical Protestant (Congregational) Church, the first organized religious group in Pittsburgh, held services in a small block-house at the corner of present Wood and Diamond streets. Reverend John William Weber was pastor.

1784 *June:* In the first real estate sale on

PITTSBURGH ACADEMY IN 1787
when Pittsburgh was an 80-acre clearing. This reconstruction was made by Architect Charles M. Stotz and Ward Hunter for Agnes Starrett's history of the University of Pittsburgh.

record, Isaac Craig and Samuel Bayard purchased three acres of land lying between Fort Pitt and the Allegheny River.
Bouquet's Redoubt—the Blockhouse—was converted into a dwelling and continued as such until April 1, 1894. The Penns' Pittsburgh Manor was laid out in lots by George Woods and Thomas Vickroy. The manor embraced the tongue of land between the two rivers as far as present Grant Street and Eleventh.

1785 *August 15:* The Supreme Executive Council of Pennsylvania ordered John Ormsby to "take possession of Fort Pitt in behalf of the Commonwealth, upon its being relinquished" by the United States.
Lodge No. 45, Ancient Order of York Masons, was organized.

1786 *July 29:* The Pittsburgh *Gazette*, first newspaper west of the Allegheny Mountains, was published as a weekly by John Scull and Joseph Hall, printers.
In the columns of the newly launched *Gazette*, Hugh H. Brackenridge wrote that, at the junction of the three rivers in the morning, "a light fog is usually incumbent." But, he observed, "inasmuch as it consists of vapor . . . which the sun of the preceding day had extracted from trees and flowers and in the evening had sent back into dew . . . it is experienced to be healthful."
Niles' Weekly Register reported that "36 log houses, one stone house, one frame house, and five small stores" extended along Chancery Lane and Market Street.
February 28: The State Legislature granted a charter for the Pittsburgh Academy "for the education of youth in useful arts, sciences and literature." Judge Hugh Henry Brackenridge was prime organizer.
September 24: The Penns donated two and one half lots each to the First Presbyterian, the German Evangelical Protestant, and the Trinity Protestant Episcopal churches.

643

September 29: The First Presbyterian Church was incorporated by an act of the Legislature.

October 5: David Redick was appointed by the Supreme Executive Council to lay out the "Town Common and lots in the reserve tract opposite Pittsburgh." The reserved tract had been authorized by the Legislature in September 1787.

The first market house was erected.

1788 *September 24*: Mainly through efforts of Hugh H. Brackenridge, lawyer and state assemblyman, Allegheny County was created out of parts of Westmoreland and Washington counties; Pittsburgh was decreed the county seat.

November 19: Lots in the reserved tract were sold at public sale in Philadelphia.

December 16: The first Quarter Sessions Court of Allegheny County convened in Pittsburgh at Andrew Watson's tavern.

Regular mail service to Philadelphia was inaugurated.

A Mechanical Society, devoted to the betterment of the workingman, was organized.

1789 *March 14*: The first Court of Common Pleas convened in Andrew Watson's tavern.

July 2: The *Gazette* reported: "Yesterday was brought to this place and buried, the bodies of two young men, named Arthur Graham and Alexander Campbell, who had gone out to fish. They were killed by the savages about two miles from this place."

Captain Thomas Hutchins, geographer of the United States, died at John Ormsby's.

1790 *April*: Army garrison officers gave a theatrical presentation—*Cato* and *All the World's a Stage*.

Population: 376; Allegheny County, 10,309.

1791 *February*: Isaac Craig was appointed quartermaster general and was given permission to repair Fort Pitt.

September 6: Robert Johnson, the revenue collector, was tarred and feathered by angered citizens.

November: An army hospital was established "in a rented house in the town," with Dr. Carmichael in charge.

Samuel Slater started a cotton mill with a staff of nine children from seven to twelve years of age.

1792 *May 1*: Captain Hughes, in command of the army garrison at Fort Pitt, occupied Fort Fayette (LaFayette), just completed near the Allegheny close to the old bastion.

General Anthony Wayne and his army arrived in town.

1793 *September 12*: The city's first fire engine was purchased at a cost of £1200, and the Eagle Fire Engine and Hose Company, the first to be organized in the town, was formed with headquarters at First Street (Avenue) between Market and Ferry.

October 14: Regular river packet service was inaugurated by Jacob Myers between Pittsburgh and Cincinnati.

Modern Chivalry, volume three, a novel by Hugh Henry Brackenridge, was printed by John Scull. It was the first book printed west of the Allegheny Mountains.

George Anshutz built a small furnace in Two Mile Run (present Shadyside). One of its first tasks was to manufacture cannon balls for General Anthony Wayne's army.

1794 *April 22*: Pittsburgh was incorporated as a borough.

May 19: George Robinson and Josiah Tannehill were chosen chief burgesses in the first borough election.

August: Farmers who protested against the collection of excise tax on whisky marched to Pittsburgh from their rendezvous at Braddock's Field.

November 12-13: Burgess George Robinson and three other Pittsburghers were among 18 southwestern Pennsylvanians arrested by General Irvine's troops during the "dreadful night" of the Whisky Insurrection.

1795 *April 18*: Weekly mail service was established between Pittsburgh and Philadelphia.

First glass factory was built by Major Isaac Craig and General O'Hara on the north bank of the Ohio River across from the Point. It manufactured bottles.

1796 A census of Pittsburgh showed a population of 1300.

The first Methodist Episcopal Church service was held in the "unoccupied meeting house" of the Presbyterians.

1797 *January 28*: Red Pole, great Shawnee Indian chief, died at Pittsburgh and was buried in Trinity churchyard.

August 5: Notice of July 8 advertised the sale of all building material remaining on the site of the abandoned Fort Pitt.

1798 *May 19*: The ship *President Adams* was launched at nearby Elizabeth; it was built in Pittsburgh and armed for service against the Spaniards on the lower Mississippi. The *Senator Ross* was built in Pittsburgh the same year. Glass was blown at O'Hara's Glassworks, the first flint glass made west of the Alleghenies.

1799 The first courthouse, a two-story brick structure, was completed. It stood on the western half of the Diamond. County, state, and federal courts convened here until 1841.

Reformed Presbyterian Church was organized.

1800 *August 16*: The city's second newspaper, *Tree of Liberty*, was published by John Israel, with Hugh Henry Brackenridge as chief backer and chief editorial writer.

Zadok Cramer, a New Jersey printer, purchased Gilkinson's Book Store, re-named it the *Sign of the Franklin Head*, began a printing and bookbinding business, and printed his first *Almanack*.

Pittsburgh commercial life revolved around 63 shops, 23 of them general stores, six shoe shops, four bakeries, and four hat shops.

Population: 1565; Allegheny County, 15,087.

Perkins store, first "department store" west of Philadelphia, was opened.

1801 *November 24*: The associate Presbyterian Church was organized.

Zadok Cramer printed the first edition of the *Navigator*, a guide to river navigation.

1802 *August 9*: The Borough Council ordered four public wells to be sunk on Market Street—the beginning of Pittsburgh's water system.

Jeffery Scaife Tin and Japanned Ware Manufactory, parent organization of the William B. Scaife & Sons Company began business in the Diamond.

A report by Zadok Cramer in the *Pittsburgh Almanack* stated that industry in Pittsburgh included one large brewery, two glassworks, one fine-glass factory, one large paper mill, several oil mills, powder works, ironworks, saltworks, saw- and gristmills, and a boat yard.

1803 *January 26*: In the first theatrical production in the city, the Bromly and Arnold traveling troupe of actors presented a tragedy, *The Gamester*, at the courthouse.

March 26: A public meeting was held to consider a proposal for a bank in the borough.

The *Pittsburgh Almanack for the Year 1803* estimated the total value of Pittsburgh manufacturing at $358,903. Of that amount, iron manufacturing accounted for $56,548 from the production of 180 tons of castings and bar iron and 40 tons of nails. Textile manufacturing was second in value with $46,825.

The rivers were beginning to be used for the shipment of coal from Pittsburgh to Philadelphia via New Orleans.

1804 *January 9*: Pittsburgh's first bank, a branch of the Bank of Pennsylvania at Philadelphia, opened for business at a location on Second Street, between Market and Ferry.

December: In the first recorded strike in Pittsburgh, traveling journeymen shoemakers "made a turnout for higher wages."

A newly established stagecoach line was offering "speedy" six-day service between Pittsburgh and Philadelphia.

Peter Eltonhead, an Englishman, founded the first large-scale cotton mill.

General Presley Neville, burgess of Pittsburgh, asked George Stevenson, president of the Council, to study smoke problems and, in particular, the possibility of higher chimneys as a smoke-control measure. His letter stated that "not only the comfort, health and, in some measure, the consequence of the place, but the harmony of the inhabitants, depends upon speedy measures being adopted to remedy this nuisance."

The Pittsburgh Foundry (predecessor of Mackintosh-Hemphill Company), first in the city, was established at Fifth and Smithfield by Joseph McClurg.

1805 *July 1:* Cornerstone was laid for the Old Round Church of St. Luke's Protestant Episcopal Congregation. Its charter was granted on September 1.
Commonwealth, a weekly newspaper, began publication.

1806 *January 21:* The *United States Gazette for the Country,* at Philadelphia, published a letter from a Pittsburgh correspondent reporting: "On Wednesday last (the 8th inst.) a duel was fought in the vicinity of Pittsburgh between Tarleton Bates, Esq., the prothonotary of Allegheny County, and a person of the name of Stewart, a storekeeper here, in which Mr. Bates was killed at the second fire. . . . The minds of the people of Pittsburgh appear much inflamed."
February: The first company prepared to build a turnpike from Pittsburgh to Harrisburg was incorporated.
April 10: A flood of 37.1 feet was recorded.

1807 George Robinson and Edward Ensel glassworks was in operation.
Anthony Beelen established the Eagle foundry.
George Miltenberger's Copper and Tinware Manufactory was established.

1808 Bakewell and Page purchased the Robinson and Ensel glassworks. In 1818 the firm furnished President Monroe "a complete set of flint glass, each piece engraved with the arms of the United States."
James B. Scott and Company (Follansbee Steel Corporation) was founded by James Park.

1809 Pittsburgh Steam Flour Mill, the first west of the Alleghenies, was established by Oliver and Owen Evans.

1810 *November 9:* The city was innundated by a flood of 35.2 feet.
Bank of Pittsburgh, second in the borough and first with local capital, was organized and operated for a time under the name of Pittsburgh Manufacturing Company.
Population: 4786; Allegheny County, **25,317.**

1811 *May 31:* The Vigilant Fire Company was organized.
June 24: First Masonic Hall dedicated.
August: Old St. Patrick's Church, the city's first Roman Catholic church, was dedicated at Liberty and Washington streets.

October 25: The *New Orleans,* which was built at a cost of $40,000 by Nicholas Roosevelt, sailed down the Ohio to establish the first regular packet service between Natchez and New Orleans and thus became the first steamboat to navigate western rivers.
The Reverend Francis Herron began a 49-year pastorate in the First Presbyterian Church.

1812 *May 7:* William Turner and Company opened what is believed to have been the city's first theater.
September 10: The Pittsburgh Blues, a military unit, left on a year's expedition in the Ohio Country, in the service of the United States.
The first rolling mill was built by Christopher Cowan.

BOAT OUTFITTER

Florence Cotter advertises in the 1819 *Pittsburgh Directory* "that he constantly has on hand, a complete assortment of Groceries and Liquors . . . which he will sell on the most reasonable terms." Boat outfitting was an important commercial activity in the city.

Rigging for Oliver H. Perry's fleet on Lake Erie was made in the borough.
Steam-engine works, built by Oliver Evans and managed by Mark Stackhouse, went into operation in May.
Christopher Cowan built a steam mill for slitting iron.
Elliott Nursery was established at Smithfield Street.

1813 *May 10:* Humane Society was organized.
November 27: First recorded meeting of the Pittsburgh Permanent Library Company.
The Comet, a stern-wheel steamboat, was built.

1814 *June 10:* A letter printed in the *Gazette* said: "Although much of the prosperity of Pittsburgh is owing to its 'Fires,' it is not be concealed that the effects of those fires have become subjects of complaint. That the evil (if it be an evil to be enveloped in smoke) is daily increasing and that relief is now universally called for."
November 23: Bank of Pittsburgh was reorganized with capital of $600,000 and George Wilkins as president.
A stern-wheel steamboat left Pittsburgh with a cargo of guns destined for General Jackson at New Orleans.

Pepin, Brishard, and Cayetano conducted the first circus.
Western Medical Society was organized.
Allegheny Arsenal was established by the federal government. It was designed by B. H. Latrobe and built in the Lawrenceville district under the direction of Colonel Abraham R. Butler at a cost of $300,000.
Anchor Steam Paper Mill, first papermill in Pittsburgh, was built by Henry Holdship.

1815 *March:* Newspapers advocated "some plan for smoke abatement."
Pittsburgh Directory for 1815, the city's first directory, was compiled and published by James M. Riddle.
The Farmers and Mechanics Bank, founded by John Scull, was incorporated.
The weekly *Mercury* began publication.

1816 *January 27:* According to the *Gazette,* Alexander Thompson, "who resides on the turnpike road 4½ miles from Pittsburgh," reported that during 1815, excluding iron shipments, a total of "5,800 road waggons laden with merchandise, etc., passed his farm for Pittsburgh. The greater part of these waggons returned loaded with cordage, salt petre, etc., to the east of the mountains."
February: Flood waters reached a stage of 36.2 feet.
March 18: Pittsburgh was incorporated as a city under an act providing for a mayor, one select and one common council, 12 aldermen, and a recorder.
July 9: Ebenezer Denny, merchant, began serving term as the first mayor of Pittsburgh; James Ross as first president of the select council; William Wilkins as first president of the common council.
August 2: The Farmers and Mechanics Bank was chartered.
Whale-oil lamps were installed as the city's first street lights.

1817 *September 5:* President James Monroe visited arsenal in the city.
First shoe-jobbing firm in United States, H. Childs and Company, was established.
A branch of the second Bank of the United States was established in Pittsburgh with John Thaw as cashier. This bank took over the business of the defunct Bank of Pennsylvania and was named Office of Discounts and Deposits of the United States.
John Darragh began his eight-year term as the city's second mayor.

1818 *March 25:* Ten thousand men, women, and children witnessed the first execution of a white man in Allegheny County, the hanging of John Tiernan, who was found guilty of killing his best friend.
April 6: In Pittsburgh's first bank

robbery, $104,000 was stolen from Farmers and Mechanics Bank; the accused robbers, Pluymart and Emmons, were captured soon thereafter.

May 20: A federal court for Western Pennsylvania was established here; Jonathan Hoge Walker was appointed first judge by President James Monroe.

The Pittsburgh-Harrisburg turnpike was opened to travel.

1819 *February 18:* Pittsburgh Academy was rechartered by the Legislature and renamed Western University of Pennsylvania; its location was on Third Avenue.

December 16: General James O'Hara, Pittsburgh's pioneer industrialist, died at his home at the Point.

The first bridge across the Allegheny River (Federal and St. Clair streets) was completed. It served till 1860, when it was replaced by a suspension bridge.

Monongahela Bridge was erected at a cost of $102,000.

Angle iron was rolled at the Union Rolling Mill, the first complete rolling mill in the United States.

The city's first steam cotton mill, James Arthurs and Sons Cotton Factory, began production.

1820 Population: 7248; Allegheny County, 34,927.

The city's Alms House was built.

1821 *June:* Pittsburgh Medical Society was organized.

Turnpike was completed from Pittsburgh to Erie, via Butler, Mercer, and Meadville.

The *Pittsburgh Recorder*, a Presbyterian journal, was first issued.

1822 N. Holmes and Sons, the city's first family-owned bank, was established.

1823 *April 28:* Henry Clay was a visitor.

The Apprentice Library was established as Pittsburgh's first free public library.

1824 Western University of Pennsylvania conferred bachelor's degrees for the first time. There were six in the graduating class.

The Councils passed an ordinance providing for a central city water system.

1825 *April 7:* Western Theological Seminary was founded in Allegheny City by Presbyterian Church.

May 30: The Marquis de Lafayette arrived at the Mansion House for a two-week visit. One of the most spectacular social events was a ball held at Colonel Ramsay's Hotel on Wood Street at Third Avenue in honor of the French statesman.

Allegheny Theological Seminary was established in Allegheny by the Associate Reformed Presbyterian Church.

1826 *July 4:* Composer Stephen Collins Foster was born at 3600 Penn Avenue.

September: The city's first water reservoir was completed on Grant's Hill.

THE WESTERN STATE PENITENTIARY
In 1818 the Assembly voted for "a penitentiary on the principle of solitary confinement of convicts" at Allegheny. After eight years and at a cost of $178,206.85½ the architecturally sumptuous building was completed.

December: Work was started on the Pennsylvania Canal.

1827 *February:* The Bethel African Methodist Episcopal Church, the first Negro church west of the Allegheny Mountains, was instituted at Water and Smithfield streets.

April: *The Albion*, first steamboat to travel up the Allegheny River as far as Kittanning, left the city.

June 20: Henry Clay, Secretary of State, visited the city again.

November 16: Western Theologicial Seminary was opened for study.

November 22: Western Penitentiary, the first state penal institution west of the mountains, was completed in Allegheny.

November 28: Contract was let to construct the Aqueduct to carry the Pennsylvania Canal over the Allegheny River to the city.

St. Paul's Church was organized under leadership of Father Charles Bonaventure Maguire, and a building, which six years later became St. Paul's Cathedral, was erected at Fifth Avenue and Grant Street.

1828 *April 14:* Allegheny was incorporated as a borough.

May 3: Foundation stone was laid for the Washington Lock, the first of four, to connect the Pennsylvania Canal and the Monongahela River.

September: The city's first water-supply system, with a reservoir on Grant's Hill and a pumping station at the foot of Cecil Alley, was ready for service.

John Irwin was elected the first burgess of Allegheny.

First museum and art gallery was opened to public.

Etna Iron Works, first iron-pipe manufacturing plant west of Alleghenies, was built by H. S. Spang and Son (Predecessor of Spang, Chalfant and Company).

1829 *November 10:* The Aqueduct carrying the Canal over the Allegheny River to the Canal basin in the city went into service.

1830 *March:* Natural gas was discovered in Saw Mill Run at depth of 627 feet.

The anti-Masonic, anti-Jackson councils elected Mathew B. Lowrie mayor. Population: Pittsburgh, 12,568; Allegheny, 2801 citizens, eight slaves; Allegheny County, 50,552.

1831 *January 12:* Pittsburgh *Times* began publication.

July 1: First steam ferry began operating at the foot of Penn Street.

Duquesne Grays, a citizens' militia, was organized.

David G. Blythe, the artist, arrived in the city to study wood carving.

John H. Mellor established on Wood Street a firm said to be the first piano house in America.

1832 *February 10:* Flood waters reached a level of 38.2 feet at the Point.

April 5: Orphan Society of Pittsburgh and Allegheny, the present Protestant Home for Children and the oldest institution of its kind in Pennsylvania, was founded. It was incorporated in 1834.

John M. Roberts and Son opened a jewelry and watchmaking establishment at Fifth Avenue and Market.

Samuel Pettigrew was chosen mayor.

The Farmer's Deposit National Bank of Pittsburgh began business as the Pittsburgh Savings Fund Company.

1833 *July 4:* Daniel Webster visited.

July 30: The *Gazette*, under management of John I. Scull and Morgan Neville, became a daily paper.

September 2: The Pittsburgh Theater, known as Old Drury and located on Fifth Avenue between Wood and Smithfield streets, opened with the play *Busy Body* and the afterpiece *Age of Tomorrow*. Tyrone Power played *Hamlet* in the third presentation at the theater.

St. Paul's Roman Catholic Church was dedicated. It was consecrated the sect's first cathedral in the city on August 7, 1843.

The City Charter was amended to provide for the election of the mayor by popular vote. Previously mayors had been chosen by the City Councils, and their choice restricted to the city's 12 aldermen.

1834 *February 27:* The first historical society was organized.

ROPE WALK IN EAST LIBERTY
The ropemakers of early Pittsburgh walked backward along a narrow roofed-in enclosure, deftly winding the strands of fiber into rope.

Spring: A route between Pittsburgh and Philadelphia via canal and railroad (Pennsylvania Canal, Portage and Columbia railroads) was opened.

August 9: William Lesky, sheriff, issued a proclamation establishing a "general system of common schools." Pennsylvania canal system from Philadelphia to Pittsburgh was completed at a cost of $10,000,000.

Samuel Pettigrew was returned to office in the first public election for mayor.

1835 *April 8:* The select and common councils authorized the first gas works to be built in the city.

September 11: Pittsburgh's first public school opened in a rented room in a Seventh Street building; five pupils attended class taught by James F. Gilmore.

The Pittsburgh, the first steam locomotive to be built west of the Allegheny Mountains, was built by McClurg, Wade, and Company.

1836 *March 26:* The Councils adopted an ordinance establishing a system of police to include one captain of the watch, two lieutenants, and 16 watchmen.

March 31: The Monongahela Navigation Company was chartered and began construction of locks and dams in Monongahela River.

May 26: A city ordinance was passed authorizing the initial grading of Grant's Hill, familiarly known as "the Hump," a cut of ten feet in Fifth Avenue hill just east of Central City.

August 6: Fourteen trade unions amalgamated to form the Pittsburgh Central Labor Union.

October 13: A cornerstone was laid for construction of the second courthouse.

Jonas R. McClintock was first successful public candidate for mayor.

N. R. Smith founded a system of lyceums which dominated the city's intellectual life for the next ten years.

1837 *April 6:* For the first time, manufactured gas lighting appeared on the streets of the city and in many stores.

May 15: All Pittsburgh banks suspended gold payments as the result of nationwide inflation caused by overexpansion of business and "disorderly currency."

A TWO DOLLAR NOTE

which the city of Pittsburgh issued in October 1847 was "bearing an interest of one per cent per annum," rather low for those days.

TRAVELLING IN 1836

A road scene painted by George Tattersall (1817–49). It is now in the Karolik Collection of the Boston Museum of Fine Arts.

November 1: The first public school for Negroes was opened.

Isaac Harris' *Directory for 1837* estimated the value of Pittsburgh manufacturing at $11,606,350.

The Orphan Society built its first orphanage.

1838 Mechanics Bridge was built over the Allegheny River at Sixteenth Street.

1839 *Spring:* Over 1400 canal boats carrying 25,000 tons of freight passed through Pittsburgh.

September: Valley Forge, the first large iron steamboat, was built by Robinson and Minis.

The bridge over the Allegheny River at Hand (Ninth) Street was completed. The roof of the bridge became a fashionable promenade.

Grogan Company, jewelers, was established.

1840 *April 13:* Allegheny was incorporated as a third-class city with a population of 10,989.

May 4: Clayton's "aerial mail packet" balloon, bound for Philadelphia, took off from Pittsburgh and landed the same evening in the vicinity of Tarentum.

July 17: William Robinson was inaugurated as first mayor of Allegheny City.

Pittsburgh developed as a coal port; in this year coal shipments out of city totaled 464,826 tons.

Peter Duff's Mercantile College (Duff's Business College) established. Population: 21,515; Allegheny City, 10,089; Allegheny County, 81,235.

1841 *January:* En route to Washington for his inauguration, President-elect William H. Harrison visited the city.

April: The hostelry Monongahela House, opened its doors.

July 31: A strike followed by riots in six cotton factories in Allegheny.

September 8: The Pittsburgh *Weekly Chronicle* began publication.

1842 *March 20:* Charles Dickens, the English author, arrived with his wife at the Exchange Hotel, Penn Avenue at Sixth, for a three-day visit.

September 10: Pittsburgh *Daily Morning Post* was first published.

The Henry Oliver family, including

2-year-old Henry William Oliver, emigrated from Ireland to Pittsburgh. The second courthouse, designed by John Chislett, was completed on Grant's Hill.

1843 *August 7:* The See of Pittsburgh was created with the Right Reverend Michael O'Connor as first bishop.

December 22: Seven Sisters of Mercy arrived from Ireland to establish their Order here.

The Aqueduct was rebuilt on the suspension principle, using wire cable made by John Roebling. This was the first great public work in which wire cable was used in place of wooden beams.

1844 *November 13:* The Monongahela River was formally opened for navigation as far as Brownsville; seven dams and 11 locks were in operation.

Joseph Woodwell, well known in the city as a wood carver of unusual ability, entered the hardware business in partnership in a store named Walker and Woodwell.

1845 *April 10:* A fire that started in the back of an icehouse at Ferry Street and Second Avenue destroyed 982 buildings, made about 12,000 persons homeless, resulted in damage estimated between $5,000,000 and $8,000,000 and left one third of city in ashes.

May 22: Mary Cassatt, noted impressionist painter, was born in Allegheny. (She died in 1926.)

Steamboats were first used here for towing coal barges.

The iron frigate *Allegheny* was built here for the United States Navy.

1846 *February 8:* The Pittsburgh *Dispatch,* first successful penny newspaper west of Alleghenies, was founded by Colonel J. Heron Foster.

April 13: The Pennsylvania Railroad was incorporated.

December 22: Duquesne Grays and Jackson Blues, first Pittsburgh regiments, left by boat for New Orleans and Vera Cruz to join in the war against Mexico.

December 29: Pittsburgh dispatched its first telegraphic message, a report from General Bowman of the Pennsylvania militia notifying President Polk that the second Pennsylvania regiment was ready to leave for Mexico.

First manufacture of a new explosive gun cotton.

Samuel M. Kier, Pittsburgh druggist, began to sell crude oil for medicinal purposes.

The covered wooden bridge over the Monongahela River at Smithfield Street was replaced by a wire suspension one, the first so constructed by John Roebling, builder of the Brooklyn Bridge.

A Society of Jews, forerunner of the Rodef Shalom Congregation, was formed.

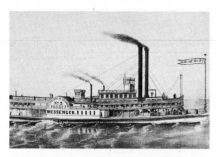

THE MESSENGER NO. 2
One of the favorite boats of the Pittsburgh & Cincinnati Packet Line. This lithograph was published by N. Currier in New York.

1847   *January 1:* The Sisters of Mercy opened their first hospital here, called it the "Mercy."
March 1: The Joseph Woodwell Company, situated at Second Avenue and Wood Street, opened its doors to the public.
March 5: The Monongahela House, rebuilt after being destroyed in the 1845 fire, was opened.
March 9: A citizens' meeting was held to plan erection of a public hospital.
July 13: The Mercantile Library Association, a union of several library groups, was founded.
The *Post* became the first city newspaper to utilize the telegraph for news coverage.
Pittsburgh-born Jane Grey Swisshelm, reformer and abolitionist, began publication of *The Saturday Visiter,* a weekly journal.

1848   *February 1:* The *Mercury* published the city's first Sunday newspaper.
March 18: Western Pennsylvania Hospital (West Penn) was chartered.
May 9: Sisters of Mercy completed a hospital on Stevenson Street with bed capacity for 60 patients.
August 17: Allegheny Medical Society was organized as a branch of the State Medical Society.
Thirteen-year-old Andrew Carnegie and his family left Scotland for Pittsburgh.
Anesthesia—in the form of chloroform—was used for the first time in Pittsburgh by Dr. William H. Wright in a tooth extraction.

1849   *February 22:* An advertisement appeared in *Daily Gazette* announcing that "J. Horne, Trimmings, Notions, Millinery and Fancy Goods," was open for business at 63 Market Street.
December 20: Puddlers and boilers in iron mills began a five-month strike in protest against a reduction in wages; this action led to later organization of the Sons of Vulcan.
Iron City Industrial Congress was organized by 23 local unions.
Pittsburgh City Glass Works was

started by Wilson Cunningham and his two brothers.
A two-hour speech by Salmon P. Chase, Ohio Free-Soil senator, at Allegheny Market House, set the trend of abolitionist thinking in Pittsburgh. First waterworks in Allegheny was completed.
A second cut, this one seven feet, was made in the "Hump."

1850   *January 7:* Joseph Barker, an itinerant reformer, was elected mayor while serving a year's term in jail for disturbing the peace.
January: Passavant Hospital, founded in 1849 under the name Pittsburgh Infirmary by the Reverend William Passavant of Zelienople, was chartered.
September 10: Pennsylvania Railroad began operating trains between Pittsburgh and Johnstown.
Colonel James Anderson established in Allegheny an Apprentices' Library and opened it to working boys. Andrew Carnegie was one of the regular boy patrons.
The value of Pittsburgh manufacturing was estimated at $50,000,000 by Samuel Fahnestock in the *Pittsburgh Directory for the Year 1850.*
B. F. Jones resigned as manager of the Pennsylvania Canal to begin operating a puddling iron works on the south bank of the Monongahela River.
Population: Pittsburgh, 46,601; Allegheny City, 21,262; Allegheny County, 138,290.

1851   *January:* Jane Grey Swisshelm, advocate of women's rights, polled only three votes in her campaign for the office of mayor.
April 25: In the city's greatest musical event of the era, Jenny Lind, under the management of Phineas T. Barnum, sang at Masonic Hall, Fifth Avenue, before 1000 persons who paid an average of $7 each for tickets sold on auction.
May 16: Evergreen Hamlet, an experiment in communal living, started.
July 30: Regular passenger service was inaugurated by the Ohio and Pennsylvania Railroad (Fort Wayne) between Allegheny and New Brighton.
December 10: The Pennsylvania Railroad formally began business in the city of Pittsburgh with its rail line extended as far as Turtle Creek. At that point passengers transferred to stagecoach, which bridged a 28-mile gap in the rail connection.
A Marine Hospital, designed to care for disabled rivermen, was established by the federal government at nearby Woods Run.
The report-card system was established in the city schools.

1852   *April 19:* The rivers went to a stage of 35.1 feet in another flood.
August: The National Free-Soil Convention, one of the first mass aboli-

tionist meetings in the country, was held in Pittsburgh.
August 19: Flood waters reached a mark of 31 feet, 9 inches.
November 17: The Ohio and Pennsylvania Railroad posted regular schedules between Pittsburgh, Alliance, Canton, Massillon, and Wooster, Ohio. It offered four trains daily, the first leaving Pittsburgh at 8 A.M. and arriving in Wooster at 3:30 P.M.
November 29: The Pennsylvania Railroad opened an all-rail route from Pittsburgh to Philadelphia, utilizing the Portage and Columbia railroads. The Pennsylvania State Teachers Association was organized at a meeting in Pittsburgh.
Pittsburgh Board of Health was created.

1853   *June:* Benjamin F. Jones formed a partnership with Bernard and John Lauth and Samuel Kier, with whom he had operated the Mechanics Line, a canal boat line from Pittsburgh to Philadelphia. They established on the south bank of the Monongahela River puddling furnaces and rolling mills under the name of Jones, Lauth and Company.
September: The *Morning Post* listed the following hotels in operation in Pittsburgh: Monongahela House, Exchange Hotel, Merchants Hotel, American Hotel, United States, Spread Eagle, Miller's Mansion House, and Broadhurst Mansion House.
The Economites, a religious society near Ambridge, Pa., completed the Saw Mill Run Railroad to Banksville, a distance of three miles.
The city's first Jewish congregation held services in a temporary synagogue located over the Vigilant Fire Engine House on Third Avenue.
The borough of West Pittsburgh was formed.
The first Pittsburgh post office and federal government building was erected at Fifth Avenue and Smithfield Street.
The Pittsburgh *Legal Journal* (second law periodical in the United States and third in the world) was published by Thomas J. Keenan and John Hastings.

1854   *February 15:* The Summit tunnel of

WESTERN PENNSYLVANIA HOSPITAL, which first opened its doors in 1853, was located at 28th Street and Liberty Avenue.

the Pennsylvania Railroad was opened, allowing continuous rail travel between Pittsburgh and Harrisburg.

March: The first bill was introduced in the Legislature to consolidate the cities of Pittsburgh and Allegheny.

September: The Pittsburgh *Post* reported a total of 400 deaths in two weeks in the city's worst cholera epidemic.

Rodef Shalom Congregation was organized.

1855 *March 24:* Andrew W. Mellon was born in East Liberty.

March: Ladies were first employed as clerks in dry-goods stores.

July 19: The Dollar Savings Bank, founded as the Pittsburgh Dollar Savings Institution, was opened for business.

August 29: The first county Republican convention adopted an abolition resolution.

September 25: The first public high school (Central) was opened in rented quarters, at 508 Smithfield Street, for 114 pupils.

A new city hall and market, at Diamond and Market, was completed.

1856 *January 29:* The Allegheny Valley Railroad was opened to Kittanning.

February 22: The first national convention of Republicans met in Lafayette Hall in Pittsburgh for a two-day session to complete national party organization.

July 29: The Pittsburgh, Fort Wayne and Chicago Railroad was incorporated and its line was opened through to Chicago from Allegheny.

Joseph L. Lowry built the first steam fire engine for the city.

John Lauth, sold his interests in Jones, Lauth, and Company to the other partners. James A. Laughlin bought into the business.

1857 *February 23:* Novelist Margaret Wade Deland was born in Allegheny. (She died in 1945.)

August: The financial panic reached a climax in Pittsburgh when all local banks, with the exception of the Bank of Pittsburgh, suspended payments "until such time as the Philadelphia banks resume."

September 22: The first railroad bridge across the Allegheny River, a

BALL OF THE DUQUESNE GRAYS
The date of it: February 14, 1860, the very year Abraham Lincoln was elected President.

wooden structure, was opened to bring the Ohio and Pennsylvania Railroad into the city of Pittsburgh.

Fall: Charlotte Jones, convicted of killing her aunt and uncle for their money in the notorious "McKeesport cabin murder," became the first woman to be hanged in Allegheny County. She said, "I did this for the great love I had for Denny Fife."

The Pennsylvania Railroad purchased the Pennsylvania Canal for $7,500,000.

The Diamond Savings Institution (predecessor of the Union National Bank of Pittsburgh) was founded.

1858 *March 10:* The first train operated from Allegheny into the city's first Union Station, located at Seventh Street and Liberty Avenue.

May 26: The United Presbyterian Church of North America was created by the merger of the Associate Reformed and the Associate Presbyterian churches. The merger took place in the old City Hall in Market Square.

Mackeown and Finley agreed to sell to the A. C. Ferris and Company of New York City two thirds of their output of carbon oil. This contract marked the beginning of the use of petroleum products in New York.

Samuel Kier set up his first commercial oil refinery or "still" in his drugstore basement at 363 Liberty Avenue.

A small group of iron puddlers, meeting in an old Diamond Street hotel, organized the Sons of Vulcan, first union movement in the iron industry in Pittsburgh. The action was the result of the financial panic of 1857, which had forced their wage to be reduced to $3.25 per ton.

In Millvale, the Kloman brothers began operating the forge works which led to the Carnegie steel organization.

The first tin plate (iron coated with tin) ever made was produced by C. G. Hussey and Company.

1859 *January 10:* The Western Pennsylvania Historical Society held its first meeting in the Merchants Exchange.

March 22: The Citizen Passenger Railway Company was granted a charter for construction and operation of first street railway in city. The first track was laid on Penn Avenue from St. Clair (Sixth) Street to 26th Street.

July: James Laughlin, a banker and merchant, built the first two Eliza blast furnaces with beehive coke ovens, on the north side of the Monongahela River, directly opposite the Jones, Lauth plant. The new plant was known as Laughlin and Company.

August 5: The first horsecar, "a single-truck vehicle, seating 14 passengers, dimly lighted at night," began operating; the fare from Butler Street to East Liberty was six cents.

August 29: The petroleum industry had its birth when Colonel Edward L.

TRAVELLING IN AMERICA
An artist of the *Illustrated London News* drew this picture for the April 6, 1861 issue.

Drake struck oil at 69 feet at Titusville about 75 miles north of the city.

September 1: The Union National Bank was organized as a successor to the Diamond Savings Institution.

November 16: Clinton, the second blast furnace built in the district, and the first to use coke for the blast, went into operation at the South Side plant of Graff, Bennett, and Company.

Cold rolling of iron and steel was invented and patented by Bernard Lauth, a partner of Benjamin F. Jones.

H. Samson began operating as a funeral director.

1860 *June 22:* An announcement was made of the opening of "books to receive subscription of stock" for construction of a "free bridge" over the Allegheny.

July 29: Professor S. Wilson ascended from Pittsburgh in his balloon, *Great Western*, disappeared from view, and landed hours later on a hill near Sharpsburg.

October 1: The Prince of Wales, the later Edward VII of the United Kingdom, was warmly greeted by Pittsburghers when he arrived at the Monongahela House for an overnight stay. He visited factories and manufacturing establishments.

November 28: Because of Civil War clouds, all Pittsburgh banks except the Bank of Pittsburgh suspended specie payments.

December: The city refused to comply with the Secretary of War's order for the transfer of guns from the Allegheny Arsenal to the South.

Allegheny Observatory was founded.

Population: 49,221; Allegheny City, 28,702; Allegheny County, 178,031.

1861 *February 15:* From a balcony of the Monongahela House, President-elect Lincoln, who had stopped in the city on his way to Washington, in a reference to the secession from the Union of southern states, declared that "notwithstanding the trouble across the river, there is no crisis but an artificial one."

April 24: Eighty men comprising "Turners Rifles" departed for Harrisburg to join Union troops; they became the first Pittsburgh soldiers to see action in the war.

ALLEGHENY ARSENAL
On September 17, 1862, a mysterious explosion blew up the Arsenal on Butler Street.

April: Camp Wilkins, near Penn Avenue and 26th Street, was established by Governor Andrew G. Curtin; a home guard was organized.

August: Bernard Lauth retired and James Laughlin bought his interest. Jones, Lauth, and Company became Jones and Laughlin's American Iron Works.

September 21: Property damage was heavy in a flood that reached a mark of 30 feet, 9½ inches.

October: United States Sanitary Commission, designed to receive donations of clothing and medical supplies for the Army, was established by the Citizens Committee of 100, which had been selected at a mass meeting in City Hall on April 15.

Baltimore and Ohio Railroad, via connecting railroads, was extended to the city.

The Trimble Construction Company began operations as the Crawford, Trimble and Gilliland Company.

1862 *January 1:* Iron City Forge Company, the parent of Kloman and Company and of the Carnegie iron and steel interests, was organized as a partnership of the Kloman brothers, Thomas Miller, and Henry Phipps.

January 4: The Home for the Friendless was chartered.

September 17: Seventy-eight persons, mostly boys and girls employed there, were killed and twice as many injured in an explosion at the Allegheny Arsenal in Lawrenceville, where munitions were being manufactured for the Union army.

November 25: Ethelbert Nevin, composer, author, and pianist, was born in nearby Edgeworth. He was the composer of "The Rosary."

1863 *March:* The Pittsburgh Trades Assembly was organized by representatives of 46 local unions.

April: The United States Christian Commission, directed by the Reverend Herrick Johnson, assumed most of work of Sanitary Commission and hospital activities of the Subsistence Committee.

June 14: In a Sunday meeting at the Monongahela House, Pittsburgh business-

nessmen and manufacturers, fearing a raid by the Confederate cavalry forces of J. E. B. Stuart, decided to suspend business and set up a defense.

June 16: Two thousand men, paid at rate of $1.25 per day by their own employers, began digging rifle pits on hills as a line of defense around the city.

June 25: Pittsburgh militia and home guard prepared for an attack on receipt of a telegraphic message that Jeb Stuart's troops had occupied McConnellsburg and were moving toward the city.

June 26: There were 11,828 men at work on 32 separate defense installations in the city.

July 4: All fortifications were completed, but the Confederate retreat after the Union victory at Gettysburg removed the threat to Pittsburgh.

August 5: Following their surrender to Union troops at Lisbon, Ohio, 118 officers of General John H. Morgan's cavalry, the only Confederate prisoners held in Pittsburgh in the Civil War, were brought to Western Penitentiary.

The iron frigates *Manayunk* and *Umpqua* were built.

The Third National Bank of Pittsburgh was founded at the corner of Wood Street and Virgin Alley (Oliver Avenue).

1864 *January 13:* Stephen Collins Foster, Pittsburgh's best-known composer, died destitute in New York.

STEPHEN FOSTER'S LAST NOTE
When the composer died in New York in January 1864, attendants found this in his pocket.

STATE SUPREME COURT IN 1868
Standing, left to right: George Sharswood and Henry W. Williams. Sitting: John M. Reed, James Thompson, and Daniel Agnew.

GREAT TUNNEL UNDER PITTSBURGH
A sketch made by Davis, published in the popular *Harper's Weekly* on December 3, 1864.

January: New city hall, market house, and weight house, bordering on the public square in Allegheny City, were completed.

March 21: Ulysses S. Grant, en route to take command of the Army of the Potomac, was the guest of honor at a dinner in the Monongahela House.

May 2: Andrew Carnegie, at 29, entered the iron-producing business by purchasing a sixth interest in the Iron City Forge Company for $8925. Other shareholders included Andrew Kloman and Henry Phipps.

June 16: Allegheny City's Sanitary Fair closed after raising $363,570 in 16 days for benefit of Union soldiers and their dependents. At the end of the war $200,000 unused funds were given to West Penn Hospital as a nucleus for an endowment.

June 30: The first train ran between Pittsburgh and Erie.

August 19: The *Quarterly Trade Circular* reported that there were 58 oil refineries in the city with a weekly capacity of 26,000 barrels.

November 11: Thurston's (oil) Stock Exchange opened on Fourth Street.

December: Newspapers reported that the wage of iron puddlers had risen from $3.56 per ton in October 1861 to $9 per ton.

The firm that was the forerunner of the A. M. Byers Company was established.

1865 *February 5:* The Pittsburgh Clearing House Association was opened for business with John Harper as president.

February: After an eight-month strike, the first trade-union agreement in America was made between the Sons of Vulcan and the iron industry. Among major provisions of the contract was a sliding wage scale on economic conditions in the industry.

THE OPERA HOUSE
A *Harper's Weekly* drawing, March 31, 1866.

Spring: Cyclops Mill, a Thomas Miller and Carnegie enterprise, was completed.

April 25: The Keystone Bridge Company was organized, designed to use iron from the Iron City Forge and the new Cyclops Mill.

May 1: Iron City Forge and Cyclops Mill were merged to form Union Iron Mills.

October 4: A tremendous ovation was given General Grant when he arrived in the city.

October 31: George Westinghouse, at 19, received his first patent for the invention of a rotary steam engine.

The new Pennsylvania Railroad Station went into service. Located at 11th Street and Liberty Avenue, it was a four-story structure with upper floors assigned to a hotel.

The Sisters of St. Francis converted a frame building into a hospital for 12 patients.

Pittsburgh Diocese of the Protestant Episcopal Church was created. John E. Kerfoot was the first bishop.

Pittsburgh School of Design was instituted.

Merchants' and Manufacturers' Bank was organized.

1866 *July 3:* Peoples Savings Bank of Pittsburgh was chartered.

August 29: The police night call, "All's well," was abolished.

August: Homeopathic Medical and Surgical Hospital and Dispensary was founded.

September 13: Once more General Grant came to Pittsburgh, this time with President Andrew Johnson and Admiral David G. Farragut.

Annual exchange clearings of the Pittsburgh Clearing House Association, reflecting the amount of business activity in Pittsburgh, totaled $83,-731,242.

Smith and Porter (H. K. Porter Company) began manufacturing locomotives in Pittsburgh. The first one operated under its own steam on street car rails across a Monongahela River bridge.

1867 *April 12:* Monongahela Incline Plane Railroad, up the face of Mount Washington, was chartered.

April: The councils of Allegheny and Pittsburgh agreed on a plan of union in the first definite step toward consolidation.

First fire-alarm telegraph system was established in Allegheny.

Samuel Pierpont Langley was appointed Director of the Allegheny Observatory.

Andrew Carnegie acquired the controlling interest in the Union Iron Mills.

Rosenbaum and Company was established at 76 Market Street as Rosenbaum and Fleischman, a retail and wholesale millinery firm.

The Peoples First National Bank and Trust Company was founded as the Safe Deposit Company.

An act of the Legislature officially transferrerd to the city of Allegheny the Allegheny Parks, the land of which was originally the gift of the Penn family.

1868 *June 30:* The city of Pittsburgh extended its eastern boundary by annexing the townships of Pitt, Peebles, Liberty, Collins, and Oakland.

August 8: Cornerstone was laid for the new City Hall on Smithfield Street.

1869 *January 9:* The Boggs and Buhl department store was opened at 512 Federal Street in Allegheny as the Boggs, Blair and Buhl notions and dry goods shop.

April 13: In the first practical demonstration, an air-brake train made a

A BLYTHE PAINTING
Art versus Law, painted by David G. Blythe (1815–65), one of Pittsburgh's greatest artists. It is owned by George D. Robinson.

THE MELLON FAMILY'S BANK
A drawing of the institution T. Mellon & Sons in 1869, the year of its foundation.

trip from Union Station in Pittsburgh to Steubenville.

June 10: The Home for Aged Protestant Women was founded.

July: George Westinghouse's first major enterprise, the Westinghouse Air Brake Company, was organized to manufacture air brakes for steam railways. The first site of the company was at 25th Street and Liberty Avenue.

September 14: President Ulysses S. Grant visited the city.

December 11: Pennsylvania College for Women, founded by the Reverend W. T. Beatty, was incorporated.

H. J. Heinz, at 25, planted in Millvale a three-quarter of an acre patch of horse-radish, and thus began the world-renowned H. J. Heinz Company.

1870 *January 1:* The Old Drury Theater closed its doors after 37 years of service.

January 2: Judge Thomas Mellon, the father of Andrew W. and Richard B. Mellon, retired from the bench to open a private banking establishment under the name of T. Mellon and Sons on Smithfield Street near Sixth Avenue.

January 17: The first professional teachers organization was established in the city.

April 6: The Pittsburgh and Ormsby Passenger Railroad Company was incorporated to construct a railway from the borough of Ormsby to a Market Street terminal.

June 13: Pittsburgh's first paid fire department was organized.

September 28: Pennsylvania College for Women opened under the auspices of the Presbyterian Church.

October 13: The first Pittsburgh Weather Bureau was established by the War Department and Signal Corps at 25 Fifth Avenue.

The 642-foot Monongahela Incline, first in the city, was completed to the top of "Coal Hill" (Mount Washington).

Jacob, Henry, Morris, and Isaac Kaufmann, German immigrants with $1500 between them, opened a men's clothing

MRS. O'DOUD'S GROCERY STORE

is the title of this Jaspar Lawman (1829-1906) painting made in 1868. The work is now in the possession of William K. Frank.

business in an 18-by-28 foot storeroom at 1918 Carson Street, primarily to serve puddlers of the nearby Jones and Laughlin steel mill (Kaufmann's Store, incorporated in 1871).

The Pittsburgh Coal Exchange was chartered for coal companies engaged in river transportation.

Allegheny Bar Association was incorporated.

The establishment of Pittsburgh titles for land belonging to the Penns was completed.

Population: 86,076; Allegheny City, 51,180; Allegheny County, 262,204.

1871 *January 24:* The retail division of the Joseph Horne Company moved into Library Hall (Penn Avenue), a building which previously had housed Mercy Hospital.

May 30: General George G. Meade, a Civil War military leader, and Governor John W. Geary were speakers at a dedication of the Soldiers Monument on Monument Hill in Allegheny.

The Pittsburgh Grand Opera House, on Fifth Avenue, was completed.

Making of steel castings from crucible steel was begun at the Pittsburgh Steel Casting Company.

Baltimore and Ohio Railroad opened continuous service from the east to Pittsburgh.

1872 *April 2:* The city of Pittsburgh annexed the boroughs of South Pittsburgh, Monongahela, Allentown, St. Clair, Lawrenceville, Temperanceville, Birmingham, Sligo, Mount Washington, West Pittsburgh, and Ormsby.

May 18: It was reported that Pittsburgh oil refineries were using about 10,000 barrels of crude oil daily from the Oil Creek and Allegheny River fields.

May 23: The new City Hall, erected at Smithfield and Oliver Way at a cost of $600,000, was officially opened.

May: The Lucy furnace of Kloman, Phipps, and Carnegie went into blast.

The Mount Oliver Incline; 1600 feet long and the first to be cable-driven, was built.

1873 *January 13:* Carnegie, McCandless, and Company, with $750,000 capital, was organized to build a steel-rail mill at nearby Braddock; Andrew

Carnegie had one-third interest.

The Duquesne Club was founded by a group of industrialists and financiers.

The Pittsburgh Art Society was organized.

1874 *May 27:* The Central District and Printing Telegraph Company was organized as the first telephone company in the city.

July 26-27-28: One hundred and fifty persons died in the "Butcher's Run Flood" which deluged Allegheny, Woods Run, West End, South Side, and neighboring communities.

October 12: Edgar Thomson Steel Company, Limited, with $1,000,000 capital, was organized and took over Carnegie, McCandless, and Company.

November: The first Exposition Society was formed to exploit Pittsburgh goods, and built several great halls on Killbuck Island.

December 5: At a meeting in the Germania Bank Building, at Wood and Diamond, the Pittsburgh Chamber of Commerce was organized, with General Thomas H. Howe as the first president.

Construction started on the Union Bridge (Manchester) to connect Allegheny with the Point.

1875 *February 19:* A "heavy smoke" entry in the daily journal of the Weather Bureau stated: "Extremely dark this morning. Had to keep all gaslights burning until 11 o'clock. Street lamps were lighted for a time after 9 o'clock (A.M.)."

May 1: The Duquesne Incline Plane Company was chartered to build an incline to the top of "Coal Hill" (Mount Washington).

September 1: The first steel rail was rolled at the Edgar Thomson works, under the supervision of Captain William R. Jones. This was the first use of the Bessemer process in the United States.

Natural gas was first used in manufacturing.

Women's Club of Pittsburgh, the first such club in Pennsylvania and the second in the nation, was organized.

Mrs. William A. Herron and Mrs. William Thaw organized the Pittsburgh Association for the Improvement of the Poor.

ROBINSON HOUSE IN THE 1870s

It stood at Duquesne Way and Seventh Ave.

THE FOURTH OF JULY

Independence Day was always a gay holiday. In this 1868 photograph, the Pennsylvania Railroad's locomotive is decorated with flags.

1876 *January 11:* The See of Allegheny was created by the Roman Catholic Church.

January 11: Writer Mary Roberts Rinehart was born. (She died on September 22, 1958.)

July 8: Pittsburgh Chamber of Commerce was chartered.

August 4: The unions of steel heaters and steel roll hands, in convention in Pittsburgh, merged to form the Amalgamated Association of Iron and Steel Workers.

Poet Richard Realf dedicated his "Hymn of Pittsburgh" to the city. The poem started with the line, "My father was a mighty Vulcan".

The Point Bridge was completed, providing an important connection between the central portion of the city and the south and west parts.

The London Bakery (predecessor of the Ward Baking Company of New York) was opened by R. B. Ward on Penn Avenue.

1877 *June:* First experiment with the telephone was made by Captain William Boylston and T. B. A. David of the Central District and Printing Telegraph Company.

July 19: Pittsburgh railroad workers struck in protest against a nationwide reduction of railroaders' wages and a Pennsylvania Railroad order cutting employment of brakemen.

July 20: Large crowds gathered at 28th Street crossing of Pennsylvania Railroad; switches and trains were blocked.

July 21: Twenty-six were killed and many wounded in the "Battle of 28th Street," which started when militiamen from Philadelphia fired on strikers.

July 22: The *Gazette* proclaimed: "Riot Law Triumphant—The Reign of Anarchy in the Smoky City." The Union Depot was burned out and Pennsylvania Railroad property was destroyed as far as 33rd Street. Damage was estimated at $5,000,000.

August 18: The See of Allegheny of the Roman Catholic Church was merged with the See of Pittsburgh.

September 4: The first exposition opened on Smoky Island, Allegheny;

the city's first telephone was in operation there.

The Pittsburgh and Lake Erie Railroad completed organization and began building its first rail line—from Pittsburgh to Youngstown.

Armstrong Cork Company was organized.

The first public exhibition of electric lights took place on Duquesne Heights.

1878 *July 21:* Pittsburgh Oil Exchange (forerunner of the Pittsburgh Stock Exchange) was organized with a membership of 180.

October 1: Order of the Holy Ghost began operating a college.

T. B. A. David strung telephone wires from his office in the First National Bank Building to the Iron Exchange on Fourth Avenue and publicly engaged in the first telephone conversation in Pittsburgh.

1879 *February 24:* The Pittsburgh and Lake Erie Railroad inaugurated rail traffic between Pittsburgh and Youngstown.

March 27: The Pittsburgh and West End Railway Company was chartered; it ran a line from Fifth Avenue near the Union Station to West End and the Washington Turnpike.

September 10: Pennsylvania Female College (now Chatham College) opened.

The new telephone switchboard provided service to 777 subscribers.

The city's water pumping station at Brilliant went into operation.

The beginning of electric street lighting.

1880 The Allegheny County Light Company, first ambitious electric light concern in the city, began operation with a generator that supplied energy to 40 lights at one time.

The F. J. Kress Box Company was founded for the manufacture of wooden boxes.

Assessed valuation of real estate in the city of Pittsburgh was set at $99,-600,000.

Population: 156,389; Allegheny City, 78,682; Allegheny County, 355,869.

TRAVELLING FOURSOME
A photograph from Miss Helen C. Frick's scrapbook, showing her father with Andrew W. Mellon and two other friends in 1881.

THE RAILROAD RIOTS OF 1877
Governor John F. Hartranft's headquarters on a car of the Pennsylvania Railroad Company at Pittsburgh. This sketch by John Donaghy was published in *Frank Leslie's Illustrated Newspaper,* on August 18, 1877.

"AT TEN TAPS OF THE BIG BELL,"
read this sign at the Allegheny Post Office during the Railroad Riots in 1877, "the Mayor requests the citizens to assemble at City Hall *Armed* to protect their homes."

1881 *Spring:* The Pittsburgh Press Club was organized by newspaper workers at a meeting in the Common Council Chambers at City Hall.

November 15-18: With Samuel Gompers a prime mover the Federation of Organized Trades and Labor Unions (American Federation of Labor) was organized, in a Pittsburgh convention, by the Knights of Labor and other trade unions, including the Amalgamated Association of Iron and Steel Workers.

November 25: Andrew Carnegie made his first move to create a free library for Pittsburgh; he offered $250,000 on the condition that the city government agree to appropriate $15,000 annually for its maintenance. The city was unable to accept the gift as it had no funds on hand for such a purpose.

November 28: Pittsburgh Catholic College of the Holy Ghost (Duquesne University) received a state charter.

The Homestead mill of the Pittsburgh Bessemer Steel Company, built by Andrew Kloman and a group of other Pittsburgh industrialists, went into operation.

The Union Switch and Signal Company, a pioneer in the manufacture of automatic signals for trains, was founded by George Westinghouse.

1882 *March 6:* The Homestead mill of the Pittsburgh Bessemer Steel Company had its first strike when millworkers refused to sign "yellow dog" contracts; violence followed.

May 5: H. C. Frick Coke Company was incorporated with $2,000,000.

May 7: The second courthouse, on Grant's Hill, was destroyed by fire.

June 1: a nationwide strike resulted from a general stoppage of work called by the Amalgamated Association of Iron and Steel Workers in a wage dispute.

July 22: Jane Grey Swisshelm, newspaper publisher, reformer, author, and one of the first nurses to accompany Union troops in the Civil war, died.

December 4: Allegheny General Hospital was incorporated.

Historical Society of Western Pennsylvania became the new name for the Old Residents' Association of Pittsburgh and Western Pennsylvania, founded in 1879 as the fourth historical society in the city.

1883 *January:* The Penn Fuel Gas Company opened a line to 16th Street from Murraysville, location of the area's first gas field opened in 1878, and thus brought the first natural gas into the city.

September 1: Western Pennsylvania Medical College was opened.

September 8: The county commissioners offered $2500 each to five outstanding architects to prepare sketches for a new courthouse and jail.

October 3: The first Exposition buildings on Smoky Island in Allegheny burned to the ground.

The 17th Street Incline was built by the Penn Incline Company.

Carnegie, Phipps and Company was

THE GREAT STRIKE IN 1882
Drawing from *Harper's Weekly,* July 1, 1882.

653

organized to purchase and operate the Homestead mill, owned by a coalition of seven Pittsburgh firms.

Jones and Laughlin's American Iron Works became Jones and Laughlin, Limited, and the first stock was issued. Officers were Benjamin F. Jones, Sr., chairman; G. M. Laughlin, secretary-treasurer; T. M. Jones, general manager.

1884 *February 1:* Henry Hobson Richardson, noted for his Romanesque architecture, was appointed by the county commisioners to design the new courthouse.

February 6: The city was flooded, the rivers reached a mark of 36.5 feet.

May: George Westinghouse drilled a gas well on his property in the Homewood district, and his home was the first in Pittsburgh to be lighted and heated by gas.

June 20: Pittsburgh *Press,* a daily newspaper, began publication as the *Evening Penny Press.*

July: George Westinghouse acquired control of the one-year-old Philadelphia Company for the development of natural gas; it became the world's largest in that field.

August 5: William F. (Buffalo Bill) Cody visited the city.

September 1: A contract for construction of the new courthouse was let to Norcross Brothers of Worcester, Massachusetts, on a bid of $2,243,024.

An incandescent lamp was used for the first time in Pittsburgh in a restaurant located at 52½ Fifth Avenue. The first school for nurses between the Allegheny Mountains and Chicago was opened at the Homeopathic Medical and Surgical Hospital and Dispensary.

George Westinghouse began the manufacture of electric lamps.

Monongahela Natural Gas Company was organized.

Benjamin F. Jones, Sr., became president of the American Iron and Steel Association, a post he held for 18 years.

A Postal Telegraph bureau was established in Pittsburgh as a rival for Western Union.

1885 *September 1:* The Pitt Medical College was opened.

October 13: The cornerstone for the new courthouse was laid on the 49th anniversary of the cornerstone laying for the previous courthouse.

October 30: The Western Pennsylvania Exposition Society was chartered for the purpose of establishing a technical school in the city, and buildings were erected on Duquesne Way; dissolved, April 10, 1934.

November: Elizabeth Cochrane (1867-1922), the Nellie Bly of the "Around the world in 72 days" fame began her newspaper career as a reporter for the Pittsburgh *Dispatch.* She investigated

the factories and public institutions of the city and reported about them.

Boggs and Buhl announced installation of a telephone. The store also introduced delivery service, utilizing a wheelbarrow and a horse and wagon.

1886 *January 8:* The Westinghouse Electric Company was established in Garrison Alley to manufacture and promote the use of equipment for the alternating electric current system.

August 19: Jones and Laughlin constructed two seven-ton Bessemer converters at the South Side plant for the job of making its first steel.

September: Western Pennsylvania Medical College was established on Brereton Street, near West Penn Hospital.

November 27: The Fidelity Trust Company was incorporated.

December: The Federation of Organized Trades and Labor Unions changed its name to the American Federation of Labor.

George Westinghouse introduced Saturday half holiday for employees and vacations with pay for salaried employees.

Riverside Penitentiary of Western Pennsylvania (Western Penitentiary) was built in Woods Run on the Ohio River to replace the old institution in Allegheny.

Andrew Carnegie offered the city of Allegheny $300,000 for a Carnegie free library, with provision that the city maintain it.

1887 *March 18:* Pittsburgh Hospital for Children was incorporated.

September 30: President Grover Cleveland visited Pittsburgh. At the sight of natural gas he remarked: "An uncanny picture, a superb spectacle".

1888 *July 31:* Under the name of the Pittsburgh Reduction Company, the first

THE SMITHFIELD STREET BRIDGE
A photograph taken in the early 1880s. The double tracks in the center were for horsecars.

aluminum-producing company was organized at the home of Captain Alfred E. Hunt, 272 Shady Lane (Avenue), by five young men, all under 35. They were Captain Hunt, a military figure; Charles Martin Hall, developer of the new metal; Romaine C. Cole, George H. Clapp, and Howard Lash.

August 7: The first electric streetcar was placed in service by the Pittsburgh, Knoxville and St. Clair Street Railways, but was destined to failure.

September 24: The new Allegheny County courthouse and jail, designed by H. H. Richardson, was dedicated on the final day of the county's centennial anniversary.

October 3: Fire destroyed Machinery Hall and other exposition buildings. *The Arabian,* the first steam locomotive to run in the United States, and Stephen Foster's piano were among the exhibits destroyed.

Thanksgiving Day: Charles M. Hall and Arthur V. Davis poured the first commercial ingot of aluminum in the Smallman Street plant of the Pittsburgh Reduction Company.

The Oliver interests were reorganized to form the Oliver Iron and Steel Company.

1889 *April 29:* The Pittsburgh Chamber of Commerce began urging construction of a Lake Erie and Ohio River canal.

May 31: Pittsburgh dispatched aid to Johnstown, where the flood toll was mounting to 2300 dead.

September 4: The Western Exposition opened.

September 12: The Fifth Avenue Horse Car System was replaced by cable cars, which reduced the running time from Downtown to East Liberty by 30 minutes to one hour. The five-and-a-half-mile system, built by the Pittsburgh Traction Company, was considered to be the city's first "rapid transit" facility.

Fall: Allegheny City's first trolley operated on Pennsylvania Avenue and was the first to run into downtown Pittsburgh.

October 2: The Pittsburgh Reduction Company, its pilot plant having demonstrated the success of the Hall aluminum-making process, was capitalized at $1,000,000, and 10,000 shares were issued.

October 26: South Side Hospital was founded.

October 28: The Union Trust Company of Pittsburgh was established in the Oil Exchange Building.

October 30: Mrs. Mary E. Schenley presented the city of Pittsburgh with 300 acres of land for park purposes, and Schenley Park, the city's first, was developed.

November 16: Playwright George S. Kaufman was born in the city. (He died in 1961.)

December 8: Hervey Allen, novelist,

was born in East Liberty. (He died on December 28, 1949.)

New exposition buildings were built at the Point.

1890 January 16: A. W. Mellon and his brother, Richard B. Mellon, acquired their first stock in the Pittsburgh Reduction Company.

January 25: Nellie Bly completed her trip around the globe in 72 days 6 hours and 11 minutes.

February 6: Andrew Carnegie repeated his original library proposal first made November 25, 1881, and offered to increase his gift to $1,000,000 to include funds for a museum of natural history and art gallery and for branch libraries.

February 13: The Carnegie Library in Allegheny, the first Carnegie Free Library, was opened to the public after being dedicated by President Benjamin Harrison.

March: Oil discovery in Westview.

June 4: Children's Hospital opened.

July 17: The city of Allegheny celebrated its Golden Jubilee.

October 15: Western Pennsylvania Institute for the blind opened in Oakland. The site was given by Mrs. Mary Schenley.

December 13: Marc Connelly, playwright, was born in McKeesport.

The Second Avenue Line, the city's first successful electric trolley line, began operating between Downtown and Glenwood.

The Joseph Horne Company was the first large store in the city to substitute electricity for gas illumination.

The Pittsburgh Incline to Knoxville was rebuilt.

Assessed valuation of Pittsburgh real estate totaled $207,300,000.

Annual clearings of the Pittsburgh Clearing House Association totaled $786,694,231.

Population: 238,617; Allegheny City, 105,287; Allegheny County, 551,959.

1891 January: Pittsburgh eyes were on nearby Youngwood, where 100 miners were killed in a mine explosion.

February 6: Andrew Carnegie gave the promised $1,000,000 to be controlled by a Board of Trustees appointed by the City Council, for a library and other buildings to be erected in Oakland.

April 2: Coke workers went on strike at the Morewood mines of the H. C. Frick Company.

April 3: City Council adopted an ordinance authorizing erection of Carnegie Library on a 19-acre tract acquired from Mrs. Schenley.

April 13: Samuel Gompers, of the AFL, hailed the "eight-hour day" during a Pittsburgh visit.

September: The Alvin Theater opened with Pauline Hall and her opera company in La Belle Hélène.

October: Three hundred delegates of

POURING METAL INTO THE MOULD, a sketch by John Beatty depicting the manufacturing of a large steel gun at the Pittsburgh Steel Casting Company. The drawing appeared in *Frank Leslie's Illustrated* in 1888.

THE RANDALL MARCHING CLUB as it posed for a picture in Washington in March 1885. The men went to the capital to see the inauguration of Grover Cleveland.

THE NORTH PUBLIC SCHOOL IN 1890 It stood at Penn and Cecil Alley, today the site of the Joseph Horne Department Store.

GLEANER'S MISSIONARY SOCIETY A photograph of the society in 1892, taken outside the Sandusky Street Baptist Church.

the American Street Railway Association assembled at the Monongahela House for their 10th annual national convention. The convention slogan was "The Mule Must Go."

December 19: First telephone line between Pittsburgh and New York City was in operation.

The United States Glass Company, one of the country's first large industrial combines, was formed; 17 flint-glass factories, most of them in or near Pittsburgh, were acquired.

A "Roads Congress" was held in Allegheny Carnegie Library lecture hall, under auspices of the Chamber of Commerce, to consider ways of improving public roads.

1892 June 30: H. C. Frick discharged the entire labor force of 3800 workers at the Homestead works after they threatened to strike for higher wages.

July 6: Three hundred Pinkerton men were engaged by millworkers in a pitched battle at the Homestead works after arriving via the Monongahela River on two barges; 16 men were killed and many more wounded.

July 6: The central branch of the Pittsburgh Young Women's Christian Association was incorporated.

July 13: National Guard troops were ordered to Homestead by the governor to prevent further violence; the strike ended soon thereafter.

The Castle Shannon Incline was built.

City Council enacted Pittsburgh's first antismoke ordinance, which proved to be a wholly ineffective instrument.

Western University of Pennsylvania instituted a Department of Medicine and absorbed the Western Pennsylvania Medical College.

1893 March 20: Ground was broken for the first Ferris wheel, invented by George Washington Ferris of the city.

July: Construction began for Carnegie Public Library in Oakland.

December 7: Phipps Conservatory in Schenley Park was completed.

Highland Park opened.

The Joseph Horne Company opened a modern new six-story building at Penn Avenue and Fifth (Stanwix).

Construction work started on "steel headquarters"—the 15-story Carnegie Building on Fifth Avenue, regarded city's first "skyscraper."

1894 March 15: Pittsburgh citizens contributed to a fund to be used to put 1000 to 2000 unemployed men to work on city projects.

April 3: The vanguard of General Coxey's army of 300,000 unemployed men reached Pittsburgh en route to demonstrate in Washington, D. C.

April: Pittsburgh Stock Exchange was in operation.

December 1: The city of Pittsburgh annexed the borough of Brushton.

Free textbooks were adopted in city schools.

Jones and Laughlin scrapped 40 puddling furnaces and discontinued a highly successful wrought-iron business.

Oliver Wire Company, a merger of all the Oliver wire interests, was incorporated.

Mrs. Mary Schenley presented to the D.A.R. the Blockhouse at the Point.

1895 *May 4:* Presbyterian Hospital was founded.

June 22: Eye and Ear Hospital received a charter to operate.

September 13: Miss Agnes Watson was the first woman admitted to the Allegheny County Bar.

November 5: The Carnegie Library building was dedicated and opened to the public in a ceremony marked by Andrew Carnegie's announcement of an additional gift for enlarging the building.

The Carnegie Steel Company moved from 48 Fifth Avenue into its new building, the steel frame of which had been allowed to stand unfinished one year to demonstrate the use of steel as a construction material.

The National Tube Works of John and Harvey Flagler became the first company in America to manufacture seamless steel tubing by the rotary piercing method for the bicycle, automobile, and pipe industries.

Women were first admitted to the Schools of Law and Pharmacy at the Western University of Pennsylvania.

1896 *February 27:* The Pittsburgh Orchestra, which developed from the "Symphony Society," presented its first concert at Carnegie Music Hall with Frederic Archer as conductor.

March 25: The 22nd Street Bridge, first toll-free bridge to be built in the city, was dedicated to public use.

April 22: Experimental Xrays were successful at Homeopathic Hospital.

May 12: St. John's Hospital was opened.

June 8: As the result of recurring typhoid epidemics, the city appointed a Pittsburgh Filtration Commission to study water problems; it subsequently recommended that the city's water be filtered.

July 25: Pittsburgh Stock Exchange officially began operating under that name.

August 24: The conversion from cable cars to electric streetcars began on Fifth Avenue.

September 7: Lumière's Cinematograph, French forerunner of motion pictures, opened in Harry Davis' Avenue Theater.

September 23: The police department organized a bicycle corps.

November 5: The First International Art Exhibition was held at Carnegie Institute with 312 paintings on display; 19 Pittsburgh artists were represented.

THE BRIDGE AT SIXTH STREET
A photograph of the bridge taken in 1890.

The city purchased the Point Bridge for $750,000 and the Smithfield Street Bridge for $1,152,583.

1897 *May 3:* Joseph Horne and Company department store was destroyed by fire.

October 29: The Union Trust Company and Pittsburgh Stock Exchange were destroyed by fire.

November 3: In a Founders Day speech at Carnegie Institute, President William McKinley praised Pittsburgh for its progressive spirit.

November 18: D. Herbert Hostetter announced that five of the largest gas companies in the city were consolidated into a new company capitalized at $5,000,000. He also announced a plan to build an $800,000 plant on the site of the Pittsburgh Gas Company on Second Avenue.

The 15-story Park Building, one of the city's earliest "skyscrapers," was erected on Fifth Avenue.

1898 *March 1:* The borough of Beltzhoover was annexed by the city.

April 29: Troops for service in the Spanish-American War entrained for camp at Mount Gretna.

November 4: The Edgar Thomson Steel Works began shipping rails to South Africa and Japan.

The Pittsburgh Chamber of Commerce opposed free and unlimited grants of street franchises, contending that they should be held by the city in trust for the people.

Victor Herbert, cellist and composer of operas, began a six-year reign as conductor of the Pittsburgh Orchestra.

Willa Cather, novelist, joined the staff of the Pittsburgh *Dispatch.* Two years later she became reporter for the Pittsburgh *Leader*, the city's leading newspaper.

Mesta Machine Company was formed by the merger of the Leechburg Foundry (George Mesta) and the Robinson-Rea Manufacturing Company.

1899 *April 4:* James Whitcomb Riley, poet, lectured in Pittsburgh.

May: The city's first six-hole golf course, known as Belmar, was laid out in Homewood, and the Western Pennsylvania Golf Association came into being.

July 4: First automobile races conducted in Schenley Park.

September: Western University began playing regular football schedules at Recreation Park; it was the first school in the city to do so.

City Council authorized a purifying system for the city water supply.

Pittsburgh Coal Company of Pennsylvania was organized.

The Duquesne Club erected a five-story building on Sixth Avenue.

National Tube Works consolidated with other pipe producers to form the National Tube Company.

1900 *April 1:* The Carnegie Company, with capitalization of $320,000,000, was formed by the merger of the H. C. Frick Coke Company and Carnegie Steel Company, Limited.

Spring: Barney Dreyfuss began a 32-year reign as owner and president of the Pittsburgh Pirates professional baseball club.

July 1: Grant Boulevard (Bigelow Boulevard), a "rapid transit" road to the east, conceived in 1891 by E. M. Bigelow and cut out of the side of Bedford Hill, was opened to traffic after three years of work.

November 14: At a dinner of Carnegie Institute trustees in the Schenley Hotel, Andrew Carnegie proposed an endowment of $1,000,000 for establishment of a polytechnic school on condition that the city provide a suitable site for it.

December 12: At a testimonial dinner for him in New York, Charles M. Schwab, president of the Carnegie Company, made a speech that impressed one of the guests, J. P. Morgan, and led later to organization of the United States Steel Corporation, the greatest steel corporation in the world.

Assessed valuation in the city totaled $321,700,000.

Annual clearings of the Pittsburgh Clearing House Association amounted to $1,615,641,592.

Isaac Seder and Jacob A. Frank formed a partnership and organized a wholesale firm known as the Pittsburgh Wrapper Manufacturing Company, the forerunner of the Frank and Seder Store.

The 12-story Empire Building was erected at 508 Liberty Avenue.

Population: Pittsburgh, 321,616; Allegheny City, 129,896; Allegheny County, 775,058.

1901 *February 1:* United States Steel was incorporated; the founding companies included Federal Steel Company, American Steel and Wire Company, National Tube, National Steel, American Tin Plate, American Steel Hopp Company, and the American Sheet Steel Company.

February 17: Ethelbert Nevin, Pittsburgh composer of "Cradle Song," "A

Day in Venice," "The Rosary," and other well-known songs, died.

March 7: The "ripper" act, changing the city charter, became law. William J. Diehl, of the Magee-Flinn "ring," was ousted as mayor; Adam M. Brown, first president of the Allegheny County Bar Association and a judge of Common Pleas Court, was named first city recorder.

March 11: Andrew Carnegie sold his steel interests to J. P. Morgan receiving value of $492,000,000 for it.

March 14: Andrew Carnegie announced a $4,000,000 pension plan for employees and a gift of $1,000,000 for maintenance of the Homestead, Braddock, and Duquesne libraries established by him.

March 17: All exposition buildings near the Point, excepting Machinery Hall, were destroyed by fire. They were soon replaced by new structures.

April 1: J. P. Morgan completed organization of the world's largest steel trust. The United States Steel Corporation was capitalized at $1,402,000,-000. Charles M. Schwab became its first president.

April 17: First automobile accident in the city was reported.

April 20-21: The Triangle had a flood equaling that of February 1884, when floodwaters reached a level of over 36 feet.

July 14: The Amalgamated Association of Iron, Steel and Tin Workers called a general strike against the U.S. Steel Corporation subsidiaries, the first steelworker's strike since 1892.

August 5: Newspapers and the general public demanded construction of a water filter system as hospitals became crowded with 266 victims of typhoid fever.

September 21: The Mellons sold their street car interests to the Philadelphia Company.

October 12: The new Pennsylvania Railroad Station, at 10th and Liberty, went into service.

October 20: The Iron City Trades Council (Pittsburgh Central Labor Union) was organized by craft and trade unions of the city.

November 10: The first *Sunday Gazette* was issued.

December 27: The Pittsburgh Railways Company was created by the merger of several city traction companies, including Southern Traction. The 18-story Arrott Building on Wood Street and the 16-story Peoples-Pittsburgh Trust Building on Fourth Avenue and Wood were completed.

1902 *January 1:* The Pittsburgh Railways Company took over properties of the Consolidated Traction Company and United Traction Company, and began operating a city-wide system of 400 miles of single track.

January 5: Andrew Carnegie an-

nounced a gift to form Carnegie Technical Schools, the present Carnegie Institute of Technology.

January 30: The notorious Biddle boys, Edward and John, convicted murderers of grocer Thomas D. Kahney and Detective Patrick Fitzgerald, sawed their way out of their cells, overpowered guards, and escaped from the county jail.

March 1: Another flood disabled the city, the rivers rising to a level of 35.6 feet at the Point.

March 15: The first tenants moved into the 20-story Frick Building, erected by H. C. Frick on Fifth Avenue.

June 21: The Daughters of the American Revolution won a legal suit to prevent removal of the historic Blockhouse from its original site at the Point.

July 4: A crowd estimated at between 75,000 and 100,000 assembled on Flagstaff Hill to hear a Fourth of July oration by President Theodore Roosevelt.

July 14: The Union Savings Bank began operations.

July: T. Mellon and Sons was incorporated as the Mellon National Bank.

October 25: Henry Steele Commager, noted historian, was born in the city. Benjamin F. Jones, Sr. died; Jones and Laughlin, Limited, and Laughlin and Company, Limited were reorganized to form Jones and Laughlin Steel Company.

The 14-story Keystone Bank Building was built at 325 Fouth Avenue.

1903 *February 24:* A "Greater Pittsburgh" bill was passed in Harrisburg to permit annexation of the territory surrounding the city of Pittsburgh.

April 23: The office of mayor was restored to the city charter; William B. Hays, who had taken office as city recorder on March 17, 1903, assumed the title of mayor.

June 9: The Pennsylvania Railroad presented plans to Councils for construction of a new passenger station in East Liberty.

October 13: The first of baseball's modern World Series ended in Pittsburgh before 7455 persons at Exposition Park; the Pirates were defeated

SQUIRREL HILL IN 1893

by Boston, 4 to 3, and lost the Series three games to five.

October 19: The Wabash Bridge over the Monongahela collapsed.

October: Three months prior to the Wright Brothers' historic Kitty Hawk flight, Samuel Pierpont Langley, director of the Allegheny Observatory and builder of the famous "Whirling Table" in the early 1880s, experimented with a man-carrying airplane, which became known as "Langley's Folly."

November 4: Mrs. Mary E. Schenley died in London.

December 7: The Nixon Theater, built by Samuel F. Nixon-Nirdlinger with support from Senator George T. Oliver and others, was described as the "world's most perfect playhouse" at its formal opening.

The 24-story Farmers Bank Building, on Liberty Avenue, and the 13-story Bessemer Building, at 100 Sixth Street, were constructed.

1904 *January 23:* The rivers reached a 32-foot flood level.

February 4: City Councils passed an ordinance permitting the Wabash Railroad to enter the city.

February 9: Henry W. Oliver, who was instrumental in opening up the Mesabi iron ore regions to Pittsburgh steel and iron manufacturers, died at the age of 64 at his home at Ridge and Grant Avenues.

March 21: Virgin Alley, one of the first streets in the city, was renamed Oliver Avenue in honor of Henry W. Oliver.

July 2: After three years' struggle and conflict, George Jay Gould's Wabash Railroad operated its first train out of Pittsburgh—a special to the World's Fair at St. Louis.

McCreery's Department Store opened for business at Sixth and Wood with 450 employees.

1905 *April 3:* On a Schenley Park site provided by the city, ground was broken for the first group of buildings for the Carnegie Technical Schools.

May 16: The world's first main-line electric locomotive was demonstrated in the East Pittsburgh railway yards.

June 19: The "Nickelodeon," the country's first all-motion-picture house, was opened by Harry Davis and John P. Harris at 433-35 Smithfield Street with the showing of two short films, *Poor but Honest* and *The Baffled Burglar.* It was a great success, with people flocking to the place and marveling at the moving figures.

July 25: The Pennsylvania Railroad began construction of elevated railroad tracks on Duquesne Way along the Allegheny River.

October 16: First Carnegie Technical Schools buildings were opened.

October 31: The "Gayety," which later became one of the best-known

FIRST U. S. MOTION PICTURE HOUSE
called the Nickelodeon, was at Smithfield
Street. The doors of this all movie theater were
first opened to the public on June 19, 1905.

burlesque houses in the nation, opened as a legitimate theater for the carriage trade.

Ground was broken 20 miles down the
Ohio River for the new Aliquippa
works of Jones and Laughlin.

The Gulf Oil Company began using
its first tank wagons in Pittsburgh to
haul gasoline and other fuel.

The 13-story Diamond National Bank
Building was erected.

George Jay Gould built his ornate
Wabash Railroad terminal and 11-story
office building on Liberty Avenue.

A special windshield glass was invented by Banker Brothers.

1906 *January 7:* The Carnegie Steel Company announced plans for a $7,000,-
000 expansion of the Homestead
works.

January 20: Historic old City Hall, in
"the Diamond," a Civil War landmark, was destroyed by fire.

February 4: The University Club was
in the process of purchasing a site on
Grant (Bigelow) Boulevard, in the
Bellefield district, for its new home.

April 2: George W. Guthrie was inaugurated as Mayor. He held office
for three years.

June 12: By a majority of 19,943 votes,
an act of the Legislature uniting the
cities of Pittsburgh and Allegheny was
approved in a public referendum.

July 1: The Pennsylvania Railroad's
elevated line on Duquesne Way was
ready for service, and the removal of
tracks from Liberty Avenue (where
since 1851 they had occupied the center strip of the street from 11th Street
to the Point) was completed.

October 24: St. Paul's Cathedral, one
of the city's most notable examples of
Gothic architecture, built at a cost of
$885,481, was consecrated.

Among the large structures built in
the city in this year were the Fort Pitt
Hotel, the 21-story Commonwealth
Building on Fourth Avenue, the 19-
story Frick Annex on Diamond, and

the 19-story Benedum-Trees Building
on Fourth Avenue.

1907 *March 15:* Duquesne Way was under
nine feet of water and River Avenue
on the North Side under 14 feet in a
flood that recorded a crest of 38.7 feet.

April 11: Andrew Carnegie formally
presented the $6,000,000 Carnegie In-
stitute in a dedication ceremony witnessed by 20,000.

April 15: An ordinance giving the
Pittsburgh Subway Company the right
to build a subway to East End was
introduced in Councils.

May 4: The historic old Union Bridge,
built about 1835 over the Allegheny
River at the Point, was closed to traffic, and dismantling of it began.

June 19: The Schenley Park oval and
matinee race track was opened.

October 21: Lillian Russell at the Nixon Theatre in the comedy, *Wildfire*.

October 23: The Pittsburgh Stock Exchange closed for a three-month period because of the effects of the nationwide depression.

November 18: The United States Supreme Court upheld the constitutionality of the Guthrie-Watson Greater
Pittsburgh bill.

December 7: Pittsburgh officially annexed Allegheny City and became a
city of 521,000 population, the sixth
largest in the nation.

The Frank and Seder organization
rented a storeroom on Fifth Avenue
and launched a retail business.

The 21-story Union National Bank
Building was erected at 306 Fourth
Avenue and the 12-story Century
Building at 130 Seventh Street.

Pittsburgh's death rate was 143.6 per
100,000 persons.

The city's first Bureau of Smoke Control was instituted. William Holdship Rea was chief inspector, 1907–9.
Pittsburgh Reduction Company was
renamed the Aluminum Company of
America.

1908 *January 4:* Beechview borough was
annexed.

February 3: Judge Thomas Mellon
died at his home on Negley Avenue
at the age of 95.

THE FLOOD OF 1907
In the middle of March 1907 the waters of
the Monongahela rose to a peak of 38.7 feet.

A CLEAR SUMMER DAY IN 1906
But the smoke rose from the chimneys and
darkened the skies. This photograph was taken
from the Union Station looking northwest.

February: Wages of millworkers at
the Homestead works were reduced
10 to 30 per cent by the Carnegie
Steel Company.

May 26: Carry Nation, the celebrated crusader against the saloons,
came for a visit.

July 11: Western University of Pennsylvania was rechartered as the University of Pittsburgh.

October 2: As a climax of the city's
sesquicentennial festivities, two cor-
nerstone-laying ceremonies were
staged in Oakland, one for Soldiers
and Sailors Memorial Hall and the
other for State Hall (School of
Mines), first building to be erected in
the new University of Pittsburgh campus.

December 18: The city's filtration
plant, undertaken in 1905, began delivering the first filtered water to
residents.

The Jones and Laughlin Steel Company built a 12-story office building on Ross Street.

The number of typhoid cases in Pittsburgh was 1853 for the year 1908,
compared with 2969 in 1905, and 5730
in 1906.

1909 *May 4:* The city's first taxicab company, organized by John Weibley, began operating with a fleet of 18 motor-
ized cabs.

May 23: Cornerstone was laid for the
$300,000 East Liberty Y.M.C.A.

May 29: President William H. Taft
arrived for a two-day visit, watched
the Pirates lose to Chicago, 8 to 3,
and participated in the dedication of
Memorial Fountain in Arsenal Park.

May 31: Gladys Schmitt, novelist,
was born in the city.

June 9: The University of Pittsburgh
began its removal from the North Side
to Oakland, where it dedicated State
Hall, laid the cornerstone for Thaw
Hall (School of Engineering) and
broke ground for the School of Medicine.

June 10: The Pennsylvania Railroad and borough of Wilkinsburg agreed on a plan for elevating the main-line tracks and thus eliminating all grade crossings in the borough.

June 27: Mayor William A. Magee, inaugurated on April 5 of this year was credited with settling the two-day strike of 2900 motormen and conductors; settlement was a blow to railroads, which had put on 400 extra cars in absence of trolley service.

June 29: In the final game played in Exposition Park, the Pittsburgh Pirates defeated Chicago, 8 to 1.

June 30: Forbes Field, named after the head of the British forces in 1758, General John Forbes, was dedicated; 30,338 persons watched the Pirates lose the opening game there to Chicago, 3 to 2.

June: Montefiore Hospital was founded.

July 15: Rioting workers of the Pressed Steel Car Company, near McKees Rocks, clashed with guards; Coal and Iron Police and State Constabulary were called out; many strikers were wounded by volleys of buckshot fired to halt their charges; state police were ordered to "shoot to kill" if attacked by strikers.

August 23: Five were killed, scores injured in two more riot battles between police and Press Steel Car strikers.

August 29: Plans were announced for a $450,000 state armory on a site in Schenley Farms.

September 12: The Pittsburgh Aero Club was organized, with Philip S. Flinn as first president, and planned an international balloon race for Pittsburgh as its first project.

October 16: The Pittsburgh Pirates, winners of 110 games in their regular season, defeated the Detroit Tigers, 8 to 0, to win the seventh and deciding game of the World Series before 17,562 fans at Forbes Field.

The Amalgamated Association of Iron, Steel and Tin Workers was eliminated as a bargaining factor in the steel industry as the result of a 14-month strike.

1910 January 23: Three were dead and communications and streetcar service disrupted in a nine-inch snowfall.

April 1: The new Henry W. Oliver Building, 25 floors high, was ready for occupancy.

October 9: Soldiers and Sailors Memorial Hall was dedicated.

Because of lack of funds, the Pittsburgh Symphony Orchestra was disbanded.

John Kowalski, marine engine maker, recorded the first flight of an airplane built in Pittsburgh when he accidentally took off in a four-cylinder plane he had devised.

The Pittsburgh *Courier* was published for the first time.

WORLD MIDDLEWEIGHT CHAMPION, Stanley Ketchel (center), came to Pittsburgh in 1909 to defend his title against Jack McGann (Kid Hubert). At Ketchel's right are promoter Jimmy Dime, and Willus Britt, the champion's manager. At his left the tall man under the bowler is the legendary Wilson Mizner, next to him Charles McLaughlin. Photograph by Frank E. Bingaman.

THE LAST GAME
at old Exposition Park was played in June 1909. The crowd was watching the Pirates at Monument Hill. Photograph by A. J. Huber who was on the staff of the *Pittsburgh Press*.

A. W. and R. B. Mellon announced that they were providing funds for creation of Mellon Institute for Industrial Research.

New 215-bed Homeopathic Hospital opened at Center and Aiken avenues.

Assessed valuation of real estate in the city rose to $745,700,000.

Annual clearings of the Pittsburgh Clearing House amounted to $2,587,325,785.

U. S. Bureau of Mines established a center in Oakland District.

Population: Pittsburgh, 553,905; Allegheny County, 1,018,463.

1911 January 1: The first old-age retirement plan for United States Steel employees was created with a fund of $12,000,000, of which $4,000,000 had been provided by Andrew Carnegie ten years before.

January 19: The Elizabeth Steel Magee Hospital, founded by Christopher L. Magee, began operation.

February 2: New St. Joseph's Hospital was opened to the public.

March 1: The Pittsburgh Catholic College of the Holy Ghost became Duquesne University and was chartered to award degrees in major educational fields.

March 16: The county commissioners formally declared the Sixth, Seventh,

Ninth, 16th, and 30th Street Bridges free to the public.

May 26: A new city charter act, replacing the Select and Common Councils with a single Council of nine members, was signed by Governor John K. Tener.

November 5: Galbraith Perry Rodgers, Pittsburgh aviator, completed the first transcontinental flight, which started at Sheepshead Bay, Long Island, on September 17. Rodgers Field in Allegheny County was later named for him.

November 23: An Art Commission was organized under a state act to pass official judgment on plans for buildings, bridges, and other structures in the city.

December 31: New West Penn Hospital was opened.

The Pittsburgh Industrial Development Commission was organized by the Chamber of Commerce for the purpose of securing diversified industries for Pittsburgh; it received contributions of $136,473 to begin work.

The Jenkins Arcade was erected on Liberty Avenue.

1912 March 22: A 28-foot crest was reached by the rivers.

April 5: A contract was let for the grading of Grant's Hill on Fifth Avenue from Smithfield Street to Sixth Avenue and from Fourth to Sixth Avenue.

April 20: The Carnegie Technical Schools were renamed Carnegie Institute of Technology.

June 12: Alexander Moore, editor of the Pittsburgh *Leader*, was married to the singer, Lillian Russell.

October 18: In a pre-election speech before 12,000 persons at Duquesne Gardens, Governor Woodrow Wilson, of New Jersey, Democratic candidate for president, attacked the government's "protective tariff."

October 19: The Pitt Panthers were defeated, 45 to 8, by Jim Thorpe and the Carlisle Indians.

October 21: William Jennings Bryan appeared before 4000 at the Lyceum and made three other speeches in the Pittsburgh district in behalf of the democratic ticket.

November 5: Although Woodrow Wilson won over Bull Moose candidate Theodore Roosevelt and regular Republican candidate William Howard Taft in the presidential election, Roosevelt carried Pittsburgh by a plurality of 8300 votes.

November 26: Andrew Carnegie, at 77, turned over all but $25,000,000 of his vast fortune to the Carnegie Corporation for charitable and philanthropic distribution.

December 11: City and county officials agreed on a joint plan to erect a City-County Building at Grant and Diamond.

The Gulf Oil Company opened on Baum Boulevard the first company-owned service station in the world, forerunner of the modern super-service station.

The Syria Mosque in Oakland was dedicated.

The 26-story First National Bank Building, the city's tallest to this date, was erected at 511 Wood Street.

1913 *January 1:* The first parcel-post deliveries were made in Pittsburgh by the post office at a rate of five cents for the first pound and one cent for each additional pound.

January 9: The rivers crested at 31 feet in another flood.

January 14: The famous evangelist Billy Sunday held a revival meeting in a tabernacle erected for that purpose on the site of the present Heinz Chapel.

November 25: A number of people were killed in a sewer explosion.

The Central District Telephone and Printing Company was incorporated with other telephone companies into the Central District Telephone Company.

The Bell Telephone Company of Pennsylvania built a 20-story office building and equipment headquarters on Seventh Street.

1914 *January 1:* Excavations of 14.9 feet at Fifth and Grant and of 16.3 feet at Fifth and Wylie completed the grading of Grant's Hill.

January 25: A public subscription campaign for the University of Pittsburgh was completed with a total of $2,000,000 collected.

March 10: The cornerstone was laid for the Masonic Temple on Fifth Avenue in Oakland.

March 12: George Westinghouse died in his country home in Lenox, Massachusetts.

June 5: Ten thousand Westinghouse workers went on strike.

July 31: The Pittsburgh Stock Exchange suspended operations (for four months) because of the economic effects of the World War.

August 6: Eugene (Wild Bill) Heth piloted a Wright biplane to Pittsburgh, the first to carry a passenger, Colonel Harry C. Fry, to the city. The Gulf Oil Company began the practice of issuing free road maps to motorists, one of the most successful promotion efforts in the country. Dr. Heinrich Koppers sold the patents for his by-product coke ovens to Andrew Mellon for $300,000, and the Koppers Company, founded in Illinois, was reorganized with main offices in Pittsburgh.

1915 *February 1:* The Carnegie Steel Company announced that it was increasing employment rolls by 8000 in order to meet increasing demands for steel.

February 26: The Mellon Institute for

POOR HOUSING CONDITIONS OF 1912
are inspected by a social worker of the city.

THIS OLD COVERED TOLL BRIDGE
was replaced in 1914 by Manchester Bridge.

THE TOLL BRIDGE
spanning the Allegheny River at Seventh Street, was demolished in the year of 1913.

THE MAILMAN
Winfield Wise collected the mail on the South Side at the beginning of the century.

THE CITY GROWS
Ground is cleared for the Kaufmann-Baer Store (now Gimbels) in the spring of 1913.

Industrial Research, on O'Hara Street, Oakland, was dedicated.

August 1: All steel mills in Pittsburgh were operating night and day to meet steel demands of nations at war.

August 9: The new Manchester Bridge, connecting the Point with the North Side, was ready for traffic.

Rosenbaum and Company moved into its new building at Sixth and Liberty.

December 24: Henry Clay Frick repaid schoolchildren the savings ($169,000) they lost when the Pittsburgh Bank for Savings closed its doors.

1916 *January:* The Pittsburgh Coal Company was created through the merger of the Pittsburgh Coal Company of Pennsylvania and the Monongahela River Consolidated Coal and Coke Company.

March 18: The cornerstone was laid for the new City-County Building.

March: The William Penn Hotel was completed on Grant Street at Sixth at a cost of $6,000,000.

April 27: A strike of 24,000 miners was settled.

May 1: Martial law was declared in Braddock following riots at the Edgar Thomson works.

May 9: Thirty thousand Westinghouse workers were on strike.

June 30: Pittsburgh troops entrained for the Mexican border as trouble increased in Mexico.

July 6: A $200,000 fire destroyed the city block bounded by Second and Third avenues and Market and Ferry streets.

August 25: The Mellons purchased a site at the corner of Smithfield Street and Oliver Avenue for construction of a new bank building.

September 16: Beginning of the last exposition held in the old Exposition Buildings.

September 17: Schenley High School in Oakland opened.

1917 *January 27:* The Grand Opera House was destroyed by fire, along with other Fifth Avenue buildings, including the Frank and Seder Store.

May 1: The new Chamber of Commerce Building, at Seventh and Smithfield, was completed.

May 5: Enrico Caruso, the great Italian tenor, gave his first Pittsburgh concert.

July 20: The first draft lists were published; many Pittsburghers were destined to go overseas in the 28th and 80th divisions.

July 25: Ex-President Theodore Roosevelt visited the city; 30,000 people listened to his address.

July 29: The University of Pittsburgh organized a hospital unit to go overseas.

December 22: Trolley fares were raised to six cents.

December 24: Twenty were killed in a Mount Washington streetcar accident in one of the city's worst transit tragedies.

The 15-story Union Trust Building, rated architecturally as one of the finest structures in the nation, was erected on a Grant Street block-square site.

1918 *March 7:* The new Grand Theater (Warner) was opened on the site of the old Opera House.

March 11: Pittsburgh branch of the Federal Reserve Bank of Cleveland began business at Ninth Street and Liberty.

April 1: Daylight-saving time, conceived and promoted by Robert Garland, of Pittsburgh, went into effect.

April 23: Sixteenth Street Bridge burned.

May 18: Explosion at nearby Etna Chemical Company killed 114 persons, many of them were residents of the city.

June 1: A Red Cross benefit show, starring George M. Cohan, established a box-office record for the city with one-night receipts of $138,000.

July 12: Pittsburgh ranked third in the nation in per capita sales of war savings stamps.

August 24: Pittsburgh fire fighters staged a strike for higher wages, leaving the city without fire protection for six hours.

October 5 to December 21: An influenza epidemic, starting at the Cantonment Hospital in Point Breeze, victimized 23,268 Pittsburgh residents. Of the total, 1374 died of lobar pneumonia and 678 of bronchopneumonia.

October 20: Allegheny County went $10,000,000 over its $165,000,000 quota in the fourth Liberty Loan drive.

October 29: A group of the city's leading citizens met and formulated the Citizens Committee on City Plan for Pittsburgh; C. D. Armstrong was elected president; R. B. Mellon, vice-president, and J. D. Hailman, secretary.

November 11: A summary at the Armistice showed approximately 60,000 Allegheny County men had seen service in the war, mostly in the 80th and 28th divisions; 1527 died or were killed in action; government war contracts executed in Pittsburgh totaled $215,405,000.

December: Frederick Bigger, one of the city's first planning engineers, was named full-time executive secretary of the Citizens Committee on City Plan; under his direction work was started toward a master plan; studies were initiated to cover playgrounds, a street plan, transit problems, parks, railroads, and waterways.

1919 *March:* The Aero Club—for Pitt and Carnegie Tech war fliers—was organized in a leather shop on First Avenue, with Barney Mulvihill as

JOHN A. BRASHEAR IN 1913
He leans against the wall of his first shop; the second, larger one is seen in the rear.

CARNEGIE UNVEILS BOBBIE BURNS
On October 27, 1914, Andrew Carnegie unveiled the Bobbie Burns statue in Schenley Park. Standing on the millionaire's left is County Commissioner Joseph Armstrong.

THE EDITORIAL STAFF
of the *Pittsburgh Times.* Left to right: Henry Hall, George Welshons, Charles Danziger, Chris Evans, Paddy Denmarsh, Austin Beech.

THE BURNING OF ST. AGNES
On January 21, 1914, the Roman Catholic Church on Fifth Avenue was destroyed by fire. The photograph is by Frank E. Bingaman.

president and Joseph M. (Hap) Slater as vice-president.

May 10: The Pittsburgh district went over the top in the fifth Liberty Loan with subscriptions totaling $117,210,350.

May 14: Henry John Heinz, founder of the H. J. Heinz Company, one of the world's largest food manufacturing firms and owner of one of the nation's outstanding private art collections, died of pneumonia at the age of 75 at his home, 7009 Penn Avenue.

May 15: The streetcar system suspended operation at midnight when motormen and conductors struck to enforce demands for a 12-cent hourly pay increase.

July 8: Pittsburgh voters authorized a $22,996,000 improvement program, including $6,000,000 for a proposed Downtown subway system.

August 1: The five-cent zone fare was discontinued; trolley fares were raised to 10 cents.

August 11: Andrew Carnegie died in his eighty-fourth year at his summer home, "Shadowbrook," in Lenox, Massachusetts, after three days of pneumonia. His philanthropies up to this time had totaled $350,000,000.

August 15: Three thousand streetcar men again walked off the job, this time in protest against War Labor Board's award of a six-cent-an-hour raise, only half of what they asked.

August 26: The Pittsburgh Railways Company attempted to operate strike-bound cars; the result was a series of riots in downtown Pittsburgh and other sections of the city; many of the strikers were injured.

August 28: The streetcar strike was broken when the national union expelled local leaders; the strikers returned to work with great reluctance.

September 21: A campaign to unionize the steel industry started in Pittsburgh when a strike was called by National Committee for Organizing Iron and Steel Workers, headed by William Z. Foster, later general secretary of the American Communist party; 365,000 steel workers struck throughout nation for union recognition and reduction of the 12-hour day.

September 29 to October 1: The United States Bureau of Mines dedicated its new $1,000,000 laboratories on Forbes Street in a three-day ceremony.

October 17: Dr. Frank Conrad began regular broadcasting of phonograph records (8XK).

October 23: King Albert of Belgium visited the city.

November 1: Forty-two thousand miners in Pittsburgh district left jobs in start of nationwide strike closing coal mines; the National Guard was alerted.

December 2: Gulf Oil Company opened its first Downtown gasoline service station, at Liberty Avenue and Water Street.

December 2: Henry Clay Frick, industrial and financial leader of Pittsburgh, died suddenly at his New York residence at the age of 69; his body was brought to Pittsburgh for burial. His philanthropies while living were said to total $60,000,000. His probated will disposed of a total estate of $143,000,000 and left $20,000,000 to public, educational, and charitable institutions of Pittsburgh. The city received a 150-acre plot for a park in Fern Hollow, below Beechwood Boulevard, in addition to a $2,000,000 endowment fund to maintain it.

December 10: The nationwide coal strike ended, but a national coal conservation order, restricting use of coal everywhere except in private homes, went into effect under rigid enforcement.

December 20: Ground was broken for the Liberty Tubes with Governor William C. Sproul participating.

Mayer Field, Pittsburgh's first commercial airport, was established in Bridgeville by Casper P. Mayer, realtor and aviation pioneer.

Air transportation was inaugurated in Pittsburgh with the organization of the Kennedy Aircraft Company.

Natural gas was discovered in nearby McKeesport.

1920 January 2 to 3: A total of 233 suspected leaders of the Communist movement in Pittsburgh were arrested by federal agents in two days as part of a nationwide roundup ordered by Attorney General A. Mitchell Palmer.

January 11: Judges wore gowns in court for the first time in Allegheny County.

January 13: The Pennsylvania Railroad announced a $100,000,000 improvement and expansion program for the Pittsburgh area.

January 15: Henry Ford came to Pittsburgh to place in person $15,000,000 worth of steel contracts in the area.

January 20: The national steel workers' organizing strike ended after the fourth month without achieving its objective.

January 22: B. F. Jones, Jr., of Jones and Laughlin Steel, purchased the old Monongahela House for $750,000 with the intention of converting it into an office building.

February 28: The great Italian tenor, Enrico Caruso, sang at the Syria Mosque.

March 1: The United States Supreme Court declined to dissolve the United States Steel Corporation and its subsidiary companies as asked by the federal government in a suit alleging violation of antitrust laws.

April 28: Dr. John Brashear, noted astronomer and maker of astronomical lenses and other scientific instruments, died at 80 at his South Side home.

June: The Citizens Committee completed the first of a series of six major studies leading toward a comprehensive city plan, issued a report analyzing the city's recreational deficiencies, and recommended a system of playgrounds.

November 2: Allegheny County women appeared at polling places to cast their first ballots.

November 2: Station KDKA, first licensed radio broadcasting station, gave the Harding-Cox election returns as its first scheduled broadcast. Allegheny County gave Harding a plurality of 105,000 over Governor Cox.

November 6 to 18: Repeated landslides occurred below Bigelow Boulevard as rainfall continued; engineers waged a losing fight in their efforts to stop the slides and protect Pennsylvania Railroad tracks.

November 20: General George W. Goethals, builder of the Panama Canal, on invitation of city officials, came to Pittsburgh and inspected the Bigelow Boulevard slide. He reported: "The situation will prevail until all has come down."

December 31: The Citizens Committee on City Plan was incorporated and chartered as the Municipal Planning Association, with a goal of promoting "orderly and efficient development of municipalities" and "scientific methods of city and municipal planning."

Population: 588,343; Allegheny County, 1,018,463.

1921 January 2: Church service was broadcast from the Calvary Protestant Episcopal Church in East Liberty—the world's first such broadcast.

February 4: Andrew W. Mellon, Pittsburgh financier, was appointed Secretary of the Treasury, and James J. Davis, former union steelworker of Pittsburgh, was named Secretary of Labor in the cabinet of President Warren G. Harding.

February 16: To relieve traffic congestion, City Council banned automobile parking on Downtown streets between 4:30 and 6 P.M. daily.

May 25: Madame Marie Curie, famed French scientist and co-discoverer of radium, arrived in Pittsburgh for a visit but was taken ill and confined to the home of Mrs. Henry R. Rea in Sewickley. Although weak from her illness, Madame Curie appeared at Memorial Hall the following day to receive her fifty-ninth honorary degree, conferred by Chancellor Bowman of the University of Pittsburgh.

June 4: The Carnegie Corporation of New York announced a $21,662,888

THE RAILWAY STATION
One of the superb etchings of Joseph Pennel (1857-1926) which the artist made of the city.

THE POINT
Another one of Pennel's Pittsburgh views.

appropriation for Carnegie Institute and Carnegie Tech.

June 29: The Reverend Hugh C. Boyle was consecrated bishop of the Catholic diocese of Pittsburgh; 100,000 persons assembled in and around St. Paul's Cathedral for the ceremony.

June 30: The $30,000,000 will of the late steel magnate, William P. Snyder, was contested in court.

July 13: The body of Thomas F. Enright, first American soldier killed in action in the World War, was brought home to Pittsburgh. The Enright Theater in East Liberty was later named in his honor.

August 8: The Boulevard of the Allies was dedicated.

October: KQV, the city's second radio station, began operation.

November 4: Secretary of War Weeks gave the county commissioners final warning to raise all bridges over the Allegheny River in order to make the river free for navigation.

November 4: Census report for 1920 listed 20,297 persons over 10 years of age in Pittsburgh as illiterate.

November 8: William A. Magee Re-

THE FIRST RADIO BROADCAST
of William Jennings Bryan at Point Breeze
Presbyterian Church in 1922 over KDKA.

OAKLAND IN WINTER
An impressive photograph of the district.

publican, was elected mayor of Pittsburgh by 50,000 votes over William N. McNair, Democrat.

November 10: Marshal Ferdinand Foch, leader of French forces in the war, was given a tremendous ovation during a daylong visit to Pittsburgh.

November 26: A. W. and R. B. Mellon presented a 14-acre H. C. Frick estate tract in Oakland, valued at $2,500,000, to the University of Pittsburgh for further development of a campus. This became the site of the Cathedral of Learning.

1922 *January 2:* Mrs. Enoch Rauh, long active in welfare work, became the first woman to hold a cabinet post in a major Pennsylvania city when she took office as head of the Department of Charities in the new Magee administration.

January 2: Westinghouse's radio station KDKA at East Pittsburgh was broadcasting nightly from 7:30 to 10 o'clock.

January 9: Mrs. Minnie Penfield was the first woman to serve on a jury in Allegheny County.

April 9: The cost of the Boulevard of the Allies, nearing completion, was expected to be $1,600,000 per mile, said to be most expensive road construction job in the world.

April 15: Hotel Chatham, a "popular hostelry" on lower Penn Avenue, was purchased by the Manufacturers Club of Pittsburgh for its headquarters.

May 11: The first Liberty Tube was completed.

June 3: Announcement was made of a $7,000,000 plan to develop the Hotel Schenley into a "galaxy of the finest and most modern metropolitan structures" by building apartments immediately adjoining the hotel.

June 5: A posse of humane agents routed 500 "cocking main" enthusiasts assembled in an amphitheater at Keller's Grove, Mount Nebo Road, a historic spot for cock fighting.

June 6: Mrs. Lillian Russell Moore, wife of Alexander Moore, died at the age of 61 at her Point Breeze home.

October 21: Part of Reserve Township was annexed to the city.

November 5: A new record for auto fatalities in a single day in Allegheny County was established when the coroner's office reported five deaths.

November 21: A $1,000,000 fire destroyed three buildings at the Duquesne Steel Foundry.

Radio Station WCAE began broadcasting.

1923 *February 13:* Henry Ford announced purchase of the Allegheny Plate Glass Company plant at Glassmere for establishment of the first Ford plant in the Pittsburgh district.

February 14: Daily newspapers *Dispatch* and *Leader* ceased publication.

March 4: Alexander Moore, of Pittsburgh, was appointed ambassador to Spain.

June 5: The Pittsburgh Skin and Cancer Foundation opened a clinic at 1901 Fifth Avenue.

June 6: Governor Pinchot created a Metropolitan Plan Commission for the city.

August: Harry Greb, of Pittsburgh, defeated Johnny Wilson in New York to win the middleweight title he held for three years.

August: The city's first zoning ordinance, one of the earliest in the United States, became effective amid claims of opposition that it would discourage construction in the city.

October 2: Boulevard of the Allies was opened to traffic.

October 24: Historic Mount Mercy Academy, on Fifth Avenue, suffered $100,000 damages in a fire which injured seven.

October 24: In a speech at Syria Mosque, David Lloyd George, wartime Premier of Great Britain, pleaded for mercy to end wars.

October 27: The last horse car on Sarah Street, suspended operation.

October: The Municipal Planning Association issued its final report; it included recommendations for canalization of the Ohio River, a river-rail terminal, greater use of wharves, and a system of water-storage reservoirs for flood protection advocated by the 1911 Flood Commission.

November 13: Twenty thousand persons attended formal opening of new banking room of Union Trust Company at Fifth and Grant.

November 13: The first unit traffic-light system was installed as an experiment at all corners intersecting the Boulevard of the Allies in the downtown area.

Jones and Laughlin became a corporation and sold its first stock on the open market.

1924 *January 1:* The Schenley Apartments, consisting of five structures in a new-type housing development, were ready for occupancy at monthly rents of $150 and up.

January 4: The rivers hit a crest of 30.4 feet causing $5,000,000 damage, heaviest from a flood in the city since 1913.

January 30: The Liberty Tubes were opened for a two-week chemical test.

February 7: Parts of lower St. Clair Township were annexed.

April 10: It was announced that the first city-county airport would be built and named in honor of Galbraith Perry Rodgers of the city, first aviator to span the U.S. on Nov. 5, 1911.

April 21: A few days after her final performance in *The Closed Door* here, Eleanora Duse, celebrated tragedienne on tour, died in her suite at the Schenley Hotel.

May 10: The city's fifth trolley strike in 15 years started; the Downtown area was jammed with automobile traffic; the Pittsburgh Railways imported 900 electric railways operators and guards from New York to run trolleys.

May 10: The Liberty Tubes were closed for further work on the ventilation system after 12 persons were overcome by gas; a trolley strike had caused a traffic jam in them.

May 12: Motormen and conductors voted to return to work, ending the 39-hour streetcar strike.

May 22: Seven police inspectors and three fire chiefs were demoted in the biggest police shake-up in 20 years.

June: Rodgers Airfield, on a 41-acre tract near Aspinwall, was completed for operation as the first city-county airport.

November 3: A total of $2,266,893 was pledged by 8341 Jewish residents of the city for construction of new Montefiore Hospital.

November 4: Calvin Coolidge, in winning the presidential election, carried Allegheny County by 75,000 votes.

November 6: Pitt Chancellor John G. Bowman announced plans for a "52-story" Gothic skyscraper to be built at a cost of $10,000,000 and known as the Cathedral of Learning.

December 1: In the face of heated protests, the county commissioners asked for bids for the razing of the Ninth Street Bridge.

Bettis Field, sponsored by Samuel Brendel, Harry Neal, and D. Parr Peat, of McKeesport, was established on the Pittsburgh-McKeesport road as a commercial flying enterprise.

1925   *February 1*: Burton W. Marsh, the city's first traffic engineer, submitted his first traffic survey to City Council, recommending strict parking regulations for the downtown area.

March 8: H. P. Davis, president of Westinghouse, urged broadcasting stations to link themselves together by short wave for simultaneous broadcasting of programs.

March 31: City Council enacted an ordinance eliminating the practice of compelling policemen to work two days a month without pay.

April 1: A city assessor's report fixed total taxable values of Pittsburgh's 28 wards of realty at $990,000,000.

April 13: A bill to create a Greater Pittsburgh by joining all boroughs and townships to the city was killed in committee at Harrisburg.

April 22: George Mesta died.

May 10: Evangeline Booth visited the city to dedicate the new Salvation Army home for business girls, located on the Boulevard of the Allies.

May 13: County commissioners tabled action on a plan to remove the county jail from its Ross Street site, purchase nearby sites, and erect a $3,500,000 county office skyscraper and jail.

May 14: The largest electric locomotive in the world, 152 feet long and weighing 1,275,900 pounds, was given a test run at Westinghouse's East Pittsburgh yards.

May 19: The fund for construction of the Cathedral of Learning reached a total of $5,597,782—more than twice as much as ever raised in the city's history for an educational or philanthropic purpose.

May 23: The Young Men's and Women's Hebrew Association in Oakland was dedicated.

June 26: The Philadelphia Company dedicated its new $3,500,000 building, on Sixth Avenue, and President Arthur W. Thompson announced a five-year, $100,000,000 utility improvement program.

June 27: The Keystone Athletic Club announced purchase of the old St. Charles Hotel property, at Third Avenue and Wood, and plans for construction of a 20-story, $3,000,000 building.

July 8: Plans were announced for

erection of another Downtown skyscraper—the Law and Finance Building.

September 26: Pitt Stadium, with a capacity of 60,000, was formally opened with the Panthers defeating Washington and Lee, 28 to 0, before a crowd of 20,000.

October 15: The Pittsburgh Pirates defeated the Washington Senators, 9 to 7, in the seventh and deciding game of the World Series before 42,-856 at Forbes Field; Downtown stores suspended business, and traffic stopped as Pittsburghers celebrated the victory.

November 6: United States Steel stock jumped 5½ points in one day to 138, highest quotation ever recorded to this date.

November 9: General W. W. Atterbury, president of the Pennsylvania Railroad, in Pittsburgh with other railroad officials to inspect the $14,000,-000 station and street improvement program, stated: "While Pittsburgh has called for all the Pennsylvania Railroad could produce, Pittsburgh itself has been our greatest producer." Motor buses were introduced on a large scale on city streets.

The United States Steel Corporation developed a process for producing seamless pipe 16 inches in diameter, more than twice the size previously possible.

1926   *January 5*: R. B. Mellon, president of the Mellon National Bank, was elected chairman of Allegheny County Planning Commission.

January 6: Marcus Loew announced plans to erect the largest theater in Pennsylvania, a 4000-seat house on the site of the old Hotel Anderson, Sixth and Penn, at cost of $2,500,000.

February 3: Twenty men were killed in an explosion that wrecked a mine of the Pittsburgh Terminal Company at Horning, near Castle Shannon.

Spring: The Pittsburgh Symphony Orchestra, reorganized and financed by its own musicians, began playing public concerts.

May 18: Pittsburgh voters approved a $19,902,000 bond issue for various city improvements.

June 12: Approximately $60,000,000 was being expended to improve steel mills in the area.

June 13: The new Seventh Street Bridge was opened.

June 28: Plans were announced for a $7,000,000 campaign for establishment of a Presbyterian "medical center."

June 28: Duquesne Light Company announced a plan to build the "largest and most modern" electric power plant in the world at Shippingport on the Ohio River at a cost of $40,000,-000.

September 27: Ground was broken for

the University of Pittsburgh's Cathedral of Learning.

November 6: Official opening was held for Armstrong Tunnels, named for Commissioner Joseph G. Armstrong.

November 13: An air show featured dedication of Bettis Field as a Pittsburgh-McKeesport airport.

November 27: Carnegie Tech upset Notre Dame, 19 to 0 at Forbes Field before 45,000.

November: Double-deck trolleys, declared too dangerous for Pittsburgh, were abandoned.

The $1,650,000 Webster Hall, on Fifth Avenue, was erected as a hotel to specialize in club residences for men.

1927   *April 1*: Forty-five thousand miners in the district joined in a nationwide coal strike.

April 21: Carrying a single pouch of mail, an open cockpit Waco belonging to Clifford Ball, Inc., the city's pioneer airline, inaugurated airmail service between Pittsburgh and Cleveland.

April 24: After a Sunday concert, which drew an audience of 4000, nine members of the executive board of the Pittsburgh Symphony were arrested on charges of violating "blue laws". All were found guilty and fined $25 each by Alderman Samuel McKinley; group included Richard S. Rauh, secretary of the society; Edward Specter, chairman of the orchestra committee; Elias Breeskin, assistant conductor, and seven others.

June 3: Carrick Borough was annexed to the city.

June 12: The Buhl Foundation was established with a $15,000,000 gift announced by Henry Buhl, Jr.

June 12: The New Point Bridge was dedicated.

June 25: Frick Park, 380 acres in Squirrel Hill willed to the city by H. C. Frick, was opened for public use.

August 2: After a series of negotiations the *Post-Gazette* came into being under ownership of Paul Block, and the *Sun-Telegraph* was organized under ownership of William Randolph Hearst.

August 3: Charles Lindbergh, the first to fly alone over the Atlantic to Europe, was fêted by the city.

August 12: The widening of Grant Street, Downtown, was started.

October 8: The Pittsburgh Pirates lost the fourth straight game of the World Series, 4 to 3, to the New York Yankees.

October 13: President Coolidge was guest speaker at the Carnegie Institute's 31st Founders Day exercises at Carnegie Music Hall. He also appeared before Carnegie Tech students in accordance with a promise made to them by Samuel H. Church, Institute president, and made a speech—a nine-word address: "I shall not break Colonel Church's promise to you."

October: The new Roosevelt Hotel, at Sixth Street and Penn, was opened.

December 27: J. P. Morgan, Jr., New York financier, became chairman of the board of the United States Steel Corporation.

Construction crews began erecting the Pittsburgher Hotel on Diamond Street.

1928 *February 27:* Stanley Theater opened.

March 27: The Liberty Bridge was dedicated and opened to public use.

May 2: Air express service was inaugurated between Pittsburgh and Cleveland by the Clifford Ball Air Line; 1000 spectators watched Pilot Dewey Noyes take off in a plane carrying first express parcels.

May 31: The National Elimination Balloon Races, witnessed by 150,000 persons at Bettis Field, resulted in the death of two balloonists—W. W. Morton and Lieutenant Paul Evert, of the United States Army.

May: The 23-story Clark Building, on Liberty Avenue, was ready for occupancy.

June 26: Allegheny County voters approved a $43,680,000 bond issue for public works, including $6,000,000 for a town hall, $2,550,000 for a county office building, and $10,930,000 for new boulevards and highways.

July 3: Fire destroyed the Cameo Theater building at 347 Fifth Avenue.

July 12: State Superior Court approved Sunday symphony concerts for Pittsburgh; Sabbath Association announced it intended nevertheless to demand enforcement of the blue laws of 1794.

July 16: The first film "talkie," titled *Tenderloin,* was introduced at the Stanley Theater. Previewers said it had less than 10 minutes' "audible" dialogue, and one commented the "project is so new that its possibilities scarcely can be gauged yet."

July 17: Called the "scenic boulevard of Pittsburgh," Mount Washington Roadway, to the top of Mount Washington, was opened with a mile-long parade followed by a celebration.

August 8: Westinghouse staged what was said to be the world's first demonstration of "motion pictures broadcast by radio"—"television"—in its East Pittsburgh laboratories. The idea was worked out by Dr. Frank Conrad, assistant chief engineer at Westinghouse.

August 15: Air passenger service from the city was instituted.

October 28: Site for a new county airport (Lebanon Church Road) was chosen.

November 6: In the election of Herbert Hoover as President, Allegheny County gave Hoover 213,681 votes, and Al Smith 159,718.

November 6: A constitutional amend-

FAMOUS VISITORS

THE DISCOVERER OF RADIUM
Madame Curie visited Pittsburgh in 1921.

THE FRENCH WAR LEADER
Marshal Ferdinand Foch came in 1921.

BRITISH STATESMAN
David Lloyd George arrived in 1923.

COMPOSER OF PORGY AND BESS
In 1933 Pittsburghers voted for Sunday baseball and concerts. On November 29 of that year George Gershwin sold the first Sunday ticket for a concert by the Pittsburgh Symphony. It was a memorable occasion. On Gershwin's left is conductor Antonio Modarelli, on his right Mrs. William Maclay Hall, president of the Symphony Society and Leo Lehman, prominent Pittsburgh businessman.

ment to permit Pittsburgh and Allegheny County to consolidate into a metropolitan district was approved by a state-wide vote.

November 19: Two thousand scientists, representing 20 different nations, assembled at Carnegie Tech for the opening of the Second International Conference on Bituminous Coal, initiated in 1926 by Tech President Thomas S. Baker.

1929 *January 11:* Declaring that the city should assume leadership in the fight against air pollution, City Council authorized installation of smoke-prevention equipment at the city's pumping station at Brilliant.

January 13: President James A. Farrell, of the United States Steel Corporation, announced a $20,000,000 expansion program for subsidiary plants at Duquesne, McKeesport, and Braddock.

February 1: The 37-story Grant Building, tallest in the city and topped by an airplane beacon spelling out Pittsburgh in Morse code, was ready for occupancy.

February 7: A metropolitan charter bill, designed to make Pittsburgh the fifth largest city in the United States with a consolidated population of 1,319,684, was prepared for the State Legislature.

March: The 32-story Koppers Building was opened to tenants.

June 25: The Pittsburgh Metropolitan District Charter, submitted to an Allegheny County vote, failed to acquire the required two thirds majority in each of 62 municipalities, a majority of the total in the county; city voters were eight to one in favor of the bill, but only 47 municipalities cast two thirds vote.

June 28: A five-day work week was adopted by the building trades of Pittsburgh.

July 12: Contract for the new airport on Lebanon Church Road was signed.

September 24: Mount Mercy College for Women was opened.

September: Freda Seund became the first woman in Pittsburgh to be instructed in flying and to solo at a Pittsburgh airfield.

October 18: A crowd of 100,000 persons viewed a river pageant marking the completion of the canalization of the Ohio River.

November 5: Pittsburgh residents voted overwhelmingly in favor of adoption of voting machines in Pennsylvania.

November 5: R. B. Mellon, president of Mellon National Bank, resigned as chairman of the County Planning Commission in order, he said, to make a trip to Europe. His action was construed as an indication that a proposal to built a $6,000,000 town hall would be delayed.

December 16: Maurice Falk announced creation of a $10,000,000 fund by the Maurice and Laura Falk Foundation for welfare and charitable purposes.

December 21: Saw Mill Run Boulevard was opened to the public.

December: The Gulf Oil Company was making final plans for erection of its 11 million dollar office building at Seventh and Grant.

1930 January 3: The United States purchased land for a new Post Office Building.

January 12: Pittsburgh taxi drivers held a mass meeting at Duquesne Gardens to begin a strike against the Green and Yellow Cab companies in protest against what they claimed was a pay cut.

January 28: United States Steel reported record peacetime profits of $197,531,349.

February 14: Police used tear-gas bombs to disperse a crowd on Center Avenue; two cabs were burned and 10 persons arrested as taxi strike violence continued.

April 16: The cornerstone was laid for the new $2,700,000 county office building at Ross and Diamond Streets.

July 9: Jones and Laughlin announced a $20,000,000 expansion program for its plants in Pittsburgh and Aliquippa.

July 10: The Better Traffic Committee recommended a ban on all Downtown curb parking; it also urged Mayor Charles H. Kline to eliminate the practice of "fixing" traffic tags.

July 11: The Baltimore and Ohio Railroad applied for a federal permit to build a river-rail terminal on the Monongahela River.

August 27: Sara Soffel was sworn in by Judge Richard Kennedy as judge of County Court, the first woman jurist in Pennsylvania.

Fall: Construction work started on the $6,000,000 Mellon Institute building at Fifth and Bellefield.

September 18: Chamber of Commerce recommended to the United States Census Bureau a Greater Pittsburgh metropolitan area with 4043 square miles in 13 counties of Pennsylvania, Ohio, and West Virginia with a population of 2,203,000.

October 2: Rear Admiral Richard E. Byrd addressed 3000 at Syria Mosque during National Safety Congress here.

October 12: Eucharistic Congress was held in Forbes Field.

October 21: City Council passed an emergency proposal to set up a fund of $100,000 to aid families in need.

October 21: McCann and Company opened for business in its new 10-story building at Diamond and Ferry Streets.

November 25: The Mississippi Valley Association, in convention at St. Louis, endorsed proposed construction of an Ohio River-Lake Erie canal at the request of Pittsburgh and Youngstown business interests.

November 25: A capacity audience filled the Stanley Theater for a benefit show for Pittsburgh unemployed and needy families; among those featured were Phil Baker, Fred Stone and Dick Powell.

December 30: A deed of trust filed by Andrew Mellon created the A. W. Mellon Educational and Charitable Trust.

December: The Gulf Oil Company was engaged in the construction of a research center at Craft Avenue and the Boulevard of the Allies.

Population: 669,817.

KDKA announced the erection of a powerful transmitter at Saxonburg.

1931 January 15: The Chamber of Commerce reported that 27 new manufacturing plants and warehouses, representing investments totaling $29,502,000, started operations in the Pittsburgh district in 1930.

January 16: Their funds exhausted, relief agencies warned that approximately 47,750 Pittsburgh district residents would "begin starving" immediately.

January 27: Gulf Oil opened a new refinery on Neville Island.

February 5: McClintock-Marshall and Bethlehem Steel Companies merged.

March 11: The Homer Smith, pleasure steamboat, burned at the North Side wharf.

March 17: The county commissioners voted $3,000,000 for construction of the Homestead High Level Bridge.

May 11: Pittsburgh's first police radio "cruisers" were patrolling the streets as WPOU, police radio station, began broadcasting.

June 3: Buhl Foundation announced plans for a 45-acre housing development on Mount Washington to be known as Chatham Village, the first low-rent community housing project in the nation.

June 14: Florenz Ziegfeld's Follies opened the new season of their 23rd edition at the Nixon Theater; among those featured in the cast were Helen Morgan, Gladys Glad, Ruth Etting, Harry Richman, and, in the chorus, two Pittsburgh girls—Zecil Silvonia and Mony Lange.

June 25: Mayor Kline was indicted with Bertram L. Succop, former director of supplies, on 49 counts of misdemeanor in office.

June 30: About 5000 hunger strikers paraded in the city streets.

July 23: Forty-two aged men and women were killed in or died from the effects of a fire that destroyed the Little Sisters of the Poor Home at Penn Avenue and South Aiken; 157 others were hurt.

July 29: Wiley Post and Harold Gatty, renowned round-the-world fliers, were given an enthusiastic welcome in Pittsburgh.

August 19: The McKees Rocks-Ohio River Boulevard Bridge was opened.

September 15: For the first time in Allegheny County, voting machines —186 of them—were used in the primary election.

September 21: The Bank of Pittsburgh announced its decision to close to conserve interests of depositors and stockholders.

September 30: The 583 feet tall Gulf Building went into construction.

October 28: The Edgar Thomson works in Braddock prepared to re-open; plans were announced to re-employ about 7000 at Homestead and Braddock.

December 4: Hunger marchers, en route in trucks and autos to Washington, D.C., to urge an unemployment insurance bill, stopped over in Pittsburgh and requested food and shelter from Helping Hand Society headquarters.

December 22: Five million dollars were distributed to various institutions by the H. C. Frick estate.

1932 January 5: Led by Father James R. Cox, a jobless army of 15,000 men left St. Patrick's Church, at Seventeenth Street and Liberty Avenue, and headed for the Capital of the nation; many were afoot in a driving rain.

January 6: The county government was reorganized, and six departments were created: Highways, Property and Supplies, Parks, Airport, Elections, and Law.

January 8: Exhausted and hungry, Father Cox's jobless army arrived home after making a plea to Congress and President Hoover for immediate relief and jobs and warning that "something must be done to avert violence."

January 17: More than 55,000 persons, in a rally at Pitt Stadium, cheered Father Cox, "Shepherd of the

THE FRUIT MARKET
Painted by Samuel Rosenberg in 1937. It is the property of Mr. and Mrs. A. Adelman.

Unemployed," as he announced formation of the "Jobless Party" and himself as its candidate for president.

January 22: Patrick T. Fagan, president of District 5, United Mine Workers, announced union acceptance of a 10 per cent wage cut for coal miners employed by the Pittsburgh Terminal Coal Corporation.

February 4: A. W. Mellon, at the age of 76, was appointed ambassador to Great Britain after serving 11 years as Secretary of the Treasury.

February 5: Barney Dreyfuss, president and owner of the Pittsburgh Pirates since 1899 and an organizer of the first World Series, died at the age of 66 at Mount Sinai Hospital in New York.

February 7: Winston Churchill visited the city.

March 28: In order to provide employment for the needy, the city began to extend the Mount Washington Road project; six stations were also set up for free food distribution.

March 28: The "Snodgrass-Herron" plan for a $5,500,000 Downtown subway to relieve traffic congestion was presented to Council.

April 26: A $5,000,000 unemployment relief bond issue was approved in the primary election by Pittsburgh voters.

May 14: Mayor Charles H. Kline and his ousted supplies director, Bertram L. Succop, were found guilty of misconduct in office in a jury trial in Butler.

June 6: A disorganized bonus army marched through Pittsburgh en route to Washington.

June 8: Students demonstrated against General Douglas MacArthur when he delivered the commencement address at the University of Pittsburgh.

June 8: Construction was started on the new $8,000,000 federal building and post office on Grant Street.

September 5: Organized labor of Pittsburgh held its first parade in a dozen years and ended it at West View Park, where William Green, president of the AFL, called for shorter working hours and a more equitable distribution of wealth.

September 10: Thirty thousand persons attended the dedication of the George Westinghouse Bridge, the $1,750,000 link in relocated Lincoln Highway over Turtle Creek.

September 15: Mayor Kline returned to City Hall and to his "political fence mending" after Judge Thomas D. Finletter reversed a jury verdict and set him free; former Supplies Director Succop was sentenced to one year in jail.

October 15: President Herbert Hoover campaigned in the city.

October 19: Speaking as a presidential candidate before 30,000 at Forbes Field, Governor Franklin D. Roosevelt, of New York, expressed opposition to payment of the soldiers' bonus "until the government has balanced the budget and has a surplus of cash in the treasury." It was his first public declaration on the bonus issue since his nomination.

November 8: Franklin D. Roosevelt carried Allegheny County by 40,000 votes in the Democratic sweep that placed him in the White House.

November 14: Distribution of free milk to 50,000 needy and undernourished children was started in 500 schools of Allegheny County.

November 14 to 15: The Duquesne National and Diamond banks closed their doors because of heavy withdrawal of deposits.

December 2: Property owners threatened a "taxpayers' strike" unless Mayor Kline reduced proposed $25,000,000 budget for 1933 by 25 per cent.

December 15: City Council lowered the mill levy and cut Mayor Kline's budget 20 per cent.

December: The Duquesne Club was building a 13-story addition to its Sixth Street headquarters.

Of the 197 homes designed on Buhl Foundation's Chatham Village, 129 were completed.

1933 *February 10:* The 10th Street Bridge was completed and opened to traffic.

March 5: The Pittsburgh Stock Exchange closed at the start of a bank holiday ordered by the President; the Pittsburgh Clearing House prepared to issue scrip.

March 9: At a rally of 2000 persons in Syria Mosque, plans were made to send a delegation to Harrisburg to fight for city-manager form of government for Pittsburgh.

March 14: Thirty-three banking institutions in Pittsburgh reopened for normal business activity and were crowded through the day with thousands of depositors.

March 31: Mayor Charles H. Kline, described as a "defeated and broken man," resigned after seven years in office; Council President John S. Herron became mayor.

April 7: The *Post-Gazette* reported: "With a whoop of joy, thousands of parched Pittsburgh throats greeted the end of the Great Dry Era at 12:01 o'clock this morning." Large crowds milled about outside Pittsburgh breweries waiting for first legalized 3.2 beer.

April 11: A group of 224 men—the first from Pittsburgh to join President Roosevelt's reforestation army—entrained for Virginia.

August 5: Relocated and widened Pittsburgh-Butler Highway (Route 8) was opened to traffic.

September 1: The Chamber of Commerce estimated that 95 per cent of all Pittsburgh businesses were enrolled under the banner of the NRA Blue Eagle.

September 20: Modern professional football began in Pittsburgh when the Pittsburgh Pirates, under ownership of Arthur J. Rooney, lost, 23 to 2, to the New York Giants before 25,000 at Forbes Field.

October 9: After President Roosevelt ordered "captive mine" owners to make peace, 75,000 miners of western Pennsylvania returned to work. Philip Murray, international vice-president of the United Mine Workers, and Thomas Moses, president of the H. C. Frick Coke Company, began negotiating differences.

October 11: Three thousand men ended a six-day attempt to "bring back prosperity" by staying on the job and producing steel while barricaded inside the Clairton by-products plant of Carnegie Steel Company.

November 7: Pittsburghers voted out the "blue laws" and voted in Sunday baseball and other sports. They also approved a constitutional amendment to permit the State Legislature to draft a new metropolitan charter for Pittsburgh.

November 7: William McNair was elected mayor.

November 10: In a conference at the White House, President Roosevelt advised Mayor-elect McNair and his campaign chairman, David L. Lawrence: "Now give the people of Pittsburgh good administration."

December 1: Richard Beatty Mellon, junior partner in the Mellon banking empire, brother of A. W. Mellon, died at the age of 75 in his Fifth Avenue mansion.

1934 *January 1:* New year reports showed Pittsburgh business in 1933 increased 18 per cent in volume over 1932.

January 2: According to news accounts, "pandemonium broke loose" at City Hall as Mayor McNair, in his first day in office, began feuding with Council over confirmation of his cabinet appointments.

SOHO
A painting by Samuel Rosenberg which was exhibited at the Carnegie Institute in 1938.

January 14: Civil Works Administrator Harry L. Hopkins ordered an investigation into trade union charges of "political favoritism" in the hiring of men for CWA jobs in Pittsburgh.

February 13: Plans were announced for a $350,000 juvenile court and detention home in Oakland.

February 26: An Akron-to-Pittsburgh passenger train of the Pennsylvania Railroad plunged off a bridge at Merchant Street as it sped into the North Side station; nine persons were killed and 39 injured.

March 27: Steel mills in the Pittsburgh district retained the 40-hour week and granted 10 per cent pay raises to 100,000 steel workers, increasing district payrolls by a total of approximately $1,750,000 per month.

June 28: The government approved a $25,000,000 loan to the Allegheny County Authority for a construction program entailing 12,000 jobs for unemployed men.

June: Hervey Allen, Pittsburgh novelist, visited in the city.

August 9: Pittsburgh artist John Kane became a controversial figure in the national art world.

October 13: Postmaster James A. Farley dedicated Pittsburgh's new $7,000,000 post office-federal building in an outdoor ceremony on Grant Street.

December 28: One of the lecturers at the meeting of the American Association for the Advancement of Science, attended by a selected group of 400 scientists, was Professor Albert Einstein; he spoke on the "equivalent of mass and energy" in the Carnegie Tech Little Theater.

1935 January 2: Business activity in Pittsburgh in 1934 was 68 per cent higher than 1933; industrial production was up 5.6 per cent over 1933 and 20 per cent over 1932, according to business summaries.

January 19: Andrew Mellon announced that he would give his art collection to the federal government to be housed in a gallery in Washington, D. C.

February 25: The United Engineering and Foundry Company of Pittsburgh received a $3,000,000 order for the Zaporoptal Steel Works in Soviet Russia—one of the largest contracts ever placed in the United States for foreign shipment.

February 26: In what was said to be the largest industrial dismantling project in the city's history, the National Tube Company began disassembling its Pennsylvania plant, Second Avenue, and Republic plant, on 24th Street, South Side.

March 1: A slight earth tremor was felt in the city.

March 4: In a Democratic caucus in Harrisburg, State Democratic Chairman David L. Lawrence demanded that the McNair ripper bill be pushed through the Legislature. While he later denied having made such a speech in the caucus, he was quoted as saying: "I put him [McNair] in, and I'll take him out."

March 21: Two Pittsburghers — William P. Witherow, representing industry, and Philip Murray, representing organized labor—were named by President Roosevelt to the NRA board.

March 21: Father Cox's Old St. Patrick's Church, a 125-year-old Pittsburgh landmark and one of the most popular churches in the city, was destroyed by fire.

April 12: The Monongahela House, where policy-making party caucuses were held prior to and during the first Republican convention in 1856 and said to be, for that reason, the "birthplace of the Republican Party," closed its doors. A plan to convert it to Jones and Laughlin office building failed to materialize.

May 12: Nearly 6000 persons gathered in and about the chapel for dedication of the East Liberty Presbyterian Church, built at a cost of more than $4,000,000 by Mr. and Mrs. R. B. Mellon as a memorial to their respective mothers.

June 3: Mayor McNair installed a bed in his office in preparation for a long siege in the event the ripper bill against him was passed by State Legislature.

June 19: The Pittsburgh Metropolitan District Charter bill, amended drastically by the House, was defeated in the State Senate.

June 23: The McNair ripper bill died with adjournment of the Legislature.

October 14: Andrew Mellon announced a gift of $10,000,000 for construction of the National Gallery of Art in Washington, D.C.; his private art collection, accumulated at a cost of $25,000,000 and valued at $40,000,000, was made immediately available to the gallery.

November 5: Pittsburgh and Allegheny County voters approved Sunday movies by a vote of three to one.

November 24: Large crowds filled theaters of the city as Sunday movies were shown for the first time.

December 16: In the city's healthiest economic signs since before the 1929 crash, Jones and Laughlin announced a $40,000,000 expansion program, including a new $25,000,000 sheet and strip mill on Second Avenue, and the Pennsylvania Railroad placed an order for 10,000 brake sets with the Westinghouse Air Brake Company.

1936 January 2: Business reviews showed a definite upturn of Pittsburgh business in 1935; general business activity was up 14.7 per cent over 1934 and 45.3 per cent over 1932; department store sales were up 6.5 per cent.

February 25: Dr. Robert E. Doherty, Yale dean and electrical researcher, was elected president of Carnegie Tech to succeed Dr. Thomas S. Baker.

February 26: An ice gorge formed in the Allegheny River and moved toward Pittsburgh; flood waters swept over many Western Pennsylvania communities.

March 17 (St. Patrick's Day): The rivers rose to 34 feet at the Point, and for the first time in 23 years water flowed over the city's low-level streets.

March 18: Floodwaters reached a crest of 46.4 feet, highest in the city's history, and began receding; some streets were inundated by 20 feet of water.

March 19: More than 60 persons were believed dead as the flood stage dropped to 32.1 feet; health, relief, and city agencies mustered support to fight disease, hunger, and cold; explosions and fires added to the peril.

March 19: Between 5000 and 7000 men, women, and children were rescued from flooded homes in the McKees Rocks "Bottoms."

March 20: The flood death toll was reported at 46 known dead and 384 injured; the Red Cross was attempting to assist 50,000 homeless persons; drinking water was restored; bandits and vandals roamed the area.

March 20: Municipal officers from 200 cities and towns in the Tri-State area met here in an emergency conference to discuss flood prevention for the future.

March 22: The Pittsburgh district struggled to get back to normal, but 110,144 men, women, and children remained homeless in Allegheny County.

March 24: City Council asked the federal government for $10,000,000 to replace and repair 1000 homes destroyed and 8000 damaged by flood waters.

THE PRESIDENTIAL

President Herbert Hoover visited Pittsburgh on October 15, 1932; asking for the people's support and their vote for a second term.

March 27: The flood death toll rose to 74. The Chamber of Commerce, representing the business interests of Pittsburgh, informed the federal government that the delay of an adequate flood-control program, sought since 1907, had cost Allegheny County between $150,000,000 and $200,000,000 in property loss.

March 30: The National Guard was withdrawn, the Triangle was reopened.

April 18: Mayor McNair was jailed for disobeying a court order directing him to return a $100 fine to an alleged numbers writer who had successfully appealed his conviction to County Court; the mayor was released from jail on agreeing to return the fine.

June 17: The Steel Workers' Organizing Committee held its first meeting in the Commonwealth Building and named Philip Murray, international vice-president of United Mine Workers, as chairman of a planned organizing campaign.

June 22: Congress passed the flood-control act, setting up funds for flood-control work in this district.

June 27: Newly completed Allegheny General Hospital was dedicated.

October 2: Addressing 50,000 persons at Forbes Field, President Roosevelt predicted a balanced budget based on an increase in national income.

October 6: With no advance notice, William H. McNair resigned and turned the office of mayor over to Cornelius P. Scully, president of Council and McNair's bitterest personal enemy in his three years in office.

October 8: The Reverend Charles E. Coughlin, Detroit radio priest and head of the National Union for Social Justice, in a speech to an overflow crowd of 4500 at Syria Mosque, charged that President Roosevelt "has adopted communistic activities."

October 11: One hundred thousand Catholic men of Pittsburgh assembled at Pitt Stadium for a eucharistic rally.

October 13: Mayor McNair repented and withdrew his resignation, but Council declined to accept it. Mayor Scully fired Leslie Johnston, public works director.

October 27: Governor Alfred M. Landon, of Kansas, appeared in Pittsburgh as the Republican presidential candidate and spoke to a crowd of 20,000 at Duquesne Gardens.

November 3: A total of 560,000 Allegheny County citizens voted in the presidential election to set a balloting record, 150,000 above the previous high. President Roosevelt carried the county by 188,478 votes; county Democrats won five seats in Congress, two in the United States Senate, and 27 in the State House.

November 8: At the conclusion of a two-day meeting of the CIO, headed by John L. Lewis, Lewis refused to meet William Green of AFL to discuss peace terms between the two union groups.

December 20: In a mass meeting at the Fort Pitt Hotel, Philip Murray, CIO chairman, declared in his keynote speech that "the company union must be put out of business." Employee representatives of 42 steel plants pledged full support to the CIO in its drive to organize all steel workers into one trade union.

1937 *January 1:* Pittsburgh business in 1936 was at its highest level since 1930, up 29.2 per cent from 1935.

January 14: With 500 business guests in attendance, the Carnegie-Illinois Steel Corporation formally opened a new $10,000,000 plant in Homestead, a 100-inch semicontinuous plate mill with a capacity of 729,000 tons per year.

January 15: William A. Irvin, president of United States Steel, and Benjamin F. Fairless, president of Carnegie-Illinois, announced plans for the expenditure of $60,000,000 for the expansion and improvement of plants at Clairton and Braddock.

January 20: Three-month strike of 6000 Pittsburgh Plate Glass workers ended with an agreement for an eight-cent hourly pay raise.

March 17: Five United States Steel subsidiaries, headed by Benjamin F. Fairless, of Carnegie-Illinois, signed the first wage contract with the Steel Workers Organizing Committee. It established in the steel industry the $5-a-day minimum wage, the 40-hour week, vacations with pay, seniority rights, and grievance procedure.

April 21: Buhl Foundation gave $750,000 to the city for a planetarium and institute of popular science on the site of the old Allegheny City Hall.

April 26: Rivers hit crest of 35.1 feet, but only low-lying areas were affected. State Senator William B. Rodgers, Jr.

demanded federal government make an immediate start on the long-delayed flood-control program.

May 4: The Better Traffic Committee endorsed Mayor Scully's plan to make Forbes Street and Fifth Avenue one-way streets and to construct a short trolley loop in the downtown area.

May 6: Andrew W. Mellon dedicated the $10,000,000 Mellon Institute at the start of a five-day program in Carnegie Music Hall, highlighted by an announcement of a new successful treatment for pneumonia, developed by Institute scientists. Among the scores of leading scientists in attendance were three Nobel prize winners —Drs. H. C. Urey, W. P. Murphy, and Irving Langmuir.

May 11: Mayor Scully proposed a $70,400,000 "pure water supply" to be brought to Pittsburgh and neighboring communities by an aqueduct system from northern creeks.

May 12: Twenty-five thousand men were idled at Jones and Laughlin's Pittsburgh and Aliquippa plants by a strike ordered by Philip Murray in the Steel Workers Organizing Committee organizational drive. Jones and Laughlin and a group of other operators were accused by the union of violating the Wagner Labor Relations Act by refusing to sign wage scale contracts.

May 20: In the nation's largest collective bargaining election, steel workers in Jones and Laughlin plants voted 17,028 for the CIO Amalgamated Association of Iron, Steel, and Tin Workers and 7207 against.

May 21: Governor Earle signed a bill to create a turnpike commission to issue $50,000,000 to $65,000,000 in bonds to finance construction of an "all-weather" toll highway from Pittsburgh to Harrisburg.

May 22: The Carnegie-Illinois Steel Corporation broke ground for its new Irvin works, in West Mifflin, estimated to cost $63,000,000 and employ 4000 men.

June 2: The Stephen C. Foster Memorial adjoining the Cathedral of Learning was dedicated.

June 4: The Westinghouse Electric Corporation was building a cyclotron.

June 7: As the climax of a week-long celebration of the 150th anniversary of its founding, the University of Pittsburgh celebrated the completion of its 42-story Cathedral of Learning a decade after construction on the building was started.

September 10: The Kelsey-Hayes Wheel Company of Detroit, nation's largest manufacturer of auto wheels, announced purchase of a Neville Island property as site for a $1,000,000 plant to employ 1500 persons.

September 13: The *Post-Gazette* initiated a series of articles by Ray

CAMPAIGN OF 1932

Governor Franklin D. Roosevelt, the Democratic standard bearer campaigned hard in Pittsburgh and the neighboring communities.

Sprigle, exposing United States Supreme Court Justice Hugo L. Black as a member of the Ku Klux Klan; the articles led to demands for Justice Black's resignation.

September 13: The PWA in Washington announced a $2,847,000 appropriation for construction of a proposed psychiatric hospital on the Pitt campus.

September 16: The AFL-Central Labor Union expelled its president, Patrick C. Fagan, for his support of Mayor Scully. The mayor had opposed the union's endorsement of the Kane-McArdle faction in the Democratic primary. All other CIO delegates were also expelled, and Fagan immediately announced formation of a "CIO-Central Labor Union" (Steel City Industrial Union).

September 20: Andrew W. Mellon, who died on August 26, left his vast estate to his son, Paul Mellon, and son-in-law, David K. E. Bruce, to be administered "as they shall deem advisable and for best interests of my estate." The will bound them only to the deed that created the A. W. Mellon Educational and Charitable Trust, under which Mr. Mellon's bequest to the public was estimated at between $100,000,000 and $500,000,000.

October 1: In a nationwide radio talk Justice Hugo Black admitted membership in the Ku Klux Klan, as charged by Ray Sprigle, but stated that he resigned after a successful primary race for the United States Senate and disclaimed all sympathy for the movement.

October 20: Chief Justice John W. Kephart, of the State Supreme Court, dedicated the new $350,000 Juvenile Court here, calling it a "monument to an enlightened judicial system."

October 20: Ground was broken at Crooked Creek dam site on upper Allegheny River, first of a network of dams to protect the Pittsburgh area from floods.

October 21: After a 10-year rebuilding job, directed by Edward Specter, the Pittsburgh Symphony Orchestra, backed by a successful public campaign for $300,000, presented its first concert as a major orchestra with Otto Klemperer as guest conductor.

October 27: Benjamin F. Fairless was elected president of the U.S. Steel Corp.

November 20: The Homestead High Level Bridge was dedicated.

December 2: Allegheny Housing Authority was established.

December 3: The famed Lucy Furnace, first blast furnace built by Andrew Carnegie and named for his brother's wife, was dismantled.

December 3: Air pilots said Pittsburgh appeared "like a ball of black ink" as one of the city's heaviest smoke screens cut Downtown visibility to 300 feet, slowed traffic, and caused lights to be turned on at high noon; home furnaces were held to be the chief cause.

December 8: Pittsburgh became the center of national steel production when United States Steel decided to move its management headquarters to Pittsburgh.

December 8: The federal government earmarked $10,000,000 for low-cost housing projects planned by the Pittsburgh Housing Authority.

1938 *January 1:* Reports showed that, despite a recession in the closing months of the year, Pittsburgh business activity for 1937 was up 8.7 per cent over 1936; the total resources of 97 banks in Allegheny County were reported to be $1,507,604,000.

January 1: At this date wage contracts between the Steel Workers Organizing Committee and the steel industry totaled 445.

January 20: *Falling Water*, Edgar Kaufmann's country home designed by Frank Lloyd Wright, was viewed by interested visitors.

January 27: A plan for creating a historic memorial park in Pittsburgh, covering a 36-acre area at the Point and including proposed restoration of Fort Pitt and Fort Duquesne on their original sites, was before the National Park Service in Washington.

January 27: The WPA fixed the cost of a proposed sewage-disposal system to end stream pollution in Allegheny County at $25,000,000.

March 3: Fritz Reiner, noted Hungarian conductor, was appointed full-time director of the Pittsburgh Symphony Orchestra.

March 26: Six hundred Pittsburgh business and civic leaders, at a dinner in the William Penn Hotel, were informed that Secretary of the Interior Harold Ickes had approved the Point as a site for a historic memorial. A Point Park commission was promoting the plan under chairmanship of Frank C. Harper.

April 5: Myron C. Taylor resigned as chairman of the board of United States Steel.

April 14: Using the same gold-plated shovel that started the grading of Grant's Hill, known locally as the Hump, Mayor Scully broke ground for the $1,050,000 Buhl Planetarium.

May 2: Ray Sprigle was awarded the Pulitzer Prize for his exposé of Justice Hugo Black's affiliation with Ku Klux Klan.

May 5: Downtown traffic was bottled up by a city-wide strike of parking-lot and garage attendants called by taxicab drivers' union.

May 11: The Pittsburgh Railways Company, which had emerged from a receivership in 1922, again went into bankruptcy.

May 12: Homeopathic Hospital changed its name to Shadyside.

May 15: A survey conducted by the city's Bureau of Smoke Regulation indicated that smog was a major factor in Pittsburgh's high pneumonia death rate.

May 17: The Allegheny and Ludlum Steel companies were merged.

June 24: Carnegie-Illinois announced a reduction in steel prices to approximately the level prior to 1938.

June: Steel Workers Organizing Committee contracts in the steel industry were increased to cover 529 mills.

September 2: Douglas "Wrong Way" Corrigan, solo transatlantic flier, was a special guest at the opening of Allegheny County's Sesquicentennial Anniversary celebration.

October 1: The Pittsburgh Housing Authority announced its first low-cost housing project would be located in the Hill District and named Bedford Dwellings, initial step in a $40,000,000 city-county slum-clearance program.

November 8: The Democrats lost heavily in Allegheny County.

November 15: In its first constitutional convention at the Grotto, in North Side Pittsburgh, the CIO became a permanent organization; it also voted for a "no compromise" stand for peace on its own terms in its three-year war with the AFL.

November 20: After five years in construction, the Heinz Chapel, topped by a 235-foot spire, was dedicated on the Pitt campus as the gift of the Heinz family.

November 21: David L. Lawrence testified in Harrisburg before a legislative committee investigating charges that he and other high officers of state had engaged in a conspiracy involving "bribery, extortion, and coercion."

December 13: The world's largest slabbing mill went into operation at the Edgar Thomson works of Carnegie-Illinois in Braddock.

December 15: Nearly 2000 business leaders attended dedication of new $60,000,000 Irvin works.

December 19: Again with the gold-plated "Hump shovel," Mayor Scully broke ground for the $3,000,000 Bedford Dwellings, low-cost housing community for 420 families.

December: The Pittsburgh Regional Planning Association, successor to the Municipal Planning Association, undertook a series of studies to attempt to find ways of halting the decline of property values in Pittsburgh.

1939 *January 3:* The effects of a business recession were felt in 1938, when business activity was down 39.3 per cent from 1937.

January: A $5,000,000 Monongahela River front improvement was started with WPA funds.

February 21: Army engineers recommended a $207,000,000 Beaver-Youngstown canal with "dead end" at Youngstown. Pittsburgh civic and business interests immediately mobilized to continue their 20-year fight for a canal extending to Lake Erie.

March 5: The University of Pittsburgh's greatest era as a national football power ended with the resignation of Dr. John B. (Jock) Sutherland as head coach.

March 10: Pitt students went on strike in protest against Dr. Sutherland's resignation and against what they called "autocratic administrative evils" and the "bungling policies" of Chancellor John G. Bowman.

March 13: The city began construction of an $890,000 incinerator plant, its first, at the foot of 29th Street in Lawrenceville.

March 14: A new metropolitan commission was created at a meeting of business, labor, and civic representatives; its purpose was to formulate a "political reorganization which will produce the maximum of efficiency under the maximum of home rule."

April 17: The newly proposed metropolitan plan of government, seeking to establish Pittsburgh as the nation's fifth city in size with a population of 1,700,000, was defeated at Harrisburg when it failed to receive the backing of Allegheny County senators, Democrats and Republicans alike.

April 27: After five years of planning, work was underway to widen and rebuild Bigelow Boulevard into a four-lane highway at a cost of $1,800,000.

April 27: Federal Court issued an injunction, sought by the Pittsburgh Railways Company, to restrain the city from enforcing a one-way traffic plan on Forbes and Fifth Avenue during closing of Bigelow Boulevard.

May 27: A 310-family project in McKees Rocks, with rents averaging $12.50 to $15 per month, was authorized by President Roosevelt for immediate construction as the first project in Allegheny County's $19,000,000 public-housing program.

June 2: Because of improved business conditions, Westinghouse made full restoration of pay cuts ordered in 1938.

June 19: State Supreme Court upheld a verdict awarding $800,000 to Pennsylvania Railroad for damages against the city as the result of 1920 Bigelow Boulevard landslide.

June: A glass house, the first of its kind to be made, was built in the city to be exhibited at the World's Fair in New York.

September 3: Thousands of persons of all faiths, attending the county fair, joined in a peace demonstration as Great Britain declared war on Nazi Germany.

October 24: Buhl Planetarium, built at a cost of $1,100,000 and containing a giant projector, was dedicated; 400 scientists were guests at the first sky show.

November 3: Pittsburgh had its first movie "world premiere" in Hollywood style, with the showing of *Allegheny Uprising* at Loew's Penn; among guests was Claire Trevor, one of the stars of the film.

November 16: After a three-month study, Robert Moses, of New York, and other leading planners unveiled their comprehensive "arterial plan" for solution of the Triangle traffic problem. At a total cost of $38,000,000, the plan included a Pitt Parkway, from a point east of Wilkinsburg to downtown Pittsburgh; a cross-town highway at upper border of the Triangle; reconstruction of Duquesne Way as the first step in a highway system to encompass the Tri-

SPRING LANDSCAPE
It was painted by Abe Weiner in the 1930s.

angle; removal of the Wabash Station and railroad tracks leading to it; improvement of Saw Mill Run Boulevard; removal of trolleys from Downtown streets; removal of the Baltimore and Ohio Railroad station to clear route for the parkway along Monongahela River. The plan discarded the proposed restoration of Fort Pitt as "impractical and undesirable."

December 8: Democratic State Chairman David L. Lawrence was acquitted by a Dauphin County jury of three counts of conspiracy, one of statutory blackmail, and one of violating election laws. Thus the politically inspired charges came to nothing. Next day five thousand cheering Democratic leaders and workers gave Lawrence an enthusiastic welcome when he arrived at Pennsylvania Station from Harrisburg.

December 26: The Duquesne Light Company announced a $16,000,000 program of expansion and construction in the Pittsburgh district.

1940   *January 2:* Pittsburgh business activity for 1939 was 34.9 per cent over that of 1938, approaching 1929 levels in the closing months.

January 5: City and county officials

announced that the $38,000,000 "Moses Plan" would be put into motion in 1940 with reconstruction of Duquesne Way, at a cost of $2,500,000, as the first project. Next on the list were a $1,400,000 Liberty Tubes grade separation plaza and a $1,500,000 extension of Saw Mill Run Boulevard to West End.

January 25: "Musical Americana," the national radio program of Westinghouse, was instituted by KDKA.

February 15: A 20-inch snowfall stopped auto and trolley traffic and forced a two-day suspension in business and trading activities.

March 26: Investigators for the Dies Congressional Committee raided Pittsburgh Communist headquarters at 305-7 Seventh Avenue following arrest of James H. Dolsen, local Communist leader, on a congressional contempt citation.

March 27: David L. Lawrence and seven other state Democratic leaders went on trial in Harrisburg on charge of conspiring to "mace" state payrolls (forcing employees to make political contributions); the original charges were made by ex-Attorney General Charles J. Margiotti. On April 12 Lawrence and his co-defendants were acquitted by a Dauphin County Court jury.

April 15: Bedford Dwellings, the first large federal public housing development, was completed.

June 4: The Pirates played their first night game in Forbes Field.

June 4: Irving S. Olds succeeded Edward R. Stettinius, Jr., as Chairman of the United Steel Corporation.

June 13: Industrial leaders met with public officials to plan mobilization of Pittsburgh district resources for the nation's $5,000,000,000 defense program.

June 28: Highland Park Zoo, completely overhauled and modernized, was reopened to the public.

August 1: A reorganization plan, consolidating 55 interlocking street transit systems into a single company, was filed in Federal Court by trustees for the bankrupt Pittsburgh Railways Company.

August 18: Spear and Company leased a Wood Street 14-story building, formerly occupied by McCreery's Department Store, and announced plans for a $1,000,000 renovation program.

August 22: Preparations were made to raze old Allegheny General Hospital and 25 other buildings in a congested North Side section, site of a huge new Sears, Roebuck and Company store and parking lot.

August 23: The two-level Water Street Bypass, built at a cost of $3,000,000 to relieve Downtown congestion, was opened to traffic.

September 16: The Mesta Machine

Company received an $8,390,000 contract for "artillery material," largest national defense order placed in the Pittsburgh district to this date.

October 1: The nation's longest toll expressway, the 160-mile, $70,000,000 Pittsburgh-to-Harrisburg "dream highway," was opened, and 1560 motorists paid tolls to use it the first day. Governor James ordered the speed limit fixed at 50 miles per hour.

October 3: Wendell L. Willkie spoke at a campaign rally in Forbes Field.

October 4: Fritzie Zivic, of Pittsburgh, won the decision from the favored Henry Armstrong to capture world's welterweight title in a bout at Madison Square Garden, New York.

October 10: Plans for a park at the Point were announced.

October 11: After inspecting the flood-control program in the area, President Roosevelt arrived in Pittsburgh for a brief visit; in a two-and-a-half hour period he toured steel mills, inspected armament plants, and personally dedicated the $13,800,000 Terrace Village, second largest public-housing project in the nation.

October 16: A total of 188,876 Allegheny County men registered for the nation's first peacetime draft; of that number, 89,069 were city residents.

November 5: A record vote of 630,000 was cast in Allegheny County which gave President Roosevelt a majority of 105,599 over Wendell L. Willkie.

November 14: Two hundred men, women, and children escaped serious injury and probable death when the roof of the 50-year-old Harris-Alvin Theater, on Sixth Street, collapsed, bringing down tons of masonry and rafters; four persons were slightly hurt.

November 14: Mayor Scully created a new Point Park commission, with Councilman Fred Weir as chairman.

November 22: Philip Murray was unanimously elected president of the CIO at the conclusion of its Atlantic City convention; in a speech he protested President Roosevelt's efforts to force a merger of the CIO and AFL.

November 25: A group of 40 young men, comprising the city's first draft contingent, passed physical examinations and entrained for Fort Meade, Maryland.

December 11: For his work in labor and national defense, Philip Murray was honored by the Junior Chamber of Commerce as Pittsburgh's "man of the year."

December 18: Crucible·Steel Company announced a $10,000,000 expansion of its Midland plant. Population: 671,659.

1941 *January 1:* Spurred by war demands for goods, business activity in the Pittsburgh district in the closing months of 1940 equaled that of 1929, according to surveys. Steel firms were operating at 100 per cent of capacity; all mills were planning major expansion; defense contracts placed with Pittsburgh district industries totaled $75,000,000.

January: An influenza epidemic caused the absence of 6000 pupils and 138 teachers from the city's schools.

February 5: Dr. I. Hope Alexander, city health director, stepped up his efforts for a smoke-abatement campaign as a black smoke pall blotted out the sun and hung over the city. The Allegheny County Medical Society endorsed efforts to obtain an anti-smoke law.

February 9: Howard Heinz, president of the H. J. Heinz Company, and son of its founder, died at the age of 63 in a Philadelphia hospital.

February 13: City Hall was flooded with mail complaints about the smog that continued to blanket the city.

February 14: The Koppers Company received orders totaling $10,000,000 for coke ovens.

February 19-21: Eight members of City Council visited St. Louis in a body to witness the effects of that city's smoke-control program. They were advised by Mayor Bernard F. Dickmann that Pittsburgh's air could be cleansed, too, "if you have the courage of your convictions."

February: Mrs. Alan M. Scaife presented a cyclotron to the University of Pittsburgh.

March 20: Dr. Joseph H. Barach of Presbyterian Hospital, in the first public hearing before the smoke commission, testified that smog increased the incidence of colds, pneumonia, and other illnesses in Pittsburgh.

March: Richard K. Mellon was elected president of Pittsburgh Regional Planning Association to succeed Howard Heinz.

April 14: A major strike in the steel industry was averted when "Big Steel" signed a pact with the Steel Workers Organizing Committee for a 10-cent hourly wage increase for 240,000.

June 22: Paul Block, publisher of the *Post-Gazette,* died at the age of 63 in the Hotel Waldorf-Astoria in N. Y.

July 5: The University of Pittsburgh Bureau of Business Research reported that business activity in Pittsburgh was at its highest level in the 57 years for which records were available.

October 1: Pittsburgh's eight major hotels were closed by a strike of 2400 AFL service employees.

October 1: A new and more stringent smoke control ordinance was passed by the City Council. Its enforcement was postponed because of the war.

October 16: The 15-day strike which closed the hotels was settled when union members voted to accept pay raises totaling $215,000 a year.

CHURCH IN THE VALLEY
A painting by Marty Cornelius which was exhibited at the Carnegie Institute in 1941.

OHIO RIVER BOULEVARD
A painting made by C. K. Ewing in 1943.

October 22: M. W. Clement, president of the Pennsylvania Railroad, announced the beginning of a program to modernize the Pittsburgh Pennsylvania Station.

December 4: W. P. Witherow, Pittsburgh industrialist, was elected president of the National Association of Manufacturers.

December 7: Pittsburgh was shocked over the Japanese attack on Pearl Harbor.

December 8: More than 1200 Pittsburgh young men volunteered for enlistment in the armed services in one day.

December 12: Dr. Frank Conrad, father of radio broadcasting, died.

1942 *January 1:* An industrial review for 1941 showed the steel industry produced approximately 18,000,000 net tons of steel ingots in 1941 to set a new production record; the output was 200 per cent greater than that of 1938 and 500 per cent over 1932. The amount of prime defense contracts awarded to Pittsburgh industries totaled $137,865,000, and industry expansion projects amounted to $137,106,000. During the previous year, 23,000 workers were added to payrolls of iron and steel industry in the area.

January 1: United States Steel prepared to move ahead with construction of a $75,000,000 mill in Homestead.

PROMENADE IN THE EVENING
A 1941 painting by Rosenberg which was exhibited at the Carnegie Institute in 1944.

THE MOVIE POSTER
A painting by Aaron Bohrod made in 1947.

February 9: Archaeologists excavating near the intersection of the Boulevard of the Allies and Liberty Avenue found what was believed to be part of the curtain of Fort Pitt.

February 16: A total of 115,000 Allegheny County men in the expanded 20-to-44-year age group registered for the draft.

March 1: Domestic use of natural gas was curtailed as a war measure.

March 3: A 17-inch snowfall, one of the city's heaviest in history, paralyzed traffic.

March 5: The Dravo Corporation became the first defense industry to receive the all-Navy "E" in a ceremony highlighted by the launching of a submarine chaser built by Dravo.

March 5: Air raid drills were organized.

April 6: An estimated 300,000 persons assembled in the Downtown area to watch 35,000 marchers in an Army Day demonstration of loyalty and patriotism.

April 7: For the first time since labor's split in 1936, CIO President Philip Murray and AFL President William Green spoke from the same platform and renewed their pledge of labor peace in a rally at Syria Mosque.

April 19: The 13- and 16-year-old sons of David L. Lawrence, national Democratic committeeman, were both

killed in an automobile crash north of Pittsburgh.

April 19: Corporal Frank Basa, wounded hero of the Japanese attack on Pearl Harbor, was welcomed home by 40,000 persons who turned out for a parade in Lawrenceville.

April 20: Following an auction sale of prize dairy herds, bulldozers began leveling an 1100-acre tract of the old Bell farm in Moon Township for a $3,000,000 defense airport.

April 29: Pittsburgh and nine surrounding counties were designated by the federal government as a defense rental area, and rents were frozen.

May 23: The United Steel Workers of America, successor to the Steel Workers Organizing Committee, in convention at Cleveland, elected Philip Murray its first president at $20,000 a year.

May 28: Philip Murray was ousted as vice-president of the United Mine Workers as result of his break with John L. Lewis; John O'Leary, of Pittsburgh, was appointed to succeed him.

May: After serving as first assistant to nine city solicitors, Anne X. Alpern was appointed city solicitor by Mayor Scully as replacement for William A. Stewart, who entered the army. She was the first woman to become the chief legal officer of a major American city.

June 8: First "blackout" practice took place.

July 3 to 8: The Army War Show was given at Pitt Stadium.

July 17: United Steel Workers' wage policy committee, meeting at William Penn Hotel, accepted a 44-cents-a-day wage increase granted by War Labor Board to employees of "Little Steel" firms.

September 11: Western State Psychiatric Hospital, a 17-story building started in 1938 and built at a cost of $2,500,000, was dedicated by Governor Arthur H. James.

September 16: The Pittsburgh and West Virginia Railroad began razing its huge steel train shed behind the old Wabash Station and consigned it to the Pittsburgh scrap drive.

November 22: Women bus drivers were first employed.

December 9: H. J. Heinz, II, president of the 1942 United War Fund, which conducted a successful $4,500,000 drive, was honored by the Junior Chamber of Commerce as the "man of the year."

December 9: John P. Busarello, a John L. Lewis follower, was elected president of District 5, United Mine Workers, defeating Patrick T. Fagan, holder of the office for 22 years and a leader of the Murray forces.

December 25: For the first time in Pittsburgh's history the steel mills operated on Christmas Day.

December 30: Allegheny and Monon-

gahela rivers overflowed, crested at 36.6 at the Point, forced war plants and Downtown theaters to close, made 7500 persons temporarily homeless, and disrupted auto and trolley traffic.

1943 *January 2:* The Pittsburgh district was recognized as the nation's No. 1 steel center after its 1942 record of having produced 20,000,000 tons of steel, chiefly for war purposes; employment was up 10 per cent.

February 1: Judge Sara M. Soffel, of Common Pleas Court, became the first woman ever to preside over an Allegheny County criminal court.

February 1: The Allegheny County War Transportation Committee appealed for "no compromise" co-operation from business in proposed plan to stagger working hours in order to prevent serious traffic congestion.

March 11: Twenty-nine German aliens living near war plants in the Pittsburgh district were arrested.

May 17: The USO-Variety Club Canteen at Pennsylvania Station was opened with 1700 servicemen as guests.

May 20 to 21: Pittsburgh police, enforcing an OPA ban on pleasure driving, stopped scores of motorists and cited a total of 403 in two days for violation of ration rules.

May 24: Drastic curtailment of bus and taxi service was required by ODT's 40 per cent cut in Pittsburgh's gasoline allotment; the city faced a serious transportation problem as Pittsburgh Railways eliminated five bus routes, curtailed nine others.

May 26: The nation's first gasoline "night court," set up by the OPA office here to speed up action against pleasure driving, opened in the Fulton Building.

June 3: Mayor Scully had his gas-ration privileges suspended for three months for violating the OPA driving ban by making a 350-mile trip to West Virginia.

July 14: A federal grand jury began a probe of an insurgent strike which hampered coal production in Western Pennsylvania for nearly a month and slowed steel mills.

July 20: Colonel Richard K. Mellon, 44-year-old Pittsburgh financier, was named director of the Pennsylvania Selective Service.

August 19: The $2,000,000 Duquesne Way improvement, another link in the planned Downtown arterial highway system, was opened to traffic. The county commissioners announced that the next step in the Moses Plan would be construction of a cross-town highway at a cost of about $10,000,000.

September 12: A "Hollywood Cavalcade" at Forbes Field sold $87,000,000 in United States war bonds; among those featured were Greer Garson, Fred Astaire, and Harpo Marx.

September: The Allegheny Conference on Community Development was incorporated as a private, nonprofit organization "to develop, stimulate, encourage, and co-ordinate" planning activities in the area.

October 1: The 19-county western Pennsylvania area went $6,567,000 over its $305,808,900 quota in the third War Loan bond drive.

October 11: Samuel Harden Church, 85, president of Carnegie Institute, died at Shadyside Hospital after he was stricken at his desk while planning the Institute's 46th annual Founders Day.

October 26: William Frew was elevated from the position of vice-president to the presidency of Carnegie Institute.

November 29: Contracts for the long planned Pitt Parkway were signed in Harrisburg but the start of construction was postponed to the end of the war; the cost for the nine-and-a-half mile road was estimated at $20,000,000.

1944 January 14: Although granted a 10 per cent raise at the first of the year, 290 city garbage collectors staged their eighth strike in three years for higher wages.

January 18: A "ceiling zero" smog blanketed Pittsburgh and prevented thousands of war workers from reaching their jobs and homes.

January 23: Private haulers, hired by the city to collect accumulation of garbage, were operating under protection of an 80-man police squad after some trucks were attacked by roving pickets.

January 24: On the 11th day of the garbage strike, City Council passed two ordinances to end the three-year-old municipal operation and to place the collection of garbage in the hands of private contractors.

February 2: The city garbage collectors voted to return to work and began hauling away 9000 tons of refuse that had accumulated during their 20-day walkout.

February 24: Pittsburgh Symphony Orchestra went on tour.

April 24: Technical Sergeant Charles E. "Commando" Kelly, Pittsburgh's first Congressional Medal of Honor winner in World War II, received a hero's welcome when he arrived home.

May 10: Mrs. Eleanor Roosevelt made her second visit to Pittsburgh in three months, spent the day touring the city.

May 30: LST-750, financed by Allegheny County residents through the purchase of $5,000,000 worth of extra war bonds, was launched at Dravo's East shipyard on Neville Island before a crowd of 25,000.

June 8: In a mass rally outside the East Pittsburgh plant, 20,000 employees of Westinghouse reaffirmed a no-strike pledge for duration of the war.

July 13: The fifth War Loan went $5,000,000 over the $334,914,500 quota for the 19-county Western Pennsylvania area.

August 7: A survey showed that war contracts completed to date or underway in Pittsburgh district plants totaled $903,398,644, with $322,000,000 of it delivered to the front lines.

October 20: Governor Thomas E. Dewey, of New York, Republican candidate for president, in a pre-election address at Hunt Armory in Pittsburgh, charged the New Deal with having "turned collective bargaining into political bargaining." While in the city he conferred with top union representatives of 65,000 coal miners in Western Pennsylvania.

November 2: Harry S. Truman, Democratic nominee for vice-president, called for the re-election of President Roosevelt at Syria Mosque.

November 8: In winning his fourth term, President Roosevelt carried Allegheny County with a 75,582 majority over Thomas E. Dewey.

November 9: As the county's first postwar project, the county commissioners scheduled construction of the $4,000,000 Dravosburg Bridge over the Monongahela River.

November 14: In one of the district's worst trolley disasters, six persons were killed and 34 injured when a Homestead-East Pittsburgh streetcar loaded with war workers crashed into the rear of an empty East Liberty-Homestead car at Munhall Junction.

December 4: Pittsburgh realty values dropped to $980,000,000, their lowest point in 25 years and about $30,000,000 under the 1941 assessment.

December 11 to 12: Thousands of Monday-night Christmas shoppers were stranded Downtown by a 15-inch snowfall; all hotels were filled to capacity and lobbies were pressed into service as shelter; mills, schools, and many other activities were forced to suspend for two days.

1945 January 3: Mayor Scully signed an ordinance setting the 1946 budget at $25,417,422—highest since 1931.

January 30: Park H. Martin, who, as chief engineer of the County Works Department, formulated the county's long-range planning program in 1936, was appointed executive director of the Allegheny Conference on Community Development by Dr. Robert E. Doherty, chairman.

January: Pittsburgh Foundation was instituted.

February 16: Dr. John G. Bowman, the nation's highest-paid educator of the day at $31,500 a year, resigned after 15 years as chancellor of the University of Pittsburgh; Dr. Rufus H. Fitzgerald, vice-chancellor, was designated his successor.

March 7: Heavy production losses resulted and 25,000 persons in industry were idled by swollen rivers which rose to a crest of 33.4 feet.

April 10: The city marked the 100th anniversary of its great fire of 1845 with a parade and pageantry.

April 12: The city and county governments, business, schools, and all other activities were suspended, all churches scheduled special prayer services, and Mayor Scully asked all amusement places to close in mourning for President Franklin D. Roosevelt.

May 30: Dr. Paul R. Anderson, dean of Lawrence College in Appleton, Wisconsin, was elected president of Pennsylvania College for Women to succeed Dr. Herbert L. Spencer.

June 8: Councilman George E. Evan, chairman of the Pittsburgh Housing Authority and a pioneer in slum-clearance planning, died at the age of 69.

June 25: One hundred thousand persons turned out to extend a hero's welcome to 64 officers and enlisted men returning home from the war.

July 25: Stockholders of the Pittsburgh Coal Company approved a merger with the Consolidation Coal Company.

August 9: Russian labor leaders arrived to tour the district's steel mills.

August 14: The city was jubilant over the surrender of Japan.

August 17: Pittsburgh district industries laid off 7000 workers as the first cancellation of a war contract became effective.

November 6: David L. Lawrence, 56-year-old Democratic state chairman, was elected mayor of Pittsburgh by a margin of 12,000 votes; five Democratic councilmen retained their seats.

November 14: At meeting of civic leaders in the Duquesne Club, Richard K. Mellon, president of Regional Planning Association, urged concerted action on plans for a proposed 36-acre $6,000,000 state park at the Point.

December 5: Council passed an ordinance setting the highest real estate levy in the city's history—28 mills on

THE CAMPAIGN IN 1944
Vice-Presidential Candidate Harry S. Truman and family with County Commissioner John J. Kane and Mayor Cornelius Scully.

land and 14 mills on buildings, a 12 per cent increase over that of 1945.

December 15: Artemas C. Leslie, son of State Senator Max G. Leslie, was elected district attorney by the judiciary to succeed Russell H. Adams, judge-elect.

December 18: The county commissioners approved a resolution to create the Allegheny County Sanitary Authority to build and operate a $50,-000,000 county-wide sewage disposal system.

December 21: Park Superintendent Ralph E. Griswold angrily resigned in protest against an "archaic administrative system" for maintaining and operating the city's $25,000,000 park system.

Work stoppages were reduced 50 per cent during the year by a United States Steel - United Steel Workers agreement on principle of a "fair day's work for a fair day's pay," setting up 32 job classifications and eliminating "speed-up."

1946 *January 7:* Sworn in as the city's 47th mayor for the start of the 13th year of unbroken Democratic rule in the city, Mayor David L. Lawrence promised that his basic objective was to make Pittsburgh "outstanding where it is now merely good."

January 10: The Commonwealth asked the city and county to contribute a total of $6,000,000 as their share of the estimated $31,000,000 cost of the Penn-Lincoln Parkway.

January 15: In the Pittsburgh district 18,000 Westinghouse employees joined a nationwide strike of 200,000 electrical industry workers seeking a $2-a-day wage increase.

January 20: In the largest single walkout in the nation's history, 800,000 CIO United Steel Workers—227,000 of them in the Pittsburgh district—closed down the steel industry after President Truman's 11th hour fact-finding efforts failed. The first picket line appeared at the Irwin works and National Tube plant.

January 21: All mills in the district

THE CAMPAIGN IN 1944
Presidential Contender Thomas E. Dewey made an eloquent appeal in Pittsburgh lashing into the CIO Political Action Committee.

were silent, steel production hit a 50-year low; Philip Murray, in nation-wide broadcast from Pittsburgh, accused American business of an "evil conspiracy" to destroy labor unions.

January 27: R. K. Mellon and Sarah Mellon Scaife announced gift of a 13½-acre tract of land at Fifth and Penn and $100,000 in cash for development by the city of a public recreation center.

February 12: Trolley service was suspended and the area was blacked out by a one-day strike of 3400 Duquesne Light employees demanding a 20 per cent cost-of-living pay increase.

February 15: Seventy thousand United States Steel employees in the Pittsburgh area began to return to work following the signing of an agreement for an 18½-cent hourly wage increase,

FROM BRADY STREET BRIDGE
A painting by C. K. Ewing made in 1945.

ending a 27-day shutdown of mills.

February 28: Attorney General James H. Duff, a Carnegie citizen, was slated as Republican nominee for governor.

March 1: Threats of a power blackout were removed when Duquesne Light's independent union agreed to arbitrate the wage dispute.

March 6: A $200,000, five-alarm fire destroyed a building-supply building at 410 Liberty Avenue, and flames spread to the nearby Pittsburgh and West Virginia Railroad trestle and to part of the old Wabash Terminal.

March 14: The county commissioners proposed a $300,000 people's bond issue for public improvements, including $8,000,000 for the Greater Pittsburgh Airport and an Ohio River Boulevard extension through the North Side into the Triangle.

March 14: The Farmers Deposit National Bank prepared to become a $200,000,000 institution with acquisition of the Pitt National Bank.

March 18: Maurice Falk, Pittsburgh philanthropist, co-founder of the Falk Chemical Company, and originator of the Maurice and Laura Falk Foundation, died at the age of 79 in Florida.

March 22: Another fire, with damages estimated at $500,000, gutted the

Wabash Terminal and railroad trestle and damaged 11 warehouses. It was this group of structures which blocked the development of the Point area.

March 22: State police moved into areas around Westinghouse plants to enforce a court order limiting picketing in the 67-day strike of Westinghouse workers.

March 25: General Brehon B. Somervell, commander of the Army Service Forces in World War II, was elected president of the Koppers Company.

April 1: Smoke-control regulations, suspended with the start of the war, were revived in a new ordinance establishing October 1 as the effective date for first half of program.

April 4: Enforcement of home provisions of the smoke-control ordinance was postponed one year as result of an agreement worked out by the Allegheny Conference on Community Development and the Western Pennsylvania Conference on Air Pollution, representing coal producers.

April 12: An 18-cent hourly wage raise was awarded to Duquesne Light workers by the arbitration board.

May 7: Federal Court ordered the Pittsburgh Railways to reorganize and find an immediate solution to its financial problems.

May 9: A 115-day strike of 75,000 Westinghouse workers—longest major walkout since the war—ended with the CIO-United Electrical accepting an 18-cent hourly wage increase; 15,000 Pittsburgh district employees approved pact and prepared to go back to work.

June 3: The Civic Light Opera, founded on a $50,000 gift from Edgar J. Kaufmann and the 10-year efforts of a civic group headed by A. L. Wolk, H. Edgar Lewis, Mrs. Clifford Heinz, and others, opened its first eight-week summer season with a performance of Victor Herbert's *Naughty Marietta* before 5000 persons at Pitt Stadium.

June 19: Pittsburgh's Billy Conn was knocked out at Yankee Stadium, New York, in the eighth round of his second attempt to win the heavyweight boxing championship from Joe Louis.

June 26: Official casualty lists of the United States War Department placed Allegheny County's World War II dead at 3982 out of a total of 26,554 for Pennsylvania.

July 8: The Mellon National Bank and Trust Company became a billion-dollar financial institution, one of the nation's largest and strongest, as the result of an approval of merger by directors of the Union Trust Company of Pittsburgh and the Mellon National Bank.

July 18: Ground was broken in Moon Township for a $10,000,000 Greater Pittsburgh Airport extension.

July 27: The first Civic Light Opera season ended as a success, with total attendance of 270,000 and gate receipts at $319,121.

August 4: The 13-story, 500-room Roosevelt Hotel was purchased by Charles M. Morris and Norbert Stern for $1,800,000.

August 8: After 47 years under ownership of the Dreyfuss family, the Pittsburgh Pirates Baseball Club was purchased, at a price reported to be about $2,250,000, by a combine headed by Frank E. McKinney, Indianapolis banker, and including singer Bing Crosby, attorney Thomas P. Johnson, of Pittsburgh, and realtor John W. Galbraith, of Columbus, Ohio.

August: Construction work started on a new bus terminal on the site of the old Monongahela House at Smithfield and Water streets.

September 3: In a move to break a deadlock in their wage dispute with the Duquesne Light Company, members of the 3800-member power union voted to strike.

September 24: The city's power supply was cut to 45 per cent when Duquesne Light Company employees failed to report for work; Union President George L. Mueller was sentenced to one year in jail for inspiring the strike in defiance of a court restraining order. Pittsburgh labor leaders, headed by County Commissioner John J. Kane, protested Mueller's arrest.

September 25: Eight thousand steel and electrical workers in the Pittsburgh district struck in protest against George Mueller's arrest; despite Mueller's plea to them to return to work, union members voted in a meeting to refuse to consider a company offer until the court lifted its anti-strike injunction. Trolley service was cut 50 per cent; many stores closed.

September 26: Negotiations were resumed and formal picketing started when the contempt citation against George Mueller was dismissed.

September 28: Trolley service was stopped by a sympathy strike.

October 1: The city's eight major hotels—William Penn, Roosevelt, Fort Pitt, Pittsburgher, Keystone, Webster Hall, Schenley, and Henry—closed at midnight when AFL hotel restaurant employees, Local 237, walked off job to enforce wage demands.

October 1: The city's smoke-control law became effective for industry, railroads, and commercial establishments.

October 7: Closed two weeks because of the power blackout, the department stores reopened and were stormed by crowds of eager shoppers.

October 14: Despite the power strike, business and social life in Pittsburgh returned to near-normal; a number of auxiliary generating plants appeared on sidewalks outside Downtown buildings; traffic into the Downtown area increased 25 per cent; steel production was running at from 80 to 100 per cent of capacity; schools opened; crime decreased.

October 14: Trolley and bus operators voted to cross the electric union's picket lines, and limited transit service was resumed.

October 21: Full street lighting was resumed after the union agreed to submit wage demands to arbitration, ending the 27-day power strike.

November 5: The Very Reverend Daniel Ivancho, 38-year-old Cleveland priest, was consecrated bishop of the Byzantine-Slavonic Rite of the Roman Catholic Church in a four-hour ceremony at St. Paul's Cathedral; he was the second American to be so honored.

November 12: City Council approved an ordinance creating a five-man Urban Redevelopment Authority as an instrument for acquiring and clearing land in the city's fight against blight and slums; Mayor Lawrence became its chairman.

November 18: In a meeting called by the United Smoke Council, a majority of municipal officers of Allegheny County demanded that the proposed county-wide smoke-control law include all railroads.

November 22: A 53-day shutdown of eight Pittsburgh hotels ended when 1700 striking employees voted to go back to work.

November 25: The city's first "brownout" became effective with a national order to curtail electric power consumption as the result of a coal shortage caused by another nationwide strike of miners.

November 26: Pittsburgh was assured funds for the Conemaugh Dam flood-control project when the Truman administration decided to spend an additional $55,000,000 for such work.

December 5: Some 120,000 steel workers, railroaders, and miners were idle in the Pittsburgh area because of the coal strike.

December 9: At the annual dinner of the Regional Planning Association in the Duquesne Club, announcement was made of the organization of the Pittsburgh Public Parking Authority and a plan to build 20 new parking garages for 25,819 cars daily at a total cost of $36,000,000.

Carnegie Institute of Technology received an $8,000,000 grant from the Carnegie Foundation.

1947 *February 11:* The Veterans Administration approved plans for a 1248-bed hospital above Pitt Stadium at a cost of $11,000,000.

February 22: Hundreds of persons were forced to seek overnight shelter Downtown when an 11-inch snowstorm hit the city and disrupted traffic.

March 17: Ben Moreell, Chief of the United States Navy Bureau of Yards and Docks in World War II and organizer and commander of the construction battalions—the famed "Seabees"—was elected president and chairman of the board of Jones and Laughlin.

March 20: Mayor Lawrence ordered all-out crackdown on railroad violators of the city's new antismoke law.

March 20: Richard K. Mellon, as president of the Regional Planning Association, expressed wholehearted support of all 10 bills in the "Pittsburgh Package" legislative program for improving the city.

March: Pittsburgh's new "Ladycops," 100 strong, appeared for the first time at school crossings to protect children from traffic.

April 2: A six-month brewery jurisdictional war ended with a truce between AFL Teamsters and CIO Brewery Workers.

April 18: Westinghouse and the United Electrical Workers signed a pact providing for an 11½-cent hourly wage increase for workers.

April 18: A record opening-day crowd at Forbes Field—38,216, including Bing Crosby—saw the Pittsburgh Pirates, under new ownership, defeat Cincinnati, 12 to 11.

April 18: The new bus terminal was opened at Water and Smithfield Streets and hailed as the first step in "the Downtown of tomorrow."

April 20: United States Steel granted a $1-a-day wage increase to 140,000 employees.

April 23: Pitt announced plans to build a $2,000,000 field house and gymnasium.

April 30: The State Senate passed, 25 to 4, a county-wide smoke-control bill covering railroads; also enacted in the Legislature was a bill to create a county-wide system of incineration.

May 6: Defeated in the House, a bill to create the Pittsburgh Parking Authority was rescued by Governor Duff and submitted for reconsideration.

May 9: A 31-day taxi strike ended when 900 members of Local 128, AFL Teamsters, agreed to a 45-cent hourly pay raise.

May 21: Philip Murray issued a two-year, no-strike order to 3000 United Steel Workers locals.

May 23: As the first step in a station improvement program, the Pennsylvania Railroad began dismantling its huge passenger train shed.

May 27: A major advancement in smoke control was represented in the Pennsylvania Railroad's announcement of a complete dieselization program, with the first 47 diesel locomotives scheduled for operation before the end of 1947.

June 4: The Allegheny Conference on Community Development, in its first "mass transit" report, branded Pittsburgh's transportation system as outmoded; it recommended an Oakland to Downtown subway, express buses, a curb parking ban, and other measures.

June 5: The Parking Authority Act became law.

June 8: In the preceding 15-year period, the A. W. Mellon Educational and Charitable Trust contributed a total of $76,000,000 to local and national institutions, a trust report showed.

June 12: The Brentwood Motor Coach strike ended after 44 days of one of the longest transportation tie-ups in city history.

June 19: The annual assessment report showed assessed valuation in the city had dropped to $957,234,801—nearly $250,000,000 below the 1936 figure.

July 31: A 60-day strike which idled 2500 truck drivers in Western Pennsylvania ended.

August 31: The Allegheny County Free Fair drew the largest one-day crowd in its history—roughly estimated at 450,000 persons.

September 2: For the first time police began enforcing the city's ban on Downtown curb parking between 8 and 9:30 A.M. and 4:30 and 6 P.M. daily.

September 9: A river excursion boat, the *Island Queen,* said to be the largest river pleasure boat in the world, exploded as it was tied to the Monongahela River wharf; 19 persons were fatally injured.

September 9: City voters approved a $21,000,000 bond issue for an assortment of municipal improvements to cover sewers, streets, parks, and other facilities.

September 23: Mayor Lawrence returned to his desk after a six-week layoff enforced by a delicate eye operation.

October 1: The city's antismoke ordinance, expected to save the city $16,000,000 a year in cleaning, health, and decorating bills, was extended to 141,788 coal-burning private homes.

October 3: A survey showed that the steel industry was spending "in excess of $100,000,000" in the Pittsburgh district for expansion and replacement of old equipment.

October 21: A three-man congressional investigating committee opened a hearing on Pittsburgh's critical housing shortage. Its climax came when the committee chairman, Senator Joseph R. McCarthy, of Wisconsin, threatened to expel City Solicitor Anne X. Alpern from the hearing room when she repeatedly called attention to the senator's failure to support public housing measures.

October 29: President Richard K. Mellon of the Pittsburgh Regional Planning Association, at its annual dinner, announced plans for redevelopment of 70 acres of the Lower Hill District and creation there of a "Pittsburgh Center," to include a sports arena for 18,000, apartment housing, a new street pattern, and other improvements.

November 4: William S. Rahauser, Democrat of Coraopolis, was elected district attorney over incumbent Artemas C. Leslie; five Democratic councilmen were re-elected; County Commissioners Kane and Rankin were re-elected; Earnest Hillman was elected minority commissioner.

November 10: A financial drive to back Henry A. Wallace for president as a third-party candidate was launched in Pittsburgh at Syria Mosque, where he spoke to an overflow crowd.

November 24: Mayor Lawrence presented to Council an all-time high budget, totaling $30,110,973 for 1948.

November 28: City Council passed the record-high budget and enacted three new special taxes—mercantile, amusement, and personal property—over the bitter opposition of business interests.

November 28: The Pittsburgh Board of Education adopted an $18,000,000 budget, an increase of $3,000,000 over 1947, and levied a new $5-a-year head tax on all city residents over 21 years.

1948 *January 5:* Trolley fares went up to 10 cents cash and three-for-a-quarter tokens were eliminated.

January 15: Secretary of State George C. Marshall spoke at the 74th annual dinner of the Pittsburgh Chamber of Commerce, warned against any cuts in United States aid to Europe.

THE INCLINE

A view from Mount Washington as it was painted by the artist Aaron Bohrod in 1947.

January 19: State Supreme Court upheld the city's new mercantile and personal property taxes.

January 20: Richard K. Mellon, the Jaycees' "man of the year," announced creation of a $6,400,000 Richard King Mellon Foundation —the seventh to be set up by members of his family.

January 29: A long-smoldering feud between left- and right-wing factions of the CIO-United Electrical flared into riot proportions during a meeting at the Fort Pitt Hotel.

January 31: Boggs and Buhl, 79-year-old North Side department store, was purchased for $2,500,000 by a group of Pittsburghers and New Yorkers and thus saved from liquidation; plans were announced for a $1,000,000 rejuvenation.

February 4: The Equitable Life Assurance Society of New York purchased the 33-story Koppers Building for $6,000,000.

February 14: Workmen Evert J. Hungerford and John E. Morse were killed in a rock fall during construction of the Squirrel Hill Tunnels of the Penn-Lincoln Parkway.

February 16: At the outset of a strike of 1100 Yellow Cab drivers, Louis Di Lembo, 28, a striker, was killed on a Downtown street by a shot fired from a passing Owl Cab.

February 24: Fritz Reiner announced his resignation after 10 years as conductor of the Pittsburgh Symphony.

February 26: The Pennsylvania Railroad announced plans to build a $4,500,000 warehouse covering three blocks between Penn and Liberty avenues.

March 9: The 24-day Yellow Cab strike came to an end.

March 11: Judge William H. McNaugher ruled invalid a 1947 city ordinance to sell the historic Diamond Market House. He held that the city had no right to sell because it never legally owned the property, which was laid out in 1784 as a "public square" by John Penn and John Penn, Jr.

March 21: Duquesne Light announced plans for a $28,000,000 power plant at Elrama, near Clairton, to serve the area.

March 31: George Hubbard Clapp, one of five men responsible for the production of aluminum, the founder of the Aluminum Company of America and the oldest alumnus of Pitt, died at the age of 90 at Sewickley Valley Hospital.

April 11: Dr. John B. (Jock) Sutherland, coach of the Pittsburgh Steelers and regarded as Pittsburgh's greatest gridiron figure, died at the age of 59 at West Penn Hospital.

April 12: Soft-coal miners of western Pennsylvania began returning to work on the 29th day of a walkout that won for them $100-a-month retirement pay.

April 14: The rivers went to 29.5 feet in a "surprise" flood.

April 15: Thomas A. Mellon, retired president of Mellon-Stuart Company and nephew of the late A. W. Mellon, died at the age of 74.

April 22: United States Steel announced a $25,000,000 price cut after rejecting demands for a pay increase.

May 24: Pennsylvania Supreme Court upheld the constitutionality of the Pittsburgh Public Parking Authority and opened the way for the start of a parking program in the city.

May 26: W. L. Mellon, at 80, retired as chairman of the board of the Gulf Oil Corporation after 45 years as the firm's active head; J. F. Drake was named his successor; S. A. Swensrud was named president. At the same annual meeting the company announced plans to spend $250,000,000 for expansion.

May 31: A five-alarm fire destroyed Pitt's chemical engineering and metallurgical laboratory on the upper campus at a loss of $500,000.

June 1: The Philadelphia Company, Pittsburgh utility holding company, was ordered by the Securities Exchange Commission to dispose of its gas and transportation properties and dissolve its business.

June 3: The University of Pittsburgh announced the greatest single expansion move in its 161-year history, a $19,500,000 program to build eight new structures, including a new medical school, nurses' home, and library. A campaign for $16,500,000 in public subscriptions was started.

June 20: Westinghouse agreed to an 8 per cent wage increase for 70,000 employees.

July 1: Wallace Richards, 44, director of Pittsburgh Regional Planning for 11 years and one of Pittsburgh's leading professional planners, became assistant director of Carnegie Museum in charge of a revitalization program for that institution.

July 20: United States Steel raised prices of finished steel product an average of $9.34 per ton.

July 22: The city hired Herbert J. Dunsmore, Michigan expert in food and milk sanitation, as its first public health engineer.

August 9: Plans were announced for a 40-story combination United States Steel-Mellon National Bank and Trust Company office skyscraper to connect with the Mellon Bank Building on Fifth at Smithfield.

August 23: The city signed a $3,475,-000 contract with the Broadway Maintenance Corporation of New York for installation and maintenance of an entirely new and modern streetlighting system.

September 1: The Veterans Administration revealed plans for a $17,000,-000 hospital to consist of 11 major buildings on a 200-acre site adjoining the city's Leech Farm Tuberculosis hospital.

September 2: Edward V. Babcock, World War I Republican mayor, former member of Council, county commissioner, and multimillionaire lumberman, died at the age of 84 at his home, 5135 Ellsworth Avenue.

September 9: William N. McNair, Pittsburgh's most publicized, most quixotic mayor and the city's best-known and most fervent single-tax advocate, died at the age of 68 when he was stricken in the St. Louis, Missouri, Union Station. He had gone to that city to address the Henry George School of Social Science.

September 15: Tens of thousands of Pittsburghers visited the Freedom Train during its stopover at Pennsylvania Station.

September 28: Bernard Nieman, president of Frank and Seder, died at the age of 68 at his home, 5405 Northumberland.

October 1: Senator Alben W. Barkley, Democratic vice-presidential nominee, campaigned in the city.

October 2: Pittsburgh Playhouse announced plans for a new theater.

October 3: Mrs. William Thaw, Jr., once the "grand matron" of Pittsburgh society, died at the age of 94 at her home, 5427 Forbes Street.

October 11: In a major campaign address before 20,000 at Hunt Armory, Governor Thomas E. Dewey offered a 12-point program for labor to strengthen "free society."

October 18: Henry A. Wallace, Progressive candidate for President, spoke to a crowd of 3100 at Duquesne Gardens.

October 22: General Motors leased the Ambridge shipyards for a metal stamping plant.

October 23: President Truman addressed 25,000 enthusiastic partisans in and around Hunt Armory. Philip Murray shared the platform and spoke in support of the President's re-election.

October 25: General Motors announced plans to build a second metal stamping plant in the Pittsburgh district after purchasing a Mifflin Township site from Carnegie-Illinois Steel for its Fisher Body Division.

October 27: Westinghouse gave $200,000 to Pitt for a science building.

October 31: A four-day smog began to lift from the Pittsburgh district after causing the death of 20 people in nearby Donora.

November 2: Allegheny County gave Truman 325,411; Dewey 252,638; Wallace 10,883 in the presidential election. Congressman John R. McDowell,

Republican member of the House un-American Activities Investigating Committee, was defeated by Harry J. Davenport in his bid for re-election.

November 19: For the second time in less than a year, the Pittsburgh Railways sought a fare increase—to 12 cents cash; the Bell Telephone Company requested a 25.5 per cent increase for private phones.

November 22: City Council authorized City Solicitor Anne X. Alpern to wage a fight against the "highly unjust advance" asked for trolleys.

November 23: The United States Public Health Service, in a 100,000-word survey report, charged that the city was deficient in its health department and recommended $1,000,-000 worth of improvements.

November 24: Captain Thomas J. Hamilton, twice football coach of the United States Naval Academy at Annapolis, was named athletic director of the University of Pittsburgh.

December 1: Edgar J. Kaufmann, president of the Civic Light Opera Association, announced plans for construction of a $1,000,000 amphitheater with a retractable roof.

December 7: The H. J. Heinz Company disclosed plans for a $15,000,000 expansion program at its North Side plant, including construction of four new buildings.

December 13: Carnegie Tech announced a $4,000,000 building and renovation program in a move to relieve overcrowding.

December 27: Thomas J. Fitzpatrick, head of the left-wing forces in Local 601, United Electrical Workers, was defeated in his bid for re-election as president. The "Rank and File" forces, headed by Phil Counahan, assumed control of the union after a long and bitter fight.

December 28: The job of building the nation's first atomic-powered engine —for use in propelling a navy ship— was assigned by the Atomic Energy Commission to the Westinghouse Electric Corporation, which immediately made preparation to employ some 600 persons in the district for the project.

1949 *January 2:* A report by the Pittsburgh Industrial Development Council of the Chamber of Commerce showed that 50 new industries were established in the Pittsburgh area in 1948.

January 4: Jones and Laughlin Steel prepared to launch a $210,000,000 postwar expansion program, including a new six-furnace open-hearth shop at the South Side works.

January 4: A report from the Building Owners and Managers Association showed the rate of occupancy in 40 Pittsburgh office buildings was 99.8 per cent.

January 11: Pittsburgh's first television station—DuMont's WDTV,

Channel 2—went on the air with a program originating on the stage of Syria Mosque.

February 2: The Aluminum Company of America announced plans for the nation's first all-aluminum office skyscraper.

February 13: The State purchased from the Pennsylvania Railroad 13 acres for the projected Point Park.

April 2: A minor riot had to be quelled by police when a crowd outside Carnegie Music Hall, North Side, closed in on 250 Communists after a rally.

April 11: More than 100,000 items went on sale at auction at the Hotel Henry preparatory to its demolition to clear the site for the new United States Steel-Mellon building.

April 13: A grant of $225,000 for revival of the International Exhibit of Contemporary Painting at Carnegie Institute was provided by the A. W. Mellon Educational and Charitable Trust.

April 23: The Mellon family gave $4,000,000 to the city for acquisition of a mid-town site and establishment of a park over a 1000-car, block-square underground parking garage.

April: The largest project in a flood-control network to protect Pittsburgh—the $44,000,000 Conemaugh Dam, near Saltsburg—went into construction.

May 17: Harry W. Fowler, 58-year-old chairman of the County Planning Commission, became the first North Sider to be named to the board of county commissioners.

May 19: Crucible Steel opened a new $18,000,000 sheet and strip mill at its Midland works.

May 21: More than 200,000 persons lined the banks of the Monongahela River to watch Carnegie-Illinois's *Homestead* defeat Jones and Laughlin's *William Larimer Jones* by inches in a modern-day race of sternwheelers.

May 28: The Pittsburgh Public Parking Authority announced a program to build four off-street parking garages Downtown to alleviate the growing traffic problem.

June 6: Carnegie Institute of Technology opened a nuclear research center at nearby Saxonburg.

June 9: Dr. J. C. Warner, chemistry department head and wartime atomic scientist, was named to succeed Dr. Robert E. Doherty on the latter's retirement July 1, 1950, as president of Carnegie Tech.

June 18: The United Engineering and Foundry, the Mesta Machine Company, and Westinghouse received major portions of a $149,360,000 contract for a French steel mill scheduled for construction under the European Recovery Administration program.

June 28: On request of the city, the State Supreme Court postponed trolley rate increases indefinitely.

August 13: The Urban Redevelopment Authority announced the first public-private project of its kind in the nation—a plan to clear 30 South Side blocks of substandard housing and small business for Jones and Laughlin's $42,000,000 South Side expansion, improve surrounding streets, and eliminate three railroad grade crossings.

September 5: President Truman addressed an estimated crowd of 200,000 at the County Fair; later, 15,000 AFL members marched through Downtown in the city's first Labor Day parade in eight years.

September 13: Following a bitter campaign, Mayor Lawrence won the nomination for re-election; his primary election opponent was AFL-backed Councilman Edward J. Leonard.

September 20: The Equitable Life Assurance Society approved plans to convert 23 acres in lower Triangle into a modern, landscaped business area, the first project consisting of three 20-story office buildings.

September 22: The Mellon Educational and Charitable Trust Fund gave $13,600,000 to the University of Pittsburgh to build and operate a Graduate School of Public Health.

November 2: Because of alleged Communist leanings, the United Electrical Workers Union was expelled from the CIO in a convention at Cleveland; United Electrical locals in the Pittsburgh area, under right-wing control, withdrew from the parent union and prepared to charter a CIO electrical union.

November 8: Mayor Lawrence was given a majority of 56,000 votes, the largest ever accorded a mayoralty candidate of Pittsburgh, in his victory over Timothy F. (Tice) Ryan for re-election to his second term.

November 11: A 42-day strike, which halted production in steel mills of the district and nation, was ended when United States Steel signed a contract with the CIO-United Steel Workers for a company-financed pension plan.

November 11: The city had its largest Armistice Day parade in 31 years, with 20,000 veterans of three wars participating.

November 16: The Pennsylvania Railroad raised district commuter fares 22 per cent.

November 20: After an eight-month trial, the *Post-Gazette* printed the final edition of its Sunday paper and returned to a six-day operation; copyrights and features were sold to the Sunday *Sun-Telegraph.*

November 23: The 12-cent trolley and 15-cent bus fare became effective; State Supreme Court refused the city's plea for a further suspension of higher rates.

December 5: Mayor Lawrence again submitted to Council a record-high budget, proposing appropriation of $34,400,000 for 1950.

December 11: Edward T. Leech, 57, editor of the Pittsburgh *Press* for 18 years, died at Mercy Hospital.

December 15: United States Steel announced a price increase averaging $4 a ton.

December 21: Charles R. Cox resigned as president of Carnegie-Illinois Steel and was succeeded by Clifford Hood.

1950 *January 4:* For the third time in two years, the Pittsburgh Railways Company announced rate increases—to 15 cents on trolleys and 20 cents on buses.

January 11: Lawsuits brought by property owners in the Lower Triangle were dismissed by State Supreme Court and the way was clear for construction of the 23-acre Gateway Center.

January 25: January heat records were shattered when the temperature went to 76.

February 10: Detailed plans were disclosed for construction of the Penn-Lincoln Parkway West with a large interchange in Carnegie.

February 14: Fifty million dollars worth of contracts were signed in the mayor's office for the start of Gateway Center. At the same time the Urban Redevelopment Authority announced purchase of the Jones and Laughlin building, on Ross Street, for use as civic headquarters. The city also announced purchase of the Peoples Gas building for $1,116,000 for demolition in the Mellon Square Park project.

February 18: After posing for nine years as a Communist party member, Matt Cvetic, 41-year-old executive secretary of the American Slav Congress of Pittsburgh, appeared before the House un-American Activities Investigating Committee in Washington and revealed himself to be an FBI undercover agent.

February 22: In testimony before the House committee, Matt Cvetic placed the number of Communist party members in Western Pennsylvania at 550, listed a number of Pittsburgh organizations as Communist "fronts," and exposed the names of many Pittsburghers alleged to be connected with the Communist party.

February 27: The Central Christian Church in Bellefield was destroyed by fire; the loss was estimated at $175,000.

March 3: A power-conserving "dim-out" ended in the Pittsburgh district as the United Mine Workers and coal-mine operators agreed on a wage increase to settle a nationwide strike.

March 21: City Council passed six

ordinances banning billboards along the route of the Penn-Lincoln Parkway, except for a portion west of Bates Street.

April 30: The Nixon Theater—47 years and 48 seasons old—closed its doors with a performance of Mae West's *Diamond Lil* before an audience of 2256.

May 2: Some 150,000 persons were without transportation after 130 drivers of the Harmony Short Line, serving the Allegheny Valley, went on strike.

May 17: Five additional bus lines were idled by a strike of 750 drivers, depriving 450,000 district residents of transportation.

May 18: Governor Duff gave the signal that set in motion an 1800-pound demolition ball that began wrecking a 103-year-old building at 110 Penn Avenue, first of many destined for destruction in the 36-acre Point Park area.

May 18: Mayor Lawrence and Ben Moreell, president of Jones and Laughlin, jointly broke ground for the start of Jones and Laughlin's $60,-000,000 open-hearth plant at its South Side works.

May 31: Allegheny County's smoke-control ordinance, covering 128 municipalities, became partially effective.

June 9: A strike of 3250 dairy drivers shut off milk supplies to seven counties of Western Pennsylvania.

June 29: Members of Local 205, AFL Teamsters, agreed to wage terms, ending a 21-day milk strike.

August 1: Western Pennsylvania's famed 28th Division was called into active service to strengthen United States ground forces in the Korean war.

August 11: State Supreme Court overrode arguments of the city of Pittsburgh for a postponement and permitted 15-cent trolley and 20-cent bus fares to take effect.

August 29: A 118-day strike of Harmony Bus Line drivers ended.

August 31: Steve Nelson, Western Pennsylvania Communist party leader, was arrested with two other party leaders on bench warrants sworn out by Judge Michael A. Musmanno and charged with sedition. Later in the day Judge Musmanno personally led a raid on Communist headquarters in the Bakewell Building.

September 4: The Senator motion-picture house on Liberty Avenue became the new Nixon Theater with the opening of *Oklahoma.*

September 10: More than 130,000 Catholic men filled Forbes Field for a Holy Name rally in one of the city's largest religious demonstrations in history.

September 13: A 119-day Brentwood Motor Coach strike ended.

September 19: Oriole Motor Coach drivers ended their 125-day strike.

September 29: At a height of 550 feet, the United States Steel-Mellon building was "topped out" in a flag-raising ceremony which made it the second tallest building in the city, 35 feet shorter than the Gulf Building.

October 1: Two hundred mailing-room employees failed to report for work because of a contract dispute, forcing the *Sun-Telegraph, Press,* and *Post-Gazette* to suspend publication and idle 2500 other employees.

October 15: Under leadership of the Pittsburgh local of the American Newspaper Guild, members of 10 unions idled by the newspaper strike published the *Daily Reporter* after two weeks of a virtual news and advertising blackout.

October 15: Ground was broken for the 16-story nurses' residence, first major project to be started in the building program for the Pitt Medical Center.

October 15: Excavation started for construction of three stainless steel office buildings in Gateway Center and a large underground parking area.

October 19: General Dwight D. Eisenhower, president of Columbia University, told a Carnegie Institute Founders Day audience at Carnegie Music Hall that "there is no such thing as a preventive war." The occasion marked the opening of the Institute's 38th International Art Exhibit, its first in eleven years.

November 6: Branch Rickey, builder of the St. Louis Cardinals and Brooklyn Dodgers, was named general manager of the Pittsburgh Pirates.

November 6: AFL Teamster delivery truck drivers began a strike against Kaufmann's, Gimbels, and Horne's.

November 8: CIO telephone workers of the district joined a nationwide strike, interrupting telephone service here.

November 18: The 47-day-old newspaper strike ended; 3000 employees returned to their jobs.

November 24: Auto, bus, and trolley traffic was brought to a standstill by a 30.5-inch snowfall — heaviest in the city's history. Snowbanks on streets were piled as high as automobile tops.

November 27: The city and its environs were snowbound. Newspapers failed to publish; most stores were closed; schools were closed; deaths resulting from the storm totaled 15.

November 29: Downtown stores reopened with National Guardsmen on hand to prevent a traffic impasse. Trolleys and buses resumed operation.

November 30: City tow trucks began removing some 5000 snowbound autos from trolley routes; snow-removal machines were also in action.

December 1: National Guard road-

blocks were removed and the Triangle was opened to all traffic.

December 18: More than 8000 members of 19 other AFL unions returned to work after AFL delivery drivers ended a 29-day strike against the three major department stores—Kaufmann's, Gimbels, and Horne's.

December 22: Bishop Hugh C. Boyle, 77-year-old spiritual leader of 800,000 Roman Catholics in the Pittsburgh diocese, died in Mercy Hospital; he was immediately succeeded by Coadjutor Bishop John F. Dearden.

Population: 676,806. Pittsburgh is listed as the 12th largest city in America.

1951 *January 2:* The State Supreme Court sustained the city's controversial "A-B-C" restaurant sanitation code, and the Department of Public Health prepared to enforce it.

February 18: Another trolley fare increase—this one raising the price of tokens one and three-quarters cents—became effective.

February 27: William Alvah Stewart, a city councilman, was appointed a federal judge by President Truman.

March 6: Koppers' Kobuta rubber plant was knocked out of defense production for three months by a $500,-000 fire.

March 26: In a message to City Council, Mayor Lawrence outlined plans for Pittsburgh's third major redevelopment program—the clearance of 100 acres of slums in the Hill District and construction of a public arena, 30 acres of housing, and other improvements.

April 1: Mayor Lawrence invited representatives of school districts and colleges and universities to meet with him to discuss organization of an educational television station for Pittsburgh.

April 16: Design of a giant lighted fountain, shooting a brilliant column of water 100 feet into the air, was approved by the Point Park committee as an appropriate decoration for the tip of Point Park.

April 19: I. W. Wilson, senior vice-president, was elected president of the Aluminum Company of America.

May 5: Mrs. Edith Oliver Rea, who pioneered in the field of Veterans' Rehabilitation (World War I) and who instituted the Grey Ladies service of the Red Cross, died in Boston, Massachusetts.

May 25: The Pittsburgh Railways Company asked the Public Utilities Commission for permission to abandon its 79-year-old Mount Oliver Incline.

June 27: A special grand jury recommended indictment of Mayor Lawrence, City Controller Edward R. Frey, and nine others as the result of an investigation into city light and coal contracts.

June: Washington Boulevard was

flooded, and one woman, trapped in her car, was drowned.

July 18: Joe Walcott, 37, knocked out Ezzard Charles in the seventh round in a heavyweight championship fight at Forbes Field before 28,272 persons —a record fight turnout for Pittsburgh.

July 25: In the primary election, Judge Michael A. Musmanno upset the Democratic leadership and won a 21-year term on the bench of Pennsylvania State Supreme Court.

August 10: In connection with the Penn-Lincoln Parkway project, the Baltimore and Ohio Railroad agreed to get its passenger station out of the way and build a new one at the foot of Grant Street.

August 10: Pittsburgh Railways asked that fares be raised to 17 cents on trolleys and 23 cents on buses.

August 17: Steve Nelson, already on trial on sedition charges, was arrested by the FBI with five other district Communist leaders in the latest of a nationwide series of raids.

August 31: After a 35-week trial, Communists Andrew Onda and James Dolsen were found guilty by a Criminal Court jury of advocating overthrow of the government by force and violence.

September 9: In a radio and television speech Mayor Lawrence denounced the management of the Pittsburgh Railways Company and appealed to the public to join the city in fighting fare increases.

September 20: Judge Timothy F. (Tice) Ryan, 1949 Republican mayoralty candidate, died at 65 at his East End home.

October 5: Mayor Lawrence was cleared by a grand jury, but seven other officials were indicted in connection with alleged discrepancies in contracts for a new city lighting system.

October 11: Kaufmann's department store announced purchase of the 19-story Frick Annex building for the start of a multi-million-dollar enlargement program.

October 24: A district epidemic of bank frauds spread to Pittsburgh; three officials of the Federal Credit Union of Kaufmann's were arrested on charges of embezzling $338,901.

October 30: Defense Mobilizer Charles E. Wilson tapped the first heat, putting into operation the new $70,000,000 open-hearth shop at the South Side plant of Jones and Laughlin Steel Corporation.

November 6: James F. Malone, Republican leader, was elected district attorney over Judge Francis J. O'Connor; Democratic County Commissioners Kane and Fowler were re-elected; State Senator John M. Walker of Oakmont was named minority commissioner.

November 26: The 67-mile $77,500,-

THE SIGNERS
On February 14, 1950, Mayor David Lawrence signed the contract between the Urban Redevelopment Authority and the Equitable Life Assurance Society. Sitting: Edgar Kaufmann, Arthur van Buskirk, Mayor Lawrence, M. D. Howell, W. A. Stewart. Standing: Jack P. Robin, Raymond H. Weims, Theodore L. Hazlett, Jr., Alexander McNeil.

DEMOLITION
of the Pennsylvania Railroad's Warehouse, a dramatic photograph taken in Sept. 1951.

000 western extension of the Pennsylvania Turnpike was dedicated at the Ohio border with Governor Frank J. Lausche, of Ohio, promising that his state would extend the expressway.

November 29: The first mass transit study made under sponsorship of the Allegheny Conference on Community Development urged reconsideration of a Triangle subway estimated to cost $65,000,000.

November: The Pittsburgh Housing Authority initiated construction of the 1089-unit St. Clair Village housing project on the South Side.

December 22: City Council, at Mayor Lawrence's request, passed another record-high budget, totaling $41,881,-900 for 1952.

1952 *January 19:* Five years after its opening, the Union Bus Terminal, Downtown, closed its doors because of bankruptcy, leaving five bus lines "homeless."

January 25: William Steinberg, director of the Buffalo Philharmonic Orchestra, was appointed conductor of the Pittsburgh Symphony; he became the orchestra's first permanent director since the departure of Fritz Reiner in 1948.

January 29: C. L. Austin, a former banker, was elected president of Jones and Laughlin; Ben Moreell relinquished that post but continued as chairman of the board.

January 31: Following a 19-day trial, a Criminal Court jury found Steve Nelson guilty of sedition.

February 6: Edward Specter, manager of the Pittsburgh Symphony Orchestra, resigned.

February 24: The Bigelow, first apartment house to be built in downtown Pittsburgh, was opened to tenants.

March 1: The Carlton House, the city's first new hotel in 25 years, received its first guests.

March 1: At midnight 100 men of the United States Steel Corporation sat around a horseshoe table in the Carnegie Building, then emptied of all tenants, and drank a toast to what had been "steel headquarters" for 57 years. At 8 A.M. demolition crews began the long and arduous task of disassembling this structure, beam by beam, to clear the site for a Kaufmann's annex.

March 3: Allegheny County reduced taxes to a 22-year low while adopting a $32,400,000 budget, highest in its history.

April 8: President Truman ordered steel mills seized, and the United Steel Workers called off a scheduled strike.

April 21: A precedent was established when Pittsburgh industry and business, through 65 of its leaders, pledged financial support to the Pittsburgh Symphony Orchestra; they approved a novel plan under which companies were to be designated sponsors with contributions of $10,000 annually.

April 23: Clifford Ball, 61-year-old aviation promoter for more than 35 years and founder of Pennsylvania (Capital) Airlines, was named director of the new Greater Pittsburgh Airport.

April 29: President Truman's seizure of the steel industry was declared illegal by Federal Court and district steel workers joined 650,000 throughout the nation in a walkout that paralyzed the industry.

May 31: The new Greater Pittsburgh Airport, completed at a cost of $33,-000,000, was dedicated, and more than 100,000 persons went to Moon Township over the holiday weekend to inspect the 1600-acre air terminal.

June 2: Commercial airlines began flying a total of 228 flights daily into and out of the new airport.

June 25: Pittsburgh Railways asked the Public Utilities Commission for permission to institute a 20-cent trolley and 25-cent bus fare—the sixth rate increase in four years and the third in less than 20 months.

June 30: Judge Henry Ellenbogan ruled out the Public Parking Authority's plan for the sale of gas, oil, and services in its parking garages.

July 24: At the White House, President Truman, flanked by Philip Murray and Benjamin F. Fairless, announced settlement of the 53-day steel strike.

August 8: Pittsburgh's Old City Hall, built in 1872 at a cost of $600,000, was sold for nearly $2,500,000 to a real estate group planning to demolish it for commercial development.

August 11: Police Superintendent Harvey J. Scott, the city's police chief for 13 years, was fired by Safety Director George E. A. Fairley for misconduct.

September 15: The Point Park Commission approved detailed plans for landscaping and developing Point Park. Wallace Richards, Parking Authority chairman, suggested a 1000-car parking garage be built on the park fringe area.

September 22: Cornelius Decatur Scully, who had served nine consecutive years as mayor, died at the age of 73 in Winchester, Virginia.

October 6: William D. Mansfield, former state senator, former county commissioner, editor of the McKeesport *Daily News,* and one of McKeesport's best-known citizens, died at 74 in McKeesport Hospital.

October 8: Senator Richard M. Nixon, Republican candidate for vice-president, charged in a speech to 3900 persons at Syria Mosque that the Communist party was aiding the Democrats.

October 22: President Truman, in an address to an overflow crowd at Syria Mosque, accused General Eisenhower of following a "straight isolationist line."

October 27: After being welcomed by huge crowds, General Eisenhower, in an address at Hunt Armory, promised that the first objective of a Republican administration in Washington would be an "honorable" peace in Korea.

October 29: City Council approved an ordinance, recommended by Mayor Lawrence, to create a municipal authority to purchase and reconstruct the city's deteriorated water-supply system at a cost of $27,000,000.

October 29: Pittsburgh's first public parking garage, a 776-car facility built at a cost of $2,100,000 at Sixth Avenue and Bigelow Boulevard, was officially opened by Mayor Lawrence and Authority Chairman Wallace B. Richards.

October 30: Governor Adlai Stevenson, of Illinois, in a final bid for votes, declared to a crowd of 25,000 at Hunt Armory that General Eisenhower was a "captive" candidate of the Republican "Old Guard," the "depression party."

November 4: In losing the presidential election to General Eisenhower, Governor Stevenson carried Allegheny County by 13,820 votes.

November 6: Special demolition crews began the delicate task of taking apart H. J. Heinz's "Little House Where We Began" to permit expansion of the North Side plant. The house was later reassembled in its original state at Ford's Greenfield Village in Dearborn, Michigan.

November 8: At its 75th anniversary celebration, Duquesne University announced a $13,300,000 program to clear blight and create a modern, 25-acre Bluff campus. Ground was broken earlier in the day for construction of a women's dormitory, the first of eight new buildings.

November 9: Philip Murray, 66-year-old president of both the CIO and the United Steel Workers, died unexpectedly in his room at the Mark Hopkins Hotel in San Francisco after addressing 350 delegates at the United Steel Workers' western regional conference.

November 14: A storm of protest from Downtown merchants prompted the city to postpone enforcement of a rigid curb-parking restriction adopted for Downtown streets.

November 20: Jones and Laughlin, the Urban Redevelopment Authority, and city officials signed contracts for their second joint industrial redevelopment project—the conversion of 30 acres of blighted land in Hazelwood into a productive plant.

November 20: The city's second parking garage, a six-level, 815-car structure on Fourth Avenue, built at a cost of $1,500,000, was opened to the motoring public.

November 24: In the first event of its kind ever staged, Pittsburgh's First International Contemporary Music Festival, a week-long series of concerts featuring works of contemporary composers, opened at Carnegie Music Hall.

December 3: The Pittsburgh Symphony Orchestra played the first of a series of experimental "industrial" concerts for 1600 persons in Scott High School auditorium in North Braddock. It was the first time that any major orchestra attempted to take its music directly to an industrial community.

December 5: Mayor Lawrence signed into law the city's first fair employment practices code, prohibiting job discrimination against minority groups; Pittsburgh thus became the 23rd city in the nation with FEPC.

December 23: Two ultra-high frequency television stations were authorized for Pittsburgh by the Federal Communications Commission; they were channels 16 and 47.

December 30: Chancellor Rufus H. Fitzgerald, of the University of Pitts-

burgh, announced that 22 Pittsburgh business and industrial firms had subscribed a total of $4,836,000 for construction of a $15,000,000 building for the schools of the health professions.

December 31: The ten-month-old Carlton House was sold to a New York syndicate for $7,400,000.

1953 *January 14:* Mayor Lawrence announced that articles of incorporation were ready to be filed for formation of Pittsburgh's "Metropolitan Educational Television Station, Inc.," WQED.

January 15: Grading and seeding started at the Point Park in time for greenness in the spring.

January 22: Mayor Lawrence announced his candidacy for election to a third term in order to see through "to its climax of achievement" Pittsburgh's rebuilding program.

January 26: Plans were announced for construction of a 2000-unit, $24,500,000 low-rent housing project in City View-Summer Hill section of the North Side. Residents of the area immediately announced plans to fight it.

February 2: A 60-day trial of rigid no-parking rules Downtown went into effect; only 17 autos were towed away by police to the city auto pound.

February 8: After obtaining Edgar J. Kaufmann's approval of the use of a $1,000,000 grant originally pledged to the Civic Light Opera, Mayor Lawrence announced plans to proceed with construction of a $7,000,000 sports-theater arena, with a retractable roof, as the key project in the Lower Hill District redevelopment area.

February 10: David J. McDonald, secretary-treasurer of the United Steel Workers since its inception in 1937 and once a prospect for Hollywood filmland, was elected, without opposition, second president of the 1,100,000 union.

March 4: The Allegheny Conference on Community Development revealed plans for a toll tunnel under Mount Washington as the most feasible way to finance that link in the Penn-Lincoln Parkway.

March 12: A $30,000,000 public-works program for new bridges, highways, and other improvements was announced by the county commissioners.

March 26: Dr. Jonas E. Salk, 38-year-old University of Pittsburgh researcher and professor, reported success of a new polio vaccine tried on 90 human beings; the vaccine was developed by him and his staff at Pitt.

April 20: Carnegie Tech announced a move to raze Carnegie Inn, a campus landmark, and build a modern $700,000 men's dormitory.

May 6: Because of Pittsburgh Railways' opposition, the city discarded its plan for making Forbes Street and Fifth Avenue one way in order to relieve traffic congestion expected with temporary closing of the Boulevard of the Allies.

May 12: The $4,500,000 Nurses' Residence for the Medical Center was dedicated and its quarters were opened for 600 student nurses and 46 staff members.

May 19: In the primary election, City Solicitor Anne X. Alpern received both the Democratic and Republican nominations to a judgeship.

June 4: Pittsburgh's most publicized and highest paid baseball player, Ralph Kiner, was traded to the Chicago Cubs.

June 5: Many state and local officials participated in a ribbon cutting opening the $18,000,000 Squirrel Hill Tunnel, the most costly single project ever undertaken by the State Highways Department. This placed in service the first eight mile stretch of the $34,000,000 Penn-Lincoln Highway.

June 8: The first and most troublesome of many detours resulting from new highway work took the Boulevard of the Allies out of service for some 30,000 motorists using it daily. This marked the start of Pittsburgh's most critical period of traffic congestion.

June 22: The Allegheny Conference on Community Development released its second citizens' mass transit study; it recommended creation of a transit authority to acquire and unify bus and trolley lines in the county.

July 5: It was announced that the Wabash Building, a city landmark, was to be demolished to make way for further development in the Gateway Center.

August 5: A building in Oakland, gift of the Pittsburgh Plate Glass to the University of Pittsburgh, was provided for the headquarters of educational television in the city.

August 25: Following a six-month trial, Steve Nelson, already under a 20-year sentence to the Workhouse, and five other Communist leaders of Pittsburgh were convicted under the Smith Act in Federal Court and sentenced to five years in prison.

September 7: John M. Phillips, pioneer industrialist and well-known conservationist, died at the age of 92 at his home at 2336 Brownsville Road, Carrick. He was the father of Pennsylvania's basic game code, used by many other states as a model.

September 15: At the start of a weeklong dedication, the Aluminum Company of America opened its new 30-story office building for public inspection. On the first night 7500 invited guests toured the skyscraper, the nation's first with an all-aluminum exterior.

September 18: Two thousand Pittsburghers and state officials traveled to Saltsburg by special train and auto to participate in the dedication of the Conemaugh Dam, $46,200,000 bulwark against floods, the largest and most important dam in a $125,000,000 flood-control system. The speaker, Major General S. D. Sturgis, Jr., chief of army engineers, warned that navigational locks and dams in the Ohio River were in desperate need of rehabilitation.

September 23: The newly constituted Metropolitan Study Commission of Allegheny County formed 10 committees to begin the job of assembling information on urban expansion under a $50,000 grant provided by Buhl Foundation.

September 28: Richard K. Mellon, head of the nation's greatest banking empire, tacitly endorsed the Democratic leader, Mayor Lawrence, for re-election. He did so in a short speech at ground-breaking ceremonies for the Mellon Square Park and underground garage, site of which was acquired with a $4,000,000 grant from the Mellon family.

September 29: Ten thousand campaign volunteers began canvassing homes in the Pittsburgh area in solicitation of 100,000 family subscriptions of $2 each for educational television station WQED; the proceeds were to supplement grants of $350,000.

October 6: Pittsburgh voters overwhelmingly defeated a proposed raise in school taxes following a bitter battle.

October 15: The $15,000,000 Penn-Lincoln Parkway West, opening up a fast route between Downtown Pittsburgh and the Greater Pittsburgh Airport and routes west, was dedicated by Governor John S. Fine and Senators James H. Duff and Ed-

CONCERT AT CARNEGIE INSTITUTE

ward Martin. All, as governors, were instrumental in various phases of its construction. The dedication ceremony was held at the interchange in Senator Duff's home town Carnegie.

October 23: The Allegheny Foundation, a new organization to aid charitable, scientific, literary, and other public activities, was chartered by the Mellon family.

October 28: The Public Auditorium Authority was created by Mayor Lawrence and the county commissioners for the purpose of building and operating an all-purpose civic arena in the Hill District. Brehon B. Somervell, president of Koppers Company, was chosen first chairman.

November 3: David L. Lawrence defeated Leonard P. Kane by 54,000 votes and became the first mayor in the history of Pittsburgh to be elected to a third consecutive term. The Democrats swept the city and county.

November 23: A brief noon-time ceremony was held at Gateway Center to inscribe into history "November 23, 1753," as the date on which George Washington first envisioned the Point as a natural site. Pittsburgh thus memorialized its distinction of being "the only city in the United States to have had its location chosen by the first president."

November 27: Five hundred delivery truck drivers of Local 249, AFL Teamsters, began a strike against the city's major department stores. The stores remained open; the Joseph Horne Company's warehouse was stoned in the first incidence of violence.

December 2: Edgar J. Kaufmann, charter financial backer of Lower Hill District civic arena project, promised to contribute $500,000, in addition to $1,000,000 already pledged, if needed on completion of fund-raising efforts.

December 2: For the first time in seven months, the Boulevard of the Allies was open to traffic on a restricted basis.

December 4: Mayor Lawrence presented to City Council what he termed the "most difficult" budget in the eight years of his administration; he also indicated reluctant approval of a wage tax as a means of raising money.

December 27: Delayed 17 months by court orders resulting from actions started by City Solicitor Anne X. Alpern, trolley and bus rate increases —to 20 and 25 cents, respectively— became effective.

December 30: Anne X. Alpern (Mrs. Irwin Swiss in private life) was sworn in as a judge of Common Pleas Court. She was the first Democratic woman in Pennsylvania elected to a judgeship.

December 31: Mayor Lawrence signed

into law another record high budget, with appropriations totaling $47,282,-991; it also committed the city to a 1 per cent tax on all earned incomes within the city.

1954 January 1: Fifty squads of policemen and detectives manned road blocks in the city to halt violence in the 36-day department store strike; earlier the homes of two store executives were stoned and "paint bombed."

January 3: The Pennsylvania Railroad unveiled a $3,611,400 plan for a new ramp and platform for trains to and from the west as part of its $27,-000,000 station modernization program.

January 4: After Mayor Lawrence was sworn in for his third term, City Council received from him a recommendation for a precedent-shattering wage tax ordinance estimated to yield the city $6,300,000 in 1954.

January 18: In one of the largest grants of its kind ever made, the Mellon family, represented by three foundations, gave $15,000,000 to the University of Pittsburgh for medical education. The money was designated chiefly for development of Pitt's first full-time medical school teaching staff.

January 21: Powered by the world's first atomic engine, built by the Westinghouse Electric Corporation, the submarine U. S. S. *Nautilus*, christened by Mrs. Dwight D. Eisenhower, was launched at Groton, Connecticut.

January 25: The city's first wage tax was adopted with March 1 as the effective date. Councilman John F. Counahan was Council's only dissenter in the vote.

January 25: State Supreme Court dismissed the Common Pleas Court conviction and 20-year sentence of Communist Steve Nelson on grounds that the case legally belonged in Federal Court under the Smith Act.

February 24: The attention of parents around the world was on Arsenal Elementary school in Lawrenceville, where Dr. Jonas E. Salk began his polio vaccine tests on a large-scale basis. In the gymnasium of that school 137 youngsters, first of 5000 Pitts-

burgh school volunteers, were given injections of the new serum.

February 25: The Chamber of Commerce and Allegheny Conference on Community Development undertook a joint campaign to form an "industrial development corporation" to bolster Pittsburgh's economy by attracting new light industry.

March 1: The wage tax of one cent on each dollar of earned income went into effect in Pittsburgh.

March 9: Frederick Bigger, Pittsburgh's "dean of planners," resigned after 31 years of membership on the City Planning Commission, which he served for 20 years as chairman. He was co-organizer of Regional Planning Association and was noted nationally as chief planner in the New Deal's famed model-town projects of "Greenbelt," Maryland, "Greenhills," Ohio, and "Greendale," Wisconsin.

March 12: The Regional Planning Association issued its first report on a suburban community under an expanded new policy. The report recommended that a planned industrial district, first in the Pittsburgh area be developed in a blighted McKeesport district at the Monongahela-Youghiogheny river junction.

March 24: Teamster delivery truck drivers ended their 113-day strike against five furniture stores—Hahn's, Spear and Company, Ruben's, Ohringer's, and May-Stern.

April 1: Station WQED, the world's first community-sponsored educational noncommercial television station, went on the air.

April 12: The Atomic Energy Commission assigned to the Westinghouse Electric Corporation and Duquesne Light Company the job of building the first atomic electric power plant in the world. It also announced the site as Shippingport, a once important river port on the Ohio River 25 miles north of Pittsburgh. Operation of the plant also was assigned to Duquesne Light.

April 28: A "schematic plan" for rebuilding 1286 deteriorating acres of North Side property was proposed by the Regional Planning Association, in

a dinner at the H. J. Heinz plant, as the fourth major redevelopment project in the city. It included recommendations for 3000 new parking spaces, an "Allegheny Center" shopping district, new housing, additional recreation, planned neighborhood and industrial districts, all compatible with the proposed Ohio River Boulevard high-speed extension through the North Side.

April: The University of Pittsburgh began demolishing 32 structures on a 10-acre Oakland site preparatory to erecting its graduate school of public health.

April: Dr. M. Graham Netting, a member of the staff for 32 years, was named director of Carnegie Museum to succeed Wallace Richards after the latter was stricken ill.

May 2: Four new buildings were dedicated on the campus of the Pennsylvania College for Women.

May 9: Dozens of traffic tie-ups occurred after bus and trolley were cut off by a strike of 2700 operators.

May 11: The Chamber of Commerce recommended the Allegheny Valley as the most practical route for the proposed Pittsburgh-to-Erie extension of the Pennsylvania Turnpike.

May 23: The garages of the Public Parking Authority were ruled tax-exempt by the State Supreme Court; the way was thus opened for construction of more garages. The same ruling held as that for taxable garage space rented to private interests for commercial purposes.

May 28: District Attorney James Malone warned against "paint bombings" after eight homes were hit by a wave of vandalism in the sixth month of the department store strike.

June 14: Trolleys and buses resumed normal operation with the settlement of the 34-day strike, longest and costliest in the history of Pittsburgh Railways Company.

June 23: The Board of Education approved a $5,000,000 bond issue for a building and renovation program and elected attorney J. Garfield Houston as its new president.

June 28: Mrs. Alan M. Scaife, wife

REGISTRATION DAY FOR UNIVERSITY STUDENTS

Outside the offices of the University of Pittsburgh in Oakland, hundreds of students line up for the annual enrollment; their line extends from Syria Mosque around the block to Fifth Avenue. A photograph taken by Paul Hunter for the *Sun-Telegraph*, Sept. 18, 1955.

Photograph by Bill Herman for the Pittsburgh Sun-Telegraph

1954, July 19: FIRST MEETING of the leaders of the Allegheny Conference with Stefan Lorant, who was to do this book.

William Penn Snyder, III, President of the Conference, Edgar J. Kaufmann, the department store owner, and Leland Haz-

ard, the "philosopher" of the Renaissance, acquaint Lorant with a pictorial representation of the projected Point State Park.

of the president of the board of trustees of the University of Pittsburgh, turned the first spade of earth to start excavation for the $15,000,000 building to house the schools of medicine, dentistry, pharmacy, and nursing.

June 29: United States Steel and the United Steel Workers union signed a contract for a five-cent hourly wage increase, forestalling a scheduled strike.

July 1: Ground was broken on Fifth Avenue site, facing the Cathedral of Learning, for Pitt's new $2,500,000 center of natural sciences. It was named in memory of George Hubbard Clapp, the noted scientist, co-founder of the Aluminum Company of America, and president of the University of Pittsburgh board of trustees for 42 years until his death in 1949.

July 11: Contracts were awarded for the basic design of the $25,000,000 Fort Pitt Tunnel through Mount Washington.

July 28: The State General Authority completed negotiations with Equitable Life Assurance Society for purchase of a Gateway Center site, at a price

of $1,041,143, for construction of a new $8,000,000 state office building to serve as capital of Western Pennsylvania.

July 28: Allegheny General Hospital broke ground for a two-story building to house a "cobalt bomb," second such cancer-treatment unit to be established in the city. The first was in process of construction at Mercy Hospital.

July 29: The State Department of Commerce issued a report showing 46 new industries or expansions in 1954 in the Pittsburgh district; investments totaled $125,000,000, and 13,448 persons were added to payrolls.

August 10: Dr. Bryn J. Hovde, executive director of the Pittsburgh Housing Association and a nationally known expert on housing, died at the age of 58 after he was stricken on a Downtown streetcar.

August 27: The Board of Education announced plans to construct four new schools in the biggest building program in many years.

September 2: The Pittsburgh Parking

Authority announced it was ready to proceed with construction of 1388 additional off-street spaces in two parking garages, to be built at a total cost of $6,000,000 and operated by Kaufmann's store primarily for the shopping convenience of customers.

September 6: In Denver, 1600 miles away, President Eisenhower waved an "atomic wand" over an electronic cabinet. He thus relayed the impulse that sent into motion huge steam shovels at the Shippingport site of the world's first atomic power plant. Some 1500 business, industrial, and scientific leaders of the Pittsburgh area attended the Labor Day groundbreaking ceremony starting construction of the $45,000,000 installation.

September 7: City Council passed an ordinance to permit erection of a $3,500,000 eight-story apartment building on the Shady Avenue site of the historical Kenmawr Hotel, a 90-year-old landmark. The ordinance upset height building regulations for this East End area.

September 11: A strike against the Westinghouse Electric Corporation was averted at the zero hour with the signing of a two-year contract.

September 12: Vice-Admiral Joel T. Boone, chief medical officer for the Veterans Administration, dedicated the new 11-story, 750-bed VA general medical and surgical hospital, situated above Oakland.

September 17: United States Steel announced a $10,000,000 expansion program for its Homestead Works.

September 21: The Peoples First National Bank and Trust Company announced plans to construct a central headquarters building in the Gateway Center.

October 10: After 16 months of restrictions, the vital Boulevard of the Allies was fully reopened to traffic.

October 18: The National Foundation for Infantile Paralysis contracted to buy the Salk polio vaccine for 9,000,000 persons in 1955.

October 27: Jones and Laughlin Steel announced a $51,000,000 program for expanding and improving its plants in 1955.

October 29: Sidney A. Swensrud, board chairman and chief executive officer of the Gulf Oil Company, became chairman of the Public Auditorium Authority following the resignation of Brehon B. Somervell. The Authority set spring of 1956 as its target date for starting construction of a civic arena in the Lower Hill District redevelopment area.

November 2: The county gave State Senator George M. Leader, 37-year-old chicken farmer, a plurality of more than 87,000 votes over Lloyd H. Woods for the governorship in a Democratic victory that ended 16 years of Republican rule in Harrisburg.

November 16: The Allegheny County Redevelopment Authority prepared to proceed with a $3,500,000 slum clearance and redevelopment project in McKees Rocks.

November 19: The Baltimore and Ohio Railroad announced a decision to abandon plans for a central office building and to construct instead a small new passenger station in connection with its Penn-Lincoln Parkway relocation project.

November 22: State Supreme Court dismissed complaints of North Side residents, enabling the Pittsburgh Housing Authority to proceed with plans for construction of a 1000-unit low-rent housing project on Summer Hill.

November 26: Teamster delivery drivers signed a contract ending their strike against five Downtown department stores on the eve of its first anniversary; but the union served notice the drivers would not resume deliveries until 11 other store unions ended their strike. It was estimated that the walkout cost the 760 drivers and helpers a total of $5,000,000 in wages.

SOUTH SIDE
Photograph by W. Eugene Smith.

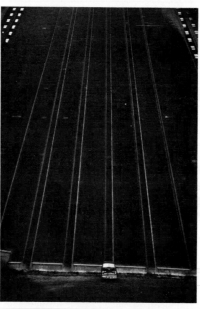

SUNDAY AT A PARKING LOT
Photograph by W. Eugene Smith.

December 3: Westinghouse Electric Corporation announced purchase of Pittsburgh's pioneer television station, WDTV, from DuMont Laboratories, Inc., for $9,750,000, highest amount ever paid for a television station.

December 3: The Pittsburgh Board of Public Education adopted an "austerity" budget of $23,882,326 for 1955, rejecting teachers' requests for pay raises but retaining kindergartens for another year.

December 5: The county commissioners made public proposed legislation, drafted by a seven-member citizens' committee, for creation of a county-wide public transportation authority to acquire and consolidate bus and trolley lines. The legislation required approval of voters in a referendum scheduled for primary election of 1956.

December 6: One hundred and eighteen business firms, schools, and hospitals 80 years or older were honored by the Pittsburgh Chamber of Commerce at its 80th anniversary dinner, attended by 900 persons in the William Penn Hotel. The speakers were William Block, publisher of the *Post-Gazette*, the city's oldest (1786), and Alan M. Scaife, chairman of the board of the Scaife Company, second oldest (1802). Each received a special plaque.

December 10: The University of Pittsburgh announced plans to build four additional structures at a total cost of $2,900,000—a 336-parking-space garage, and physicians' office building to serve the Medical Center, a student union, and men's dormitory.

December 12: Dr. John C. Warner, Carnegie Tech president, was named national president of the American Chemical Society for the year 1956. He was the second Pittsburgher to be so honored. The first was Dr. E. R. Weidlein, director of the Mellon Institute, in 1937.

December 15: Equitable Life Assurance Society of New York announced it had decided to construct a parking garage in Gateway Center for at least 600 cars.

December 22: Duquesne University announced it was ready to build the third structure in its $13,000,000 campus expansion program—a hall of law and business, featuring a moot courtroom made possible by a $100,000 grant from the Maurice and Laura Falk Foundation.

December 24: Mayor Lawrence signed a $48,320,473 budget for 1955, the eighth record high appropriation ordinance in eight consecutive years.

1955 *January 4:* Five employes at the Westinghouse Electric Corporation's East Pittsburgh plant were fired as "undesirable" following hearings at

Photograph by Steubgen for the Pittsburgh Post Gazette

1955, January 13: STARTING WORK. Stefan Lorant, who in the Fall of 1954 took up residence in Pittsburgh, plans the initial layout for his book in his Mt. Washington studio. It took ten years of research and writing before the volume was done

Washington by Senator McCarthy's investigations subcommittee.

January 18: The Allegheny County School Board approved working plans for a $1,300,000 new school construction program.

February 1: The Board of Public Education supported redevelopment of the Lower Hill area by indicating they would relinquish several vital properties situated in the heart of the district.

February 14: General Brehon Somervell, Koppers Company board chairman and president, died at 62.

February 22: James J. Thomas, director of District 15, CIO United Steel Workers, and veteran organizer in the steel industry, died.

March 1: Pittsburgh's new housing code—an attempt to upgrade the city's residential property—became effective. Every residential unit was required to have electricity, effective heating facilities, hot and cold running water, kitchen sink, a flush water closet, lavatory basin, and either a bathtub or a shower.

March 9: W. F. Munnikhuysen was elected chairman of the board of Koppers Company, and Fred C. Foy was named president and chief executive officer at a special meeting of the board of directors.

March 10: The Defense Department announced that $15,000,000 would be spent during 1955 for antiaircraft defense of Pittsburgh. Half of the sum was to pay for installation of Nike missiles, the rest for support of the 18th AAA Group.

March 13: Henry Kaufmann, 94, pioneer Pittsburgh merchant, one of the four founders of Kaufmann's Department Store, died in New York City.

March 17: AFL Teamsters prepared to roll delivery trucks at the five Downtown department stores for the first time in nearly 16 months. Pickets were removed although some differences remained to be negotiated.

April 15: Edgar J. Kaufmann—merchant prince and pioneer planner of Pittsburgh's physical and cultural redevelopment—one of the city's outstanding citizens, died suddenly at 69 in his Palm Springs, California home.

April 25: Bell Telephone Company announced that its new headquarters building—the fifth structure to be added to Pittsburgh's Gateway Center—was going into construction.

April 28: Jones and Laughlin Steel Corporation added $86,000,000 to its expansion program, including new mills to be constructed in the Pittsburgh area.

May 2: Benjamin F. Fairless resigned as board chairman and chief executive officer of the United States Steel Corporation; he was succeeded by Roger M. Blough.

May 3: It was announced that construction on the Baltimore and Ohio Railroad's new passenger terminal, at the foot of Grant Street, would begin within the next month.

May 23: A capital improvement program for 1955, amounting to almost $6,000,000, was submitted to City Council by Mayor Lawrence. Plans

SYRIA MOSQUE

SPRING COMES TO MELLON PARK

FORBES FIELD

included a start on rehabilitation of the city's water system, construction of new fire stations, a fire-police training center, street and sewer repairs, and grants to the Auditorium Authority and Carnegie Library.

June 1: Approximately 10,000 Westinghouse Electric Corporation workers voted to stay away from their jobs in protest against disciplinary furloughs given 1100 East Pittsburgh workers.

June 8: The strike at East Pittsburgh and three other Westinghouse plants was settled.

June 13: General Matthew B. Ridgway was appointed chairman of the board of Mellon Institute. Dr. E. R. Weidlein remained as president and member of the board.

June 20: The Regional Industrial Development Corporation, a nonprofit organization, was created.

June 22: T. M. Girdler resigned as chief executive officer of Republic Steel Corporation, but remained as board chairman. C. M. White, the firm's president, was named chief executive officer.

July 1: A nationwide steel strike began, but ended 12 hours later when agreement was reached.

July 8: At a hearing conducted by the Public Utility Commission, it was decided to remove the Pennsylvania Railroad's last Downtown elevated, leaving Fort Duquesne Boulevard free to be developed into a sunlit, landscaped, riverside drive.

July 14: County Commissioners adopted broad revisions in the smoke-control ordinance, giving industry an additional two to four years to comply.

July 15: Pittsburgh's fourth municipal parking garage, at Boulevard of the Allies and Smithfield Street, was opened.

July 29: Greyhound Lines announced plans for a new bus terminal covering more than two and one-half acres, bounded by 11th Street, 12th Street, Penn Avenue, and Liberty Avenue.

August 8: More than 2200 members of Local 601, CIO International Union of Electrical Workers, struck at Westinghouse Electric Corporation in protest against the company's time-study program.

August 15: The city's first heliport was established atop the Gateway Parking Garage, at Fourth Avenue and Stanwix Street, in anticipation of regular helicopter service between Downtown and the airports.

August 24: Thousands of persons gathered at Greater Pittsburgh Airport for the dedication of a spectacular fountain as a memorial to the county's dead of all wars.

August 30: H. J. Heinz Company announced plans for immediate construction of one of the world's most advanced food research centers at a cost of $3,000,000.

September 6: Plans for construction of a new $3,000,000 chemical plant on Neville Island were made by Pittsburgh Coke and Chemical Company.

September 9: Dr. James Purdy Kerr, 91, the oldest active surgeon in the country, died at St. Joseph's Hospital, which he had helped to found.

September 12: At the annual dinner of the Allegheny Conference on Community Development, Commissioner James W. Follin of the Urban Renewal Authority, Washington, as-

sured Pittsburgh of $17,386,610 for slum clearance and redevelopment of the Lower Hill District.

October 17: Forty-four thousand members of the CIO International Union of Electrical Workers started another strike against the Westinghouse Electric Corporation.

October 18: Mellon Square Park—the most spectacular in the city's expanding park system—formally became a possession of the citizens of Pittsburgh.

October 24: Harry W. Fowler, a member of the board of Allegheny County Commissioners since 1949 and long a leader in the county's highway planning and designing, died at 64.

October 25: A contract signing set the stage for the four-year four-month job of moving families out of the 100 acres of Lower Hill District scheduled for redevelopment. The Housing Authority of Pittsburgh agreed to handle relocation of 1800 families.

October 27: Jones and Laughlin Steel Corporation announced it would enlarge its 1955–56 expansion program to an expenditure of $250,000,000 covering 1955–58.

November 14: Dr. Charles F. Lewis, director of the Buhl Foundation since it was organized in 1928, announced his retirement, effective June 30, 1956.

November 15: The National Steel Corporation planned to spend a minimum of $200,000,000 on additions to existing plants within the next three and one-half years.

November 30: Pennsylvania College for Women was renamed Chatham College and announced a $12,000,000 development program.

688

Photograph in 1955 by W. Eugene Smith

1955, February 5: REMINISCING. David L. Lawrence visited Stefan Lorant often in the author's studio at 718 Grandview Avenue, where Lorant interviewed him a number of times.

The Mayor's words were recorded on an old fashioned tape recorder; the tapes given by Lorant to the Carnegie Library, where they mysteriously disappeared.

December 14: Dr. Charles B. Nutting, vice chancellor of the University of Pittsburgh, was named director of the Buhl Foundation.

1956 *January 20:* Contracts totaling $10,-333,062 for two major projects on the Penn-Lincoln Parkway—the Downtown link and the Fort Pitt Bridge—were awarded by the State Highways Department.

March 8: The University of Pittsburgh's Cathedral of Learning was officially dedicated to President Honorarius John G. Bowman, who served as Pitt's Chancellor from 1921 to 1946.

March 19: Dr. Edward R. Weidlein, long-time president of Mellon Institute, announced his retirement.

March 20: The long and bitter Westinghouse strike came to an end after 156 days.

April 1: Twenty-two persons were killed when a twin-engined TWA plane crashed just after taking off from Greater Pittsburgh Airport. This was the first disaster at the airport

and the worst in the history of local commercial aviation.

April 4: Mayor Lawrence recommended a new and broader attack against neighborhood blight under a $4,740,250 capital improvement program. Included was more than $800,-000 to represent the city's first cash commitments to the Lower Hill redevelopment and Crosstown Boulevard projects.

April 18: Irwin D. Wolf, 61, who succeeded Edgar J. Kaufmann as president and general manager of Kaufmann Department Store, a civic and philanthropic leader, died at his Fifth Avenue home after a long illness.

May 8: United States Steel Corporation formally opened its newly built Research Center, consisting of four buildings and covering 142 acres in Monroeville.

May 9: The Koppers Company revealed plans for a multimillion-dollar research center in the borough of Monroeville.

May 10: Rodef Shalom Congregation observed its 100th anniversary and dedicated its new Temple at Fifth and Morewood avenues.

June 11: Hilton Hotels Corporation announced that it would build a $15,000,000 hotel next to Point Park.

July 1: A nationwide steel strike began. Federal Mediation and Conciliation Service entered the dispute which idled 600,000 United Steelworkers.

July 16: The last canvas tent performance of Ringling Brothers and Barnum & Bailey Combined Shows was given at Heidelberg Raceways, marking the end of an era of entertainment.

July 27: A master settlement, providing a three-year, no-strike agreement, ended the strike which shut down 85 per cent of the nation's steel productive capacity for 27 days.

August 9: The United Steelworkers and the Aluminum Company of America signed a three-year no-strike

AT PHIPPS CONSERVATORY

SPRING FESTIVITIES AT THE UNIVERSITY

agreement ending a nine-day strike of 18,000 members of 12 of the company's 21 plants.

August 13: Razing of the Gardens, historic landmark and scene of sports events for more than 50 years, was begun, to make room for an eight-story apartment house containing 127 luxury-type dwellings.

August 16: A program to expend $81,304,000 for additions to the National Tube Division of United States Steel in McKeesport was announced.

September 5: According to a Navy announcement, an atomic reactor for the world's first nuclear powered surface warship would be built by Westinghouse.

October 3: Democratic presidential candidate Adlai E. Stevenson spoke in the city and made a network television broadcast from KDKA-TV.

October 3: The last steam engine in the Pittsburgh area was sent to the scrap heap.

October 8: Ex-President Harry S. Truman campaigned in Pittsburgh for the Democratic ticket.

October 9: President Dwight D. Eisenhower made a major campaign speech at Hunt Armory for the Republican ticket.

October 17: Admiral Benjamin Moreell, chairman of Jones and Laughlin Steel Corporation, received the John Fritz Medal—one of the nation's highest awards for scientific and engineering achievement—at the National Convention dinner of the American Society of Civil Engineers in the Penn-Sheraton Hotel.

October 31: The Pittsburgh Department of Public Health revealed that nine of every ten North Side houses examined by city housing inspectors were in violation of the new code.

October 31: More than 12,000 jammed into Hunt Armory to hear a major address by the Democratic presidential candidate, Adlai E. Stevenson.

November 1: Theodore L. Hazlett, Jr., executive director of the Urban Redevelopment Authority, warned that a critical shortage of housing for relocation of families threatened to undermine Pittsburgh's ambitious program for eliminating blight.

November 5: The Commission on Human Relations announced the for-

NEAR FORBES FIELD

HARVARD-PRINCETON-YALE CLUB

AT SCHENLEY PARK

Photographs especially taken for this book in 1955 by W. Eugene Smith.

690

mation of a Citizens Committee for Integrated Housing, to be composed of about 150 persons from all segments of community life, and a subcommittee of builders and mortgage bankers, to work on plans for a pilot integrated housing project.

November 6: President Eisenhower was re-elected for a second term. He won a smashing victory in Allegheny County, moving the area into the Republican column for the first time since 1928. Adlai E. Stevenson carried the city of Pittsburgh.

November 8: Final totals for the Allegheny County United Fund Drive, the county's first combined charity appeal, amounted to 107.8 per cent of the goal, a total of $9,564,222.

November 20: Mayor Lawrence recommended an all-time high city budget of $44,273,292, but at the same time called for a slight reduction in real estate taxes.

November 30: H. K. Porter Company made it known that it would build a 17-story, $7,000,000 office building at the corner of Sixth and Grant streets.

December 11: Equitable Life Assurance Society announced plans for a 15- to 22-story office building in the Gateway Center, costing between $9,000,000 and $12,000,000.

1957 *January 23:* Western Pennsylvania's heavy construction industry and the Laborer's District Council ended a three-week strike by signing a two-year wage contract.

February 4: Paul H. Martin, retiring head of the Pittsburgh Regional Planning Association, urged comprehensive planning on a regional basis for the Pittsburgh area.

March 19: The Board of Education voted to spend another $10,000,000, most of it within the next five years, to build new schools and modernize a number of others. Money was to be raised by selling general obligation bonds.

April 1: A federal grant for construction of a new east-west runway at the Pittsburgh Airport was announced.

April 8: Carnegie Institute of Technology embarked on a $26,000,000-plus plan of progress.

April 9: Six industrial concerns were named as violators of the country's smoke-control ordinance.

April 13: Public Works Director James S. Devlin said that $2,850,000 would be spent in street resurfacing and rebuilding projects during 1957.

April 14: Thomas E. Kilgallen, former president of City Council, died at 64.

April 17: Ground was broken for construction of the $17,000,000 Fort Pitt Tunnels under Duquesne Heights, to provide the final link between the eastern and western sections of the Penn-Lincoln Parkway.

April 26: The State Office Building in Gateway Center was dedicated.

May 11: Dr. Edward H. Litchfield was inaugurated as the 12th chancellor of the University of Pittsburgh.

May 21: The Allegheny Conference urged state, county, and city governments to join in a long-range highway program to meet traffic requirements.

June 4: The last three contracts were awarded for construction of an east loading dock, the first major expansion of the terminal building at Greater Pittsburgh Airport.

June 21: The University of Pittsburgh announced plans for a new graduate program to train engineers in all phases of air pollution control in keeping with the city's pioneering advances in that field.

June 26: Plans were made for the merger of Pittsburgh Xenia Theological Seminary (Presbyterian), North Highland Avenue, and the Western Theological Seminary (Presbyterian), Ridge Avenue, North Side.

June 26: Ernest T. Weir, 81, long a "rugged individualist" in the well-organized steel industry and former chief executive of the National Steel Corporation, died in Philadelphia.

July 25: Television City, Incorporated, was granted authority by the Federal Communications Commission to operate a Pittsburgh television station on Channel 4.

July 25: Avery C. Adams, president and chief operating officer of Jones and Laughlin Steel Corporation, was

elected chief executive officer, effective October 1. Admiral Benjamin Moreell remained as board chairman and chairman of the executive committee.

August 1: Carnegie Institute of Technology was purchasing eight acres of property fronting on Forbes Street near Morewood Avenue for faculty and student residences.

August 14: The National Steel Corporation elected George M. Humphrey, former Secretary of the Treasury, as its chairman of the board.

August 28: Drilling began on the $17,000,000 Fort Pitt Tunnels.

September 1: Pittsburgh's Channel 4, WIIC, began broadcasting as the nation's newest and most powerful VHF television station.

September 10: The city was assured of a federal grant of nearly $11,000,000 with which to begin urban renewal in East Liberty and the North Side's Manchester District.

September 20: Ground was broken at Gateway Center by Conrad N. Hilton for the new Hilton hotel.

October 14: A strike by operators of the Pittsburgh Railways Company began.

October 18: A Pittsburgh to Erie extension of the Pennsylvania Turnpike became a definite prospect with the announcement that it had been added to the National Interstate Highway System.

November 5: Mayor Lawrence won a fourth term victory by a 59,500 vote majority over his Republican opponent, John Drew.

December 2: A total municipal budget of more than $54,000,000 for 1958 was proposed by Mayor Lawrence.

December 9: The transit strike ended and within hours the trolley and bus lines were in operation.

December 18: Pittsburgh started receiving electricity generated by atomic power from Shippingport, Pennsylvania, site of the world's first full-scale atomic electric power plant.

December 18: Westinghouse was awarded a $46,050,000 Navy contract for nuclear power plant components for the world's first atomic-powered

GUARDING THE TREASURES!
Photograph by W. Eugene Smith.

AT THE CHILDREN'S ZOO
Photograph by Margaret Bourke-White.

60,000 AT PITT STADIUM.
An aerial photograph by Lee D. Renick.

aircraft carrier.

1958 *January 17:* Penn-Lincoln Parkway, in its 12th year of construction, was directly linked to the Downtown Triangle with the opening of a new Grant Street outbound ramp.

January 27: Mayor Lawrence presented his 1958 capital improvements budget to City Council, calling for expenditure of $13,221,300.

February 12: Boggs and Buhl, one of Pittsburgh's oldest department stores, announced it would go out of business after 89 years of operation.

March 3: Mayor Lawrence agreed to run for the Democratic nomination for governor in order to end a contest that threatened to split the Democratic party.

March 5: Spear and Company, which had operated a department store in the city since 1893, was sold to the Hahn Furniture Company.

March 18: Mrs. John M. Phillips, for more than 40 years an outstanding figure in Pittsburgh life, and a militant fighter for the rights of others, died in Mercy Hospital at 76.

March 31: Mayor Lawrence and Governor George M. Leader set off a charge that created an opening in the upper arc of Fort Pitt Tunnel's north portal, above West Carson Street.

May 8: Allegheny County's Common Pleas Court judges ordered a drastic reform in court procedure and urged the Legislature to create four new judgeships to reduce the ever-increasing backlog of civil cases in the court.

May 9: Common Pleas Court judges extended their battle to speed up justice to the year-and-one-half backlog in Criminal Court.

May 28: The United Presbyterian Church of the United States of America was formed by the merger of the Presbyterian Church USA and the United Presbyterian Church of North America in ceremonies at Fifth Avenue and Bigelow Boulevard. Dr. Theophilus Mills Taylor of Pittsburgh Xenia Theological Seminary was elected moderator.

June 3: Allegheny County prepared to start on a public improvement program authorized in the May primary. Projects included a $9,575,000 Glenwood Bridge over the Monongahela, a new high-level bridge over the Allegheny and a $5,000,000 viaduct to span Turtle Creek in East Pittsburgh.

June 17: It was revealed that the Mellon family foundations had paid $3,000,000 for 3650 acres in six strategic locations in Allegheny County. The land was to be sold to the county at cost for a regional park system for Pittsburgh's suburbs.

July 11: The United States Steel Corporation announced that production at its Edgar Thomson Works would be curtailed because of declining demand. About 1500 men were to be laid off.

July 24: Alan M. Scaife, a leader in Pittsburgh's cultural life, died at 58.

July 30: Leland Hazard, vice-president and general counsel of the Pittsburgh Plate-Glass Company and one of the sparkplugs for Pittsburgh's renaissance was named professor of industrial administration and law at Carnegie Institute of Technology.

August 3: The Urban Redevelopment Authority began final planning for the $15,000,000 Chateau Street-West renewal project in the Manchester District of the North Side.

August 6: The federal government assured Pittsburgh of aid for the proposed $15,000,000 redevelopment project for substandard areas at East Liberty.

August 6: The State Highway Department approved plans for a new Glenwood Bridge, thereby making it possible for the county to receive $10,000,000 in federal aid.

August 29: Jones and Laughlin Steel Corporation was to spend $35,000,000 on mill improvements at its Pittsburgh and Aliquippa plants, increasing planned projects for 1958-1959 to $93,000,000.

September 5: By switching WQEX, the new educational outlet, from channel 22 to channel 16, the Federal Communications Commission assured the operation of a second educational television station in Pittsburgh.

September 9: Chancellor Edward H. Litchfield of the University of Pittsburgh unveiled a huge long-range, multimillion-dollar campus development plan, which would require eviction of the Pittsburgh Pirates from Forbes Field.

September 21: Judge A. Marshall Thompson, 86, oldest member of Allegheny County Common Pleas Court, died. A former dean of the University of Pittsburgh Law School, he was serving his third 10-year term on the court.

September 22: Mary Roberts Rinehart, 82, a native of Pittsburgh, died in New York City.

October 22: A 22-day strike at Pittsburgh's five major hotels ended.

October 27: President Dwight D. Eisenhower campaigned for the Republican ticket in an address at the Syria Mosque.

October 28: Carnegie Institute of Technology received a gift of $2,800,000 from Mr. and Mrs. Roy A. Hunt for the construction of a campus library.

November 4: Mayor Lawrence was elected governor of Pennsylvania over Republican Arthur T. McGonigle.

November 9: The General Services Administration announced that Pittsburgh's new Federal Building would be constructed near the Greyhound Terminal, ending a three-year debate over location.

November 9: Dr. I. Hope Alexander, director of the Pittsburgh Health Department for 20 years before retirement in 1956, died at 79.

November 20: The Crosstown Boulevard moved nearer reality when the State Highway Department awarded two contracts for $3,349,690 to start its construction.

November 27: Thousands assembled in Point State Park, at the very spot where Fort Duquesne once stood, to hear Mayor David Lawrence and General Matthew B. Ridgway begin the city's bicentennial celebration. It was two hundred years ago that the French abandoned Fort Duquesne (on November 24, 1758) and General Forbes' army took possession of the area.

THE PITTSBURGH SYMPHONY ORCHESTRA WITH ITS WORLD-RENOWNED CONDUCTOR, WILLIAM STEINBERG.

GROUNDBREAKING
Mayor David Lawrence with other city officials at the site where the Civic Arena was to be built. The date is April 25, 1958.

November 28: Sale of Forbes Field to University of Pittsburgh is approved; the Pirates will stay on for five years, until new Northside stadium is built. In reality, the Pirates stayed on not for five but for twelve years, until 1970 when the new stadium opened.

December 1: Red Manning began as coach of Duquesne University's basketball team.

December 16: A. W. Mellon Educational and Charitable Trust gives $12 million to the University of Pittsburgh.

December 17: John Dearden, Roman Catholic bishop of Pittsburgh, is appointed archbishop of Detroit.

December 23: City Solicitor Anne X. Alpern named attorney general of Pennsylvania.

1959 *January 1:* The 51-year-old Frank & Seder's department store will have a going-out-of-business sale.

January 16: City Council President Thomas Gallagher sworn in as mayor of Pittsburgh, replacing David Lawrence, who on January 20 will be inaugurated as governor.

January 31: In a trade that will later be credited with making the Pittsburgh Pirates pennant winners in 1960, the baseball team obtains Harvey Haddix, Don Hoak, and Smoky Burgess from the Cincinnati Reds.

February 7: Art Rooney, president of the Steelers, is dissatisfied with Pitt Stadium and wants to return his club to Forbes Field.

February 9: Governor David Lawrence will ask the state legislature for a law banning racial discrimination in housing.

February 16: The Democratic slate of candidates for May primary includes Joseph M. Barr for mayor; John Kane and William McClelland for county commissioners.

February 19: Thirteen men are arrested in a raid on the headquarters of the alleged numbers-racket boss Tony Grosso.

February 25: Industrialist Paul Reinhold enters race for mayor on the Republican ticket.

March 18: John J. Wright is installed as Roman Catholic bishop of Pittsburgh in St. Paul's Cathedral.

March 27: David J. McDonald, president of the United Steelworkers asserts that big-steel management is "hell-bent" on fomenting a strike when contract expires July 1.

April 10: A consensus is forming for legislation to provide for public ownership of mass transit.

April 11: United Steelworkers refuse one-year extension of their contract.

April 17: A mock air-raid is a failure; passersby laughingly refuse to take cover.

April 21: The Allegheny Conference on Community Development urges support for publicly-owned mass transit.

May 1: Jones and Laughlin an-

THE NEW BISHOP
John J. Wright blesses the faithful in St. Paul's Cathedral after his installation.

nounces a $234 million capital expenditure program.

May 6: Walter A. Munford becomes president of United States Steel.

May 13: A bill establishing public ownership of mass transit is reported out of committee in Harrisburg.

May 19: In the primary election, Joseph Barr and Paul Reinhold win nominations for mayor on the Democratic and Republican tickets respectively.

May 21: Peoples First National Bank and Trust and Fidelity Trust approve the merger of their institutions.

June 1: Pittsburgh becomes second city in the United States to ban discrimination in residential renting or purchasing, due to a new "Fair Housing Practices Ordinance."

June 4: Up to $60 million in residential and commercial construction, designed for the Pittsburgh of tomorrow, is envisioned for the Lower Hill District in bids from eleven developers. The development did not materialize.

THE 116 DAY LONG STEEL STRIKE
I. W. Abel, the International Secretary of the Steel Workers, at the Second Avenue Hazelwood Mill Gate No. 18 in July 1959.

June 4: Alcoma Golf Club suffers considerable fire damage.

June 8: The Public Utility Commission authorizes shift from trolleys to buses, on a temporary basis, as the tracks may not be removed.

June 8: Possibility of a $722,000 federal loan for Allegheny County's new Northside sports stadium is announced.

June 11: Allegheny County Boroughs Association votes to oppose the mass transit bill in its present form. The bill, bitterly attacked by spokesmen for the Independent Bus Operators and others, is sent back to House committee for further amendments.

June 19: Fort Pitt Bridge, vital link in Penn-Lincoln Parkway, is opened.

June 23: Allegheny County's transit bill is passed by House; goes to state Senate for final action.

June 24: H. I. Casteel, businessman, dies.

July 1: Four members of Pittsburgh Pirates picked for All-Star Game: Smoky Burgess, Dick Groat, Elroy Face and Bill Mazeroski.

July 7: Pittsburgh hosts All-Star Game (National League wins 5-4; Vice President Richard M. Nixon throws out first ball).

July 14: Pickets at the steel mills, as another steel strike begins.

July 15: John J. Kane announces his withdrawal from race for re-election as county commissioner.

July 21: Steel strike slows down construction of the Civic Arena.

July 28: United Steelworkers union extends contracts with nation's major aluminum producers, averting walkout of 30,000 members.

July 30: Michael L. Benedum, multi-millionaire oil wildcatter dies two weeks after his 90th birthday.

August 4: 2,000 striking steelworkers in a rally at Memorial Hall voice all-out support to union leadership in their fight for wage increase and benefits.

KHRUSHCHEV VISITS PITTSBURGH
During the steel strike in September, 1959 Premier Nikita Khrushchev arrived in the city. He emphasized the eagerness of his country to coexist peacefully with the U.S.

August 23: In violent storms, three city buildings were damaged.

August 25: Steelworkers President McDonald declares that the USW will stay on strike.

September 2: Two officials of the Russian embassy are in Pittsburgh to arrange details of Nikita Khrushchev's forthcoming tour.

September 19: The unfinished East Hills Shopping Center is offered to highest bidder at auction ("largest sheriff's sale ever"). The center is worth $8 million.

September 20: Religious services mark a protest against Khrushchev's visit. Khrushchev arrives and speaks of eagerness for peace. Thousands of Pittsburghers are on hand to see him.

September 25: Steelworkers Union breaks off talks in 73-day steel strike.

September 29: Dr. Jonas Salk gets a March of Dimes grant of $413,439 to continue his study at the University of Pittsburgh of viruses and cells.

October 1: Sam Grosso and ten of his racketeers are found guilty.

October 9: President Eisenhower invokes the Taft-Hartley Act to break the deadlock between management and labor in the steel industry.

October 20: The Carnegie Institute of Technology gets $2.25 million grant from the Ford Foundation.

October 23: The new Port Authority (mass transportation) gets off to a shaky start.

November 3: Joseph M. Barr, Democrat, elected mayor. Barr—124,500; Reinhold—71,202.

November 8: After striking for 116 days, steelworkers return to the mills.

November 13: A new site, closer to Allegheny River, is chosen for the stadium.

November 23: Representatives of trolley operators and representatives of the Pittsburgh Railways negotiate.

November 31: Pittsburgh Railways rejects new union contract offer.

December 2: Joseph M. Barr sworn in as 51st mayor of the city.

December 4: Mayor Barr invites trolley union and management to a meeting.

December 8: After the Mayor's proposal is rejected by management and labor, trolley strike begins.

December 13: Vote of 914—11 ratifies a 26 cent-per-hour increase in wages, as trolley strike ends after six days.

1960

January 11: The eight-year-old stalemate about trolley-to-bus conversion in West End routes threatens to jeopardize key "Renaissance" projects near Point State Park.

January 21: The Public Auditorium Authority announces that Deeter and Ritchey Architects of Pittsburgh, Michael Baker Jr. of Rochester, and Osborn Engineering of Cleveland are commissioned to design the Northside stadium.

February 2: Racketeer Sam Grosso sentenced to 16—32 months in Western Penitentiary.

February 14: Twelve-inch snowstorm closes airports and schools.

February 21: KDKA performers, members of the American Federation of Television and Radio Artists, go on strike.

March 1: A $500,000 fire destroys ten downtown businesses.

March 11: Announcement is made of the departure in 1961 of Dr. Jonas Salk from the University of Pittsburgh. He will become the head of a research institute in San Diego, California.

March 14: A $20 million new construction work in Pittsburgh district highway program will begin in the spring. Included is the linkage of the Penn-Lincoln Parkway with the turnpike.

March 23: $170 million is set for improvement expenditures at the University of Pittsburgh within the next ten years.

April 14: Three Pittsburgh bishops — John Wright, Roman Catholic, Austin Pardue, Episcopal, and Nicholas T. Elko, Byzantine Catholic — oppose ballot issue to allow betting on harness racing.

April 18: A new chapter in Pittsburgh redevelopment begins with Sampson Brothers' plan to build private homes.

PIRATES WIN WORLD SERIES
On a memorable day in October, 1960 the Pirates won the seventh game against the Yankees through Bill Mazeroski's homer in the ninth inning. Pittsburgh went wild.

April 22: The afternoon *Sun-Telegraph* is purchased by the *Post-Gazette.*

April 26: The issue of harness racing, opposed by the bishops (see above) is defeated — 219,509 people voted "No"; 167,195, "Yes."

May 14: General Matthew B. Ridgway, the chairman and chief executive officer of Mellon Institute, retires.

May 25: City Safety Director Louis Rosenberg orders halt to all bingo games, even those sponsored by churches.

June 9: AFL and CIO merge.

June 19: Northside "Lower Belt" plan for $99 million interstate expressway wins formal support of State Highway Secretary Park H. Martin.

June 31: 17,000 baseball fans crowd Greater Pittsburgh Airport to welcome 1st-place Pirates home from Chicago.

September 1: Fort Pitt Tunnel is opened.

September 25: Pirates win National League pennant, even though losing 4—2 to Braves. (St. Louis Cardinals' loss on same day gives Pirates the victory.)

October 5: World Series begins. Pirates beat Yankees in first game, 6—4.

October 10: Senator John F. Kennedy, the Democratic presidential candidate, speaks in the city.

October 13: With World Series even, three games each, the Pirates win the seventh game 10—9 with a home run by Bill Mazeroski in the ninth inning.

October 24: Richard Nixon the

1963, October 17: LORANT PRESENTS THE FINISHED "DUMMY" TO MAYOR LAWRENCE AND TO THEODORE HAZLETT.

Republican presidential candidate, speaks in the city.

October 25: University of Pittsburgh will buy five blocks in Oakland to build new dormitories.

November 3: President Eisenhower and former President Harry Truman speak in Pittsburgh for their party's nominees.

November 8: Allegheny County joins in Pennsylvania's support of John F. Kennedy, who is elected to the presidency.

December 5: The six-year battle for the "Lower-Belt" system in Northside is won.

1961 *February 18:* North Park ice skating rink opens.

February 24: East Liberty urban renewal project is approved.

March 2: Conversion from trolleys to buses is discussed again.

March 5: John J. Kane, retired county commissioner, dies at the age of 70.

March 20: The Carnegie Institute of Technology receives grant by Ford Foundation to help raise the standards of the American theatre.

April 6: Yellow Cab drivers and mechanics go on strike.

May 5: Alcoa joins with a Kansas City real estate developer to rebuild the 79-acre commercial area, part of Northside renewal.

June 15: After 70 days, cab strike is settled.

June 18: Liquor sales at hotel bars on Sunday become legal.

July 16: Jones and Laughlin plans a quarter of a billion dollar expansion program.

July 30: The *Post-Gazette* celebrates its 175th birthday.

August 25: Port Authority rejects Pennsylvania Railroad's bid for public subsidies to keep its commuter trains running.

September 17: Civic Arena opens for the public.

October 1: Plans for a 55,000-seat, $22 million sports stadium go before the city and county officials.

October 6: Plans for the thirteen story IBM building in Gateway Center is approved.

November 7: Democrats sweep elections in city and county. Barr elected to his first full term as mayor.

November 28: Allegheny County voters will have the final say on unified mass transit for the county.

1962 *January 1:* Benjamin Fairless, former president of US Steel, dies at 71.

March 20: Civic Arena reaches agreement over jurisdiction with unions. Agreement insures that the arena will

be the summer home for the Civic Light Opera.

April 11: United States Steel sets increase of $6 a ton as a "catch-up adjustment."

May 20: Troubles at the Civic Arena as air conditioning cooling system fails during the Western Pennsylvania Kennel show.

June 14: An $84 million rebuilding plan for the Golden Triangle is announced.

October 12: President Kennedy assails Republicans in the city. 300,000 Pittsburghers welcome him.

November 6: William Scranton elected governor of Pennsylvania.

November 19: Allegheny County Port Authority has acquisition agreements with 23 of 30 local bus companies.

1963 *January 9:* City and county oppose merger of Pennsylvania Railroad and New York Central system.

January 11: An outer space research center will be built in Oakland by the University of Pittsburgh.

January 21: McClelland and McGrady announce re-election drive for county commissioners.

January 23: Chancellor Litchfield of University of Pittsburgh says Pirates baseball team may remain at Forbes Field, now owned by Pitt.

January 29: Seven Northside buildings were destroyed by fire.

January 31: William H. McNaugher resigns from the Common Pleas bench, to be succeeded by Henry Ellenbogen.

February 1: David L. Lawrence sworn in as chairman of President's Commission on Equal Opportunity in Housing.

February 14: The University of Pittsburgh leaves up to its individual schools whether they will boycott clubs that practice racial discrimination.

February 21: Child Welfare Services of Allegheny County approved by the county commissioners.

March 28: Mayor Joseph Barr criticizes County Commissioner William McClelland in his continuing controversy over Northside stadium.

April 2: Stadium financing plan deemed dead.

April 28: Two more major fires add to previous wave of fires; arson again suspected.

May 7: Pittsburgh Pirates reject demand that they give $3,830,000 to Northside stadium project.

June 28: US Steel announces that cutbacks will result in 1,000 workers being laid off.

July 8: Pittsburgh building trade unions (except Brotherhood of Electrical Workers) agree to accept black men in their ranks.

July 29: Milk strike starts; the main reason for it: job security.

September 23: Westinghouse offers its four major unions a 14 cent raise and a five-year pension improvement.

October 27: After a record drought, showers bring relief to the city.

November 5: Democratic victory in the Allegheny County election. Re-elected are Commissioners McClelland and McGrady. The only Republican to be elected to major office is the new district attorney, Robert W. Duggan.

December 11: Mayor Barr announces that he is "looking into" the possibility of imposing an occupation tax on all working in Pittsburgh.

December 11: Avery Adams, chairman of Jones and Laughlin's executive committee, dies at age 65.

December 19: Earl Belle, "financial wizard," returns from Brazil to face trial.

1964 *January 28:* Former Judge William H. McNaugher dies at age 72.

February 2: Dapper Dan banquet gives top award to Pitt football coach John Michelosen.

February 28: Port Authority wins control of the Pittsburgh Railways Company.

March 11: In the worst flood of the past decade, water reaches 31.6 foot crests.

March 17: Fire destroys the Pittsburgher Motel.

April 5: Sabin anti-polio vaccine is administered to 800,000.

June 29: Police Detective Ralph Barnett sworn in as city's first black police inspector.

September 1: Pittsburgh's WIIC-TV, Channel 11, sold by *Post-Gazette* and Brennan family to the Cox Broadcasting Company for more than $20 million.

October 20: Groundbreaking ceremonies at Chatham Center.

October 27: President Lyndon B. Johnson arrives for rally in Civic Arena.

October 29: Republican presidential candidate Barry Goldwater speaks at the Civic Arena.

November 3: In the presidential election, the Johnson-Humphrey ticket wins, defeating the Republican ticket of Goldwater-Miller.

November 6: I. W. Abel, United Steelworkers secretary-treasurer will oppose USW President David J. McDonald in the forthcoming election of the Steelworkers.

1965 *April 30:* I. W. Abel wins the presidency of USW.

May 6: John W. Galbreath plans a 60-story building at a cost of $50 million to house U. S. Steel offices.

July 27: Edward Litchfield resigns as chancellor of the University of Pittsburgh.

September 5: United Steelworkers accept new 35-month wage agreement.

November 2: Mayor Barr and his five City Council running mates are re-elected, with new councilman Peter Flaherty leading the ticket.

1966 *January 11:* Sarah Mellon Scaife's bequest of $7.9 million to institutions is announced. The University of Pittsburgh will receive $5 million.

January 20: Bill Austin named new Pittsburgh Steelers head coach.

January 26: Dr. Stanton C. Crawford, acting chancellor of the University of Pittsburgh, dies. He is succeeded by David Kurtzman.

February 9: Pittsburgh is granted National Hockey League franchise.

April 5: K. C. Morrissey named as first president of Allegheny County Community College. Monument Hill, Northside, will be the site of the college's first campus.

April 19: Pittsburgh board of public education takes first steps in a $50 million construction program.

April 22: Court ends roadblock to construction of new stadium brought about by taxpayers' suit.

May 25: The creation of UHF television Channel 53 is announced.

June 10: Harry Keller is appointed fire chief, succeeding Steven Adley.

June 30: "Commuter bandit" hits the Oakland Western Pennsylvania National Bank branch for $9,554. This is the "commuter's" 14th robbery.

July 6: Pittsburgh Symphony is given a $2.5 million grant by the Ford Foundation.

July 11: Stadium Authority declares that the projected stadium as designed is too costly. It asks for alternative designs.

August 9: The University of Pittsburgh appropriations bill — $19,757,-200 — passes the state House and Senate and is sent to the governor for his signature. It will enable Pitt to reduce tuition for full-time Pennsylvania residents to $450 annually.

August 25: The new stadium plans are unveiled; it is similar to stadiums in St. Louis and Atlanta and it will cost $12 million less than the original design.

September 14: A plan to merge Mel-

lon Institute and Carnegie Institute of Technology is announced by Paul Mellon and Aiken Fisher, the respective board chairmen of the two institutions.

September 19: Classes began for some 950 students at the Community College's Allegheny Campus and at Boyle Campus, then named East Campus on October 6.

October 21: Roy Arthur Hunt, 85, retired president and chairman of Alcoa's executive committee and member of its board of directors since 1914, dies.

November 14: Richard K. Mellon retires as chairman of the Board of Mellon National Bank and Trust Co.

November 17: The State Highway Department discloses that a bridge might be built over the Ohio River parallel to the West End Bridge.

"COMMUTER BANDIT"
William Zeiler, a Northside grocer, turned out to be the man who was responsible for numerous bank robberies. He was found guilty and sentenced to 15 years in prison.

November 21: David L. Lawrence, who on November 4 suffered a heart attack while attending a political rally at the Syria Mosque, dies.

December 1: Maury Wills traded to Pittsburgh Pirates.

1967 *January 13:* Wesley Posvar named chancellor of the University of Pittsburgh.

February 27: Mrs. Henry Hillman elected county Republican party chairman.

March 15: US Steel breaks ground for its new skyscraper headquarters, the world's second largest high-rise office building.

March 19: H. J. Heinz II, and the Howard Heinz Endowment acquire the Penn Theater for the Pittsburgh Symphony.

April 9: "Secret" project entailing new wing for Carnegie Institute financed by Scaife family is reported.

April 21: State Highway Commission says that the finishing of the "Bridge to Nowhere" will start shortly.

May 17: "Commuter Bandit" hits the Bloomfield branch of the Pittsburgh National Bank for the second time.

June 11: A master plan for a new $200 million terminal and cargo complex for Greater Pittsburgh Airport that would accommodate 12 million passengers by the year 2000 is unveiled. The first phase of the extension is planned to be completed by 1980.

June 23: A Northside grocer William Zeiler, arrested. FBI agents and city police believe him to be the "Commuter Bandit," who is responsible for sixteen robberies totaling more than $200,000.

June 29: U.S. attorney's office announces that "Commuter Bandit" Zeiler will be charged with committing five bank robberies. His alleged accomplice, Richard P. Chiocca, surrendered to police.

July 20: State Senator John Devlin, minority leader, dies.

August 14: County Commissioner McClelland, rejected by the Democratic party, will run on the Constitutional party ballot with George Shankey as the other candidate.

September 11: An 11-mile, $160 million superhighway that will cut through Oakland to link major highways in the North and South Hills is under consideration.

September 18: Plans for a second Skybus to run between downtown and the South Hills have shelved survey work on an $800 million regional-rapid transit system for all of Allegheny County. The new system, different from its predecessor at South Park, will cost $60 million in state, federal, and local funds.

November 7: Leonard C. Staisey and Thomas J. Foerster elected new Democratic majority commissioners. Robert Duggan, Republican, re-elected as district attorney. Robert Friend, former Pirate pitcher, new county controller.

November 14: Canon Robert Appleyard elected new bishop of Episcopal Diocese of Pittsburgh to succeed Bishop Austin Pardue who will retire in August of 1968. More than 70 clerics and 220 lay Episcopal deputies cast their votes in separate elections.

December 29: A report for the Allegheny County Port Authority states that Skybus would be cheaper than a conventional "steel on steel" mass transit system, spreading over 60 miles, but would be more costly to run. Either could be in operation in seventeen years.

A survey conducted in 1967 by the American Insurance Association

THE STADIUM DEAL
John Galbraith of the Pirates and Mayor Joseph M. Barr shake hands with Art Rooney of the Steelers and John Stabile, the parking concessioner of the Stadium.

gave the city's fire defenses the worst rating in Pittsburgh's history.

1968 *January 12:* Pittsburgh Stadium Authority approves final plans and specifications for the 52,000-seat stadium on the Northside that could be built for $28,000,000.

January 23: "Commuter Bandit" Zeiler is sentenced to 15 years.

February 20: The Penn Sheraton Hotel goes on the auction block after Local 327 Hotel and Restaurant workers refuse to accept the management's terms to end their 43-day old strike.

February 29: Pittsburgh Federation of Teachers (AFL-CIO) goes on strike despite injunction against union leadership.

March 8: A plane crash into Lake Michigan takes the lives of Dr. Edward Litchfield, former chancellor of the University of Pittsburgh, his wife, his mother, and his two sons.

March 10: Teachers' strike ends. Board of Education must accept elected bargaining agent as exclusive bargaining agent for teachers.

March 14: Carnegie-Mellon President H. Guyford Stever discloses proposals for the University for the next three years. CMU will broaden its scope by creating a Graduate School of Urban and Public Affairs and a College of Humanities and Social Sciences.

April 5: Groups of black youth cause unrest in the Hill District and in the city following April 4 assassination of Martin Luther King, Jr., the black civil rights leader.

April 7: Mayor Barr imposes a five-day curfew for Pittsburgh.

May 10: Ling-Temco-Vought, Inc. of Texas offers $85 a share for up to five million shares of Pittsburgh's Jones and Laughlin Steel. The deal would give LTV 63 percent of J and L stock.

May 22: Hotel Penn Sheraton is sold to Pittsburgh investors. Local 327 and Bartenders Union Local 188 reaches agreement with new owners.

June 6: Dr. Sidney Marland resigns as superintendent of the city school system and is succeeded by Bernard J. McCormick.

September 11: William K. Whiteford, retired chairman and chief executive of Gulf Oil Corp., killed in traffic accident.

October 12: State Supreme Court Justice Michael Angelo Musmanno, 71, one of the prosecutors in the Nürnberg trials, dies.

1969 *January 16:* Pittsburgh Federation of Teachers reaches agreement preventing teachers' strike in city schools.

February 24: The Democratic Policy Committee unanimously endorses Judge Harry Kramer to run for Democratic nomination for Mayor against City Councilman Peter Flaherty who announced his candidacy earlier.

March 2: John Tabor accepts Republican nomination for mayor.

March 28: Pope Paul appoints Bishop John Wright of Pittsburgh a cardinal. He will be a member of the Curia at the Vatican.

May 16: Dr. Louis Kishkunas is named to succeed Dr. Bernard McCormick as school's superintendent.

May 20: Councilman Peter Flaherty wins Democratic nomination for mayor, in an upset victory against the Democratic machine.

June 4: Vincent M. Leonard, the auxiliary bishop to Wright becomes the new bishop of the Diocese.

September 23: Democratic majority commissioners approve PAT's Skybus-PATway (Early Action) mass transit plans.

October 9: Danny Murtaugh named to manage Pittsburgh Pirates for the 1970 season.

November 4: Peter Flaherty elected mayor over Republican John Tabor. Cyril Wecht, lawyer-doctor, elected county coroner.

December 30: Penn Theater approved as new home for Pittsburgh Symphony.

1970 *January 2:* Mayor-elect Flaherty replaces Police Supt. James Slusser with Inspector Stephen Joyce. The city council holds over confirmation of Mayor Flaherty's cabinet appointments: Joseph W. Cosetti for City Treasurer, Ralph Lynch, Jr. for City Solicitor and Bruce D. Campbell for Director of Lands and Buildings.

January 7: Flaherty the new mayor, freezes city jobs.

February 18: The Flaherty administration fires 71 rank-and-file pay-

UNREST IN THE CITY
Following the assassination of Dr. Martin Luther King, Jr. in the spring of 1968 there were steady rioting in Pittsburgh. The Mayor had to impose a five day curfew.

rollers; begins its austerity plan.

March 2: Flaherty threatens to close Pittsburgh Zoo.

April 1: Attorney John H. Bingler named Director of Public Safety.

May 4: Allison Krause of nearby Churchill was among four Kent State University students killed by National Guardsmen.

June 3: Richard King Mellon, 70, the key figure in Pittsburgh's Renaissance, dies.

June 23: Board of Public Education votes to abandon "Great High School" plans.

July 16: After many delays, the Three Rivers Stadium on Northside opens with Pirates losing to Cincinnati 3–2.

August 27: William R. Roesch named Jones and Laughlin Steel president and chief operating officer.

September 11: Robert J. Paternoster named City Planning Director; Bruce D. Campbell the interim planning director becomes Executive Secretary to the mayor.

November 13: John F. Counahan, president of City Council, dies.

1971 *January 2, 1971:* The elimination of city truck drivers from driving plumbers to install water meters leads to a ten day strike of the city's non-uniformed employees.

January 17: Pressmen at the *Pittsburgh Press*, on strike for twelve days, are back at work.

February 4: Thomas Kennelly succeeds Harry Keller as Fire Chief.

February 10: Mayor Flaherty replaces Stephen Joyce with Robert E. Colville, as superintendent of police.

February 16: Two police inspectors retire; demoted Joyce replaces one of them.

February 17: First moves toward correcting a system by which police collected unearned witness fees is taken by Robert Peirce, the new county clerk of courts.

February 25: Peirce announces the introduction of new witness-fee system.

April 25: U.S. Representative Robert Corbett, 65, who had represented the 18th district in Congress for half his lifetime, dies.

May 15–September 19: Because of the pressmen's strike at the *Post-Gazette,* both Pittsburgh's daily newspapers cease to appear.

September 10: Heinz Hall for the Performing Arts opens.

September 20: John Bingler resigns as city's safety director, because he finds the position unnecessary. Henceforth, Mayor Flaherty will act as his own safety director.

September 20: In a July 28 letter the state Department of Commerce urged Flaherty to abandon his administration's support of the Mon Plaza site for the proposed convention center.

September 21: Allegheny County files suit to get back more than $41,000 in witness fees allegedly collected by 34 Pittsburgh policemen.

September 22: The Flaherty administration serves notice in court that it will resist any attempt by PAT to renovate the old Wabash Tunnel, which is a vital link to the Early Action phase of the Skybus lines to the South Hill.

October 6: Pittsburgh Pirates win National League pennant.

October 6: James Fulton, Dormont Republican, dies.

October 22: In a defeat for the Mayor, city council votes unanimously in private caucus to throw full support behind PAT's Early Action mass transit plan.

October 26: Robert R. Dorsey, president of Gulf Oil, will become chief executive officer of the company.

November 2: In the election, Robert Duggan is re-elected district attorney. Republican William Hunt, a Skybus opponent, wins largest vote for county commissioner; Straisey and Foerster also re-elected. Robert Peirce, county clerk of courts by appointment, is also elected.

November 8: Mrs. Gladys McNairy, a black woman, elected president of the Pittsburgh Board of Public Education.

November 23: Danny Murtaugh who retired as Pirate manager is replaced by Bill Virdon.

December 1: Mayor Flaherty announces that the second annual surplus will allow a reduction in taxes.

December 23: County commissioners again refuse to hold a referendum on Skybus issue.

INAUGURATION OF "PETE"
The newly-elected Mayor Peter Flaherty makes his inaugural speech in January, 1970 before his supporters and opponents.

December 27: PAT and the John F. Casey Company went to court to seek relief from malicious interference by the City of Pittsburgh to halt renovation of the Wabash Tunnel.

December 28: Mayor Flaherty lifts tunnel blockade.

1972 *January 10:* Flaherty, Commissioner William Hunt and the mayors of 14 communities file suit to enjoin PAT from spending any money on Early Action (Skybus) program until it complies with six specific legal requirements PAT allegedly ignored.

January 12: Flaherty, saying that the city must have tighter control over the Highland Park Zoo and aquarium, cancels all existing agreements with the Pittsburgh Zoological Society for the operation and maintenance of the facility.

February 22: PAT formally charges that anti-Skybus suit is a delaying tactic without legal foundation.

March 10: Pittsburgh Zoological Society sues Mayor Flaherty to enjoin him from taking control of Zoo.

March 16: Common Pleas Court order re-establishes Zoological Society as operator of Highland Park Zoo.

March 16: Harold Joseph (Pie) Traynor, third baseman and former Pittsburgh Pirates' star, dies.

April 6: Arthur Van Buskirk, 76, leader in Pittsburgh's postwar renaissance, dies.

April 13: Eugene Coon elected Democratic party chairman of Allegheny County.

May 8: Skybus trial comes to an end after 69 days.

May 10: Carnegie-Mellon University chooses Dr. Richard Cyert as its sixth president.

May 26: J. F. Hillman, 83, prominent coal operator and philanthropist, dies.

The survey of the American Insurance Association indicates that Pittsburgh's fire protection services are the best since World War II.

June 24: Flood water crests at 35.82 feet, about eleven feet over flood level.

July 17: Commonwealth Court rules that the mayor must sign over to PAT parcels of land at both ends of the Wabash Tunnel.

July 24: Judge Anne X. Alpern orders the halt of further spending on the Early Action transit program.

August 14: Pittsburgh-born pianist Oscar Levant dies in Hollywood at the age of 65.

October 3: Gladys Schmitt, novelist and Carnegie-Mellon faculty member, dies at age 61.

November 6: Judge Alpern issues a permanent injunction halting financing and construction of the proposed rapid transit system. Decree moves case closer to final adjudication in the state Supreme Court.

November 29: E. B. Speer elected chairman of the board of US Steel.

December 1: Mayor Flaherty announces that the 13.5 million surplus in 1972 will allow the elimination of the wage tax imposed in 1954, adjustment in the amusement tax and tax on parking lot operators. He also announces a 60 million dollar Capital Improvement Program.

December 31: Roberto Clemente, Pirates outfielder, died in the crash of a cargo plane on mercy mission to Managua, Nicaragua.

1973 *January 19:* The State Supreme Court by 6–1 vote overturns Judge Alpern's injunction and puts Skybus back on the track.

February 13: City Councilman Richard Caliguiri announces candidacy for Democratic nomination for mayor.

February 24: After Mayor Flaherty's announcement that he will seek re-election, the Democratic city committee endorses Richard Caliguiri.

May 15: Flaherty wins both the Democratic and Republican nominations for re-election.

July 24: Federal grand jury opens investigation into business activities of Allegheny County District Attorney Robert W. Duggan.

September 6: Bill Virdon fired as Pirates' manager; he will be succeeded by Danny Murtaugh.

October 12: Mayor Flaherty unveils his transit plan, which will cost $82 million. He would utilize the existing rail lines and would upgrade trolley lines to southern suburbs.

October 29: Pittsburgh "numbers boss" Tony Grosso testifies that former county racket squads chief Samuel G. Ferraro had received payments from him.

November 2: Ferraro found guilty by federal jury; sentenced to six years in prison and a $30,000 fine.

November 6: Mayor Flaherty, Sheriff Coon, Coroner Wecht are re-elected.

November 6: It is revealed that District Attorney Duggan had married Cordelia Scaife May, a Mellon heiress, on Aug. 29.

November 9: According to a *Post-Gazette* story, Duggan's marriage took place less than a week after his new wife was to appear before the Internal Revenue Service. Duggan calls the newspaper story "sick."

December 2: Patrick Fagan, ex-city councilman, dies.

1974 January 21: The end of the Professional Theater at Pittsburgh Playhouse had been decided.

January 30: State Crime Commission charges that District Attorney Robert W. Duggan concealed $68,000 in contributions and expenditures, squeezed more than $36,000 from employees, and falsified election records in his 1971 re-election campaign. Duggan replies that the mistakes happened because of "poor bookkeeping practices."

February 22: Grand jury demands Duggan's financial records.

March 5: Robert W. Duggan found dead in his Westmoreland County home. Not long after his death, the federal grand jury charges against him becomes known. He supposedly evaded $93,000 in income taxes.

March 12: The Westmoreland County coroner closes investigation of Duggan's death without ruling.

April 1–May 15: Strike at the *Post-Gazette* and the *Pittsburgh Press*. For six weeks the city is without newspapers.

HILL HOUSE AUDITORIUM
The Oliver Kaufmanns place a plaque in the auditorium which came into being through their generosity. The black leader Nate Smith (left); Allen H. Berkman, Lorenzo A. Hill, Russell Shelton (right).

ROBERT W. DUGGAN,
the District Attorney who, after the State Crime Commission started investigating his affairs was found dead in his home.

May 21: In the primary, the home-rule charter for Allegheny County is defeated. Mayor Flaherty wins nomination for the senatorial race over ex-insurance commissioner Herbert S. Denenberg.

June 13: Gulf Building shaken by dynamite explosion, causing a million dollars damage. No one was hurt. A caller identifying himself as member of the terrorist Weather Underground said the bomb had been planted by his group. Another caller told Associated Press that the bombing was to protest Gulf's "racist policies" in the Portuguese colony of Angola.

July 8: James Higgins becomes board chairman of the Mellon National Corporation.

September 5: A smaller and cheaper Penn Central site between Ft. Duquesne Blvd. and Penn Avenue is recommended by Mayor Flaherty for the city's convention center.

August 30: Dedication of the Point State Park Fountain. After three decades of planning and construction Point Park is finally completed.

September 9: President Ford visits Pittsburgh among cheers and boos — booed for giving pardon to ex-President Nixon.

September 27: County Commissioner Thomas Foerster pronounces Skybus "deader than a doornail."

October 15: Urban Mass Transportation Administration says Skybus is feasible. It says local governments must resolve conflict over the plan or lose federal funds.

October 25: Colorful inaugural reception is held at the magnificent Sarah Scaife gallery in Oakland.

November 5: In the senatorial race, Peter Flaherty is defeated by incumbent GOP Senator Richard S. Schweiker.

November 12: Mayor Flaherty announces balanced budget for 1975. There won't be a tax increase.

December 10: City of Pittsburgh and Allegheny County settle their differences about the construction of the convention center; they will go jointly to the state agencies to seek approval of plan.

1975 January 9: Mayor Flaherty increases exhibit space of proposed convention center from 104,000 to 135,000 square feet.

January 12: Steelers win Super Bowl in New Orleans, 16–6 over Minnesota Vikings. 10,000 people invade Downtown area after victory; 224 were arrested for drunkenness.

January 19: William Steinberg, because of ill health, resigns as Director of the Pittsburgh Symphony.

January 31: John Robin calls for independent engineering study of proposed mass-transit systems (rail vs. rubber tire).

February 3: County Democratic chairman Eugene L. Coon calls for federal investigation of U.S. Atty. Richard L. Thornburgh, whom Coon says was motivated by partisan politics in his investigation of alleged official corruption.

February 4: PAT directors authorize creation of 8-member task force to develop independent engineering study. Mayor Flaherty, county commissioners included. Decision comes after Federal Urban Mass Transportation administrator Herringer sets deadline for new attempt to resolve mass-transit controversy.

February 4: Thornburgh defends himself against Coon's charges of partisan politics.

February 6: NAACP, state attorney general and minority groups sue City

PROTESTING THE PARDON
At President Ford's arrival in Pittsburgh in September, 1974 students wave posters deploring his pardon for ex-President Nixon. The President was under guard and kept away from the demonstrators.

of Pittsburgh charging race and sex discrimination in police hiring and promotion. Similar charges had been filed with regard to hiring in the Bureau of Fire in 1972 and subsequent year, charges which consequently were dismissed.

February 7: The Mayor and county commissioners agree on convention center proposal. Proposal is for a 130,000–140,000 sq. foot site center on site bounded by Penn Avenue, Tenth Street and Ft. Duquesne Blvd.

February 11: I. W. Abel, United Steelworkers president who will retire in June of 1977, says he will refuse election to George Meany's job as head of AFL-CIO.

February 14: Staisey and Foerster announce they will run for renomination as county commissioners, as a team, in May 20 primary election.

February 16: Mayor Flaherty will cooperate with Allegheny Conference on Community Development in exploring possibilities for a 1984 World's Fair in Pittsburgh.

February 28: Robert Coll replaces Robert Colville as Superintendent of Police. Colville resigned to run for the office of District Attorney.

March 17: Perle Mesta, the fabulous hostess, dies. She will be buried in Homewood Cemetery.

April 9: Port Authority Transit (PAT) begins construction route from Downtown through Mt. Washington Trolley Tunnel and up Sawmill Run Boulevard.

April 21: University of Pittsburgh receives $1 million from Japan Iron and Steel Federation as an endowment for Pitt's Asian Studies Program. It would finance a rotating visiting professorship in Japanese studies and an Asian library.

April 28: Zoological Society will quit all operations by August 1, charging "senseless, irrational interference and harassment by City officials."

May 4: Mayor Flaherty plans three new structures in the Zoo to replace 80 year old main Zoo building.

May 14: André Previn appointed as the new Director of the Symphony.

May 18: The city administration hires Illinois firm of McFadzean and Everly to design new plan for Zoo.

May 20: Leonard Staisey denied renomination as county commissioner by Democratic voters. Ticket will be Thomas J. Forester and James Flaherty, brother of the Pittsburgh mayor. Republicans nominate Robert N. Peirce and Dr. William Hunt, incumbent GOP commissioner.

May 21: James Flaherty, the Mayor's brother, and Thomas J. Foerster win in primary election for County Commissioners.

May 25: University of Pittsburgh School of Medicine will graduate Elaine Morris, the first black woman.

June 3: Jones and Laughlin will lay off 1200, bringing total to 2600 out of work at its Pittsburgh Works.

June 4: Mayor Flaherty and the State agree on a six-lane East Street Valley Expressway.

June 9: City policemen sent home for having long hair. They do eventually get it cut before returning to duty.

June 16: DeLeuw, Cather & Company will study Skybus concept. The firm of engineers chosen by Transit Task Force will receive for the study $446,745.

June 20: A great fire destroys part of Kennywood Amusement Park, causing $400,000 damage. Roadrunner, Ghost Ship and the 75 year old dance hall burn down.

June 25: David M. Roderick is elected President of United States Steel Corporation. He will replace W. A. Walker on August 1st.

June 27: As Teamsters Local 211 calls a strike, the City of Pittsburgh is without newspapers till July 28.

July 3: The top floors of the old Duquesne University Administration building are destroyed by fire, apparently caused by lightning.

July 4: Pittsburgh celebrates the country's 199th birthday with fireworks and firecrackers.

Photographed specially for this book by A. Church

THE EXECUTIVE COMMITTEE OF THE ALLEGHENY CONFERENCE AND THE COMMITTEE'S STAFF IN 1975:

On the right behind the railing, from l. to r.: Robinson F. Barker, Robert B. Pease, Robert Dickey III, Carl B. Jansen, Fletcher L. Byrom, Benjamin R. Fisher, John D. Harper, Roger S. Ahlbrandt.

On the stairs from left to right in the first row: John J. Grove, John M. Arthur, John T. Ryan, Jr., Theodore L. Hazlett, Jr.

Behind them: William H. Rea, George A. Stinson, James M. Walton, Leon Falk, Jr., Wesley W. Posvar, John P. Robin, Adolph W. Schmidt, H. J. Heinz, Jr.

In the back row: Henry L. Hillman, W. P. Snyder III, Bernard H. Jones, James H. Higgins, Roscoe C. Haynie and Merle E. Gilliand.

1975 July 27: The month-long strike of the teamsters against the *Pittsburgh Press* and *Post Gazette* comes to an end.

July 28: The conviction of former State Senator Frank Mazzei on federal extortion charges is upheld by the Third Circuit Court of Appeals.

Aug. 7: "Medic One" superambulance begins its operation.

Aug. 21: Jones and Laughlin Steel Corporation signs a $200 million pollution control agreement with the Environmental Protection Agency, assuring J & L's continued operation and jobs for its 6,000 workers.

Aug. 30: The wildcat strike by West Virginia and Western Pennsylvania coal miners spreads, in spite of union and court demands.

Sept. 8: Pittsburgh School Board announces a $45 million school desegregation plan.

Sept. 25: Governor Milton Shapp joins the race for the 1976 Democratic Presidential Nomination.

Sept. 29: Pittsburgh Symphony musicians go on strike for the first time in the orchestra's 49-year history.

Oct. 8: The School Board announces a 113 million dollar budget.

Oct. 30: Radio Station KDKA and the Pittsburgh Pirates fire Bob Prince and Nellie King, their longtime baseball announcers.

Nov. 5: Control of the Board of County Commissioners is retained by the Democrats when Thomas Foerster and Jim Flaherty defeat their Republican opponents Robert Pierce and William Hunt.

Nov. 13: The 46-day strike of the Symphony musicians ends.

Dec. 1: City Public School teachers vote overwhelmingly for a strike.

Dec. 10: H. John Heinz III announces his candidacy for the U.S. Senate.

Dec. 15: Milo Hamilton is chosen as Pirate announcer, replacing Bob Prince.

Dec. 27: At Three River Stadium the Steelers defeat the Baltimore Colts 28–10 in the Super Bowl playoff before a crowd of 50,000.

Dec. 30: Gulf Oil's own fact-finding committee confirms that the corporation's executives had a multimillion dollar political "slush fund."

1976 Jan. 8: A 7-inch snowfall snarls traffic in the city.

Jan. 12: The striking teachers are ordered by the court to return to work.

Jan. 16: The Steelers beat the Dallas Cowboys 21 to 17, retaining their title as World Champions. Three days later the city celebrates the victory in bitter cold weather with a downtown parade.

Jan. 26: School strike ends; teachers ratify a compromise contract.

Feb. 27: James R. Maloney becomes executive director of the Pittsburgh Port Authority (PAT).

March 1: A 10¢ fare increase goes into effect on PAT buses and trolleys.

March 12: Governor Shapp withdraws as a Democratic Presidential candidate.

March 19: The two young daughters of banker Seward S. Mellon are abducted. Their abduction is a part of the battle between the banker and his wife.

March 24: City Civil Service Committee asks for the hiring of equal numbers of whites and minorities in the fire department.

April 13: The Pirates rout the St. Louis Cardinals 14–0 in the season opener with 40,937 fans in attendance at the Three River Stadium.

April 27: City voters, by a 3 to 2 margin, retain an *elected* school board.

May 12: Demonstrators stage a sit-in at Rockwell International headquarters, protesting the corporation's involvement with the B-1 bomber.

June 15: Helped by a $5 million grant from the Allegheny Foundation, City authorities will rehabilitate the Pittsburgh and Lake Erie R.R. Station.

June 25: U.S. Steel Corporation will reduce the level of air pollution at its Clairton coke works.

July 4: A giant Bicentennial Fourth of July celebration with fireworks from atop the US Steel Building.

July 9: Jones and Laughlin will install new electric blast furnaces which will reduce pollution and increase productive capacity; it will also cost 700 jobs.

July 13: In a wildcat strike pickets close down the East Pittsburgh plant of Westinghouse Electric.

July 18: Two more unions representing 28,000 workers join a nationwide strike against Westinghouse.

Aug. 2: Thirteen-year-old Terry Ford is killed in his Sewickley home when a bomb, intended for his brother, blows up in his face.

Aug. 5: Most of the mines in the district are closed by a wildcat strike.

Aug. 27: A federal grand jury indicts 38 district magistrates charging them with conspiracy and racketeering.

Sept. 3: Two of the three Cleveland gunmen convicted of murdering UMW leader Jock Yablonski, his wife and daughter are sentenced to life imprisonment.

Sept. 15: Governor Shapp signs an agreement with the Volkswagen Corporation of Germany ensuring the establishment of the firm's American assembly plant at New Stanton.

Sept. 30: Members of the State's General Assembly receive a 20% pay raise, while the pay of the city's firemen is boosted by $1,000.

Oct. 1: Duquesne Light Co. ask the Public Utility Commission for a rate increase which would raise the average residential electric bill by 31.6%.

Oct. 8: Mayor Flaherty orders all rookie policemen to walk the beat instead of riding in patrol cars.

Oct. 12: The county's "flu clinics" close and an investigation is launched into the cases of three residents whose illnesses were related to their "swine flu" inoculations.

Oct. 28: Assistant District Attorney Jo Ann D'Ariggo is dismissed from the courtroom by Judge Nicholas Papadakos who refused to hear her because she was dressed in a pantsuit.

Nov. 2: In the presidential election of 1976 Democrat Jimmy Carter narrowly defeats Gerald Ford.

John Heinz (R) is successful in his Senate bid.

Nov. 17: The State Superior Court upholds the legality of the Sunday "Blue" laws which prohibit most retail stores from doing business on Sunday.

Dec. 1: Allegheny County's mass transit system grinds to a halt as Port Authority Transit workers shut down all public transportation.

Dec. 2: A snowstorm snarls traffic.

Dec. 30: A $600 million "cleanup" pact is signed by U.S. Steel and county and state officials. It provides for an extensive anti-pollution rehabilitation of the Clairton Coke Works.

1977 Jan. 1: Pitt Panthers beat Georgia 27–3 in the Sugar Bowl to tighten their grip on the 1977 National College Football Championship.

Jan. 17: Record low temperatures of −17° F and gas shortages force the closing of the public school system.

Jan. 20: A blast at Langley Hall, on the University of Pittsburgh campus caused by a gas leak kills three and injures 22.

Jan. 23: As ice-packed rivers rise to danger levels the river towns brace for floods.

Feb. 1: A gaping crack threatening its collapse was found in the $50 million bridge on Interstate I-79, which was completed in 1976 as part of the Bicentennial celebration.

Feb. 2: Richard Karp, 94, musical director of the Pittsburgh Opera for 35 years dies of cancer in Montefiore Hospital.

Feb. 9: In the election for president of the United Steelworkers of America, AFL-CIO Lloyd McBride, the organization candidate, turns back Edward Sadlowski, the candidate of the rank and file reform movement.

Feb. 18: Four city policemen who moonlighted as "security guards" at a North Side "pornography warehouse" are suspended.

Feb. 21: President Carter names Pittsburgh Mayor Pete Flaherty as Deputy U.S. Attorney General.

Feb. 25: George E. Lee, whose massage parlor operations are under investigation, shot dead in a parking lot on Seventh Street.

March 8: City Democrats choose County Commissioner Thomas J. Foerster for Mayor.

April 1: An Oakland cobbler arrested for bookmaking invented an ingenious method for taking bets. He wrote them on the soles of shoes which he repaired.

April 9: A tentative three-year contract which includes some lifetime income security is approved by the Steelworkers Union.

April 11: Richard S. Caliguiri is sworn in as Mayor in City Hall, replacing Pete Flaherty who resigned.

April 25: Eleanor Cutri Sneal, a housewife from Mt. Lebanon, is elected president of the National Organization of Women.

May 10: Striking Teamsters block installation of voting machines for the upcoming primary elections.

May 17: Thomas Foerster wins the Democratic Mayoral primary and prepares to campaign against Joseph Cosetti, the Republican nominee, and Richard Caliguiri who runs on the independent ticket.

May 20: The nude body of 18-year-old Brenda Lee Ritter is found on a hill, the fourth young woman to be slain in Washington County during the past six months.

June 21: Thirty-nine suspected heroin pushers are arrested in a drug bust.

July 25: Flooding and explosions kill 45 people in Johnstown.

July 27: The Board of Education rejects a plan to reinstate corporal punishment in the city's schools, a measure backed by the Teachers' Union.

Aug. 1: The strike of 14,000 steelworkers is the first major walkout in the basic steel industry during the past eighteen years.

Aug. 7: Seventeen prisoners escape from the Allegheny County jail.

Aug. 19: Thousands of state employees, including guards at several prisons and aides in hospitals, join a "sick out," protesting the state's failure to pay their salaries because of the budget crisis in Harrisburg.

Aug. 20: The state budget is passed and paychecks go out to state employees.

Aug. 26: The PAT board, by an 11–1 vote, approves application for $93 million in federal funds to construct a $110 million busway from downtown to the eastern suburbs.

Sept. 8: The report by Sheriff Eu-

gene Coon about the deterioration of the County jail stirs the prison board into approving sweeping reforms.

Sept. 19: Jones and Laughlin Corporation lays off some 500 workers.

Sept. 29: West View Park, an amusement attraction for over four decades, will close its doors.

Oct. 6: Over the next six months U.S. Steel intends to lay off 4,500 of its white collar employees.

Nov. 8: In the mayoral election Richard Caliguiri defeats Thomas Foerster. Democrats sweep the contested City Council seats.

Nov. 14: Mayor Caliguiri announces plans for a no-tax-hike budget and for the beginning of "Renaissance II," to revitalize the city.

Dec. 16: Massage parlor operator Anthony Robert Pugh is found shot to death at his suburban apartment.

Dec. 27: Webster Hall Hotel, a landmark in Oakland, will be converted into luxury apartments.

1978 *Jan. 20:* Another big snowfall made January the snowiest month since the "Big Snow" of 1950.

Jan. 22: Former Mayor Pete Flaherty announces his Democratic candidacy for Governor.

Jan. 24: A blizzard strikes the area, knocking out power and disrupting telephone service. Rivers crest two feet below flood level at the Point.

Jan. 29: UMW President Arnold Miller declares that the miners' strike might go on indefinitely.

Feb. 6: UMW strikers stage a large rally downtown; they demonstrate before the U.S. Steel and Duquesne Light buildings.

Feb. 27: Thirty-five-year-old Phyllis Wyberg, from the North Side, becomes the third million dollar winner in the Pennsylvania lottery.

March 1: Bus driver Rosie Lee and her passengers are routed from their No. 87 Ardmore bus by a rat.

March 2: A large group of truck drivers stage a slowdown to protest the huge potholes on I-70 between the Turnpike and the Pennsylvania border.

March 6: UMW rank and file rejects a proposed contract; President Carter invokes the Taft-Hartley Act; miners must return to work.

March 7: The miners vow to defy the Taft-Hartley injunction.

March 14: Jennifer Lee Wesner, a former topless model, draws the top spot in the Democratic primary for governor.

March 17: School officials confiscate knives, guns, baseball bats and an ax after a racial brawl at Brashear High School.

March 25: Area miners prepare to return to work under a new contract which they first opposed but

which had been accepted by the majority of the UMW's members.

March 28: Schenley High School's Spartans win the Pennsylvania Triple A Basketball Championship, defeating Lebanon High 51–50 at Hershey, Pa.

March 30: The state government authorizes over $55 million in federal, state and local funds to pay for the first phase of the proposed East Busway in Allegheny County.

April 4: The City Council overrides Mayor Caliguiri's veto of an anti-pornography referendum designed to provide a mandate for "cleaning up" Liberty Avenue and other pornography retail areas.

April 6: The FBI and the District Attorney's Office begin their investigation of Community Action Pittsburgh, the Agency which is dispensing federal anti-poverty funds.

April 9: The majority in the county commission votes against putting the anti-pornography referendum on the May 16 primary ballot.

April 23: PennDot seeks a three-year guarantee from all asphalt contractors.

May 16: William Steinberg, 78, music director emeritus of the Pittsburgh Symphony who was conductor of the Symphony for more than a quarter century, dies in New York.

May 17: Peter Flaherty and Richard Thornburgh win the respective Democratic and Republican gubernatorial nominations.

May 23: After being pinned by his legs for two hours atop the Brady Street Bridge, a screaming construction worker is freed by a physician who climbs to the top of the bridge and amputates his leg.

June 6: Bail Bondsman David Wander and Edward Reddington are convicted on a sex-blackmail scheme against County Commissioner Robert N. Peirce.

June 19: Mayor Caliguiri, speaking before the U.S. Conference of Mayors, throws his support behind a plan which would make it easier for cities to annex their suburbs.

June 27: State legislature approves the death penalty.

July 5: Nathaniel Rosen, the Pittsburgh Symphony's first cellist, wins the Tschaikovsky Gold Medal in Moscow.

July 5: Edward Suratt, wanted for two murders, is arrested in Florida.

July 6: A major urban renewal project in Market Square will be spearheaded by the 40-story Pittsburgh Plate Glass Building.

Aug. 6: The Greater Pittsburgh Airport reports a $2.3 million profit.

Aug. 8: Parkway East is "papered" with money for the second consecutive day. After a messenger's car becomes involved in an accident, scores of welfare checks are strewn on the road. Another accident a day later, on August 8th, littered a mile-long stretch with canceled Series E government savings bonds.

Aug. 11: The State Supreme Court unanimously upholds a Commonwealth Court order requiring the city to submit a desegregation plan to the Pennsylvania Human Relations Commission before fall, 1979.

Aug. 15: Parents and community groups charge the city School Board with promoting a racially segregated system.

Sept. 7: Thomas Ware, a city detective with fifteen years service, is charged with the murder of a city fireman in the Hill District.

Sept. 21: Edward Suratt of Aliquippa, already charged with three murders and a suspect in 17 others, is convicted of the rape of a woman and her daughter in Vilano Beach, Florida.

Sept. 25: Northview Heights public housing project wins a $10 million federal grant to rehabilitate its deteriorating North Side complex.

Oct. 23: The federal government charges Westinghouse Corporation with making false statements to cover up overseas bribery.

Nov. 2: Pittsburgh is allocated $23.9 million and Allegheny County $27.19 million to operate the Comprehensive Employment and Training Act (CETA) programs in the coming fiscal year.

Nov. 8: Richard Thornburgh upsets Peter Flaherty by 200,000 votes to become Governor of Pennsylvania. In 25 Congressional races, the Democrats lose three seats and gain one. Allegheny County voters overwhelmingly reject a home rule charter.

Nov. 28: Sixteen-year-old Dorene Crawford is shot to death in the stairway of her Terrace Village apartment. City homicide detectives search for her boyfriend, twenty-six-year-old Fred Mahaffey.

Dec. 13: Alcoa Corporation intends to spend $5.1 million on an "extensive renovation" of the William Penn Hotel.

Dec. 23: "Lonesome George," the Pittsburgh Zoo's only gorilla, dies.

Dec. 31: The Steelers defeat the Denver Broncos 33–10 before a crowd of 48,921 and advance to the final game of the Championship, Super Bowl XIII.

1979 *Jan. 4:* The sexually assaulted and strangled body of Monica Renee Jones, an 18-year-old Pitt coed is found in the basement of her dormitory.

Jan. 16: Governor Richard Thornburgh is sworn in in Harrisburg, pledging "integrity, frugality, sim-plicity and humanity."

Jan. 19: Members of the Fraternal Association of Steel Handlers (FASH) vote to end their violence-torn strike as a result of a court-ordered injunction.

Jan. 22: The Steelers defeat the Dallas Cowboys 35–31 in Miami to retain their World Championship title for a third consecutive year.

Jan. 26: Duquesne Light, having just implemented a billing increase, announces another which will increase the average monthly electric bill by $5.70.

Feb. 2: An estimated 7,000 fans join in a Steelers' victory celebration at Market Square.

Feb. 11: Controller John P. Lynch begins an investigation of the county morgue in connection with private bank accounts used for deposit of out-of-county autopsy receipts.

March 5: Controller John P. Lynch indicates that Coroner Cyril Wecht and members of his staff might be liable under theft of service statutes for the private autopsy work which they performed at the county morgue.

March 7: The $10.8 billion state budget will be financed in part by an increase in the gasoline tax.

March 14: According to the county's law department, Coroner Wecht's private autopsy work was illegal.

March 28: A cooling failure in the Three-Mile Island nuclear plant results in its shutdown as radiation begins leaking in the Harrisburg area. Pittsburghers worry about the implications for nuclear facilities in the city and its vicinity.

April 4: 3,500 Volkswagen workers at New Stanton are laid off.

April 15: An investigating grand jury will crack down on the massage parlor industry.

April 18: Police and paramedics work for more than 3½ hours to free a driver from his wrecked truck which hung precariously from a Fort Pitt Bridge ramp.

April 30: Steel trucks begin to roll as steel haulers vote to end their three-week strike.

May 1: The strike at the Pittsburgh Brewing Company stops the production of Iron City Beer.

May 7: The federal government formally commits $265 million to PAT for the proposed light-rail transit system that will connect the South Hills with Downtown.

May 10: The unexplained failure of a 23,000-volt line ignites sewer gas, touching off a series of electrical explosions, setting overhead wires on fire and knocking out power in 25,000 East End homes.

June 4: The U.S. Attorney's office loses its second major Medicare fraud case when a federal judge acquits Dr.

Leonard Merkow of Squirrel Hill.

June 9: An Erie jury finds former Allegheny County Manpower director Robert L. Hawkins guilty of payroll frauds totaling $80,000.

June 21: Independent truckers launch a nationwide shutdown; gunfire erupts on the highways.

June 25: Shots are fired at produce trucks on a highway near the city, as the striking truckers attempt to shut down the shipment of food.

June 28: The strike by service station owners, resulting in long lines at the few open stations, lulls. A new "odd-even" gas rationing plan eases the run on gasoline.

July 3: Hope fades for an early resolution of the state budget deadlock which has already ended payments to thousands of state workers and families on welfare.

July 8: Theodore L. Hazlett, President of the A. W. Mellon Educational and Charitable Trust, and the legal architect of the city's Renaissance, dies.

July 14: Only 11% of the area's service stations are open. Pittsburgh motorists are hit hard by the shutdown of the independent station operators.

July 16: An eleventh-hour attempt by federal mediators fails to avert a strike by 38,000 Westinghouse workers.

July 25: The City Council gives preliminary approval to a P.P.G. Industries plan to build its $100 million headquarters in Market Square, but area merchants are fighting the plan.

Aug. 2: An 11-year-old girl and her teenage panderer are arrested on a downtown street on prostitution charges.

Aug. 3: A woman jogger told police she was attacked under Panther Hollow Bridge near the area where Carol Jursik, a Pittsburgh University graduate student, disappeared.

Aug. 7: The body of Carol Jursik is found. Her murderer is never apprehended.

Aug. 15: Allegheny County Health Agency might lose $197,000 in federal air pollution aid as a result of bureaucratic bungling.

Sept. 4: Mt. Lebanon schools are the latest to be closed in a rash of teacher's strikes affecting more than 30,000 pupils in ten Western Pennsylvania school districts.

Sept. 11: Lawyers, businessmen and office workers are routed from the Law and Finance Building, as flames race through its 14th floor.

Sept. 17: The illegal numbers racket is doing well in spite of the state lottery's success.

Oct. 6: The Pirates win the National League penant by defeating the Cincinnati Reds 7–1 at Three Rivers Stadium.

Oct. 9: Over strong objections by two city school directors, the school board held its fifth closed meeting of the year on desegregation.

Oct. 11: The Pittsburgh Pirates defeat the Baltimore Orioles 3–2 in the second game of the World Series.

Oct. 12: A tentative agreement is reached in the six-weeks-old Mt. Lebanon school teachers' strike.

Oct. 13: Edgar B. Speer, President of U.S. Steel Corporation, dies.

Oct. 16: The Pirates tie up the World Series 3–3 by beating the Orioles 4–0.

Oct. 17: The Pirates defeat the Baltimore Orioles 4–1 to win the 1979 World Series.

Oct. 19: 25,000 fans welcome the World Champion Pirates at Market Square.

Oct. 22: Coroner Cyril Wecht files a seven million dollar suit against Controller John P. Lynch because of Lynch's alleged defamatory remarks on a radio show.

Oct. 25: The crash of a PAT bus on Centre Avenue injures forty people. A massive probe into Pittsburgh organized crime is launched by state and local authorities.

Nov. 2: The Hillman Company was to take back a chemically contaminated Ohio River Park site on Neville Island which the firm had donated to the county in 1976.

Nov. 7: Democrats are assured control of the County Board of Commissioners as Thomas J. Foerster and Cyril Wecht are elected to majority seats on the Board. Most of the other county offices in the election were also won by Democrats.

Nov. 13: Mayor Caliguiri asks the City Council for a 1% wage tax hike.

Nov. 26: The State Human Relations Commission allows the Pittsburgh School Board 18 days to submit a plan for desegregating.

Nov. 27: U.S. Steel announces massive cuts in production; 13,000 jobs will be lost, 1,800 of them in Western Pennsylvania.

Dec. 1: State Labor and Industry Secretary Charles J. Lieberth declares that Pennsylvania would have to borrow $350 million from the federal government to cope with the projected layoffs by U.S. Steel.

Dec. 5: Moments after the newly-elected Pittsburgh School Board takes office, its members agree to begin school desegregation.

Dec. 10: The Wheeling-Pittsburgh Steel Corporation presents its employees with an ultimatum: accept cuts in their "excessive" incentive pay or see the firm's Allenport plant closed.

Dec. 14: Controller Lynch asks for the dismissal of Coroner Wecht's lawsuit against him.

Dec. 28: Workers at U.S. Steel's Ambridge Works vote to accept a paycut in order to keep the plant from closing.

Dec. 31: The City Council overrides Mayor Caliguiri's veto of its 28-mill land tax increase.

1980 *Jan. 7:* The Steelers dump the Houston Oilers 27–13 to get their fourth shot at the Super Bowl.

Jan. 9: The newly installed County Commissioner Cyril Wecht announces his resignation as County Coroner.

Jan. 14: A large crowd sends the Steelers off to their fourth consecutive Super Bowl game in Miami.

Jan. 20: The "Super Steelers" rally three times in a close contest to defeat the Los Angeles Rams 31–19 and win Super Bowl XIV, the fourth Super Bowl victory in six years.

Jan. 23: University of Pittsburgh students make hundreds of dollars worth of free long distance calls when the pay phones in a dormitory lobby malfunction.

Jan. 30: U.S. Steel reported a loss of $293 million, the largest quarterly decline in the firm's history.

Feb. 1: A jury orders the electrocution of Bennie Graves, a Homewood-Brushton man convicted in the strangulation killing of two children for whom he had been babysitting.

Feb. 6: Contract negotiations continue between the United Steelworkers and the "Big 9" companies.

Feb. 8: PAT's Board of Directors approve a 10¢ fare increase.

Feb. 11: Robert L. Hawkins, Jr., former Allegheny County Manpower Director, receives a 6-16-year prison sentence and is ordered to pay a $10,000 fine and $79,000 restitution on 83 counts of payroll fraud.

Feb. 17: A Carnegie Mellon University study asserts that the outlook for the steel industry in Pittsburgh is brighter than expected because the firms will invest $1.1 billion dollars updating equipment, building new facilities and installing environmental controls.

Feb. 18: A record number of speakers and spectators packed the school board's public hearing to oppose the board's desegregation plan.

Feb. 21: Six days before the deadline set by the state Human Relations Commission the school board remains divided over desegregation.

Feb. 28: The County Commissioners offered a $18.3 million plan to line the Allegheny River with parks.

March 1: PAT bus and trolley fares are raised 10¢ despite a last-ditch court battle by a community group.

March 4: Dozens of couples line-up in the pouring rain for more than 24 hours at the doors of the Catholic Social Services of Allegheny County in the hope of adopting children.

March 10: Penn Dot's "pot hole patching team" begins its season under a new Director, District Engineer Roger Carrier.

April 8: Senator Edward Kennedy, campaigning at the Cyclops Steel Corporation plant in Bridgeville, accuses President Carter of reneging on his promise to protect steel jobs.

April 11: A State Supreme Court Justice orders a halt to P.P.G. Industries' $100 million downtown development plan until the court can decide on the legal issues raised by five Market Square merchants opposing the plan.

April 14: Vice President Mondale attacks the policies of Senator Kennedy in a campaign visit to the city.

April 15: Leaders of the United Steelworkers ratify a 3-year contract providing an estimated $2.85 hike in wages and fringe benefits.

April 17: Senator Kennedy, Republican candidate George Bush and Rosalyn Carter are in the Pittsburgh area campaigning for votes in the Pennsylvania presidential primary.

April 19: Jail terms and fines against striking Western Penitentiary guards are ordered by a Commonwealth Court judge.

April 22: The federal Nuclear Regulatory Commission declares that a low-level radioactive leak, at a nuclear plant in nearby Shippingport is not dangerous.

April 23: In the Pennsylvania presidential primary, George Bush defeats Ronald Reagan and Senator Edward Kennedy wins over President Carter.

May 10: The steel lay-offs might reach 60,000 by September.

May 22: Penn Dot announces that an $8 million reconstruction project on the Parkway West will begin in June.

May 27: U.S. Steel will temporarily shut down its third and last furnace at the Edgar Thomson Works in Braddock.

May 31: Oxford Development Company reveals plans for a 46-story $100 million office-commercial building on Grant Street.

June 19: Independent presidential candidate John Anderson campaigns in the city.

June 21: The six-week strike by moving van drivers ends.

June 25: The School Board announces a lay-off of 141 teachers as a result of declining enrollment, low attrition and the pending desegregation plan.

June 26: Oliver Tyrone Corporation will build a 20-story office tower at Stanwix Street.

June 27: The PAT board reveals plans for a downtown transit center at the old B&O railroad depot.

June 30: Unemployment in the area reaches 7.8%.

July 18: An agreement between the Market Square merchants and PPG Industries is made. The merchants will get space for their stores elsewhere. The agreement clears the way for the construction of the PPG skyscraper.

July 18: The State Human Relations Commission asks the Commonwealth Court to stop the city's Board of Education from implementing its desegregation plan.

July 21: On the first day of the draft registration there is widespread vandalism at the city's post offices.

July 24: The Commonwealth Court rules against school desegregation, paving way for the School Board busing plan.

July 27: The University Health Center announces a $250 million expansion plan for city hospitals.

August 6: Richard Wallace is named city school superintendent.

August 18: Leland Hazard—the philosopher of the Pittsburgh Renaissance—dies at the age of 87. His Autobiography "Attorney for the Situation" was published in 1975.

August 20: U.S. Steel will recall 800 furloughed employees to the Edgar Thomson works.

August 31: The 28-year-old Carlton House, one of the city's great hotel buildings, is demolished, to make way for the Dravo skyscraper which later was named *One Mellon Center.*

September 2: Desegregation plan affecting 12,000 students begins.

September 4: The County Grand Jury recommends the filing of six criminal charges against County Commissioner Cyril Wecht, who allegedly used the morgue when he was coroner "to the benefit of his private laboratory."

September 8: "I have not committed any crime or engaged in any misconduct," responds Wecht to the charges.

September 12: PAT approves a 15-cent increase in base transit fares.

September 19: An investigating grand jury determines that the April 24 drawing of the Daily Number "666" has been fixed. Six persons including WTAE-TV's popular Nick Perry are charged with conspiracy.

September 29: Gipsy, the monkey, an escapee from the Zoo for over a week, pelts officers who try to capture him with a barrage of crabapples.

October 4: Sihugo "Si" Green, who played on the Duquesne University basketball team, that won the national invitation tournament in 1955, dies of cancer at the age of 46.

October 29: Urban Redevelopment Authority designates Grant Liberty Development Corporation to build a $26 million Hotel Complex across from the Convention Center.

November 5: Former California Governer and movie actor Ronald Reagan defeats President Carter in the presidential election. Republican Arlen Specter is elected to the U.S. Senate. Leroy Zimmermann wins the race for State attorney general.

November 10: Mayor Richard Caliguiri announces a balanced budget for 1981 without raising taxes.

November 13: J & L Steel will close the continuous strip and sheet department of its Pittsburgh works. Thousands of steelworkers will lose their jobs.

December 6: A contaminated water systems leaves 20,000 South Hills residents without fresh water.

DR. THOMAS DETRE, since 1986 President of the Medical and Health Care Division of the University of Pittsburgh is one of the instigators of the city's Nuclear Magnetic Resonance Center for Biomedical Research, the Pittsburgh Cancer Institute, and he played a vital part in the establishment of a comprehensive program in Geriatric Medicine and Psychiatry, in the Epilepsy Research and Treatment Center, in the Sports and Preventive Medicine Institute.

His wife Katherine, a renowned researcher in Cardiology, is Professor of Epidemiology at the University of Pittsburgh.

December 17: The Mellon Stuart Company announces the construction of an office building for its headquarters on the North Shore.

December 18: A grand jury identifies WTAE-TV's personality Nick Perry as the planner of the $1.18 million lottery fix. Perry supposedly netted $35,000 as his share of the winnings.

December 19: Allegheny County's 1981 budget includes a 5-mill increase in the real estate tax.

December 21: The playright Marc Connelly, best known for his play "The Green Pastures," dies at the age of 90. He was born in McKeesport.

December 27: Allegheny Ludlum Steel is purchased by a local investment group for $195 million.

1981 *January 29:* Gulf Oil settles its fight with Westinghouse Corporation over monopolistic activities with a payment of $25 million.

February 3: Mayor Caliguiri plans to increase the city's $10 annual occupation tax to $40.

February 7: The David L. Lawrence Convention Center opens with a ribbon-cutting ceremony.

February 13: Duquesne Light receives from the Public Utility Commission the approval of a $47.5 million annual rate increase.

February 20: The 13-week strike of the Steel Valley teachers comes to an end, enabling 2,700 pupils to return to the classrooms.

February 24: The Pirate organization files suit for the annulment of their 40-year lease with the Three Rivers Stadium Authority.

March 2: After the state Supreme Court refused to allow Dr. Joshua A. Perper to keep his post, Sanford H. Edberg becomes Allegheny County Coroner.

March 3: Penn-DOT launches a two-year construction program for Parkway East.

March 15: Plans for 400 condominiums and apartments, 60,000 square feet of office and retail space, and a 600-car parking garage are proposed for Mt. Washington. The development will cost $60 million.

March 18: Because of a wildcat strike, twelve Southwestern Pennsylvania coal mines are closed.

April 14: Striking Mesta Machine Company workers end their 45-day walkout at the West Homestead plant.

April 16: According to a grand jury report the Allegheny County Jail was a haven of administrative corruption, drug trafficking, sexual assaults during the five-year administration of former warden James Jennings.

April 27: Mayor Caliguiri sues the city of New Orleans and the Louisiana Superdome in Federal court to stop interference with Pittsburgh's contract dispute with the Pirates.

April 28: A federal judge orders the school districts of Churchill, Edgewood, Swissvale, Turtle Creek and General Braddock to consolidate their desegregation plans.

May 17: After the 380 striking employees of the Pittsburgh Brewing Company accepted the company's offer, the only remaining brewery in the city will continue operations.

May 18: Striking United Mine Workers block the entrances to the headquarters of Consolidation Coal Company in Upper St. Clair.

May 19: Former coroner Cyril Wecht is acquitted of the charges that he used the city morgue for private gain.

May 19: A new building and fire code is passed by the City Council. Houses in Pittsburgh must install smoke alarms.

DR. THOMAS STARZL

One of the world's outstanding surgeons, he came to Pittsburgh in 1981. A pioneer in transplant operations, he transplanted 119 hearts, 903 kidneys, 384 livers, 19 sets of hearts and lungs, and eight pancreas glands in the first half of the decade. In November 1987 he performed the dramatic five organ transplant operation on Tabatha Foster, a three-year-old little girl, who survived her ordeal for 192 days.

May 20: The voters of Allegheny County approve a plan for a harness racing track.

May 26: Common Pleas Court orders PAT to roll back base fare to 60 cents and transfers to 10 cents; also to realign bus and trolley zones and eliminate all savings on pass purchases.

May 28: A fire at a Lawrenceville industrial building forces the closing of the 62nd street bridge.

July 29: End of the twenty-two-day-old strike by county employees.

July 31: End of the fifty-day-old major league baseball strike.

August 5: Thousands of air traffic controllers across the country (including 58 from Pittsburgh) get their pink slips after defying the President's back-to-work order.

August 20: As part of an adjustment to population changes, three Allegheny County House seats are eliminated by the Reappointment Commission in Harrisburg.

August 25: Mayor Caliguiri proposes a 15 percent cut in capital spending for 1982. Inflation hits 15.2% for July.

DR. PETER SAFAR

A pioneer in the field of resuscitation, his researches brought profound changes to emergency and critical care medicine. His methods are accepted all over the world. In his opinion "intensive care is not intensive unless critically ill or injured patients needing moment-to-moment monitoring and life support have a multi-disciplinary team of physicians as babysitters". Dr. Safar is since 1961 head of the Anestheology and Critical Care Department at the University of Pittsburgh and since 1978 Director of its International Resuscitation Center.

DR. BERNARD FISHER

Distinguished Service Professor of Surgery of the University of Pittsburgh, one of the 11 of the 2400 University Faculty Members so honored.

He has devoted his 35-year-long career to cancer research. His pioneering studies have led to a dramatic improvement in survival and in quality of life for more than 75,000 women with breast cancer in the United States each year. A dynamic and highly respected individual, he is the leader of the largest breast cancer study group in the country.

JOHN GILBERT CRAIG, JR.

Born in 1933, Craig is editor of the *Pittsburgh Post-Gazette* since 1977. Before coming to Pittsburgh he was a partner of Arts Development Advisors of Wilmington, Delaware, and Washington D.C. historic preservation company and executive editor of the News-Journal in Wilmington.

He declared his ambition for his newspaper in this single sentence:

"My aim since taking over as editor of the *Post-Gazette* has been to develop a local newspaper that covers the region thoroughly and is, at the same time, worldly in its outlook and entertaining in its writing and approach to news coverage."

ANGUS McEACHRAN

Born in 1939, became the editor of the *Pittsburgh Press* in 1983. He started out at *The Commercial Appeal* in Memphis as a copy clerk in 1959 and by a decade later he was already the paper's assistant managing editor. His second big job was the editorship of the *Birmingham Post-Herald* in Alabama.

His self-characterization: "I play a fair hand of poker, a lousy round of golf and some of my friends call me the worst racketball player in America."

He would like to be remembered: "If there is ever an epitaph to my newspaper career I hope it would read: He could be a SOB but he was a fair SOB."

September 4: PAT eliminates buses running between 1:30 A.M. and 5 A.M. With this the "night coach era" comes to an end.

September 8: A school desegregation plan combines five east suburban districts into one.

September 11: Six thousand Nabisco women employees are awarded $5 million in damages in their discrimination suit against the company.

October 3: The federal government's plan to build 100 B-1 bombers by Rockwell International will add $400 million to the company's profits in the next seven years.

October 10: The eight-block area between the Monongahela River and the Boulevard of the Allies (from Grant to Stanwix Streets) is proposed to become "Firstside."

October 16: Dr. Joshua Perper is cleared of perjury charges.

October 21: Governor Thornburgh's proposed private enterprise liquor

WILLIAM BLOCK,

the eternally young publisher of the *Pittsburgh Post Gazette,* the oldest newspaper in the city. There is no visible difference between his picture taken in 1975 (see page 493) and the one above taken 12 years later in 1987.

He steered his paper's destiny over the past four and a half decades.

October 16: Dr. Joshua Perper is cleared of perjury charges.

October 21: Governor Thornburgh's proposed private enterprise liquor store system fails in its first test vote.

October 28: Governor Thornburgh and Mayor Caliguiri announce that two of the four "missing link" highways will be built. The East Street and

North Shore Expressways get the green light. Crosstown Boulevard and North Hills Expressway will be built later.

November 4: Mayor Caliguiri is re-elected; the Democratic party keep their domination in Pittsburgh and in Allegheny County.

December 24: Abortion bill is vetoed by Governor Thornburgh.

December 29: The city's budget for 1982 will be $229 million.

1982 *January 6:* Rand McNally's *Places Rated Almanac,* names Pittsburgh as the third most livable city in the country.

January 7: US Steel obtains 51 percent of Marathon Oil stock.

February 7: The budget of the state government is $13 billion.

February 8: At the Wheeling-Pittsburgh Steel Company, 40% of the work force is laid off.

March 10: The Crucible Steel Plant in Beaver County is up for sale.

March 19: Penn-DOT asks a federal court to free $302 million in highway funds frozen by a judge because the state failed to put an auto emissions inspection program into effect. Twenty-four hours later the freeze is lifted.

April 17: The cost of living in the city is ranked $700 below the national average in a year.

April 20: The city's public schools are ordered to improve the racial balance in three high schools and ten elementary schools.

April 25: Federal prosecutors investigate bid-rigging and anti-trust violations by contractors who were handling public roadway work in Western Pennsylvania.

May 19: State police and city detectives complete a large sting operation. They arrest fifty people in connection with a stolen goods operation.

June 8: Colt Industries will sell its Crucible Stainless & Alloy Division in Midland to Cyclops Corporation.

June 16: Ground is broken for the East Street Valley Expressway.

June 18: The city asks additional millions in taxes to improve Three Rivers Stadium so the Pirates can be kept in Pittsburgh. $11 million will be needed to renovate the stadium.

June 29: Allegheny Ludlum will spend $12 million on modern equipment at its West Leechburg plant as a trade-off for contract concessions from its employees.

July 17: A 150,000-pound hydraulic drill press falls off a truck on the Parkway West and levels a Scott Township house.

July 21: The City Council gives a tentative approval to the proposed takeover of Three Rivers Stadium by the city.

July 22: Colt Industries refuses to sell its Crucible plant to Cyclops Corporation.

July 26: A last-minute contract settlement averts a nationwide strike by 30,000 Westinghouse employees, half of them Pittsburgh residents.

July 29: Colt Industries begins closing its Crucible Steel plant. 400 employees will lose their jobs.

July 29: The USW rejects the steel industry's plea for concessions from 300,000 basic-steel employees.

August 2: Mellon Bank agrees to merge with Girard, a Philadelphia holding company.

August 3: Toxic waste halts the construction of Bloomfield Bridge.

August 27: The basic fee for riding PAT buses and trolleys will be raised to $1 beginning October 3, 1982.

August 31: Mayor Caliguiri announces a six-year, $504 million capital spending plan that stresses street, bridge, water and sewage systems.

September 9: After more than a decade of planning, the redevelopment of the North Shore begins.

September 14: Common Pleas Judge Silvestri refuses to order the McKeesport Area School District to resume the busing of 1,900 high school students.

September 21: The National Football League players go on strike.

October 6: State police in Homewood arrest 25 people involved in drug operation.

October 20: Carnegie-Mellon University concludes an agreement with IBM to become an experimental computer center, with more than 10,000 interconnected PCs.

October 25: A desegregation plan is agreed to by city schools.

October 26: After 20 months of repairs costing $58,million, the Parkway is at last opened to full traffic.

October 27: US Steel has an $82 million loss in its third quarter and cuts its dividend from 50 cents to 25 cents.

November 3: Election Day: Republican Governor Thornburgh wins a second term in a close race against Alan Ertel. John Heinz is re-elected to the U.S. Senate, defeating his Democratic opponent, Cyril Wecht, by 700,000 votes.

November 5: Unemployment in Pennsylvania hits 11.5 percent.

November 17: The 57-day NFL players' strike ends.

December 11: "Spectacor," a Philadelphia management firm, has been chosen to run the Three Rivers Stadium.

December 16: University of Pittsburgh football player Todd Joseph Becker is killed in a fall from his dorm window.

December 17: PAT agrees to a record budget of $133.5 million, $8 million more than the year before.

1983 *January 24:* City inspectors charge Warner Cable with electrical safety violations.

February 9: Mesta Machine files for bankruptcy after a foreclosure by three local banks.

February 12: The East is buried by three feet of snow.

February 13: Mrs. Henry Hillman ("Elsie") is named by the Pittsburgh Chapter of Vector International as "Woman of the Year."

February 17: A rock and mud slide on Saw Mill Run Boulevard closes the road for three weeks.

March 1: City government will spend $1.7 million in surplus funds to create short-term jobs for the unemployed.

March 3: U.S. Steel will start up the No. 2 blast furnace at the Edgar Thomson works and recall 300 employees.

March 10: The city sues the state to implement auto emissions inspection.

March 15: Aldege "Baz" Bastien, general manager of the Penguins, is killed in a motor car accident.

April 6: President Reagan visits Pittsburgh and makes a reassuring speech about the survival of the steel industry. Four thousand protestors boo him.

April 23: City officials launch a multi-million dollar reclamation project along the Monongehela and Allegheny Rivers.

May 10: County Commissioner Cyril Wecht is ordered to pay back $172,000, the sum he allegedly made through the misuse of the morgue.

May 11: USW head Lloyd McBride announces that the steelworkers' organization will sue US Steel to prevent the corporation from importing foreign steel.

May 18: In the primary election the voters of Allegheny County oust County Commissioners Cyril Wecht and William Hunt.

May 25: Cyrus C. "Cy" Hungerford, whose cartoons brightened newspaper pages for over 70 years, died in his 95th year, four days after the death of his wife Dorothy. Until his retirement in 1977 Hungerford drew regularly three cartoons a week for the *Pittsburgh Post-Gazette.*

June 21: Flash floods hit Bedford, Somerset and Cambria counties, causing a large amount of damage.

July 1: A window washer plunges 34 stories to his death from One Oxford Centre when his scaffolding falls. The life of his coworker was saved by his safety belt.

Rebecca Stafford is elected president of Chatham College.

July 20: Copperweld Corporation closes its Glassport plant. 200 men lose their jobs.

July 22: Power failures at the Greater Pittsburgh Airport delay flights for up to 12 hours.

August 27: In a Turnpike pileup, caused by a tractor trailer, four persons are killed, ten injured.

September 29: The city will lose J & L Steel headquarters when parent

PAUL LONG

For over forty years Long is one of the foremost radio and television newscasters in the city. Clever, erudite, well-versed, intelligent, he is an outstanding reporter of events, forever seeking the truth.

He comments on his beloved Pittsburgh: "This is a unique city. The mix of ethnicity makes it the most colorful municipal personality in the world. No more smoke, but sunshine. No more grime, but clear and fresh air—a lovely place to live. But—please don't tell anybody about it. They might want to come and live here and we are already overcrowded." Of course he is only joking.

company LTV Steel buys Cleveland-based Republic Steel.
October 1: The University of Pittsburgh is assigned a key role in the national fight against AIDS with a $4 million grant.
November 3: The 650 employees of the forty-four Giant Eagle Markets end their three-week long strike.
November 6: Lloyd McBride, president of the United Steel Workers of America, dies at the age of 67.
November 14: Mayor Caliguiri makes it known that his $263.7 million budget will have no tax increase or reduced spending.
December 28: US Steel cuts 5,574 district jobs—3,827 in the Mon Valley.
1984 *January 2:* Democrats Tom Foerster and Pete Flaherty and Republican Barbara Hafer are installed as Allegheny County Commissioners.
January 9: Plans are unveiled for a 36-story skyscraper—the Hillman-First Federal Tower—to be built on the site of the Jenkins Arcade near the Hotel Hilton.

January 13: Westinghouse phases out its switch gear production in East Pittsburgh. 950 workers lose their jobs.
January 15: Veteran Pittsburgh Press news photographer Raymond Gallivan, who worked for the newspaper for fifty years, died. He was 88 years old.
January 24: Alcoa will renovate the 70-year-old William Penn Hotel. The estimated cost is $20 million.
January 26: The Pittsburgh Steelers sue Three Rivers Stadium Authority for exclusive pro-football use of the stadium. The United States Football League's Maulers had signed a four-year lease with the Stadium.
February 4: Charles H. "Chuck" Cooper, former Duquesne University All-American who joined the Boston Celtics in 1950 to become the first black to play in the National Basketball Association, dies at age 57.
February 10: Kroger Company sells all of its 45 Pittsburgh-area stores. The 2,845 union employees who had been on strike since January 19 will be out of jobs.
February 10: According to Roger Ahlbrandt, Assistant Provost at the University of Pittsburgh and Co-Director of the Western Pennsylvania Advanced Technology Center, the new center has already spawned four new companies in its first year, and is expected to bring to Pittsburgh within the next four years 80 more companies creating 6,000 new jobs.
February 14: Dr. Henry T. Bahnson and Dr. Thomas Starzl perform a simultaneous 16-hour liver and heart transplant operation on a six-year-old girl at Children's Hospital.
March 9: U.S. Steel and National Intergroup cancel their merger plans.
March 21: After strong criticism from the National administration, LTV Corporation, owner of J & L Steel, is allowed to buy Republic Steel for $700 million.
March 21: Warner Cable reaches an agreement to sell its city cable operations to TCI for $93 million.
March 23: Thirty-six-year-old William W. Millar becomes the youngest executive director of the Port Authority.
March 27: The Dixmont State Hospital and Western Restoration Center, two state-run mental health facilities in Allegheny County, will be closed.
April 1: WQED, the nation's first community owned television station, celebrates its 30th anniversary.
April 5: The future of the steel indus-

try is the focus of the debate between Democratic presidential candidates Walter Mondale, Gary Hart, and Jesse Jackson at the Convention Center.
April 6: Senator Gary Hart, Rev. Jesse Jackson and Vice President Walter Mondale have a televised Democratic presidential candidate debate at the Convention Center.
April 7: A federal judge prohibits U.S. Steel from forcing employees to sign away their rights to file age discrimination suits in return for big pensions.
April 12: U.S. Labor Secretary Raymond Donovan and Governor Thornburgh bring $1.5 million in grants to Midland to retrain 4,100 unemployed workers.
April 13: The South Hills street car junction at the Overbrook and Mt. Lebanon-Beechview trolley lines closes after 80 years in operation.
April 14–15: Timothy Johnson, the first local patient, receives a heart and kidney transplant. In separate operations at the Presbyterian-University Hospital, Dr. Bartley Griffith and Dr. Alfredo Trento give Johnson a new heart, while Dr. Rodney Taylor and Dr. Thomas Rosenthal provide him with a new kidney.
April 26: Louis Mason Jr., the first black president of the City Council, dies at the age of 69.
April 29: André Previn, music director of the Symphony since 1976, will leave Pittsburgh to take over the direction of the Los Angeles Philharmonic.
April 30: Fortune magazine lists Pittsburgh as the nation's third largest corporate headquarters center. Fifteen of Fortune's 500 companies have their headquarters in the city.
May 4: Wiretapping leads to gambling and conspiracy charges against 15 area residents who were involved in a $1 million a year betting ring.
May 31: The former Union Trust Building—since 1946 a national historic landmark—is sold to the Edward J. DeBartolo Corporation.
June 14: Gurdon Flagg, manager of the Duquesne Club for 50 years (from 1931 to 1981) and president of the Pittsburgh Opera for 25 years (from 1952 to 1981), died in his 83d year.
July 10: Dr. Joseph C. Maroon and three other doctors perform a pioneer brain surgery at Allegheny General Hospital.
September 6: Allegheny County jurors are allowed to question witnesses during a criminal trial. It is the first time in the area's history. Common Pleas Court Judge Henry R. Smith Jr. said "the purpose of a trial is to find the

truth, and some of us feel that in order to do that, jurors should be permitted to ask questions."

September 11: David B. Shakarian, founder and chairman of the board of General Nutrition, the health food company, dies of cancer at the age of 70.

September 16: The 56-year-old Stanley Threatre will become the Benedum Center for the Performing Arts as a result of a $5 million gift from the Benedum Foundation. The new center will be the permanent home of the Pittsburgh Ballet Theatre, the Pittsburgh Opera and the Civic Light Opera.

September 17: Forbes magazine's annual listing of America's 400 wealthiest people includes six Pittsburghers; Henry L. Hillman, 62; Richard Mellon Scaife, 52; Henry John Heinz II, 76; William Block, 68, and his brother Paul Block, Jr., 73; the late David B. Shakarian and Helen Clay Frick, 95.

September 19: A $230 million development plan for the Three Rivers Stadium area is announced. A Science and Technology center will be part of the project.

October 2: Three Carnegie Mellon University scientists—Raj Reddy, Allen Newell and H. T. King—receive a $19 million grant from the Defense Department to develop a new "super computer" for symbolic processing that is 100 times as fast as those currently available.

October 31: The 64-story U. S. Steel Building is sold to a Connecticut partnership for $292.2 million, constituting the largest real estate sale in Pittsburgh.

October 31: Philanthropist Alfred M. Hunt dies at the age of 65.

November 9: Helen Clay Frick, the daughter of steelman Henry Clay Frick, dies at the age of 96.

November 14: Carnegie Mellon University is awarded a five-year $103 million Defense Department contract for a new Software Engineering Institute. It is expected that the Institute will provide 250 new jobs.

November 20: The Galbreath family, after 38 years of association with the Pittsburgh Pirates, decided to sell its 51% interest in the team. The Pirates, with a lease of the Stadium until 2011, will remain in the city.

December 6: Groundbreaking for the $135 million building complex across from the David L. Lawrence Convention Center. The project will include the 615-room Vista International Hotel and a 31-story office building.

1985 *January 17:* Rockwell International will acquire Allen-Bradley Company, a Milwaukee-based industrial automation equipment manufacturer, for $1.65 billion.

February 4: "Clayton," the Point Breeze home of Helen Clay Frick, according to her will, will be opened to the public.

February 20: The city of Pittsburgh will sever financial ties with companies which are doing business with South Africa.

February 27: Rand McNally's *Places Rated Almanac* lists Pittsburgh as the most livable of the nation's 329 metropolitan areas.

April 1: Gulf Oil Corporation will donate its Harmarville Research and Development Center to the University of Pittsburgh. The huge center expected to procure jobs for 2,000 scientists and technicians.

April 4: Carnegie-Mellon University will open a research center that will use fluorescent materials to study living cells. Researchers from the biology, chemistry, physics, engineering and computer sciences departments will participate in the program.

April 15: Charles Robinson "Chick" Davies, 84, the legendary Duquesne University basketball coach, dies.

May 2: J. Bruce Johnston, chairman of the Coordinating Steel Companies Committee says the steel industry will resume company-by-company bargaining in 1987 after the expiration of the present labor agreement.

May 5: A married couple, Ken and Lisa Martin of Mesa, Arizona, win victories in the first Pittsburgh Marathon.

May 8: The 10½-mile Light Rail Transit line between South Hills Village and Downtown receives a $19.7 million grant from the Urban Mass Transportation Administration. The money will pay for the completion of the line.

May 10: Arson was suspected in two simultaneous fires, one in the City-County Building, the other in the basement of the County Office Building.

May 29: AGV Enterprises will purchase the 34-story Gulf Building—a national historic landmark—from the Chevron Corporation.

June 12: A special device developed by University-Presbyterian Hospital surgeons Dr. Bartley Griffith, Dr. Robert Hardesty and Dr. Alberto Trento is revealed after a heart-lung transplant at the hospital.

June 21: Professor Ralph Z. Roskies of the University of Pittsburgh plans to give Pittsburgh a new supercomputer which will make the city the computing center of America.

June 29: Dr. Ronald B. Herbermann, a federal science administrator and tumor researcher, will head the newly formed Pittsburgh Cancer Institute.

July 3: The city's first subway opens to traffic. It cost $90 million dollars to build.

July 4: Judge Henry Ellenbogen, 85, dies in Miami, Florida. He served on the Pittsburgh Common Pleas Court bench for 39 years and in the U.S. House of Representatives for 5 years.

July 19: Prime parking places in Downtown cost two dollars per hour, twice as much as in the nation's 25 largest cities.

August 2: National Intergroup buys Permian Corporation of Houston, the crude oil gathering company for $172 million.

August 4: The 8th annual Three Rivers Regatta is watched by over a hundred thousand people.

August 28: Willeen Benedum, niece of the legendary oil wildcatter Michael Benedum, dies of pneumonia at the age of 80.

September 11: The Pittsburgh Foundation celebrates its 40th anniversary by commemorating Pittsburgh's achievements over the past 40 years that "shaped the city's renaissance."

September 13: A Port Authority study outlines the economic advantages of extending the subway north to Allegheny Center and east to Oakland and Squirrel Hill. The proposed $400 million expansion would replace buses with trolleys and would help PAT save $2 million a year.

RICHARD C. WALLACE, JR.
He became superintendent of the Pittsburgh School System in 1980. Dr. Wallace's educational rebuilding efforts in the city turned out enormously successful.

September 26: George A. Ferris, the new Chief Executive Officer of the Wheeling-Pittsburgh Steel Corporation, orders layoffs and pay cuts for management and vows to work without pay until the 69-day labor dispute involving 8,200 workers is settled.

October 2: A private-public partnership led by Malcolm Prine, the Chairman of Ryan Homes Inc., buys the Pittsburgh Pirates for $22 million from the Galbreath family. The public and private partners will contribute $50 million, while Mayor Caliguiri plans to raise the city's share—$25 million—through selling Three Rivers Stadium.

October 8: Roger Miles Blough, former U.S. Steel Chairman of the Board and Chief Executive Officer, dies at age 81.

October 28: Dr. Bartley Griffith leads a three-man surgical team at Presbyterian-University Hospital that gives Pittsburgh's first artificial heart recipient, Thomas J. Gaidosh, a new heart which replaces the Jarvik-7 artificial heart that had kept the patient alive for 4 days.

November 5: Mayor Richard Caliguiri is elected to a third consecutive term.

November 6: The Monongahela River is closed from Pittsburgh south to the West Virginia border after floodwater dislodged 62 barges from their moorings.

November 8: The Pittsburgh City Council unanimously approve Mayor Caliguiri's proposal to sell Three Rivers Stadium, thus enabling the Pirates to remain in Pittsburgh.

November 20: Kimberly Fuller, 9, becomes the youngest American to undergo lung-heart transplant surgery in a 5½-hour operation performed by Dr. Bartley Griffith and Dr. Robert Hardesty at the Children's Hospital.

December 6: Mark Di Suvero's 90-foot-tall steel sculpture for a traffic island in Gateway Center is approved by the city's Art Commission.

1986 *January 8:* Westinghouse Electric celebrates its 100th Anniversary.

January 17: A supercomputer consortium (Westinghouse Electric Corp., Carnegie-Mellon University and the University of Pittsburgh) receives the CRAY X-MP/48 supercomputer capable of performing 840 million operations per second. The Pittsburgh group is part of a national supercomputer consortium along with Cornell University, Princeton University, the University of Illinois and the University of California in San Diego.

January 22: 15 million passengers travelled through the Greater Pittsburgh International Airport in 1985, a 1.6 million increase over the previous year.

January 28: All 7 crew members, including 1970 Carnegie-Mellon University graduate Judith Resnick, die as the Space Shuttle Challenger explodes after takeoff from Cape Canaveral.

January 31: An earthquake shakes Pittsburgh for the first time in 23 years.

JAMES C. RODDEY
After working for thirty years in radio, television and advertising, Roddey came to Pittsburgh in 1978. Here he served for four years as Chairman of the Port Authority Transit.
His wife, Elin, is on the Women's Committee of the Carnegie, a member of the Magee Women's Hospital Foundation, and on a number of other boards.

February 7: A $28 million merger offer by Australia's Swan Brewing Co. to the Pittsburgh Brewing Co. is accepted by the city's only beer maker.

February 11: U.S. Steel Chairman David Roderick announces the completion of a $3 billion merger agreement between U.S. Steel Corporation and Texas Oil and Gas Company.

February 21: Marilyn, the Pennsylvania Holstein Association Auction's prize cow, is sold for $9,500.

February 28: Seven major league baseball players, including former Pirates Dale Berra and Dave Parker, had to pay fines and perform community service to avoid drug-related suspensions handed down by Commissioner

Peter Ueberroth. Former Pirates Lee Lacy and Al Holland are given 60-day suspensions; Willie Stargell and Bill Madlock were absolved of any wrongdoing.

March 17: The City Council approves a $21 million loan to keep the Pirates in the city.

March 19: Sentry, a new security robot developed by Remming Mobile Robotics, with the help of Carnegie-Mellon University and the Massachusetts Institute of Technology, is presented in the city.

April 1: The Allegheny Tower apartments will be converted into a 273-room hotel.

April 6: Retired President of Jones and Laughlin Steel Corporation William P. Getty, 76, dies of cancer in West Penn Hospital.

April 7: Mellon Bank assumes ownership of the Trimont condominium complex's 115 apartments and 44,900 square feet of office space to settle a $30 million debt owed to the bank by Washington Heights Associates.

April 9: Stanley C. Ellerspan, vice president of human resources at National Steel Corporation, announces the company's intentions to dismiss 3,500 of its employees during the next five years.

April 11: After losing nearly $9 million during the past five years, Pittsburgh Spirit Owner Edward J. DeBartolo Sr. folds the city's Major Indoor Soccer League team.

April 17: Pittsburgh Press reporters Mary Pat Flaherty and Andrew Schneider win the Pulitzer Prize for their series, "The Challenge of a Miracle: Selling the Gift," in which they investigated the organ transplantation program.

April 21: William Moore, a 35-year veteran of the police force is appointed as the city's police chief. He is the first black appointed police chief in Pittsburgh.

May 1: President Anthony O'Reilly of H.J. Heinz Company is the highest paid executive in the city. In 1985 he earned $1.96 million in salary and in bonuses.

May 18: Two parachutists, Don Sulkowski and Alan Danko, jump off the roof of the 64-story U.S. Steel building and land safely on the parking lot of the Civic Arena. They were immediately arrested.

May 27: Mayor Caliguiri and Pittsburgh Penguins Vice-President Paul Martha announce a city and county sponsored $11.4 million renovation of the Civic Arena that will keep the National Hockey League Club in the city.

May 30: Thunderstorms bring about flash flooding causing $20 million damages.

June 2: University of Arkansas third baseman Jeff King is chosen by the Pirates as the first pick in the 1986 major league baseball amateur draft.

June 4: Lawyer John G. Buchanan, who practiced law in Pittsburgh for 74 years, dies in his Shadyside home at age 97.

June 30: The University of Pittsburgh receives a $4.6 million federal grant for a research center in which drugs against AIDS will be tested.

July 1: The state budget gives Carnegie-Mellon University $30 million to build a High-technology Center. Private investors and the University will combine forces to raise an additional $10 million for a National Center for Advanced Manufacturing and Software Engineering.

July 8: U.S. Steel Corporation, formed in 1901, changes its name to USX Corporation and plans a major corporate restructuring.

July 14: With gross revenues of $53 million, the law firm Reed, Smith, Shaw and McClay ranks 48th in a survey of the 75 highest grossing law firms in America.

July 14: Legendary football coach Peter Dimperio ("Mr. Pete"), who led Westinghouse High School to 17 City League championships, dies in his 81st year.

July 15: The merger of Buhl Science Center and the Carnegie was approved by Buhl's Board of Trustees.

July 27: Broadcaster Joseph G. Tucker, the voice of the Steelers for 32 years, dies at the age of 76.

July 29: The *Pittsburgh Post-Gazette,* the city's oldest newspaper, celebrates its 200th anniversary.

August 19: Federal Aviation Administration rates the Greater Pittsburgh International Airport as the fifth best of the nations' large airports.

August 28: After 62 years, the YMCA Health Club on Wood Street closes its doors.

September 10: The Ritz-Carlton Hotel Company plans to build a 350-room hotel at Grant and Ross Streets.

September 11: Lorin Maazel will be the music director of the Pittsburgh Symphony in 1988.

September 13: The downtown department store of Gimbels closes after 61 years in business.

September 28: 12,000 runners run in

the 10th annual Great Race.

October 8: Dartmouth Medical School Chairman Dr. George Matthew Bernier is named Dean of the University of Pittsburgh's School of Medicine.

October 11: Gail Lawson Campbell is elected as President of the Chatham College Alumnae Association.

October 14: Louise Pershing Berlin, founder of the Pittsburgh Center for the Arts, dies.

JAY APT
(born 1949), the son of Jerome and Joan Apt, is the first Astronaut from a Pittsburgh family. A graduate of Shady Side Academy and Harvard College, he received a doctorate in Physics from the Massachusetts Institute of Technology in 1976. He qualified for assignment by NASA in July 1986 as a mission specialist on Space Shuttle flightcrews.

October 15: Carnegie-Mellon University and the University of Pittsburgh unveil a new $900,000 nuclear magnetic resonance instrument which will conduct research on cancer and organ transplants.

October 29: The University of Pittsburgh receives the Smithsonian Institution's radiocarbon dating laboratory.

November 22: Site was chosen for new $36 million Buhl Science Center. Ground breaking next to the Stadium will be in the Spring of 1988.

December 1: Jake Milliones is elected to a fourth consecutive one-year term as President of the Pittsburgh Board of Education.

December 8: Harvey Adams is elected to his sixth consecutive term as Presi-

dent of the Pittsburgh chapter of the NAACP.

December 11: The Pittsburgh Cancer Institute begins researching OK-432, a Japanese drug reported to shrink tumors and lengthen the life of cancer patients.

December 16: Carnegie-Mellon University received an $11.8 million corporate research grant for the fiscal year 1985.

December 30: Presbyterian-University Hospital officials announce a $230 million renovation project that will provide more space for the hospital's transplant center and the Cancer Institute.

1987 *January 7:* The county commissioners approve the appointment of Janet Hutchinson, director of the National Resource Center on Family Based Services, as deputy director of Allegheny County's Department of Children and Youth Services.

January 8: The Western Pennsylvania School for Blind Children in Oakland celebrates 100 years of service with a $9 million construction and renovation project to be completed in 1988.

January 9: Former Urban Redevelopment Authority official David J. Panza is indicted by a federal grand jury on charges of embezzlement.

January 31: United Steelworkers negotiator James McGeehan announces the ratification of a four-year concessions pact with the USX Corporation. The agreement brings to an end the longest shutdown at a major steelmaker in U.S. history.

February 16: A Common Pleas jury awards an injured youth $1.2 million in damages after he was electrocuted while trespassing at a closed USX Corporation steel mill.

February 22: Pop artist Andy Warhol, who was born in Pittsburgh, dies at age 58. He is buried at St. John the Baptist Byzantine Catholic Church Cemetery.

February 23: Chairman of the H. J. Heinz Corporation Henry J. Heinz II dies in his winter home on Jupiter Island, Florida, at the age of 78.

March 4: Duquesne Light, is ordered by the Public Utility Commission to reduce rates by $18.6 million.

March 7: A cancelled male strip show at the Monroeville Howard Johnson's ends in a two-hour melee as angry women litter the disco with broken glass and furniture.

March 15: Co-publisher of the *Pittsburgh Post-Gazette* Paul Block Jr. dies in Monterey, Cal. at the age of 75.

March 25: A 152-page report released by the Mon Valley Commission outlines a $333 million plan for county officials to take over and redevelop the idled McKeesport and Duquesne USX Corporation mills.

April 4: Mayor Caliguiri proposes a $105 million expansion of the David L. Lawrence Convention Center that would increase its exhibit space by 50%, double its meeting space and add five times as much storage room.

April 12: 15,000 Lawrenceville and Bloomfield residents, evacuated when toxic gas seeped out of a train's derailed tanker car, could return to their homes.

April 16: The *Pittsburgh Press* wins its second consecutive Pulitzer Prize, for a series by Andrew Schneider and Matthew Brelis that revealed inadequacies in Federal Aviation Administration screenings of airline pilots.

April 26: Monroeville's Vivel Rao finishes first out of 700 contestants at the National High School Chess Championship in Pulaski, Virginia.

April 29: Jack M. Brewer, Sr., Pittsburgh's first black assistant superintendent of public schools and Pennsylvania's first black principal, dies at the age of 69.

May 1: Westinghouse Electric Corporation announces the "phasing out" of its 94-year-old East Pittsburgh turbine plant. Because of it eight hundred workers will lose their jobs.

May 10: Fifteen-year-old Yvette Taylor of Stanton Heights graduates from the University of Pittsburgh.

May 11: Pittsburgh's first black chief of police, William H. Moore, after a year on the job, retires.

May 20: The Duquesne Heights Incline celebrates its 110 years of ascents and descents.

May 22: Urban Mass Transit Administration opens the final segment of the Port Authority's $542 million Light Rail Transit system through South Hills.

May 28: Bethel Park's 13-year-old Stephanie Petit, by correctly spelling "staphylococci," wins the National Spelling Bee.

June 2: University of Pittsburgh officials urge the Planning Commission to accept their $230 million expansion proposal.

June 7: "Fences," a family drama written by the Pittsburgh native August Wilson, set in the Hill District, wins four 1987 Tony Awards, including best play, best actor, and best director.

June 15: Four days after an audit reveals abuses at the Allegheny County Sanitary Authority, executive director James E. Creehan offers his resignation.

June 19: 12,177 fans pack Pittsburgh's Civic Arena to watch the Pittsburgh Gladiators defeat the Washington Commandos 48–46 in the first regular-season game of the newly formed Arena Football league.

June 26: Ground is broken for construction of the $503 million Greater Pittsburgh International Airport's new midfield terminal.

June 28: Plans for the construction of a new $500 million retail and industrial complex for Robinson Township were announced.

Actress Elizabeth Hartman died. Nominated for an Academy Award in 1965 as best actress for her performance in "A Patch of Blue," she committed suicide at her Oakland apartment.

June 29: Three tornadoes downed trees, damaged homes, and caused power outages as thunderstorms ripped through southwestern Pennsylvania.

Local pilot Joseph Longo arrived home after spending more than two months as a prisoner of the government of Angola.

July 1: University of Pittsburgh trustees voted to divest the university of its investments in U.S. companies that do business in South Africa.

July 3: Allegheny County reported an increase in syphylis cases from 30 to approximately 75 over last year.

July 8: Mrs Cheryl Towers resigns after six years as the executive director of the Pittsburgh Center for the Arts, ending three months of controversy.

July 9: Poet Sara Henderson Hay died at her Squirrel Hill home at the age of 80. She was the widow of the composer Nikolai Lopatnikoff.

July 14: Mellon Bank reported losses of $566.3 million during the second quarter of 1987.

July 16: President Reagan awarded Pittsburgh the status of an All-American City.

July 17: Duquesne University's Board of Directors refused to accept the resignation of their president, Reverend Donald Nesti.

30,000 Jehovah Witnesses gathered at Three Rivers Stadium in a three-day convention.

July 18: Anti-nuclear demonstrators gathered on the Bloomfield Bridge on the first anniversary of shipments of radio-active waste from Three Mile Island through Pittsburgh.

July 22: Gideon Toeplitz will become in October the new managing director of the Pittsburgh Symphony.

According to the U.S. Bureau of the Census, Pittsburgh has lost 18,300 people since 1985.

July 23: The Allegheny County Board of Commissioners has declared there will be no county tax increase next year.

The Ben Franklin Partnership approved a $6.9 million grant to a university sponsored center in Pittsburgh that funds jobs-creation efforts in the fields of robotics, computers, and advanced medical technology.

July 27: County Controller Frank Lucchino said he will push for a new hiring policy requiring all county employees to live in Allegheny County.

July 29: The Carnegie is restoring the "Noble Quartet" statues in the front of the museum and music hall.

July 30: The Reverend Donald Nesti resigned as President of Duquesne University, ending weeks of public controversy.

July 31: Margaret "Peggy" Kutz, former editor and publisher of the *Oakland News*, died July 28 after open heart surgery.

August 3: The Chicago West Pullman Transportation Corporation announced that it will be buying the Pittsburgh & Lake Erie Railroad.

Former Pittsburgh Congressman William Moorhead died of cancer.

August 9: The Three Rivers Regatta held its Champion Spark Plug Grand Prix race on the Allegheny River. It was won by Ben Robertson in a Formula One boat with an average speed of 111.59 miles per hour.

August 13: Community Activist Nate Smith was shot and wounded during an argument in a Point Breeze Diner.

In a 12 page statement Bishop Anthony Bevilacqua opposed the idea of sex counseling health clinics in the public schools.

August 19: The East Street Valley Roadway opened. It runs between the I-79 junction and downtown.

August 20: The Regional Industrial Development Corporation, with the University of Pittsburgh and Carnegie-Mellon University, received a $150,000 contract to coordinate plans for a new High Technology Park on the site of the old J & L steel plant.

August 25: The Reinhold Ice Cream Company will market the world's first microwavable milkshake, the "D'Frosta Shake."

August 27: Pittsburgh School Board President Jake Milliones was arrested in the Hill District for interfering with an arrest in progress.

August 27: In the Allegheny County jail the prison population increased by 40% over last year.

U.S.X.'s National Plant in McKeesport closed. Once giving work to 4,600, it was down to 189 employees.

August 31: 17 months after the opening of the county jail annex, the jail and the annex are filled to capacity.

September 1: The population of Allegheny County declined by 5.3%.

September 6: City Controller Tom Flaherty criticised three school board members for having relatives on their payroll.

The University of Pittsburgh received $49 million in Federal research funds during 1985.

September 7: The Reverend Jesse Jackson walked in the city's Labor Day parade and disclosed that he will become a Democratic candidate in the forthcoming presidential campaign.

September 7: Transplant doctors and patients from around the world gathered in the city in honor of Dr. Thomas Starzl, regarded as a leader in the field of transplant surgery.

September 10: The City will spend $4 million to improve the appearance of Fifth Avenue.

September 11: The Duchess of Devonshire visited the opening of her family's art exhibition, "Old Masters Drawings from Chatsworth," at the Frick Museum.

September 14: Unions representing 750 employees of the Pittsburgh and Lake Erie Railroad struck today attempting to stop the sale of the P & L E to a Chicago based group.

September 15: Vandals disturbed the skeletal remains at the Voeghtly cemetery site uncovered this summer by highway construction workers.

September 16: In the wake of the toxic waste spill during last April's train derailment, City Council adopted speed limits of 10 to 60 miles per hour for trains passing through Pittsburgh.

September 21: The parent companies of West Penn Hospital and the Forbes Health System will merge in 1988.

"Command in Hell" is the latest movie being shot in Pittsburgh.

September 23: La Roche College celebrated its 25th anniversary with the opening of a new $4.2 million College Center.

The former Braddock Public Library, the oldest Carnegie Library in America, has received donations of $80,000 to restore the closed building.

September 24: The state announced that removal of the 744 bodies from

the 120-year-old Voeghtly cemetery accidentally uncovered last summer by highway construction workers will cost $1.1 million.

September 25: The city held its 11th annual Great Race this week-end, run through the streets of Pittsburgh.

The Benedum Center for the Per-

SULTAN, THE GORILLA
One of the great crowd pleasers at the Pittsburgh Zoo. Local foundations and corporations contributed $15 million to the creation of a new Zoo, in which the animals could live in natural environment.

forming Arts opened.

September 29: The Caliguiri administration is seeking $28 million in new state monies for four major development projects: the Convention Center, Station Square, the Riverside Festival Market, and the crosstown bridge ramp project.

September 30: The Western Pennsylvania Conservancy will add a 76-acre pine forest to its holdings in Warren County.

October 1: Mayor Caliguiri stunned the city by announcing he is suffering from amyloidosis, a rare and incurable disease that attacks vital body tissues and organs.

October 6: Luciano Pavarotti starred in the Pittsburgh Opera's first performance at the Benedum Center.

October 14: Carrick native Danny

Seemiller with five other table tennis players will play for the U.S. team in the 1988 Summer Olympic games in South Korea.

October 15: The 24-day National Football League players strike ended.

October 20: Firefighters battled a blaze at a Wood Street building which formerly housed the YMCA downtown.

October 23: The Fort Pitt Tunnel was closed during the morning rush hour after a truck carrying 40,000 pounds of bananas lost its brakes.

Herr's Island was renamed Washington's Landing. Ground was broken for a $130 million development leading to a new marina, park, stores, offices, and industrial buildings.

Malcolm Prine, President of the Pittsburgh Pirates, resigned in a dispute with Syd Thrift, the team's General Manager.

November 7: The George Westinghouse Museum opened.

November 9: 1,200 cafeteria and custodial workers struck the Pittsburgh School district when negotiations failed to produce a new contract.

November 11: Vice-President George Bush marched through downtown in the annual Veteran's Day Parade.

November 21: Volkswagen's Westmoreland County Plant, dedicated with fanfare on October 5, 1976 will close. 2500 people will lose their jobs.

November 23: An ordinance known as the no-smoking law was enacted by City Council for areas in public and private buildings.

December 7: Jake Milliones was reelected president of the Pittsburgh School Board for a fifth straight year.

December 8: Pittsburgh Bishop Anthony Bevilacqua was named to succeed John Cardinal Krol as Archbishop of Philadelphia.

December 11: Israeli Foreign Minister Shimon Peres visited the city to sign an agreement of cooperation with Carnegie-Mellon University, with five Israeli universities to share information about computer research.

December 18: James G. Roddey stepped down after four years as Chairman of the Board of the Port Authority Transit.

December 24: Mayor Caliguiri, in a 45-minute operation, had a pacemaker implanted in his chest to regulate his heartbeat. He died, 56 years old, on May 6, 1988.

December 31: The estimated population of Pittsburgh for the past year was 387,499; that of Allegheny County 1,373,600.

BIBLIOGRAPHY

AARON, DANIEL (ed.), *America in Crisis* (1952).
Contains an essay by Henry David, "Upheaval at Homestead."

ABERNETHY, THOMAS PERKINS, *Western Lands and the American Revolution* (1937).

ADAMS, HENRY, *Life of Albert Gallatin* (1879).

ADDLEMAN, A. N., *Early Presbyterianism in Westmoreland County before 1800* (M.A. thesis, 1937).

AGNEW, DANIEL, *A History of the Region of Pennsylvania North of the Ohio and West of the Allegheny River* (1887).

ALLEGHENY CONFERENCE ON COMMUNITY DEVELOPMENT, *A Civic Clinic for Better Living* (1943).

———, *Pittsburgh and Allegheny County — an Era of Progress and Accomplishment* (1956).

———, *Pittsburgh — Challenge and Response* (1947).

ALLEGHENY COUNTY: A SESQUI-CENTENNIAL REVIEW, 1788–1938, edited by George E. Kelly (1938).

ALLEGHENY COUNTY CENTENNIAL SOUVENIR BOOK (1888).

ALLEGHENY COUNTY, PA., CENTENNIAL COMMITTEE, *Allegheny County: Its Early History and Subsequent Development*, by A. A. Lambing and J. W. F. White (1888).

ALLEN, FREDERICK LEWIS, *The Great Pierpont Morgan* (1949).

ALSHOUSE, H. S., and KLEIN, PHILIP, *Pennsylvania Pioneers* (1951).

ALVORD, C. W. (ed.), *The Critical Period, 1763-1765* (1915).

AMERICAN IRON AND STEEL INSTITUTE, Annual Statistical Reports.

AMORY, CLEVELAND, *Who Killed Society?* (1960)

ANDREWS, J. CUTLER, *Pittsburgh's Post-Gazette: The First Newspaper West of the Alleghenies* (1936).

ANNUAL REPORT OF THE ADJUTANT GENERAL OF PENNSYLVANIA (1878).
Contains reports of the military on the 1877 railroad riot.

BABBITT, E. L., *The Allegheny Pilot, Containing a Complete Chart of the Allegheny River* (1855).

BACON, EMERY F., *United Steelworkers of America: These Are Our People* (1956).

BAILEY, KENNETH P., *The Ohio Company of Virginia and the Westward Movement, 1748-1792* (1939).

——— (ed.), *The Ohio Company Papers, 1753–1817* (1947).

———, *Thomas Cresap, Maryland Frontiersman* (1944).

BAKEWELL, MARY ELLA, *Of Long Ago: The Children and the City* (1949).

BALDWIN, LELAND D., *The Keelboat Age on Western Waters* (1941).

———, *Pittsburgh: The Story of a City* (1937).

———, *Whiskey Rebels: The Story of a Frontier Uprising* (1939).

BEATTY, CHARLES, *Journal of a Two Months' Tour: With a View of Promoting Religion Among the Frontier Inhabitants of Pennsylvania* (London, 1768).

BEHRMAN, SAMUEL N., *Duveen* (1952).

BENTON, C. C., *Pittsburgh in Ye Olden Time* (1908).

BIGHAM, K. Q., *Major Abraham Kirkpatrick and His Descendants* (1911).

BINING, A. C., *Pennsylvania Iron Manufacture in the Eighteenth Century* (1938).

BISSONNETTE, WESLEY SMITH, *Pittsburgh, Songs of the Mother's Sons* (1926).

BLAIR, WALTER, and MEINE, FRANKLIN J. (eds.), *Half Horse, Half Alligator: The Growth of the Mike Fink Legend* (1956).

BOUCHER, JOHN N., *A Century and a Half of Pittsburgh and Her People* (1908).

BOUQUET, HENRY, *The Papers of Henry Bouquet*, edited by S. K. Stevens and D. H. Kent (Harrisburg, 1940–41; mimeographed).

———, *Papers of Henry Bouquet*, edited by S. K. Stevens and others (1952; vol. 2, Forbes Expedition).

BOWMAN, JOHN G., *The Cathedral of Learning of the University of Pittsburgh* (1925).

———, *Inside the Cathedral, the University of Pittsburgh* (1925).

———, *Nationality Rooms of the University of Pittsburgh*, with illustrations by Andrey Avinoff and Louis Orr (1947).

BRACKENRIDGE, HENRY M., *History of the Western Insurrection, Called the Whiskey Insurrection, 1794* (1859).
A vindication of the author's father for his part in the event.

———, *Recollections of Persons and Places in the West* (1834; enlarged and rev. ed., 1868).
Contains a description of Pittsburgh about 1800.

BRACKENRIDGE, HUGH H., *Gazette Publications* (1806).

———, *Incidents of the Insurrection in the Western Parts of Pennsylvania, in the Year 1794* (1795).

BRANTZ, LEWIS, *Memoranda of a Journey in the Western Parts of the United States in 1785 . . .* (1853).

BRASHEAR, JOHN A., *John A. Brashear: The Autobiography of a Man Who Loved the Stars* (1925).

BRIDGE, JAMES HOWARD, *The Inside History of the Carnegie Steel Company* (1903).

BROWN, LLOYD A., *Early Maps of the Ohio Valley* (1959).

BRUCE, ROBERT, *The National Road* (1916).

BUCK, SOLON J. and ELIZABETH H., *The Planting of Civilization in Western Pennsylvania* (1939).

BUHL FOUNDATION, *A Report by the Director upon Its Work to June 30, 1955* (1955).

BURGESS, ELLIS B., *Memorial History of the Pittsburgh Synod of the Evangelical Lutheran Church* (1926).

BURGOYNE, ARTHUR G., *All Sorts of Pittsburghers* (1892).

———, *Homestead. A Complete History of the Struggle of July 1892 . . .* (1893).

CARNEGIE, ANDREW, *An American Four-in-Hand in Britain* (1883).

———, *Autobiography*, edited by John C. Van Dyck (1920).

———, *The Empire of Business* (1902).

———, *The Gospel of Wealth* (1901).

——, *Problems of To-day* (1908).

——, *Triumphant Democracy* (1886; rev. ed., 1893).

CARNEGIE ENDOWMENT FOR INTERNATIONAL PEACE, *A Manual of the Public Benefactions of Andrew Carnegie* (1919).

CARNEGIE LIBRARY, PITTSBURGH, *Pittsburgh in 1816*, edited by Rose Demorest (1916).

——, *Pittsburgh 1758–1958*, by Rose Demorest (1958).

CARR, CHARLES C., *Alcoa, an American Enterprise* (1952).

CASSON, HERBERT N., *The Romance of Steel* (1907).

CÉLORON DE BLAINVILLE, P. J., "Journal," in Pierre Margry, *Exploration des affluents du Mississippi (Découvertes et établissements des Français dans l'ouest et dans le sud de l'Amérique septentrionale*, vol. 6; Paris, 1886). — English trans. in *Fort Pitt and Letters from the Frontier*, edited by Mary C. Darlington (1892).

CENTURY CYCLOPAEDIA OF HISTORY & BIOGRAPHY, "History of Western Pennsylvania Previous to the Civil War" (1910).

CHALFANT, ELLA, *A Goodly Heritage: Earliest Wills on an American Frontier* (1955).

CHANDLER, ALFRED D., JR., *Strategy and Structure: Chapters in the History of the Industrial Enterprise* (1962).

CHEVALIER, MICHEL, *Society, Manners and Politics in the United States* (1839).

CHURCH, SAMUEL HARDEN, *A Short History of Pittsburgh, 1758–1908* (1908).

CITY CHARTER CENTENNIAL EXHIBITION OF PORTRAITS AND VIEWS OF EARLY PITTSBURGH (1916). — Catalogue.

CIVIC CLUB OF ALLEGHENY COUNTY, *Fifteen Years of Civic History, October, 1895–December, 1910* (1911).

CLARK, VICTOR S., *History of Manufactures in the United States, 1607–1860* (rev. ed., 3 vols., 1929).

CLELAND, HUGH, *George Washington in the Ohio Valley* (1956).
Contains Washington's Journal of 1753 in facsimile.

COLDEN, CADWALLADER, *The History of the Five Indian Nations* (London, 3rd ed., 1755).

COLLOT, GEORGES H. V., *Voyage en Amérique septentrionale* (2 vols., Paris, 1826).
Contains a description of Pittsburgh. — English trans., *A Journey in North America (1796)* (Paris, 1826).

COMMAGER, HENRY STEELE, *The American Mind* (1950).

CONNOLLY, JOHN, *A Narrative of the Transactions, Imprisonment, and Sufferings of John Connolly, an American Loyalist* (London, 1783).

COTTER, ARUNDEL, *Authentic History of the U. S. Steel Corporation* (1916).

COWAN, JOHN P. (ed.), *Great Men: Their Esteem for a Great City* (1919).

COXE, TENCH, *A View of the United States of America, Written between 1787 and 1794* (1794).

CRAIG, NEVILLE B., *Exposure of a Few of the Many Misstatements in H. M. Brackenridge's History of the Whiskey Insurrection* (1859).

——, *The History of Pittsburgh* (1851; reprinted 1917).

——, *Lecture Upon the Controversy Between Pennsylvania and Virginia, about the Border Line* (1843).

—— (ed.), *The Olden Time* (1846–48).

CRAMER, ZADOK, *The Navigator . . . 1802–1824* (1802–24).

CROGHAN, GEORGE, *Journal of His Trip to Detroit in 1767*, edited by Howard H. Peckham (1939).

——, "Journal," in *Pennsylvania Archives*, first series, 3:560-563.
This journal describing a trip from Pittsburgh to the Beaver River is erroneously ascribed to Christian F. Post.

CUMING, FORTESQUE, *Sketches of a Tour to the Western Country (1807–1809)* (1810; reprinted in *Early Western Travels*, vol. 4, 1904).

DAHLINGER, CHARLES W., *Fort Pitt* (1922).

——, *Pittsburgh, a Sketch of Its Early Social Life* (1916).

DANIEL, DOROTHY, *Cut and Engraved Glass, 1771–1905* (1950).

DARLINGTON, M. C. (O'HARA), *Fort Pitt and Letters from the Frontier* (1892).

DAY, GEORGE C., *Sixty-one Years of Friendly Industrial Relationship* (1930).

DENNY, EBENEZER, *Military Journal of an Officer in the Revolution and Indian Wars, with Memoirs* (1859).

DENNY, WILLIAM H., *Suc-co-tash* (1858).

DENTON, FRANK R., *The Mellons of Pittsburgh* (1948).

DEUTSCHBERGER, PAUL, *Interaction Patterns in Changing Neighborhoods: New York and Pittsburgh* (1947).

DICKENS, CHARLES, *American Notes* (London, 1842).

DICTIONARY OF AMERICAN BIOGRAPHY, edited by Allen Johnson and Dumas Malone (20 vols., 1928–36).

DODDRIDGE, JOSEPH, *Notes on the Settlement and Indian Wars of the Western Parts of Virginia and Pennsylvania, from 1763 to 1783* (1824).

DOWNES, RANDOLPH C., *Council Fires on the Upper Ohio* (1940).

EAVENSON, HOWARD NICHOLAS, *The First Century and a Quarter of American Coal Industry* (1942).

——, *Map Maker & Indian Traders: An Account of John Patten . . .* (1949).

EGLE, WILLIAM H., *An Illustrated History of the Commonwealth of Pennsylvania . . .* (1876).

EPSTEIN, ABRAHAM, *The Negro Migrant in Pittsburgh* (1918).

ERRETT, RUSSEL, "Pittsburgh in 1829," in *Magazine of Western History* (1887-88).

EVANS, HENRY O., *Iron Pioneer: Henry W. Oliver* (1942).

EVANS, LEWIS, *Geographical, Historical, Political, Philosophical and Mechanical Essays. The First, Containing an Analysis of a General Map of the Middle British Colonies* (1755).

EYRE, JEHU, "Diary," in *Pennsylvania Magazine of History and Biography* (1879).

FAULKNER, HAROLD U., *The Decline of Laissez-Faire* (1951).

FERGUSON, RUSSELL J., *Early Western Pennsylvania Politics* (1938).

FERNOW, BERTHOLD, *The Ohio Valley in Colonial Days* (1890).

FINDLEY, WILLIAM, *History of the Insurrection, in the Four Western Counties of Pennsylvania in the Year 1794* (1796).

FISHER, SAMUEL J., *The Romance of Pittsburgh or Under Three Flags and Other Poems* (1916).

FLEMING, GEORGE T., *History of Pittsburgh and Environs* (4 vols., 1922).

——, *Pittsburgh, How to See It* (1916).

"FLEM'S" VIEWS OF OLD PITTSBURGH (1905).

FLINT, TIMOTHY, *Recollections of the Last Ten Years* (1826).

FREY, LAURA C., *The Land in the Fork: Pittsburgh 1753–1914* (1955).

GALBRAITH, JOHN K., *The Great Crash, 1929* (1954).

GALBREATH, CHARLES BURLEIGH (ed.), *Expeditions of Céloron to the Ohio Country in 1749* (1921).

GAUL, HARRIET A., and EISEMAN, RUBY, *John Alfred Brashear* (1940).

GERRY, ELBRIDGE, JR., *The Diary of Elbridge Gerry, Jr.*, with notes by Claude G. Bowers (c. 1927).
The account of a journey in 1813 by horseback from Massachusetts to Pittsburgh and into Ohio.

GIDDENS, P. H., *The Beginnings of the Petroleum Industry* (1941).

GIST, CHRISTOPHER, "A Journal of Christopher Gist's Journey from Col. Cresap's . . . on Potomack River . . . down the Ohio," in Thomas Pownall, *A Topographical Description of North America* (London, 1776).

———, *Journal of His Second Journey to the Ohio.*

———, "Journal of Mr. Christopher Gist, Who Accompanied Major George Washington in His First Visit to the French," edited by John Mease, in *Massachusetts Historical Collections* (3rd series, 1836).

The journals of Gist mentioned above are also printed in William M. Darlington (ed.), *Christopher Gist's Journals, with Historical, Geographical and Ethnological Notes* (1893).

GOMPERS, SAMUEL, *Seventy Years of Life and Labor* (1925).

GRACE, E. G., *Charles M. Schwab* (1947).

GREGG, O. ORMSBY, *Pittsburgh, Her Advantageous Position and Great Resources as a Manufacturing and Commercial City* (1845).

GRIDLEY, JARED, "An Ancient Letter — Journeying by Raft and Boat in Early Days," in *Firelands Pioneer* (new series, Dec. 1900).

An account of rafting on the Allegheny River to Pittsburgh and down the Ohio in 1818.

HALL, J. MORTON, *America's Industrial Centre: Pittsburgh's Great Industries . . .* (1891).

HARPER, FRANK C., *Men and Women of Wartime Pittsburgh* (1945).

———, *Pittsburgh: Forge of the Universe* (1957).

———, *Pittsburgh of Today: Its Resources and People* (4 vols., 1931).

HARRIS' PITTSBURGH BUSINESS DIRECTORY, FOR THE YEARS 1837-1844.

HARTZ, LOUIS, *Economic Policy and Democratic Thought* (1948).

HARVEY, GEORGE, *Henry Clay Frick, the Man* (1928).

HAYS, SAMUEL P., *The Response to Industrialism 1885-1914* (1957).

HENDRICK, BURTON J., *The Age of Big Business* (1921).

———, *History of the Telephone* (1910).

———, *The Life of Andrew Carnegie* (2 vols., 1932).

HICKS, JOHN D., *Republican Ascendancy 1921-1933* (1960).

HISTORICAL STATISTICS OF THE UNITED STATES (1960).

HISTORY OF ALLEGHENY COUNTY (L. H. Everts & Co., publishers, 1876).

HISTORY OF ALLEGHENY COUNTY (A. Warner & Co., publishers, 1889).

HODGES, FLETCHER, *A Pittsburgh Composer and His Memorial* (1938).

HOFSTADTER, RICHARD, *Social Darwinism in American Thought* (1944).

HOLBROOK, STEWART H., *The Age of the Moguls* (1953).

HOLLISTER, ISAAC, *A Brief Narration of the Captivity of Isaac Hollister* (1767?); reprinted in William H. Egle, *Contributions to Pennsylvania* (1890).

HONEST MAN'S EXTRA ALMANAC, THE (1813-24). — Pittsburgh. Almanacs under different titles: Cramer's Pittsburgh Almanack, Franklin Magazine Almanac, etc.

HUNTER, LOUIS C., *Steamboats on the Western Rivers* (1949).

INDUSTRIES AND WEALTH OF PITTSBURGH . . . (1890).

IRON CITY, THE: A COMPENDIUM OF FACTS CONCERNING PITTSBURGH AND VICINITY . . . APRIL, 1867 (1867).

JAMES, ALFRED P., and STOTZ, CHARLES M., *Drums in the Forest* (1958).

JOHNSON, WILLIAM GRAHAM, *Life and Reminiscences from Birth to Manhood* (1901).

JONES, ELIOT, *The Trust Problem in the United States* (1929).

JONES, SAMUEL, *Pittsburgh in the Year 1826* (1826).

JOSEPHSON, MATTHEW, *The Politicos, 1865-1896* (1938).

———, *The Robber Barons* (1934).

KANE, JOHN, *Sky Hooks: The Autobiography of John Kane* (1938).

KELLOGG, PAUL U., *Civic Responsibilities of Democracy in an Industrial District* (1908).

KELLY, J. M., *Handbook of Greater Pittsburg* (1st annual ed., 1895).

KENNY, JAMES, "Journal," in *Pennsylvania Magazine of History and Biography* (1913).

———, "Journal to Ye Westward," in *Pennsylvania Magazine of History and Biography* (1913).

KILLIKELLY, SARAH H., *The History of Pittsburgh* (1906).

KING, J. TRAINOR, *Pittsburgh, Past and Present* (1868).

KING, SIDNEY A. (compiler), *The Story of the Sesqui-Centennial Celebration of Pittsburgh, July 4, Sept. 27 to Oct. 3, and Nov. 25, 1908* (1910).

KIRKLAND, EDWARD C., *Dream and Thought in the Business Community* (1956).

———, *A History of American Economic Life* (1947; 3rd ed., 1951).

KLEIN, BENJAMIN (ed.), *The Ohio River Handbook and Picture Album* (1950; new edition, with Eleanor Klein, 1954).

KLEIN, PHILIP, *A Social Study of Pittsburgh: Community Problems and Social Services of Allegheny County* (1938).

KOCH, THOMAS WESLEY, *A Book of Carnegie Libraries* (1917).

KUSSART, SAREPTA, *The Early History of the 15th Ward of the City of Pittsburgh* (1925).

LAMBING, ANDREW A., and WHITE, J. W. F., *Allegheny County: Its Early History and Subsequent Development, from the Earliest Period till 1790* (1888).

LATHROP, ELISE, *Early American Inns and Taverns* (1926).

LEE, RICHARD HENRY, *Life of Arthur Lee* (1829).

LELAND, WALDO G., "Lesueur Collection," in *Mississippi Valley Historical Review* (1923).

LEWIS, VIRGINIA E., *Russell Smith: Romantic Realist* (1956).

LIEB, FREDERICK G., *The Pittsburgh Pirates* (1948).

LOEWENBERG, BERT J., and others, *Darwinism — Reaction or Reform?* (1957).

LOIR, ADRIEN, *Charles A. Lesueur, Artist et savant français en Amérique de 1816-1839* (Le Havre, 1920).

LONG, HANIEL, *Pittsburgh Memoranda* (1935).

LORANT, STEFAN, *The Presidency* (1951).

———, *F.D.R., a pictorial biography* (1950).

———, *The Life and Times of Theodore Roosevelt* (1959).

LOVE, PHILIP H., *Andrew W. Mellon* (1929).

McCAFFERTY, E. D., *Henry J. Heinz* (1923).

MACARTNEY, CLARENCE E., *Right Here in Pittsburgh* (1937).

McCLINTOCK, CHARLES A., *Pittsburgh, Her Industrial Adolescence, 1760-1840* (1947).

McNAIR, H. V., *Pittsburgh: A Sonnet Sequence* (1925).

MAGAZINE OF WESTERN HISTORY; 1884-1892. The Oct. 1885 issue contains sketches of early Pittsburgh and western Pennsylvania; growth of the iron and steel business.

MARSH, DANIEL L., *The Challenge of Pittsburgh* (1917).

MARTIN, EDWARD W. (pseud. for J. D. McCabe), *The History of the Great Riots* (1877).

MATHEWS, PHILIP, *History of the Pittsburgh Bureau of Governmental Research* (1936).

MELISH, JOHN, *Travels through the United States of America, in the Years 1806 & 1807; and 1809, 1810, & 1811* (1818).

MELLON, THOMAS, *Thomas Mellon and His Times* (1885).

MERCER, GEORGE, *George Mercer Papers Relating to the Ohio Company of Virginia*, edited by Lois Mulkearn (1954).

MERCY HOSPITAL, *The Footprints of Mercy, 1847–1947* (1947).

MICHAUX, FRANCOIS ANDRE, "Portions of the Journal of André Michaux," edited by C. S. Sargent, in American Philosophical Society *Proceedings* (1889). — English trans. in part in *Early Western Travels*, 3:25–104.

    An account of the travels of a botanist from Philadelphia to Pittsburgh and thence down the Ohio.

———, *Travels to the Westward of the Allegany Mountains in Ohio, Kentucky and Tennessee and Return to Charlestown Through the Upper Carolinas, 1802.* — Trans. from the French by B. Lambert (London, 1805).

MILLER, ANNIE C., *Chronicles of Families, Houses and Estates of Pittsburgh and Its Environs* (1927).

———, *Early Land Marks and Old Names in Pittsburgh* (1924).

MILLER, DOROTHY, *The Life and Work of David G. Blythe* (1950).

MILLER, JAMES M., *The Genesis of Western Culture, the Upper Ohio Valley, 1800–1825* (1938).

MILLER, WILLIAM, and COCHRAN, THOMAS C., *The Age of Enterprise* (1942).

MOORHEAD, ELIZABETH, *Whirling Spindle: The Story of a Pittsburgh Family* (1942).

MORGAN, GEORGE, "Journal," in *Trade and Politics, 1767–1769*, by Clarence W. Alvord and Clarence E. Carter (*Illinois Historical Collections*, 1921).

    Morgan was a member of the firm of Bayton, Wharton, and Morgan; his journal describes a trip from Philadelphia to Fort Pitt.

MORISON, S. E., and COMMAGER, H. S., *The Growth of the American Republic* (2 vols.; 5th rev. ed., 1963).

MORNEWECK, EVELYN F., *Chronicles of Stephen Foster's Family* (2 vols., 1944).

MOSES, ROBERT, *Arterial Plan for Pittsburgh* (1939).

MUHLENBERG, PETER, "Journal," in *The Life of Major-General Peter Muhlenberg of the Revolutionary Army*, by Henry A. Muhlenberg (1849).

MULKEARN, LOIS, and PUGH, EDWIN V., *A Traveler's Guide to Historic Western Pennsylvania* (1954).

    The volume contains an excellent detailed bibliography.

MYERS, GUSTAVUS, *History of the Great American Fortunes* (1936).

NATIONAL URBAN LEAGUE, *Social Conditions of the Negro in the Hill District of Pittsburgh* (1930).

NEVIN, ADELAIDE MELLIER, *The Social Mirror: A Character Sketch of the Women of Pittsburgh and Vicinity during the First Century of the Country's Existence* (1888).

NEVIN, THEODORE W., *Pittsburgh and the Men Who Made It* (1904).

NEVINS, ALLAN, *The Emergence of Modern America 1865–1878* (1927).

NEWLIN, C. M., *The Life and Writings of Hugh Henry Brackenridge* (1932).

O'CONNOR, HARVEY, *Mellon's Millions* (1933).

OLMSTEAD, FREDERICK, *Pittsburgh, Main Thorofares and the Down Town District* (1911).

ORME, ROBERT, "Journal," in *The History of an Expedition against Fort Du Quesne, in 1755*, edited by Winthrop Sargent (1855).

PALMER, R. M., *Palmer's Pictorial Pittsburgh and Prominent Pittsburghers Past and Present 1758–1905* (1905).

———, *Palmer's Views of Pittsburgh* (1903).

PARKE, JOHN E., *Recollections of Seventy Years and Historical Gleanings of Allegheny, Pa.* (1886).

PARKMAN, FRANCIS, *The Conspiracy of Pontiac and the Indian War after the Conquest of Canada* (1898).

———, *Montcalm and Wolfe*, (2 vols., 1884). — Reprinted in *France and England in North America* (3 vols., 1915).

PARRISH, JOHN, "Extracts from the Journal of John Parrish," in *Pennsylvania Magazine of History and Biography* (1892).

    The journal of a Quaker missionary describing religious conditions of western Pennsylvania.

PASSER, HAROLD C., *The Electrical Manufacturers 1875–1900* (1953).

PENNSYLVANIA WRITERS' PROJECT, *Guide to the Keystone State* (1940).

———, *Pennsylvania Cavalcade* (1942).

PEN PICTURES OF EARLY WESTERN PENNSYLVANIA, edited by John W. Harpster (1938).

    Contains reprints from the Journal of Conrad Weiser, 1748, from the Account of Father Bonnecamps, 1749, from the Journal of George Washington, 1753, from the Account of James Smith, 1775, from the Journal of James Kenny, 1759–63, from the Journal of William Trent, 1763, from the Journal of Arthur Lee, 1784, the description of Pittsburgh in 1829 by Russel Errett, and other contemporary accounts.

PERLMAN, SELIG, *A History of Trade Unionism in the United States* (1922).

PHILLIPS, MARIE, *Pittsburgh Saga: Braddock's Defeat, Bouquet's Victory, 1748–1764* (1951).

———, *Ten Thousand Candles: A Souvenir of Pittsburgh* (1931).

PINKERTON'S NATIONAL DETECTIVE AGENCY . . . (1892).

    A reprint of testimony presented before the House and Senate committees, together with other material.

PITTSBURGH AND ALLEGHENY ILLUSTRATED REVIEW: HISTORICAL, BIOGRAPHICAL AND COMMERCIAL (J. M. Elstner & Co., publishers, 1889).

PITTSBURGH CHAMBER OF COMMERCE, *Characteristics of Population in the Pittsburgh District* (1927).

———, *Fifty Years of the Chamber of Commerce of Pittsburgh, 1874–1924* (1924).

———, *Greater Pittsburgh* (Feb. 1949).

    A seventy-fifth anniversary issue commemorating the founding of the Chamber of Commerce.

———, *Pittsburgh and the Lake Cities: The St. Lawrence Seaway and Its Potential Impact* (1956).

———, *Pittsburgh and the Pittsburgh Spirit, 1927–1928* (1928).

———, *Pittsburgh and the Seaway* (1956).

———, *Pittsburgh and Western Pennsylvania: Their Institutions and Commerce, Resources and Prospects* (1885).

———, *Pittsburgh, the Gateway between East and West: The Convention City* (1918).

———, *Pittsburgh the Powerful*, edited by Edward White (1907).

PITTSBURGH CHRONICLE-TELEGRAPH, *The Cities of Pittsburgh and Allegheny and Their Resources* (1889).

PITTSBURGH DIRECTORY for 1813; also for 1815, compiled by James M. Riddle, continued to 1847.

PITTSBURGH GAZETTE TIMES, *The Story of Pittsburgh and Vicinity* (1908).

PITTSBURGH INDUSTRIAL DEVELOPMENT COMMISSION, *Pittsburgh: Municipal Improvements Recently Completed, under Construction, and Provided for* (1913).

———, *The Real Pittsburgh: Facts and Figures* (1913).

———, *Where Business Centers* (1913).

PITTSBURGH POST-GAZETTE, *Cinderella City* (special section, June 30, 1953).

———, *A Pittsburgh Album, 1758–1958,* edited by Roy Stryker and Mel Seidenberg (1959).

———, *1786–1936: One Hundred Fifty Years of Papers* (anniversary issue, Sept. 26, 1936).

———, *The Tri-State Story* (special supplement, June 15, 1957).

PITTSBURGH PRESS, *Pittsburgh's Renaissance 1936–1953: The Story of Sixteen Years of Progress* (special supplement, Dec. 13, 1953).

———, *First 200 Years . . . from Fort Pitt to Point State Park* (bicentennial issue, Jan. 18, 1959).

PITTSBURGH PRESS CLUB, *Prominent Men of Pittsburgh and Vicinity, 1912–1913* (1914?).

PITTSBURGH REGIONAL PLANNING ASSOCIATION, *North Side Study* (April 1954).

PITTSBURGH STOCK EXCHANGE, *1894–1929* (1929).

PITTSBURGH SUN-TELEGRAPH, *This Is Pittsburgh — 1953* (special supplement, Nov. 8, 1953).

———, *Yesterday, Today & Tomorrow — 1758–1958 Pittsburgh Bicentennial,* (special supplement, Dec. 9, 1958).

PITTSBURGH SURVEY — FINDINGS IN SIX VOLUMES, edited by Paul U. Kellogg (1909–14):

The Pittsburgh District, by various authors.

Wage-Earning in Pittsburgh, by various authors.

Women and the Trades, by Elizabeth B. Butler.

Work-Accidents and the Law, by Crystal Eastman.

Homestead: The Household of a Mill Town, by Margaret F. Byington.

The Steel Workers, by John A. Fitch.

POWER, TYRONE, *Impressions of America* (2 vols., 1836).

PROUT, HENRY G., *A Life of George Westinghouse* (1926).

REID, W. J., *History of the First United Presbyterian Church of Pittsburgh, Pa., 1801–1901.*

REISER, CATHERINE ELIZABETH, *Pittsburgh's Commercial Development 1800–1850* (1951).

ROLLING MILLS, ROLLS, AND ROLL MAKING: A BRIEF HISTORICAL ACCOUNT OF THEIR DEVELOPMENT FROM THE FIFTEENTH CENTURY TO THE PRESENT DAY (Mackintosh-Hemphill Company, publishers, 1953).

ROYALL, ANNE, *Mrs. Royall's Pennsylvania, or, Travels Continued in the United States* (2 vols., 1829).

RUPP, I. D., *Early History of Western Pennsylvania* (1846).

SARGENT, WINTHROP, *The History of an Expedition against Fort Du Quesne, in 1755* (1855).

SCHLESINGER, ARTHUR M., *The Rise of the City 1878–1898* (1933).

SCHOEPF, JOHANN DAVID, *Travels in the Confederation 1783–1784* (2 vols., Erlangen, 1788). — Trans. and edited by Alfred J. Morrison (1911).

SCHOOLCRAFT, HENRY R., *The American Indians, Their History, Condition and Prospects* (1850).

SCHOYER, WILLIAM T., *A Century of Saving Dollars 1855–1955: Being the True and Unusual Story of How The Dollar Bank Pioneered in Making Thrift Practical for Pittsburghers* (1955).

———, *Scaife Company and the Scaife Family, 1802–1952* (1952).

SCHRIFTGIESSER, KARL, *Families* (1940).

SEARIGHT, THOMAS B., *The Old Pike: A History of the National Road* (1894).

SHANNON, FRED A., *The Farmer's Last Frontier* (1945).

SHEPPARD, MURIEL EARLEY, *Cloud by Day: The Story of Coal and Coke and People* (1947).

SIPES, WILLIAM B., *The Pennsylvania Railroad* (1875).

SLATTERY, C. L., *Felix Reville Brunot, 1820–1898* (1901).

SMELTZER, WALLACE G., *Methodism on the Headwaters of the Ohio: The History of the Pittsburgh Conference of the Methodist Church* (1951).

SMITH, COLONEL JAMES, *An Account of the Remarkable Occurrences in the Life and Travels of Colonel James Smith during His Captivity with the Indians in the Years 1755, '56, '57, '58 & '59* (Lexington, 1799).

SMITH, PERCY FRAZER, *Memory's Milestones: Reminiscences of Seventy Years of a Busy Life in Pittsburgh* (1918).

SMITH, WILLIAM, *An Historical Account of the Expedition against the Ohio Indians, in the Year 1764, under the Command of Henry Bouquet* (1765; reprinted in *Ohio Valley Historical Series,* 1868).

This account of an expedition from Fort Pitt to the Muskingum has also been ascribed to Thomas Hutchins.

SOULE, GEORGE, *Prosperity Decade* (1947).

STARRETT, AGNES L., *Through One Hundred and Fifty Years: The University of Pittsburgh* (1937).

STARRETT, MARY M., *Pioneer Women of Western Pennsylvania* (thesis, 1931).

STEFFENS, LINCOLN, *The Shame of the Cities* (1904).

STOCKING, GEORGE, *Basing Point Pricing and Regional Development: A Case Study of the Iron and Steel Industry* (1954).

STOTZ, CHARLES M., *The Early Architecture of Western Pennsylvania* (1936).

STOWELL, M. R., *"Fort Frick", or, The Siege of Homestead* (1893).

STRONG, JOSIAH, *Our Country* (1885).

SULLIVAN, MARK, *Our Times* (6 vols., 1926–35).

SULLIVAN, WILLIAM, *The Industrial Worker in Pennsylvania 1800–1840* (1955).

SWANK, EDITH ELLIOTT, *The Story of Food Preservation* (1942).

SWANK, J. M., *History of the Manufacture of Iron in All Ages* (1892).

SWETNAM, GEORGE, *The Bicentennial History of Pittsburgh and Allegheny County* (1958).

———, *Pitsylvania Country* (1951).

———, *Where Else but Pittsburgh!* (1958).

Mr. Swetnam has contributed numerous articles on the city's history and on prominent Pittsburgh personalities to the *Family Magazine* and to the *Roto Magazine* of the *Pittsburgh Press.* The range of his subjects is wide, and he writes well and knowledgeably on his themes.

SWISSHELM, JANE GREY, *Half a Century* (1880).

TAFT, PHILIP, *The A F of L* (2 vols., 1957–59).

TARBELL, ARTHUR W., *The Story of Carnegie Tech* (1937).

TAYLOR, GEORGE R., *The Transportation Revolution* (1951).

THURSTON, G. H., *Allegheny County's Hundred Years* (1888).

———, *Pittsburgh and Allegheny in the Centennial Year* (1886).

———, *Pittsburgh as It Is* (1857).

———, *Pittsburgh's Progress, Industries and Resources* (1886).

THWAITES, REUBEN G. (ed.), *Documentary History of Dunmore's War, 1774* (1905).

———, *Early Western Travels* (1904).

——— (ed.), *Frontier Defense on the Upper Ohio*, (1912).

——— (ed.), *The Revolution on the Upper Ohio*, (1908).

TOWN & COUNTRY, *Pittsburgh: A Man's Town* (special issue, March 1959).

TRENT, WILLIAM, *Journal of . . . 1752*, edited by A. T. Goodman (1871).

TURNER, FREDERICK J., *The Frontier in American History* (1920).

UNITED STATES WORKS PROGRESS ADMINISTRATION, *The Story of Old Allegheny City* (1941).

UNITED STATES WORKS PROGRESS ADMINISTRATION OF PITTSBURGH, *Tales of Pioneer Pittsburgh* (1937).

UNIVERSITY OF PITTSBURGH, *The University and the War* (1918).

———, *Training to Win*, by Agnes L. Starrett (1943).

VAIL, R. W. G., *The American Sketchbooks of Charles Alexander Lesueur 1816–1837* (1938).

VAN VOORHIS, J. S., *The Old and New Monongahela* (1893).

VEACH, JAMES, *Mason and Dixon's Line, a History* (1857).

———, *The Monongahela of Old* (1858-92).

VERMORCHEN, ELIZABETH M., *Pittsburgh Portraits* (1955).

VOLWILER, A. T., *George Croghan and the Western Movement, 1741–1782* (1926).

WADE, RICHARD C., *The Urban Frontier* (1959).

WAINRIGHT, NICHOLAS B., *George Croghan: Wilderness Diplomat* (1959).

WALLACE, P. A. W., *Conrad Weiser, 1696–1760, Friend of Colonist and Mohawk* (1945).

WALLER, J. H., (ed.), *Rafting Days in Pennsylvania* (1922).

WASHBURN, W. S., *Sketches, Serious and Otherwise: Men of Pittsburgh and Vicinity* (1914).

WASHINGTON, GEORGE, *The Diaries of George Washington, 1748–1799*, edited by J. C. Fitzpatrick (1925).

———, *The Journal of Major George Washington . . . to the Commandant of the French Forces on Ohio* (Williamsburg and London, 1754).

WEINBERG, ARTHUR and LILA, *The Muckrakers* (1961).

WEISER, CONRAD, "The Journal of Conrad Weiser," in *Early History of Western Pennsylvania, and of the West*, by Israel D. Rupp (1846).

WESTERN PENNSYLVANIA HISTORICAL MAGAZINE (Pittsburgh, 1918 to the present).

———, Addresses celebrating the 125th anniversary of the incorporation of Pittsburgh as a borough (vol. 2).

———, Anderson, Edward Park, "The Intellectual Life of Pittsburgh, 1786–1836" (vol. 14).

———, Benswanger, William E., "Professional Baseball in Pittsburgh" (vol. 30).

———, Crall, F. Frank, "A Half Century of Rivalry between Pittsburgh and Wheeling" (vol. 13).

———, Ewing, Robert M., "Washington's Western Journeys and their Relation to Pittsburgh" (vol. 5).

———, McKeever, E. M., "Earlier Lawrenceville" (vol. 5).

———, Oliver, John W., "Pittsburgh's Reawakening One Hundred Years Ago" (vol. 13).

———, Potter, J. E., "The Place of Pittsburgh in History" (vol. 9).

———, Sheedy, Morgan M., "Ten Years on Historic Ground. Early and Late Days at the Pittsburgh Point" (vol. 5).

———, Siebert, P. W., "Old Bayardstown" (vol. 9).

———, Simpson, Mrs. C., "Reminiscences of Early Pittsburgh" (vol. 4).

———, Tefft, B. F., "Pittsburgh in 1848" (vol. 17).

WESTERN PENNSYLVANIA HISTORICAL SURVEY, *Guidebook to Historic Places in Western Pennsylvania* (1938).

WHITE, EDWARD, *One Hundred and Fifty Years of Unparalleled Thrift* (1908).

WILEY, RICHARD T., *The Whiskey Rebellion* (1912).

WILLIS, WILLIAM G., *The Pittsburgh Manual: A Guide to the Government of the City of Pittsburgh* (1950).

WILSON, ERASMUS (ed.), *Standard History of Pittsburg* (1898).

WILSON, MARGARET B., *A Carnegie Anthology* (1915).

WINKLER, JOHN K., *Incredible Carnegie* (1931).

WRIGHT, J. E., and CORBETT, DORIS S., *Pioneer Life in Western Pennsylvania* (1940).

WRIGHT, J. E., SELLERS, ELISABETH M., and SHIRK, JEANETTE C., *With Rifle & Plow* (1938).

YELLEN, SAMUEL, *American Labor Struggles* (1936).

ZINK, HAROLD, *City Bosses in the United States* (1930).

PUBLICATIONS BETWEEN 1963 AND 1987

ALBERTS, ROBERT C., *The Good Provider, H. J. Heinz* (1973).

———, *Pitt, The Story of the University of Pittsburgh 1787–1987* (1986).

———, *The Shaping of the Point: Pittsburgh's Renaissance Park* (1980).

ANDREWS, J. CUTLER, *Pittsburgh History 1865–1971* (1971).

ARKUS, LEON ANTHONY (comp.), *John Kane, Painter* (1971).

ACADEMY OF TRIAL LAWYERS OF ALLEGHENY COUNTY, *Court of Common Pleas of Allegheny County, Pa.*

———, *Federal Court System in Western Pennsylvania* (1972).

BOROWSKI, JOSEPH A. (comp.), *Historical Highlights and Sites of Lawrenceville Area* (1969).

BRIGGS, ADRIAN J., *A Chronological History of Allegheny County* (1969).

BUNI, ANDREW, *Robert L. Vann of the Pittsburgh Courier* (1974).

BURTT, RICHARD L., *The Pittsburgh Pirates: A Pictoral History* (1977).

BYRNE, KATHLEEN D., *Chrysalis, Willa Cather in Pittsburgh, 1896–1906* (1980).

CAREY, JOSIE (Illustrated by Marty Wolfson), *This is Pittsburgh and Southwestern Pennsylvania* (1963–64).

CHASS, MURRAY, *Pittsburgh's Steelers: The Long Climb* (1973).

COUVARES, FRANCIS G., *The Remaking of Pittsburgh: Class and Culture in an Industrializing City, 1877–1919* (1984).

DIDINGER, RAY, *Pittsburgh Steelers* (1974).

EDMUNDS, ARTHUR J., *Daybreakers, the story of the Urban League of Pittsburgh: The First Sixty-Five Years* (1983).

ELKUS, LEONORE R., *Famous Men and Women of Pittsburgh* (1981).

GAGETTA, VINCE, *Pittsburgh, Fulfilling its Destiny* (1986).

GAY, VERNON, *Discovering Pittsburgh's Sculpture* (1983).

HAZO, SAMUEL, *The Pittsburgh that starts within you* (1986).

HILLER, JACK L., *Morningside: An Urban Community* (1969).

HOFFMAN, WILLIAM S., *Paul Mellon* (1974).

HORSBROUGH, PATRICK, *Pittsburgh Perceived* (1963).

JOHNSTON, WILLIAM GRAHAM, *Life and Reminiscences from Birth to Manhood of William G. Johnston* (1968).

KAUFMANN, EDGAR JR., *Fallingwater: A Frank Lloyd Wright Country House* (1986).

KENNET, ANDREA AND SHANGLE, ROBERT D., *Beautiful Pittsburgh* (1979).

Kidney, Walter C., *The Three Rivers* (1982).

Klein, Barbara and Roscow, Judith, *Dining in—Pittsburgh* (1982).

Krause, Corinne Azen, *Isaac W. Frank, Industrialist and Civic Leader, 1855–1930* (1984).

Lubove, Roy, *Twentieth Century Pittsburgh* (1969).

Maloney, Margaret E., *Fag on bealach: The Irish Contribution to America and in Particular to Western Pennsylvania* (1977).

Morris, Carl, *Black Mood in Pittsburgh* (1968).

Ohler, Samuel R., *Pittsburgh Inclines* (1972).

———, *PittsburGraphics: Graphic Studies in Paragraphs and Pictures Pertaining to Pittsburgh, Pennsylvania* (1983).

Pattison, Ric and Sutherland, Neil, *Pittsburgh, a Picture Book to Remember Her By* (1986).

Peebles, Sheila, *History of the Pittsburgh State, 1891–1896* (1973).

Pittsburgh Renaissance: *Transcription of Interviews on the Pittsburgh Renaissance, oral history program financed by Buhl Foundation* (1973).

Pittsburgh History and Landmarks Foundation, *Stones of Pittsburgh, No. V* (1967).

Rimmel, William M., *The Allegheny Story* (1981).

Spencer, Ethel, *The Spencers of Amberson Avenue: A Turn-of-the-Century Memoir* (1983).

Stave, Bruce M., *The New Deal and the Last Hurrah: Pittsburgh Machine Politics* (1970).

Szala, John R. B., *Flags of the City of Pittsburgh* (1970).

Toker, Franklin, *Pittsburgh: An Urban Portrait* (1986).

Van Trump, James Denholm, *Life and Architecture in Pittsburgh* (1983).

Vexler, Robert I., *Pittsburgh: A Chronological and Documentary History, 1682–1976* (1977).

Williams, Melvin D., *Community in a Black Pentecostal Church: An Anthropological Study* (1974).

Photographs in 1987 by Norman W. Schumm

SENIOR CITIZENS AT THE BAPTIST OLD AGE HOME IN NEW LEBANON

Photograph by Pamela Z. Bryan

THE OLD AND THE NEW AT MARKET SQUARE IN DOWNTOWN

PITTSBURGH
The Story of an American City
by
Stefan Lorant

Reviews of the first edition:

ALABAMA

"Few books of this nature have impressed us as has this magnificent study of Pittsburgh, an immense and breath-taking work by an outstanding author, Stefan Lorant.

"One cannot argue that it probably is the most beautiful book ever produced on an American city with its more than 1000 illustrations (many in full color) and some 200,000 words of text." — *Anniston Star*

CALIFORNIA

"Mr. Lorant, an artist with discernment and skill, has managed . . . to show that Pittsburgh has been a city of achievement, a place in which a powerful sense of public duty has brought enormous advancements and an example of American civic potentiality. The book is a large and tastefully composed work, of importance for an historic view point, and one that will be useful as a reference work on the growth of municipal pride and accomplishment." — *Bakersfield Californian*

". . . this is more than the history of one city; it is the story of most American cities. Those who want to find out how a city can transform itself will be captivated by the book. Those who want good stories, entertainment and solid, readable history can find them here. Lorant's volume is a thoroughly researched tale of an American city, a thrilling account of growth and greatness." — *San Bernardino Sun*

"It is hard not to speak in superlatives about this volume. While it tells the story of Pittsburgh's progress and accomplishments, it does not flatter and it does not bend the truth. The blemishes are here along with the glories." — *Altadena Pasadenan*

"As a history, it is a magnificent presentation of a city's rise to greatness." — Fresno *Bee*

"*Pittsburgh* is not only a history of that city, but also an anthology of excellent historical writing, a portfolio of over 1000 pictures and, in quintessence, the story of America itself . . . a king-sized volume in all respects . . . a must for any Pittsburgher — wherever he may live now. It is also an impressive contribution to history in general." — *Los Angeles Herald-Examiner*

". . . *Pittsburgh* is a heroic editorial approach to an important American region as well as a spirited social, cultural and industrial history." — *San Francisco Chronicle*

COLORADO

"All right, you beautiful cities of America, Make room for Pittsburgh. . . . For it is more than a history of a city. It is, in a larger sense, the history of a nation." — *Denver: Rocky Mountain News*

CONNECTICUT

"Stefan Lorant successfully condenses many volumes of material to create a work that has more life and interest than a pure history could achieve." — *New Haven Register*

"This is a remarkable and beautiful book. It is the story of a city in prose and pictures, and it is probably the best piece of work ever done on an American community. . . . Lorant has done a magnificent job in this mammoth book." — *Hartford Courant*

DELAWARE

". . . it has just about everything there is to be known about Pittsburgh, past and present. . . . To assemble this magnificent collection of illustrations Lorant spent years of research both here and abroad and it was time well spent." — *Wilmington News*

DISTRICT OF COLUMBIA

". . . one hardly needs to be madly in love in Pittsburgh or a collector of bibliophile's treasures (in this case at a remarkably low price) to find the book interesting and well worth the time one must invest in it. . . ." — *Washington Star*

FLORIDA

". . . it is superb. This is a fabulous book, and perhaps the forerunner of books about other cities." — *Melbourne Times*

"Stefan Lorant has created a magnificent monument to Pittsburgh, the great steel city." — *Pensacola Journal*

GEORGIA

"*Pittsburgh, the Story of an American City* is the story of our century, its mistakes, its fashions, its ambitions, its disappointments, its shame, its greed and its great triumphs. And somehow our generation gains stature and dignity from the Book." — Dorothy Daniel: *The Quitnam Free Press*

IDAHO

"People can learn much from such a book. With intelligent planning we can avoid many of the mistakes of the older communties and lay the groundwork for sensible and constructive development." — *Pocatello State Journal*

ILLINOIS

"It is dangerous, but irresistible, to say that the book has everything in it . . . a monumental work." — Robert Cromie, *Chicago Tribune*

". . . surprisingly successful in its integrated portrayal of an industrial city. The development of the encyclopaedic story, with its kaleidoscope of disparate factors and influences, is always controlled and focussed. — *Chicago Daily News*

"This book is extraordinary for several reasons . . . all the contributors, but especially Lorant, write with verve, and complement their offerings with a stunning profusion of well-selected art and photos. . . . In short, this is undoubtedly the finest biography of a city I've encountered." — Roy Newquist, *Chicago American*

"Surely one of the most beautiful and comprehensive

books ever compiled about any American city, it is a monumental accomplishment. . . ."
— *Quincy Herald-Whig*

INDIANA

"Probably the handsomest book ever devoted to one American city is called, oddly enough, *Pittsburgh, the Story of an American City.* . . . Those interested in urban renewal, history and a lively, entertaining biography of a city may find it here."
— *Evansville Press*

". . . a heroic editorial approach to an important American region as well as a spirited social, cultural and industrial history."
— *Indianapolis Times*

". . . a magnificent history, well edited, beautifully illustrated, wrapped up in an attractive, forceful layout. Even readers with no personal interest in the city will find the book interesting."
— *LaFayette Journal & Courier*

IOWA

"The story behind the forces motivating creation of a volume so bold and colorful as to pale into insignificance similar ventures. . . .
— *Sioux City Morning Journal*

". . . a history book that tells a vivid story on every page. . . . What happened in Pittsburgh is the story of America all over again, of course, and there is no more thrilling story in the history of the world."
— *Cedar Rapids Gazette*

LOUISIANA

"The volume is carefully and painstakingly put together; it is exquisitely printed and well and skillfully written . . . a thrilling account of modern day America's way of meeting its problems."
— *Baton Rouge Advocate*

MARYLAND

"This handsome history of Pittsburgh was ten years in the making and is worth every bit of the time. .

"This book is more than a history of Pittsburgh — it is a miniature but rich chronology of industrial America."
— *Baltimore Evening Sun*

MASSACHUSETTS

". . . a beautifully executed book . . . a remarkably fine job."
— Alice Dixon Bond, *Boston Sunday Herald*

"Not only Pittsburgh natives but anyone who reads it will be proud of this book and the civic spirit it celebrates."
— *Boston Traveler*

". . . this monumental and amazing book . . . demolishes the ugly duckling image of Pittsburgh among American cities which still lingers in the imaginations or residents of the Eastern coastal plain . . . a terrific book about an American city."
— Cardinal John Wright, *Boston Morning Globe*

". . . remarkable."
— *Springfield Republican*

". . . not a whitewash or propaganda job; it describes both the glorious and not so glorious parts of Pittsburgh's record. . . ."
— *The Cambridge Chronicle*

"It is a great book that Stefan Lorant has given us."
— *Provincetown Advocate*

"It is, from start to finish, a fascinating account of an American city."
— *Christian Science Monitor*

"It's history with an extraordinary sheen, blended with stuff easy on the eye and firm with the truth."
— *Worcester Telegram*

"*Pittsburgh* is a majestic book comprising a superlative effort in editing, compilation, research and writing. . . .
— *Holyoke Transcript-Telegram*

MICHIGAN

"Former residents of the Pittsburgh area or anyone interested in the portrayal of a great city will find this work of exceptional interest. . . . A great salute, done with taste and intelligence, to one of America's great communities."
— *Detroit News*

MINNESOTA

"For residents of Pittsburgh the book is a personal treasure. For residents of every city in the country it is an inspiring history."
— *St. Paul Pioneer Press*

MISSOURI

". . . a magnificent bouquet to a magnificent city, of interest to non-Pittsburghers as well as the natives because of its study in depth. Stefan Lorant . . . with a magic touch for publications, was somehow induced to spend 10 years on the story and it is bountifully illustrated. . . ."
— *St. Louis Post-Dispatch*

"Anyone who may be planning a story of Kansas City should look into this to see how magnificently it can be done."
— *Kansas City Star*

NEBRASKA

". . . a tremendous one-volume history that probably is unmatched by any other American city today. The book is a contribution to scholarly history and to the graphic arts. It is an example of American enterprise at its very best."
— *Lincoln Journal-Star*

NEW HAMPSHIRE

". . . superlative erudition, editorial finesse and exuberant art . . . a superlative book. . . ."
— *Union Leader*

NEW JERSEY

". . . the most beautiful book ever produced on an American city."
— *Hudson Dispatch*

"Few, if any, modern cities can boast of such a comprehensive account of its past, present and future . . ."
— *Morristown Record*

NEW YORK

"The whole tumultuous story of Pittsburgh, magnificently illustrated . . . is presented in this volume . . . the story of the metamorphosis is all here — the bloody struggles of the 19th century, the grit and smoke, the politics, the toil, the sweat — the imagination."
— Harrison E. Salisbury, *The New York Times*

"A giant of a book . . . a skillful compilation of reproductions from many sources, all covering Pittsburgh's eventful 200-year history."
— Jacob Deschin, *The New York Sunday Times*

"Pittsburgh is a storied city, and its story is brightly told in this book big in text and pictures."
— *New York World-Telegram*

"It is certainly one of the most fascinatingly detailed pictures histories yet attempted of any city anywhere. For readability, thoroughness (ten years of research went into it), graphic quality, and broad scope (it covers political and social history, daily life, labor, problems, architecture and what have you), this is a model history of an American city."
— *Publishers' Weekly*

"A fascinating panoramic view of Pittsburgh's history from the early 18th century to the present."
— *New York Post*

". . . a gripping piece of literature."
— *Scientific American*

". . . there will be some who despair of ever making a dent in the mountain of city deterioration. For these 'doubting Thomases,' a corrective exists in *Pittsburgh, the Story of an American City . . .* a magnificent review."
— *America,* National Catholic Weekly

"The format and documentary illustrations are superb . . . it is an achievement to be welcomed."
— *The Reporter*

". . . exceptionally attractive and informative . . . it is the most elaborate, complete and interesting book ever produced on an American city.

"It is a book which every Pittsburgher will enjoy reading and studying; one which every Pennsylvanian will want to explore; and one which even the periodic visitor to Pittsburgh would be proud to have in his library."
— *Watertown News*

"Those who read the easy flowing text and study the more than 1,000 pictures, many in color, contained in the quarto size volume will know Pittsburgh past and present."
— *Niagara Falls Gazette*

NORTH CAROLINA
"This magnificent volume by Stefan Lorant and his collaborators is no shallow exercise in civic self-congratulations. It is a meticulously researched, compellingly written chronicle of the birth, growth, decline and rejuvenation of a great American city. And it is more than that. The story of Pittsburgh is, in microcosm, the story of industrial America."
— *Charlotte Observer*

OHIO
"A superbly illustrated history of Pittsburgh. . . ."
— *Newark Ohio Advocate*

". . . a vivid picture of the city. . . ."
— *Columbus Citizen-Journal*

"Spectacular in the true sense of the word."
— *Frederickstown Citizen*

". . . a fascinating biography of the city, illustrated by equally fascinating photographs."
— *Cleveland Plain Dealer*

"It would not be an exaggeration to say that no other city has ever been presented in such a factual and fascinating way as Pittsburgh. . . . The result is something that is worth its weight in gold."
— *William Feather Magazine,* Cleveland, Ohio

". . . monumental. . . ." — *Elyria Chronicle-Telegram*

OREGON
"Seldom has an American city been so lavishly and comprehensively presented." — *Portland Oregonian*

PENNSYLVANIA
"This is a gem of a book, perhaps the finest volume of its kind ever written on a subject of Pennsylvania history. The critics usually grit their teeth when they must lavish praise, but if they don't praise this work they are being inaccurate and misleading. It is a superb book."
— *Sunday Patriot-News,* Harrisburg

"This profusely illustrated and meticulously documented story of the growth of Pittsburgh from a village to a truly great city combines entertainment, history and a record of improvement and development in balanced proportions to present one of the most readable and exciting books to come to notice in a long time. . . ."
— *Chambersburg Public Opinion*

"It is a city unusual enough to deserve an unusually good biography, and Stefan Lorant has provided just that. . . . The history of Pittsburgh is given straight, and the book is testimony both to the city and to Lorant's ability as writer and editor." — *Philadelphia Bulletin*

"This beautiful volume does justice to its subject. . . . It will give the reader hours of enjoyment and impart much information and lore concerning our neighboring metropolis." — *Johnstown Tribune-Democrat*

"The grandeur of Mr. Lorant's editorial concept is such that he has produced a book of which Pittsburgh, and the whole country, can be proud. . . . As Pittsburgh has played a large part in American history, this book too is a major work of American history."
— *Du Bois Courier-Express*

". . . material of interest to everyone."
— *Uniontown Herald*

"Lorant has produced a beautiful big book which you wouldn't mind both owning and reading!"
— *Norristown Times-Herald*

". . . excellent . . . a tremendously handsome volume."
— *Sunday Call-Chronicle,* Allentown

"The book offers not only fascinating and authentic history, but a how-to plan for American cities. It's a thriller, too, and all along the way . . . is good reading."
— *Bethlehem Globe-Times*

PENNSYLVANIA: PITTSBURGH
"Once a reader starts through the pages, he is hard-put to stop. . . . It is not an ordinary book, to be put on a shelf and looked at seldom. It is a book which should be put open on the table and used like a dictionary, frequently, with the anticipation that every page contains a new facet of interest . . . 'de luxe' is exactly the right word for it. It is a magnificent tribute to a city. Bravo."
— James E. Alexander, *Post-Gazette*

"It's a big, glossy book, in general beautifully done . . . should brighten this community's image, at home and abroad, for many years to come." — *The Pittsburgh Press*

"Be proud, Pittsburghers. The big picture book about your city is being read and acclaimed all over the country." — Gilbert Love, *The Pittsburgh Press*

"The book is a superb example of the art of producing a pictorial history . . ."
— Ralph Munn, *Carnegie Magazine*

"BEG, BORROW OR BUY THIS BOOK — IT IS WORTH ANY PRICE"

— Letter in *The Pittsburgh Press*

SOUTH CAROLINA

"A magnificent history . . . a colorful adition for any student of America's development."

— *Charlotte News & Courier*

TENNESSEE

". . . should be put on the list for 'must reading' . . ."

— *History News*, Nashville

". . . an elaborate textual and pictorial record. . . ."

— *Memphis Commercial Appeal*

TEXAS

"Anyone who is interested in history, particularly that of the United States, will find this book fascinating. . . ."

— *Beaumont Texas Journal*

"*Pittsburgh* is a massive, beautiful book about a big city that is becoming more and more beautiful. . . . It is a big, heartening story. . . ."

— *Waco News-Tribune*

". . . this book represents such a bargain in sheer bulk alone that one's investment is safe in paper and ink. . .

Not many American cities have been given such detailed, historical treatment as this and even fewer have had so much told of them and told so well."

— *Dallas Times-Herald*

WASHINGTON

". . . a fine and weighty book. . . . This is a book of which the citizens of Pittsburgh can well be proud; but it is also a thing of beauty and far more than just a regional book. It is a masterpiece of printing and illustrating crafts. . . . It is no paean of praise to satisfy local pride; it's a literary masterpiece." — *Seattle Post-Intelligencer*

WEST VIRGINIA

"Nominated for one of the most beautiful books of the year. . . . The book is a vivid picture of the city through 200 years." — *Huntington Herald-Dispatch*

PUERTO RICO

"The whole tumultuous story of Pittsburgh, magnificently illustrated."

— *San Juan Star*

1975: HENRY J. HEINZ II with Stefan Lorant after an interview for the second edition of the book.

1980: ARTHUR J. ROONEY with Stefan Lorant after an interview for the third edition of the book.

INDEX

Ridl, Buzz (coach at Duquesne), 549
Rieck, Margaret, 513
Riley, James Whitcomb, 656
Riley, Martin, 285
Rinehart, Mary Roberts, 322, 330, 652, 692
Rinehart, W. & D., 105
Ripper Act (1901), 261–264
Ritter, Brenda Lee, 703
Riverfront Center, 554, 576
River traffic, 54–55, 68, 84
Robert Morris College, 493, 549, 628
Roberts, John M., 646
Roberts, Mary Brunot, 294
Robertson, Ben, 714
Robin, John P., 373, 377, 384, 403, 431, 437, 454,
    553, 554, 562, 681, 701
Robinson, George D., 60, 64, 548, 594, 645, 651
Robinson, James, 63
Robinson, William, 647
Robotic Institute, 634
Rockefeller, John D., 234
Rockwell, Willard F., 527
Rockwell International, 532
Roddy, James C., 712, 715
Rodef Shalom Temple, 587
Roderick, David M., 557, 701, 702
Rodgers, Calbraith Perry, 659, 663
Rodgers, William D., 669
Rodman, Thomas Jackson, 132
Roebling, John, 129, 647
Roebling, Washington, 129
Roenigk, A. J., 205
Roesch, William R., 698
Roessing, Frank M., 363
Rogers, Bennett, 405
Rogers, David, 643
Rogers, Mahlon, 76
Rogers, Robert, 38
Rogers, Will, 332
Rooney, Arthur J., 482, 537, 539, 545, 667, 726
Rooney, George W., 426
Rooney, Jim, 537
Roosevelt, President Franklin D., 322, 336, 348,
    353, 371, 442, 537, 667–676 passim
Roosevelt, Nicholas, 72, 79, 645
Roosevelt, President Theodore, 187, 240, 260, 261,
    266, 289, 320, 364, 537, 657, 659, 660
Roseman, Jack, 617
Rosen, Nathaniel, 703
Rosen, Sandra H., 617
Rosenberg, Samuel, paintings by, 349, 350, 351,
    352, 666, 667, 673
Rosenbloom, Charles J., 110, 439
Rosenman, Sam, 353
Rosenstock, Sarah, 248
Rosenthal, Dr. Thomas, 710
Roskies, Ralph Z., 711
Ross, Alexander, 643
Ross, James, 63, 75, 78, 645
Rossin, Peter C., 616
Rowe, Wallace H., 269
Royal American Regiment, 520–521
Ruffin, Sidney M., 427
Russell, Charles Edward, 203
Russell, John, 466, 468
Russell, Lillian, 300, 315, 658, 659, 663
Russian Orthodox Male Chorus, 183
Ryan, John T., Jr., 428, 442, 526, 701
Ryan, Timothy F. (Tice), 402, 679, 681

Sabata, Victor de, 362, 407
Sadlowski, Edward, 702
Safar, Dr. Peter, 707
Sage Foundation, Russell, 272, 276, 287, 295
Sahadi, Lou, 549
St. Clair, Arthur, 45, 46, 48
St. Clair, Sir John, 23
St. Gaudens, Mrs. Augustus, 293
St. Nicholas Serbian Orthodox Male Chorus,
    183
St. Paul's Cathedral, 120, 129, 586
Salk, Jonas Edward, 408, 445, 682, 684
Sammartino, Bruno, 552

Samson, H., 545
Sanguillen, Manny, 549
Sanitary Commission, U. S., 140
Sarni, Vincent A., 614
Scaife, Alan M., 181, 383, 686, 692
Scaife, J. Verner, 181
Scaife, Jeffery, 70, 107
Scaife, Mr. & Mrs. Richard Mellon, 471
Scaife, Sarah Mellon (Mrs. Alan M.), 361, 406,
    468, 672, 675, 684–685, 697
Scaife, William B., 106–107, 141, 644
Scaife Gallery, 468, 501
Schenley, Edward W. H., 104
Schenley, Mary E., 104, 654, 655, 656, 657
Schenley Park, 293, 300
Schildhouse, Evelyn, 486
Schmidt, Adolph W., 357, 383, 404, 419, 428,
    429, 440, 481, 594
Schmitt, Gladys, 392, 658, 699
Schneider, Andrew, 712, 714
Schoepf, Johann, 50, 52
Schools in Pittsburgh, 118, 245, 246. See also under
    name of institution
Schoonmaker, S. L., 266
Schoyer, S., Jr., 240
Schriftglesser, Karl, 375
Schwab, Charles M., 226, 236, 256, 258, 266, 279,
    310–311, 656, 657
Schwaebischer Saengerbund, 183
Schweiker, Senator Richard S., 700
Scott, Harvey J., 682
Scott, Hugh, 70, 74
Scott, James B., 541
Scott, Thomas A., 135, 156, 170, 221
Scranton, William, 696
Scull, John I., 49, 52, 63, 66, 643, 644, 645, 646
Scully, Cornelius Decatur, 377, 380, 384, 419, 669–
    674 passim, 682
Seder, Isaac, 656
Seemiller, Danny, 552, 715
Sellers, Robert Emory, 106, 107
Semmelbrock, William, 226
Semple, William, 60, 74
Semples, Samuel, 63
Seund, Freda, 665
Sewall, Charles L., 628
Sexton, Regina, 317
Seymour, Robert E., 526
Shadyside Academy Club, 274
Shafer, John D., 305
Shakarian, David B., 710
Shaktman, Ben, 513
Shame of the Cities (Steffens), 193
Shannopin's Town, 17
Shapp, Milton, 702
Sharswood, George, 650
Sheedy, Father, 204
Shelby Steel Tube Company, 254
Sherman, James S., 294
Sherrill, Jackie, 549
Shinn, William M., 106, 107
Shippen, Joseph, 26
Shiras, George, Jr., 240
Shirley, Governor, 22
Shoemaker, George A., 429
Simon, J. Matthew, 629
Simon, Joanna, 508
Sims, Walter, 535
Sinclair, Upton, 266
Singer, William, 266
Skidmore, Owings and Merrill, 556
Skolnick, Irene, 617
Slater, Joseph M. (Hap), 661
Slater, Samuel, 540
Slavery, 108, 126
Slusser, James, 698
Smeal, Eleanor Cutri, 703
Smith, Alfred E., 665
Smith, B. F., Jr., 113
Smith, Elmer, 249
Smith, Joseph, 70
Smith, Lee, 294

Smith, Nate, 714
Smith, Nathaniel, 200
Smith, Robert, 537, 549
Smith, Russell, paintings by, 88, 96, 97, 98, 99
Smith, Thomas J., 560
Smith, William, 42
Smithsonian Institute, 200
Smoke and soot in Pittsburgh, 55, 78, 79, 81–82,
    93, 168, 177, 289, 322–323, 326, 327, 364, 370,
    374–390
Smoke Control Ordinance, 370
Snyder, Harold, 285
Snyder, William P., 558
Snyder, William P., III, 383, 428, 429, 442, 685,
    701
Social Gospel Movement, 204, 214
Soffel, Sara M., 322, 666, 673
Solid State Measurements, Inc., 616
Solomon, Emilie, 317
Somervell, Brehon B., 447, 675, 683, 686, 687
Song of Pittsburgh (Thurston), 177
Sons of Vulcan, 155, 211
Spahr, Charles B., 212, 214
Spang, Chalfant & Company, 150
Spang, Charles N., 240
Sprang, H. S., 542
Spanish-American War, 251, 260
Spear, Mrs. Nathaniel, 317
Specter, Arlen, 706
Spector, Edward, 362, 406, 664, 670, 681
Speer, Edgar B., 473, 699, 705
Spencer, Herbert L., 184, 225, 230, 272, 674
Spitzer, David M., 616
Spock, Benjamin McLane, 408
Sprigle, Ray, 670
Sproul, William C., 662
Stackhouse, Mark, 76, 78, 645
Stafford, Rebecca, 629, 708
Stalworth, John, 540
Stanley, Dorothy, 317
Stanley, William, 248, 249
Stanwix, John, 32, 34, 642
Stargell, Willie, 548, 552, 712
Starzl, Dr. Thomas, 707, 710, 715
Station Square, 562, 564
Steamboats, 72, 79, 82, 93, 129, 236, 294
Steel and iron founding, 68, 70, 92, 93, 96, 129,
    137, 145–148, 162, 175, 178, 197, 198, 199,
    207, 212–218, 222–223, 254–258, 260, 274–
    296, 370, 396
Steel strike of 1919–20, 337
Steelers, 537, 546–547, 704, 705, 710
Steffens, Lincoln, 168, 193, 201, 261, 266
Stein, Gertrude, 330
Steinberg, William, 362, 406, 407, 681, 692, 700,
    703
Stenzel, Jake, 249
Stephes, Luther, 76
Stettinius, Edward R., Jr., 671
Stever, H. Guyford, 485, 698
Stevenson, Adlai, 441, 682, 690, 691
Stevenson, George, 78, 644
Stewart, Howard B., 427, 437, 442
Stewart, William Alvah, 427, 673, 680, 681
Stinson, George A., 527, 594
Stobo, Robert, 19, 641–642
Stone, Fred, 666
Stone, Governor, 264
Stotz, Charles M., 33, 643
Stovey, Harry, 539
Strauss, Richard, 276
Street railway in Pittsburgh, 102, 160–161, 192,
    193, 198, 225
Stuart, J. E. B., 141, 401, 650
Sturgis, S. D., Jr., 683
Subway system, 600–601
Succop, Bertram L., 666, 667
Sugden, Joe, 249
Sulzberger, Cyrus L., 343–348
Sumner, Charles, 164
Sumner, William Graham, 184
Sunday, Billy, 660